JOSEPH CORNELL / MARCEL DUCHAMP ...IN RESONANCE

Joseph Cornell/Marcel Duchamp...

THE MENIL COLLECTION, HOUSTON

PHILADELPHIA MUSEUM OF ART

CANTZ

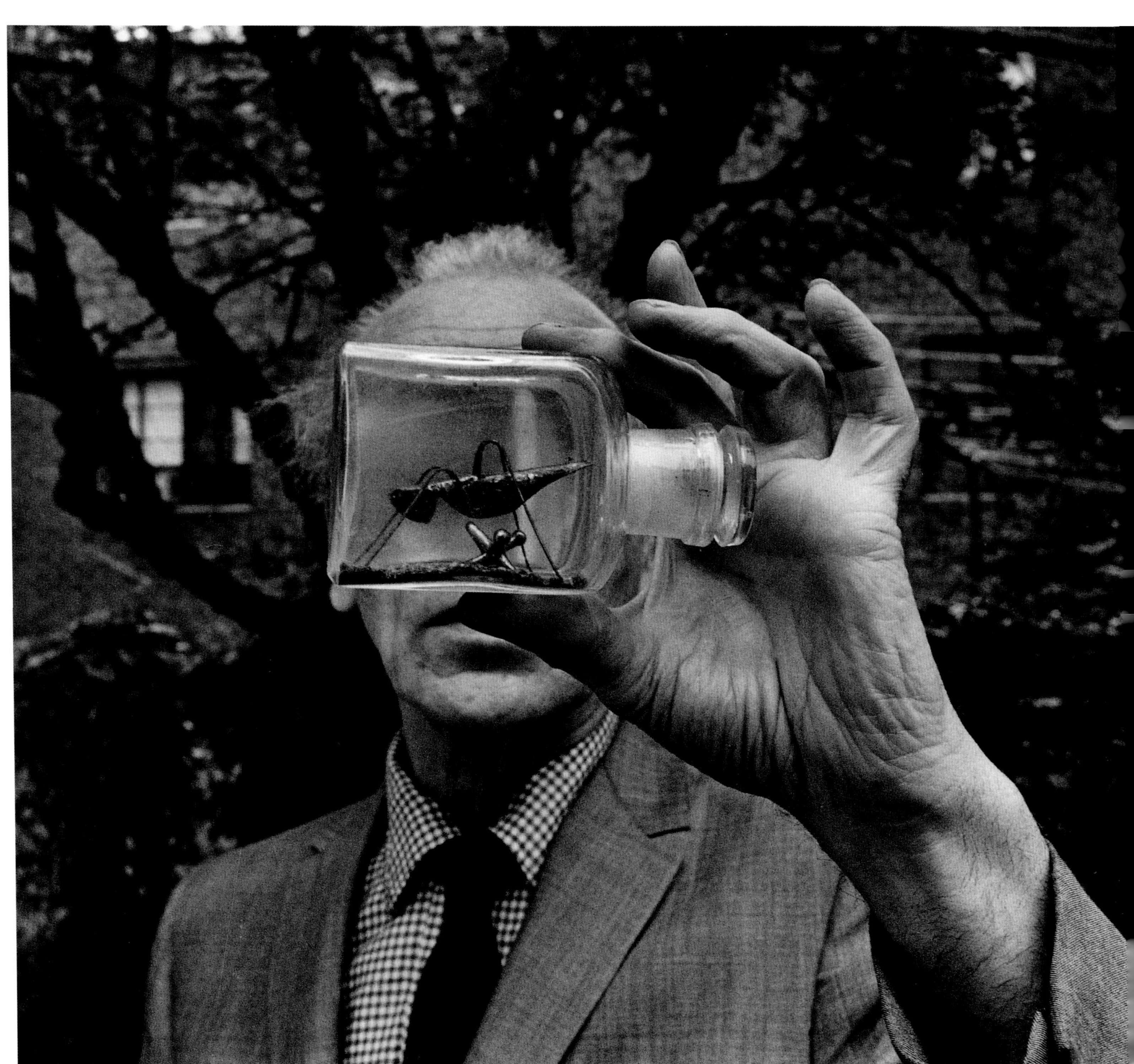

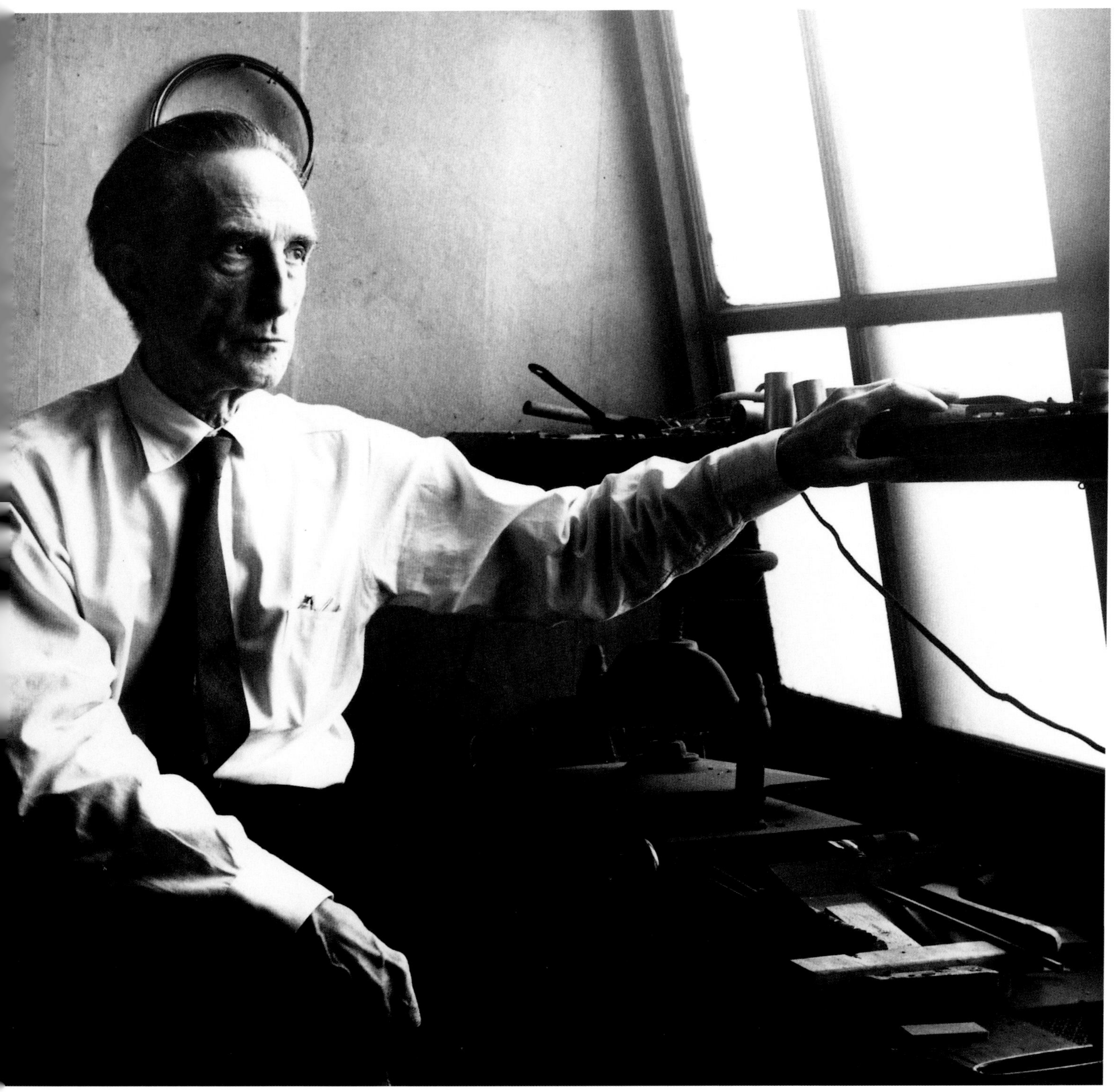

...in resonance

Introduction

ANNE D'HARNONCOURT

Texts

ECKE BONK

LYNDA ROSCOE HARTIGAN

WALTER HOPPS

DON QUAINTANCE

ANN TEMKIN

Chronology

SUSAN DAVIDSON

This catalogue accompanies the exhibition
"Joseph Cornell/ Marcel Duchamp ... in resonance"
and is supported by grants from the National Endowment for the Arts
and The Andy Warhol Foundation for the Visual Arts.
In Philadelphia, additional support has been received from the Pew Charitable Trusts.

Exhibition Itinerary

Philadelphia Museum of Art
October 8, 1998–January 3, 1999

The Menil Collection, Houston
January 22–May 16, 1999

Design: Don Quaintance, Public Address Design; Ecke Bonk, typosophic society

Editor: Polly Koch
Production: Elizabeth Frizzell
Photography: Paul Hester, Hester + Hardaway
(*Duchamp Dossier* Plates and Inventory)

Typography: Composed in Berthold Akzidenz and Adobe Caslon
Printing: Dr. Cantz´sche Druckerei, Germany
Separations: Repromayer, Reutlingen, Germany

Cover: Joseph Cornell, *Duchamp Dossier* (detail), c. 1942–53. Philadelphia Museum of Art.
Gift of The Joseph and Robert Cornell Memorial Foundation

Mention of the Marcel Duchamp Archive in the figure captions is an abbreviated form of:
Philadelphia Museum of Art. Marcel Duchamp Archive, Gift of Jacqueline, Paul and Peter Matisse,
in memory of their mother, Alexina Duchamp.

Mention of the Natl. Museum of American Art, Smithsonian, in the figure captions is an abbreviated form of:
National Museum of American Art, Smithsonian Institution, Washington, D.C..

Library of Congress Catalog Card Number: 98-87794
ISBN 0-939594-47-1 (SOFTCOVER)

ISBN 3-89322-431-9 (TRADE)

Trade edition published by:
Cantz Verlag
Senefelderstrasse 12
73760 Ostfildern-Ruit, Germany
tel (0049) 711.440 50
fax (0049) 711.440 5220
Internet: www.hatje.de

Distributed in North and South America by:
D.A.P., Distributed Art Publishers
155 Avenue of the Americas, 2nd floor
New York, N.Y. 10013
tel 212.627 1999
fax 212.627 9484

Printed in Germany

pp. 5–6
Joseph Cornell holding an Untitled Bottle Object, 3708 Utopia Parkway, Flushing, New York, c. 1969 Photograph by Duane Michals.

Marcel Duchamp, 210 West 14th Street studio, New York, c. 1956. Photograph by Waintrob-Budd. Philadelphia Museum of Art, Marcel Duchamp Archive.

Contents

Lenders to the Exhibition

Lindy Bergman, Chicago
Janice and Mickey Cartin
Dr. and Mrs. M. Michael Eisenberg
Richard L. Feigen, New York
Virginia Green, New York
Mr. and Mrs. Robert Lehrman, Washington, D.C.
Jacqueline Matisse
Christophe de Menil
Jose Mugrabi
Alice Saligman, New York
Arno Schefler
Michael Senft, New York
Ronny Van de Velde, Antwerp, Belgium
and anonymous lenders

The Archives of American Art, Smithsonian Institution
The Art Institute of Chicago
Beinecke Rare Book and Manuscript Library, Yale University
The Joseph and Robert Cornell Memorial Foundation
Joseph Cornell Study Center, National Museum of American Art, Smithsonian Institution
The Jean-Noël Herlin Archive, New York
Hirshhorn Museum and Sculpture Garden, Smithsonian Institution
The Menil Collection, Houston
Achim Moeller Fine Art, New York
Musée National d'Art Moderne, Centre Georges Pompidou, Paris
The Museum of Modern Art, New York
National Gallery of Canada, Ottawa
National Museum of American Art, Smithsonian Institution
Philadelphia Museum of Art
San Francisco Museum of Modern Art
Staatliches Museum Schwerin
Yokohama Museum of Art
The Young-Mallin Archive, New York

Preface / Acknowledgments

Dedicated to the memory of

Alexina Duchamp and

Dominique de Menil

The *Duchamp Dossier,* a little-known and until now undocumented cross between a work of art and an idiosyncratic archive, is the starting point for this exhibition and publication, which chronicle the friendship and working relationship between two of the twentieth century's most innovative and influential artists—Joseph Cornell and Marcel Duchamp. The evidence of their collaboration is chiefly contained in Cornell's elaborate file on Duchamp, one of the most intimate of the compilations that Cornell termed "explorations." Following Cornell's death in December 1972, Walter Hopps discovered the *Duchamp Dossier* among Cornell's effects in his house on Utopia Parkway. Soon thereafter, Hopps conceived of an exhibition exploring the affinities between the two artists through a focused selection of works using the *Duchamp Dossier* as a centerpiece. *Joseph Cornell/Marcel Duchamp ... in resonance* is the fulfillment of that initial impulse.

In his role as adviser to The Joseph and Robert Cornell Memorial Foundation, Hopps was instrumental in shepherding the Foundation's gift of the *Duchamp Dossier* in 1990 to the Philadelphia Museum of Art. As the greatest repository of Duchamp's work, the Philadelphia Museum of Art was the natural choice for the *Duchamp Dossier*'s permanent home. The Menil Collection with its substantial holdings of Cornell's work, collected by John and Dominique de Menil beginning in the early 1950s, provides a useful springboard for engagement with this artist's oeuvre. As the directors of these two institutions, we are delighted to take full advantage of close collaboration for the creation of an exhibition to explore the resonances between these two artists.

Collaboration began at the curatorial level. Hopps' first step was to involve Ecke Bonk in the early planning stages of the exhibition. As the exhibition took shape, they welcomed the participation of additional colleagues, enabling the project to profit from a formidable army of veterans in Duchamp and Cornell studies. In 1963, Hopps gave Duchamp his first major museum exhibition to be presented in the United States during his lifetime, at the Pasadena Museum of Art; four years later, Hopps organized a comprehensive tribute to Cornell at the same institution. Ecke Bonk's research into the history and production of Duchamp's *Boîte* edition (a major area of concern in the *Duchamp Dossier*) led to the publication of one of the most insightful books written on Duchamp in the past decade. They have been joined in formulating the concept of the exhibition and selecting its contents by three other committed partners: Lynda Roscoe Hartigan is the founding curator of the Joseph Cornell Study Center at the National Museum of American Art, which has supported her ongoing research for a Cornell catalogue raisonné, and Susan Davidson, associate curator at The Menil Collection, and Ann Temkin, The Muriel and Philip Berman Curator of Twentieth-Century Art at the Philadelphia Museum of Art, are both involved closely with the special Cornell and Duchamp collections in their respective institutions. This talented crew, together with the catalogue's co-designer, Don Quaintance, have contributed insightful essays to this book, which brings together the first scholarly thoughts on the meaning of the *Duchamp Dossier*.

Two substantial grants provided an impetus for realizing *Joseph Cornell / Marcel Duchamp ... in resonance.* Early on, the National Endowment for the Arts contributed funding toward its research and development. Realizing the importance of this exhibition to contemporary artists, The Andy Warhol Foundation for the Visual Arts expanded its usual purview to provide funding for the project. In Philadelphia, additional support has been received from the Pew Charitable Trusts.

The decision of lenders to partipate was made that much more difficult by the inherent fragility of the works of art in their collections, which include in several cases rarely exhibited ephemera. We are therefore especially indebted to the individuals and institutions, listed on page 10, whose enthusiasm and willingness to allow cherished artworks to travel made this exhibition possible.

Many people provided crucial assistance in locating artworks and securing loans. In particular, the curators would like to express their gratitude to Brooke Alexander, E. John Bullard, Tracey Bashkoff, Jeffery Bergen, Kornelia von Berswordt-Wallrabe, Bernard Blistène, Jim Corcoran, Marcel Fleiss, Gerhard Graulich, Virginia Green, Karsten Greve, Jorge Helft, Signe Howard, Robert Lehrman, Nora Lobo, Kynaston McShine, Francis M. Naumann, Alexandra O'Brian, Joyce Pomeroy Schwartz, Catherine Raphael, Daniel Schulman, Brydon Smith, Werner Spies, Jeremy Strick, Daniel Varenne, Kirk Varnedoe, Joseph Veres, Jennifer Vorbach, Patricia C. Willis, and Nancy Wooten.

Over the years, many individuals have shared their thoughts and remembrances of either Cornell or Duchamp—or, in many cases, both artists. These include Dore Ashton, Helen Batcheller, Joella Bayer, Mrs. John A. Benton, Enrico Donati, the late Alexina Duchamp, Charles Henri Ford, Howard Hussey, Helen Jagger, Lillian Kiesler, Alexander Liberman, William S. Lieberman, Jacqueline Matisse, Kiriki de Diego Metzo, James Ogle, Harry Roseman, Dorothea Tanning, Marjorie Watkins, and Donald Windham. Their recollections and perceptions have served as a primary source for the curators' understanding of both the artists' lives and their working methods.

The curators would like to thank the staffs at the following institutions for their help in reconstructing the activities of both Cornell and Duchamp: Archives of American Art, Smithsonian Institution; Beinecke Rare Book and Manuscript Library, Yale University; Joseph Cornell Study Center, National Museum of American Art, Smithsonian Institution; The Getty Research Institute for the History of Art and the Humanities; The Museum of Modern Art, New York; New York Public Library; Harry Ransom Research Center, The University of Texas at Austin; and Ryerson Library, The Art Institute of Chicago. The curators are also appreciative of the number of specialists who have shared their knowledge, in particular Dawn Ades, Dore Ashton, Joan Banach, the late Edwin A. Bergman and Mrs. Lindy Bergman, Jennifer Blessing, William Camfield, Jennifer Culvert, Anne Doran, Virginia Dortch, Michelle Elligott, Gay Ellis, Betty Freeman, Beth Ann Guyunn, Richard Hamilton, Jodi Hauptman, Vivian Horan, Mark Kelman, Maureen Lasko, Deidre E. Lawrence, Kynaston McShine, Francis M. Naumann, Catrina Neiman, Molly Nesbit, Frances Pernas, Joanna R. Roche, Rona Roob, Naomi Sawelson–Gorse, Ingrid Schaffner, Deborah Solomon, Lorraine Stuart, Catherine Tack, Dickran Tashjian, Judith Throm, Calvin Tomkins, Deborah Treisman, Joan Washburn, Mary Woolever, Judith Young-Mallin, and Judith Zilczer.

The publication has brought together a substantial number of photographs, many previously unpublished. Susan Davidson, Lynda Roscoe Hartigan, and Don Quaintance carried out this extensive research, with the assistance of Geraldine Aramanda and Carol Shanks of

The Menil Collection. We are grateful to many individuals for their guidance in locating documentary photographs and/or providing materials: Ginny Beadle, Joshua Beadle, Carole Callow, Pat Canaday, Mikki Carpenter, Geoffrey Clements, Crosby Coughlin, Lynne Crowle, Enrico Donati, Anne Easterling, Monte and Betty Factor, James Farmer, Jeffrey Figley, Kate Garmeson, Ursula Haberle, Morgan Hare, Pamela S. Johnson, Lillian Kiesler, Steven Koch, Frank Kolodny, Alexander Liberman, George Platt Lynes II, Michelle Martin, Elizabeth McGrath, Duane Michals, Mary Morel, Peter Namuth, Arnold Newman, James Ogle, Helaine Pardo, Yuki Puar, Marie-Françoise Rose, Harry Roseman, Jeffrey Ryan, Martica Sawin, Ingrid Schaffner, Lothar Schirmer, Robert Sink, Michael Stiete, Pam Stuedemann, Mrs. Soichi Sunami, Lance Thompson, Daniel Varenne, Julian Wasser, Taki Weiss, and Helen Wright. Conna Clark at the Philadelphia Museum of Art and Ann M. Brose at the National Museum of American Art each handled innumerable requests for photographic material from their respective collections. Paul Hester of Hester + Hardaway photographed the *Duchamp Dossier* specifically for this publication.

For the design of this publication, Ecke Bonk and Don Quaintance forged a rewarding collaboration to meet the unique challenges of integrating the work of Cornell and Duchamp. In Houston, Polly Koch provided an expert editorial voice while bringing consistency to the mass of material, and Elizabeth Frizzell deftly managed the complicated production parameters.

Staging an exhibition of this intricacy depends on several key persons within each museum. To their immediate colleagues, we join the curators in thanking at The Menil Collection: Buck Bakke, Julie Bakke, Deborah Brauer, Phil Heagy, Doug Laguarta, Elizabeth Lunning, Carol Mancusi-Ungaro, Bear Parham, John Peters, and William Steen; and at the Philadelphia Museum of Art: Nancy Ash, Kathleen Brown, Caroline Cassels, Abby Donovan, Jamye Jamison, Stephen Keever, George Marcus, Danielle Rice, Susan Rosenberg, Lynn Rosenthal, Jack Schlechter, Innis Howe Shoemaker, Andy Slavinskas, Michael Taylor, Suzanne Wells, Ashley West, Graydon Wood, and Faith Zieske. Remi Spriggs (The Menil Collection), Adina Loeb (Philadelphia Museum of Art), and over the years Jeana Foley, Libby Karlinger, Janna Leepson, Sandra Levinson, Ann-Louise Marquis, Joanna Marsh, Micaela Mendelsohn, Harvey Overton, and Jessica Porter, who served in various research capacities at the National Museum of American Art, also contributed to the making of this project. Above all, the curators have relied upon the dedication of Rachael Arauz at the Philadelphia Museum of Art, whose enthusiasm was unfaltering.

The boards of trustees at both The Menil Collection and the Philadelphia Museum of Art are central to the support of every exhibition presented at their respective institutions, and they have embraced the project wholeheartedly. A special homage is due Dominique de Menil, The Menil Collection's founder, who warmly endorsed the exhibition prior to her death in December 1997.

From the inception of the exhibition, Cornell's sisters, Mrs. John A. Benton and Helen Jagger, and his niece, Helen Batcheller, have eagerly anticipated our results. Richard Ader and Donald Windham, trustees of The Joseph and Robert Cornell Memorial Foundation, along with their associate Platt Ketcham, have offered kind and valued support. Significantly, both Mme Duchamp and her daughter, Jacqueline Matisse, were close friends of Cornell. Mme Duchamp's spirited engagement has been continued by Jacqueline, Duchamp's last collaborator on the assembly of his *Boîte* edition. Before her death in December 1995, Alexina derived much enjoyment from the idea of bringing together these two artists so dear to her heart, and her enthusiasm has been an inspiration to us all.

Paul Winkler
Director
The Menil Collection, Houston

Anne d'Harnoncourt
The George D. Widener Director
Philadelphia Museum of Art

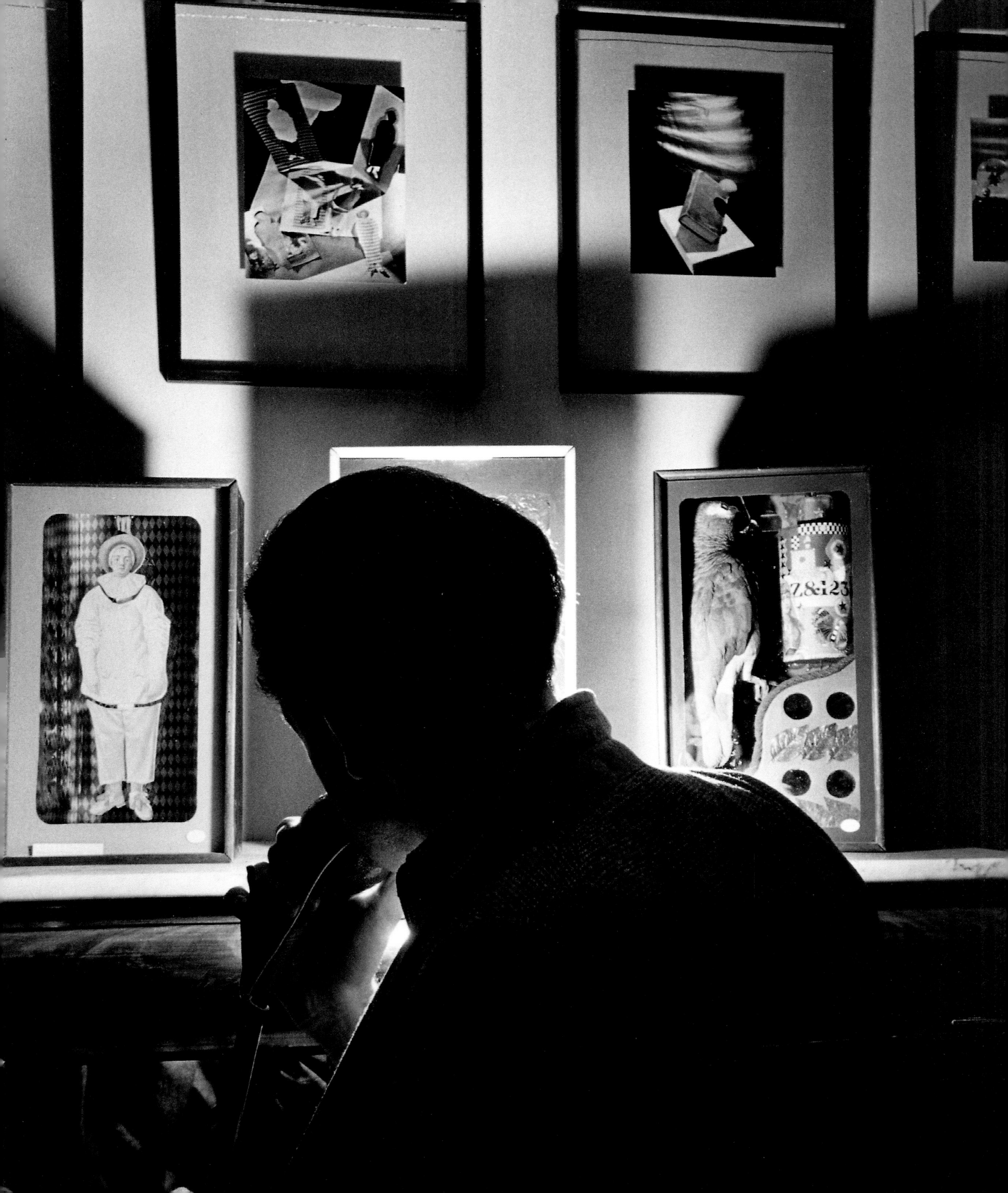
Z&123

Introduction

ANNE D'HARNONCOURT

What an unlikely pair—the charming, ironic, profoundly sophisticated Frenchman, whose acquaintance with the art world on both sides of the Atlantic was encyclopedic (encompassing Alfred Stieglitz and Gertrude Stein, Morton Schamberg and Constantin Brancusi, Louis Eilshemius and Piet Mondrian), and the shy, reclusive American who inhabited Utopia Parkway and haunted the secondhand book and curio stores of Manhattan. Marcel Duchamp and Joseph Cornell (figs. 2 and 1), brought together again in this exhibition, were nevertheless friends and, for a time and to an extent still happily beyond our ken, coconspirators, who surely found each other quite exotic yet recognized mutual interests and affinities.

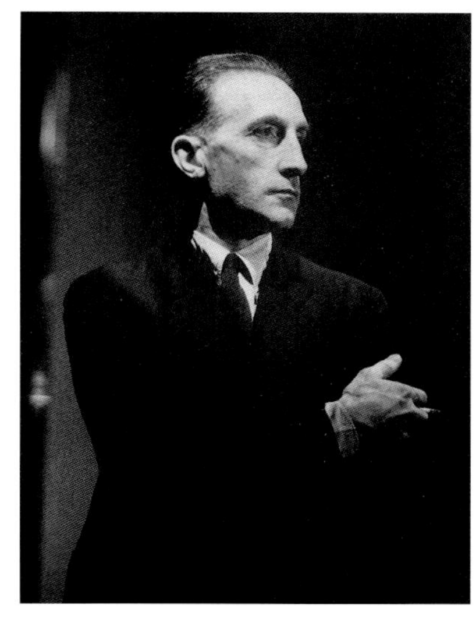

No operation is more delicate than to juxtapose the work of two complex artists and to observe affinities without belaboring them. Perhaps what these two very different twentieth-century characters had most in common was their deep sense of discretion, verging on hermeticism. They each created and occupied highly individual spheres of thought and image, borrowing freely from the world at large, yet they had little desire to impose their views on others. The essentially solitary nature of their archival pursuits made them kindred spirits.

What drew Cornell to Duchamp was surely in good part his Frenchness, the offhand ease with which he could speak of Paris, city of dazzling lights that harbored so many of Cornell's romantic heroines and dreams. A shared admiration for the poetry of Stéphane Mallarmé, a love of language and a penchant for the flotsam and jetsam of everyday life, a mutual attraction to the mysterious worlds behind shop windows (whether filled with chocolate grinders or with mannequins in bridal gowns)—Cornell could have discovered all of these connections with this debonair personage who was himself a "star." And what might Duchamp have seen in Cornell? A true "original," an idiosyncratic artist devoted to his own dreams rather than the latest fad, a lanky, quintessentially American character whose own encyclopedic acquaintance sprang not from firsthand experience and wide-ranging travel but from avid reading, film-going, and listening to music.

Here they are, then, in the decades leading up to and into World War II in New York, itself a fairy metropolis to Duchamp in the way that turn-of-the-century Paris was to Cornell. And here is a box of ephemera that tells us something, but by no means everything, about a friendship valued by both artists. We'll never know what they said to each other, or how much they left unsaid but understood. Perhaps the greatest reward of bringing two old friends together is that it makes us look at each of them anew. We are reminded of Duchamp's youthful enchantment with funfairs, eccentric machines, and poetic

1 **Cornell with *A Dressing Room for Gille* (1939), *Fortune Telling Parrot* (c. 1937–38), and James Ogle's photographs of Cornell's arrangements** including materials after Watteau's *Portrait of Gilles* and possibly *Revolving Book with Red Ball* (1934), probably Julien Levy Gallery, 602 Madison Avenue, New York, c. 1940. Photograph by James Ogle.

2 **Duchamp photographed for *Vanity Fair*,** New York, 1934. Photograph by Lusha Nelson.

(as well as erotic) wordplay, and of Cornell's amazingly intimate knowledge of French Romantic literature and his talismanic use of snippets of film and photographs. Of the many American artists Duchamp encountered over decades of transatlantic roaming, Cornell must have been among those most familiar with the nuances of the nineteenth-century literary and artistic milieu in which Duchamp came of age. Their taste for old-fashioned children's games, new-fangled popular science, amusing advertisements, and the treasure trove of ordinary objects to be found in the Bazar de l'Hôtel de Ville, the penny arcade, or a Sears, Roebuck catalogue rooted the work of these two apparently esoteric artists in the popular culture of their time.

This exhibition, which presents Cornell's *Duchamp Dossier* to the public for the first time, also assembles clusters of each artist's work that in some sense resonate together. No literal influence or borrowing is implied, only suggestions of shared fascinations. Odd materials (glass, dust, sand, torn and faded papers) and odd formats (a cage of marble cubes, a box of apothecary jars) combine with obsessive images (a doll among branches, a woman reclining on a bed of twigs) and notes, notes, and more notes—written, recopied, and carefully preserved.

Duchamp and Cornell were both in search of the marvelous, and they both knew it to be persistently elusive (fig. 3). Duchamp made fewer and fewer works, seeking never to repeat himself, while Cornell made more and more, accumulating a dusty treasure house of spare parts and half-finished efforts. Duchamp's difficult and enigmatic category of measurement for infinitesimal qualities—the *inframince*—suggests Cornell's attempt to capture the ineffable with the utmost precision and delicacy. At heart *bricoleurs*, scribblers, and tinkerers, they were absorbed in making fresh magic out of the vast plethora of things around them, and their works have a lingering perfume that even now eludes description while continuing to enchant.

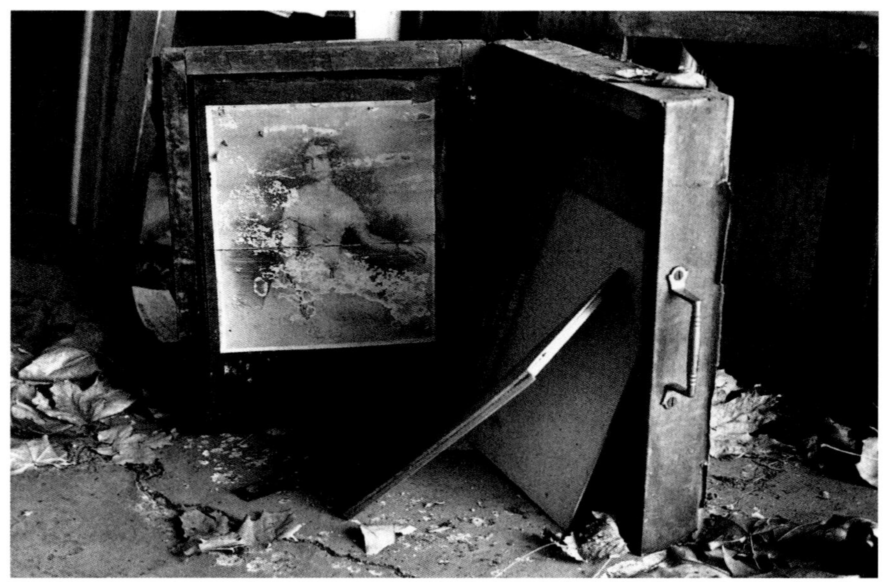

3 ***Ballerina in the Box,*** 3708 Utopia Parkway, Flushing, New York, February 1970. Photograph by Harry Roseman. Cornell's abandoned suitcase for *Portrait of Ondine* (c. 1940–late 1960s) in his garage.

Joseph Cornell: *Duchamp Dossier*

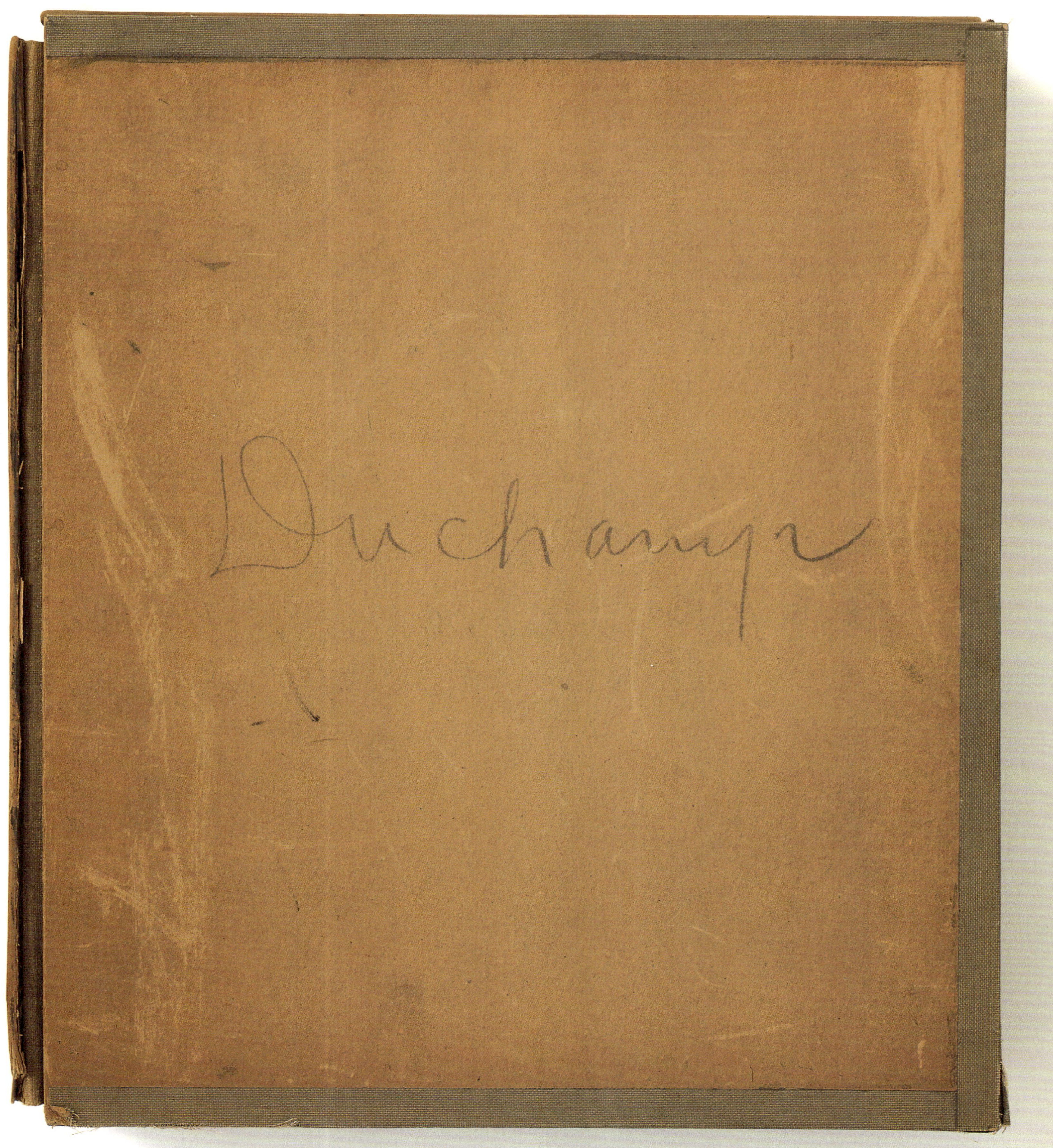
Duchamp

A

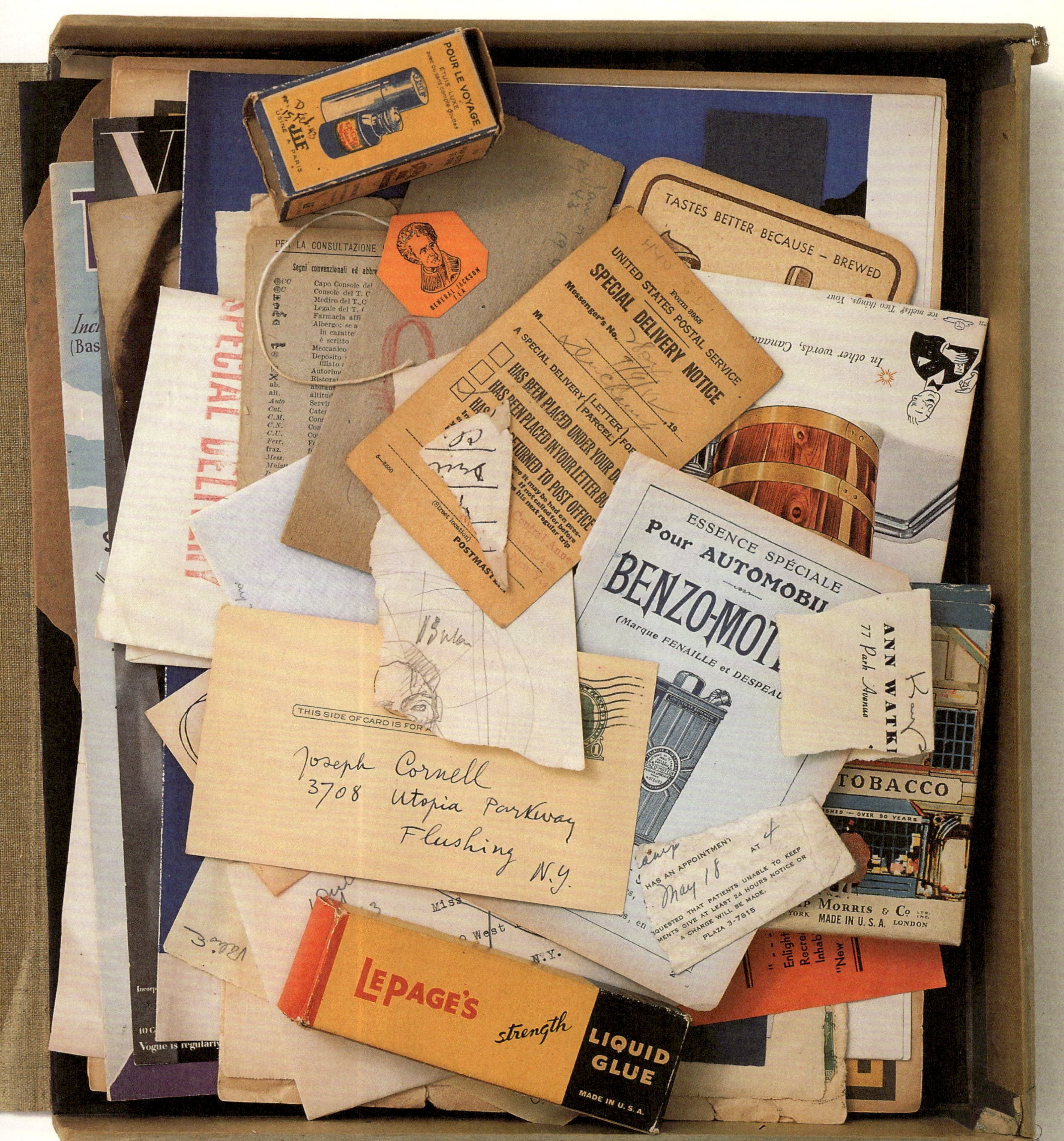

POUR LE VOYAGE
TASTES BETTER BECAUSE – BREWED
GENERAL JACKSON
Form 3905
UNITED STATES POSTAL SERVICE
SPECIAL DELIVERY NOTICE
Messenger's No.
A SPECIAL DELIVERY LETTER PARCEL
HAS BEEN RETURNED TO POST OFFICE
POSTMASTER
In other words,
ESSENCE SPÉCIALE
(Marque FENAILLE et DESPEAU
77 Park Avenue
TOBACCO
OVER 50 YEARS
MADE IN U.S.A. LONDON
THIS SIDE OF CARD IS FOR
Joseph Cornell
3708 Utopia Parkway
Flushing N.Y.
HAS AN APPOINTMENT AT 4
May 18
PLAZA 3-7815
LEPAGE'S
strength
LIQUID GLUE
MADE IN U.S.A.
Vogue is regularly

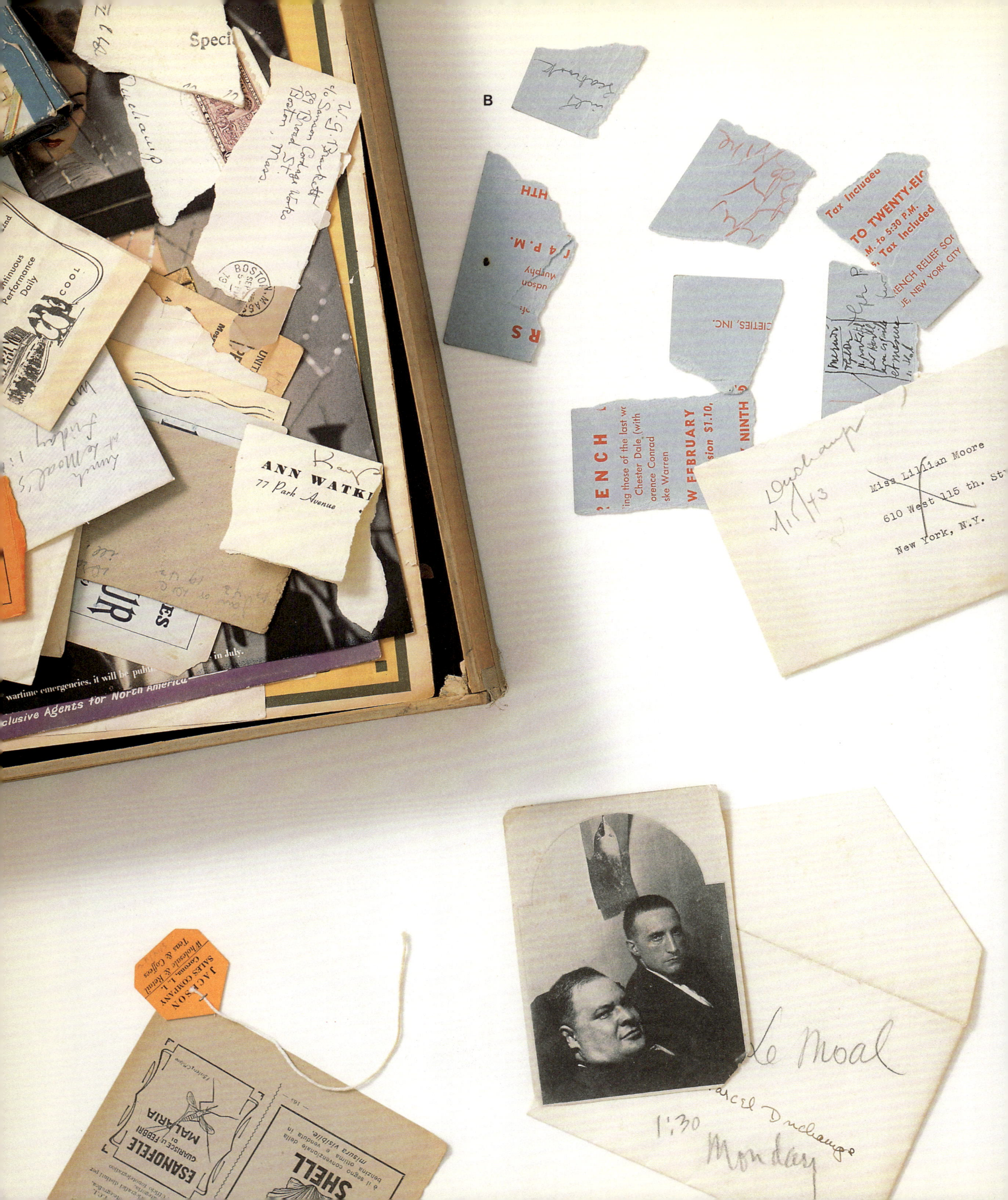
B
W. G. Brackett
% Samson Cordage Works
89 Broad St.
Boston, Mass.
BOSTON, MASS.
Duchamp
Continuous Performance Daily
COOL
ANN WATKI
77 Park Avenue
wartime emergencies, it will be publ
in July.
Exclusive Agents for North America
Tax Included
TO TWENTY-EI
M. to 5:30 P.M.
Tax Included
RENCH RELIEF SO
UE, NEW YORK CITY
CIETIES, INC.
ing those of the last w
Chester Dale (with
orence Conrad
ske Warren
W FEBRUARY
sion $1.10,
Y NINTH
Duchamp
Miss Lillian Moore
610 West 115 th. St
New York, N.Y.
JACKSON
SALES COMPANY
Wholesale & Retail
Teas & Coffees
ESANOFELE
GUARISCE LE FEBBRI
MALARIA
SHELL
Le Moal
Marcel Duchamp
1:30
Monday

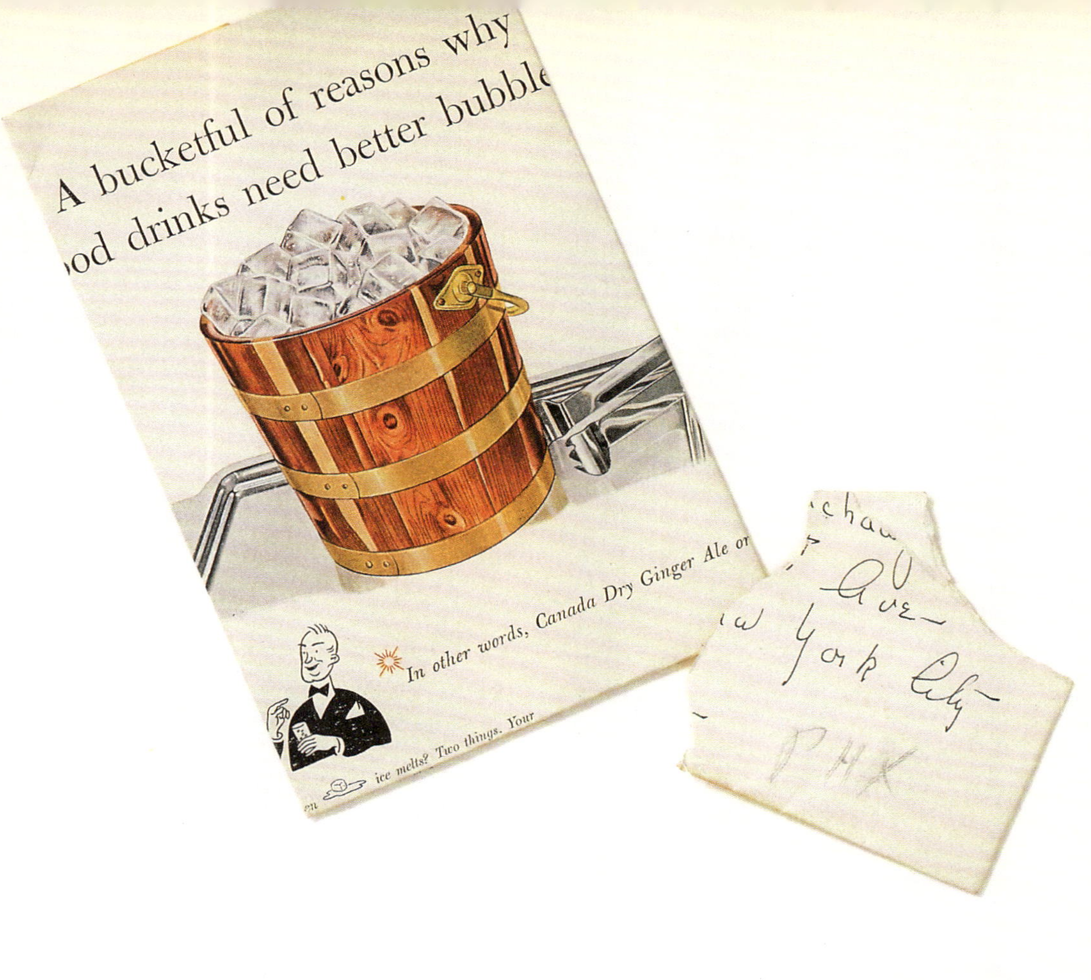
A bucketful of reasons why
od drinks need better bubble
In other words, Canada Dry Ginger Ale or
ice melts? Two things. Your

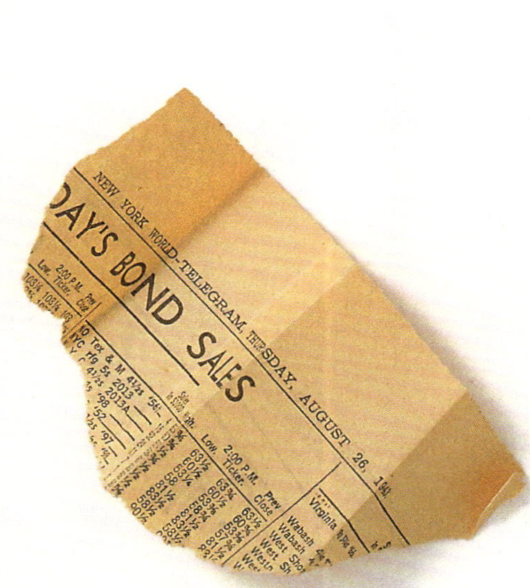
NEW YORK WORLD-TELEGRAM
DAY'S BOND SALES

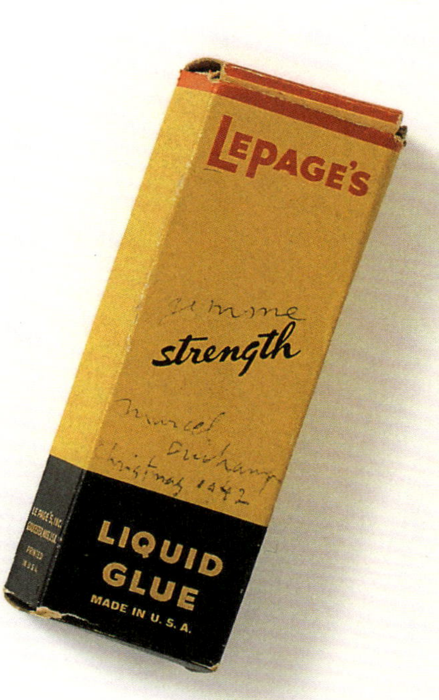
LEPAGE'S
strength
LIQUID GLUE
MADE IN U.S.A.

THERE'S AN INTERESTING MESSAGE ON THE OTHER SIDE
SOLELY OF MALT AND HOPS

C

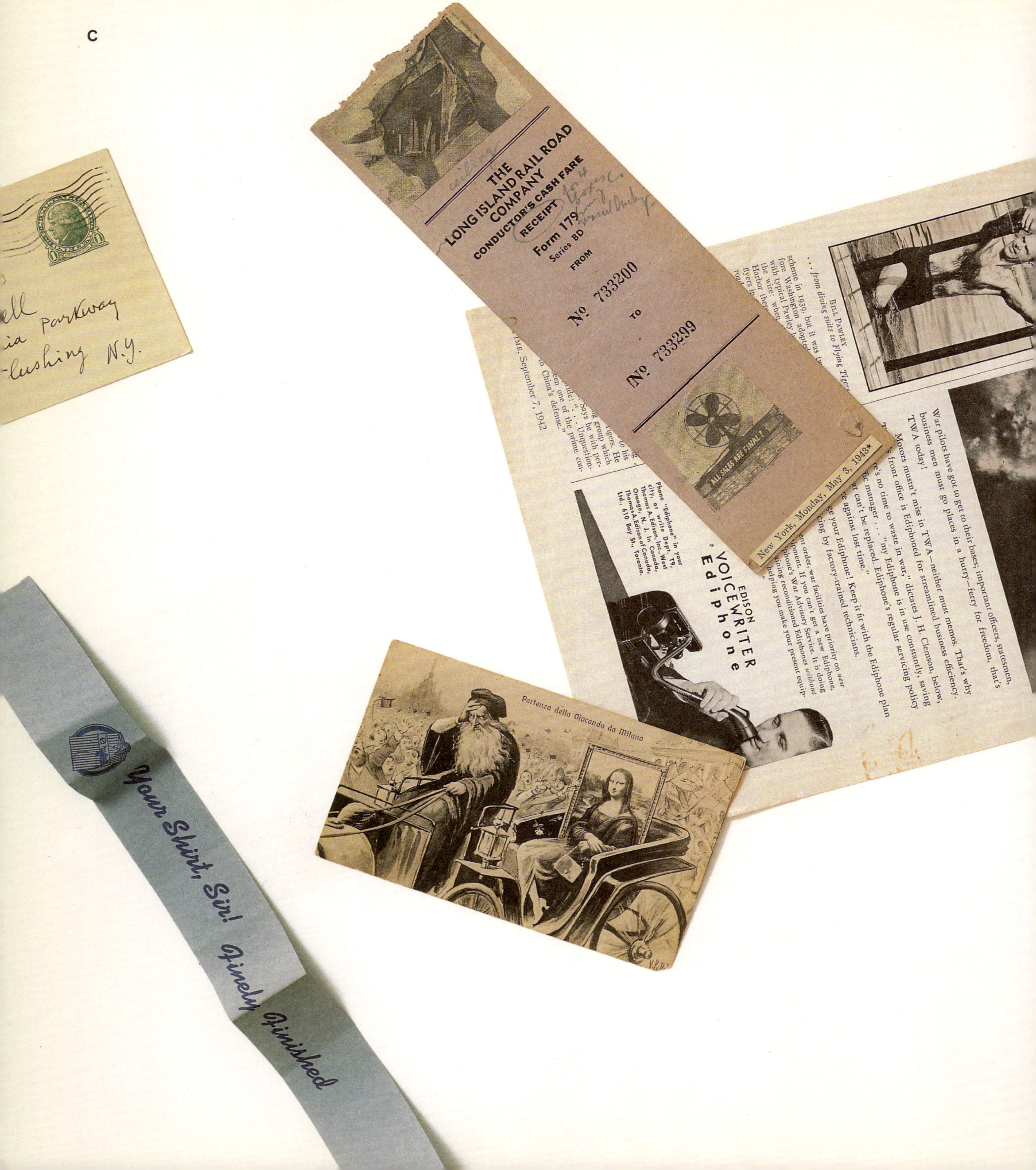

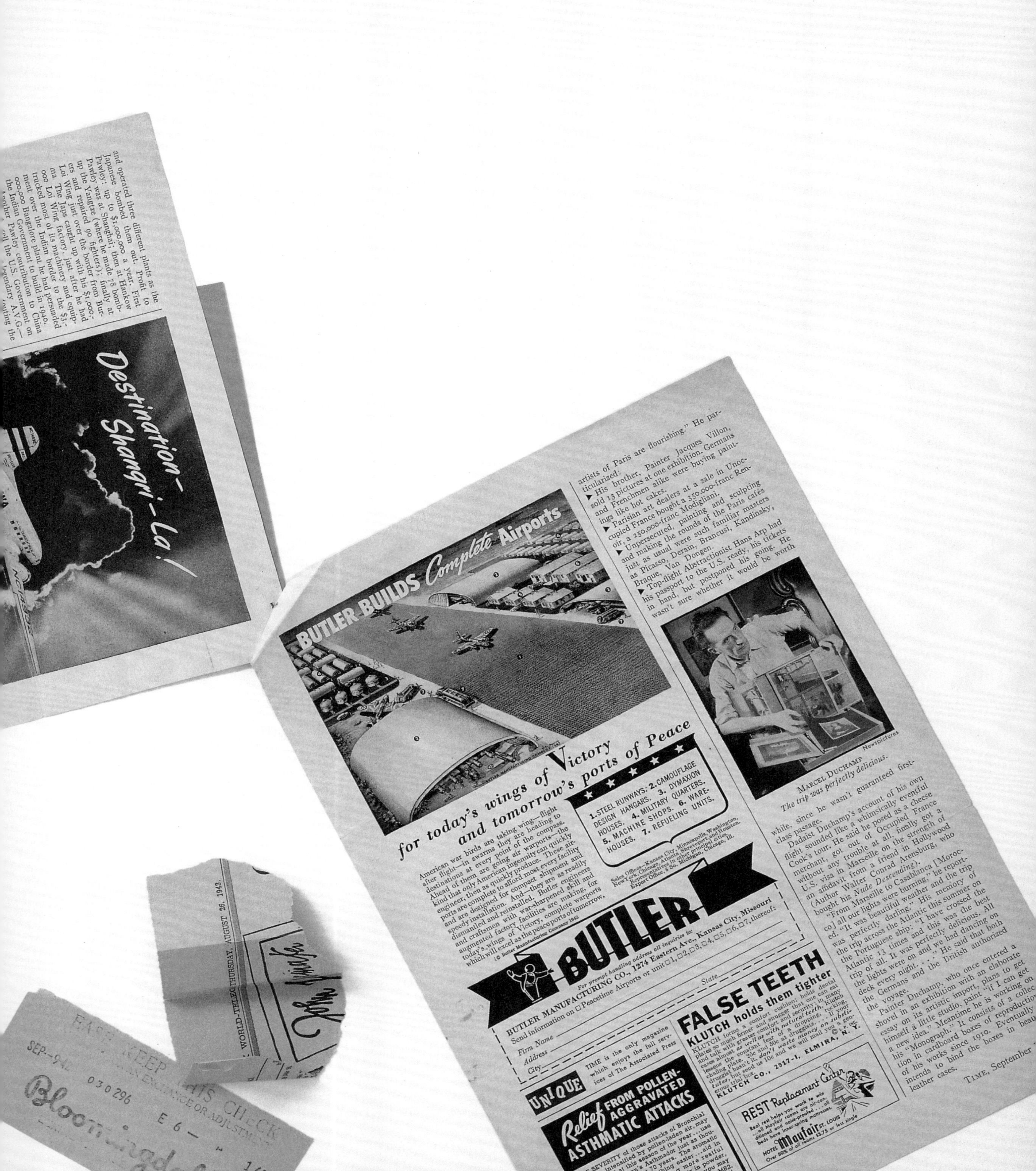

artists of Paris are flourishing." He particularized:

▶ His brother, Painter Jacques Villon, sold 13 pictures at one exhibition. Germans and Frenchmen alike were buying paintings like hot cakes.

▶ Parisian art dealers at a sale in Unoccupied France bought a 350,000-franc Renoir, a 250,000-franc Modigliani.

▶ Unpersecuted, painting and sculpting and making the rounds of the Paris cafés just as usual were such familiar masters as Picasso, Derain, Brancusi, Kandinsky, Braque, Van Dongen.

▶ Top-flight Abstractionist Hans Arp had his passport to the U.S. ready, his tickets in hand, but postponed his going. He wasn't sure whether it would be worth while, since he wasn't guaranteed first-class passage.

Dadaist Duchamp's account of his own flight sounded like a whimsically eventful Cook's tour. He said he posed as a cheese merchant, got out of Occupied France without any trouble at all, finally got a U.S. visa in Marseille on the strength of an affidavit from a friend in Hollywood (Author Walter Conrad Arensburg, who bought his *Nude Descending*).

"From Marseille to Casablanca [Morocco] all our lights were burning," he reported. "It was beautiful weather and the trip was perfectly darling." His memory of the trip across the Atlantic this summer on the Portuguese ship: "I have crossed the Atlantic 13 times and this was the best trip of all. It was perfectly delicious. All the lights were on and we had dancing on deck every night. . . ." He said that both the Germans and the British authorized the voyage.

Painter Duchamp, who once entered a shovel in an exhibition with an elaborate essay on its artistic import, plans to get himself a little studio, paint "if I can get a new idea." Meantime he is working on his "Monograph." It consists of a collection in cardboard boxes of reproductions of his works since 1910. Eventually he intends to bind the boxes in beautiful leather cases.

Newspictures

MARCEL DUCHAMP
The trip was perfectly delicious.

D

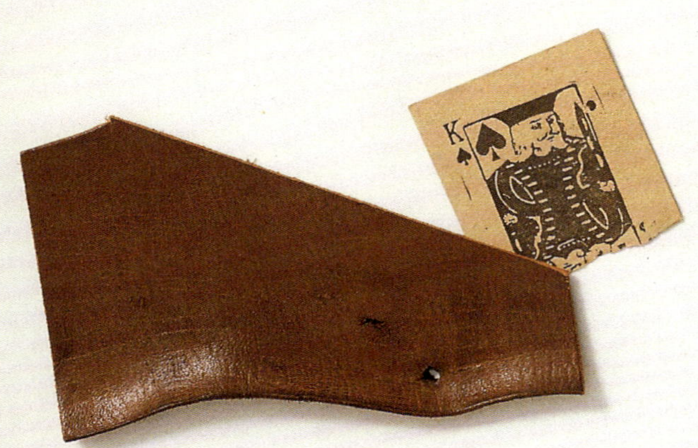

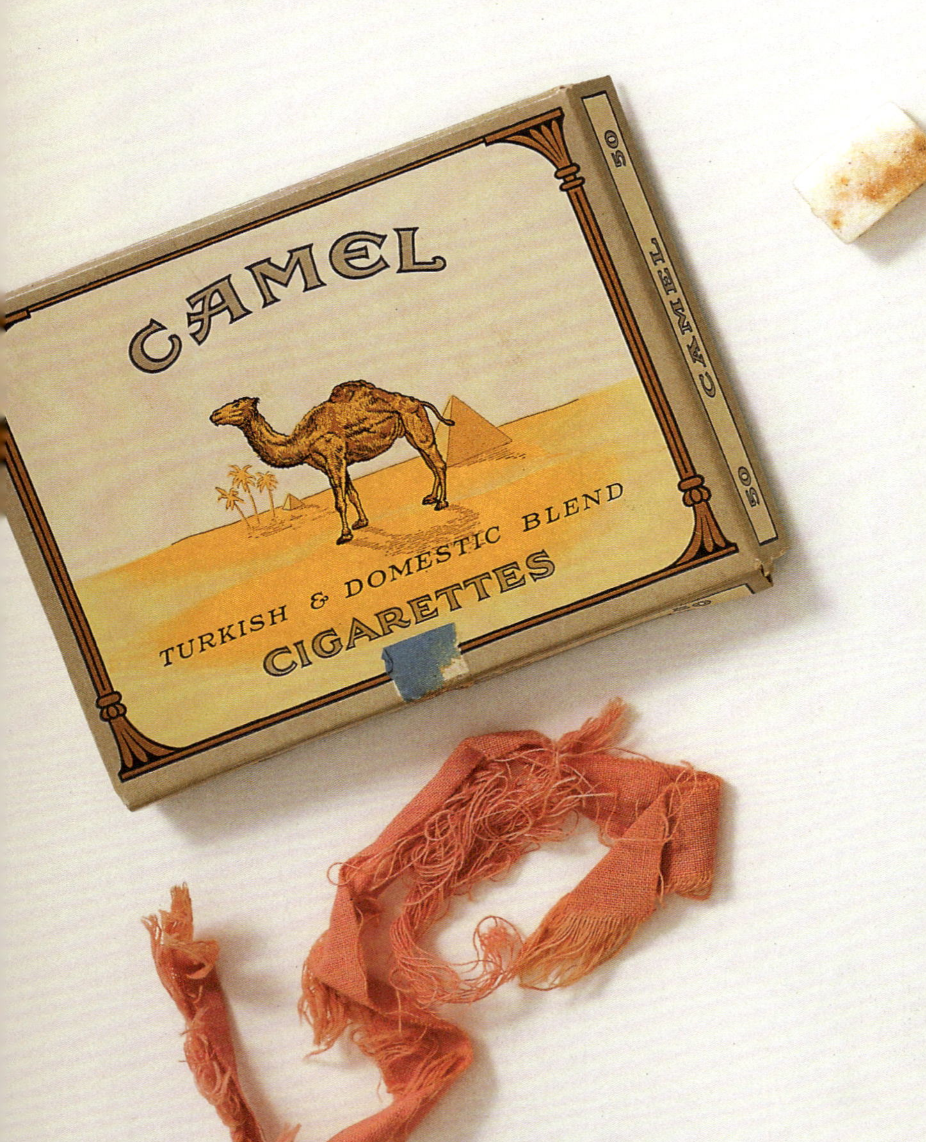

Bulletin de Souscription

Veuillez m'adresser
_______ exemplaires
de la boîte contenant les fac-simile et reproductions en couleurs de notes manuscrites, dessins, peintures ayant servi à la composition de

LA MARIÉE MISE A NU
PAR SES CÉLIBATAIRES, MÊME
par Marcel Duchamp

Ci-joint le montant en chèque barré ou en mandat-poste.

Nom et prénoms(1) _______
Adresse(1) _______
Date et Signature _______

(1) Prière d'écri

Adresser ce bulletin à
Rrose Sélavy
18 rue de l
P

en hors-texte,

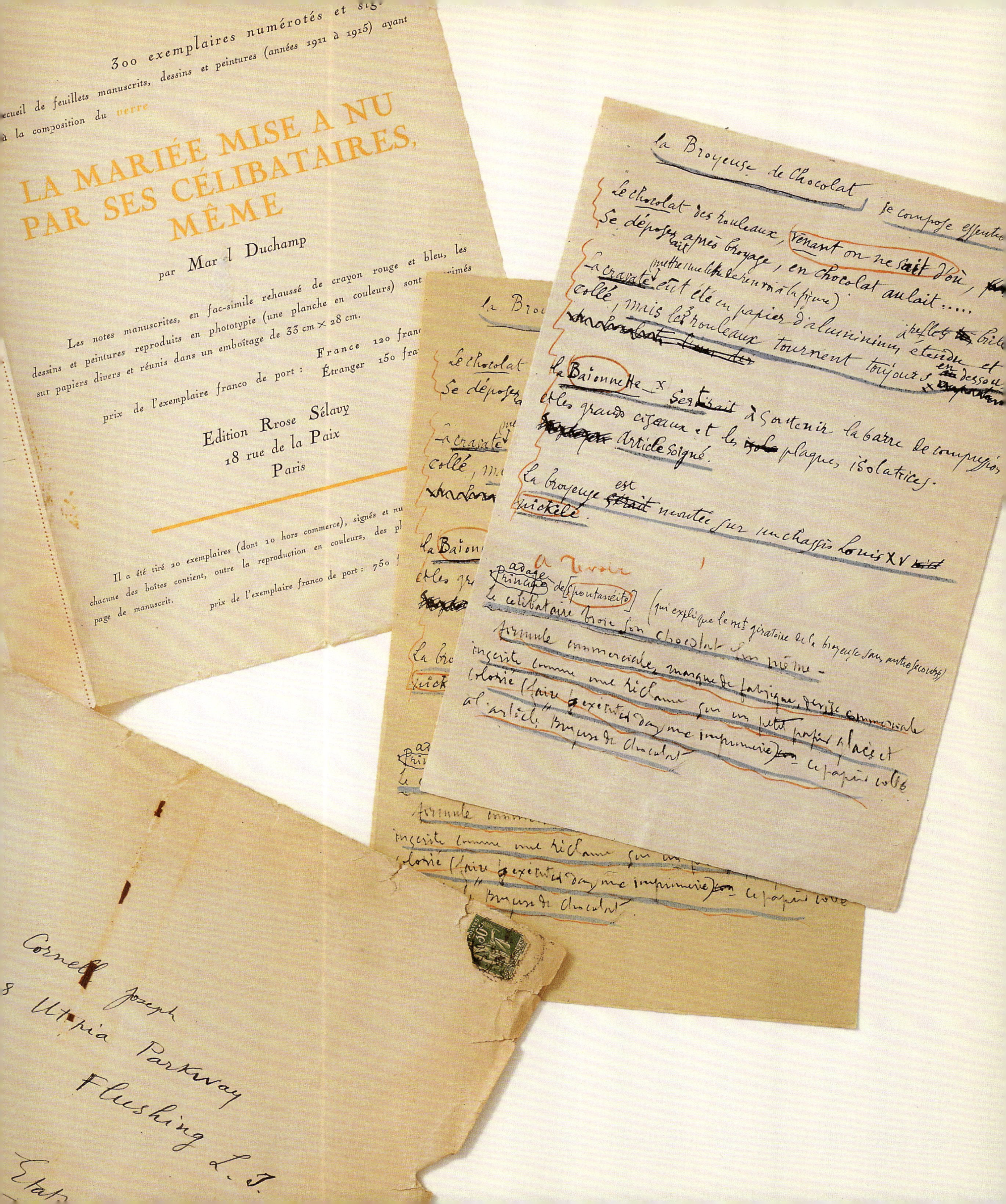

300 exemplaires numérotés et sig

ecueil de feuillets manuscrits, dessins et peintures (années 1911 à 1915) ayant à la composition du verre

LA MARIÉE MISE A NU PAR SES CÉLIBATAIRES, MÊME

par Mar l Duchamp

Les notes manuscrites, en fac-simile rehaussé de crayon rouge et bleu, les dessins et peintures reproduits en phototypie (une planche en couleurs) sont imprimés sur papiers divers et réunis dans un emboîtage de 33 cm × 28 cm.

prix de l'exemplaire franco de port : France 120 franc Étranger 150 fra

Edition Rrose Sélavy
18 rue de la Paix
Paris

Il a été tiré 20 exemplaires (dont 10 hors commerce), signés et nu chacune des boîtes contient, outre la reproduction en couleurs, des pl page de manuscrit.

prix de l'exemplaire franco de port : 750

la Broyeuse de Chocolat

Le chocolat des rouleaux, venant on ne sait d'où, se compose essentie
se déposerait après broyage, en chocolat au lait.....
(mettre une lettre de renvoi à la figure)
La cravate eût été en papier d'aluminium, étendu et collé, mais les rouleaux tournent toujours en dessous

La Baïonnette x servirait à soutenir la barre de compression et les grands ciseaux et les plaques isolatrices.
Article signé.

La broyeuse est nickelée montée sur un chassis Louis XV

A revoir

adage
Principe de spontanéité (qui explique le mvt giratoire de la broyeuse sans autre secours)
Le célibataire broie son chocolat lui-même –
Formule commerciale, marque de fabrique, devise commerciale inscrite comme une réclame sur un petit papier glacé et colorié (faire exécuter dans une imprimerie) — ce papier collé à l'article "Broyeuse de Chocolat"

Cornell Joseph
8 Utopia Parkway
Flushing L.I.
Etat

E

FRAGILE
JACKSON SALES COMPANY Corona, L. I. Wholesale & Retail Teas & Coffees
HAS AN APPOINTMENT
May 18 AT 4
A CHARGE WILL BE MADE.
PLAZA 3-7815
BEVERLY
THEATRE
50th STREET and 3rd AVENUE
Mid-Town's Most Comfortable Theatre
PHONE, Eldorado 5-8790
Program
WEEK BEGINNING SATURDAY, AUGUST 15th to SATURDAY, AUGUST 22nd
Continuous Performance Daily
COOL
Coming Sat.-Sun.-Mon. Aug. 22-23-24
Henry FONDA Lynn BARI Don AMECHE in
The Magnificent DOPE
ALSO
ANTON WALBROOK SALLY GRAY
SUICIDE SQUADRON
BALL OF FIRE
ALSO
"Simply magnificent."
1.0
1.2
1.4

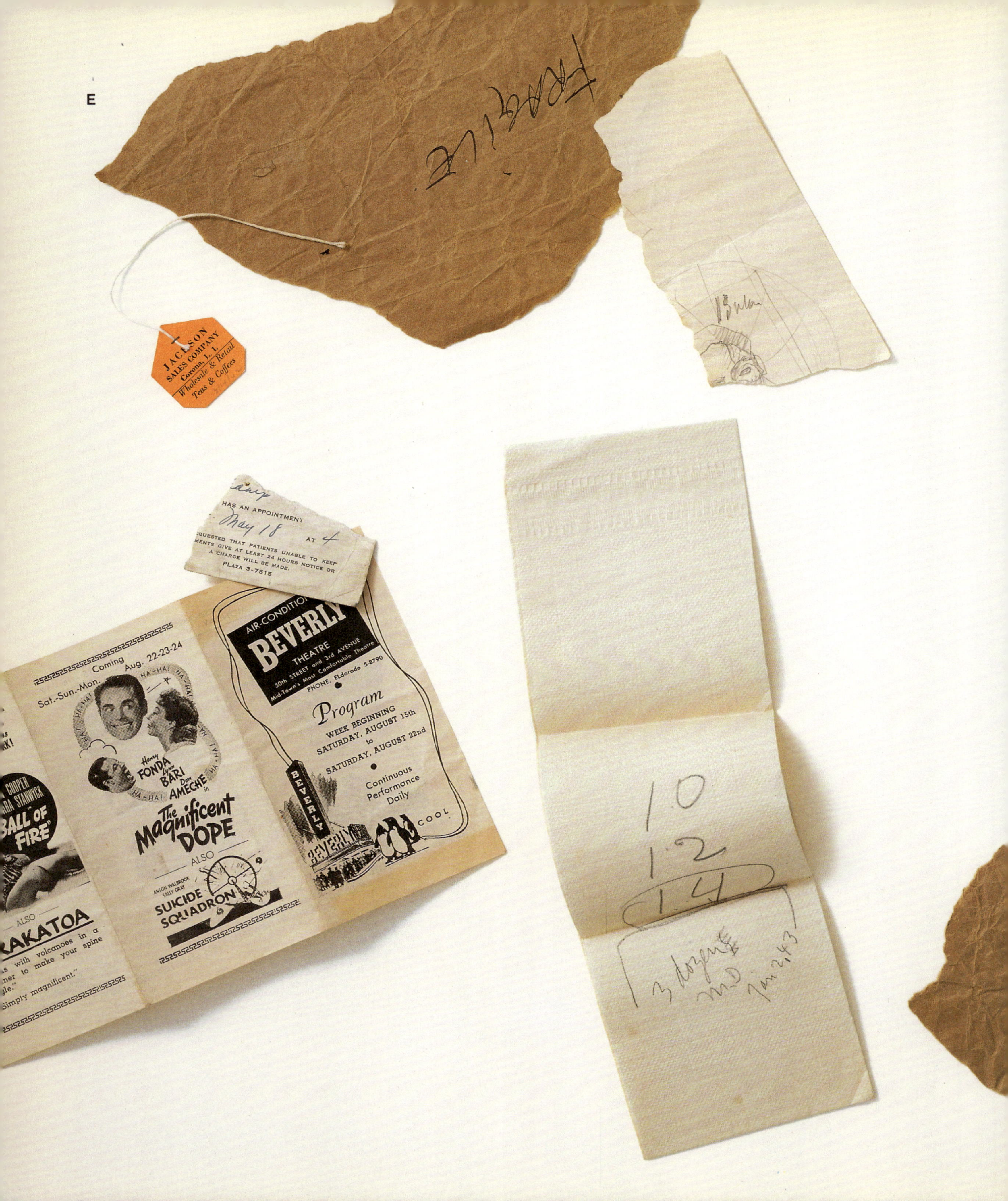

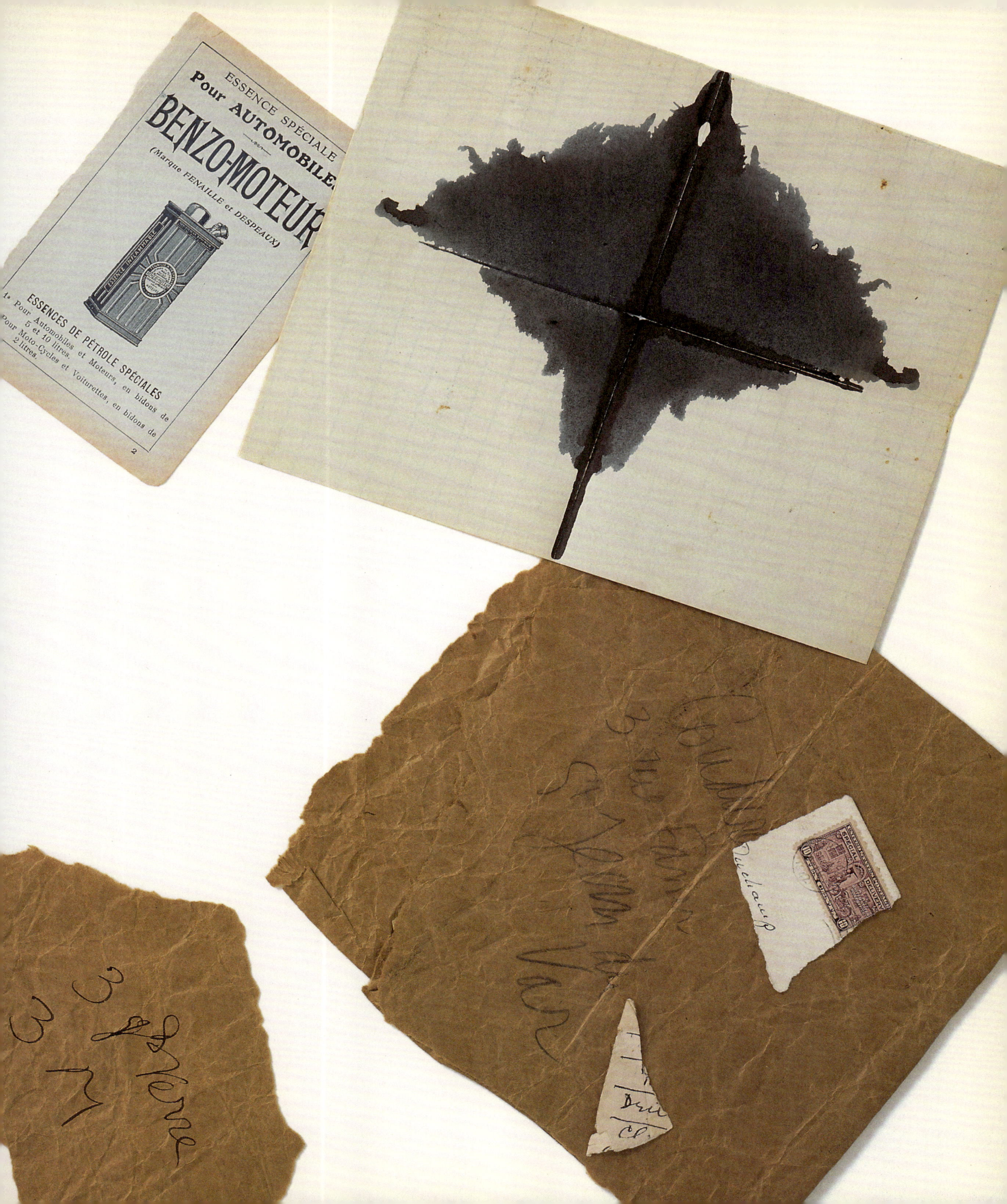
ESSENCE SPÉCIALE
Pour AUTOMOBILES
BENZO-MOTEUR
(Marque FENAILLE et DESPEAUX)
ESSENCES DE PÉTROLE SPÉCIALES
1° Pour Automobiles et Moteurs, en bidons de 5 et 10 litres.
Pour Moto-Cycles et Voiturettes, en bidons de 2 litres.
2

F

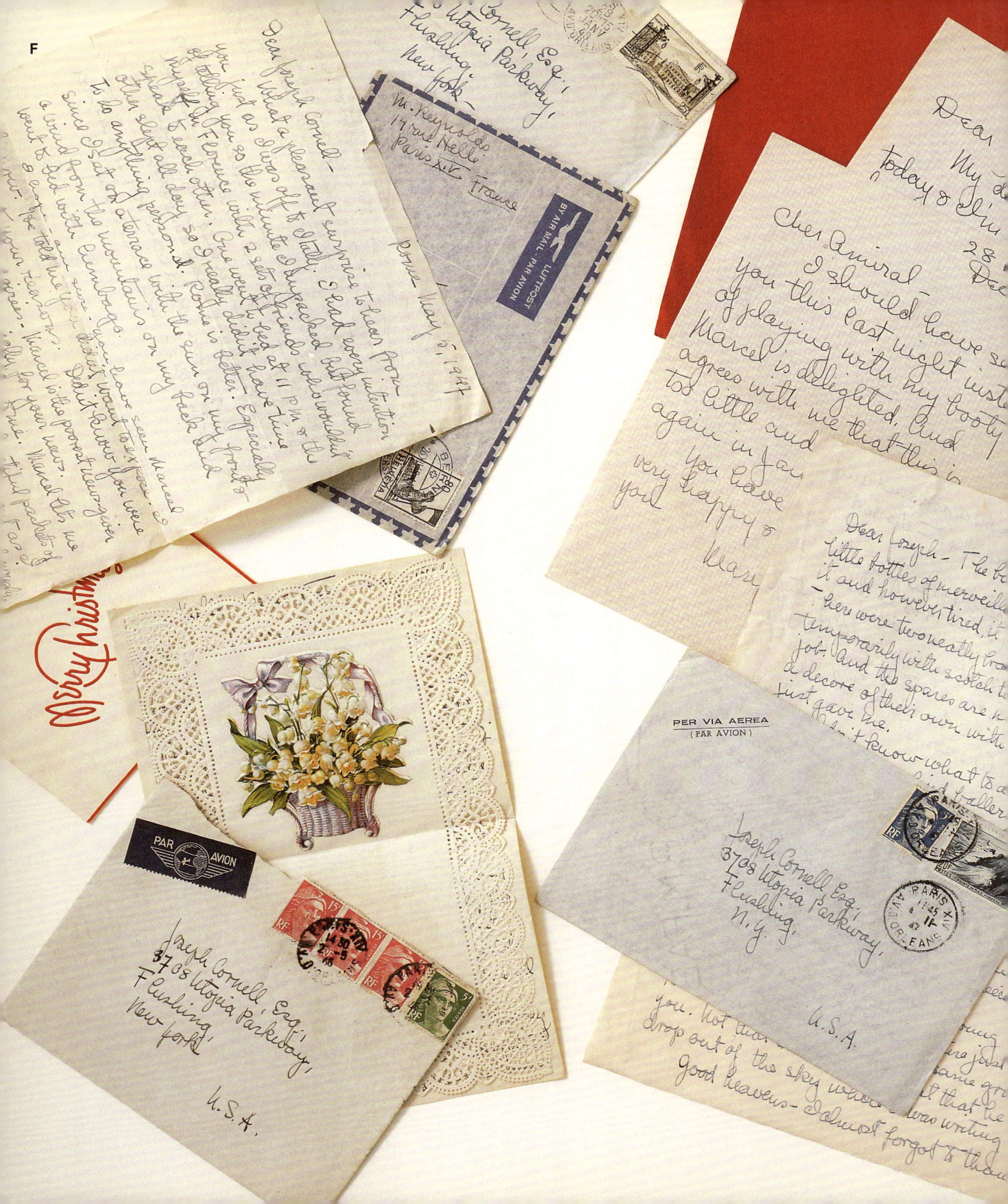

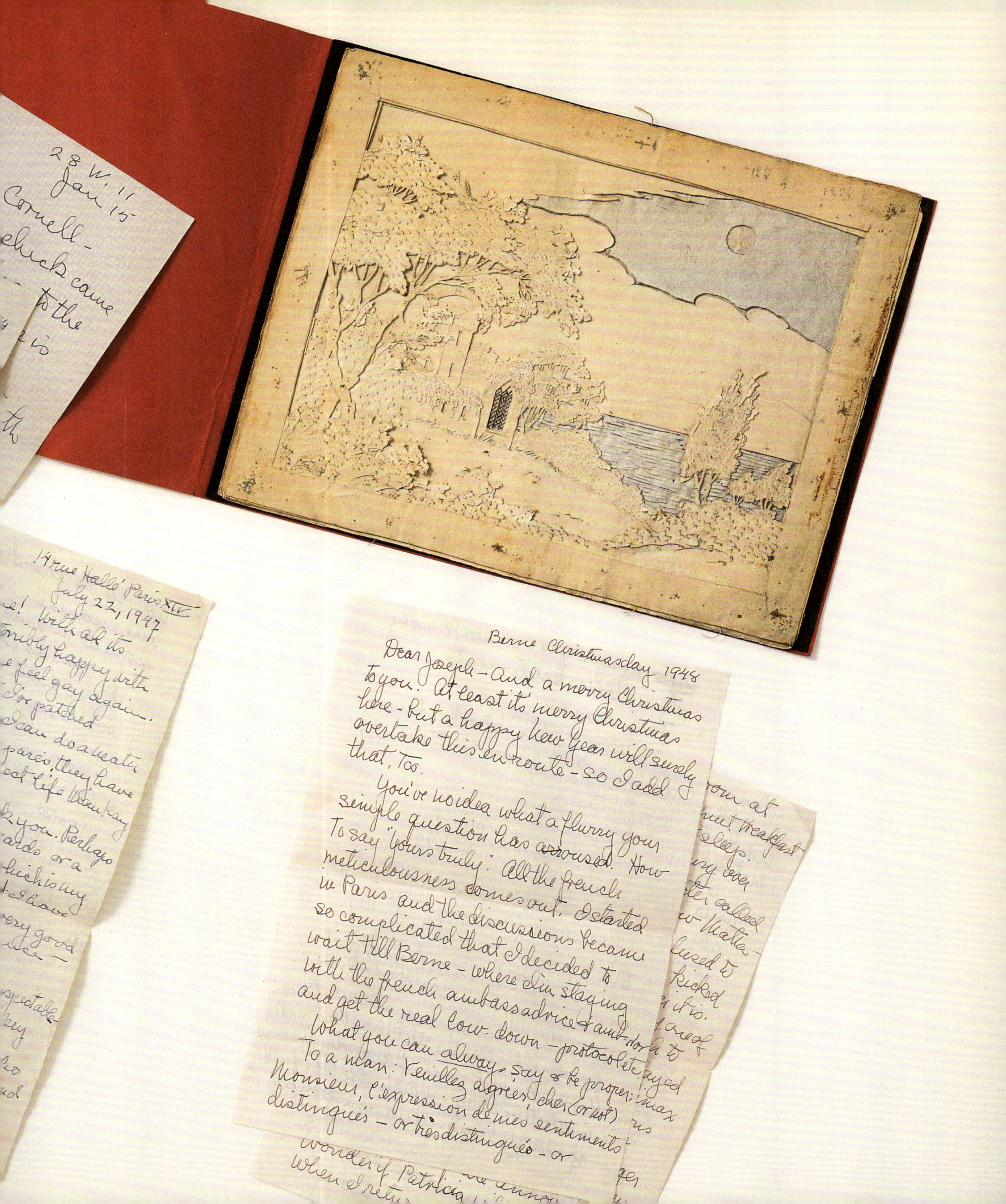

28 W. 11
Jan 15

14 rue Hallé Paris XIV
July 22, 1947

Berne Christmasday 1948

Dear Joseph - And a merry Christmas to you. At least it's merry Christmas here - but a happy New Year will surely overtake this en route - so I add that, too.

You've no idea what a flurry your single question has arroused. How To say "Yours truly". All the french meticulousness comes out. I started in Paris and the discussions became so complicated that I decided to wait till Berne - where I'm staying with the french ambassadrice & amb-dor & to and get the real low-down - protocolet. What you can always say & be proper: To a man: Veuillez agréer, cher (or not) Monsieur, l'expression de mes sentiments distingués - or très distingués - or

G

TELL ME WHY YOU SMILE, MONA LISA?
(Based on "Warum lächelst du, Mona Lisa?")
Including "JUST A CORPORAL"
(Based on "Du Dummer Kleiner Korporal)
From the
Super Production
der raub der
"MONA LISA"
(THE THEFT OF THE MONA LISA)
Distributed by
TOBIS FORENFILMS INC
Music by ROBERT STOLZ
Lyrics by WALTER REISCH
American Lyrics by
RAYMOND B. EGAN
Copyright 1931 by
International Cop
Published in Amer
56 COOPER
Sole and Exclusive
20 RALEIGH CIGARETTES
Received
from J. Cornell
one package
Aug. 26. 1943
Marcel Duchamp
Oct. 9 by proxy
BROWN & WILLIAMSON TOBACCO CORP. - LOUISVILLE, KY. U.S.A.
MADE IN U.S.A.
BURGOYNE'S SURRENDER—1777
—Mary Louise Lawser

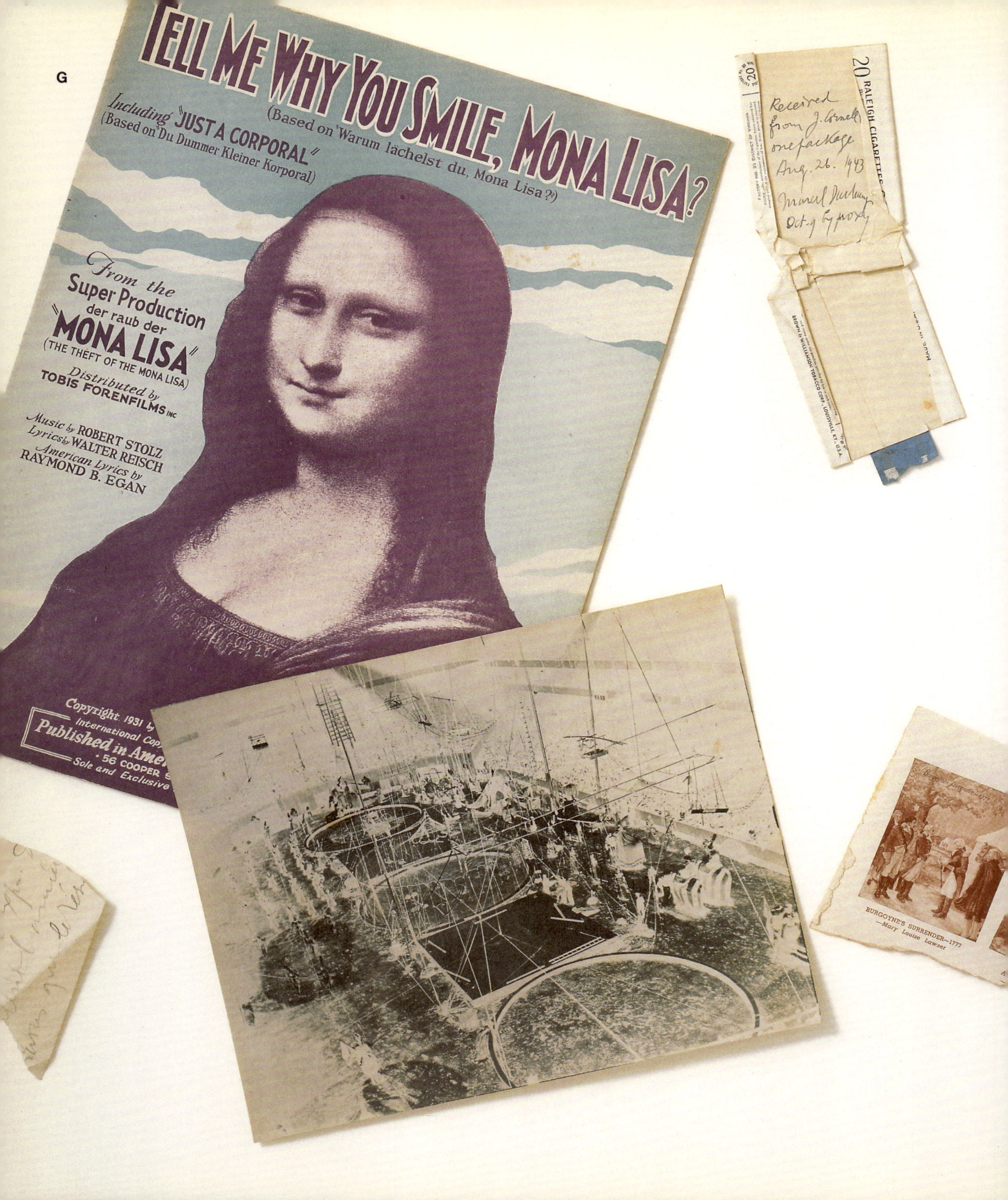

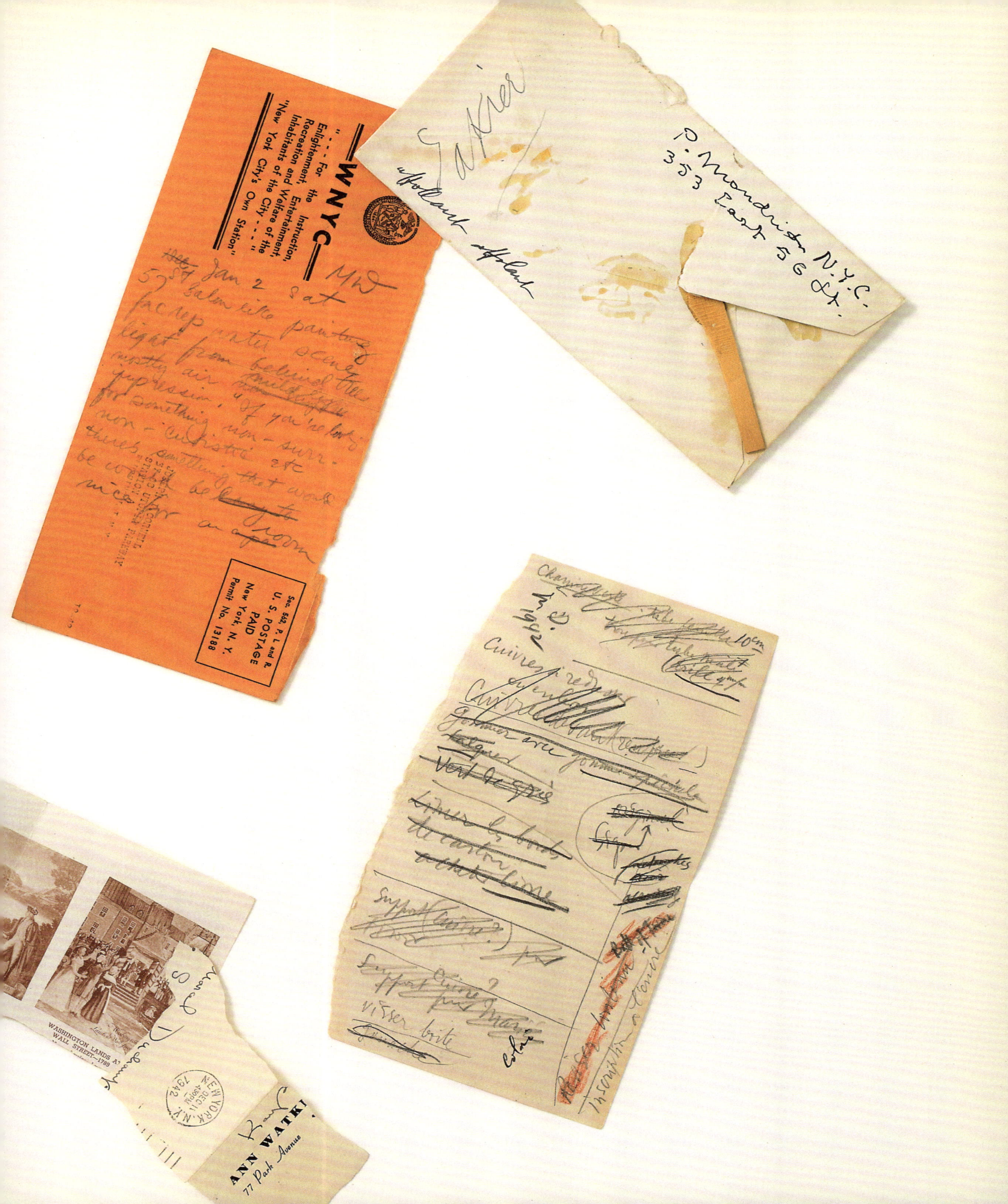
WNYC
"... For the Enlightenment, Instruction, Recreation and Entertainment, Inhabitants of and Welfare of the City ..."
"New York City's Own Station"
Sec. 562, P. L. and R.
U. S. POSTAGE
PAID
New York, N. Y.
Permit No. 13188
Jan 2 Sat
P. Mondrian N.Y.C.
353 East 56 St.
Holland
WASHINGTON LANDS A
WALL STREET—1789
NEW YORK, N.Y.
DEC 11 4:30PM
1942
ANN WATKI
77 Park Avenue

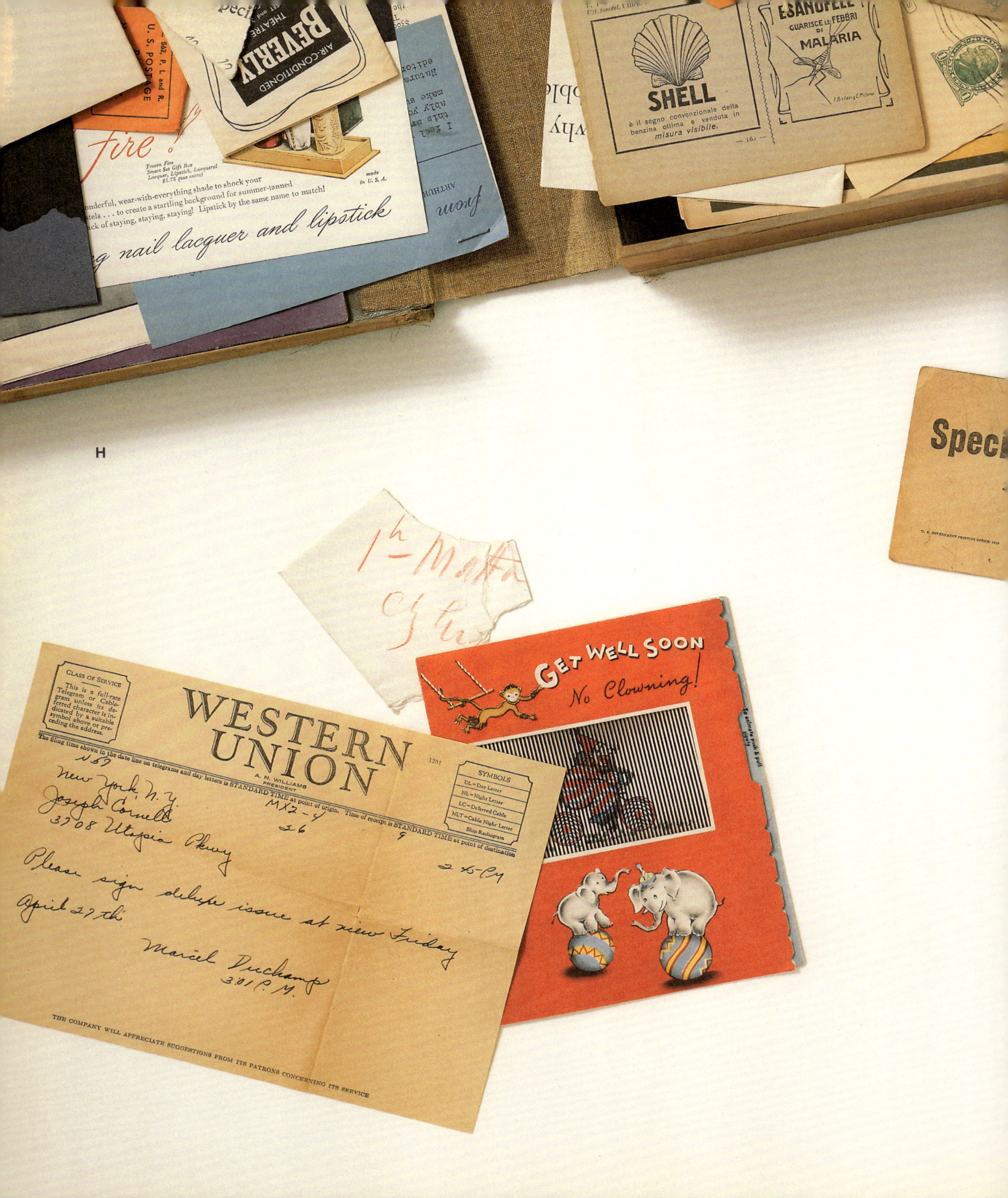

H

WESTERN UNION

A. N. WILLIAMS
PRESIDENT

CLASS OF SERVICE
This is a full-rate Telegram or Cablegram unless its deferred character is indicated by a suitable symbol above or preceding the address.

SYMBOLS
DL = Day Letter
NL = Night Letter
LC = Deferred Cable
NLT = Cable Night Letter
Ship Radiogram

The filing time shown in the date line on telegrams and day letters is STANDARD TIME at point of origin. Time of receipt is STANDARD TIME at point of destination

N57
MX2-4
26 9
New York, N.Y.
Joseph Cornell
3708 Utopia Pkwy

Please sign deluxe issue at view Friday April 27th.

Marcel Duchamp
3.01 P.M.

THE COMPANY WILL APPRECIATE SUGGESTIONS FROM ITS PATRONS CONCERNING ITS SERVICE

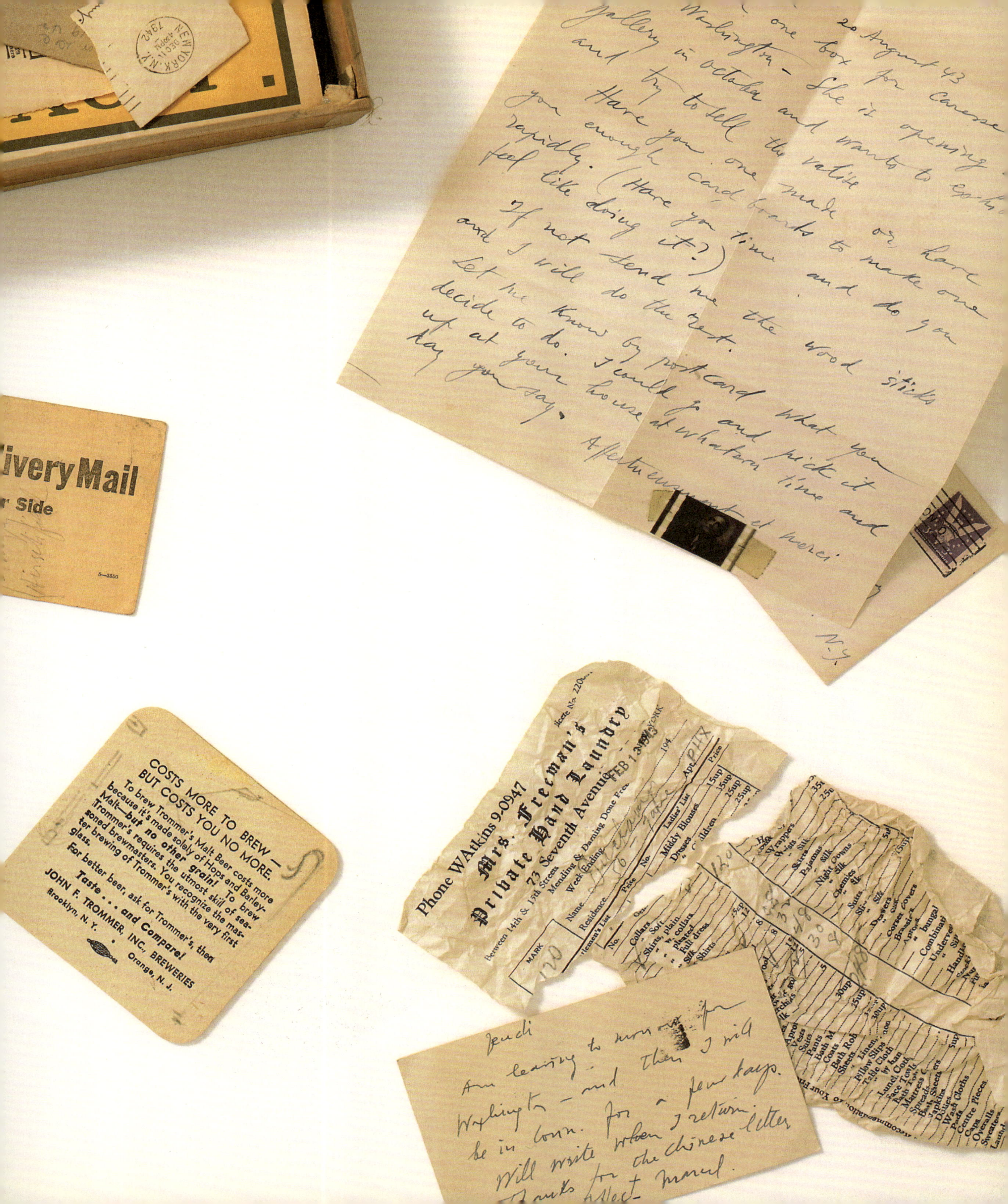
20 August 43
one box for Caresse
gallery in Washington - She is opening
and in October and wants to
try to sell the valise
Have you one made or have
you enough cardboards to make one
rapidly. (Have you time and do you
feel like doing it?)
If not send me the wood sticks
and I will do the rest.
Let me know by postcard what you
decide to do. I could go and pick it
up at your house at whatever time and
day you say.
Affectueusement et merci
COSTS MORE TO BREW — BUT COSTS YOU NO MORE.
To brew Trommer's Malt Beer costs more because it's made solely of Hops and Barley-Malt—but no other grain! To brew Trommer's requires the utmost skill of seasoned brewmasters. You recognize the master brewing of Trommer's with the very first glass.
For better beer, ask for Trommer's, then Taste . . . and Compare!
JOHN F. TROMMER, INC., BREWERIES
Brooklyn, N.Y. Orange, N.J.
Phone WAtkins 9-0947
Mrs. Freeman's Private Hand Laundry
73 Seventh Avenue
Between 14th & 15th Streets
Mending & Darning Done Free
Jeudi
Am leaving to morrow for
Washington - and then I will
be in town for a few days.
Will write when I return.
Thanks for the chinese letter
affect. Marcel

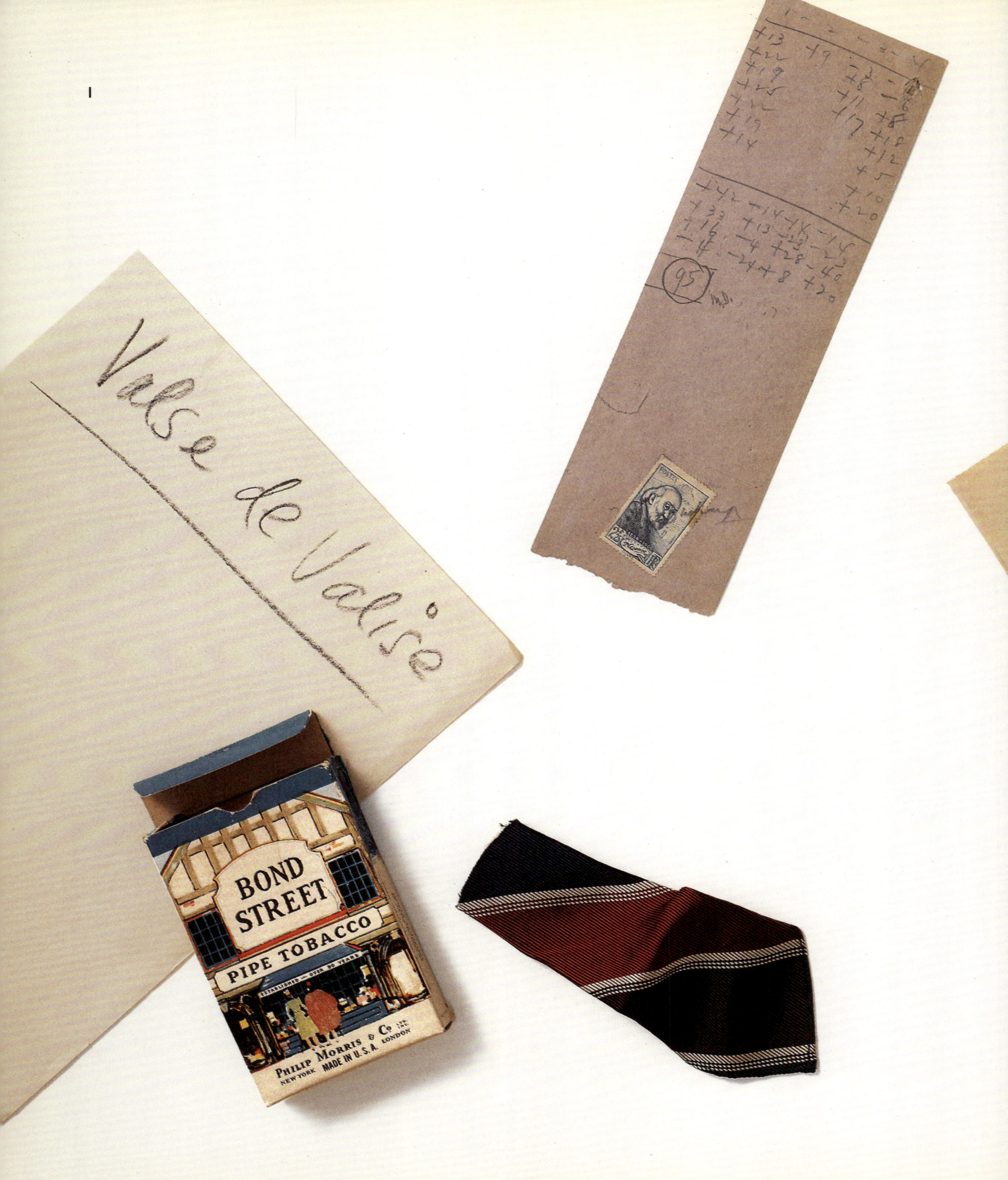
Valse de Valise
BOND STREET
PIPE TOBACCO
PHILIP MORRIS & Co
NEW YORK
MADE IN U.S.A.
LONDON
95

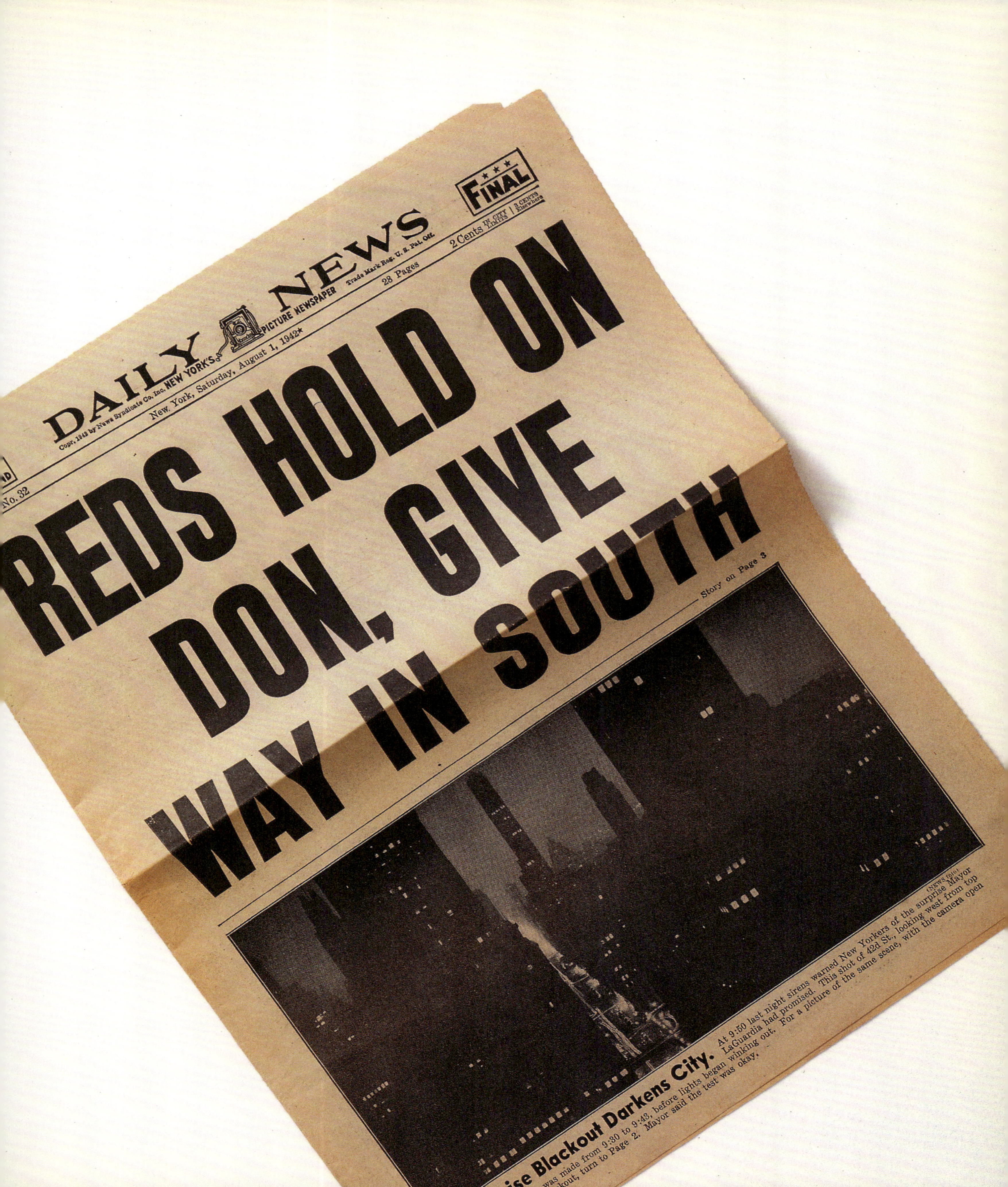

DAILY NEWS

NEW YORK'S PICTURE NEWSPAPER

Copr. 1942 by News Syndicate Co. Inc. Trade Mark Reg. U. S. Pat. Off.

No. 32 New York, Saturday, August 1, 1942★ 28 Pages 2 Cents IN CITY LIMITS | 3 CENTS Elsewhere

★★★ FINAL

REDS HOLD ON DON, GIVE WAY IN SOUTH

Story on Page 3

rise Blackout Darkens City. At 9:50 last night sirens warned New Yorkers of the surprise Mayor LaGuardia had promised. This shot of 42d St., looking west from top was made from 9:30 to 9:43, before lights began winking out. For a picture of the same scene, with the camera open lackout, turn to Page 2. Mayor said the test was okay.

(NEWS foto)

J

MUSÉE DU LOUVRE.
LEONARD DE VINCI. - LA JOCONDE.
notice nose tip
DELMONICO HAND LAUNDRY
Dry Cleaning Exclusive Hand Service
Tel. MUrray Hill 4-2080
835 SECOND AVENUE, NEW YORK
Bet. 44th & 45th Streets
AUG 22 1942
Week Ending
Name
Residence
Apt.
MARK
No.
Gentlemen's List
Price
Ladies' List
Collars, starched
" soft
Collarettes

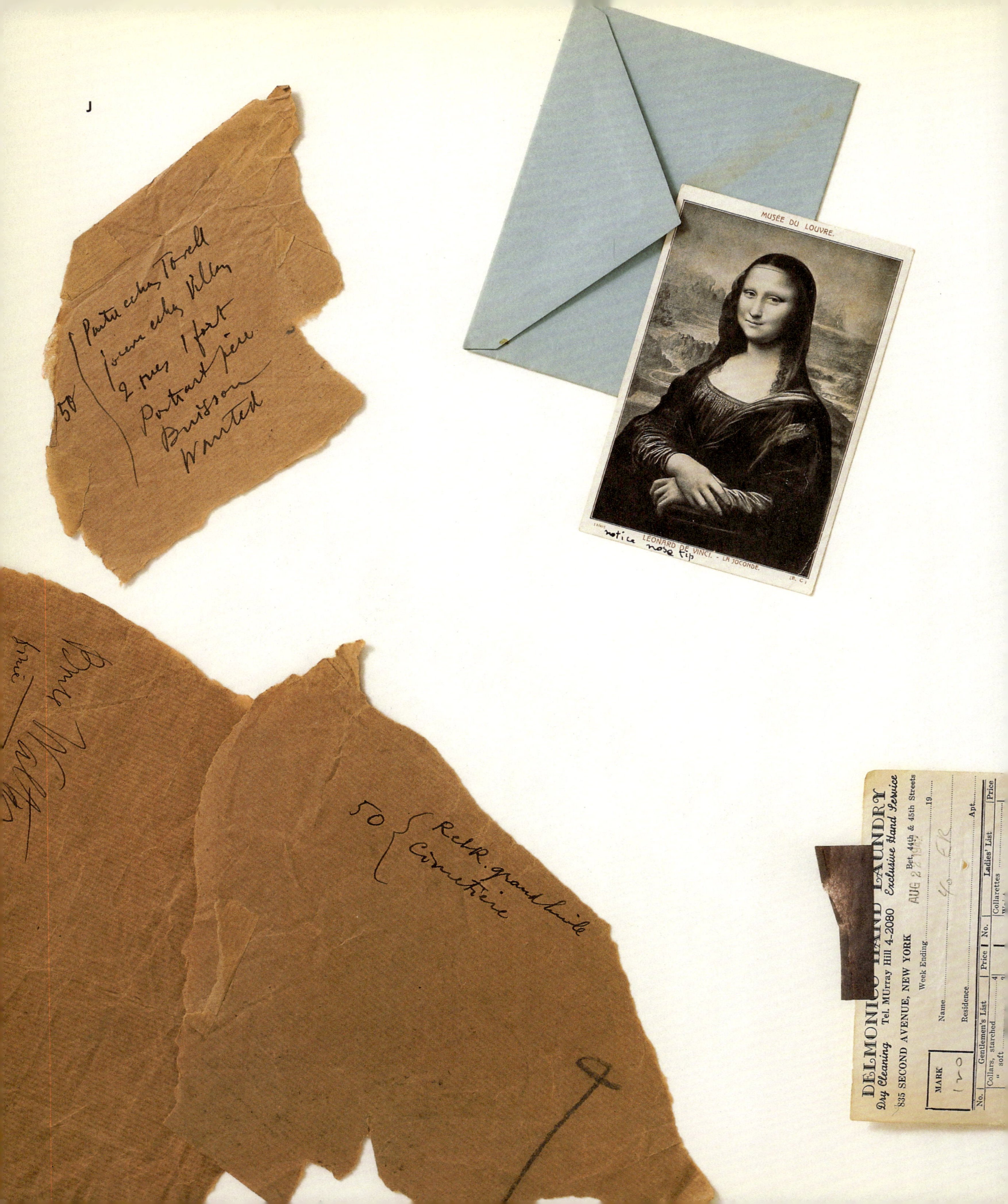

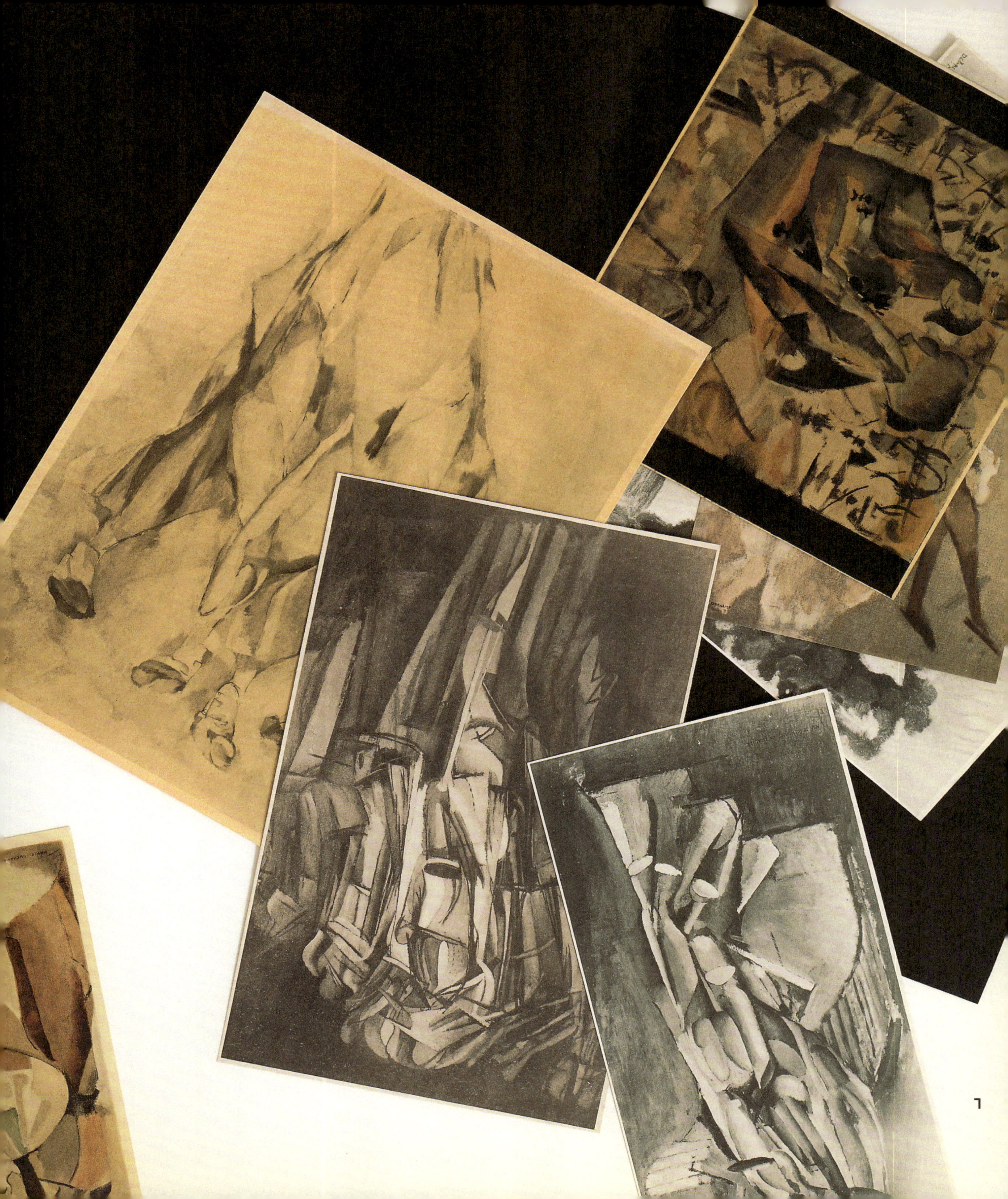

7

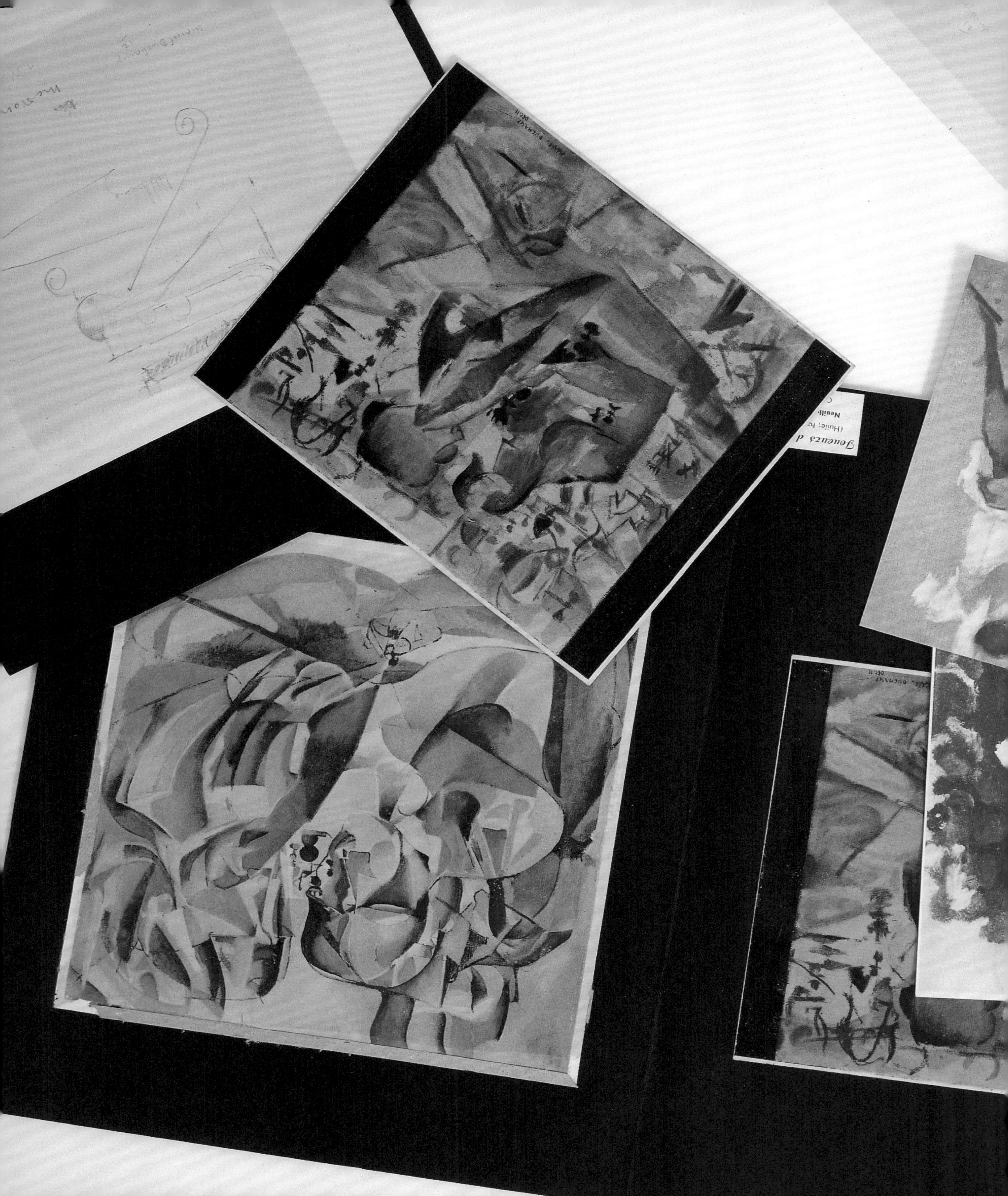

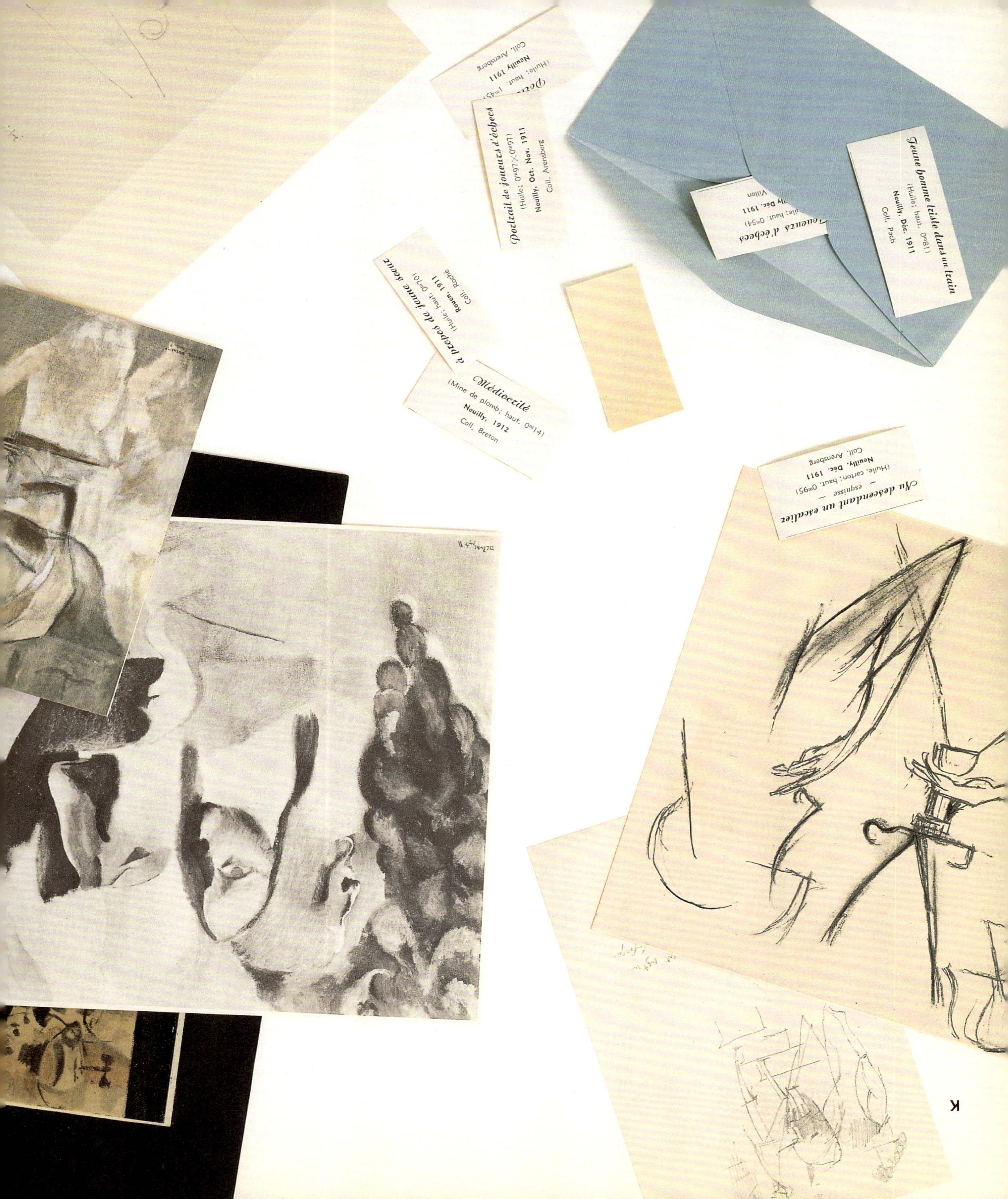

Portrait de joueurs d'échecs
(Huile; $0^{m}97 \times 0^{m}97$)
Neuilly, Oct. Nov. 1911
Coll. Arensberg
Jeune homme triste dans un train
(Huile; haut. $0^{m}81$)
Neuilly, Déc. 1911
Coll. Pach
oueurs d'échecs
(Huile; haut. $0^{m}54$)
Déc. 1911
Villon
(Huile; haut.
Neuilly 1911
Coll. Arensberg
A propos de jeune sœur
(Huile; haut. $0^{m}70$)
Rouen, 1911
Coll. Roche
Médiocrité
(Mine de plomb; haut. $0^{m}14$)
Neuilly, 1912
Coll. Breton
Nu descendant un escalier
— esquisse —
(Huile, carton; haut. $0^{m}95$)
Neuilly, Déc. 1911
Coll. Arensberg
K

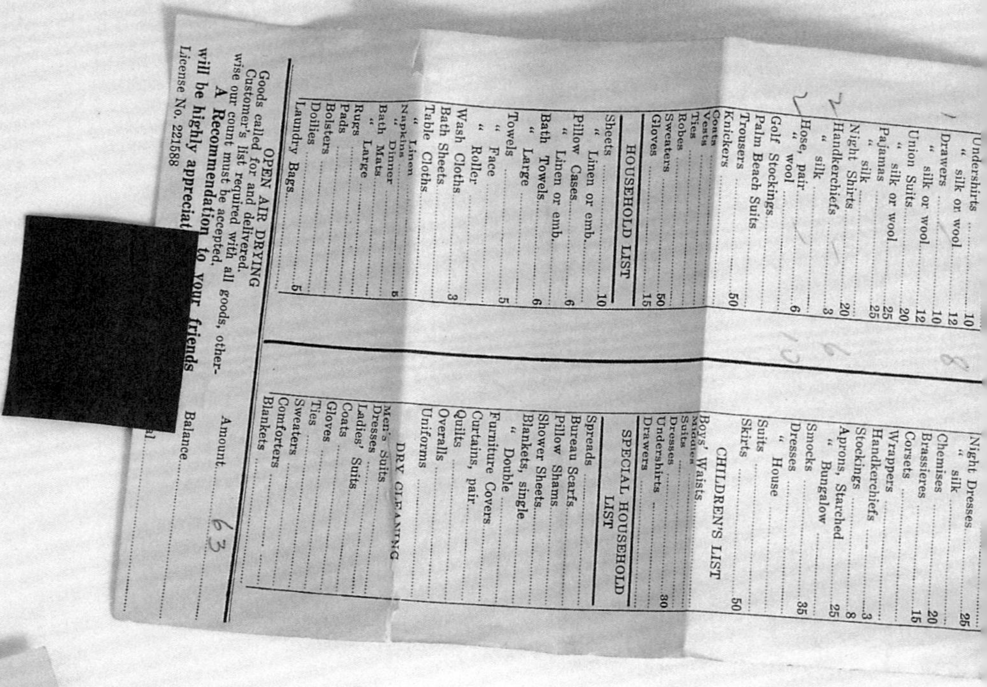

Item	Price
Undershirts	10
" silk or wool	12
Drawers	10
" silk or wool	12
Union Suits	20
" silk or wool	25
Pajamas	25
" silk	
Night Shirts	20
Handkerchiefs	3
" silk	
Hose, pair	6
" wool	
Golf Stockings	
Palm Beach Suits	
Trousers	
Knickers	50
Coats	
Vests	
Ties	
Robes	
Sweaters	50
Gloves	15

HOUSEHOLD LIST

Item	Price
Sheets	10
" Linen or emb.	
Pillow Cases	6
" Linen or emb.	
Bath Towels	6
" Large	
Towels	5
" Face	
" Roller	
Wash Cloths	3
Bath Sheets	
Table Cloths	
" Linen	
Napkins	5
" Dinner	
Bath Mats	
" Large	
Rugs	
Pads	
Bolsters	
Doilies	
Laundry Bags	5

Item	Price
Night Dresses	25
" silk	
Chemises	20
Brassieres	15
Corsets	
Wrappers	
Handkerchiefs	3
Stockings	8
Aprons, Starched	25
" Bungalow	
Smocks	
Dresses	35
" House	
Suits	
Skirts	50

CHILDREN'S LIST

Item	Price
Boys' Waists	
Middies	
Suits	
Dresses	30
Undershirts	
Drawers	

SPECIAL HOUSEHOLD LIST

Item	Price
Spreads	
Bureau Scarfs	
Pillow Shams	
Shower Sheets	
Blankets, single	
" Double	
Furniture Covers	
Curtains, pair	
Quilts	
Overalls	
Uniforms	

DRY CLEANING

Item	Price
Men's Suits	
Dresses	
Ladies' Suits	
Coats	
Gloves	
Ties	
Sweaters	
Comforters	
Blankets	

OPEN AIR DRYING

Goods called for and delivered.
Customer's list required with all goods, otherwise our count must be accepted.
A Recommendation to your friends will be highly appreciat
License No. 221588

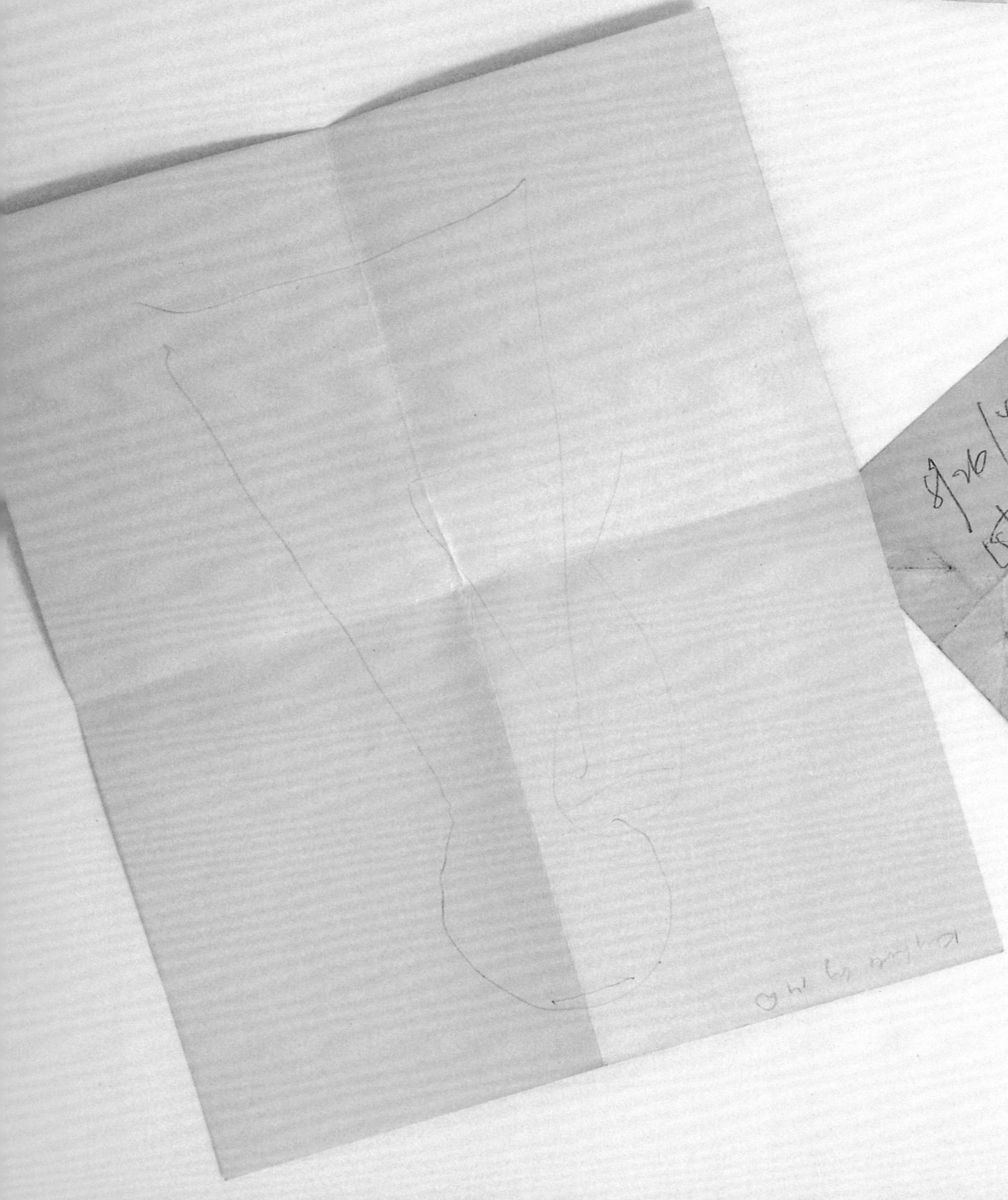

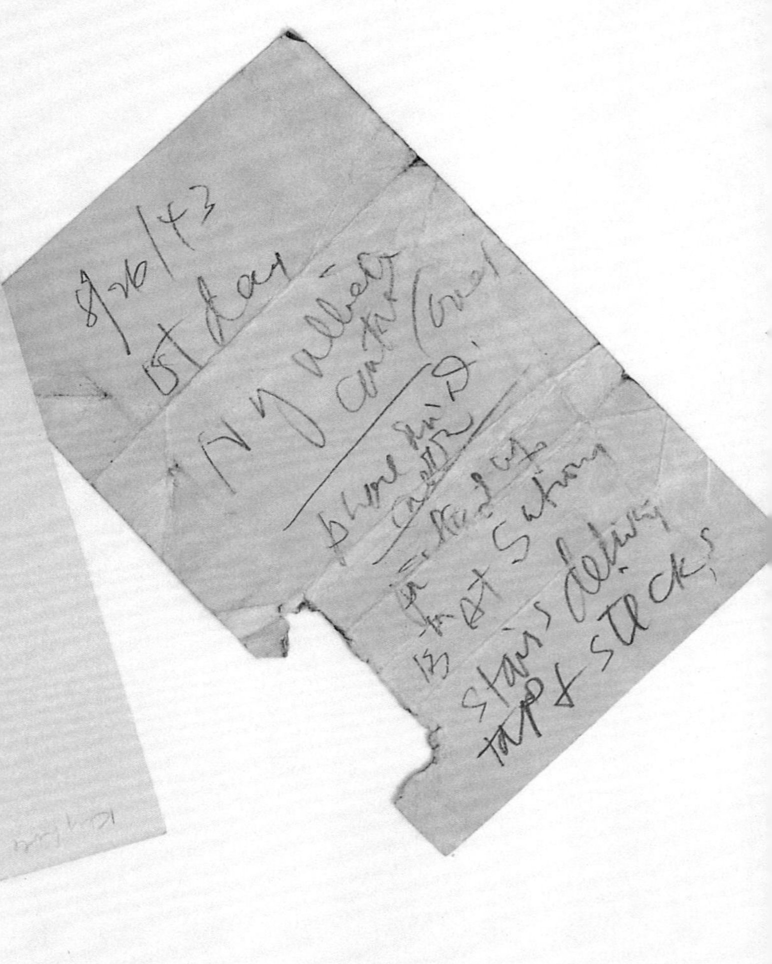

Amount 63
Balance
al

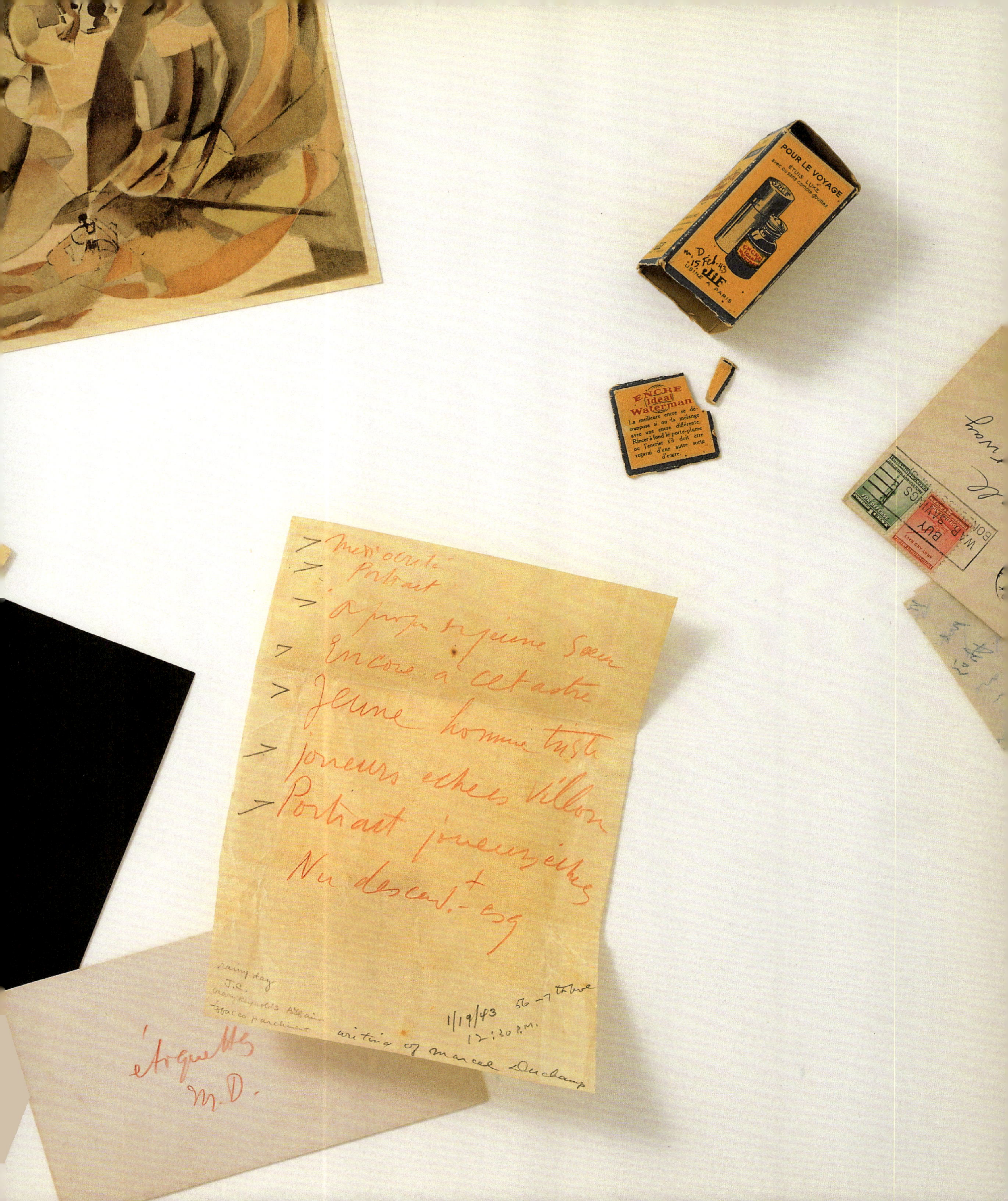
POUR LE VOYAGE
ETUIS LUXE
USINE A PARIS
ENCRE
Idéal
Waterman
La meilleure encre se décompose si on la mélange avec une encre différente. Rincer à fond le porte-plume ou l'encrier s'il doit être regarni d'une autre sorte d'encre.
Médiocrité
Portrait
à propos de jeune sœur
Encore à cet astre
Jeune homme triste
joueurs échecs Villon
Portrait joueurs échecs
Nu descent. + esq
1/19/43
12:30 A.M.
writing of marcel Duchamp
étiquettes
M.D.

M

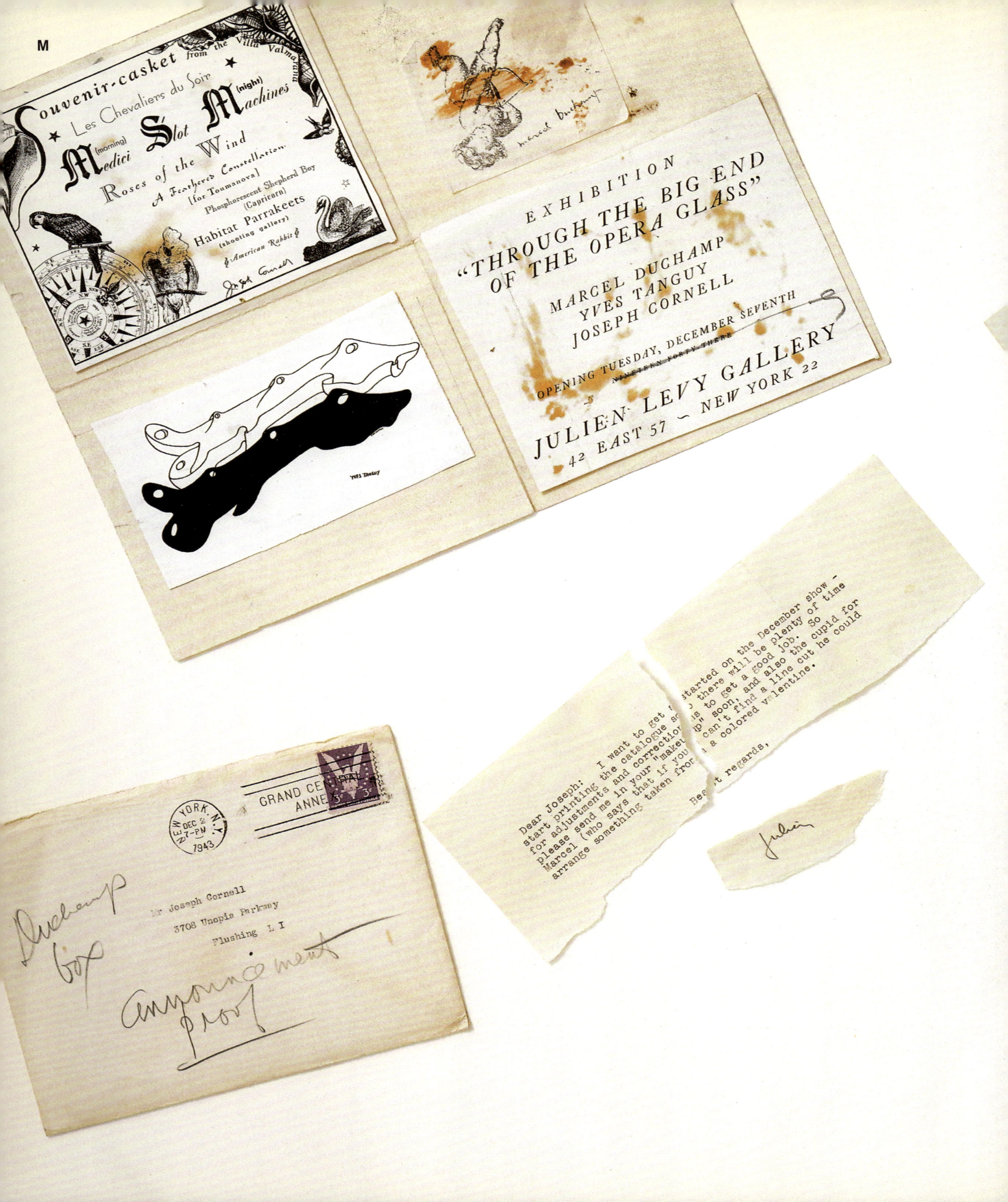

Souvenir-casket from the Villa Valmarana
Les Chevaliers du Soir
Medici (morning) Slot (night) Machines
Roses of the Wind
A Feathered Constellation
[for Toumanova]
Phosphorescent Shepherd Boy
(Capricorn)
Habitat Parrakeets
(shooting gallery)
American Rabbit
Joseph Cornell

Marcel Duchamp

EXHIBITION
"THROUGH THE BIG END
OF THE OPERA GLASS"
MARCEL DUCHAMP
YVES TANGUY
JOSEPH CORNELL
OPENING TUESDAY, DECEMBER SEVENTH
~~NINETEEN FORTY-THREE~~
JULIEN LEVY GALLERY
42 EAST 57 ~ NEW YORK 22

YVES TANGUY

GRAND CENTRAL ANNEX
NEW YORK, N.Y. DEC 2 7-PM 1943

Mr Joseph Cornell
3708 Unopia Parkway
Flushing L I

Duchamp box
announcement proof

Dear Joseph: I want to get started on the December show - start printing the catalogue so that there will be plenty of time for adjustments and corrections to get a good job. So please send me in your "makeup" soon, and also the cupid for Marcel (who says that if you can't find a line cut he could arrange something taken from a colored valentine.

Best regards,

Julien

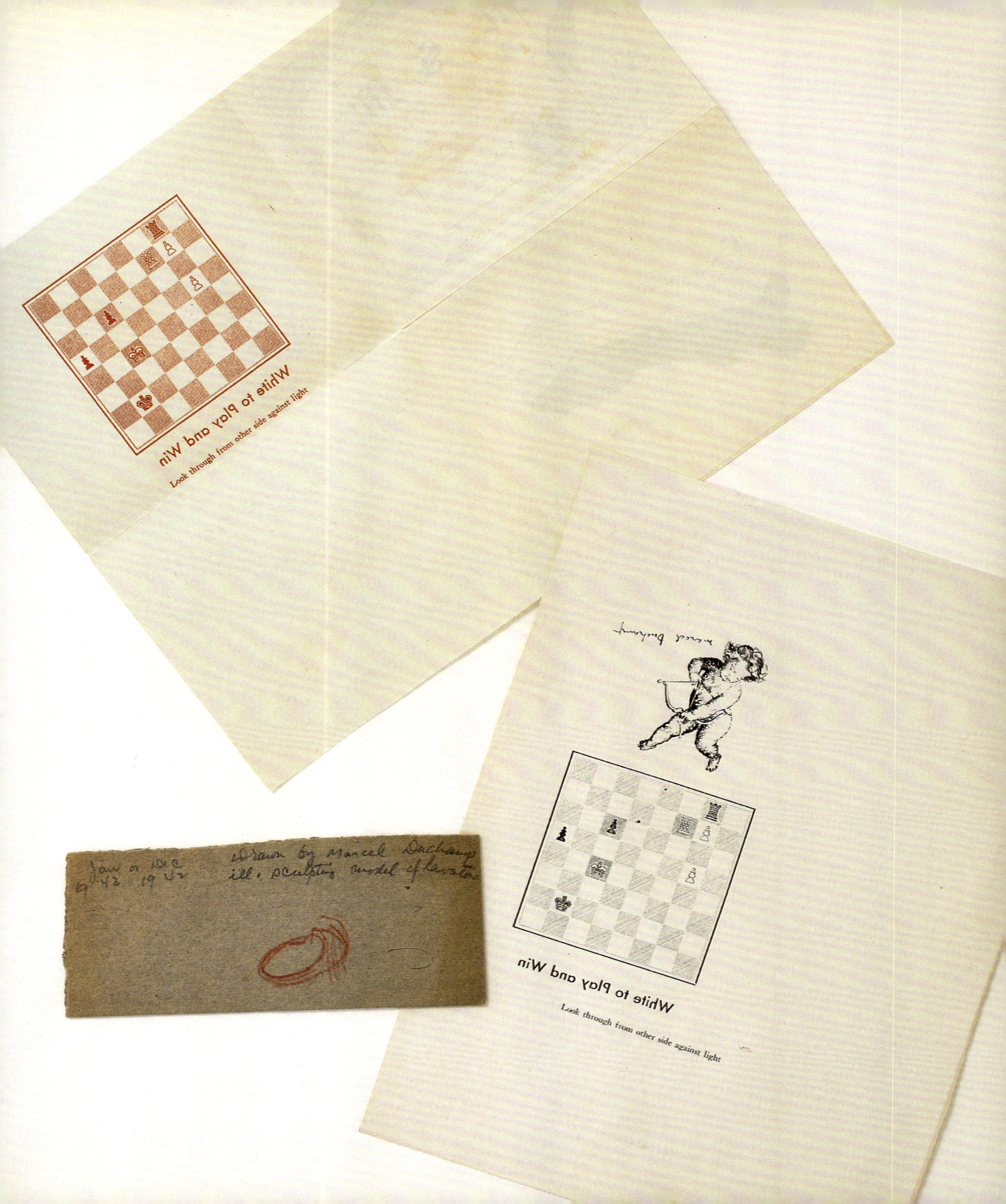

White to Play and Win

Look through from other side against light

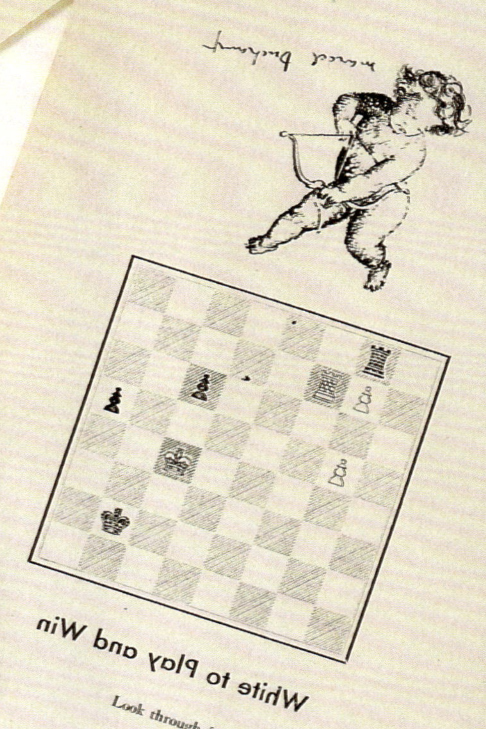

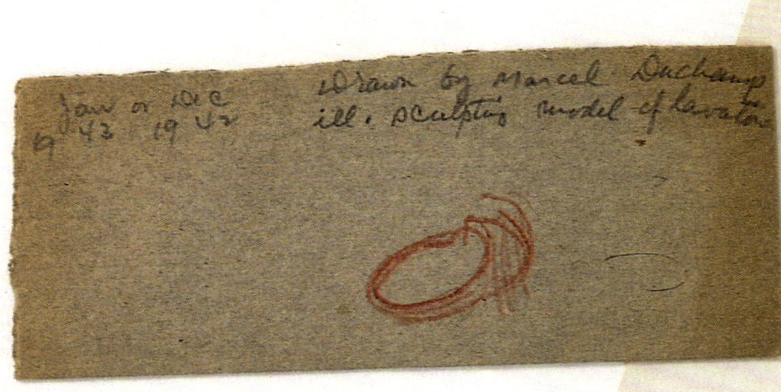

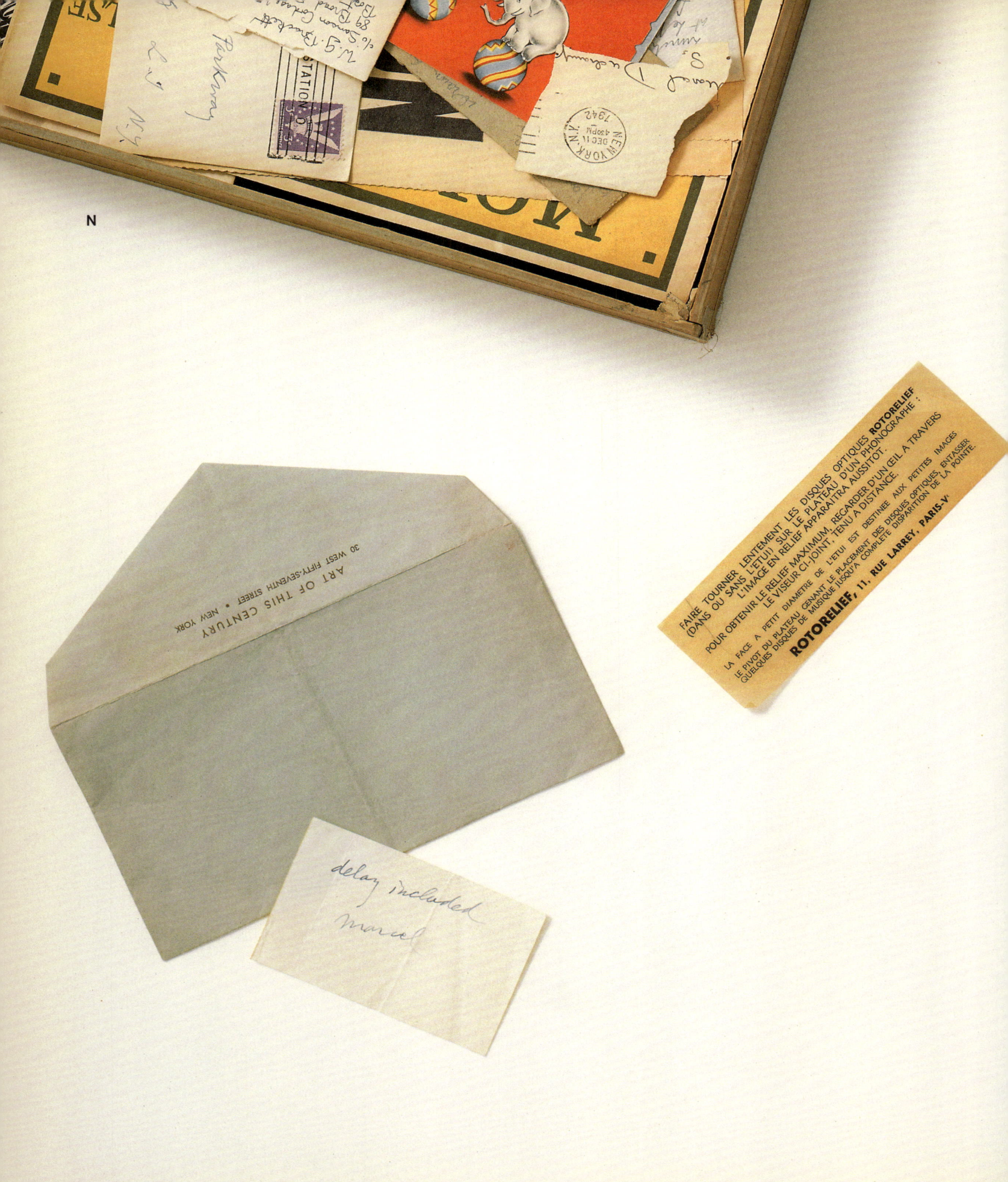
NEW YORK, N.Y. DEC 11 4:30PM 1942
ART OF THIS CENTURY
30 WEST FIFTY-SEVENTH STREET • NEW YORK
delay included
marcel
FAIRE TOURNER LENTEMENT LES DISQUES OPTIQUES ROTORELIEF
(DANS OU SANS L'ETUI) SUR LE PLATEAU D'UN PHONOGRAPHE :
L'IMAGE EN RELIEF APPARAITRA AUSSITOT.
POUR OBTENIR LE RELIEF MAXIMUM, REGARDER D'UN ŒIL A TRAVERS
LE VISEUR CI-JOINT, TENU A DISTANCE.
LA FACE A PETIT DIAMETRE DE L'ETUI EST DESTINEE AUX PETITES IMAGES
LE PIVOT DU PLATEAU GENANT LE PLACEMENT DES DISQUES OPTIQUES, ENTASSER
QUELQUES DISQUES DE MUSIQUE JUSQU'A COMPLETE DISPARITION DE LA POINTE.
ROTORELIEF, 11, RUE LARREY, PARIS-V

N

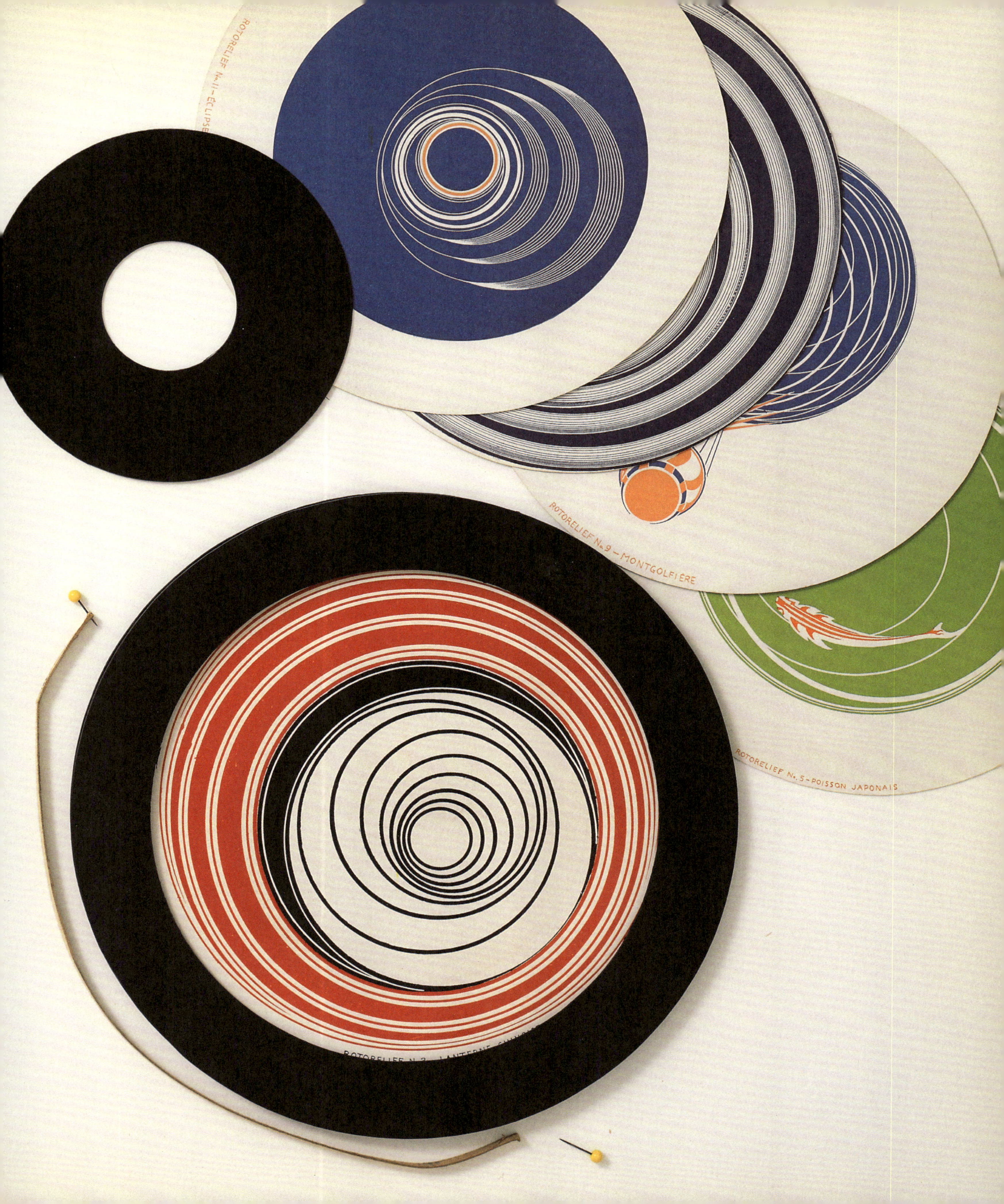
ROTORELIEF N.o 11 – ÉCLIPSE
ROTORELIEF N.o 9 – MONTGOLFIÈRE
ROTORELIEF N.o 5 – POISSON JAPONAIS

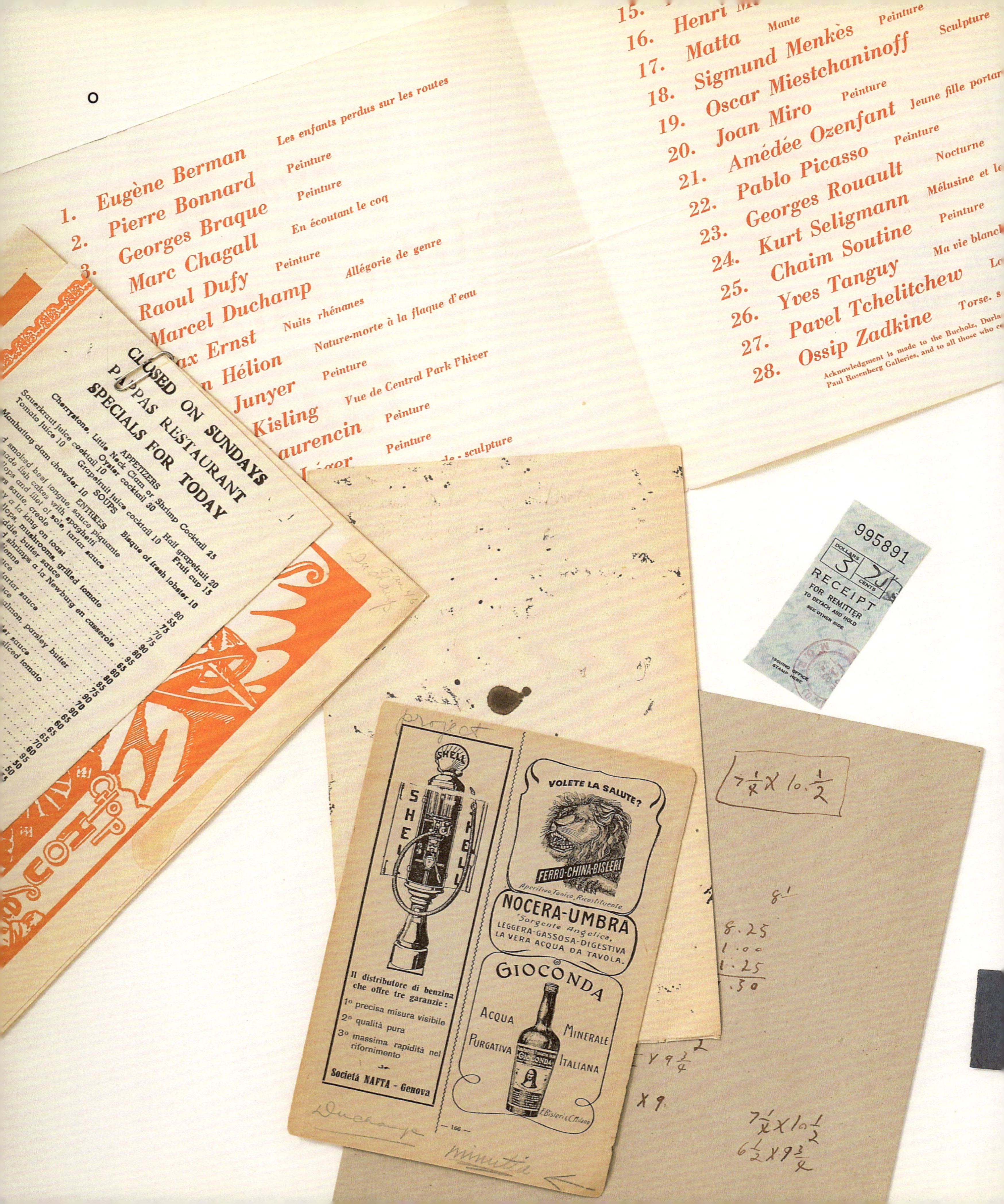

1. Eugène Berman Les enfants perdus sur les routes
2. Pierre Bonnard Peinture
3. Georges Braque Peinture
Marc Chagall En écoutant le coq
Raoul Dufy Peinture
Marcel Duchamp Allégorie de genre
ax Ernst Nuits rhénanes
n Hélion Nature-morte à la flaque d'eau
Junyer Peinture
Kisling Vue de Central Park l'hiver
aurencin Peinture
Peinture
16. Henri
17. Matta Mante
18. Sigmund Menkès Peinture
19. Oscar Miestchaninoff Sculpture
20. Joan Miro Peinture
21. Amédée Ozenfant
22. Pablo Picasso Peinture
23. Georges Rouault Nocturne
24. Kurt Seligmann
25. Chaim Soutine Peinture
26. Yves Tanguy
27. Pavel Tchelitchew
28. Ossip Zadkine Torse.
CLOSED ON SUNDAYS
PAPPAS RESTAURANT
SPECIALS FOR TODAY
APPETIZERS
Cherrystone, Little Neck Clam or Shrimp Cocktail 25
Sauerkraut juice cocktail 10 Oyster cocktail 30 Half grapefruit 20
Tomato Juice 10 Grapefruit juice cocktail 10 Fruit cup 15
SOUPS
Manhattan clam chowder 10 Bisque of fresh lobster 10
ENTREES
995891
DOLLARS 3 CENTS
RECEIPT
FOR REMITTER
TO DETACH AND HOLD
SEE OTHER SIDE
ISSUING OFFICE STAMP HERE
project
SHELL
Il distributore di benzina che offre tre garanzie:
1° precisa misura visibile
2° qualità pura
3° massima rapidità nel rifornimento
Società NAFTA - Genova
VOLETE LA SALUTE?
FERRO-CHINA-BISLERI
Aperitivo, Tonico, Ricostituente
NOCERA-UMBRA
"Sorgente Angelica"
LEGGERA-GASSOSA-DIGESTIVA
LA VERA ACQUA DA TAVOLA.
GIOCONDA
ACQUA MINERALE PURGATIVA ITALIANA
— 166 —
Duchamp
minutia
7 1/2 X 10 1/2
8.25
1.00
1.25
.30
7 1/2 X 10 1/2
6 1/2 X 9 3/4

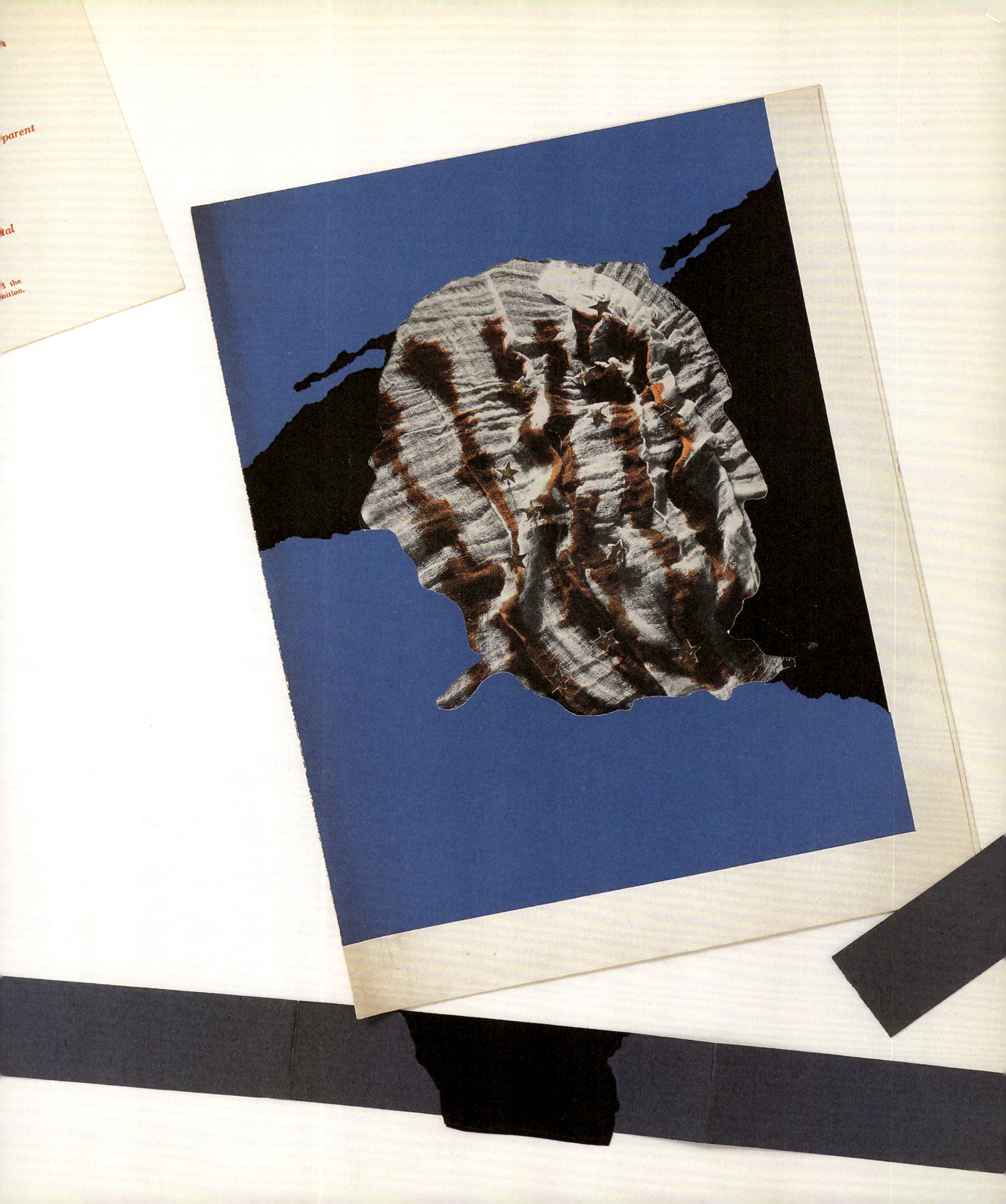

P

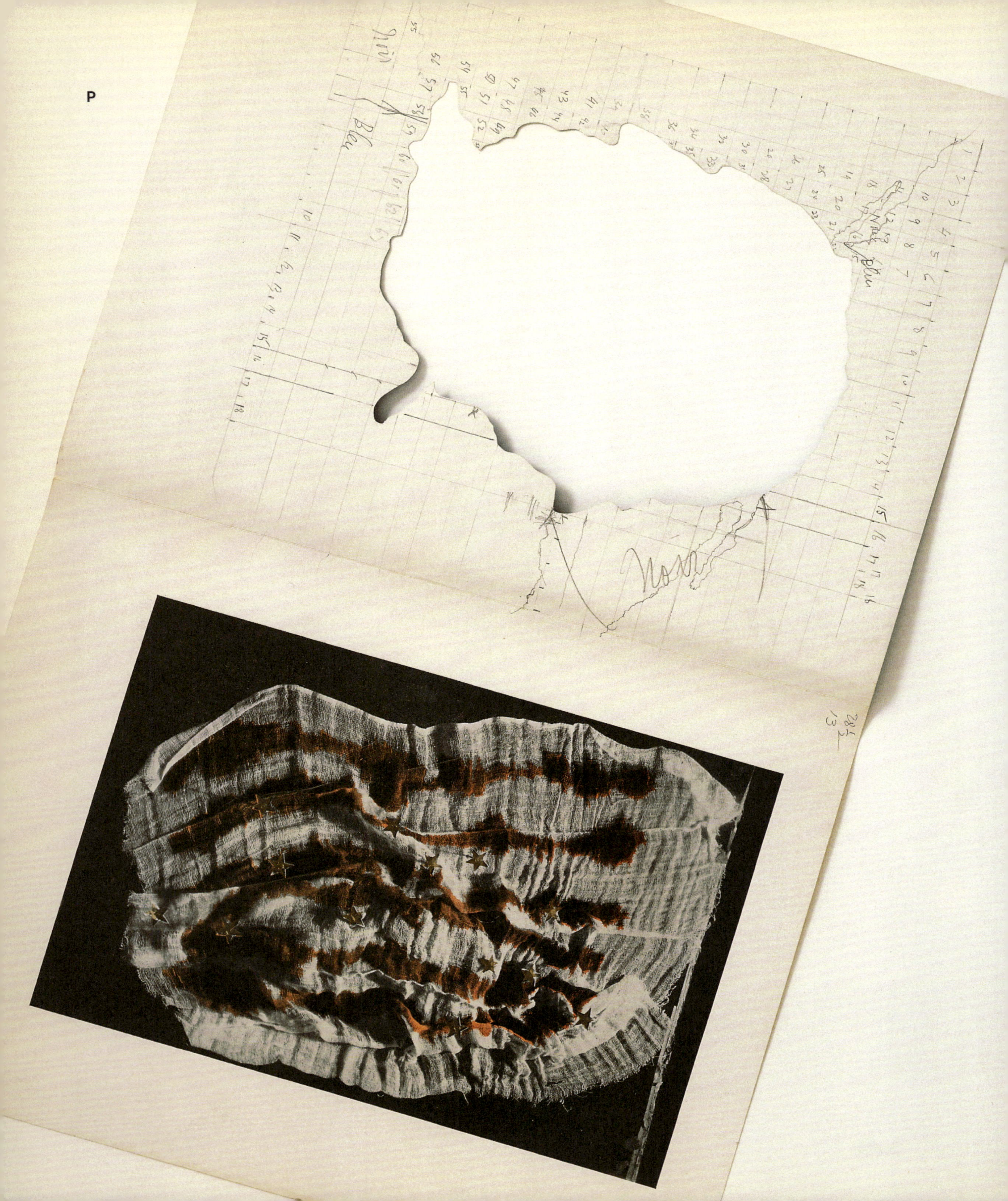

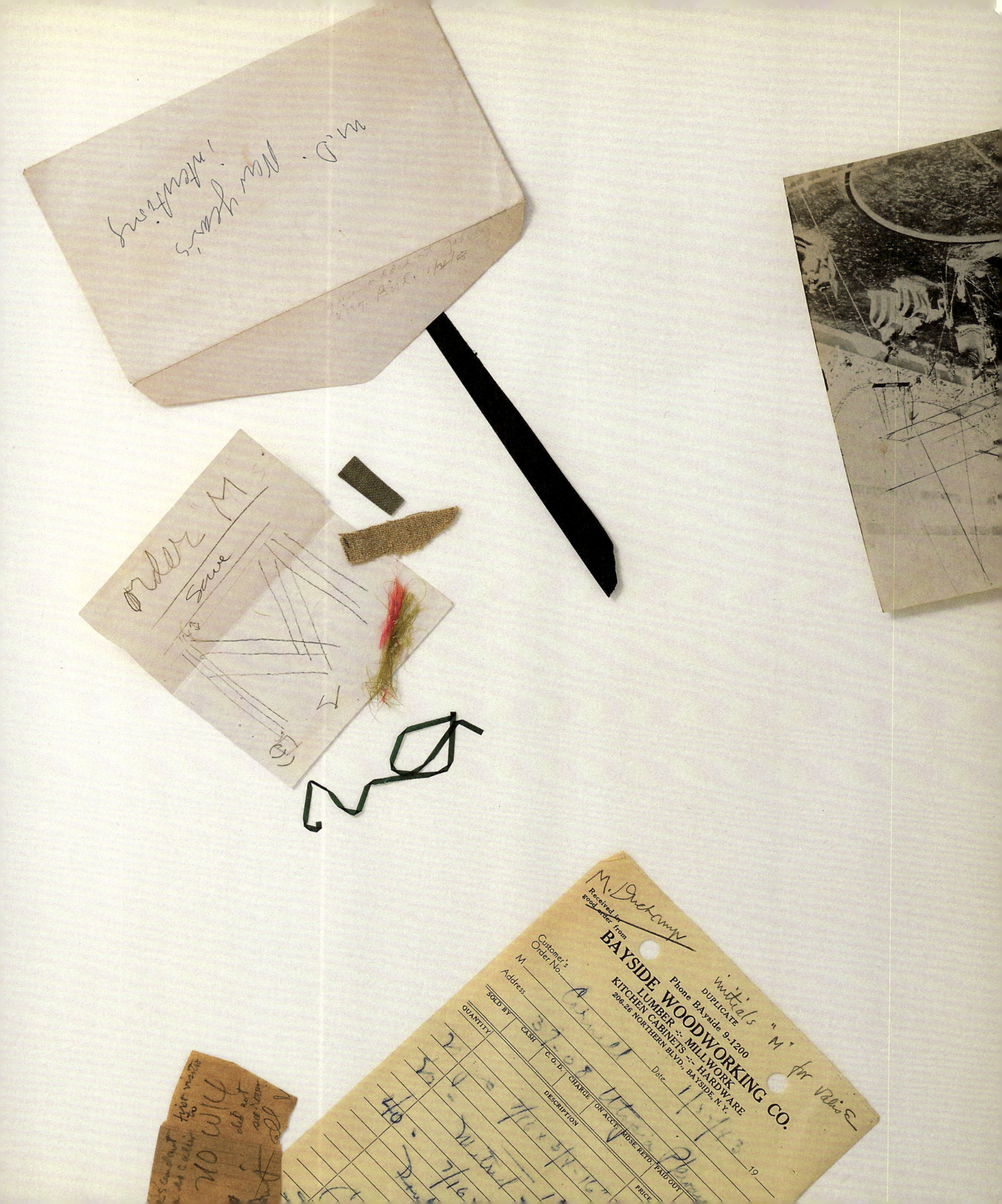
BAYSIDE WOODWORKING CO.
LUMBER :: MILLWORK
KITCHEN CABINETS :: HARDWARE
206-26 NORTHERN BLVD., BAYSIDE, N.Y.
Phone BAyside 9-1200
DUPLICATE

Q

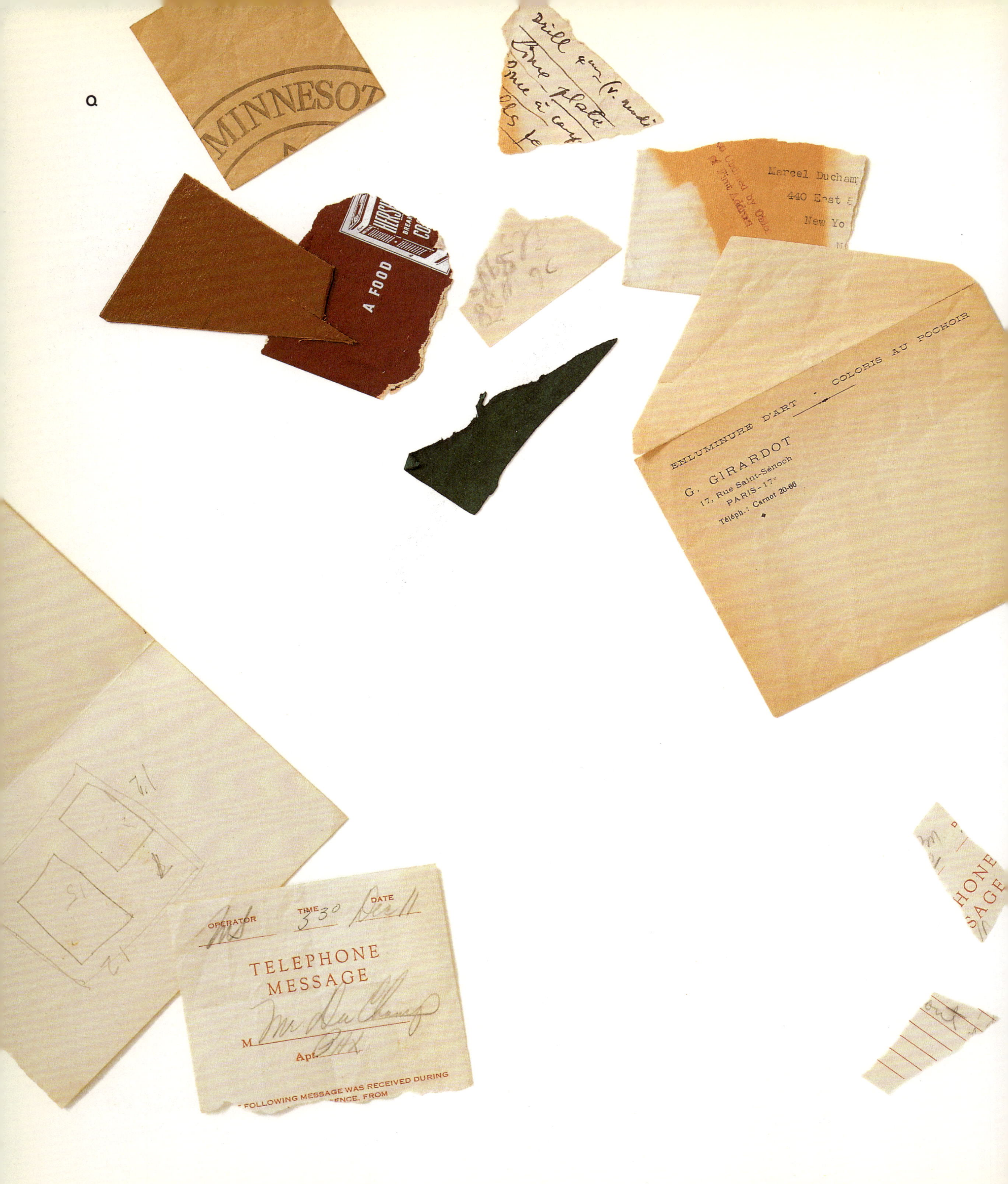

MINNESOT

A FOOD

Marcel Ducham
440 East 5
New Yo

ENLUMINURE D'ART - COLORIS AU POCHOIR
G. GIRARDOT
17, Rue Saint-Sénoch
PARIS-17e
Téléph.: Carnot 20-66

OPERATOR
TIME
DATE
TELEPHONE
MESSAGE
M
Apt.
FOLLOWING MESSAGE WAS RECEIVED DURING
ENCE. FROM

HONE
SAGE

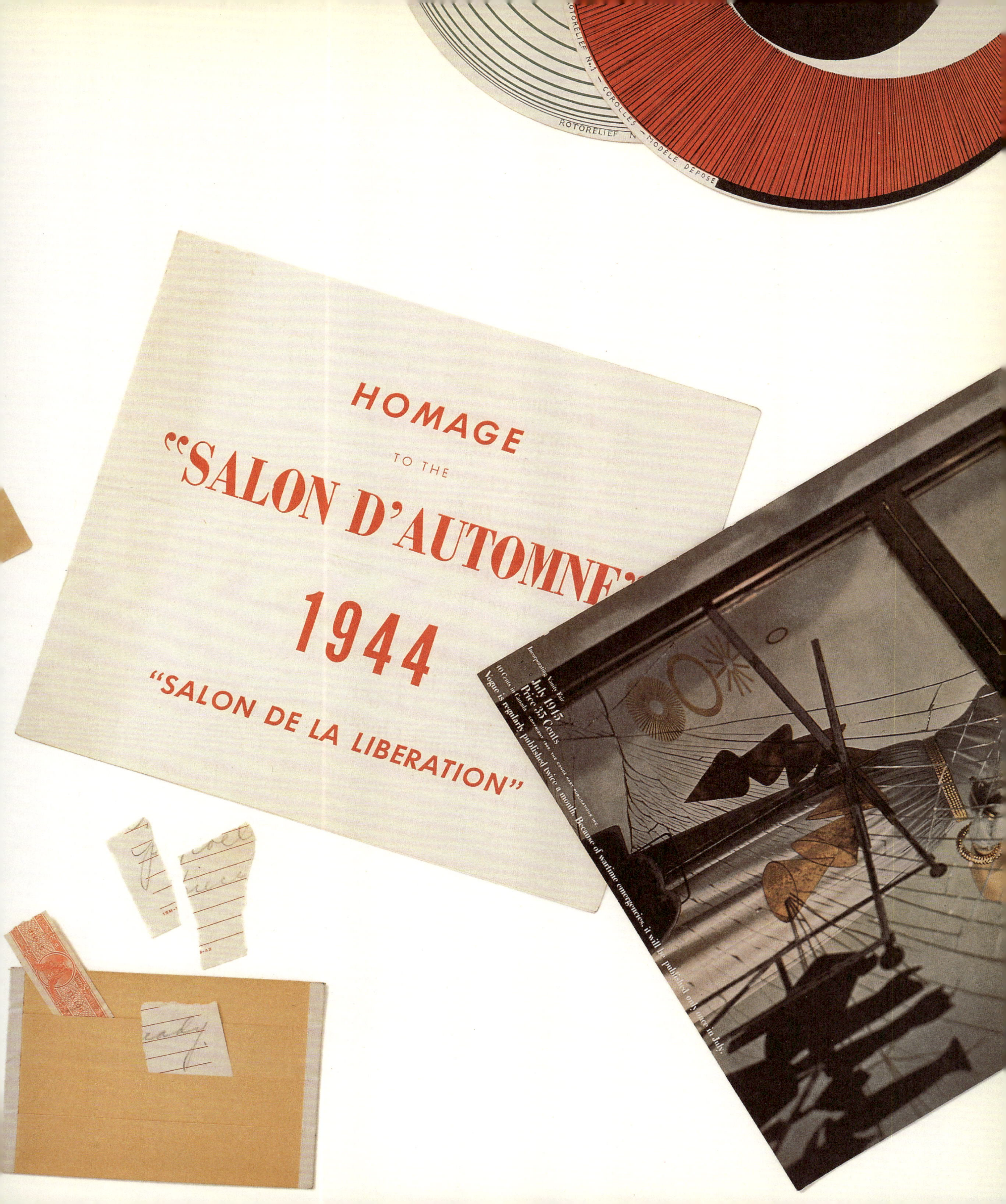
ROTORELIEF N°1 – COROLLES – MODÈLE DÉPOSÉ
HOMAGE
TO THE
"SALON D'AUTOMNE"
1944
"SALON DE LA LIBERATION"
Incorporating Vanity Fair
July 1945
Price 35 Cents
40 Cents in Canada
Vogue is regularly published twice a month. Because of wartime emergencies, it will be published only once in July.

R

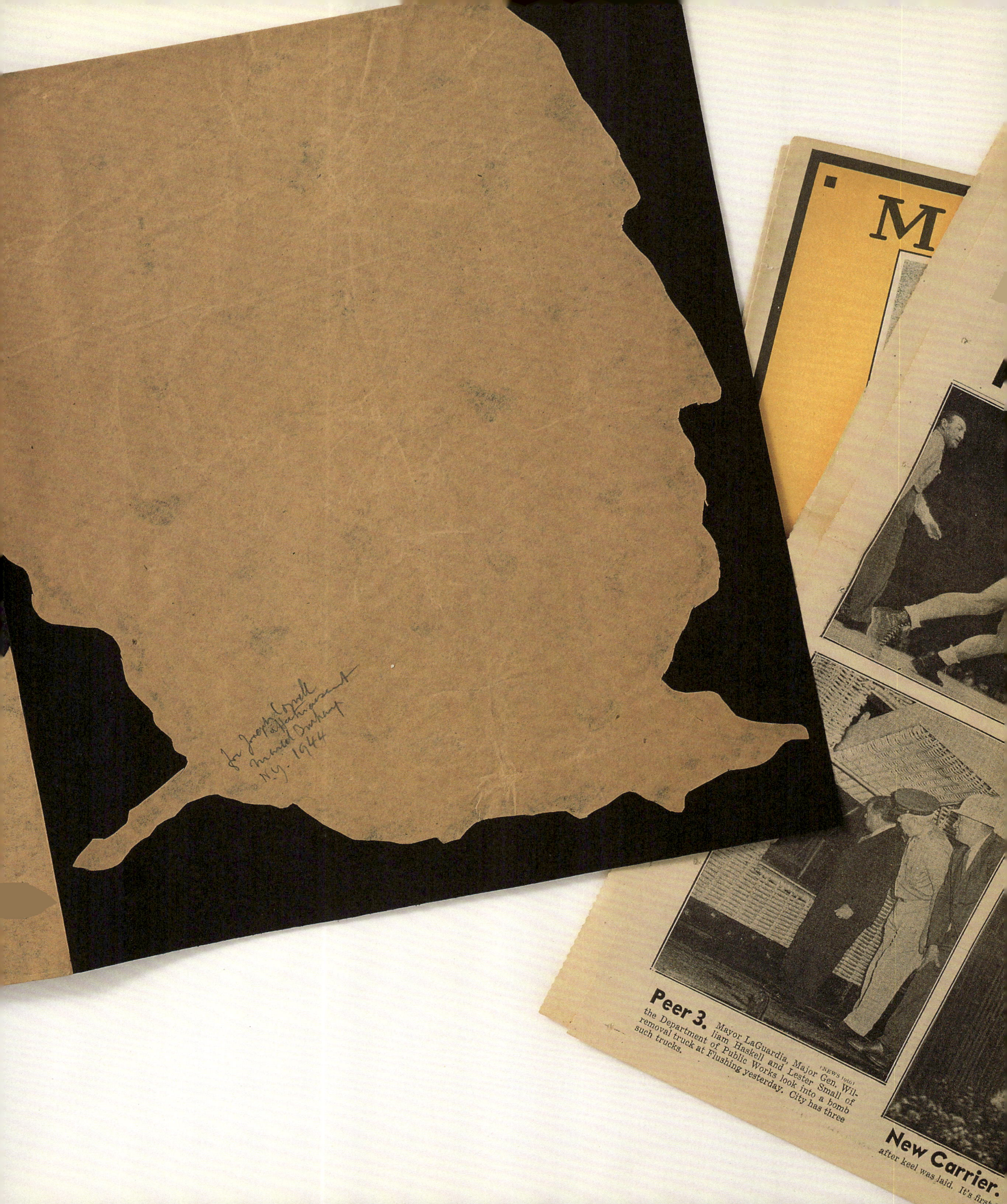
M
Peer 3. Mayor LaGuardia, Major Gen. William Haskell and Lester Small of the Department of Public Works look into a bomb removal truck at Flushing yesterday. City has three such trucks.
(NEWS foto)
New Carrier.
after keel was laid. It's first
for Joseph Cornell
N.Y. 1944

S

Duchamp
SPECIAL DELIVERY
Vogue
Vogue's Eye-view of the Museum of Modern Art
Midsummer Fashions
Lunch at Le Moal's Friday 1 P.M.
M.D.
Incorporating Vanity Fair
July 1945
Price 35 Cents
10 Cents in Canada
Vogue is regularly published
emergencies, it will be published only once in July.
Domino
Pressed Tablets
American Sugar Refining Company
UN COIN DE BRETAGNE A NEW YORK
TELEPHONE EL. 5-8554
LE MOAL
FRENCH RESTAURANT
811-3RD AVE
NEW YORK CITY

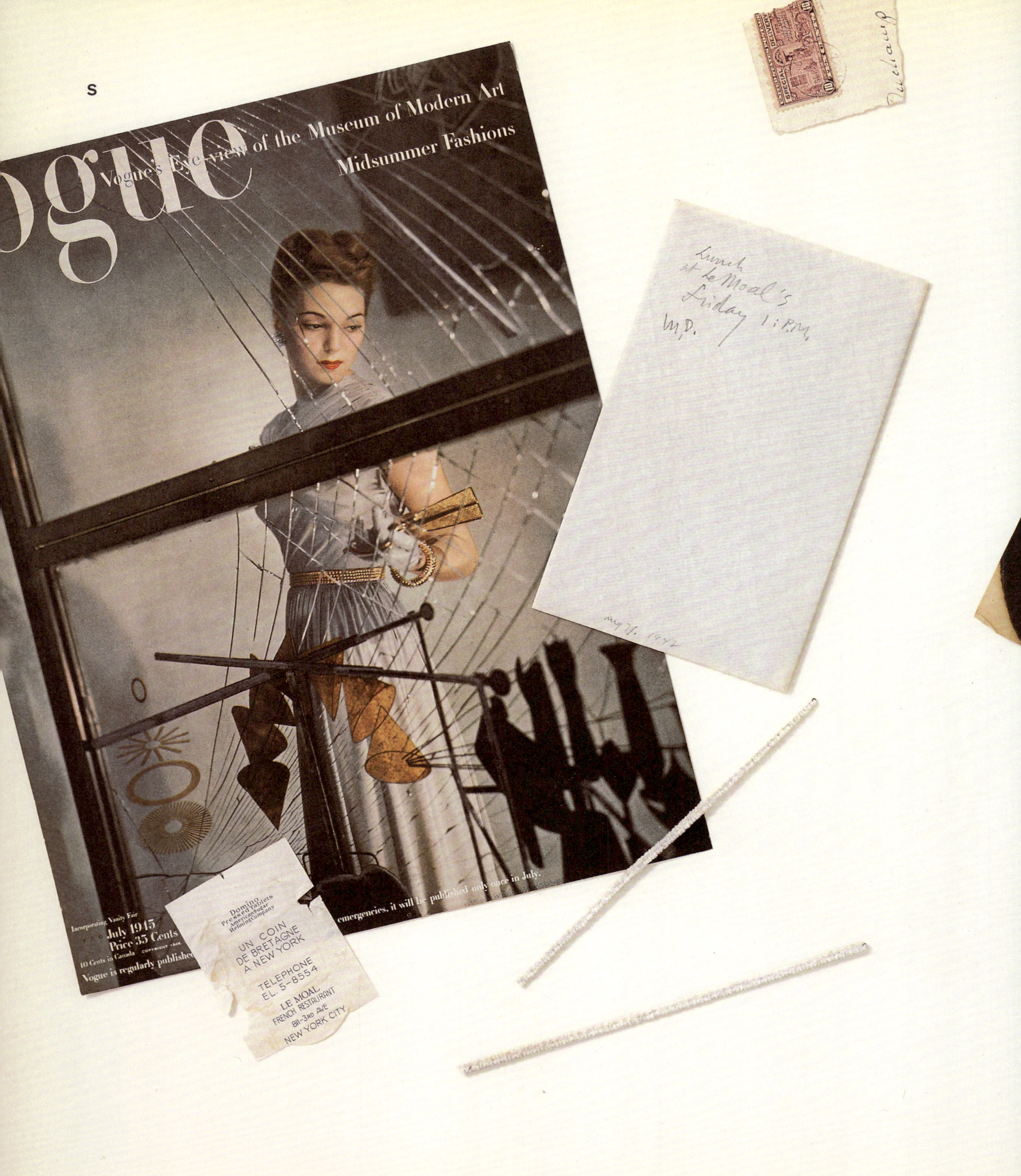

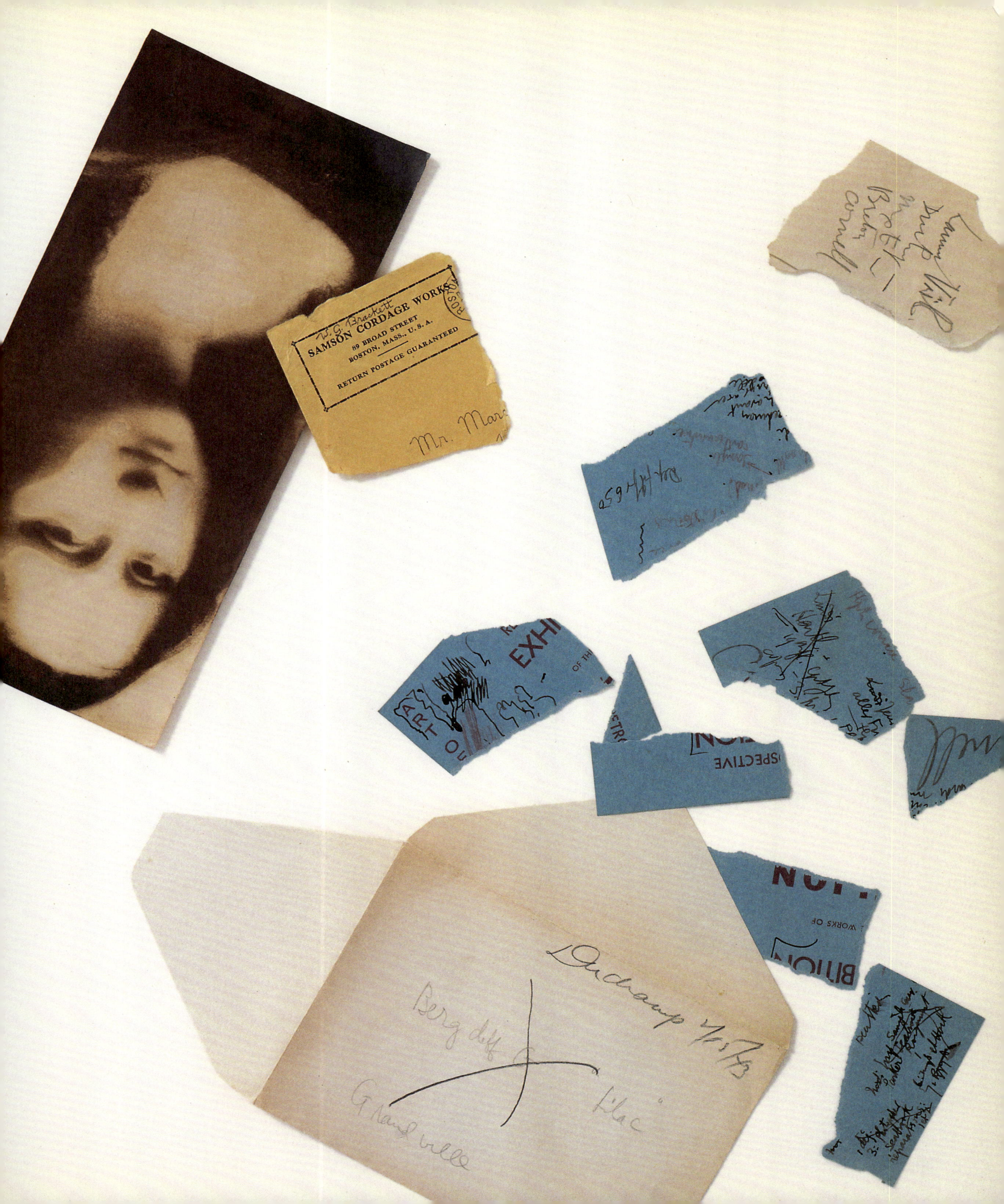
SAMSON CORDAGE WORKS
89 BROAD STREET
BOSTON, MASS., U.S.A.
RETURN POSTAGE GUARANTEED
EXHI
SPECTIVE
Duchamp

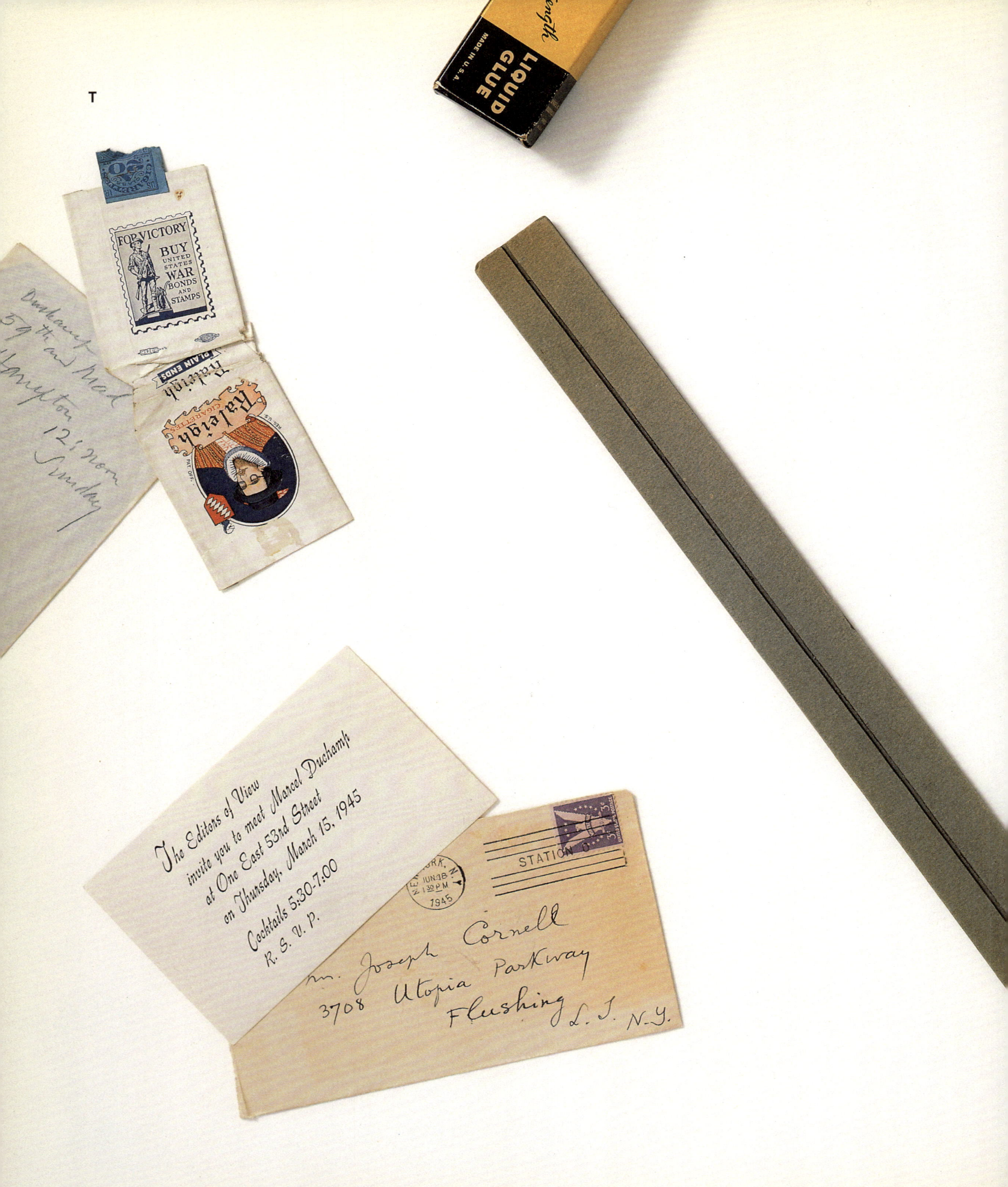
T
LIQUID
GLUE
MADE IN U.S.A.
FOR VICTORY
BUY
UNITED STATES
WAR
BONDS
AND
STAMPS
PLAIN ENDS
Raleigh
CIGARETTES
Duchamp
59th and Mad
Hampton
12 noon
Sunday
The Editors of View
invite you to meet Marcel Duchamp
at One East 53rd Street
on Thursday, March 15, 1945
Cocktails 5:30-7:00
R. S. V. P.
STATION O
NEW YORK, N.Y.
JUN 18
1:30 PM
1945
Mr. Joseph Cornell
3708 Utopia Parkway
Flushing L. I. N.Y.

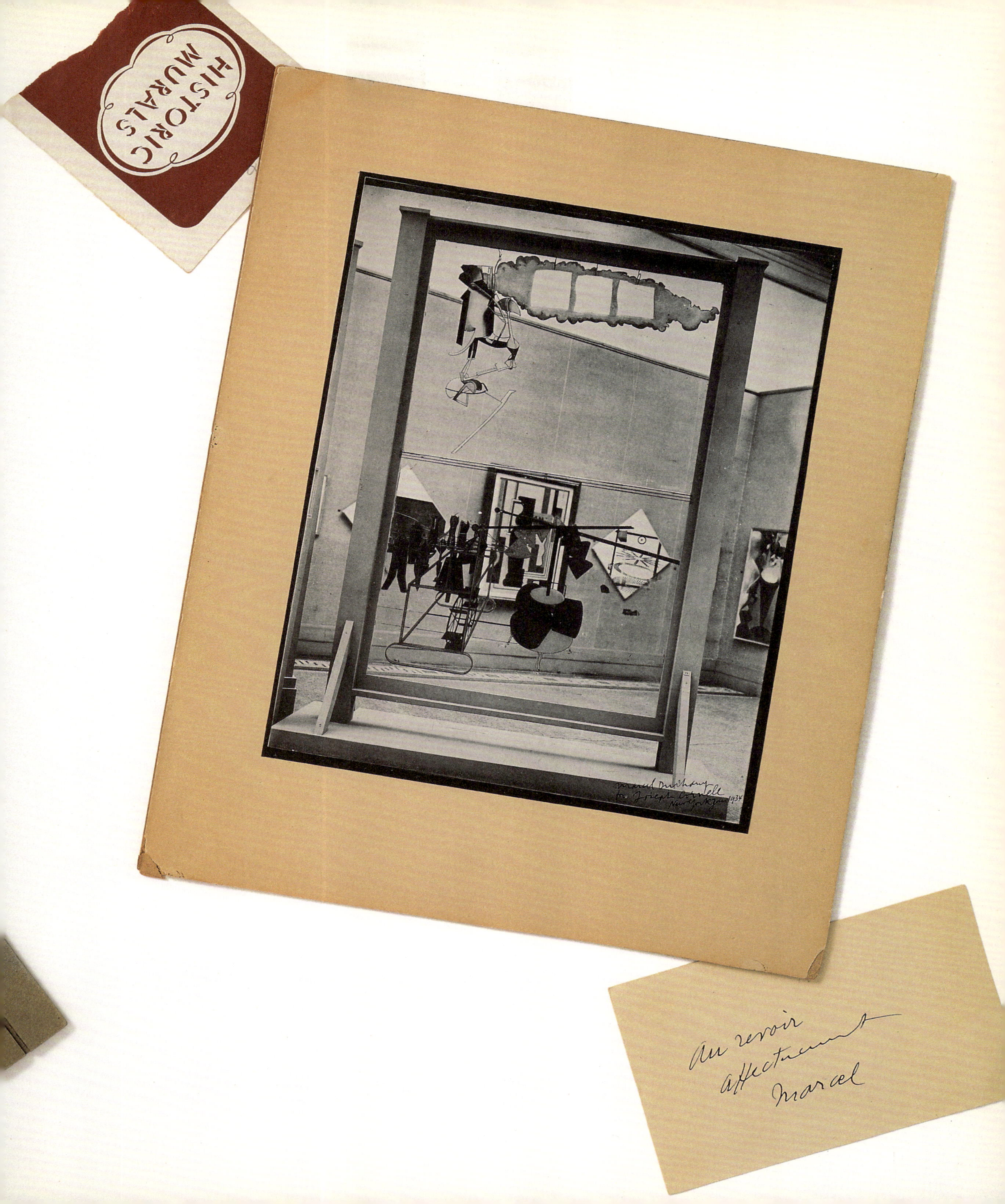

HISTORIC MURALS

Marcel Duchamp
for Joseph Cornell
New York Jan 1934

Au revoir
affectueusement
Marcel

Duchamp Dossier c. 1942–53
Philadelphia Museum of Art.
Gift of The Joseph and Robert Cornell Memorial Foundation
pp. 17–59

Duchamp Dossier Plates

In the preceding plates (pp. 17–59), the dossier box and its contents are reproduced at the same ratio, sixty percent of actual size. The illustrations do not represent any sequence or hierarchy given by Cornell. Some items of related subject matter have been grouped together (for example, letters from Mary Reynolds or parts related to the assembly of the *Boite* edition). Individual boxes and envelopes are reproduced in proximity to their contents. Certain items or details of items are repeated. Not all items are reproduced here, but all are reproduced and their complete descriptions are given in the *Duchamp Dossier* Inventory (pp. 304–31).

Individual items are identified by their inventory numbers in the *Duchamp Dossier* Pictorial Index (pp. 300–303) where thumbnail versions of the plates are labeled by a capital letter that corresponds to the letter in the upper left corner of the matching double-page spread.

Editorial Note

Titles appear in their original language, with translations provided in the first text reference. Commonly used titles, such as *Large Glass* or *Green Box*, are cited for brevity. *de ou par Marcel Duchamp ou Rrose Sélavy [by or of Marcel Duchamp or Rrose Sélavy]* is referred to as the *Boite* edition. An example of the deluxe edition of this work is referred to as a *Boite-en-valise [Box-in-a-Valise]*, and an example of the regular edition is referred to as a *Boite*.

Images in both the text and the plate sections are most often identified left to right, top to bottom.

Items in the *Duchamp Dossier* are referenced by the capital letters "DD" and the item's number, as given in the *Duchamp Dossier* Inventory (pp. 304–31); for example, (DD *25*).

In the two artists' plate sections, all works are by Marcel Duchamp or Joseph Cornell, unless otherwise noted. The plates are arranged chronologically except where thematic groupings have been introduced. Multiple illustrations of a single work have been assigned the same plate number, followed by an additional digit; for example, (**1.1**).

pp. 61–65

4 ***Manhattan Bridge,*** November 11, 1936. Photograph by Berenice Abbott, Federal Arts Project, "Changing New York." Museum of the City of New York.

5 ***Manhattan I, From Pier 11, East River,*** March 26, 1936. Photograph by Berenice Abbott, Federal Arts Project, "Changing New York." Berenice Abbott/Commerce Graphics Ltd, Inc.

6 **Times Square** (Broadway between 42nd and 43rd Streets), New York, 1943.

7 **Elevated train tracks,** New York, 1940.

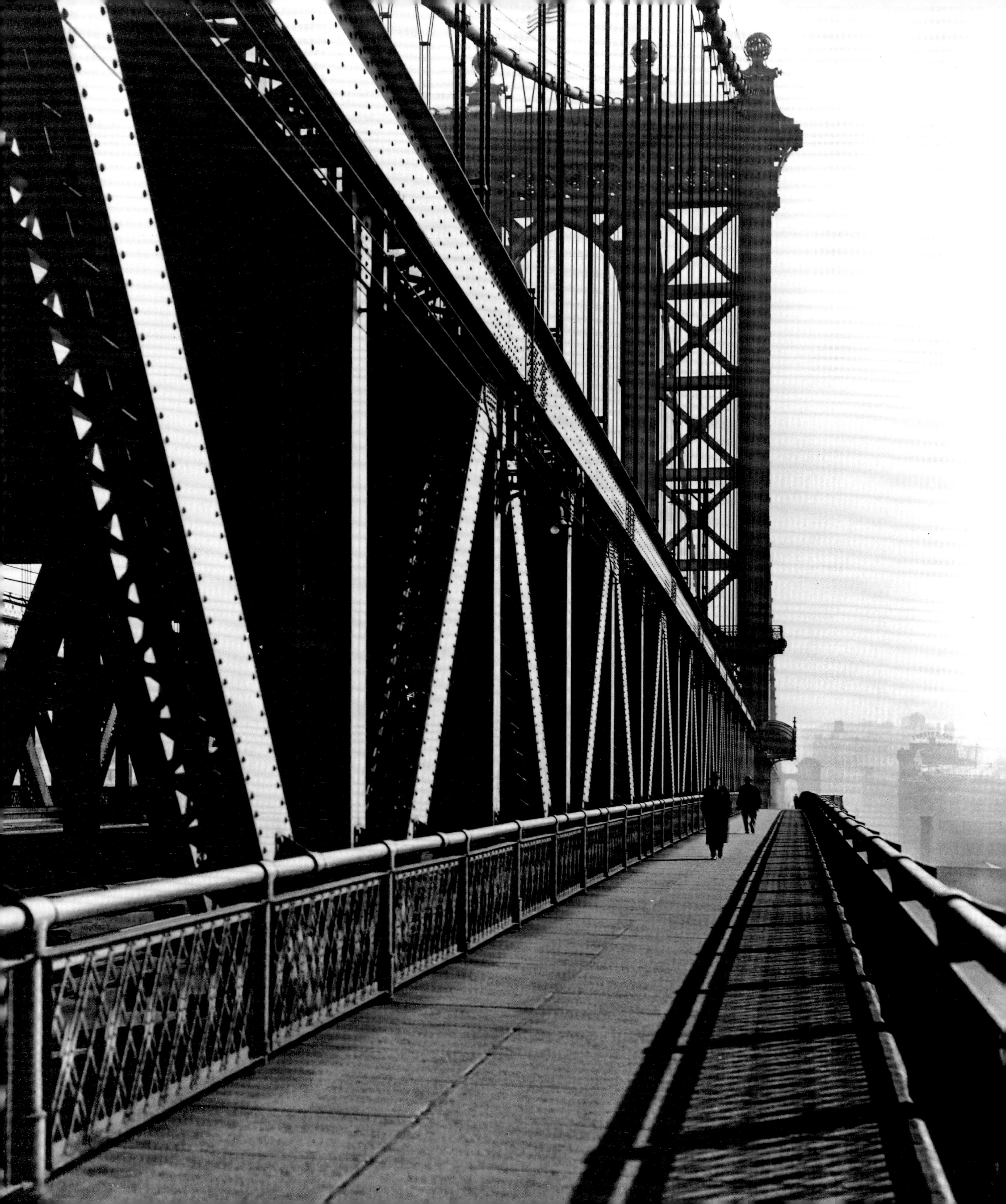

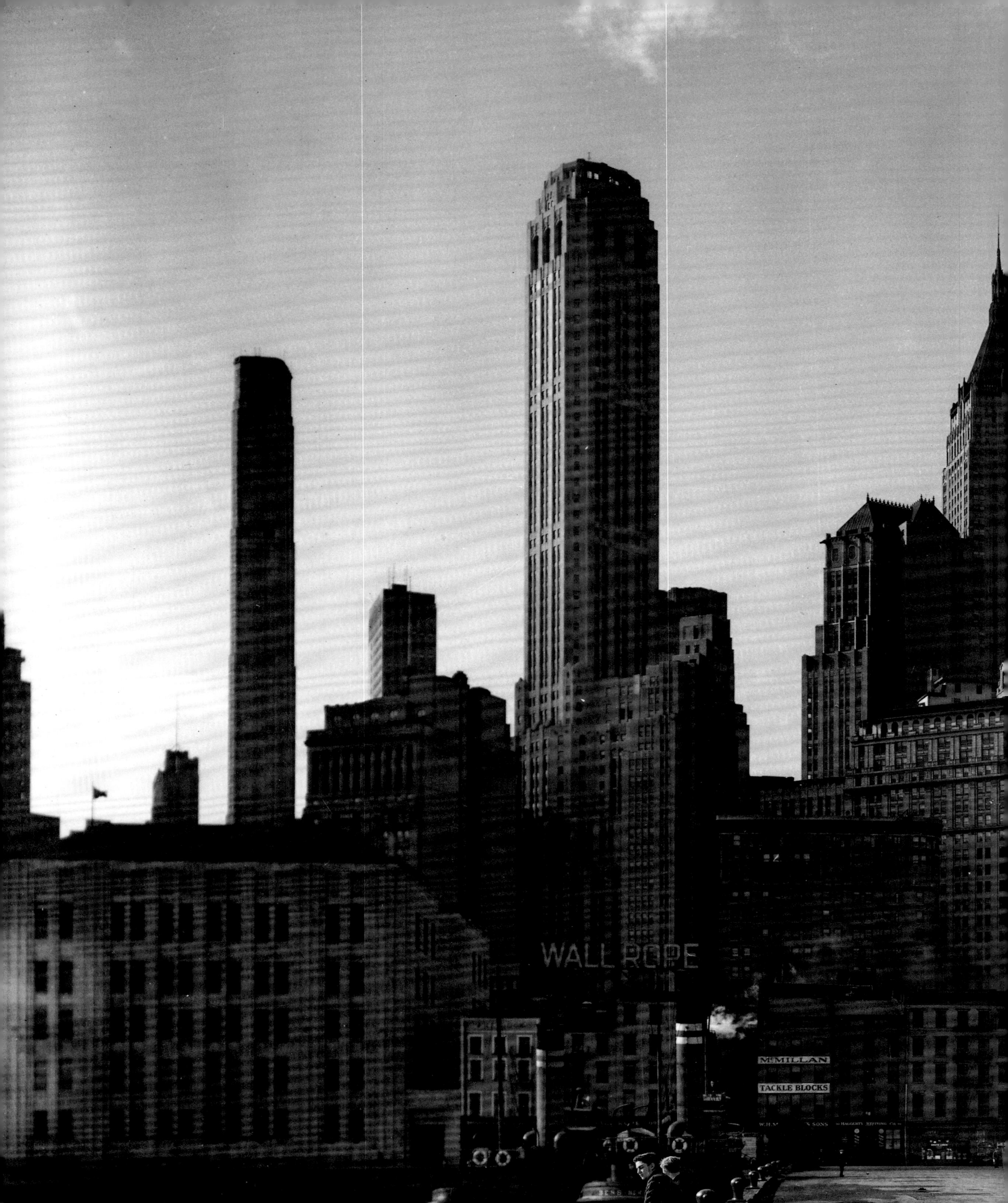
WALL ROPE
McMILLAN
TACKLE BLOCKS

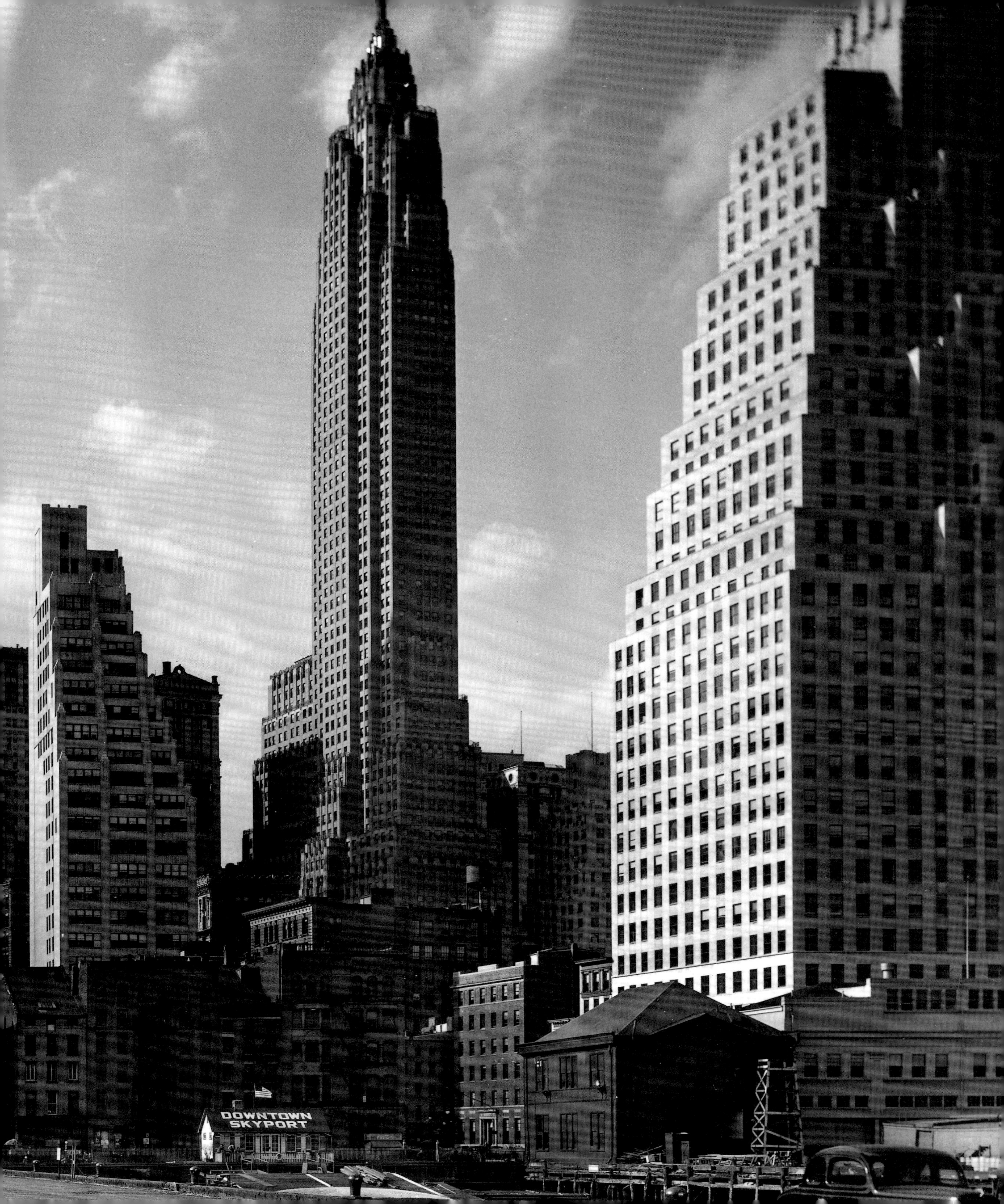
DOWNTOWN
SKYPORT

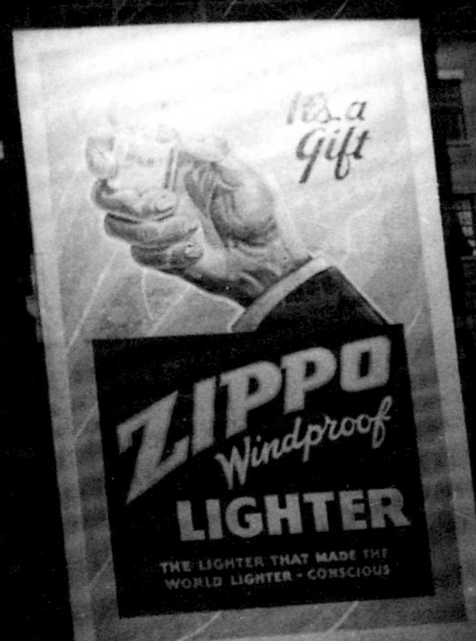
It's a Gift
ZIPPO
Windproof
LIGHTER
THE LIGHTER THAT MADE THE WORLD LIGHTER-CONSCIOUS

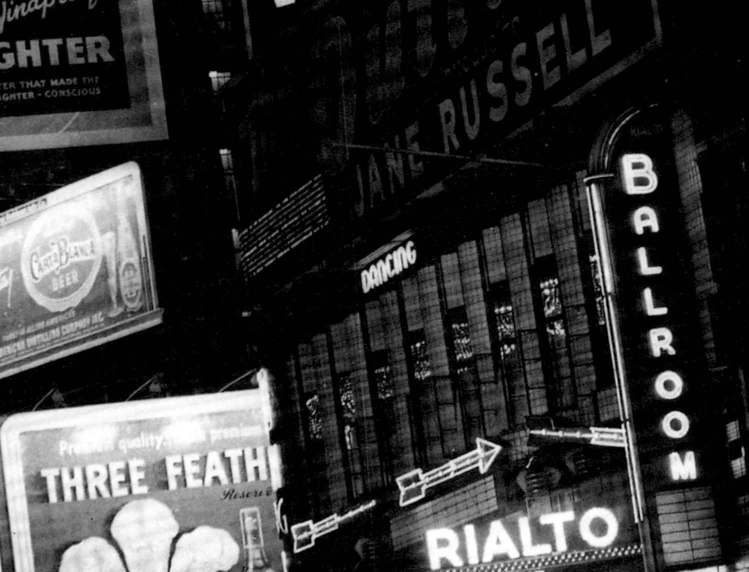
JANE RUSSELL
DANCING
BALLROOM
RIALTO

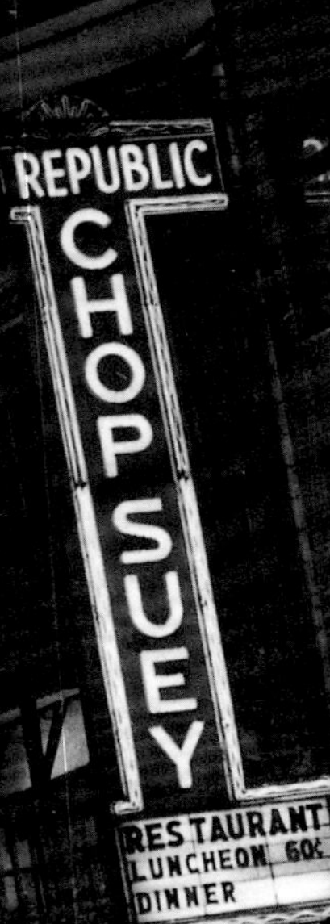
REPUBLIC
CHOP SUEY
RESTAURANT
LUNCHEON 60¢
DINNER

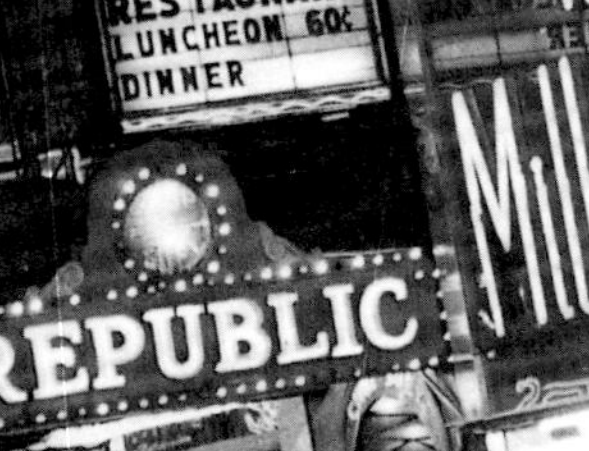
REPUBLIC

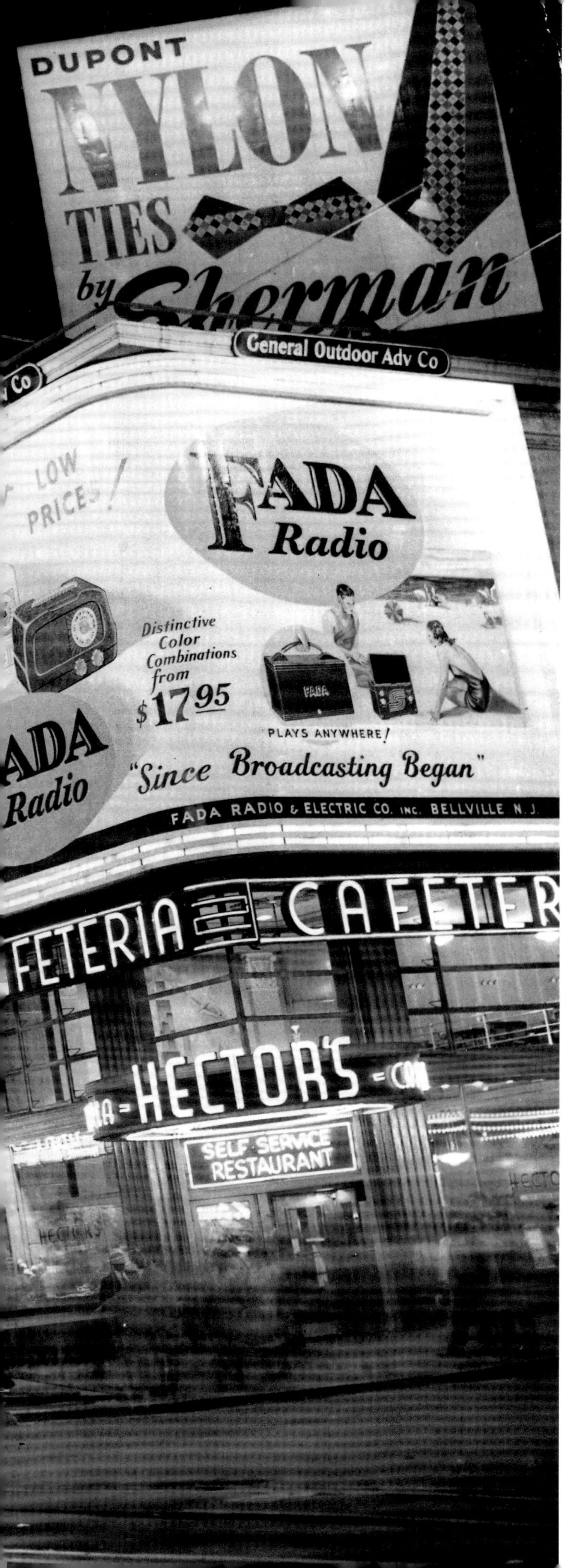

DUPONT
NYLON
TIES
by Sherman
General Outdoor Adv Co
LOW PRICES!
FADA
Radio
Distinctive Color Combinations from $17.95
PLAYS ANYWHERE!
"Since Broadcasting Began"
FADA RADIO & ELECTRIC CO. INC. BELLVILLE N.J.
FETERIA
CAFETER
HECTOR'S
SELF SERVICE RESTAURANT

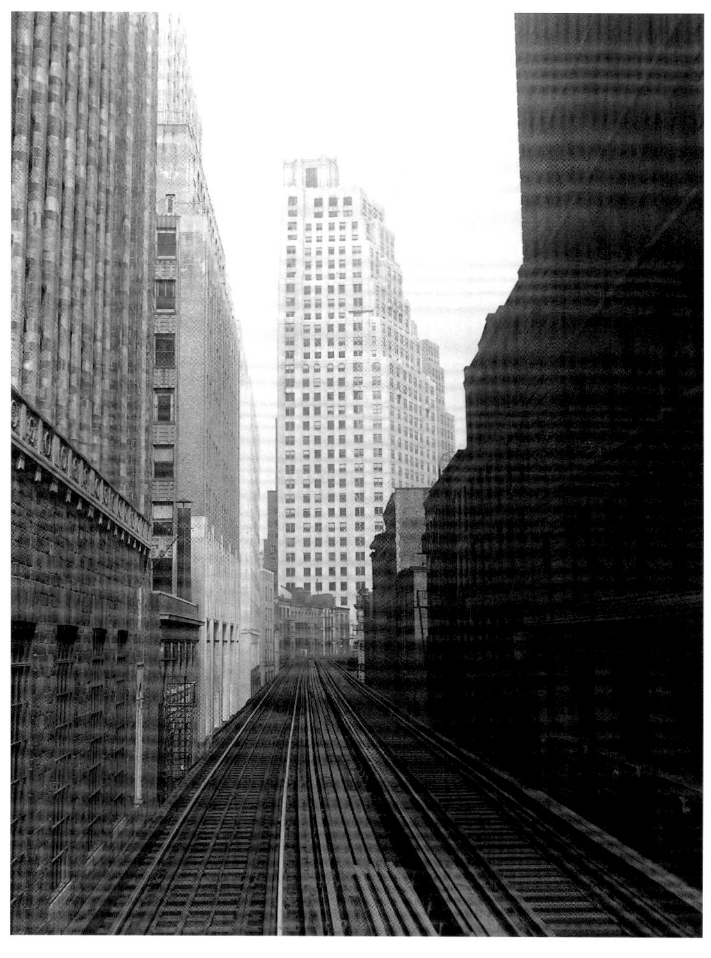

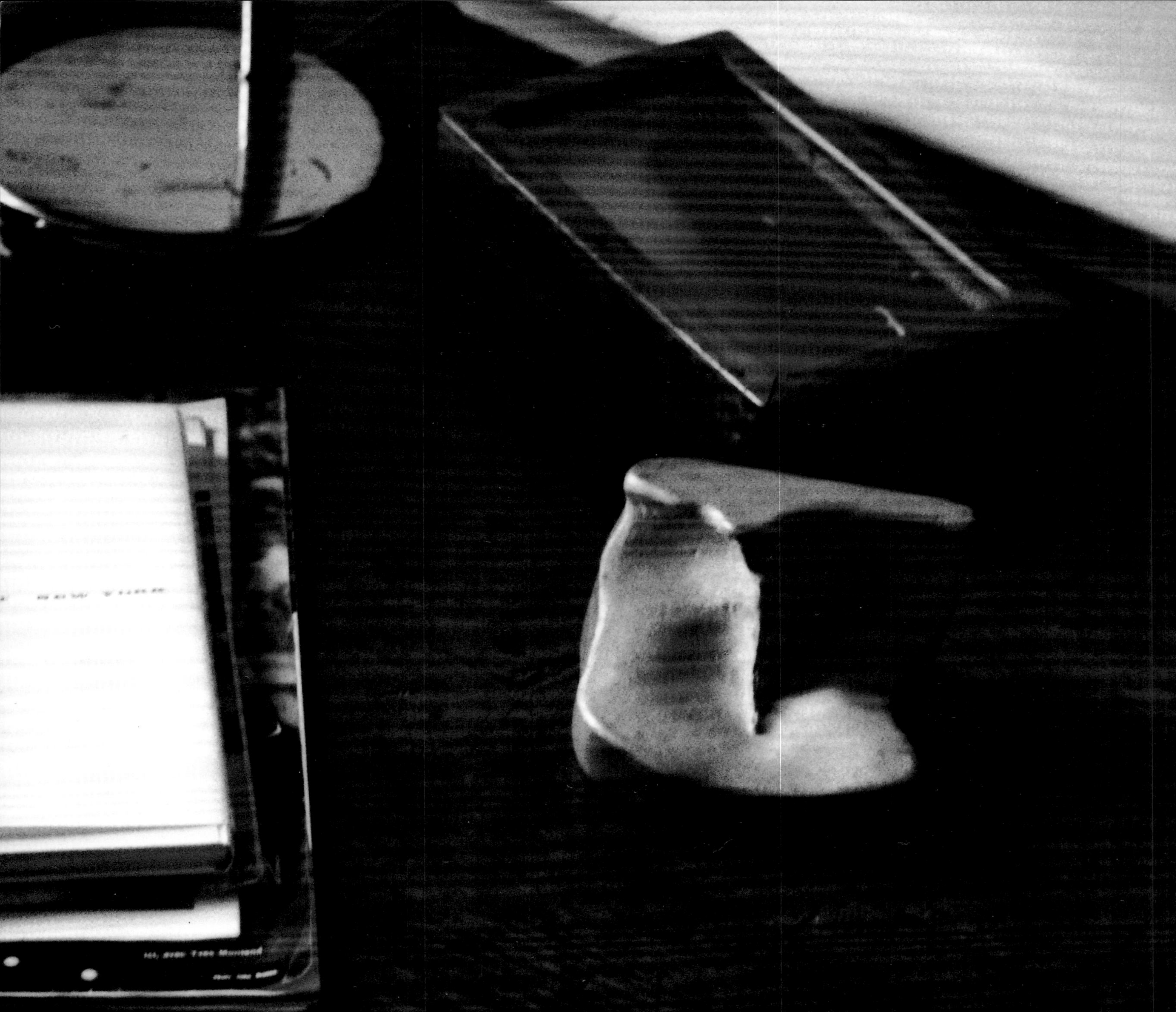

Gimme Strength: Joseph Cornell and Marcel Duchamp Remembered

WALTER HOPPS

I first became aware of Joseph Cornell's work in 1948, while I was still in high school, when I saw a show of it at William Copley's Beverly Hills gallery—which was devoted to Surrealist art and showed the work of Cornell, Ernst, Magritte, Man Ray, Matta, and Tanguy before shutting down after less than a year. Then in 1955, while I was visiting New York, I went to Eleanor Ward's Stable Gallery to see more of Cornell's work. Ward showed me work after work, then suddenly she pulled out the 1943 *Habitat Group for a Shooting Gallery* (pl. 82; fig. 9). I was just astounded by it. It was considerably more expensive than anything else there, but I immediately wrote out a check for $750, which basically wiped out my account.

I was also in high school when I first saw Marcel Duchamp's work—on a field trip to the Hollywood home of Walter and Louise Arensberg. Once I'd seen their collection of modern art—which featured the work of Duchamp and Brancusi—that was it. I would go there every weekend, and it was like a secret world for me. They'd leave me alone to look at the work, and then I would have lunch with the two of them.

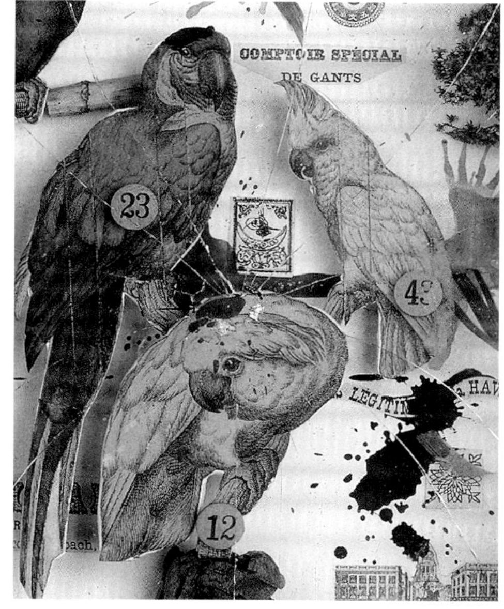

My first meeting with Cornell, in 1959, was to acquire work for a show at Ferus Gallery in Los Angeles, which I ran with Irving Blum. I also had a side deal with Edwin Janss, an adventurous collector from Southern California; he would advance the money to buy work for the gallery, and when it was sold, we'd split the profit. I showed him some images of Cornell's work, and he said, "That's interesting-looking stuff. What can you get it for?" I said, "Well, maybe about $500 apiece." He said, "Okay."

I arranged to meet with Cornell at his house, a two-story, gabled Yankee house with a sizable attic and an enclosed porch, on Utopia Parkway in Queens. It was full of things—very neat, but stuffed to the point where it could make some people nervous. Cornell was quiet and serious; for him to smile was a rare event, so you really noticed it when he did. At times, he seemed almost otherworldly.

After our first meeting, he told me to come back in two days to pick up some works. When I went back, he had them packed up in newspapers and brown paper bags. I said, "Do you think these are safe?" "Oh," he said, "sometimes I just wrap them up like groceries. I think they will be." Later, I brought a foam rubber-lined case with straps and a handle, like photographers carry, to transport his work. But the first time Cornell saw that black box, he shuddered. It sort of scared him.

Cornell and I would sit at his dining room table and talk. Or we'd sit in the kitchen while he made endless cups of tea and toast, which we'd eat with cheese or honey (fig. 10). I never could get him to go out—so I never had a meal with him anywhere except at his house.

8 Duchamp's *Female Fig Leaf* (1954) and Cornell's Untitled (Sand Tray) (c. 1954) on a table in Duchamp's apartment, 28 West 10th Street, New York, May 1959. Detail of photograph by Alexander Liberman.

9 Cornell, *Habitat Group for a Shooting Gallery* (detail), 1943. Box construction, 15½ x 11⅛ x 4¼ in. Des Moines Art Center, Iowa. Purchased with funds from the Coffin Fine Arts Trust; Nathan Emory Coffin Collection.

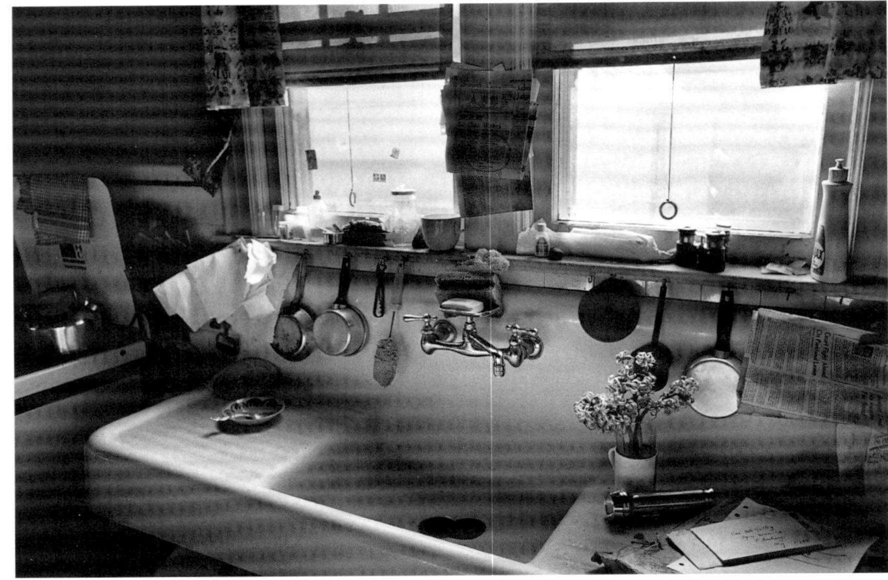

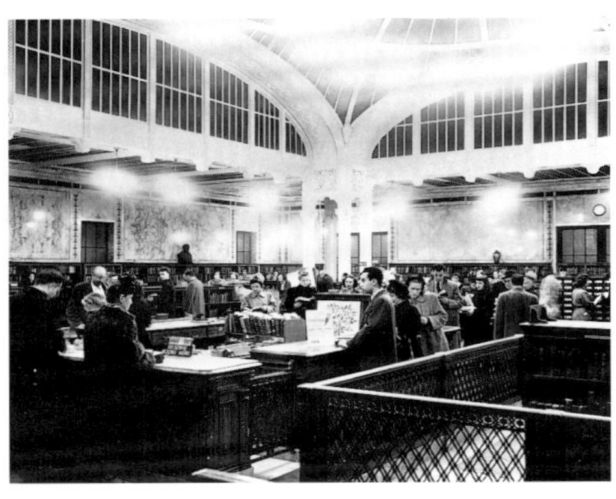

By that time, he had been hurt by a good many people, including some of his young assistants. One of the women he'd had a real crush on robbed him of some boxes, and then was stabbed to death in Manhattan. So there was all that unhappy history.

At one point, he asked me if I knew Susan Sontag. He had acquired a copy of Sontag's first novel, *Benefactor*, and the book had disturbed him, but he loved the picture of her on the dust jacket. I said, "By all means, I know her"—I had met her when we were both in high school in L.A. He was practically swooning. He had to leave the room. This often happened. He got very emotional and said he needed to go upstairs and lie down. He asked me to arrange a meeting with Sontag, which I did. Later, he gave me a collage that he regarded as an imaginary portrait of her as a young girl.

He loved beautiful women, ballet dancers especially. He'd go to all the performances, even though he had very little money—he'd buy standing-room-only tickets—and would sometimes get himself backstage to meet the dancers. He even took little snippings of their costumes to put into his talisman boxes. Possessed of a different temperament, he might have staged ballets, and I think his boxes are in some ways a sublimation of this impulse—a simulacrum of theatrical production.

Cornell was an enormously cultivated man even though he never went to Europe or even west of the Allegheny Mountains. His interest in French culture—particularly from the Symbolist through the Surrealist periods—was acute. He collected postcards and Baedeker travel guides, and I suspect he would have known exactly where in Paris to get Proust's favorite madeleines and a cup of tea. He lived like an eighteenth-century gentleman and acquired a very sophisticated understanding of the arts. From the twenties on, although he had an extremely modest budget, he availed himself of all the cultural offerings of New York City, haunting the galleries and museums, the theaters and public spaces. He spent a great deal of time in the New York Public Library (fig. 11), and the book as object became very important to him—the book literally became an armature for the art in some of his works.

10 **Cornell's kitchen,** 3708 Utopia Parkway, Flushing, New York, 1969. Photograph by Duane Michals.

11 **Central circulation desk, New York Public Library,** 42nd Street at Fifth Avenue, New York, December 1948. New York Public Library Archives.

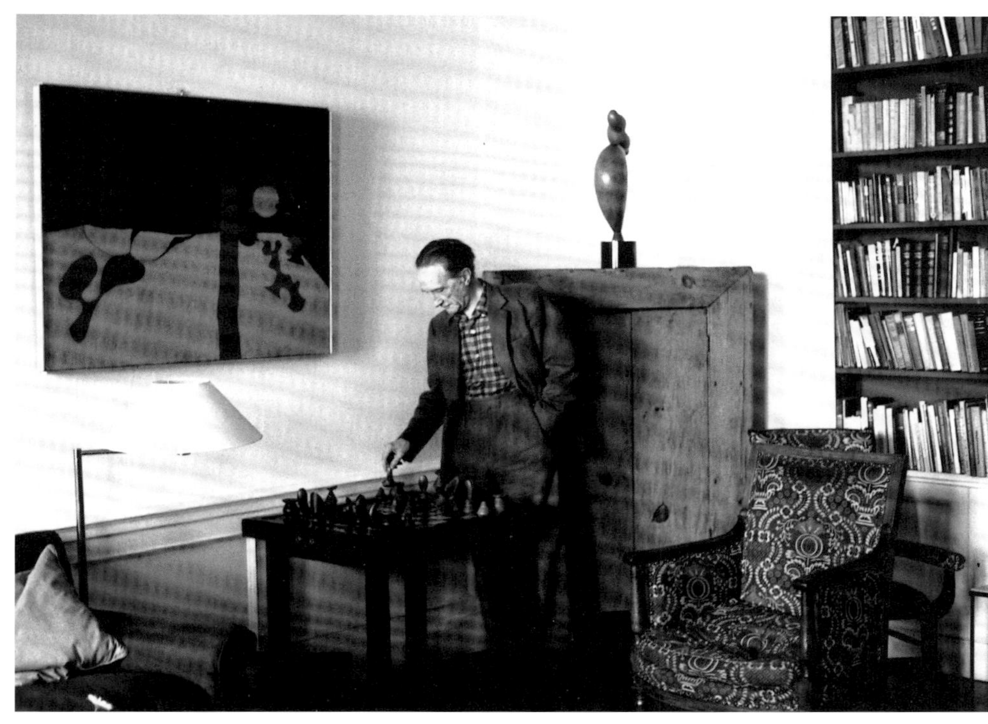

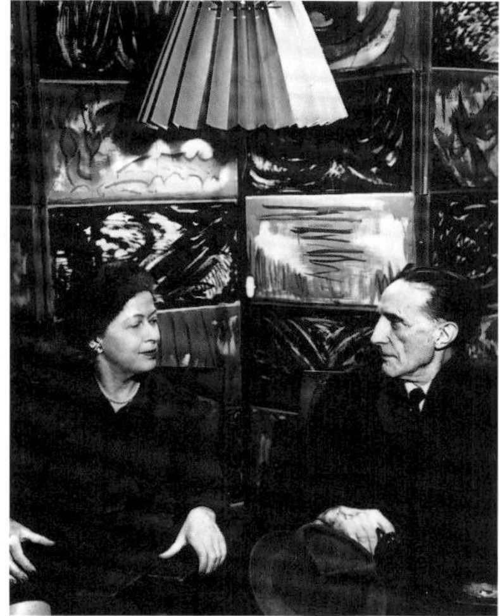

When I became the curator for the Pasadena Art Museum in 1961, I decided I wanted to organize a retrospective of Marcel Duchamp's work.[1] Bill Copley was then living in New York, pursuing his own art under the pseudonym CPLY. He was very close to Duchamp, so he invited us both to his apartment on East 69th Street and introduced us. Soon afterward, I went to visit Marcel at his home on West 10th Street. He had the work of several artists on view in his apartment, among them Balthus, Brancusi, Braque, Matisse, and Tanguy. Two of the artists were Americans: Alexander Calder and Cornell (fig. 8). The Calder was a wonderful little red-and-black miniature mobile. It sat on a Shaker bench that was being used as a coffee table. On top of a cabinet was a Brancusi, the wooden version of *Nancy Cunard* (1925–27; fig. 12).

I knew that the bedroom was beyond the bathroom, down the hall, and I noticed that Duchamp was watching me. He said, "Go on. Go on. Take a look in there." He was incredibly generous about letting me explore. There were two Cornell works on a shelf in the bedroom, and I was delighted to see them. He said, "Oh, I like him very much. I admire him." Cornell and Duchamp had met in 1933, at a show of Brancusi's work that Duchamp organized at the Brummer Gallery in New York, and they became closer after Duchamp's return to New York in 1942. In 1954, Duchamp married Teeny—Alexina Sattler Matisse—who was very fond of Joseph herself (fig. 13). She would often spend time with him on her own—Marcel was just not the type to meet in a New York department store restaurant to share the sweet little cakes that Cornell seemed to subsist on.

I visited Duchamp as often as possible while we were preparing his retrospective. On one of those visits, a young reporter appeared unexpectedly at the door. Marcel, very uncharacteristically, must have mixed up the appointment times. He said, "Oh, *merde, merde*." I could see that he was annoyed with himself for having forgotten that this person was coming, and I had a feeling things weren't going to go well. Duchamp asked him why

12 **Duchamp in his apartment, Constantin Brancusi's *Nancy Cunard* (1925–27) on cabinet,** 28 West 10th Street, New York, May 1959. Photograph by Alexander Liberman.

13 **Teeny and Duchamp at Man Ray's studio,** 2 bis rue Férou, Paris, c. 1955. Photograph by Man Ray. Philadelphia Museum of Art, Marcel Duchamp Archive.

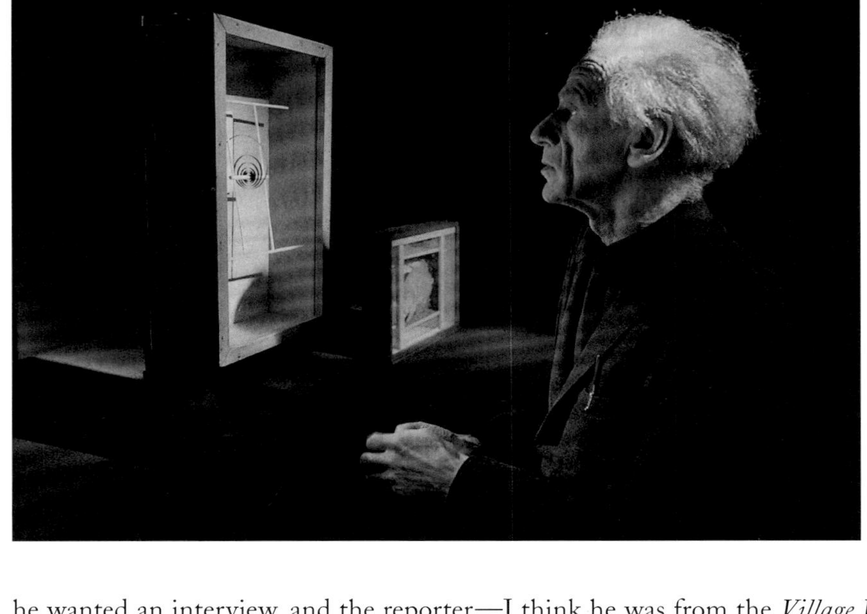

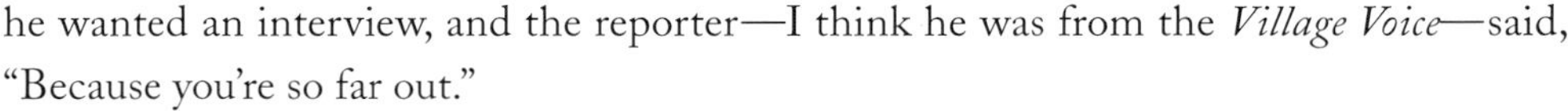

he wanted an interview, and the reporter—I think he was from the *Village Voice*—said, "Because you're so far out."

Duchamp leaned back and took a drag on his cigar. He always pulled out one of his cigars when he found himself in a less-than-perfect social situation. "Far out," he said finally, meditating on it. "Far out."

The reporter started fumbling to explain what "far out" meant.

And Duchamp said, "No, no, I understand 'far out.'" Then after a minute, he said, "I want to show you something really far out. Walter, would you go into the bedroom and bring in one of the Cornells to show this young man."

The guy was saying, "Cornell? Cornell who?" And Duchamp started to talk to him about Cornell. I came back in with the work—it was from the Pharmacy series—and the reporter stared at it, trying to take notes. Duchamp kept talking about it, using everyday language: "Look at this. Look at how marvelous it is. See? He works with *things*."

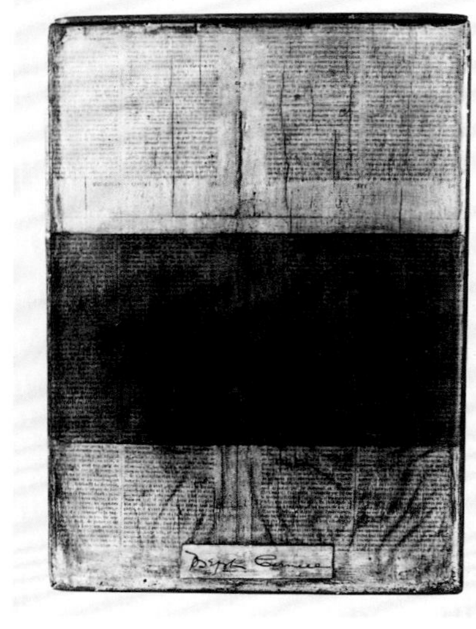

Cornell and Duchamp were artists whose imaginations and techniques transcended any number of the physical and conceptual boundaries of the art of their time. No other artists in the first half of the twentieth century were as involved with employing or assembling everyday objects for the purposes of art. By 1913, Duchamp had pioneered the art of what he called readymades. Certain of these readymades, such as the *Bottle Rack* (1914), were commercially fabricated objects he simply selected. Others, such as *With Hidden Noise* (pl. 2), were "adjusted" readymades, made up of various off-the-shelf parts put together.

This was a very radical turn away from the traditional forms of visual art based in drawing. Nonetheless, Duchamp was a superb draftsman. He made all sorts of drawings and studies on paper. Cornell, on the other hand, relied almost totally on found objects, assemblage, and collage. He is perhaps the most important twentieth-century artist who did not, in any conventional sense, draw. (He referred to his little aggregates of three-dimensional material as "sketchboxes.") The only things he produced in that regard, as far as I know, were some Rorschach-like ink patterns on paper or within the pages of books that anticipated the large Rorschach paintings that Andy Warhol made several decades later.

14 Cornell viewing his work in Walter Hopps' installation for "New York Painting and Sculpture 1940–1970" (October 18, 1969–February 8, 1970), The Metropolitan Museum of Art, New York, October 1969. Photograph by Duane Michals.

15 Cornell, Untitled (Dovecote), c. 1951–52. Box construction, 14 1/8 x 9 7/8 x 3 1/8 in. Private collection.

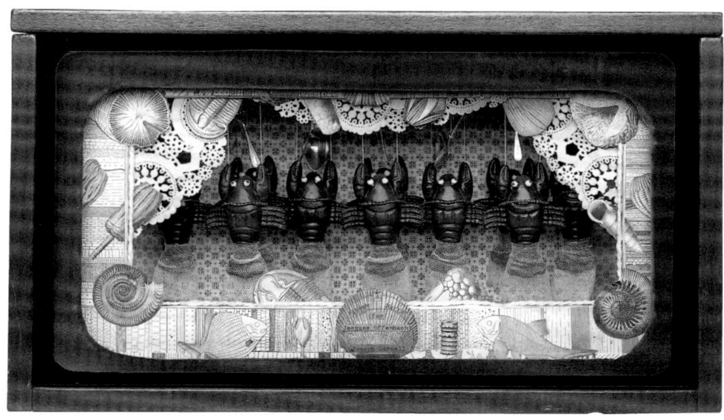

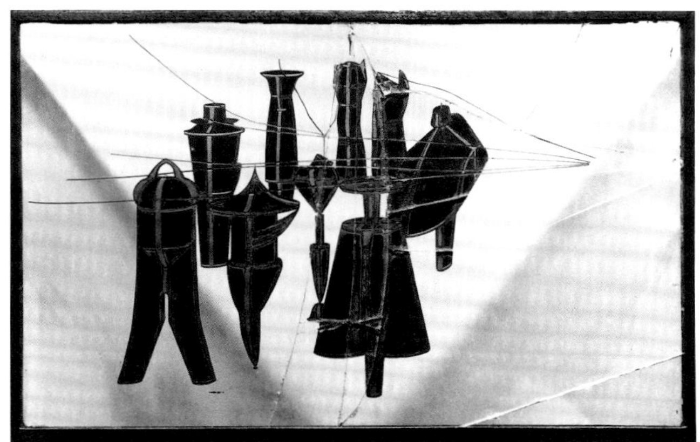

When I asked Cornell who was his favorite abstract artist of his time, he responded, "What do you mean 'my time'?" "The abstract painters who work in New York now. Born around the same time you were. Do you care for any of those?" There was a long thoughtful silence. Finally, he said, "I think Mark Rothko's paintings are very beautiful." And when you look at the backs of some of Cornell's boxes and collages, with all those blended and stained colors—sometimes rose, sometimes blue, or blue to black—they often resemble Rothkos (fig. 15).

Cornell didn't only "work with things"—he transformed them. His cosmology was one of everyday parts, a reality that was both quotidian and somehow mysteriously other (fig. 14). I think of his work as a kind of unselfconscious alchemy. And that is the quality to which I believe Duchamp responded most strongly. Duchamp was, of course, extremely interested in the history of alchemy, as were his patron Walter Arensberg and his colleague Robert Lebel. Cornell, for his part, acknowledged that he liked Duchamp's art, but found some Surrealism frightening. About Max Ernst, he said, "Oh, he is often very disturbing to me." I said, "Why is that?" "Well, it seems to involve a kind of black magic. And I'm interested in white magic."

THE

Eye Test, Not a "Nude Descending a Staircase."

By Marcel Duchamp

If you come into * linen, your time is thirsty because * ink saw some wood intelligent enough to get giddiness from a sister. However, even if it should be smilable to shut * hair whose water writes always in * plural, they have avoided frequency, meaning mother-in-law; powder will take a chance; and* road could try. But after somebody brought any multiplication as soon as * stamp was out, a great many cords refused to go through. Around the wire's people, who will be able to sweeten * rug, that is to say why must every patents look for a wife? Pushing four dangers near * listening place, * vacation had not dug absolutely nor this like-ness has eaten.

* *the*

Appartenant a' Marcel Duchamp, depuis Novembre, 1915

Duchamp and Cornell had very different sensibilities. Duchamp worked conceptually, putting art "in the service of the mind," as he would say, while Cornell tended to work poetically. His artworks were not conceptual machines; they were small, imaginary theaters. Duchamp was always the wise man, and Cornell was forever the wise child. Even the titles of their works illustrate this difference: Duchamp's *9 Malic Molds* (fig. 17) versus Cornell's *A Pantry Ballet (for Jacques Offenbach)* (fig. 16), for example.

Duchamp's interest in language was acute. In 1912, he spent a crucial period in Munich, where there were modern art shows beyond what he could see in Paris. While he was there, he studied German so that he could read what was being written about Kandinsky and what Kandinsky was writing about art. He improved his English on the boat to America in 1915. Once in New York, he made a wonderful small conceptual work called "*The*" for which he wrote a little text in English, and every time the article *the* came up, he

16 Cornell, *A Pantry Ballet (for Jacques Offenbach)*, 1942. Box construction, 10 1/2 x 18 1/8 x 6 in. The Nelson-Atkins Museum of Art, Kansas City, Missouri. Gift of the Friends of Art.

17 Duchamp, *9 Moules Mâlic [9 Malic Molds]*, 1914–15. Oil, lead wire, and sheet lead on glass, mounted between two glass plates, 26 x 39 7/8 in. Private collection.

18 Duchamp, "THE, Eye Test, Not a 'Nude Descending a Staircase,'" 1916. *Rogue* 2, no. 1 (October 1916): p. 2.

would put a star instead of the word (fig. 18). He was also a connoisseur of slang, and he really understood the Americanness of Man Ray. People who had a vernacular quality appealed to Duchamp. That's clearly what he liked about CPLY, the Pop-Surrealist who was one of the most quintessentially American figures I've ever known.

Duchamp's use of language often involved the kind of labeling one would find in a museum of science. It was pointedly technical. Even the complete title of *Étant donnés* (1946–66) is written like a curious kind of theorem:

Étant donnés: 1° la chute d'eau
2° le gaz d'éclairage

[Given: 1. The Waterfall /2. The Illuminating Gas]. These two essential elements resonate with a sign that sometimes appeared on new apartment buildings in Paris at the beginning of this century—*EAU & GAZ À TOUS LES ETAGES* [WATER AND GAS ON EVERY FLOOR]—and which Duchamp, in 1958, had selected as a readymade artwork.

Cornell also responded to signs in the world—on buildings, shops, stores, or theaters—but they were the kind one would have seen in the turn-of-the-century Paris of his imagination (or in the photographs of Eugene Atget, with which Cornell was familiar). He used examples of French typography in some of his boxes, not because he was trying for a Dadaist or Cubist effect but because he liked the language. The words and phrases in Cornell's work float alone, rather than being built into the composition as they are in the work of Braque or Schwitters. Sometimes he would throw in a line from a Verlaine poem, or a description of what the weather was like that day, or he'd glue a whole page of text from an old book in Latin onto the back of a box.

For Cornell, even small experiences could be virtually overwhelming. He would fill a pillbox with pink sand, then stare at it as if it contained a whole universe of events. The critic Nicolas Calas once told me that he had spotted Cornell alone at a department store bakery, examining a slice of angel food cake with a magnifying glass as if he were exploring the surface of the moon. Either Cornell had a great interest in tiny phenomena, Calas thought, or he was a complete madman.

One of the most perfect existential expressions of sexual feeling and its surrogates is the poem by Wallace Stevens called "The Emperor of Ice Cream." It has a line about "concupiscent curds," which I take to mean sweet little nuggets, bonbons, or sugar cubes. One of Duchamp's works with which Cornell undoubtedly was familiar is *Why Not Sneeze Rose Sélavy?*, a small white bird cage filled with marble cubes that look like sugar cubes—Rose Sélavy's ejaculatory sneeze (pl. 9). In Cornell's Dovecote series, the small white cube takes on a singularly chaste aspect. In his life, though, sweets were a passion, and I think it's fair to say that his inordinate sweet tooth was partially a sublimation of erotic impulse.

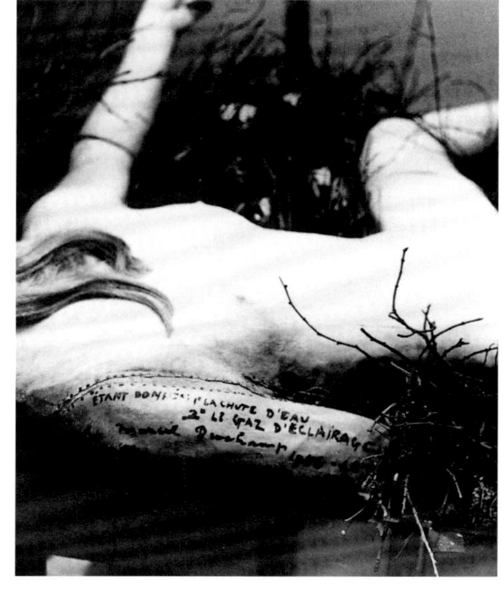

19 Duchamp's inscription on *Étant donnés* figure (1946–66), 80 East 11th Street studio, New York, c. 1966. Photograph by Denise Brown Hare.

Cornell was very interested in Duchamp's 1963 retrospective (figs. 22–25), and the fact that I had done it played well with him. (I discovered later that he had saved the announcement as well as the catalogue for the show.) In 1966, I was able to present Cornell's first major retrospective, also at the Pasadena Art Museum (figs. 20 and 21).[2] I had hoped he would come out to see it, but he didn't travel long distances.

During the first serious conversation I had with him about his show, he asked me if I had ever been to the observatory on Mount Wilson, just north of Pasadena. As it hap-

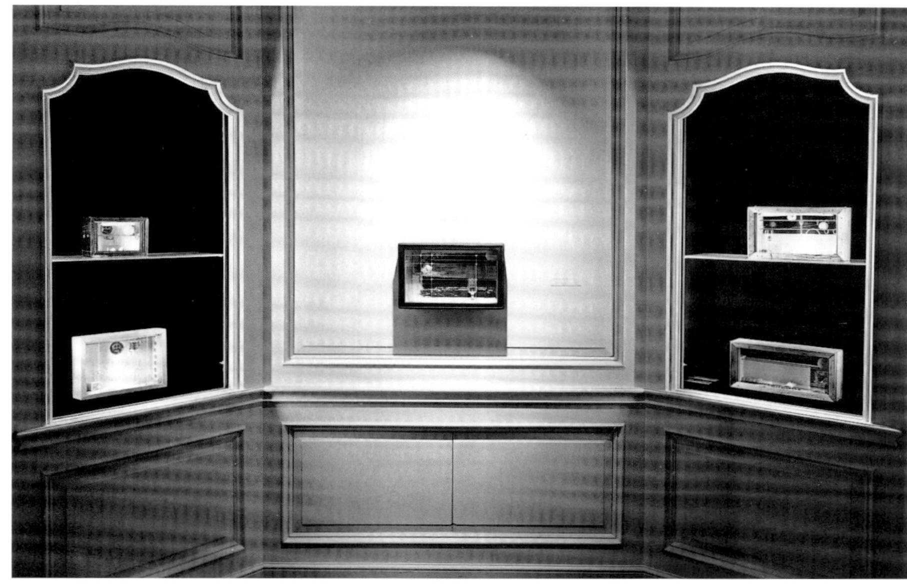

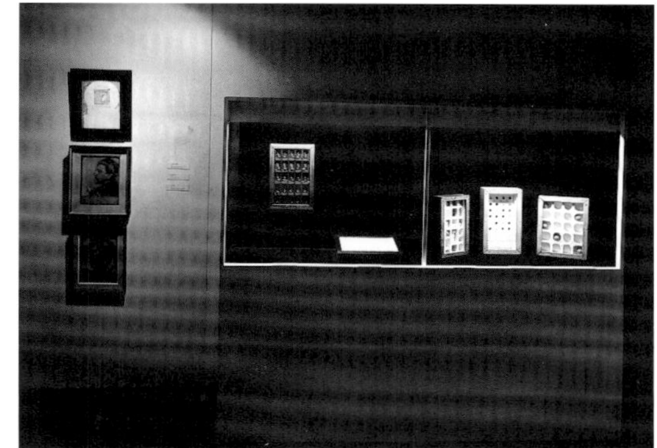

pened, I had often gone there as a child. Sometimes when it was just too hot at home, my mother would take me and my brother up there, and we would stay overnight in a cabin. Somehow she talked her way into the observatory world, and we got to know the people who worked with the great telescopes and the solar tower. We'd go in and watch them working at night and eat the marvelous banana cream pies from their commissary.

So, I said, "Let me tell you about an amazing artifact I saw up there."

And Cornell said, "What was that?"

"Doctor Albert Abraham Michelson did an experiment in the twenties to measure the speed of light in a vacuum. And sections of his mile-long tube, with mirrors at each end that trapped the pulse of light, are stored there." I went on describing it since Cornell seemed to be interested, but as I was talking, he pulled a book off the shelf and began to read it. I stopped. He said, "Go on, Mr. Hopps"—he was very courtly and he always called me "Mr. Hopps"—"I'm just following the story here as you're recounting it." The book he had in his hands was *Michelson and The Speed of Light*. He had pasted an epigraph from it onto the back of one of his boxes: "The light dove, piercing in her easy flight the air and perceiving its resistance, imagines that flight would be easier in empty space."[3]

Cornell and Duchamp were both interested in science. But while Cornell loved its poetic imagery, Duchamp was more interested in concepts that could not be depicted in any obvious way by drawings or objects. He was a serious student of advanced thought in physics. Interestingly, one reason that Duchamp didn't come over to New York for the 1913 Armory Show, where his *Nude Descending a Staircase* (1912) caused a sensation, was that he was working (for a modest salary) in the mathematics and physical science section of the Bibliothèque Sainte-Geneviève in Paris. Certain of his notes concern themselves with his idea of the *inframince* and refer to the geometry of *n*-dimensions. Late in his career, Duchamp made studies for a conceptual readymade *The Clock in Profile* (1964). He posed the question: "What time is it when you look at a clock in profile?" And he imagined a standard round clock face that is set up to be viewed from the side: the clock is functioning but—since one cannot read it—it no longer tells the time.

20, 21 Cornell retrospective exhibition (December 27, 1966–February 11, 1967), Pasadena Museum of Art, Pasadena, California, installation views. Photographs by Frank J. Thomas.

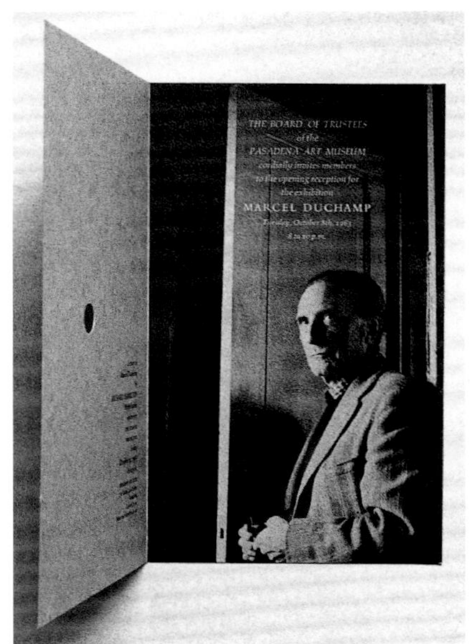

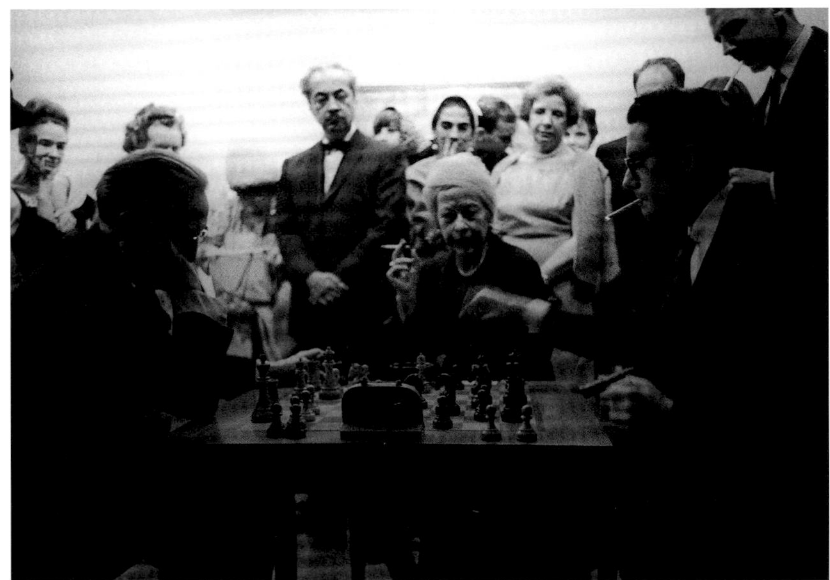

Duchamp had an ironic way of referring to himself as lazy—as a "*respirateur*," or "breather"—but, in fact, he was a very efficient man. His friend Henri-Pierre Roché once said that Duchamp's finest work was his use of time.

He was, accordingly, very particular about his collaborators. At times, a collaboration meant someone else carrying out his plans meticulously—as when Man Ray photographed *Dust Breeding* (fig. 28). Duchamp worked with Breton on several projects that interested him. Then there was Lebel, who was one of Duchamp's favorite people and with whom he probably had the greatest intellectual rapport after Arensberg. Duchamp chose him to produce the first catalogue raisonné of his work and worked closely with him on it. A particular coconspirator in Europe was Francis Picabia, whose early mechanomorphic works were strongly influenced by Duchamp.

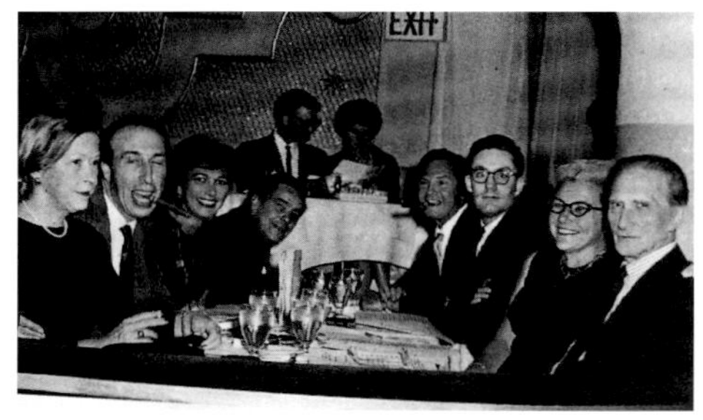

Duchamp had a special fondness for Americans, and his interaction with American artists is more significant, I think, than has been acknowledged. I believe he had a hand in *God* (1918), an extraordinary adjusted readymade attributed to Baroness Elsa von Freytag Loringhoven and Morton Schamberg, who was one of Duchamp's confidants and a relative of Arensberg's. Duchamp was also involved in the creation of a crazy headdress of von Freytag Loringhoven's, which looks like the great-grandmother of Jean Tinguely's sculpture.

There were claims that Duchamp suggested the mobile form to Calder. In the thirties, Calder was in Paris, making his wire portraits of Josephine Baker and others. Clay Spohn, a very curious artist from San Francisco who was a conceptual *bricoleur* and who did some of the first assemblage art in California, was also in Paris at that time, and he knew both Calder and Duchamp. Spohn told me that he had actually been the one to suggest the idea of the mobile to Calder. I had heard that it was Duchamp, and asked Marcel about that. He laughed and said, "Oh, people have always misunderstood. Spohn, this strange American whom I enjoyed very much, suggested to Calder that he take the little parts and balance them on wires to make these contraptions. What I did was to name it. What I invented was the word *mobile*."

When Duchamp returned to New York in 1942, he needed help producing the boxes

22 **Invitation for retrospective exhibition "by or of Marcel Duchamp or Rrose Sélavy"** (October 8–November 3, 1963), Pasadena Museum of Art, Pasadena, California.

23 **Duchamp, Teeny, and Walter Hopps playing chess** during retrospective exhibition "by or of Marcel Duchamp or Rrose Sélavy," Pasadena Museum of Art, Pasadena, California, October 1963. Photograph by Julian Wasser.

24 **Teeny, Richard Hamilton, Betty Factor, Bill Copley, Monte Factor, Walter Hopps, Betty Asher, and Duchamp,** Stardust Hotel, Las Vegas, October 1963.

of miniature artworks for his *Boîte* edition. He had sent fifty sets of all the primary parts to America beforehand, and Cornell was the first person he hired to assemble them. Cornell was clearly used to working in a miniature scale, and Duchamp must have had an appreciation for his finesse. Duchamp himself wasn't a great carpenter. That was one of the first things I noticed when I saw *Étant donnés* in his studio after he died. I was in there with Bill Copley and Teeny, looking at the woodwork and the armature, and I said, "My God, there are a lot of nails that he couldn't pound all the way through back here, and they're all bent."

It is my notion that *Étant donnés* is the final manifestation of Duchamp's masterwork, *The Bride Stripped Bare by Her Bachelors, Even* (1915-23). The first manifestation is the poetic narrative in conceptual language that is contained in the *Green Box* (pls. 16 and 17). Although they were not published until 1934, some of the notes in the *Green Box* date back to before 1915, when Duchamp started fabricating the *Large Glass*. These notes are the complete schema for, and literary form of, the *Large Glass*, which is itself like a circuit diagram or cybernetic abstraction. In *Étant donnés*, *The Bride Stripped Bare by Her Bachelors, Even* becomes a strange and magical three-dimensional tableau, and Duchamp's magnum opus is now complete: a work that exists in conceptual, diagrammatic, and figurative form.

When I was organizing Duchamp's retrospective five years before I saw *Étant donnés*, I remember asking him a question: "If you had been making a work in secret that was important to you, would this show be the occasion when you would want to have it seen?" The answer came with a nice smile: "Were it the case that such a work had been made,"—I was thrilled immediately because I knew that there was one—"this would not be the occasion."

I don't believe that Cornell knew about *Étant donnés* while Duchamp was working on it from 1946 to 1966. Both men had unusually private studio lives—very few people got down into Cornell's basement workroom, and Duchamp did most of his later work in a secret studio that perhaps only three people even knew about. But I think that Duchamp's decision to present *Étant donnés* as a tableau was probably greatly influenced by the three-dimensional theatrical space that exists, on a smaller scale, in all of Cornell's boxed assemblages.

It was not until after Cornell had died that I saw *Bébé Marie* (pl. 81; fig. 26), a work from the early 1940s, and realized that there was another, more imagistic resonance there. I had seen some of Cornell's little dolls in boxes—works such as *Mélisande* (pl. 97)—at his house when he was still alive, but *Bébé Marie* was not in his studio. The work consists of a very realistic, bisque-faced doll standing amid a suffusion of twigs and branches in a large, glass-fronted box. What is so stunning is that the female figure in *Étant donnés* lies on a similar bed of twigs and branches (fig. 19). It seems to be another instance where the things that Cornell did in innocence reverberated for Duchamp.

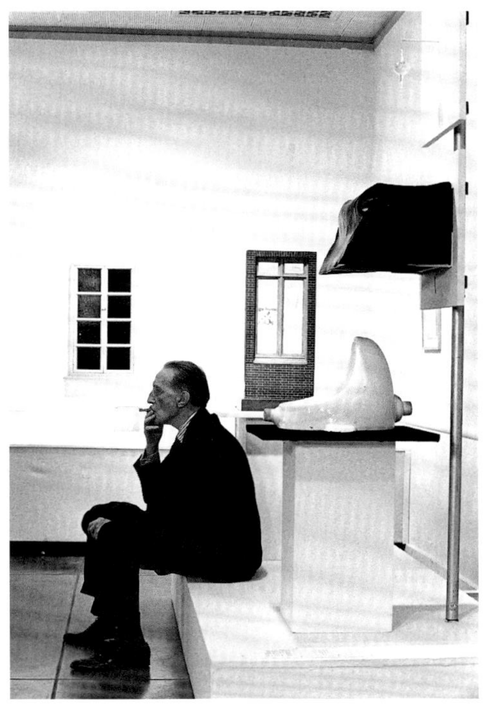

25 Duchamp at his retrospective exhibition "by or of Marcel Duchamp or Rrose Sélavy," Pasadena Museum of Art, Pasadena, California, October 1963. Photograph by Julian Wasser.

After Cornell died in 1972, the law firm of Greenbaum, Wolff and Ernst took over his estate. It was an august old firm that had also defended James Joyce's writing against pornography charges. A friend had recommended this firm to Cornell after he had made innumerable attempts to develop idealized plans for the preservation of his work. Cornell occasionally gave work away. He also had a habit of making "sanctuary loans," as he called them, to people and institutions, and there was little in the way of records for these transactions. It was a daunting task for Richard Ader—the attorney in charge—to unravel it all. Beyond this, there was the job of determining which of the boxes in Cornell's studio were finished, and of differentiating his dossier artworks from boxed accumulations of working materials. In the course of his research, Ader spotted my name and wrote to me. Eventually, he took me to Cornell's house to go through the studio.

I had seen Cornell's basement workroom, but while he was alive, I never did get up in the attic, where he stored all kinds of things, nor did I get into the garage. When I saw what was there, I got on the phone with Joshua Taylor, the director of what is now the National Museum of American Art, and told him that it was vital we pack all these things up to save for a study center. This was clearly going to require time and unbudgeted money. Taylor had one question, and he put it very succinctly. He said, "If you don't do what you are suggesting here, is it *the furnace*?" And I said, "I'm afraid it is." He said, "Well, I don't know what it all entails, but I authorize you to go ahead." Everything that was considered incunabula or ephemera—and eventually all the incomplete dossiers and unfinished boxes—went to the Smithsonian Institution and became, ultimately, the Joseph Cornell Study Center.

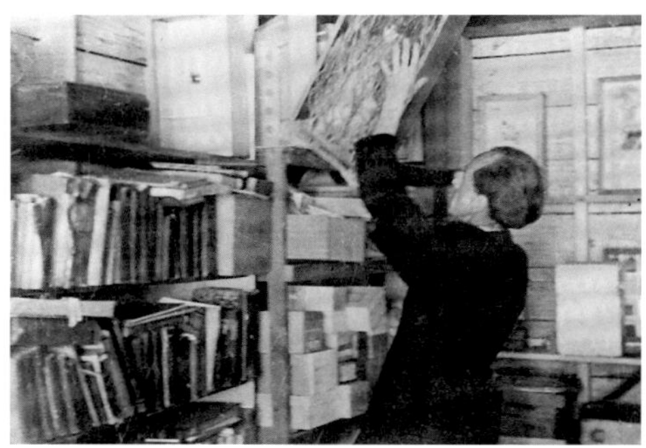

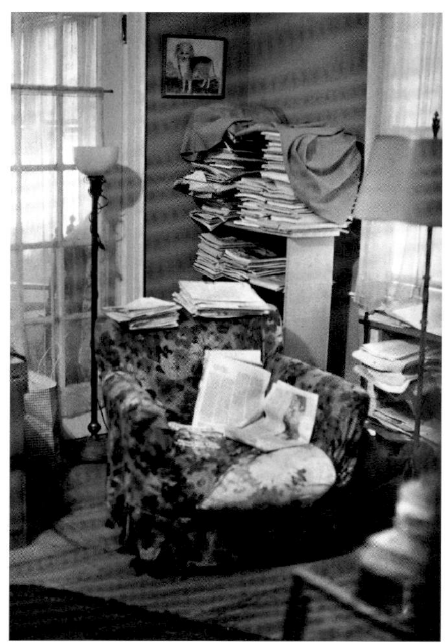

As I sorted through Cornell's studio, I discovered that although he had failed to keep a complete inventory of artwork, he did categorize and label much of his working material. He had gone farther than any other artist in the twentieth century, save Schwitters, in collecting archives of materials to turn into art. In Cornell's basement, I found a small shoebox labeled "Mouse Material," and I wondered out loud about what it could be. Ader said, "That sounds disgusting." I said, "But I have to look at this." So I opened it up and said, "Oh, dust bunnies."

Ader said, "What?"

"You know," I said. "Everyone has their own nickname for them. Cornell called it 'Mouse Material.' I call them dust bunnies. The little things that collect under beds and couches."

During one of the evaluating and packing sessions, and there were any number of these, we began to go through Cornell's books. In what was the library or dining room, there were simple bookshelves—just cinder blocks and boards, up to counter height—all the way around the walls (fig. 27). I happened to know that Cornell sometimes made collages inside books. I looked in each of the books to see what was in there, and I found two extraordinary things. One was volume XXII of a set of French agricultural journals: there were innumerable cutouts and collages integrated into it. On one of its pages was a collage portrait of Duchamp, and the book as a whole had become an extended symbolic portrait of him (pl. 51). The other unique object I found was the *Duchamp Dossier*, which was filed upright among the books (pp. 17–59).

Cornell's dossiers were boxed collections of clippings and other material that surrounded a given subject. Sometimes they centered around a place, but more often around a person or the idea of someone. The private world of the dossier had always been an important link between Duchamp and Cornell. These boxes were not just repositories for drawings or studies; they involved a curious kind of arcane and obsessive private research. The *Duchamp Dossier* was an informal dossier. Its housing, which Cornell had stained inside a lavender-blue color, appears to be a prototype for the housing of the *Boîte* edition[4]—dating probably from the time that Cornell was working for Duchamp assembling them.

26 Cornell lifting Untitled (Bébé Marie) (c. 1943), 3708 Utopia Parkway, Flushing, New York, 1960s. Joseph Cornell Study Center, Natl. Museum of American Art, Smithsonian. Gift of Mr. and Mrs. John A. Benton.

27 ***Cornell's Easy Chair,*** 3708 Utopia Parkway, Flushing, New York, May 1970. Photograph by Harry Roseman.

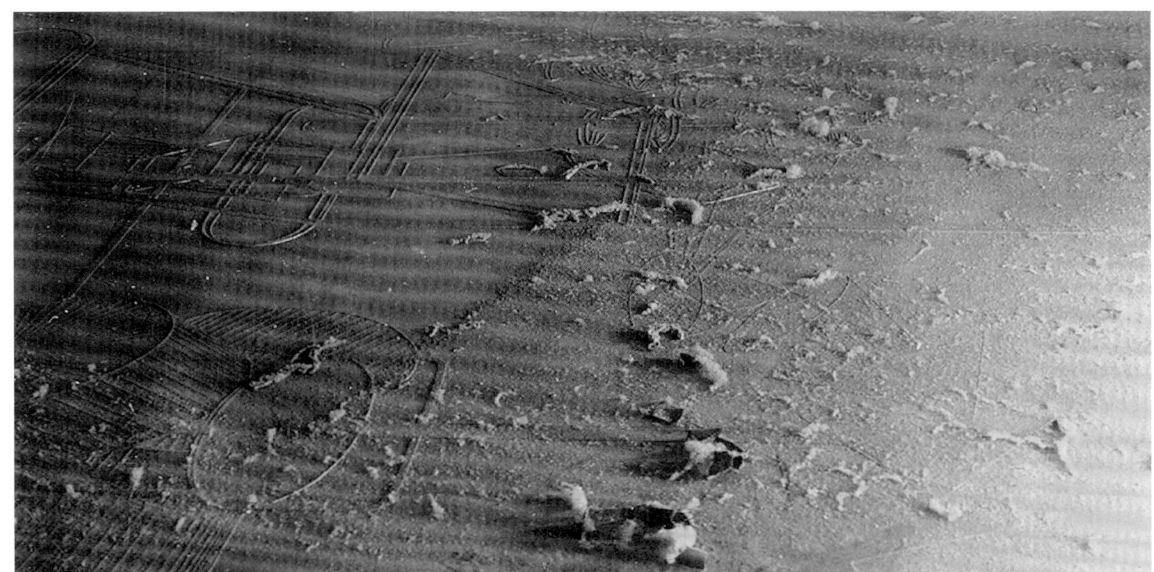

There's no way of knowing whether this dossier was made in collaboration with Duchamp, or whether Duchamp knew of it at all, although it seems likely that he may have suspected it existed. It contained various things that Duchamp had clearly given to Cornell. Others Cornell probably bought, like his copies of *Vogue* that show a model posing next to the *Large Glass* (DD 103 and 104). Duchamp always solved the problem of filing by throwing away most of the letters he received: read it, absorb it, tear it up, and throw it away. I think that Joseph sometimes might have been in a position to fish one out of the wastebasket. Most interestingly, the *Duchamp Dossier* also contained some signed Duchamp ready-mades, including the adjusted LePage's glue box. On the box where it says "strength," Duchamp had added the word "gimme," knowing that "gimme strength" was a slang phrase in America. He then signed it and gave it to Cornell, because he knew that for both of them, given the nature of their work, glue was essential (fig. 29; DD 67).

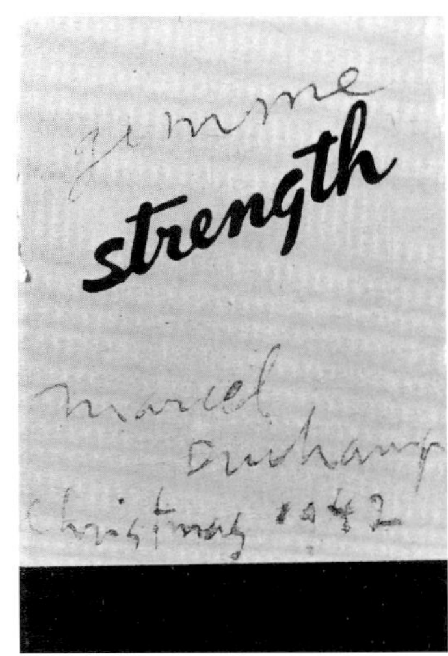

I believe it is no coincidence that Cornell chose to create his portrait of Marcel in a book on French agriculture. Duchamp, after all, once described himself as a horticulturalist—the proprietor of a "dust-breeding farm." As John Cage put it, "The rest were artists: Duchamp collected dust."

28 Man Ray, *Dust Breeding*, 1920. Vintage gelatin-silver print, 2¼ x 4⅜ in. Jedermann Collection, N.A.

29 Duchamp, cardboard box [Gimme Strength] (detail), December 21, 1942 (DD 67), from Cornell, *Duchamp Dossier*, c. 1942–53. Philadelphia Museum of Art. Gift of The Joseph and Robert Cornell Memorial Foundation.

Notes

This text is based on extensive conversations with Lynda Roscoe Hartigan on December 10, 1997, and February 5, 1998, in Houston. Additional material was taken from telephone conversations with Anne Doran in May, June, and July 1998; she and Deborah Treisman edited the transcriptions. I wish to acknowledge them all for their valuable assistance.

1. "by or of Marcel Duchamp or Rrose Sélavy," retrospective exhibition, October 8–November 3, 1963, Pasadena Art Museum, Pasadena, California.

2. "An Exhibition of Works by Joseph Cornell," December 27, 1966–February 11, 1967, Pasadena Art Museum.

3. Immanuel Kant, quoted in Bernard Jaffe, *Michelson and The Speed of Light* (Garden City, N.Y.: Doubleday & Company, Inc., 1960), epigraph.

4. See *Duchamp Dossier* Inventory (DD 0) for comments concerning the origin of this container.

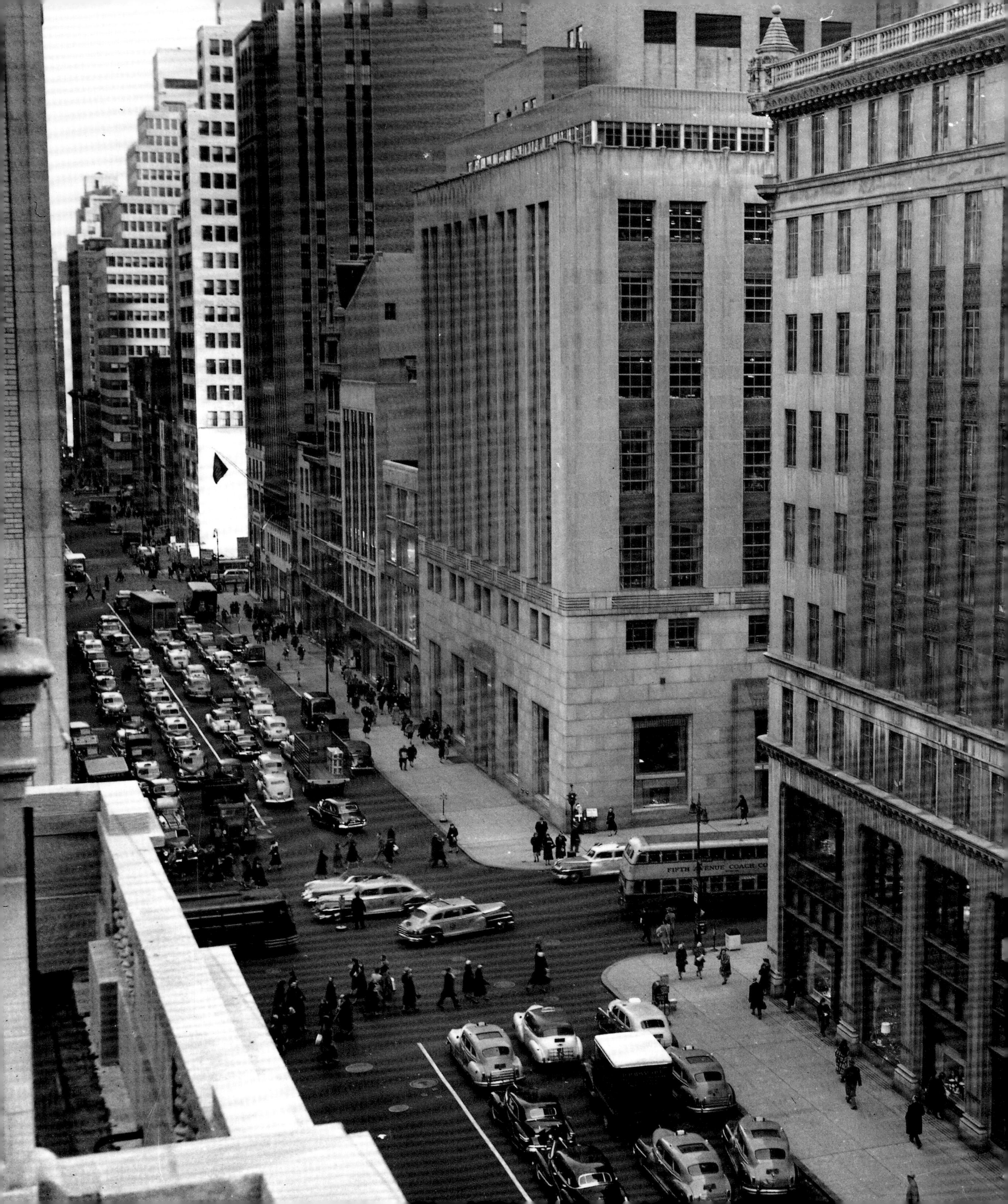
FIFTH AVENUE COACH CO

Habitat for a Dossier

ANN TEMKIN

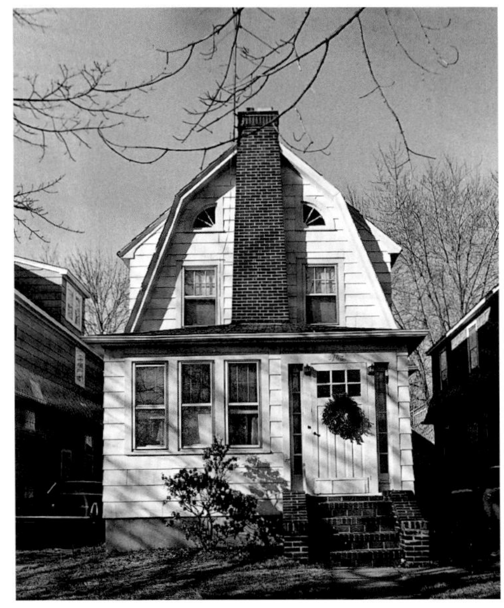

With most of its contents dating from the early 1940s, Joseph Cornell's *Duchamp Dossier* (c. 1942–53) brings an armchair traveler to New York City at one of the most remarkable moments in its history. Across the Atlantic the horrors of modern warfare and genocide continue unabated, while in New York the war is both far away and ever present. Offices are short of workers, and stores are empty of merchandise; meat and liquor are tightly rationed. Yet the city serves as "the Christmas tree of the world," and a mass influx of émigré artists and intellectuals has produced an uncanny convergence of genius.[1] The *Duchamp Dossier* thus maps a time and place of rampant creativity and cultural adventure, a climate of crowded marvels amid privation. In a world at war, Manhattan is truly an island, renewed and reshaped by its shipwrecked travelers and their hosts (fig. 30).

The *Duchamp Dossier* provides an admirable guide for navigating a route through this particular metropolis. Rand-McNally might sneer at its faded bits and pieces, but they lead us to the people and places Cornell and Duchamp share during the four years of their closest alliance, following Duchamp's June 1942 arrival in New York. Choosing for our tour the season of Christmas 1943, when Cornell turns forty (Duchamp is sixteen years his elder), we will visit the locales crucial to their story, and those specifically memorialized in the *Duchamp Dossier*.

The journey begins at Cornell's house at 3708 Utopia Parkway in Flushing, Queens, the easternmost borough of New York City. This small two-and-a-half-story, white-shingled house, with a brick chimney and front stoop, has been home to Cornell, his mother, and his brother, Robert, since 1929 (fig. 31). Flushing had its moment of glory in 1939 and 1940 as host to the spectacularly successful World's Fair. Cornell's house lies five miles northeast of the fairgrounds, which occupy a reclaimed garbage dump.[2] Cornell is a veteran of many visits to the Fair, whose attractions ranged from the carnality of Salvador Dalí's *Dream of Venus* pavilion to the utopian grandeur of the Trylon and the Perisphere (fig. 32).

Cornell's middle-class neighborhood may as well be a planet away from the art world. But it is actually a short bus or bicycle ride to Main Street, the commercial hub of Flushing, where one can board the number 7 subway to Grand Central Station, a twenty-minute trip that costs five cents. Emerging onto the Concourse, we gaze up into a Cornellian skyscape: Paul Helleu's deep blue map of the zodiac fills the huge vaulted ceiling of the station.

We walk up Lexington Avenue directly to 57th Street, the reigning capital of the international art market (figs. 33 and 34). Extending from Lexington to Sixth Avenue, its heart is at the corner of Madison and 57th. The French gallery Durand-Ruel was the first to move to East 57th Street (number 12) in 1913, and M. Knoedler and Company, the

30 **57th Street at Fifth Avenue looking east,** New York, 1940s.

31 **Cornell home,** 3708 Utopia Parkway, Flushing, New York, 1970. Photograph by Hans Namuth.

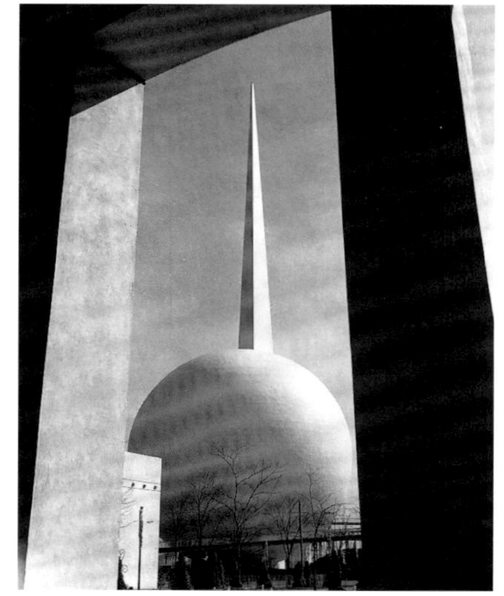

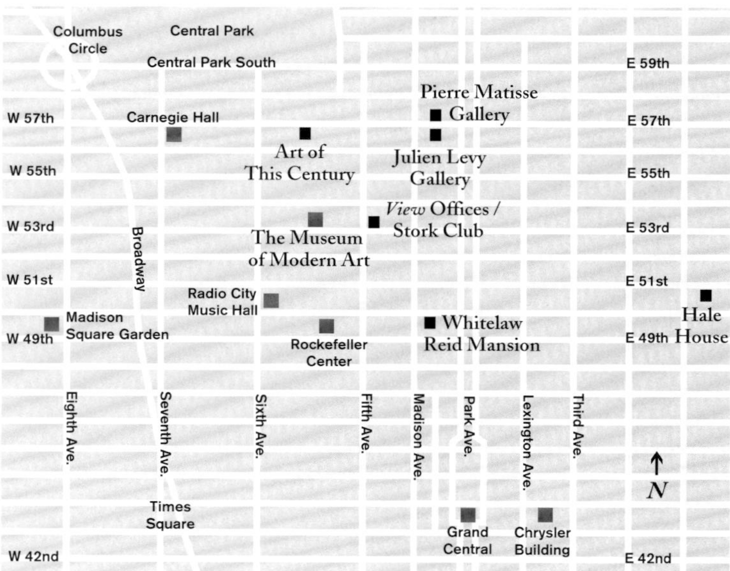

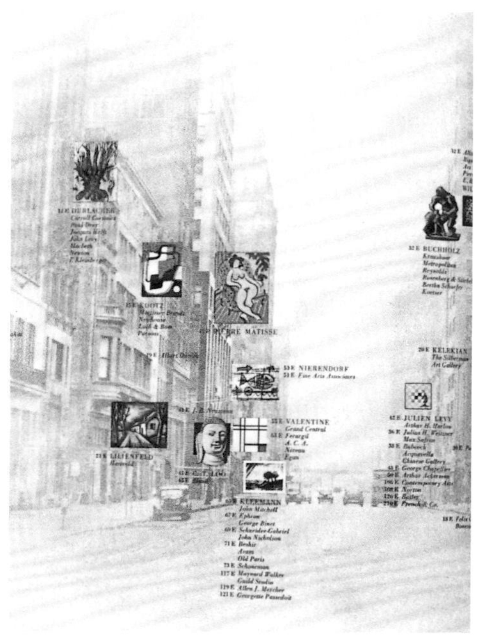

32 Perisphere and Trylon, New York World's Fair, Flushing Meadows, New York, 1939.

33 Midtown Manhattan, 1943, indicating sites of interest for Cornell and Duchamp.

34 "Two blocks of '57th' from Fifth to Park Avenues are the hodgepodge center of U.S. Art." "57th Street," *Fortune* (September 1946): p. 146.

oldest American dealer, joined them next door at number 14 in 1924. The auction house Parke-Bernet acquired new quarters in 1939 at 30 East 57th Street. By 1943 well over a hundred galleries line the broad, bustling street, or spill over into the few blocks immediately adjacent. Given that the war has dissolved most art business in Europe, "the Street" has become something of a United Nations, and since 1940 it has experienced an unprecedented boom.[3] The acknowledged dean of modern art, Paul Rosenberg, who came from Paris in 1940, joins other recent émigrés such as J. B. Neumann, Karl Nierendorf, and Curt Valentine. It is into this microclimate of galleries, the early champions of avant-garde art, that Cornell's *Duchamp Dossier* escorts its tourists.

Walking west on 57th Street, along the north side of the street between Park and Madison, we arrive at number 55, a building that formerly housed the Brummer Gallery. Hungarian-born Joseph Brummer, now based on 58th Street, is best known for his superb taste in antiquities, medieval art, and Old Masters, but he is also devoted to the French art of his time. Thus he has hosted two exhibitions of sculpture by Constantin Brancusi, both of which Duchamp arranged and installed in the 57th Street gallery (fig. 35). It was here at number 55, during the second of these exhibitions (November 17, 1933–January 13, 1934), that Cornell met Duchamp for the first time. Cornell will reflect on the occasion after Duchamp's death in 1968: "Brummer Gallery / I recall so easily an esp. cherished one, first brief meeting (as a stranger), the piquant flavor of contact with / a unique personality. . . ."[4] The *Duchamp Dossier* contains a precious memento of that meeting: a reproduction of *La Mariée mise à nu par ses célibataires, même [The Bride Stripped Bare by Her Bachelors, Even] (Large Glass)* (1915–23) at the Brooklyn Museum in 1926, inscribed by Duchamp: *for Joseph Cornell* and dated: *January 1934* (DD 108). Cornell has saved it much as he would a glossy pinup of a Hollywood starlet, kindly signed and sent to an earnest admirer.

Crossing 57th Street to the south side and taking a few steps further west, we reach the Julien Levy Gallery at 42 East 57th Street, housed in a handsome five-story brownstone. A tiny passenger elevator brings visitors to the gallery's quarters on the fourth floor; Levy lives above the gallery, Old World style, on the fifth. He opened at this location in April 1943 upon his return from a year of U.S. military service.

Since its founding in 1931, the Julien Levy Gallery has been a vortex of avant-garde art, photography, and film (fig. 36). Self-consciously following in the footsteps of Alfred Stieglitz as a champion of the new, Levy began importing the products of the newest generation of Parisian artists. They work in a post-Cubist vocabulary and belong to either the Neo-Romantic or the Surrealist camp. By 1943 most of the artists are here in New York, but they fraternize only under the aegis of Levy's gallery. The Neo-Romantics, led by Russian-born Pavel Tchelitchew, are a high-society, largely homosexual group, much involved with the theater and dance worlds. The Surrealist artists socialize primarily among themselves and favor more esoteric intellectual pastimes.

In December 1943 the gallery is host to "Through the Big End of the Opera Glass," a three-man exhibition of elaborate small-scale items (pl. 66). Cornell has sent new boxes; Yves Tanguy, a series of tiny gouaches; and Duchamp, a group of miniatures related to the fabrication of *de ou par Marcel Duchamp ou Rrose Sélavy [by or of Marcel Duchamp or Rrose Sélavy]* (*Boîte* edition; 1935–41). As usual, Levy has relied on Cornell to design the announcement for the exhibition: a small quarto with one section for each artist and the fourth for the show's title, place, and date. Tanguy is represented by a simple ink drawing, while for himself Cornell has designed a gaily decorated list of his objects. Duchamp's corner features a gray, stamped upside-down image of Cupid, signed: *Marcel Duchamp.* Holding the paper up to the light reveals a red chessboard behind the Cupid labeled: *White to play and win.*[5] This project yields some valuable material for Cornell's *Duchamp Dossier,* the announcement, the maquette, and a torn letter from Levy urging Cornell to send in the "makeup" for the exhibition, all neatly folded in an envelope with a three-cent WIN THE WAR postage stamp (DD 14).

"Through the Big End of the Opera Glass" continues Levy's tradition of staging Cornell exhibitions at Christmastime, celebrating both the fairy-tale quality of his work and his Christmas Eve birthday, while also marketing his objects as attractive gifts. Because of the war, art has become a popular substitute for now-unavailable jewelry and other luxury goods (fig. 37), leading the current issue of *The New Yorker* to obligingly list the galleries, including Levy's, "that have made definite efforts to meet the Christmas demand."[6] The miniature items of Tanguy, Duchamp, and Cornell are inexpensive enough to work as holiday ornaments. Duchamp's *Air de Paris* (pl. 4) would gladden the heart of any homesick émigré, while a tiny urinal strikes just the right note for an avant-garde Christmas tree.

The three collaborators for "Through the Big End of the Opera Glass" all have close associations with Levy, although only Cornell belongs to the gallery's stable. In 1936 Levy gave Tanguy his first show in the United States, and while Tanguy did not join the gallery when he moved here in 1941, the two have stayed dear friends. Levy first met Duchamp, whom he considers one of his "godfathers" or an "elder brother," at the Brummer Gallery in 1926, where Duchamp was installing the first Brancusi exhibition.[7] When Duchamp eventually invited Levy, an aspiring filmmaker, to sail back to Paris with him, the two established a warm bond. Levy's filmmaking career did not go far, but when he returned to New York and opened a gallery, Duchamp's guiding spirit remained strong. Levy briefly and proudly owned *Mariée [Bride]* (1912), and he has handled the sales of several other Duchamp paintings.

The new location of the Julien Levy Gallery is a few steps from the brownstone at 602 Madison Avenue where Levy first opened for business in 1931 at the age of twenty-five,

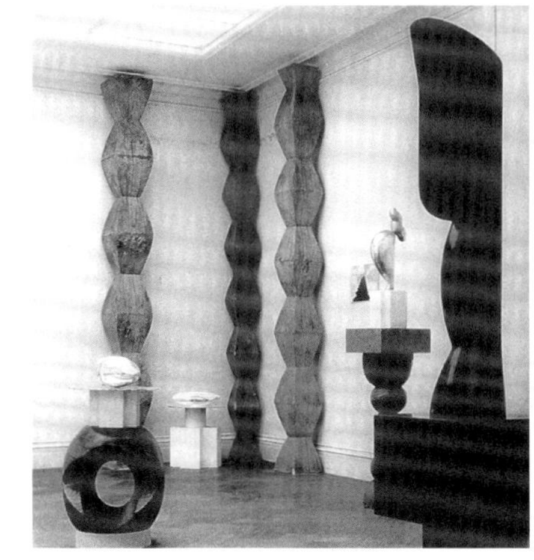

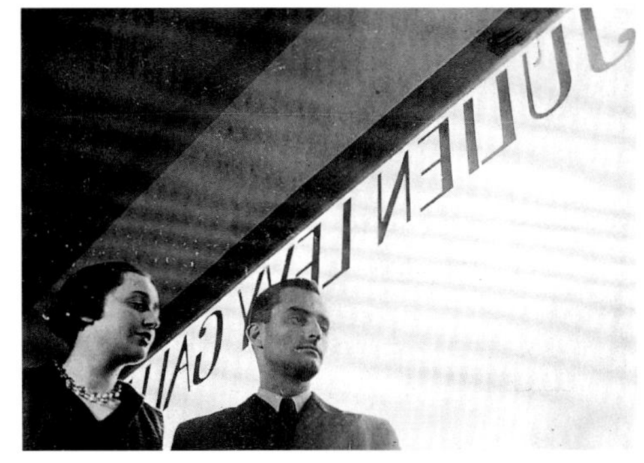

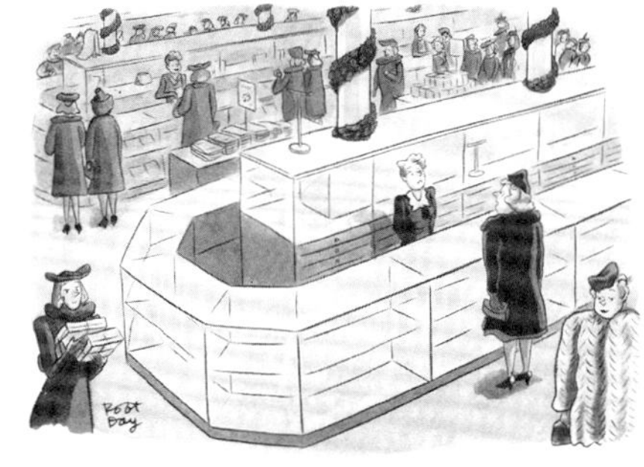

"What department is this?"

35 Duchamp's installation of Brancusi exhibition (November 17, 1933–January 13, 1934), Brummer Gallery, 55 East 57th Street, New York. Photograph by Soichi Sunami.

36 Joella and Julien Levy inside Julien Levy Gallery, 602 Madison Avenue, New York, c. 1935.

37 "What department is this?" *The New Yorker* (18 December 1943): p. 21. Cartoon by Robert Day. © The New Yorker Collection 1943, Robert J. Day

using funds inherited from his mother. Initially planning to focus on photography, he opened with a show of American photographs in the front room, while the back room, dramatically painted a deep red, held stacks of other photographs for browsing. A great photography enthusiast, Cornell quickly but unobtrusively became a habitué of the new gallery and soon introduced himself as an artist. Joella, Levy's first wife and his colleague in the gallery, later will remember Cornell bringing a collage to her desk as "he was frightened to show it to Julien first."[8] This was during the gallery's first season, when Levy was in the midst of preparing the exhibition "Surréalisme" for the coming January of 1932, following its premiere at the Wadsworth Atheneum in Hartford, Connecticut. Levy promptly added Cornell to his roster of artists for the New York showing and had him design the show's announcement (pl. 49). By the end of 1932, Levy had organized Cornell's debut exhibition, beautifully pairing his objects with Pablo Picasso's etchings for an edition of Honoré de Balzac's "The Unknown Masterpiece."

Cornell's two subsequent solo shows at the Julien Levy Gallery did not take place until 1939 and 1940 (pls. 60 and 61), in its second location at 15 East 57th Street, but he has stayed a favorite of Levy's and a dear friend of the Levy family (particularly of Joella's mother, the London-born poet and artist Mina Loy, a fellow Christian Scientist). In 1936, Cornell designed the cover of Levy's book *Surrealism*, basing it on his announcement for Levy's 1932 Surrealist exhibition (pl. 48; fig. 38). Levy ended the book's introductory text with the statement: "Finally Joseph CORNELL must be mentioned as one of the very few Americans at the present time who fully and creatively understands the surrealist viewpoint."[9] By 1943, he is one of the gallery's finest success stories.

A fellow champion of Surrealism and Levy's friendly rival, the dealer Pierre Matisse has a gallery across the street from Levy at 41 East 57th Street, on the northwest corner of Madison Avenue. It is located in the 1929 Fuller Building (fig. 39), an Art Deco masterpiece that at forty stories towers handsomely over its neighbors, boasting a sculpture by Elie Nadelman on its facade. Son of the artist Henri Matisse, Pierre came to New York in 1925 to learn the art business. He opened on the seventeenth floor of the Fuller Building in 1931, the same year that Levy founded his gallery, to market the work of his father and other Europeans such as André Masson and Joan Miró.

Pierre Matisse is ending the 1943 autumn season with an exhibition of paintings by Picasso from 1905–37; it is impossible to import recent work. The bulk of his schedule is dominated by the émigré artists who now live in or near New York (fig. 41), such as Fernand Léger, Marc Chagall, Tanguy (a schoolmate), and Roberto Sebastian Matta Echaurren. Over the last three years, Matisse and his American wife, Alexina (Teeny), have been helpful in all sorts of ways to the "artists in exile," as an exhibition at the gallery in March 1942 christened them (fig. 40). While Matisse himself has no close dealings with either Cornell or Duchamp, Teeny will become a cherished friend of the former and, in 1954, the wife of the latter.[10] From that time forward, she will be a key figure in the friendship between the two artists.

From Matisse's gallery, we continue west on 57th Street to Fifth Avenue. Crossing to the south side of the street once again, we walk half a block toward Sixth Avenue and stop at 30 West 57th Street. In the small foyer alongside Hicks tea shop and café, we take an elevator to the top of the seven-story building. There we enter the year-old galleries of Peggy Guggenheim's Art of This Century, designed by the Vienna-born architect Frederick

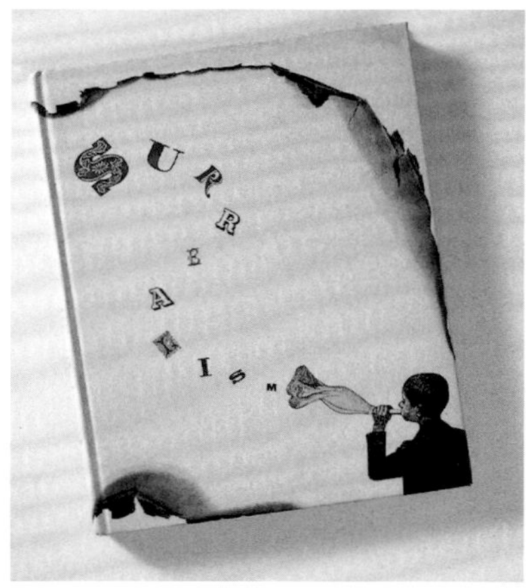

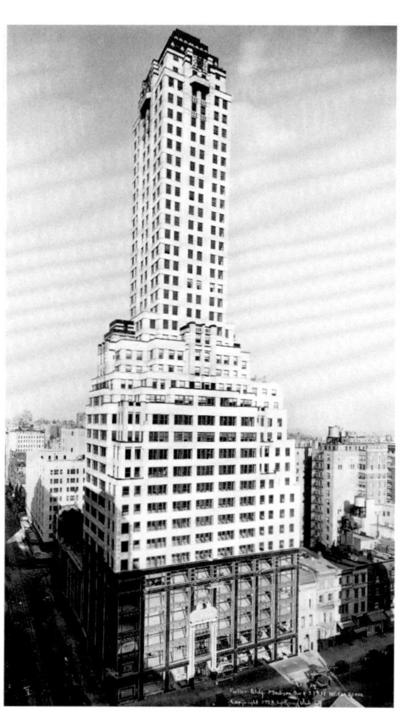

38 Cornell, cover design for Julien Levy's ***Surrealism*** (New York: The Black Sun Press, 1936).

39 Fuller Building, 41 East 57th Street at Madison Avenue, New York, 1929.

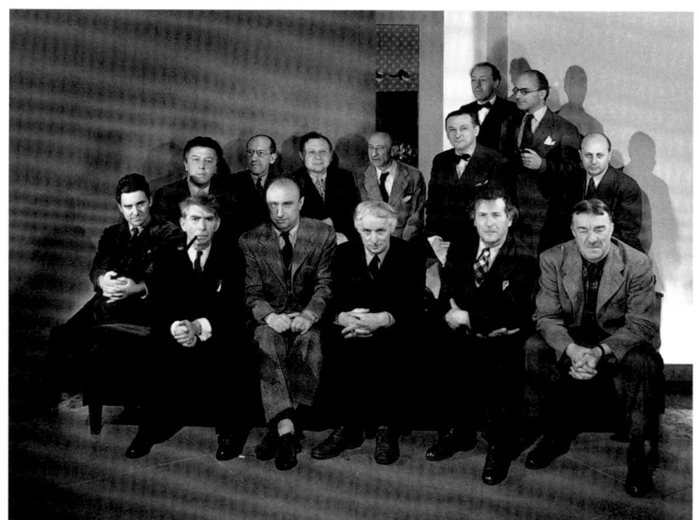

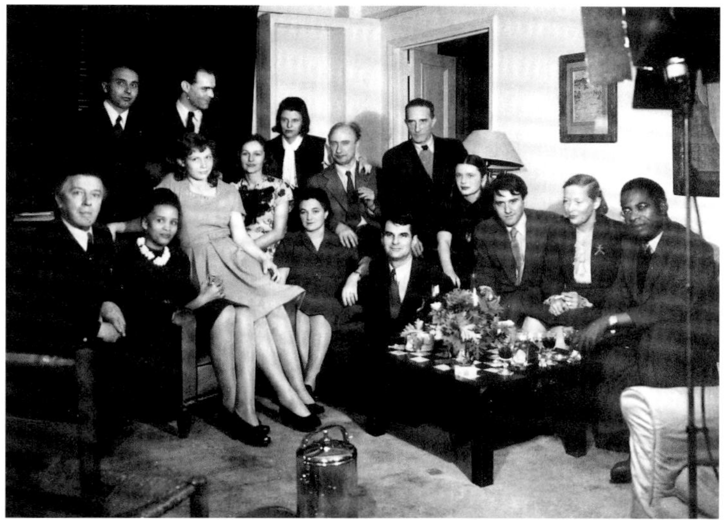

Kiesler to be more memorable than the art itself.[11] Since moving to New York in 1926, Kiesler had discussed building plans with modern art patrons Katherine Dreier and Louise and Walter Arensberg, but it was left to Guggenheim, a newly returned expatriate, to entrust Kiesler with the construction of a home for her splendid collection of modern art. In commissioning Kiesler to make a museum for her, Guggenheim surely thought to outdo the Museum of Non-Objective Art, which her uncle, Solomon Guggenheim, established in 1939 in a townhouse at 24 East 54th Street.

Guggenheim's collection represents a five-year buying frenzy that began in 1937, when she decided to open an art gallery in London. Since Guggenheim knew nothing about modern art, she enlisted her friend Duchamp as chief adviser, as had the Arensbergs and Dreier before her. After little over a year as a gallery owner, Guggenheim decided to plan a museum, and in 1939 she left London for Paris to buy "a picture a day."[12] Guggenheim's art appetite kept her in France well past a prudent departure date, but in 1941 she finally decided to bring her museum idea to New York. Her collecting continued apace and included the purchase of at least two boxes by Cornell in early 1942.[13] Around that time, she began work on a collection catalogue and hired Kiesler to design a gallery space.

Kiesler's architecture for Art of This Century seeks to redefine the viewing experience, based on his belief that the spectator's act of seeing is "a participation in the creative process no less essential and direct than the artist's own."[14] The gallery includes two main rooms, a Surrealist Gallery and an Abstract Gallery. The Surrealist Gallery (fig. 42) is equipped with concave walls and a dropped gumwood ceiling; these are set against the original walls and ceiling, which are painted black. Unframed paintings and sculptures are installed away from the walls on adjustable supports, and biomorphic furniture serves as both pedestals and flexible seating units. The Abstract Gallery (fig. 43) is painted turquoise blue on the floor, with darker blue canvas lining the walls. A passageway provides an additional Kinetic Gallery in which, among other entertainments, viewers can rotate a large wooden wheel that delivers to a peephole the individual components of a Duchamp *Boîte-en-valise [Box-in-a-Valise]* (fig. 44).

The public debut of the *Boîte* edition at Art of This Century pays a fitting tribute

40 **"Artists in Exile," Pierre Matisse Gallery,** 41 East 57th Street, New York, March 1942 (front row, left to right: Matta, Ossip Zadkine, Yves Tanguy, Max Ernst, Marc Chagall, Fernand Léger; back row, left to right: André Breton, Piet Mondrian, André Masson, Amédée Ozenfant, Jacques Lipchitz, Pavel Tchelitchew, Kurt Seligmann, Eugene Berman). Photograph by George Platt Lynes.

41 **Gathering at Pierre Matisse's apartment,** New York, 1945 (front row, left to right: André Breton, Mrs. Césaire, Jacqueline Matisse, Elisa Breton, Mrs. Calas, Nicolas Calas, Matta, Teeny Matisse, Aimd Césaire; back row, left to right: Esteban Francis, Denis de Rougemont, Sonia Sekula, Yves Tanguy, Duchamp, Patricia Matta). Philadelphia Museum of Art, Marcel Duchamp Archive.

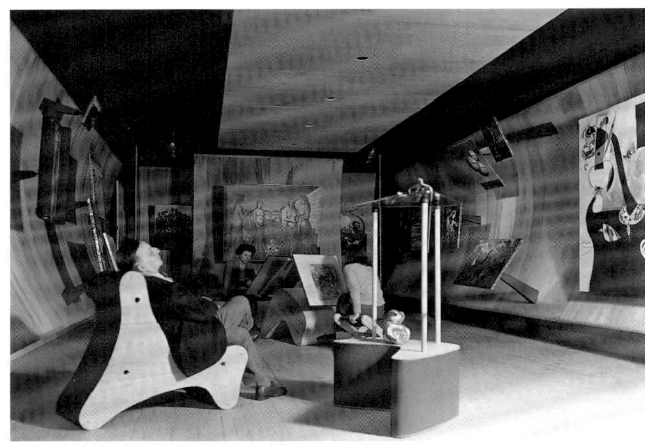

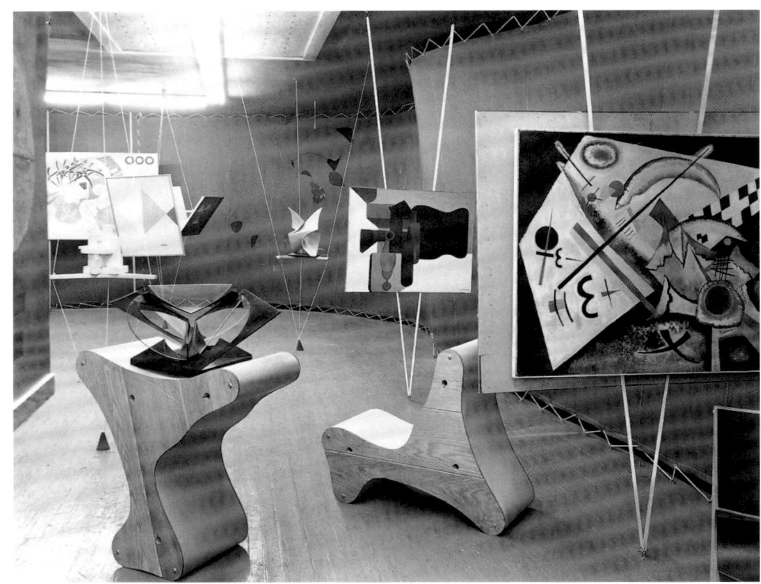

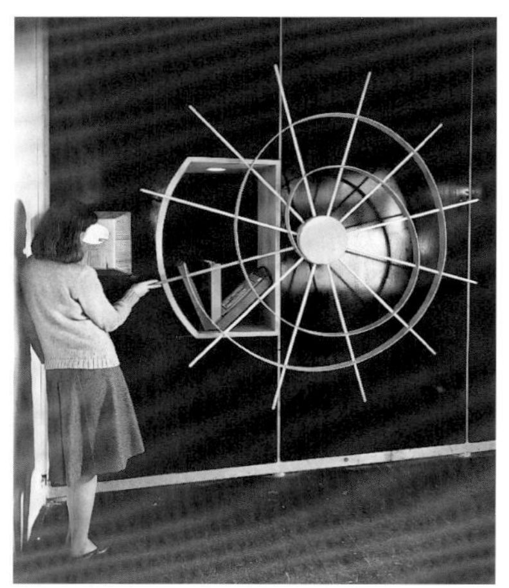

42 Frederick Kiesler, Peggy Guggenheim, and unidentified woman in the Surrealist Gallery, Art of This Century, 30 West 57th Street, New York, 1943. Photograph by Berenice Abbott. Berenice Abbott/Commerce Graphics Ltd, Inc.

43 Abstract Gallery, Art of This Century, 30 West 57th Street, New York, 1943. Photograph by Berenice Abbott. Berenice Abbott/Commerce Graphics Ltd, Inc.

44 Unidentified woman viewing Duchamp's *Boîte-en-valise* I/XX, Kinetic Gallery, Art of This Century, 30 West 57th Street, New York, 1943. Photograph by Berenice Abbott. Berenice Abbott/Commerce Graphics Ltd, Inc.

to Guggenheim, who purchased the first finished *Boîte-en-valise* in 1941 and carried it as hand luggage on her flight to New York. Moreover, when she shipped her possessions here, prior to her own departure from France, she allowed individual elements of fifty examples of the *Boîte* edition to join as "stowaways." Duchamp was reunited with these makings of the *Boîte* edition when he reached New York a year later; the edition is available on order from Guggenheim's gallery for prices ranging from $125 to $200.

Duchamp has engaged Cornell, since summer 1942, to assist in the labor-intensive assembly of these commissioned *Boîtes-en-valise* and *Boîtes*. Cornell, in turn, has squirreled away inside his own *Duchamp Dossier* many souvenirs of that enterprise. These include the documentation of his services: Duchamp's requests for more boxes and his records of payments to Cornell, the latter including a collage based on the "readymade" cover of a Long Island Railroad conductor's receipt booklet (DD 98). Cornell also has appropriated for his *Duchamp Dossier* individual elements from the *Boîte* edition, such as a number of the collotype reproductions of Duchamp's paintings, some printed labels with gummed backs, and the black paper folios onto which the collotypes and labels were applied for display in a finished box (DD 110, 111, 115, and 116). Cornell's work on Duchamp's *Boîte* edition has heightened his ambition for marketing his own art. He now fondly imagines selling limited-edition reproductions of several of his "dossiers," his accumulations of notes and souvenirs on particular subjects. Astounded by the price Guggenheim has attached to a single *Boîte-en-valise*, Cornell dreams more modestly of editions available for sale at the neighborhood five-and-dime.[15]

In a sense Art of This Century is more museum than gallery: the works on view are those of Guggenheim's private collection, published late in the summer in a book of the same title, now on sale for three dollars at the desk at the gallery entrance.[16] Only a small front room overlooking 57th Street is set aside for temporary exhibitions, doubling as what Kiesler has called a Painting Library due to its racks for perusing works of art in quantity, including those of children and the insane. Given its open mandate, this room is the most conventional, with its white walls and a chiffon curtain to diffuse the light from the window. In this gallery a year ago, two months after her grand opening, Guggenheim installed a special exhibition of objects by Cornell (priced from $12.50 to $95), Duchamp's *Boîte-en-valise*, and painted bottles by her former husband, Laurence Vail (pl. 65).[17]

Clement Greenberg, writing in *The Nation*, gave this exhibition its most important review, making the bold assertion that "Cornell could construct landscapes ten feet square inside his boxes."[18] Indeed Cornell has already designed his solo shows at Julien Levy Gallery as self-contained fairy-tale environments. In their diminutive scale, they shared the theatrical spirit of the many Surrealist installations Duchamp has masterminded. While Cornell will never take up Greenberg's challenge, it is one that uncannily anticipates Duchamp's secret creation of *Étant donnés: 1º la chute d'eau / 2º le gaz d'éclairage [Given: 1. The Waterfall / 2. The Illuminating Gas]* (1946–66).

The 1943 season has been a busy one for Guggenheim; she is ending it with the group show "Natural, Insane, and Surrealist Art," following the debut exhibition of the young American artist Jackson Pollock. Before the fall season opened, the gallery provided a shooting location for *Witch's Cradle*, a never-completed project by the filmmaker Maya Deren inspired by Kiesler's spectacular interior and Guggenheim's collection. Anne Matta Clark and Duchamp co-starred, Duchamp having last acted in a film nearly two decades ago, playing rooftop chess with Man Ray in René Clair's and Francis Picabia's *Entr'acte* (1924). In *Witch's Cradle*, Deren had Duchamp entangle himself in various cat's cradle games (fig. 46), a probable nod to his spectacular string installation for the "First Papers of Surrealism" exhibition the previous year (fig. 45). A year later, Duchamp will participate in another film sponsored by Guggenheim, Hans Richter's *Dreams That Money Can Buy*. Cornell's *Duchamp Dossier* bears witness to Duchamp's brief New York movie career: on a letter dated August 20, 1943, asking Cornell to supply a *Boîte* for the art patron and gallery owner Caresse Crosby, Duchamp taped, in place of a signature, a frame of film showing a close-up image of his face (fig. 47; DD 54).[19]

Duchamp knows Cornell to be an avid collector and maker of movies. Indeed, Cornell's filmmaking activity owes a great deal to Duchamp, given his 1926 film *Anémic Cinéma* (pl. 14) and the inspiration he provided with his concept of the readymade. Cornell's first film scenario, *Monsieur Phot* (pl. 50), was built around five "found" stereopticon images, while his first film, *Rose Hobart* (pl. 55), was made from cut and altered strips of an early talkie, *East of Borneo* (1931), rescued by Cornell from the trash.

Cornell is always looking for venues to screen his own work as well as his superb collection of early French and American films. He relies on this resource for much-needed income, informing his colleagues that "my collection of old films for use at parties, etc. is modest but hand picked. I am willing to let them out gratis for causes, war relief, etc. but would like to get a decent rental where possible."[20] Although Cornell has shown them at the Julien Levy Gallery, the film soirées now primarily occur at the homes of close friends.

These include the Spanish artist Julio de Diego, a character as flamboyant as Cornell is timid; although there could not be "two persons more opposite," they are true kindred spirits.[21] While de Diego's paintings have a Surrealist flavor, like Cornell, he has no wish to become an official member of the group. He lives and works in a large studio at the top of a four-story building at 65 West 56th Street, a block south of Art of This Century. There, for a charge of one or two dollars per person, Cornell treats de Diego's guests to films by Charlie Chaplin, Georges Mélies, and others. De Diego's lovely teenage daughter Kiriki, in charge of serving coffee, will later recall that "they'd play boogie-woogie records

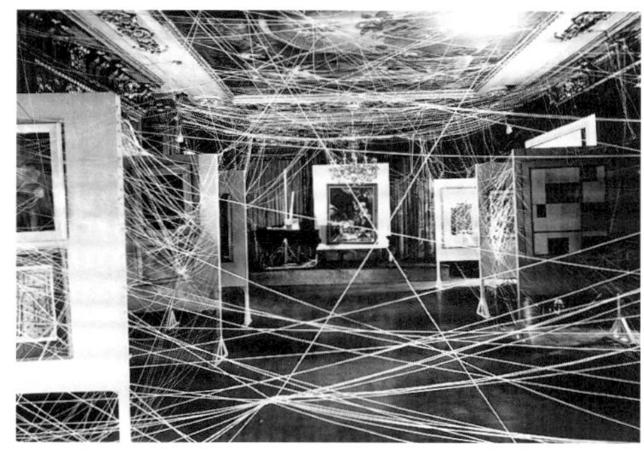

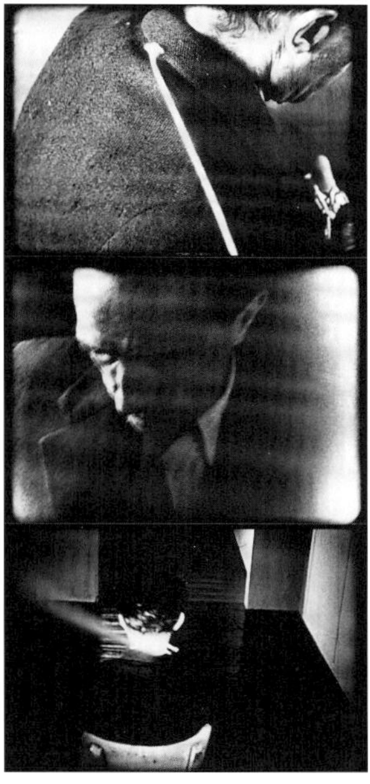

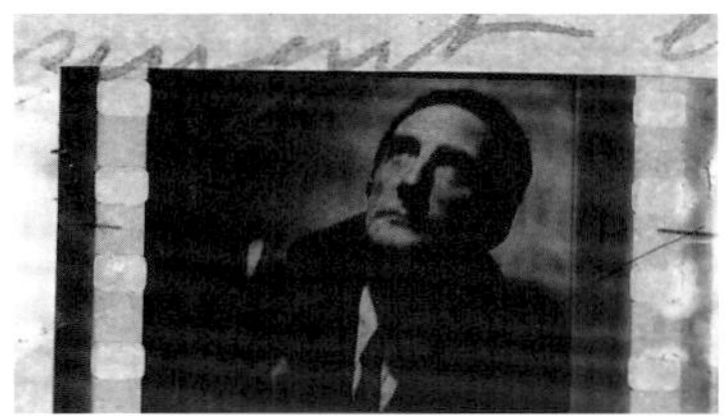

45 **"First Papers of Surrealism"** (October 14–November 7, 1942), Whitelaw Reid Mansion, 451 Madison Avenue, New York, installation view. Photograph by John D. Schiff.

46 **Film stills of Duchamp from Maya Deren's unfinished film *Witch's Cradle***, New York, August 1943.

47 **Duchamp letter to Cornell, detail showing 35mm film frame substituted for signature, August 20, 1943 (DD 54)**, from Cornell, *Duchamp Dossier*, c. 1942–53. Philadelphia Museum of Art. Gift of The Joseph and Robert Cornell Memorial Foundation.

while the films were playing."[22] The artist Enrico Donati, a regular guest at the parties, will guess that Cornell "probably picked up $10, $12, maybe $15" per evening, while giving everyone present a grand time.[23] Many of the viewers know Cornell only as a filmmaker and film connoisseur, unaware of the archives he husbands and the boxes he creates in the house on Utopia Parkway.

André Breton lives in a studio apartment a few doors from de Diego, at 45 West 56th Street.[24] This places him in easy reach of Art of This Century, where Guggenheim, who funded his passage to America, relies on him as a close adviser. Among other things, Breton took charge of the text and images published in the catalogue *Art of This Century*, including the artists' photographs cropped to show only each person's eyes. Breton's apartment is also convenient to his job as an announcer for the Voice of America; the Office of War Information produces the broadcasts in the Argonaut Building at 224 West 57th Street. Every evening, happily speaking the French he refuses to forfeit to English, Breton reports the American perspective on events to Francophones the world over.

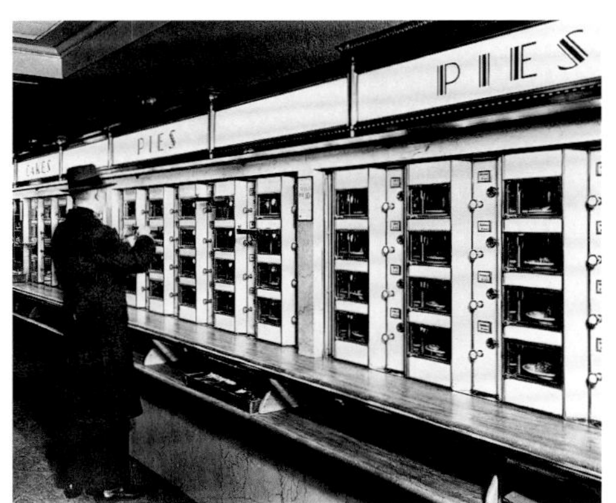

Across the street from Breton's apartment, Larré, a French restaurant, serves as the Surrealists' unofficial headquarters in New York: gathering at the family-run, white-tablecloth establishment for regular lunches at one long table, the Surrealists strive to replicate their café gatherings in Paris. It was at Larré that Duchamp, on his arrival in New York, first appeared to Breton. According to Donati, Breton was seated facing the outside window as usual, to greet his friends. He "suddenly got up like he had a spring under his seat," and as the new arrival walked in, he "started to bow in front of him, Japanese style. Several times he was bowing in front of this guy coming in. Who the hell was that, I was wondering." Duchamp had found his way: he "was in touch with everybody so automatically he came to Larré to lunch."[25]

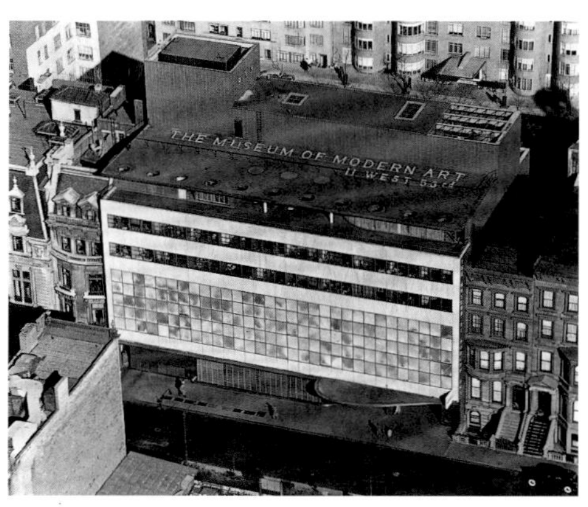

Convivial communal meals at Larré, however, hold little appeal for the reticent Cornell. His restaurant of choice remains the Automat, where the glass-doored cases framing casseroles and cakes echo his own box constructions (fig. 48). Almost fifty Automats are scattered throughout the city, including one at 57th Street between Sixth and Seventh Avenue and another on Eighth Avenue at 58th Street. Many artists living in the neighborhood meet at the 57th Street Automat for informal and multilingual breakfasts, as well as for individual rendezvous. Cornell has tucked into his *Duchamp Dossier* a folded paper napkin from a meal with Duchamp at Horn & Hardart on January 2, 1943 (DD 19). Another note and a sugar packet in the *Duchamp Dossier* testify, respectively, to further meals with Duchamp at the Hampton Cafeteria at 59th and Madison, another favorite haunt of Cornell's, and at Le Moal (described on the sugar packet as "a corner of Brittany in New York") at 811 Third Avenue, near 50th Street (DD 5 and 24).

As we walk east back to Fifth Avenue and turn downtown, it is three short blocks to The Museum of Modern Art at 11 West 53rd Street. Boldly greeting the world with a long, unmodulated facade of stone and Thermolux, a new and inexpensive alternative to glass, the 1939 building is the work of museum trustee Philip Goodwin and a young associate named Edward Durell Stone. The museum proclaims its functionalism and urbanity, free of fluted columns or grand staircases, and for neighbors aloft in new midtown skyscrapers, its name and address are lettered across the flat roof (fig. 49).

Duchamp's and Cornell's involvement at the museum dates back to 1936 when Alfred Barr's ambitious "Fantastic Art, Dada, Surrealism" exhibition (figs. 50 and 51) included

48 ***Automat,*** 977 Eighth Avenue, New York, February 10, 1936. Photograph by Berenice Abbott, Federal Arts Project, "Changing New York." Museum of the City of New York.

49 The Museum of Modern Art, 11 West 53rd Street, New York, 1939, aerial view. Photograph by Andreas Feininger.

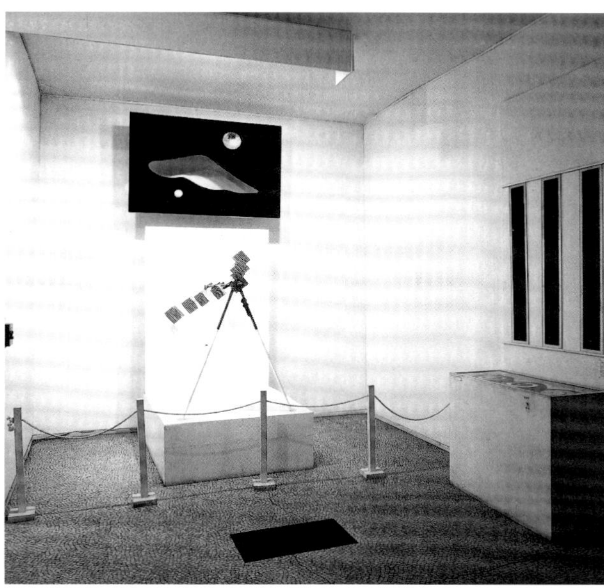

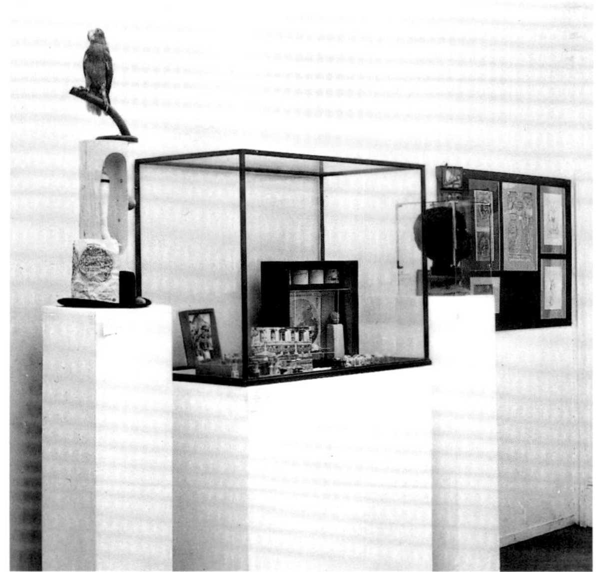

eleven items by Duchamp and two of Cornell's first boxes (pls. 52 and 53) among the show's approximately seven hundred works of art. By that time eminently stylish, Surrealism provided the occasion for "the first really grand, chic opening" at the seven-year-old Modern, still housed in the five-story townhouse of John D. and Abby Aldrich Rockefeller.[26] Neither Duchamp nor Cornell were perfectly comfortable as part of any "ism," of course. Concerned about Barr's text for the catalogue, Cornell delivered what would become his best-known comment on Duchamp: "... I have never been an official surrealist, and I believe that surrealism has healthier possibilities than have been developed. The constructions of Marcel Duchamp who the surrealists themselves acknowledge bear out this thought, I believe."[27] By 1943 Cornell's respect for Duchamp has blossomed into a working relationship and a warm friendship.

Life at the Modern at the end of 1943, however, is far from normal. Barr, the museum's guiding force, has been eased aside with the title "advisory director," and recent arrival James Thrall Soby is trying to fill his shoes. Budget, staffing, and programming all reflect the impact of the war. Having joined the patriotic cause, the museum often stages installations such as the current one featuring battle drawings by U.S. Marines. Behind the scenes, Barr and his wife, Marga, have played central roles in bringing refugees to the United States, Duchamp prominent among them. They have worked closely and covertly with the Emergency Rescue Committee in Marseilles, an American team trying to deliver endangered intellectuals and artists to safety.

Despite the museum staff's distractions, throngs of visitors flock to the Alexander Calder exhibition that is closing the 1943 fall season, along with the show "American Romantic Painting." In the permanent collection on the third floor, Duchamp's *Large Glass* resides in the area devoted to sculpture. Installed perpendicular to the wall, it stands near such works as *Standing Youth* (1913) and *Kneeling Woman* (1911) of Wilhelm Lehmbruck.[28] Katherine Dreier, the owner of the *Large Glass*, has placed it on extended loan to the museum. Remaining there for two and a half years, it will appear on the cover of *Vogue* in July 1945 in a special issue devoted to the museum, its transparency revealing an alluring model in a Hattie Carnegie evening dress. Attracted by the irresistible combination of glass

50 **Duchamp's artwork installed in "Fantastic Art, Dada, Surrealism"** (December 9, 1936–January 17, 1937), The Museum of Modern Art, 11 West 53rd Street, New York. Photograph by Soichi Sunami.

51 **Cornell's "Elements of Natural Philosophy and Soap Bubble Set" installed by Cornell in "Fantastic Art, Dada, Surrealism"** (December 9, 1936–January 17, 1937), The Museum of Modern Art, 11 West 53rd Street, New York. Photograph by Soichi Sunami.

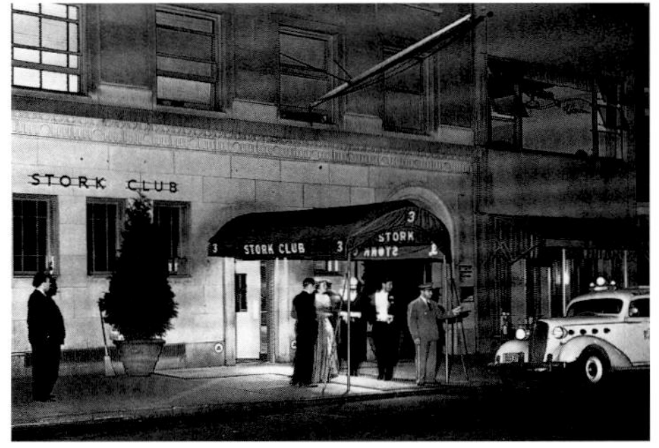

and woman, Cornell will keep two of the covers for his *Duchamp Dossier* (DD 103 and 104).[29]

Heading back to Fifth Avenue once more and crossing the street, we find two top-hatted storks at 3 East 53rd Street marking the gilt doorway to the highly fashionable Stork Club ("the New Yorkiest place in town," according to gossip columnist Walter Winchell) (fig. 52).[30] A side door at number 1 gives access to elevators to the building's sixteenth-floor penthouse and the offices of *View* magazine. *View* (fig. 53), the preeminent avant-garde publication in New York, was founded in September 1940 by two Mississippians: the poet Charles Henri Ford, returning from a decade in Paris, and the writer Parker Tyler. Both are close friends of Cornell's, who has been peripherally involved with the magazine from the start.[31] Though he refused an invitation to submit something for the first issue, the editors could not resist teasing readers of the second issue with a lengthy reference to Cornell's new ballet boxes.[32] Over the course of the magazine's seven-year life, Cornell will often stop by *View*'s headquarters, loaning a variety of his boxes to decorate the office and tempt potential buyers.

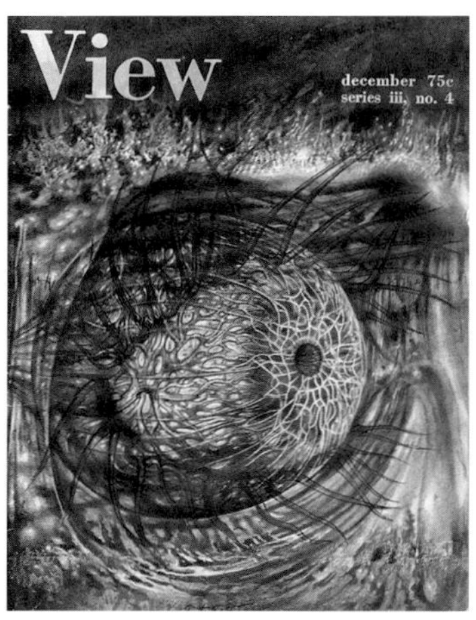

Initially, *View* was not especially focused on Surrealism; its first issue featured an interview with, and poetry by, Wallace Stevens. But with the arrival of the Europeans and the returning American expatriates, the magazine has acquired a fine Surrealist accent. The first issue following Breton's arrival in 1941, as *View* entered its second year, was an "all Surrealist" number that contained a long interview with Breton.[33] It featured as well a communiqué from Duchamp, written on a postcard issued by the French military for soldiers' correspondence with their families (fig. 54). Duchamp informed its recipients, who now included all *View* readers, that he and his companion Mary Reynolds were in fine form, and they hoped to be able to reach the United States.

Après avoir complété cette carte strictement réservée à la correspondance d'ordre familial, biffer les indications inutiles. — Ne rien écrire en dehors des lignes.
ATTENTION. — Toute carte dont le libellé ne sera pas uniquement d'ordre familial ne sera pas acheminée et sera probablement détruite.
Paris le 17 Janvier 1941
mary et moi en bonne santé à peine fatigué.
~~légèrement, gravement~~ malade, ~~blessé~~.
~~tué~~ ~~prisonnier~~.
~~décédé~~ reçu ~~sans~~ nouvelles.
de vous merci - ~~La famille~~ va ~~bien~~.
~~besoin de provisions~~ d'argent.
~~nouvelles, bagages~~ ~~est de retour à~~
je travaille à ma boite qui est finie ~~va entrer~~
à ~~l'école de~~ a été reçu
Si vous allez à New York le trouvez
moi une mission artistique (sic) pour que
j'y aille faire un tour
Affectueuses pensées. Baisers. et tout de tous deux à tous deux
Signature.
M Duchamp

By 1943 Cornell has become a solid contributor to *View*, which published his "*Enchanted Wanderer*": *Excerpt from a Journey Album for Hedy Lamarr* (pl. 64), its beautiful full-page text surrounding a photographic overlay of Lamarr's striking face onto a portrait of a young man by Giorgione.[34] But Cornell's most prominent appearance in print was in *View*'s "Americana Fantastica" issue at the beginning of 1943.[35] He contributed the cover, a seven-page "excerpt" from his album *THE Crystal Cage [portrait of Berenice]* (pl. 54), and several photographs, including a haunting composition titled *Spent Meteor: Night of Feb. 10, 1843 (For E. A. Poe)* (fig. 149; c. 1938), and on the "Children's Page," an eerie image of a doll lying face up, strewn with confetti (fig. 55).

Since the summer of 1942, *View*'s dominance of the literary landscape has been challenged by Breton's launch of an explicitly Surrealist publication called *VVV*. Supported by the New York collectors Bernard and Becky Reis, the magazine uses Reis' accounting office at 10 East 40th Street as its office address, and meetings are held at their home on Central Park West. In open rivalry with *View*, the magazine explains the three V's of its name as "a synthesis, in a third term," of "the View around us" and "the View inside us."[36] Breton appointed the American sculptor David Hare as editor, and Max Ernst joined on as editorial adviser. Just after the magazine's first issue appeared, Duchamp arrived in New York, and Breton promptly enlisted him for the editorial board. In 1943 Duchamp has designed the second issue's front and back covers, the latter in collaboration with Kiesler (pl. 25).

VVV will survive for only one more issue, which will appear in February 1944 and include a reproduction of a complex assemblage by Duchamp titled *Allégorie de genre* [*Allegory of Genre*] (pl. 31). A double image that reads as either George Washington in pro-

52 **Stork Club,** 3 East 53rd Street, New York, 1940.

53 ***View* (December 1943),** cover featuring Pavel Tchelitchew's *The Flower of Sight*.

54 **French military correspondence card from Duchamp to André Breton,** Paris, 1941. *View* (October–November 1941): p. 5.

file or a map of the United States, the work was made for the February 1943 "Americana" issue of *Vogue*, which was devoted to the theme of Presidents. The silhouette is filled with white gauze, stained in stripes the color of dried blood, and pierced by gilt stars. Predictably rejected, it has spent the year awaiting publication and ultimately will enter Breton's private collection. Cornell's *Duchamp Dossier* provides a permanent home for an uncut proof of the *VVV* reproduction and a unique variant of the head/map double image, constructed with heavy brown and black paper and inscribed with affection by Duchamp (pl. 30; DD 112 and 113).

Cornell has never affiliated himself with the strictly Surrealist agenda of *VVV*, preferring to stay in contact with *View*, while Duchamp characteristically straddles both camps. From the early days of *View*, the editors have nurtured the idea of a special Duchamp number. Billed as "the first complete survey of his life and work," it finally will appear in March 1945, *View*'s most expensive and ambitious venture ever.[37] Duchamp will design the cover for the issue, a beautiful composition of a wine bottle shooting smoke into a starry deep blue sky (pl. 35). The issue will feature tributes in both text and image, including a "space poem" by Kiesler that fuses photographs of the *Large Glass* and Duchamp's current studio. Cornell similarly will use montage in his more modest contribution, *3/4 Bird's-Eye View of 'A Watch-Case for Marcel Duchamp'* (pl. 74), a composition based on repeating images of a small round box lined with French text and filled with watch springs and gears. Though the Duchamp number of *View* will not be included in the *Duchamp Dossier*, it will twice make an indirect appearance: Cornell will save a telegram that asks him to come to *View*'s offices to sign the deluxe issue, as well as a note from Duchamp written on the back of a printed invitation to cocktails celebrating its publication (DD 57 and 58).

As we walk from the *View* offices toward the East River, the neighborhood gradually turns more residential. Guggenheim's townhouse is at 440 East 51st Street, on the corner of Beekman Place, a charming tree-lined street that runs only two blocks (fig. 56). Named Hale House after Nathan Hale, the house occupies the supposed site of the patriot's execution by hanging. When she discovered it in early 1942, Guggenheim imagined Hale House as a site for her museum but was foiled by New York's zoning laws. She decided instead that it would make a fine home for herself and Max Ernst, her husband at the time. The house, with its remarkable two-story living room facing the river, complete with a giant stone fireplace and a clerestory overhead, has proven to be a magnificent gathering place for the European émigrés—Guggenheim's yen to entertain having overwhelmed her famous parsimony (fig. 57).

Indeed Duchamp lived at Hale House during the summer of 1942, soon after his arrival in New York. This stay led to his chance encounter with Cornell almost a decade after their first meeting. As Cornell recorded in his diary: "Marcel Duchamp answered the telephone at Peggy Guggenheim Ernst's during a cloudburst. It was at once one of the most delightful and strangest experiences I ever had. He is coming out Friday which should prove a much needed inspiration to get some of the objects finished."[38] Duchamp's effect on Cornell is not unique. Since arriving in New York, he has stepped easily into the guiding role at which he is so adept, and in such demand. The other newcomers rely heavily on his familiarity with the city and his relish for improvisation under whatever circumstance life brings.

Duchamp could hardly afford to remain in Guggenheim's expensive neighborhood.

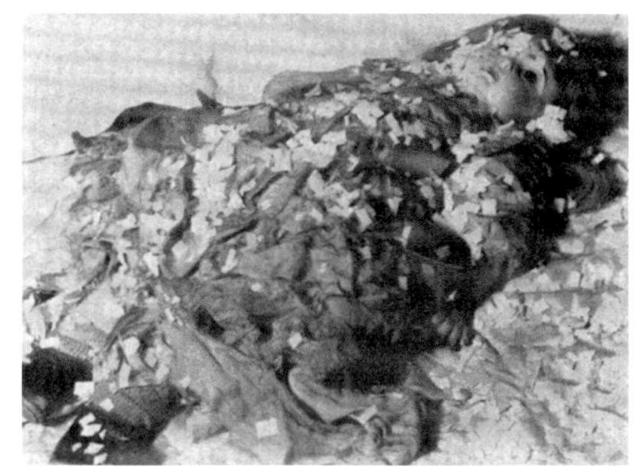

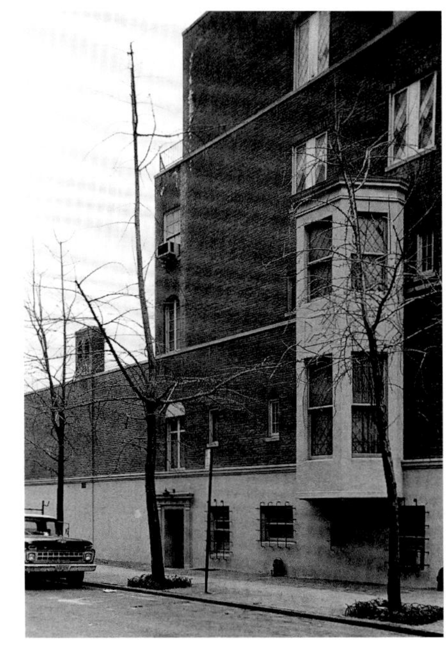

55 Victorian "Bébé Marie" doll arranged by Cornell and photographed by James Ogle, 1938. *View* (January 1943): p. 38.

56 Peggy Guggenheim's townhouse, Hale House, 440 East 51st Street, New York. Photograph by Peter Hujar, 1973.

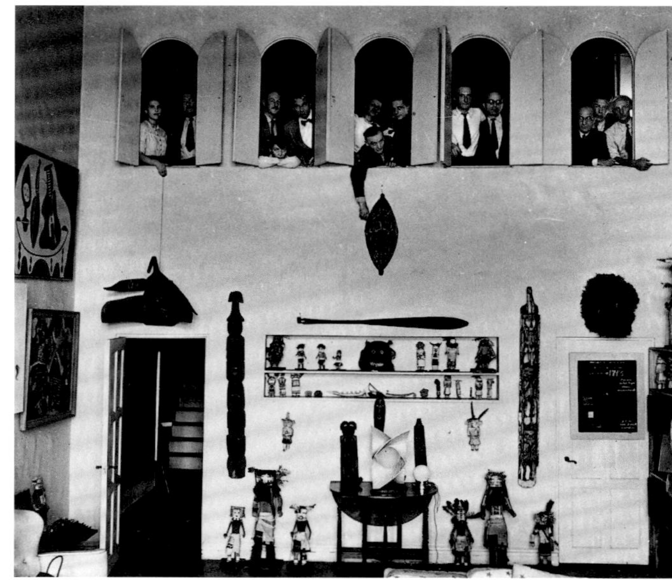

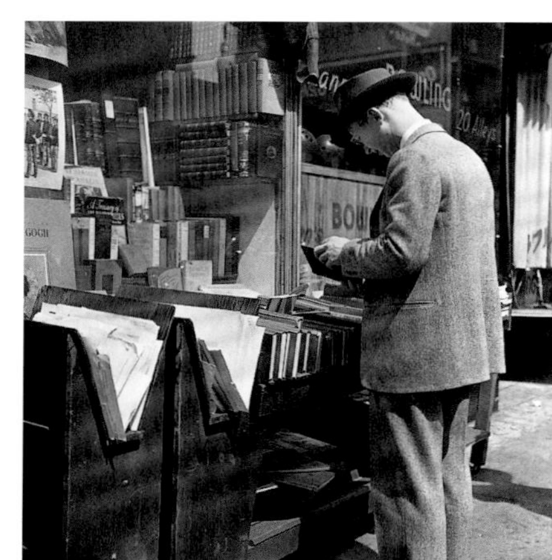

Greenwich Village presents an attractive, more practical alternative, and it is here that the *Duchamp Dossier* finally leads its tourists. As we follow Fifth Avenue downtown, the architectural scale shifts back to that of the eighteenth and nineteenth centuries; the pace of life seems to slow accordingly. Long known as a haven for literary and artistic sorts, the Village had its heyday in the 1910s during Duchamp's first sojourn in New York. The emigration brought on by the Second World War has triggered a new boom in its cultural population, giving Cornell many new reasons for coming downtown besides his beloved secondhand bookstores along Fourth Avenue (fig. 58). Artists such as Tanguy and Masson first found their bearings here, although by 1943 they have moved on to form something of a Surrealist colony in northwestern Connecticut. Matta, who will become one of Cornell's close friends, resides at 47 West 12th Street.

Kiesler lives in the penthouse apartment of a twenty-story brick building at 56 Seventh Avenue, on the southwest corner of 14th Street. The penthouse has become a mecca for the new arrivals. Kiesler and his wife, Stefi, who have lived at this address since 1933, are experienced New Yorkers and generous, gregarious hosts. In the fall of 1942, they provided Duchamp with a rent-free room and bath, where he stayed for a year.[39] Kiesler and Duchamp have known each other since the mid 1930s, and in 1937 Kiesler published an article in the journal *The Architectural Record,* describing the *Large Glass* as "architecture, sculpture, and painting in ONE."[40] He has been the proud owner of Duchamp's *Large Glass*-related painting of 1914, *Réseaux des stoppages [Network of Stoppages].*

The penthouse at 56 Seventh Avenue has a prominent presence in the *Duchamp Dossier*. Several items of correspondence from Duchamp to Cornell carry this return address, which also appears on scavenged receipts of various kinds including a telephone message and an itemized laundry bill (DD 16 and 21). The *Duchamp Dossier* also contains a cardboard box for LePage's liquid glue on which Duchamp has scrawled the Americanism *gimme* above the printed word *strength* (describing the glue) (DD 67). It was while they were together in his room at the Kieslers' on December 21, 1942, that Duchamp concocted this Christmas gift, an example of what Cornell called a "'ready-made' done on spot."[41] Much of the construction work on Duchamp's *Boîte* edition has occurred in this small

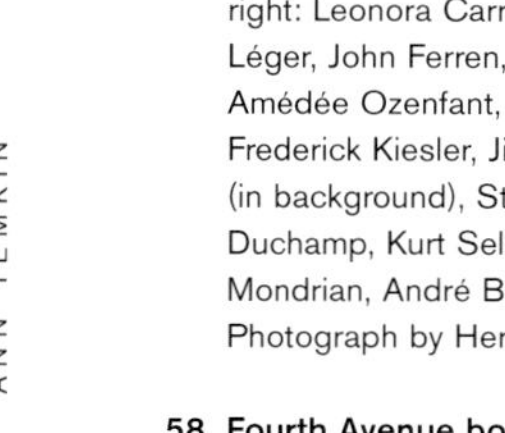

57 Surrealist artists at Peggy Guggenheim's townhouse, 440 East 51st Street, New York, Fall 1942 (left to right: Leonora Carrington, Fernand Léger, John Ferren, Berenice Abbott, Amédée Ozenfant, Guggenheim, Frederick Kiesler, Jimmy Ernst (in background), Stanley William Hayter, Duchamp, Kurt Seligmann, Piet Mondrian, André Breton, Max Ernst). Photograph by Herman Landshoff.

58 Fourth Avenue bookstalls, New York, 1945. Photograph by Sidney Latham.

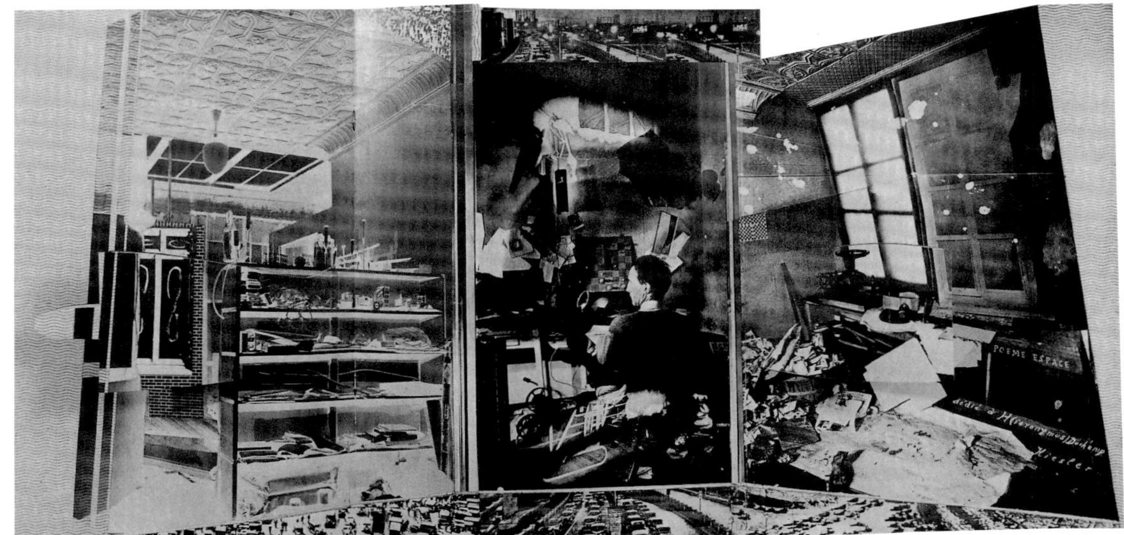

space, which Cornell's diary describes as "a mess with debris but pleasant looking out over East from the elevation."[42]

In October 1943 Duchamp moved from his penthouse aerie to a rented apartment at 210 West 14th Street, just around the corner from the Kieslers'. It is a humble fifth-floor walk-up, but it offers a full wall of slanting windows that face north onto 14th Street (fig. 60). While the room has no kitchen and only a shared bath, it nonetheless serves as a fine base of operation for Duchamp's work on his *Boîtes* and *Boîtes-en-valise*, and soon, the early formulations of what will become *Étant donnés*. Kiesler's montage for the Duchamp number of *View* will portray this studio as a private intellectual headquarters, with shots taken by the photographer Percy Rainford to emphasize the tangle of papers, tools, and supplies (fig. 59). Kiesler will dedicate the triptych to "H(ieronymus) Duchamp," presumably in reference to the study chamber of Saint Jerome, while also calling to mind the artistic alchemies of Bosch. With no telephone, it is indeed a hideaway, its privacy assured by Duchamp's practice of meeting friends at neighboring restaurants. According to a fragment of brown paper in the *Duchamp Dossier*, inscribed with the date of *10-2-43* and the 14th Street address, Cornell paid a call on Duchamp just after he moved to the new apartment. But his notation makes the honest admission that "first visitors / to / did not / see room" (DD 20).[43]

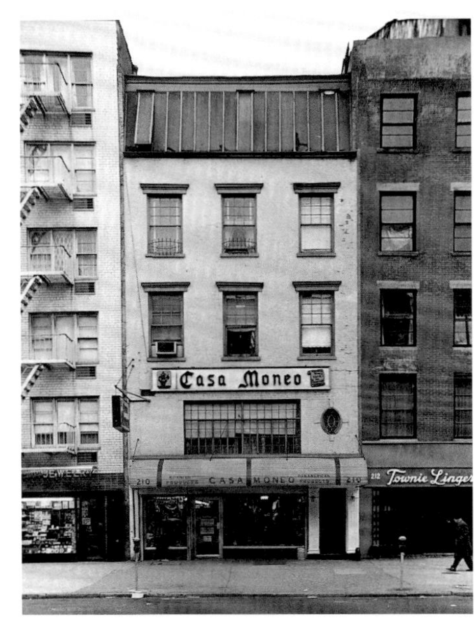

Leaving 14th Street and walking four blocks further downtown on Seventh Avenue brings us to Perry Street. Turning right and proceeding west, we arrive at the brownstone apartment of Mary Reynolds at number 73. Although she has been Duchamp's loyal companion for the last two decades, the two have never shared an address. Reynolds arrived in New York only in January 1943, after a long and difficult escape from France, where she stayed on until the last possible moment as a key figure in the Resistance. A courageous and sophisticated American, Reynolds moved to Paris in the early 1920s after being widowed at the age of thirty-three. There she became a great friend of fellow expatriates such as Guggenheim and Virgil Thomson, who crowned her "the queen of American Montparnasse."[44] In 1929 Reynolds took up the art of bookbinding and became an artist in her own right, collaborating with Duchamp and others to produce petite masterpieces in exotic materials.

59 **Frederick Kiesler, photomontage of Duchamp's 210 West 14th Street studio,** New York, 1945. *View* (March 1945): pp. 24-30. Photographs by Percy Rainford.

60 **Duchamp's 5th floor studio,** 210 West 14th Street, New York. Photograph by Peter Hujar, 1973.

A group of nine letters in the *Duchamp Dossier* reveals that Reynolds will become a warm friend of Cornell's, both receiving gifts from him and buying his work.[45] Like many of Cornell's correspondents, she will assume in her letters to him a cheerfully conspiratorial tone of shared intimacies. The letters will continue when she goes back to Paris in spring 1945, taking on the post of *View*'s foreign correspondent. A letter dated May 1, 1946, thanks Cornell for a package that "arrived at the same time as a wire from Marcel saying he was really sailing" (DD 80). Apparently Duchamp will bring with him two Cornell boxes to join those she has already with her. Reynolds goes on to thank Cornell for a treasured package of gingerbread mix: "with courage, fortitude, and unparalleled generosity I shall wait for Marcel to MIX." Cornell will also learn of Duchamp's departure from New York firsthand. The *Duchamp Dossier* preserves a postcard postmarked ten-thirty p.m., April 30, 1946 (fig. 61; DD 33). It has no image on the front, just space for writing, and contains a farewell that is as economical as the rest of their friendship: *Au revoir affectueusement Marcel.*

Duchamp's goodbye to Cornell will be only a temporary one, as he will return to settle in New York the following year. But with the end of the war in 1945, the climate that nurtured their collaboration will begin to evaporate, and the sites they shared in common will vanish one by one. The European "artists in exile" will for the most part return gratefully to their various homes, Breton leading the way back to Paris in April 1946, his passage booked by an ever-helpful Duchamp.[46] That same month, the *Large Glass* will travel safely from New York to Dreier's new house in Milford, Connecticut. With its funding exhausted and vitality gone, *View* will cease publication in spring 1947. That will also be the final season for Art of This Century; off to Venice, a restless Guggenheim will sell Kiesler's furnishings straight from the gallery at fire-sale prices. Levy will struggle along nobly but finally close the gallery in 1949 as he finds himself outdistanced by newer dealers.

The itinerary traced by the *Duchamp Dossier* is thus a highly evanescent one. The *Duchamp Dossier* itself draws toward a close at this juncture, as both artists move on to new pursuits and friends. It includes a few letters from Reynolds from the late 1940s, carrying friendly transatlantic gossip, and a postcard sent or given by Duchamp in 1953. But whereas the two artists will remain cordial, and their mutual admiration strong, the energy that animates the *Duchamp Dossier* wholly depends on the specific moment of its invention. Its tattered fragments summon back that extraordinary moment, the people who together made it happen, and the places that provided them a stage.

61 Duchamp, postcard to Cornell, April 30, 1946 (DD 33), from Cornell, *Duchamp Dossier,* c. 1942–53. Philadelphia Museum of Art. Gift of The Joseph and Robert Cornell Memorial Foundation.

Notes

1. Jacqueline Breton to Varian Fry, 24 June 1941, quoted in Mark Polizzotti, *Revolution of the Mind: The Life of André Breton* (New York: Farrar, Straus and Giroux, 1995), p. 499.

2. "I have been going by the old garbage dumping grounds for twenty years, and thought it was just a plaisanterie when I read in the papers that the Fair site would be established there." Joseph Cornell to Charles Henri Ford, 27 September 1939, Getty Research Institute, Los Angeles, Archive #880205.

3. "57th Street," *Fortune* (September 1946): pp. 144–51, 197–202.

4. Draft of condolence note from Joseph Cornell to Alexina Duchamp, 9 October 1968, Joseph Cornell Papers, Archives of American Art, Smithsonian Institution, Washington, D.C., microfilm, 1056:679–681.

5. An allusion to the chess problem and caption that open Lewis Carroll's *Through the Looking Glass* (1871).

6. "Art for Christmas," *The New Yorker* (20 November 1943): p. 82. *Art News*, the previous Christmas, specifically recommended giving art "since few priority materials need go into its fashioning." "Christmas Guide for Gallery Shoppers," *Art News* 41, no. 15 (15–31 December 1942): p. 30.

7. Julien Levy, *Memoir of an Art Gallery* (New York: G.P. Putnam's Sons, 1977), pp. 17, 20. The Brummer Gallery was then located at 27 East 57th Street.

8. Joella Bayer, interview with author, Montecito, Calif., January 1997.

9. Julien Levy, *Surrealism* (New York: The Black Sun Press, 1936), p. 28.

10. Matisse did purchase from Levy at least one work by Cornell, Untitled (Pharmacy) (1943).

11. Peggy Guggenheim, *Out of This Century: Confessions of an Art Addict* (1946; reprint, New York: Universe Books, 1979), p. 270.

12. Ibid., p. 209. Guggenheim, Jeune, Inc. in London operated from January 1938 to June 1939.

13. In a letter of 12 March 1942, Cornell answers Guggenheim's questions about the dates of a "Fortune Telling parrot," a "Revolving book with red ball," and a "Thimble box." Peggy Guggenheim Papers, Archives of American Art, Smithsonian Institution, Washington, D.C., microfilm, ITVE 1:149. However, Guggenheim's catalogue cites only the last two works. Peggy Guggenheim, ed., *Art of This Century* (New York: Art of This Century, 1942), p. 149.

14. Frederick Kiesler, "Notes on Designing the Gallery," quoted in Lisa Phillips, *Frederick Kiesler* (New York: Whitney Museum of American Art, in association with New York, London: W.W. Norton & Company, 1989), p. 114.

15. Donald Windham, interview with Rachael Arauz, New York, N.Y., 24 February 1998.

16. Guggenheim, ed., *Art of This Century*. Cornell was mentioned in the catalogue's appendix of works on paper and objects (p. 149). The section on Duchamp ("now on his way to America") reproduced the painting *Sad Young Man on a Train* (1912) and the first ever illustration of the *Boite-en- valise*, not yet so titled (pp. 57, 59).

17. Prices listed in "The Passing Shows," *Art News* 41, no. 15 (15–31 December 1942): p. 34.

18. Clement Greenberg, "Joseph Cornell and Laurence Vail: Objects and Bottles," *The Nation* (26 December 1942): p. 728.

19. The source of the frame is unclear; it does not match that used by Deren, who shot solely in 16 mm.

20. Joseph Cornell to Charles Henri Ford, 2 October 1939, Getty Research Institute, Los Angeles, Archive #880205.

21. Kiriki de Diego Metzo, telephone interview with author, May 1998.

22. Ibid.

23. Enrico Donati, interview with author, New York, N.Y., January 1997. When de Diego married Gypsy Rose Lee in 1948, the film soirées moved to her townhouse on East 63rd Street.

24. He first lived at 265 West 11th Street with his wife, Jacqueline Lamba, but he moved uptown when their marriage dissolved.

25. Enrico Donati, interview with author, New York, N.Y., January 1997.

26. Allen Porter, former secretary at the Julien Levy Gallery, quoted in Russell Lynes, *Good Old Modern* (New York: Atheneum, 1973), p. 144. Duchamp had already been shown at The Museum of Modern Art, represented by five objects in the "Cubism and Abstract Art" exhibition in spring 1936.

27. Joseph Cornell to Alfred Barr, 13 November 1936, The Museum of Modern Art, Department of Registration, "Fantastic Art, Dada, Surrealism," Exhibition No. 855, exhibition file, New York.

28. William Lieberman, telephone interview with author, May 1998.

29. Later that year, in November 1945, Cornell had his own moment at The Museum of Modern Art, when his dossier *Portrait of Ondine* (c. 1940–late 1960s) was displayed in the gallery outside the auditorium; he also designed the museum's Christmas card that year.

30. Jan Morris, *Manhattan '45* (New York: Oxford University Press, 1987), p. 146.

31. Tyler, a great admirer of Cornell's objects and films, wrote the essay for his 1939 show at the Julien Levy Gallery; Cornell collaborated on the design of *ABC's*, a collection of Ford's poetry published in 1940.

32. *View*, series 1, no. 2 (October 1940): p. 4. See also Joseph Cornell to Charles Henri Ford, 27 July 1940, Getty Research Institute, Los Angeles, Archive #880205.

33. Nicolas Calas, "Interview with André Breton," *View*, series 1, nos. 7–8 (October–November 1941): pp. 1–2.

34. Joseph Cornell, "Enchanted Wanderer," *View*, series 1, nos. 9–10 (December 1941–January 1942): p. 3. Duchamp employed the same tactic when he gave the Statue of Liberty the face of Breton for the cover of Breton's anthology *Young Cherry Trees Secured Against Hares*, published by *View* in 1946.

35. *View*, series 2, no. 4 (January 1943).

36. From "Declaration VVV" by André Breton, which appeared on the title page of each issue of *VVV*.

37. *View*, series 5, no. 1 (March 1945).

38. Diary entry, 28 June 1942, Cornell Papers, AAA, 1058:883.

39. Stefi Kiesler's records contain no evidence of rent checks. Lillian Kiesler, interview with Rachael Arauz, New York, N.Y., 24 February 1998.

40. Frederick Kiesler, "Design-Correlation," *The Architectural Record* 81, no. 5 (May 1937): p. 54.

41. Diary entry, 21 December 1942 [entered 2/17/47], Cornell Papers, AAA, 1058:890.

42. Ibid.

43. The *Duchamp Dossier* also contains an entire menu from the Pappas Restaurant at 254 West 14th Street, a record of a visit in January 1946 (DD 97).

44. Virgil Thomson, *Virgil Thomson* (New York: E.P. Dutton, 1966), p. 110.

45. The letters in the *Duchamp Dossier* from Mary Reynolds are from 28 West 11th Street, where she lived both prior to and after her stay at 73 Perry Street, which lasted from October 1943 to spring 1944.

46. Polizzotti, p. 533.

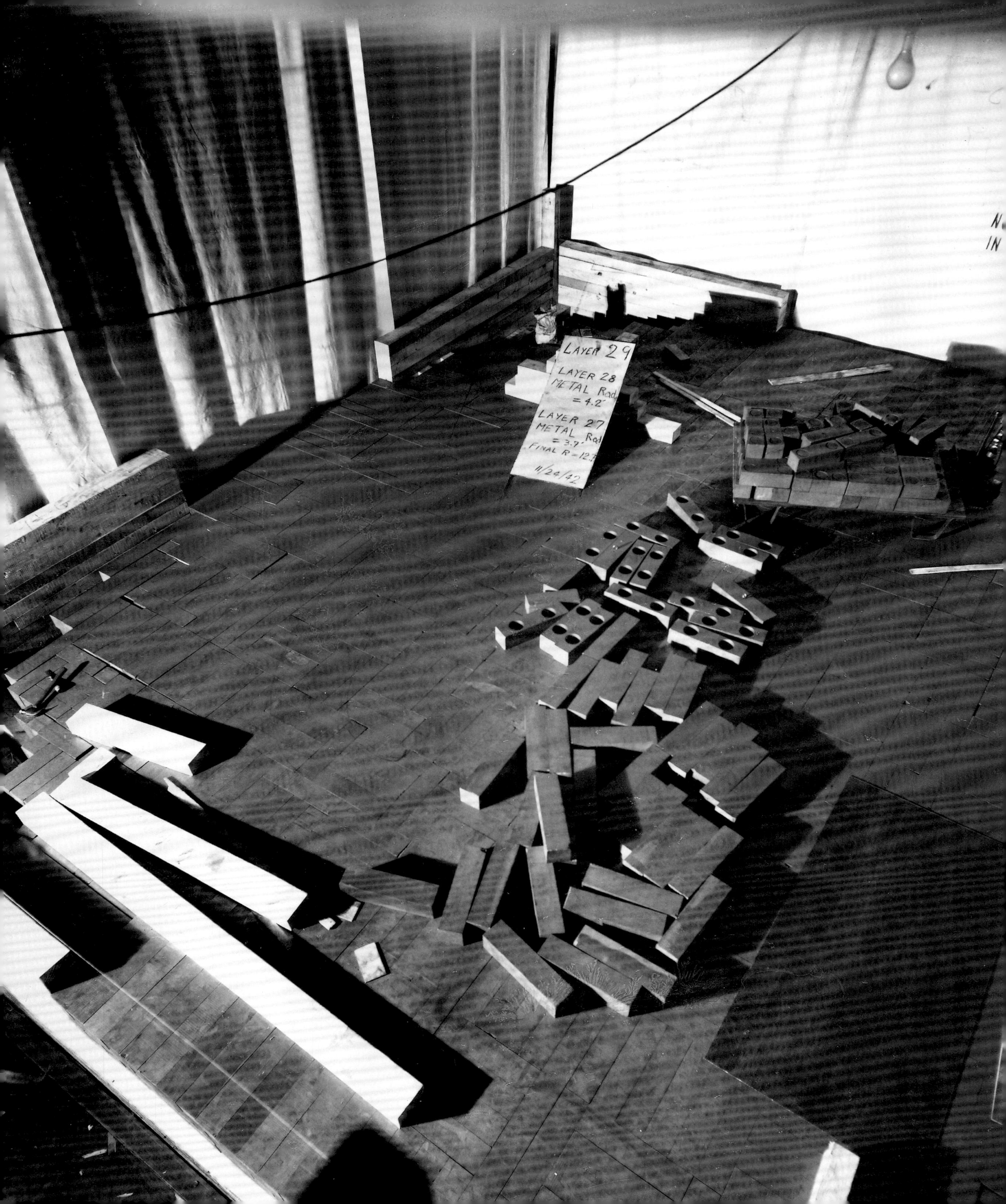
LAYER 29
LAYER 28
METAL Rad
= 4.2'
LAYER 27
METAL Rad
= 3.7'
FINAL R = 12.
11/24/42

delay included

ECKE BONK

centennial fragments. beware of critical mass The turn of our century experienced the dramatic consequences of a great quest toward a new level of perception. As the gap between the perceivable and the perceiver widened, the explored microcosms revealed an unbridgeable abyss. At the same time, language and the limits of expression itself came under scrutiny as the inherent problems of denotation and the denoted, of signifier and signified, were dissected and analyzed.

Attempts in physics to describe matter in an atomic state had to overcome the impossibility of following the individual atom's random walk. A generalized statistical mode and method seemed to work best. This introduction of probability is crucial since performance of a single atom can be described in neither the past nor the future. As a result, calculated probability and carefully conducted chance operations would develop into an important hermeneutic feature of twentieth-century science (fig. 63).

When in December 1900 Max Planck published the discovery of the quantum *(h)* as the natural limit of emission, he proved that not only is matter granular, but energy is emitted in irreducible packages *(quanta)*. A few years later, Albert Einstein posited the speed of light *(c)* as another universal, unsurpassable, unalterable constant of nature: it was the base upon which he built his special, and later the general, theory of relativity. But the respective conceptual consequences of quanta and the speed of light in relation to understanding nature as a whole produced puzzling paradoxes. Already by 1927 Niels Bohr had introduced *Complementarity* as an explanatory principle that could pacify the contradictions between the chance-governed microcosms of quantum mechanics and the obviously deterministic macrocosms of everyday life.

The statistical description of matter, laws of probability, and game theory were employed as tools to understand atomic and subatomic vistas, the indeterminate path of a single pollen under a microscope, the mathematical mastering of radioactive decay, and alpha particles bombarding a sheet of gold leaf. All these investigations on simple laboratory tables deeply influenced the immediate environment and perceptions of certain gifted individuals before leaving their imprint on the cultural periphery: the course of our century has been primed by them.

And now at the very end of this century, we find ourselves contemplating the fractal contents of a ragged, dilapidated box, found in the estate of Joseph Cornell, the so-called *Duchamp Dossier* (c. 1942–53). If we read the constellation of included items correctly, they not only illuminate the work relation between two artists but, on a more general level, seem to provide a unique instrument to scan the artificial horizon of our century.

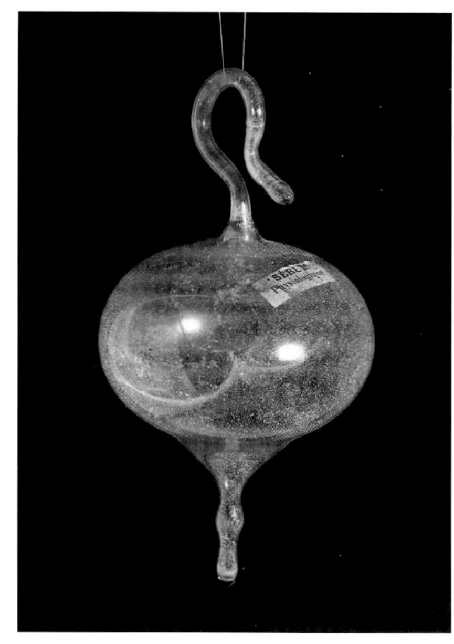

62 **First nuclear reactor during assembly,** Stagg Field, The University of Chicago, November 24, 1942.

63 **Duchamp, *Air de Paris*, 1919.** Readymade: glass ampoule (broken and later restored), 5¼ x 8⅛ in., diameter. Philadelphia Museum of Art. The Louise and Walter Arensberg Collection.

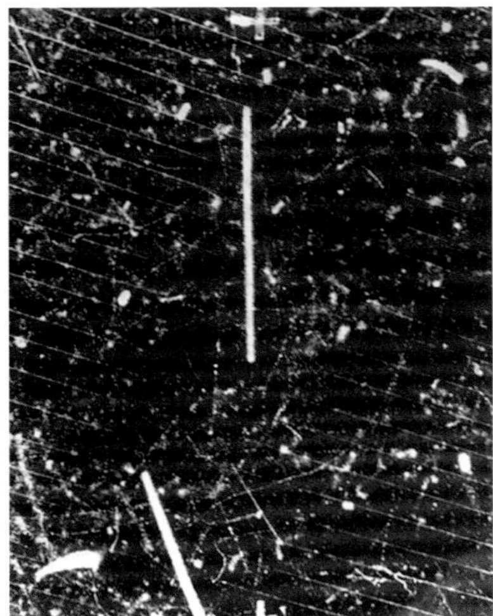

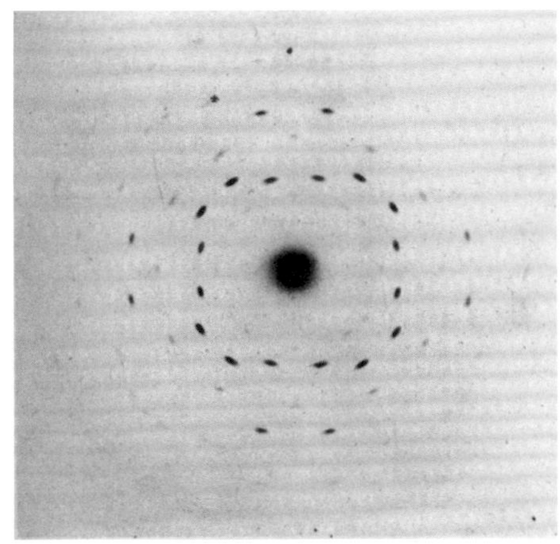

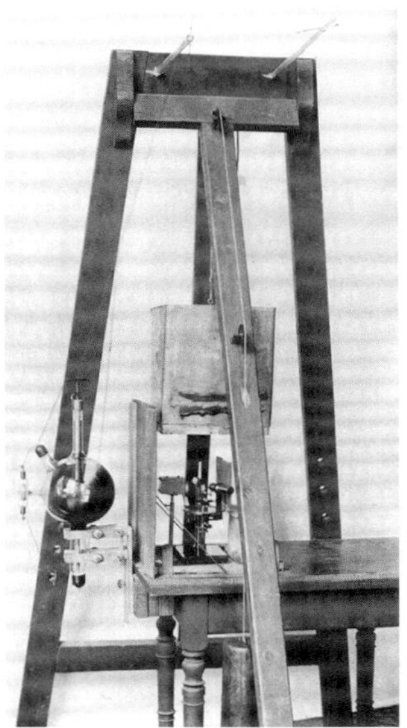

instant exposure – ultra rapid 1912: On the night of April 15, the SS *Titanic* sank. In Japan, Emperor Meji, who had opened Japan to the West, died. In Scotland, C. T. R. Wilson built his first cloud chamber to record the tracks of passing particles (fig. 64). In Munich, a group around the German physicist Max von Laue investigating the optical properties of X-rays discovered crystallography (figs. 65 and 66). Einstein published on photochemistry and light-quantum, and Wassily Kandinsky's book *Concerning the Spiritual in Art* appeared. A young Austrian self-taught philosopher schooled in engineering named Ludwig Wittgenstein—heir to a steel industry empire—started to work on what would be known as the *Tractatus Logico-Philosophicus*. In Dublin, James Joyce was preoccupied with June 16, 1904, while in Paris, Marcel Proust was halfway through his magnum opus *À la recherche du temps perdu [Remembrance of Things Past]*. Also in Paris, in a small studio an artist who was almost twenty-five finished one of his larger canvases: *Le roi et la reine entourés de nus vites [The King and Queen Surrounded by Swift Nudes]*. Marcel Duchamp was planning a long stay abroad. He felt the necessity to retreat from the buzzing beehive climate of Paris.

"The disorder (xaos) of today is the order (kosmos) of tomorrow."

A highly intuitive understanding of chaos theory was brought to our world by the young new republicans of revolutionary France in the late eighteenth century.

Spring 1914: The artist was now almost twenty-seven, two years past his dramatic, and yet very private, turn away from the prevailing currents of contemporary art. During his 1912 stay in Munich, he developed the outline and scheme for *La Mariée mise à nu par ses célibataires, même [The Bride Stripped Bare by Her Bachelors, Even] (Large Glass)* (1915–23), a work that would occupy him for the next eleven years before being abandoned in New York, described in his own words as *definitifment inachevé*. But it seems that even before he began to work on this new project, before he actually conceived it, he had prepared for himself a set of axioms, or guiding principles, that would propel him beyond the beaten tracks of the art world and outside traditional methods of art-making. The axioms he formulated—such as *beauté d'indifférence, peinture de prècision*, or *hazard en conserve*[1]—radically contradicted the avant-garde standards of his day. He stood on the verge of developing his own personal software ... *une sorte de nominalisme pictural (contrôler)*.[2]

Until now, Duchamp's key medium had been oil on canvas, but the formal language he employed deviated from any known or practiced variation of Cubism. And the strange poetic quality of his nontitles, written sometimes directly onto his canvases, generated a

64 Cloud chamber, Brookhaven National Laboratory, Long Island, New York, 1949.

65 X-ray crystallography by M. von Laue, 1912. Niels Bohr Library, Copenhagen.

66 Apparatus used to record X-ray diffraction, built by W. Friedrich, P. Knipping, and M. von Laue, April 1912. Deutsches Museum Munich.

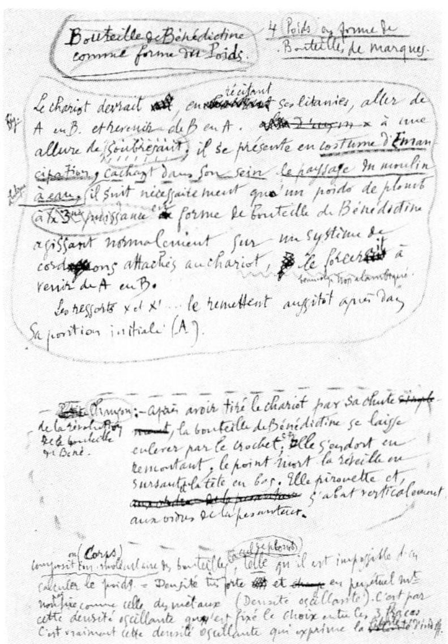

3 Stoppages Etalon =
du hasard en Conserve

1914.

textual realm that was totally his own. Turning from his previous research in painting, Duchamp now began to use a more dissociative technique that would become a prolific source for all his future projects and, in fact, a lifelong obsession. In terms of technique alone, his choice was the most personal imaginable, far removed from contemporary artistic endeavors. Obsessed with the idea of eliminating the presence of the artist in the work of art, he decided to approach the metaphorical artist's hand as literally as possible: he started to collect his handwritten scribbles and notes, his manu/scripts. Without any hesitation, he realized their dormant potential as visual, graphic elements, in particular the calligraphic quality (*callios*=beautiful) of the autograph (figs. 67 and 68). Handwriting, the scribbled note with all its corrections, rewriting, and underlining—the visualization of a thought process—became in his hands a refined, precise instrument.

The casual, fragile quality of these random notes was recharged and transformed into a new artistic concept, a kind of reference manual. Duchamp established an equilibrium between the recognizable hand of the artist in his personal handwriting and the strict elimination of any detectable artist's touch in his other works, or mani/festations. The activity of handwriting was able to filter and absorb the detested presence of the *pâte d'artiste*. At the other extreme, Duchamp positioned the anonymous readymade object—art by virtue of the mere choice of the artist—which would become the necessary counterweight to this growing codex of notes, the opposite end of Duchamp's personal spectrum of artistic expression: . . . *et qui libre?* [3]

By 1914, personalized "autography"—Duchamp's newly established outpost of artistic territory—had revealed its working potential. Even as he experienced from his transatlantic haven the *succés de scandale* of his painting *Nu descendant un escalier [Nude Descending a Staircase]* (1912) in the triple-venue 1913 "International Exhibition of Modern Art" (Armory Show), Duchamp already had passed the point of no return: most of the details and the first complete drafts of the *Large Glass*—as a whole—were finished. Meanwhile, the scheme for a different type of project had materialized in which he contemplated a dry and technical solution that would position his handwriting within his expanding universe. Familiar with documentary photography through his own work, he had experience with

Ludwig Wittgenstein
(1889–1951)

During his lifetime he published only his *Tractatus*—five years after he had finished the typescript—and the *Wörterbuch für die Volksschule [German Dictionary for Primary School]*.

All other philosophical projects were developed through multiple manuscript and typescript stages, left for ambitious, posthumous editions and publications. In his estate, a box was found in which Wittgenstein had kept notes and text fragments scribbled on *Zettel* [small pieces of paper].

67 Duchamp, original note *(Bouteille de Bénédictine,* 1913–14), from the *Green Box,* 1934, deluxe edition VI/XX. The Menil Collection, Houston.

68 Duchamp, facsimile note *(3 stoppages étalon,* 1913–14) from the *Green Box,* 1934, deluxe edition VI/XX. The Menil Collection, Houston.

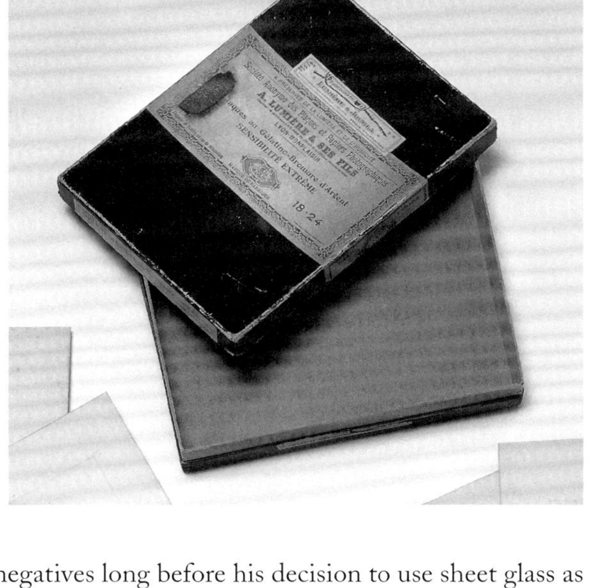

the use of large photographic glass negatives long before his decision to use sheet glass as the surface and background for his studies of the *Large Glass*. The technical term employed for photographic plates—*plaques extra rapides*—in fact, was stripped to a poetical level in a note from 1914: "*Pour repos instantané: faire entrer l'expression extra rapide.*"[4]

Not only by rotating two-dimensional elements but simply by the accumulation of them, one can traverse into the three-dimensional world. The almost nonexisting thickness of a sheet of paper—when stacked or piled up—allows passage to the next dimension.

"Through inframince we get from one dimension to the next."
—Marcel Duchamp, 1945

The applied production formula was simple and straightforward: a group of notes and the drawing *Avoir l'apprenti dans le soleil [To Have the Apprentice in the Sun]* (1914) were selected, photographically reproduced, printed, mounted, and boxed (pl. 1; fig. 69). As Duchamp would later write on May 28, 1961, from New York: "No, not a theme in the *Box of 1914*, simply a reunion of notes written at random."[5] Reproduced individually close to their original size as contact prints on paper, these 1:1 reproductions were then mounted on thick mat board and placed in a standard 18 x 24 cm box used for photographic plates. As the intention was to avoid the production of a singular object that could be mistaken for an original, Duchamp manu/factured probably five sets: "There has been no edition, just a box with the originals and 2 [sic] other boxes with the photographs of these originals."[6]

The secondhand readymade boxes, originally for photographic plates (by manufacturers Kodak, Jougla, or Lumière), bear no hint of their altered contents—except one example where the small typeface inscription of the readymade label has been changed from *Union Photographique Industrielle* to *15/16 Photographes Industrielles*. There is no signature, no date, not even a dedication in or on any of the known boxes. While the signature and date on the original drawing *Avoir l'apprenti dans le soleil* are visible on the glass negative, both are cut off on all mounted contact prints. The artist's signature is not necessary to certify its authenticity: neither in the facsimiles nor in the original. This devaluation has to be avoided. Only one of the sixteen notes—*Idée de la fabrication*—refers to a specific work outside the box: *3 stoppages étalons [3 Standard Stoppages]* (1913–14). Two of the boxes include three small photographs of this work, the ultimate result of Duchamp's research on the cultivation of chance—the *hazard en conserve*.

69 Duchamp, *Box of 1914* (detail), 1913–14. Commercial photographic supply box containing facsimiles of sixteen manuscript notes and one drawing, 1 1/2 x 7 1/2 x 9 7/8 in. Philadelphia Museum of Art. Gift of Mme. Marcel Duchamp.

To place sixteen documents, and/or their photographic facsimiles, into readymade (industrially produced) boxes is a highly personal and challenging concept—not only for the spring of 1914. On the one hand, the *Box of 1914*—as it would later be called—is very

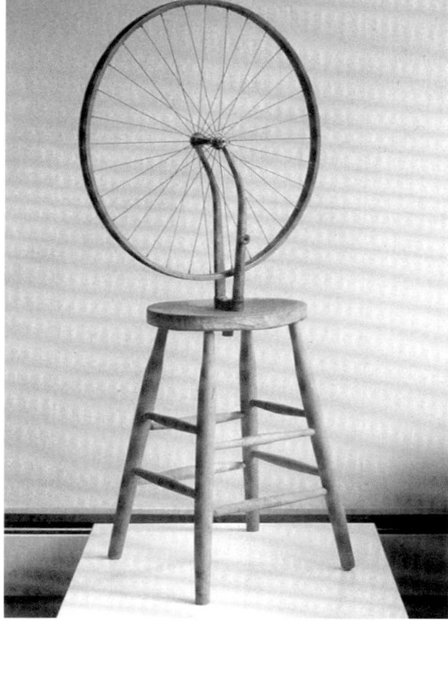

restrained, dry, and impersonal, while on the other, it suggests the primacy of individual endeavor over the normative social conventions demanded by Max Stirner, the nineteenth-century anarchist/philosopher, in his *Der Einzelne und sein Eigentum [The Ego and His Own].*

At the same time that Duchamp was investigating the effects of artist's choice through a selection of anonymous industrial objects, *Bicycle Wheel* (1913; fig. 70) and *Bottle Rack* (1914), he was using his "non-edition" of sixteen facsimile photographs of notes to synthesize his guiding principles of *beauté d'indifférence*, *hazard en conserve*, and the "transindividual" concept of the readymade. These aspects-in-opposition were reconciled by—and so belong to *(sind Eigentum von)*—the same artist who reflected his individualized approach in several inscriptions on his productions of around 1914:

"*appartenant à Marcel Duchamp* [belonging to Marcel Duchamp]."

70 **Duchamp, *Bicycle Wheel*, 1913/5th version, 1963.** Readymade: bicycle wheel and fork mounted upside down on a painted kitchen stool, 50¾ in., height. Collection of Richard Hamilton (present whereabouts unknown).

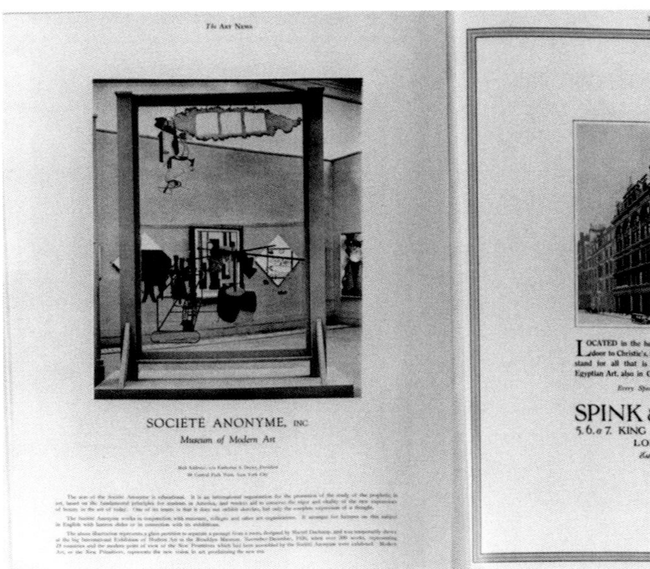

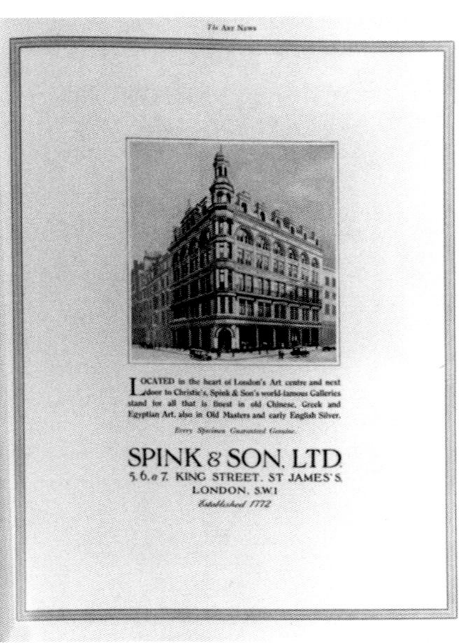

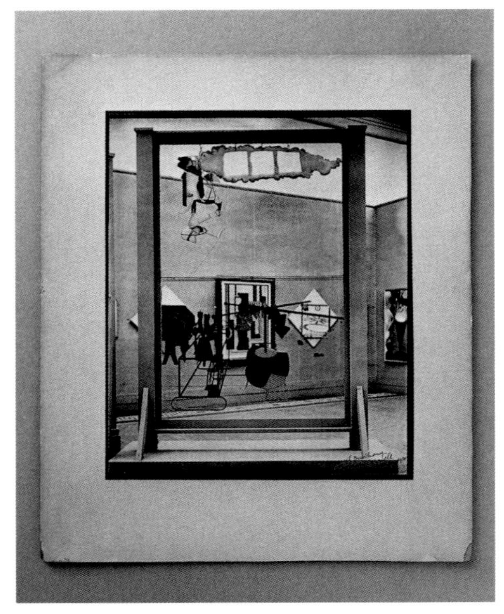

71 **Advertisement for Société Anonyme in *Art News* (14 May 1927)** reproducing Duchamp's *Large Glass* in "International Exhibition of Modern Art" (November 19, 1926–January 1, 1927), Brooklyn Museum.

72 **Mounted magazine reproduction of *Large Glass* from *Art News* (14 May 1927), 1934 (DD 108),** from Cornell, *Duchamp Dossier,* c. 1942–53. Philadelphia Museum of Art. Gift of The Joseph and Robert Cornell Memorial Foundation.

in a green box In 1934, more than twenty years after he had scribbled those first notes in the summer of 1912 and a little more then ten years after he had abandoned work on the *Large Glass*, Duchamp started to make a second edition of his personal calligraphy. This new publication venture could have been sparked by—at least it curiously overlaps with—the information that the *Large Glass* lay shattered in Katherine Dreier's barn in Connecticut. When Duchamp visited the site at the end of 1933, he could not then determine the extent of the overall damage to the work nor the necessary operations for its repair. A resolution developed that the *Large Glass* (certainly inaccessible and maybe even beyond recovery) should gain legibility and visibility through the publication of facsimile notes—appropriate for an object that was conceived as being *non-retinal* from the outset. For the envisioned project, acknowledging the unknown extent of the damage and the impossibility of securing a quality vintage photograph of the *Large Glass*, Duchamp obtained from Dreier a copy of *Art News* from May 14, 1927, depicting a full frontal view of the *Large Glass* in its unbroken state as presented in the 1926 Brooklyn Museum exhibition of the collections of the Société Anonyme, which he gave, signed and dedicated, to Cornell (figs. 71 and 72). In Paris, Man Ray rephotographed this installation view as a preparation for the publication—according to Duchamp's instructions—obliterated the background to emphasize the details of the *Large Glass* (figs. 73 and 74).

Throughout 1934, Duchamp continued with the facsimile re/production of a careful selection from his jottings dealing with the metaphorical mechanisms and the factual making of the *Large Glass*. His plan was not to create—as in 1914—four or five copies, but to produce three hundred sets. Although the use of photographic prints for reproduction purposes would have been costly and time-consuming, Duchamp was determined to replicate the originals as closely as possible. He eventually decided to use another expensive and labor-intensive technique, the collotype, whose continuous (no grain) tone, versus the halftone screen, allows printing from an ordinary film negative. Since Duchamp employed various coloring techniques in his calligraphy—underlinings and X-ings out in red and blue pencils, and the use of different inks (blue, red, sepia, and purple)—he sought a method to reproduce these colors in the facsimiles. To add this extra color to the

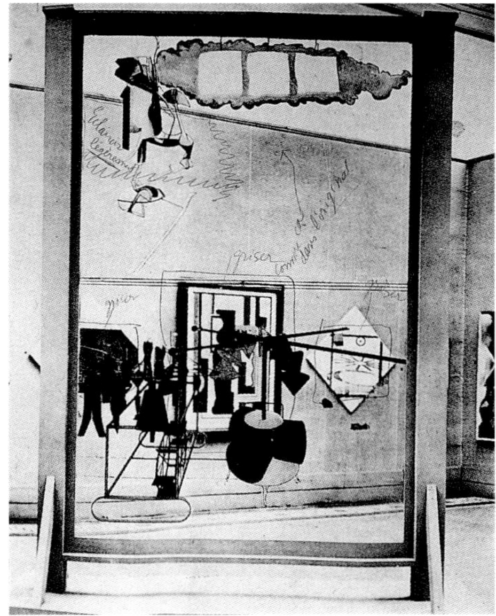

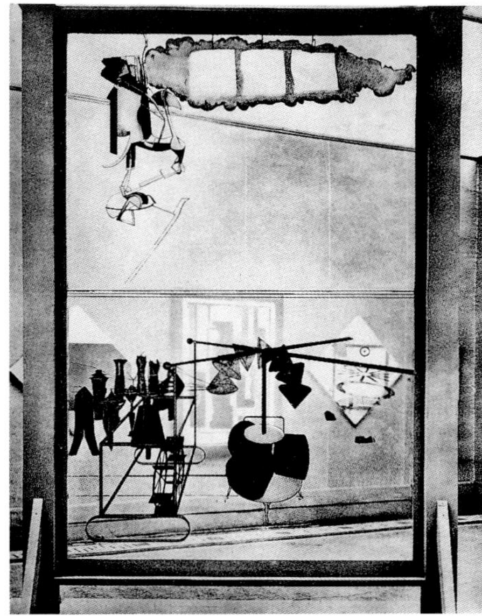

monochromatic collotype printing, Duchamp hired a pochoir studio, which applies colored washes to printed images in an assembly line process. For coloring his notes, the studio had to cut individual metal stencils for each underlining. To match the notes' torn edges, individual metal templates were necessary to recreate the single random edge of each torn piece of paper. The next step was to tear more than three hundred individual pieces of printed notes along each of these different tear-templates. Duchamp would inform later interviewers that he had created jobs by giving this assignment to the concierge in his apartment. Knowing a little bit of Duchamp's patience and working principles, one can assume that a great deal of this hand/work (manu/facturing) was eventually done by the artist himself, maybe with help from Mary Reynolds.

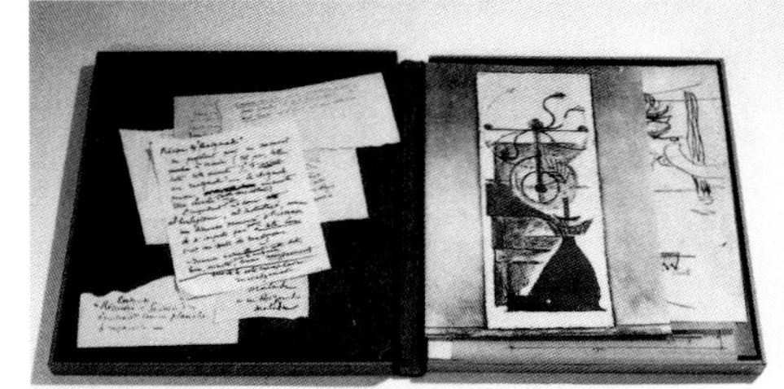

In addition to facsimiles of handwritten notes and the above-mentioned reproduction of the *Large Glass*, the publication holds a number of carefully reproduced studies and diagrams, a portrait of the artist with *Glissiere contenant un Moulin à Eau (en métaux voisins) [Glider Containing a Water Mill (in Neighboring Metals)]* (1913–15), and a pochoir-colored reproduction of *9 moules mâlic [9 Malic Molds]* (1914–15)—all printed in collotype as well. Two different box containers were conceived, prototyped, and then manufactured: a deluxe version with the initials MD in copper and a standard one with green, flocked paper. The title appears in mirror-image perforation on the deluxe examples and in a simulated form *en pochoir* on the regular versions. The chosen color for the latter supplied the edition's short colloquial title: *Green Box* (pls. 16 and 17; fig. 75).[7] The contents ended up, by Duchamp's own counting, numbering 93 + 1, thus reflecting the number three as one of the guiding structural axioms governing the elements of the *Large Glass*.

In fall 1934, Duchamp sent out an elaborate subscription bulletin (DD 90) for his new edition, including a specimen of its contents: one facsimile note concerning the *Broyeuse de chocolat [Chocolate Grinder]* (1913). The return address that he used seems slightly counterproductive: it was neither his studio nor a recently rented office but 18, rue de la Paix, Paris. The location given for the Editions Rrose Sélavy, publisher of the *Green Box*, was a financial institution, a bank—today it is, appropriately, a jewelry shop.

73 **Duchamp's retouching instructions for *Large Glass* as rephotographed by Man Ray** for reproduction in the *Green Box*, 1934. Vintage gelatin-silver print, 21 x 15 3/4 in. Private collection, courtesy Sotheby's.

74 ***Large Glass* as reproduced in the *Green Box*, 1934.**

75 **Duchamp, *La Mariée mise à nu par ses célibataires même [The Bride Stripped Bare by Her Bachelors Even] (Green Box)*, 1934**, deluxe edition VI/XX. 1 x 11 x 13 1/8 in. The Menil Collection, Houston.

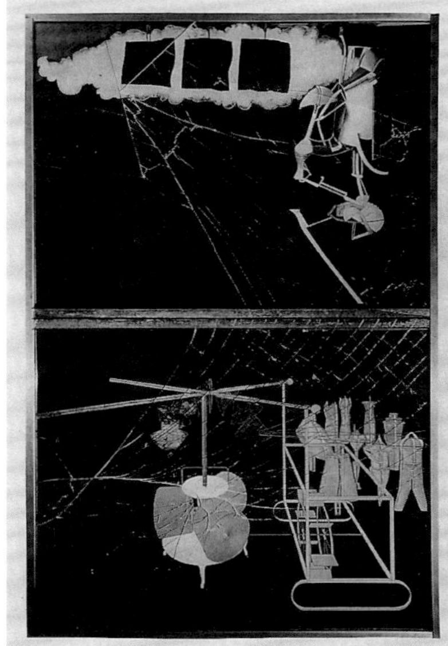

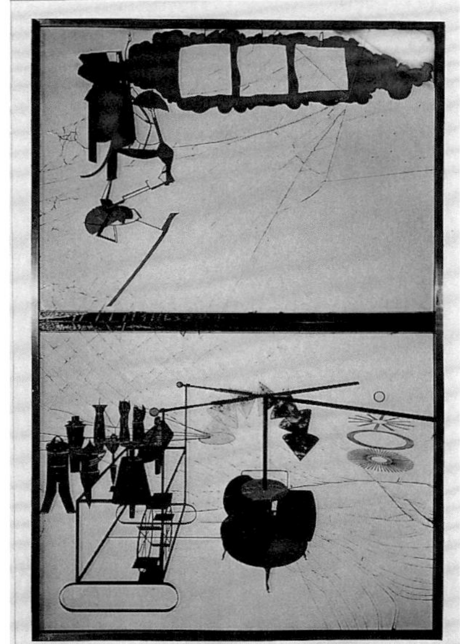

Walter Benjamin
(1892–1940)

The German essayist and philosopher, who was working in the Reading Room of the Bibliothèque Nationale in Paris on his incompleted and finally lost dossiers *Das Passagenwerk [The Passages]*, noted in his diary in late spring 1937: "Saw Duchamp this morning, same Café on Blvd. St. Germain.... Showed me his painting: *Nu descendant un escalier* in a reduced format, colored by hand en pochoir. breathtakingly beautiful. maybe mention...." (Walter Benjamin Archive, Institut für Sozialforschung, Goethe Universität, Frankfurt)

Benjamin brought most of his notes, collected images, and a final draft of *Das Passagenwerk* in a suitcase to the Spanish town of Port Bou near the French-Spanish border. Fearing deportation by the Gestapo, Benjamin committed suicide in late September 1940. None of his personal belongings including *Das Passagenwerk* was recovered.

76, 77 Photographs by Robert Coates of *Large Glass* according to Duchamp's specifications (against black for detail and against white for figure) for reproduction in the *Boîte* edition, 1938.

the album. facsimile as art The final sequence of work on the *Large Glass*, undertaken between 1920 and 1923 in New York, had been accompanied by an increased interest in purely optical phenomena: Duchamp made the first of his drawings intended to be seen in rotation about the time when work on the *Large Glass* came to an end. Similarly, just after he finished work on the *Green Box*, Duchamp embarked on a limited edition of his *Rotorelief (disques optiques)* (pl. 18), registered and patented as *Modèle déposée* on May 9, 1935. It was concurrently with the *Green Box* and the *Rotorelief (disques optiques)* that Duchamp began considering yet another publication project. He decided to accomplish "an album of approximately all the things I produced."[8]

Rather than use the faster reproduction techniques that were available, such as offset lithography, Duchamp opted for the same method he had already explored in the production of the *Green Box*, turning again to a combination of collotype printing and pochoir coloring. These techniques in the end would blur the boundaries between the unique art object and the multiple, between the specific original and its mechanical reproduction, creating a number of transitional stages that are hard to define and/or to distinguish (figs. 76 and 77). Nevertheless, Duchamp always delegated the execution of the actual handwork involved to a workshop or special studio and maintained precise distinctions between his own preparatory studies and the multiplied sets of the individual reproductions.

His part consisted principally of orchestrating a large number of successive operations as he maneuvered the sixty-nine items through each stage until a single item had been reproduced in an edition of more than three hundred copies. He dissected and disseminated his originals, ensuring a sufficient number of graphical steps to enable their reassembly as multiplied re/productions. In order to maintain the authentic appearance of the readymade postcard used for *L.H.O.O.Q.* in 1919 (pl. 5), Duchamp opted for its meticulous reproduction *en pochoir*, a process requiring presumably twenty to thirty individual color templates, before the mustache and goatee were added in actual graphite—employing a precisely cut minute little stencil (pl. 7; see also fig. 82).

Finally, the new edition, rather then presenting its contents in the linear sequence of a book, instead uses a box container to simulate the horizontals and verticals of an exhibition

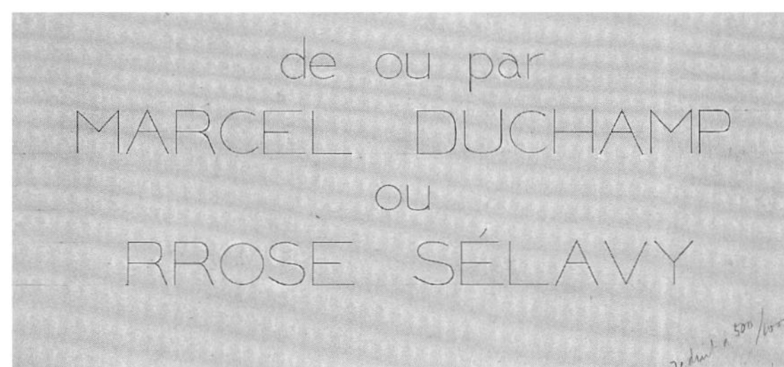

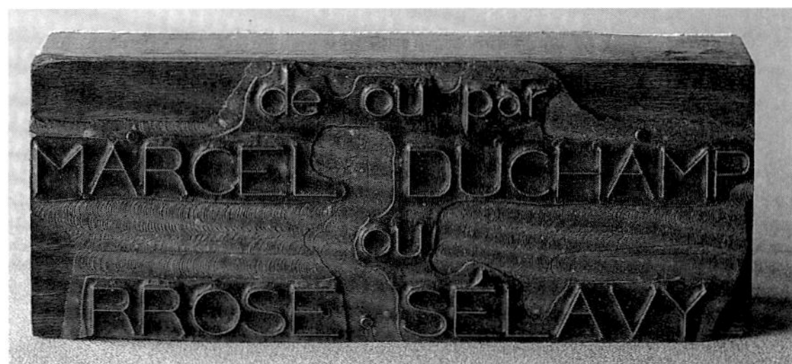

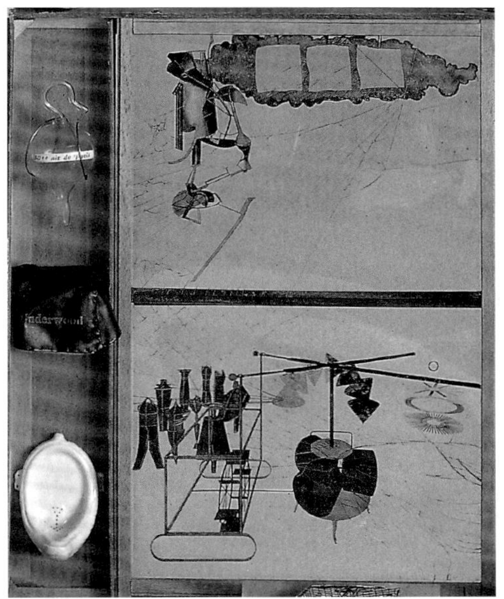

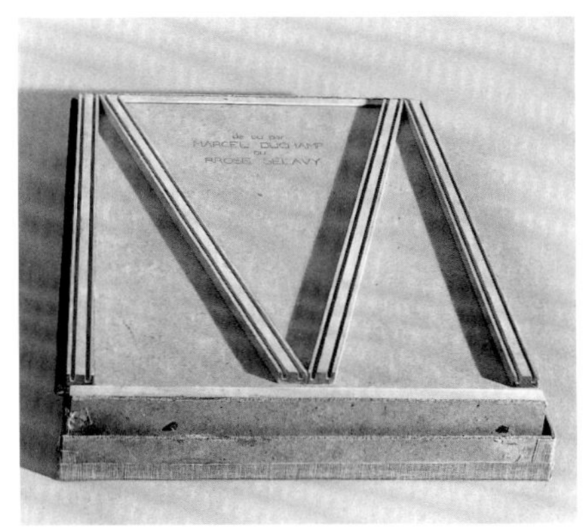

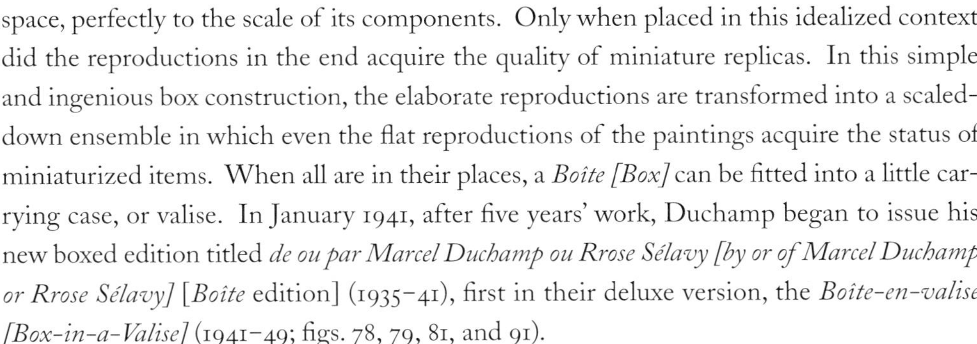

space, perfectly to the scale of its components. Only when placed in this idealized context did the reproductions in the end acquire the quality of miniature replicas. In this simple and ingenious box construction, the elaborate reproductions are transformed into a scaled-down ensemble in which even the flat reproductions of the paintings acquire the status of miniaturized items. When all are in their places, a *Boîte [Box]* can be fitted into a little carrying case, or valise. In January 1941, after five years' work, Duchamp began to issue his new boxed edition titled *de ou par Marcel Duchamp ou Rrose Sélavy [by or of Marcel Duchamp or Rrose Sélavy]* [*Boîte* edition] (1935–41), first in their deluxe version, the *Boîte-en-valise [Box-in-a-Valise]* (1941–49; figs. 78, 79, 81, and 91).

In effect, Duchamp had been working since the beginning of 1934 almost exclusively on collecting, reproducing, and publishing his own work. *Green Box*, *Rotorelief (disques optiques)*, and the *Boîte* edition underlined the inaccessibility of the originals, while at the same time offering a cross-referential galaxy to the cognoscenti. It was not until years later, in 1954, when the Arensberg Collection was installed in the Philadelphia Museum of Art with Duchamp's assistance, then opened to the public, that the originals acquired a status comparable to what they had already achieved, *en miniature*, in the *Boîte* edition. The permanent installation in the museum, centering on the *Large Glass*, appears as a delayed 1:1 simulation of the multiple miniature ensemble (fig. 80). The *Boîte* edition represents the artist's flexible matrix from which the ideal presentation could be formed.

The magnitude of the logistics of the whole album project is hard to comprehend, and it is significant that Duchamp never betrayed the extent of his efforts. But an imaginary group photo of all the parties, collaborators, and participants involved including the artist would change the still-dominant perception of the portable museum project as an amusing aperçu, a mere passing gesture. Despite this successful camouflage of his monumental endeavor, Duchamp never before or after conducted an enterprise depending on so many people and different kinds of professionals—comparable in scale and the required precise choreography only to a film production. The necessary preparations and decisions were manifold and highly differentiated, requiring complex strategies. Duchamp compiled lists providing information on locations and owners of individual works. Letters of

78 Lettering for title of *de ou par Marcel Duchamp or Rrose Sélavy [by or of Marcel Duchamp or Rrose Sélavy]* (*Boîte* edition), 1940.

79 Letterpress block plate for title of *de ou par Marcel Duchamp or Rrose Sélavy [by or of Marcel Duchamp or Rrose Sélavy]* (*Boîte* edition), 1940.

80 Duchamp, *Boîte* edition, interior detail.

81 Title and M initial on *de ou par Marcel Duchamp or Rrose Sélavy [by or of Marcel Duchamp or Rrose Sélavy]* (*Boîte* edition).

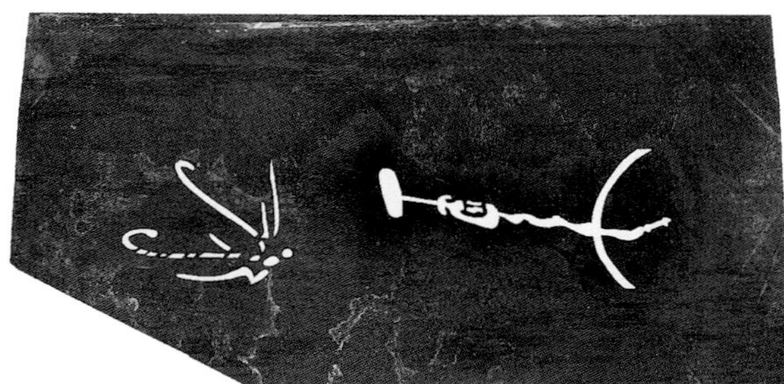

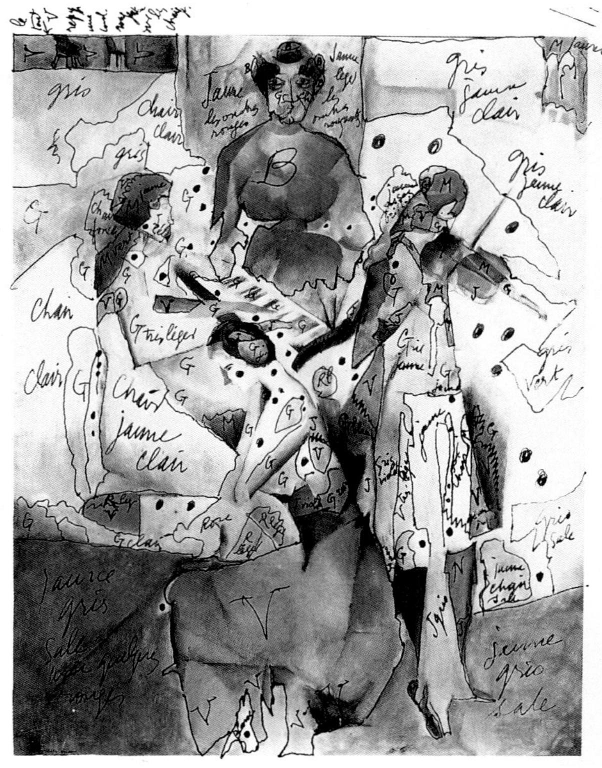

82 Zinc pochoir [stencil] used for coloring shadows of readymades on reproduction of *Tu m'* (1918), 1939.

83 Photograph of *Sonate* (1911) with Duchamp's color specifications for reproduction in *Boîte* edition, 1936.

requests and inquiries had to be written. In more than one case, work did not exist anymore or could not be located in time. With a few exceptions, the essential source material for the reproductions was photographs. Even so, hardly any existing photography was of a sufficient quality for the new project. Since color photography was not in common use, Duchamp had to find a way that would allow him to record all the necessary color information for the high-quality reproductions the album would require. Unbelievable to our Fujichrome world and its ubiquitous four-color reproduction technique, Duchamp reconstructed the colors of his paintings he intended to re/produce from memory and with the help of shorthand notations (fig. 83). The fact that almost all the key entries for the album happened to be in American collections made a field trip necessary. And most problematic of all, the primary object was unavailable for photography: the *Large Glass* was still subject to intensive care.

Sources tapped for the album project included photographers, several printshops, typesetters, paper merchants, two or three pochoir studios, dye-cut specialists, bookbinders for the standardized cardboard parts and assorted binding materials, carpenters for the framing parts, glassblowers, vitreous china craftsman, and ceramicists. Not to mention oilcloth suppliers and suitcase-makers for locks and leather.

Sixty-nine reproductions, their labels, black paper folders, customized and mitred cardboard strips for the mock-framing of several reproductions of paintings, specially designed wooden frames for the replicas of the *Large Glass* and *9 moules mâlic*, wooden sliding elements, different metal items necessary for the final assembly, small screws, metal rods—together more than 180 individual pieces belonged to a single *Boîte*. Each had to be decided on, designed, ordered, and manufactured in advance. The assemblage of a single *Boîte*

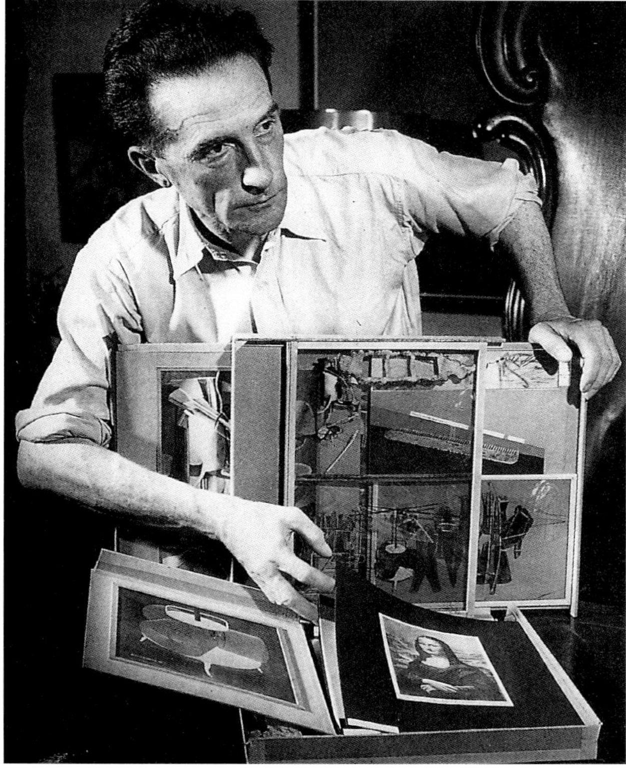

could take easily ten days or more and certainly involved boring, repetitive work. Between January 1941 and summer 1942, only four or five copies of the new edition became ready.

The *Boîte* edition constitutes a model in three dimensions of Duchamp's ironic Cartesian view. His profound skepticism—"I doubt the words *to be*"—permitted him to relentlessly concentrate on artistic forms that bore no resemblance to any conventional expression. The works he produced throughout his long life—many of them involving extraordinary delays—are pared down, attenuated by doubt. All his boxed artworks—published and edited by the artist himself—represent a multiplied embodiment of this *personalized* fragility—*appartenant à Marcel Duchamp*.

Doubt served as a common denominator, in a sense as a vanishing point, of Duchamp's pseudo-paradoxical, constantly reversible principles: chance and precision were not the only incompatibles that he reconciled. Convinced of the absence of purpose and meaning in existence, he was free to concentrate on the most minute and "useless" distinctions, differences, and nuances. Thus he reached a plateau where even the conventional categories of visibility and invisibility lost their accepted validity. Parallel to and in synchronicity with all his different publishing ventures throughout the 1930s, Duchamp developed a speculative perceptual model of his own: the *inframince*, a concept that allowed his mind to muse on the indiscernible.

Armand Schulthess
(1901–1972)

Employee of a Swiss insurance company, Schulthess left his job at age fifty and retreated to a remote part of Ticino. Here he started with an elaborate distribution of calligraphic tinplate (from flattened food tins) in the trees of his property. Subjects and quotes ranged from astronomy, philosophy, and psychoanalysis to medicine and chemistry, from literature to art and classical music. Schulthess collected for over twenty years literally tons of printed matter and stored it in a derelict old house on the premises. There seemed to be hardly space to move by the time of his death. In his estate, medical books were found where every page had been altered and amended by Schulthess, female anatomy being his preferred subject.

84 **Duchamp with a *Boîte-en-valise* (in progress),** Peggy Guggenheim's townhouse, 440 East 51st Street, New York, August 1942. Photograph by Allan Grant for *Time* (7 September 1942).

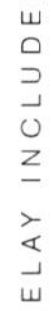

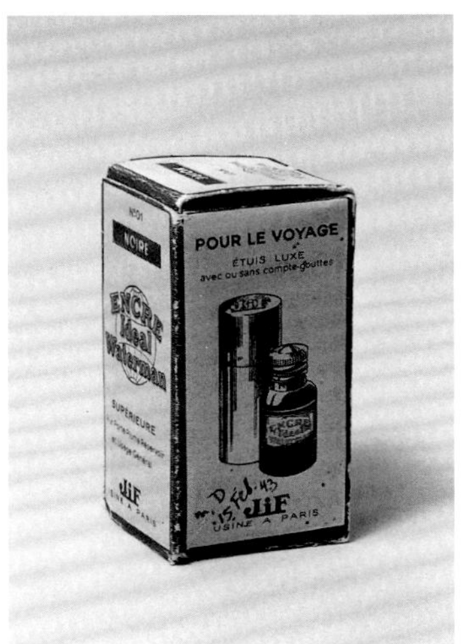

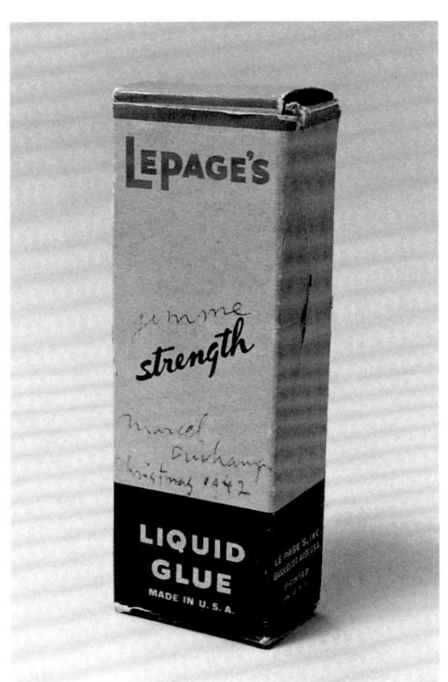

85 Duchamp, cardboard box [Encre Ideal Waterman] (detail), February 15, 1943 (DD 17), from Cornell, *Duchamp Dossier,* c. 1942–53. Philadelphia Museum of Art. Gift of The Joseph and Robert Cornell Memorial Foundation.

86 Duchamp, cardboard box [Gimme Strength], December 21, 1942 (DD 67), from Cornell, *Duchamp Dossier,* c. 1942–53. Philadelphia Museum of Art. Gift of The Joseph and Robert Cornell Memorial Foundation.

imaginary glue and virtual ink Before he boarded the boat in Marseilles in May 1942, Duchamp gave to Henriette Gomes the *Boîte-en-valise* IV/XX as a farewell present. Material for the assembly of fifty more boxes had already gone on a year earlier, declared as "household goods" with Peggy Guggenheim's furniture and art collection shipped from Grenoble to New York. Guggenheim had hand-carried her *Boîte-en-valise* I/XX in April 1941 to New York.

On June 25, the SS *Serpa Pinto,* calling at Casablanca and Lisbon, arrived in New York. After staying with the Robert Allerton Parkers for about a month, Duchamp moved to Guggenheim's townhouse. Here he began to unpack the material he had had shipped from Europe and eventually finished a *Boîte* he had started in Marseilles. At the end of July, Duchamp visited Cornell's house on Utopia Parkway for the first time, taking a *Boîte-en-valise* to him and his brother, Robert, for close inspection.[9] By August 14, the two artists were engaged in the organization of their soon-to-come work relationship.

Meetings and work lunches leave their traces in the collections of Cornell. These first Duchamp mementos of the most ephemeral kind would germinate into the *Duchamp Dossier*: cigarette packages without cigarettes, sugarcubes without wrappers, wrappers without the sugar, a tea tag without a tea bag, pipe cleaners without the pipe, a chocolate tin label without its chocolate. Following these early items, additions to the *Duchamp Dossier* would change into condensed matter directly related to Cornell's intended work on the *Boîte* edition: a glue spatula on a discarded envelope, a note about "1 yard of Belgian linen," a drawing that numbers components, an envelope from Paris, stationery of one of the pochoir studios involved, leather samples, and squares of 3M sandpaper.

Toward the end of August 1942, Duchamp was photographed by a Newspictures staff

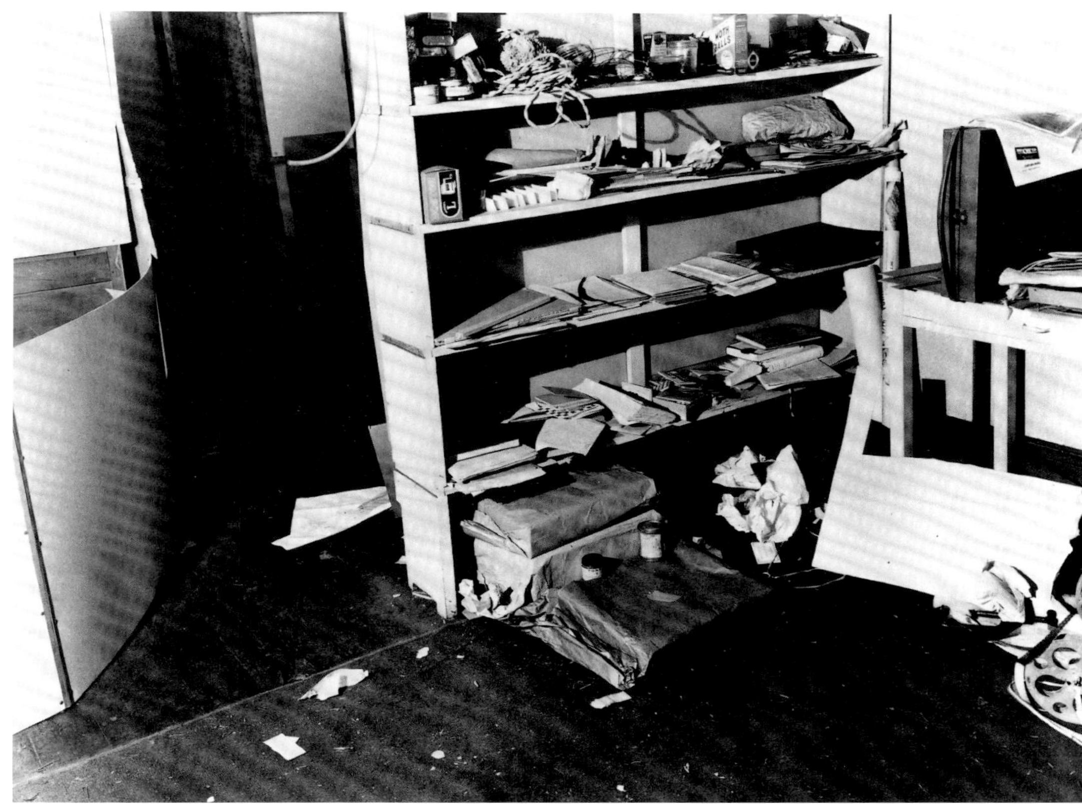

photographer in Guggenheim's townhouse (fig. 84), working on what the accompanying article called his "Monograph." The article continued: "It consists of a collection in cardboard boxes of reproductions of his work since 1910. Eventually he intends to bind the boxes in beautiful leather cases."[10] In fast succession between that time and early 1943, Duchamp produced, with Cornell's help, at least six of his *Boîtes-en-valise*. Around Christmas 1942, Duchamp turned an empty LePage's glue box into a signed and dated votive offering to the overall challenge and success of the project, amending the slogan to read "gimme strength" (fig. 86). Only two months later, by February 1943, his favorite blue Encre Ideal Waterman ink he had brought from Paris, used for dedicating, dating, and signing the *Boîtes-en-valise,* was spent (fig. 85). The Ideal Waterman package, turned into another signed token of Duchamp's friendship with Cornell and their ongoing enterprise, was transferred to the growing complex of the *Duchamp Dossier* project.

A philosopher often describes his "entry into the world," his "being in the world," by using a familiar object as a symbol. By describing his ink bottle phenomenologically, Duchamp turned a paltry thing into the janitor of the wide world.

> The man with the magnifying glass—quite simply—bars the every-day world. He is a fresh eye before a new object. The botanist's magnifying glass is youth recaptured. It gives him back the enlarging gaze of a child.... Thus the minuscule, a narrow gate, opens up an entire world. The details of a thing can be the sign of a new world which, like all worlds, contains the attributes of greatness.... Miniature is one of the refuges of greatness.[11]

Enrico Fermi
(1901–1954)

In the late fall of 1942—as part of a highly classified operation in a racquet court under the West Stands at Stagg Field, The University of Chicago—a team led by Enrico Fermi constructed the first nuclear "pile" using 400 tons of purified graphite and 22,000 pseudospheres of uranium stacked in 57 layers of cadmium sheets. Its final height was slightly under 20 feet. The pile occupied an approximate 24-foot-square area and weighed 432 tons. A cadmium strip regulated the rate of the reaction, and another cadmium bar tethered by a rope acted as an emergency shutdown. Also three physicists stood ready with buckets of cadmium sulphate in case all else failed and the reaction was uncontrolled. When at 3:25 p.m. on December 2, 1942, the cadmium strips were removed, the pile reached criticality and the chain reaction became self-sustaining. This procedure initiated the first controlled release of nuclear energy: a privileged and isolated few were eyewitnesses to the first man-made atomic reactor at work. The reactor, which operated for 28 minutes, generated 200 watts of power (fig. 62).

87 **Duchamp's studio,** 210 West 14th Street, New York, 1945. Photograph by Percy Rainford.

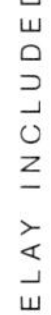

Aby Warburg
(1866–1929)

Warburg worked for many years on a project, incomplete at the time of his death. His *Bilderatlas*, also called Mnemosyne, represented a visual thesaurus relating to his concept of the *Pathosformula* (figs. 88 and 89).

Trying to apply his strict research principles to verify the flood of published pictures of World War I, he encountered disquieting paradoxes and contradictions. The obviously propaganda-oriented manipulations of the source material disoriented him to the degree that treatment in the clinic of Dr. Binswanger in Kreuzlingen, Switzerland, became necessary. His demand for an essential truth to reside in images and the dawn of the age of mass media had created unwanted turbulences.

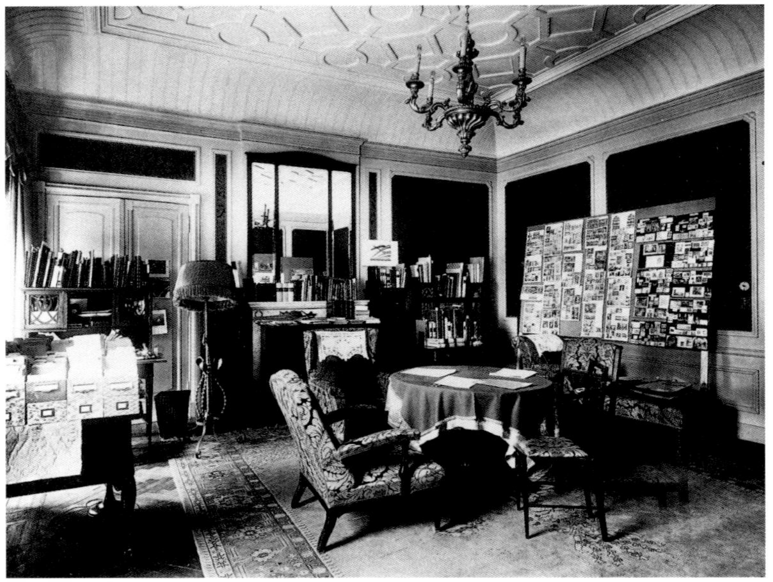

88 Aby Warburg's Mnemosyne project (photographic arrangements and reference card files), Rome, 1929.

compiled and discompleted All items/fragments/objects in the *Duchamp Dossier* seem to represent both the provocative meandering of an aimless stroll and the deterministic result of a careful, selective filtering process—allied in paradoxical harmony. The *Duchamp Dossier* does not include everything related to Duchamp that Cornell could have laid his hands on or come in close contact with (fig. 87). We do not know when he last "worked on" and shifted its contents, and there is no way to find out whether all the items that at one point were included are still in the container.

This is the "uncertainty principle" of posthumous objects in general and Cornell's dossiers in particular, when there has been no previous exposure to the public. The *Duchamp Dossier* was never exhibited by the artist, and even in its place in the Utopia Parkway studio, very few individuals ever saw it. It thus *maintains* an air (fragrance) of being incomplete. The radiance of being open-ended is an inherent feature of the pile-in-a-box format. Incompleteness is the medium of a dossier.

Evaluating the specifics of the *Duchamp Dossier*, one finds Cornell's selection m(eth)ode fairly homogeneous at its core (the filtered fragments). All the collectibles united in the *Duchamp Dossier* seem to refer to a particular kind of cultural periphery, representing a borderline aesthetic. Only a few items retain their self-contained state. In particular, the unfragmented inclusions (i.e., the *Rotorelief (disques optiques)*, *Vogue* covers, and reproductions from the *Boîte* edition) seem oddly "healthy," even somewhat "sturdy," compared to the feel and appearance of the other torn and tattered matter. As scattered and disassembled as most of its items seem, even at their most aloof and elusive, the dossier format nonetheless appears as a vehicle for successful reentry to the cultural discourse. Everything that is recycled is a re/minder of our quintessential amnesia: the unforeseeable turbulences of the centripetal and centrifugal dynamics of cultural oblivion are difficult to follow, much less to record, as the vortexes of deletion and frequent chance-operations control the re/dis/coursing. Cultural dynamics manipulate the valves of the value system and operate the shifting differentiations between trash and artifact; how to retrieve, select, refine, and regenerate the relevant elementary particles of the cultural process from the refuse and rejects, the garbage and the litter, the flotsam and jetsam of our societies? How

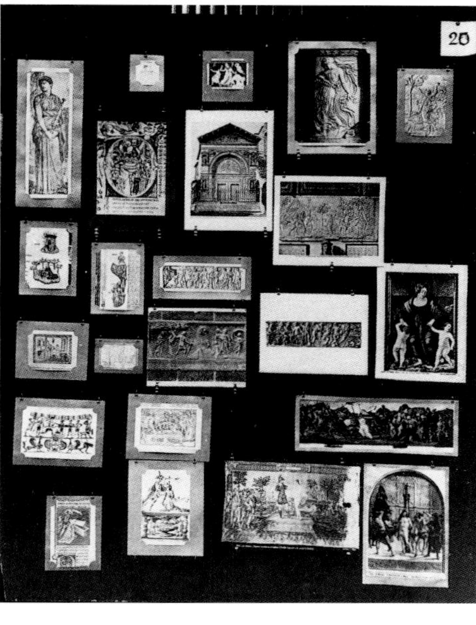

89 **One of sixty-three photographic arrangements, Aby Warburg's Mnemosyne project**, Rome, 1929.

Mnemosyne, daughter of Heaven and Earth, bride of Zeus, in nine nights becomes the mother of nine muses: Clio (History), Euterpe (Music), Thalia (Comedy), Melpomene (Tragedy), Terpsichore (Dance), Erato (Love Poetry), Urania (Astronomy), Calliope (Epic Poetry), and Polyhymnia (Heroic Hymns).

to convert the retrieved matter into cultural energy that feeds back into the system? To the cultivators of dust, like Duchamp, and compilers of "mouse material," like Cornell, residue becomes a discipline.

The fractal disorder of the accumulated pile characterizes its critical potential. By a virtually endless succession of selective steps—the cycloidal waltz of the on/off, in/out decisions—material for the dossier is collected until the pile reaches criticality. Since no stable hierarchy is possible, the pile represents a time-warp, a condensation of space. When the pile is spread out, the white areas between individual items—indivisible, no more reducible—function in the same way as the leading (line space) between typeset text. The empty interval becomes significant. Accumulated archival piles can be regarded as the plastic (pictorial and/or sculptural) dialectic representation of memory.

Intended as a celebration of memory—the most luxurious feature of cellular and neuronal evolution—these accumulations are at the same time a massive monument to memory's prime defunct mechanism: its inescapable tendency to dissolve into the vast nebula of oblivion or else to turn into something like the towering calcified structures of coral reefs.

> We think of creation as a bringing forth. But the making of equipment, too, is a bringing forth. Handicraft—a remarkable play of language—does not, to be sure, create works, not even when we contrast, as we must, the handmade with the factory product.... The creation of a work requires craftsmanship. Great artists prize craftsmanship most highly. They are the first to call for its painstaking cultivation, based on complete mastery.... It has often enough been pointed out that the Greeks, who knew a few things about works of art, use the same word, *techne*, for craft and art and call the craftsman and the artist by the same name: *technites*.... it never means a kind of practical performance.... denotes rather a mode of knowing.[12]

delay included
marcel

90 **Duchamp, note, April 19, 1943 (DD 15),** from Cornell, *Duchamp Dossier,* c. 1942–53. Philadelphia Museum of Art. Gift of The Joseph and Robert Cornell Memorial Foundation.

the memory cloud Unique to the 1,300 grams of human wetware (gray matter) encapsulated in cerebral bone is its critical mass potential: a certain surplus of neurons and brain tissue provides a neuronal networking capacity. At its origin, conscious perception and memory must have set in as a chain reaction.

Though we observe and treasure it, leaving aside its daily deficiencies, it is not necessary for our nor any other life-sustaining system. Three and a half billion years of geological time passed without a hint of this recalling function, save that of some carbon crystals, only very recently designated diamonds.

Memory as a highly efficient selection process and structuring format is incomplete by definition. The selective sensory mode suppresses, eliminates, and deletes raw data in order to gain cohesion. Memory thus is a refined residue of information, filtered from data-detritus. The constant flow and flux acquires structure (a formation) only by radical subtraction: our perceptive apparatus (utensil) only works by massive data-sewers.

On the side of life-sustaining objectives, the copy mechanisms of genetic information work by suppressing selective potential: both molecular mechanisms and conscious memory functions are rarified evolutionary extremes. From the ultimate exactitude of atomic standards (a given isotope of neon [nobel gas] has the same properties wherever it is found in this universe) to the nearly flawless propagation of the genetic code—all these orders of precision provide a foil to the conditional incompleteness of our conscious perception and memory. The selective powers of the sensory apparatus is the biochemical complementary principle to the perfection of the genetic code: no matter, never mind.

All our libraries, collections, museums, depots, archives, and storage facilities—including all the digital formats, all our inherited and preserved manuscripts, and finally the thousands of miles of printed matter stored in the libraries of the world—are massive accumulated monuments dedicated to our source meta-material *per se*, to INFORMATION. All cultures in recorded history are trying to approach critical mass by piling up such cultural detritus, constantly struggling with the perplexing consequences of the value system. These operators are directed toward preventing complete disintegration, defying the info-void (fig. 90). Stemming the tide requires constant epistemological research into the puzzling hermetic proceedings of recovering the rejected and balancing the ever-present de/instability of order—delaying the final descent past the event horizon.

In Paris in 1913, Duchamp jotted on a small piece of paper: "Can works be made which are not 'of art?'"[13] Aptly Duchamp hid this sentence in his arsenals for fifty-four years. In 1967 this art-*koan* was among the 120 facsimile notes published as *à l'infinitif [In the Infinitive]* (1967), commonly called the *White Box.* It encapsulates the quality of those Zen-Buddhist questions guiding the disciple through endless hours of *zazen* until finally reaching a state of personal *satori.*

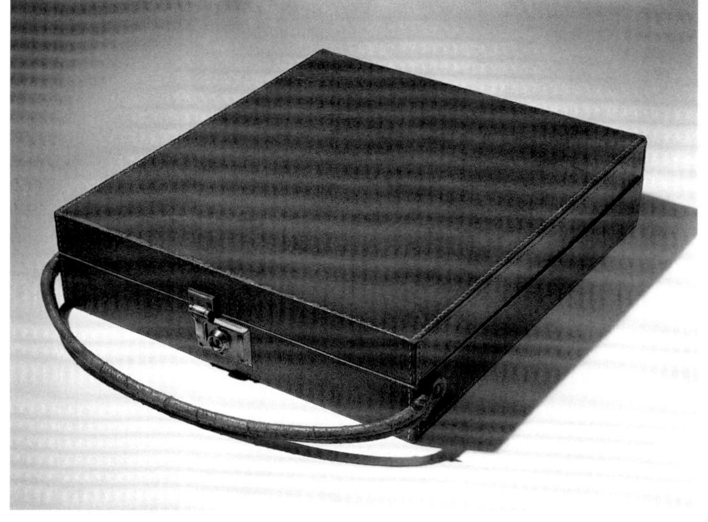

Notes

1. "Beauty of indifference / precision painting / canned chance" appear on notes in *La Mariée mise à nu par ses célibataires même [The Bride Stripped Bare by Her Bachelors Even]* (*Green Box*), Paris: Editions Rrose Sélavy, 1934.

2. ". . . a type of pictorial nominalism (check)" is a note in *à l'infinitif [In the Infinitive] (White Box)*, New York, 1967. English translation from Richard Hamilton and Ecke Bonk, *Marcel Duchamp, in the infinitive–White Box: A Typographic Rendering* (forthcoming).

3. ". . . and who is free" is a wordplay on *equilibrium*. See Duchamp's illustration for a 1917 poem by Francis Picabia, "L'Equilibre," Paris: Pierre-André Benoit, 1958.

4. "For the instant repose = bring in the term extra-rapid" is a Duchamp note in the *Green Box*.

5. "*Non, pas de thème dans la* Boîte de 1914, *simple reunion de notes écrits au hazard*," Marcel Duchamp to Serge Stauffer, 28 May 1961.

6. "*Il n'y a pas eu d'edition, seulement une boite avec les originaux et 2* [sic] *autres boites contenant la photo de ces originaux,*" Marcel Duchamp to Serge Stauffer. Duchamp states erroneously that only two copies were made. Five copies of the edition are known today: Philadelphia Museum of Art; The Art Institute of Chicago; Dina Vierny, Paris; the Estate of Teeny Duchamp; and one location at present unknown.

7. The full title of the edition is *La Mariée mise à nu par ses célibataires même [The Bride Stripped Bare by Her Bachelors Even] (Green Box)*.

8. Marcel Duchamp to Katherine Dreier, 5 March 1935, Katherine Dreier Papers, Yale Collection of American Literature, Beinecke Rare Book and Manuscript Library.

9. Robert Cornell, diary entry, 31 July 1942, courtesy Mrs. John A. Benton.

10. "Artist Descending to America," *Time*, 60, no. 10 (7 September 1942): p. 102.

11. Gaston Bachelard, *The Poetics of Space*, translated by Marie Jolas (Boston: Beacon Press, 1969), p. 155.

12. Martin Heidegger, "The Origin of the Work of Art," in *Basic Writings*, edited by David Farrell Krell,(New York: Harper & Row, 1977), p. 181*f*.

13. "*Peut-on faire des œuvres qui ne soient pas 'd'art'?*" is a note in *à l'infinitif [In the Infinitive]* (*White Box*), 1967. English translation (see note 2).

91 Duchamp, *de ou par Marcel Duchamp or Rrose Sélavy [by or of Marcel Duchamp or Rrose Sélavy] (Boîte* edition).

pp. 112–13

92 Duchamp in his twine installation for "First Papers of Surrealism" exhibition (October 14–November 7, 1942), Whitelaw Reid Mansion, 451 Madison Avenue, New York, with his *Réseaux des stoppages [Network of Stoppages]* (1914) to his left. Photograph by Arnold Newman.

93 Duchamp's studio, 210 West 14th Street, New York, 1945. Photograph by Percy Rainford.

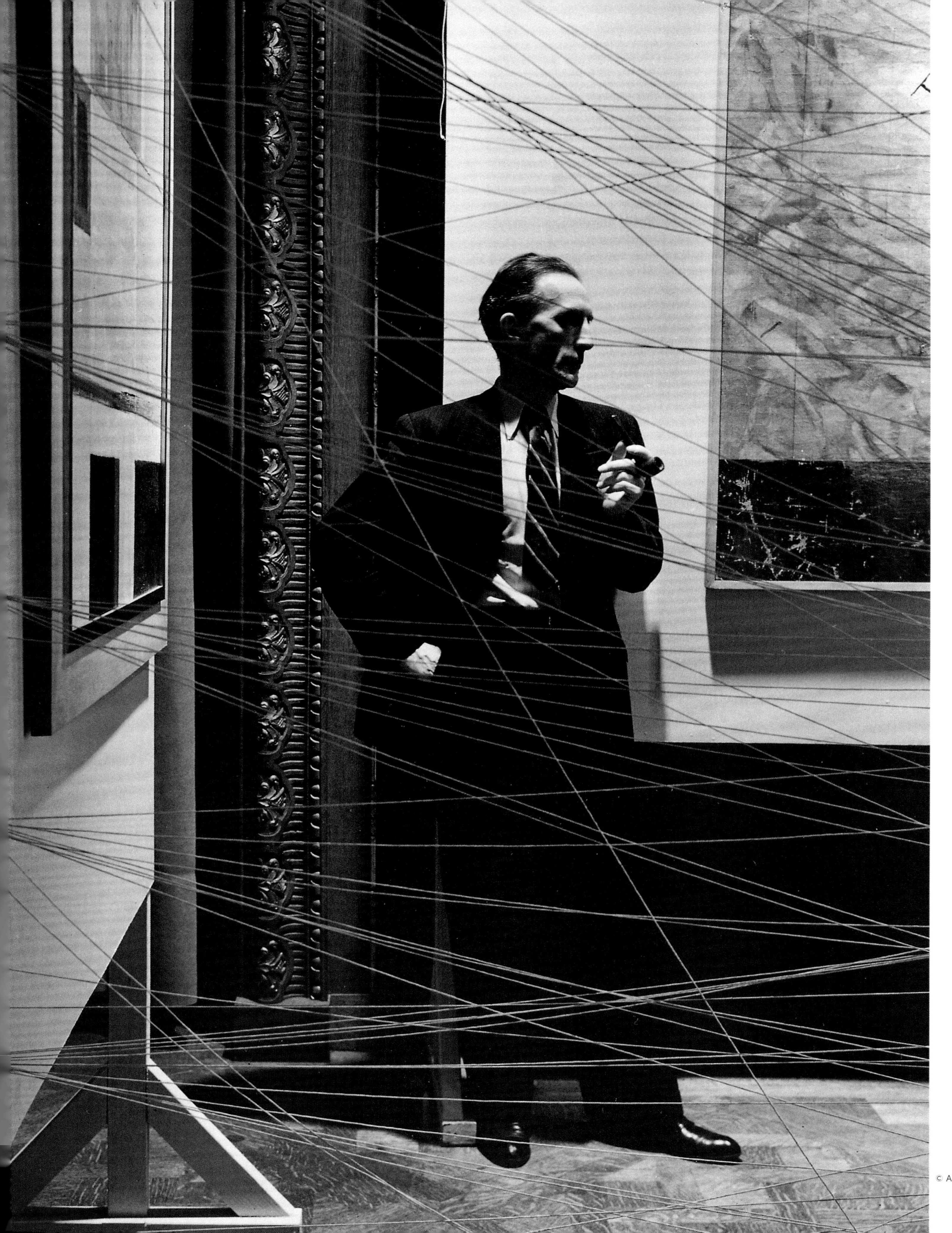

© Arnold Newma

Marcel Duchamp Plates

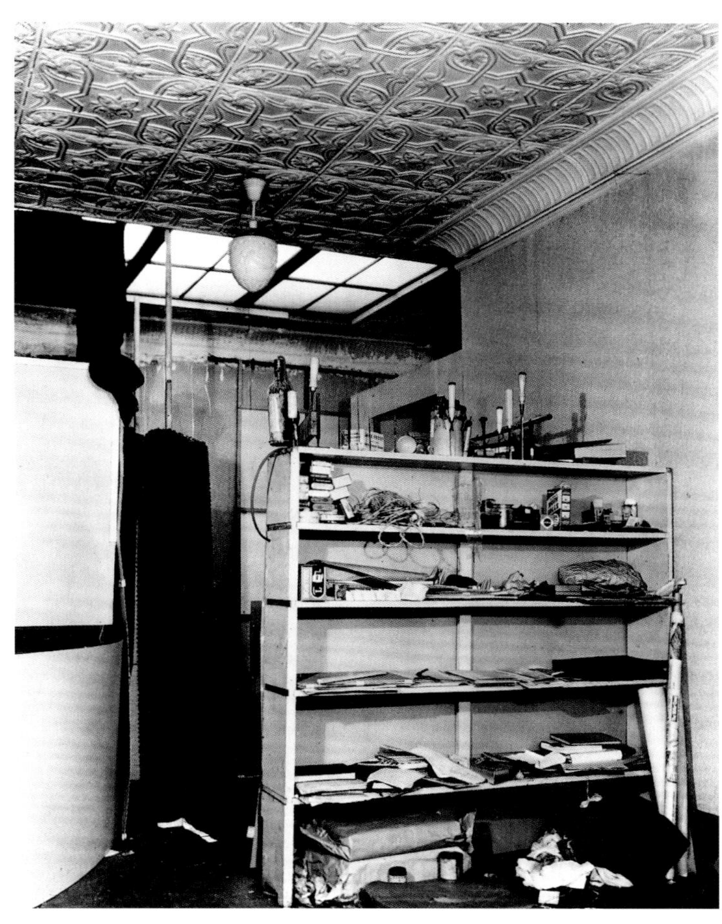

1 ***Box of 1914*** 1913–14
Philadelphia Museum of Art.
Gift of Mme. Marcel Duchamp

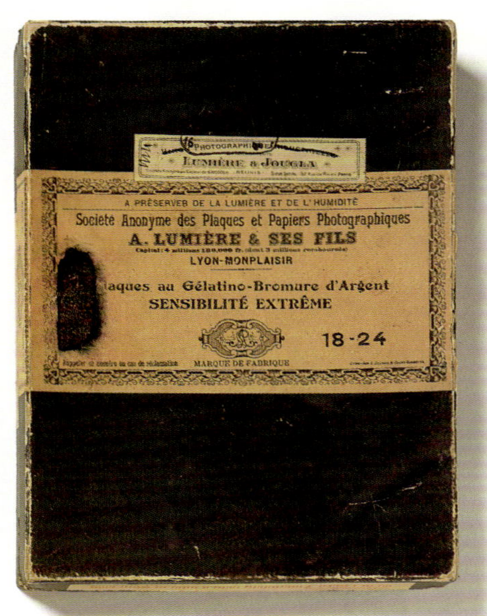

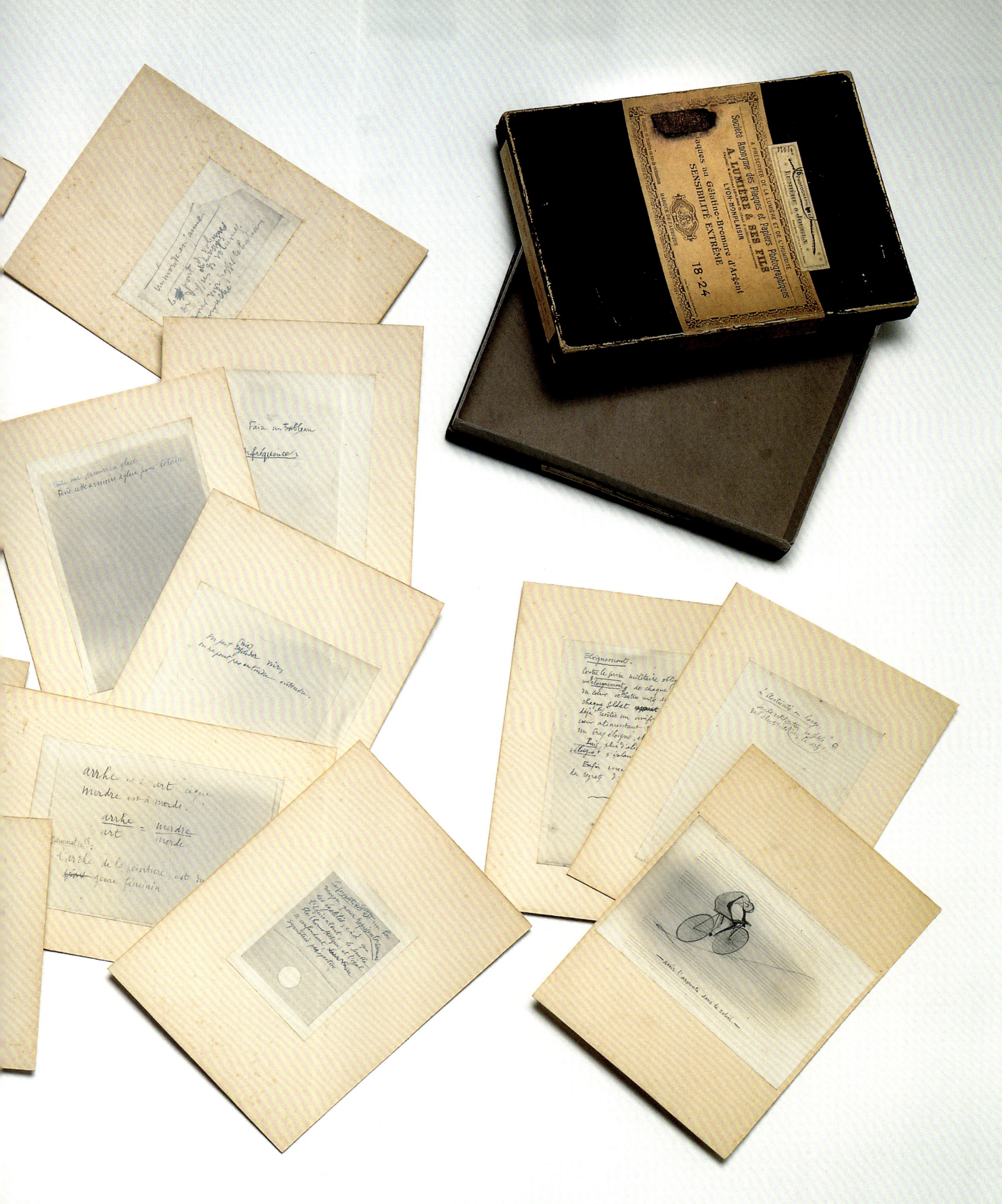

À PRÉSERVER DE LA LUMIÈRE ET DE L'HUMIDITÉ
Société Anonyme des Plaques et Papiers Photographiques
A. LUMIÈRE & SES FILS
LYON-MONPLAISIR
Plaques au Gélatino-Bromure d'Argent
SENSIBILITÉ EXTRÊME
18·24
arrhe est à art ce que merdre est à merde.
arrhe / art = merdre / merde

2 ***A Bruit Secret [With Hidden Noise]*** 1916
Philadelphia Museum of Art.
The Louise and Walter Arensberg Collection

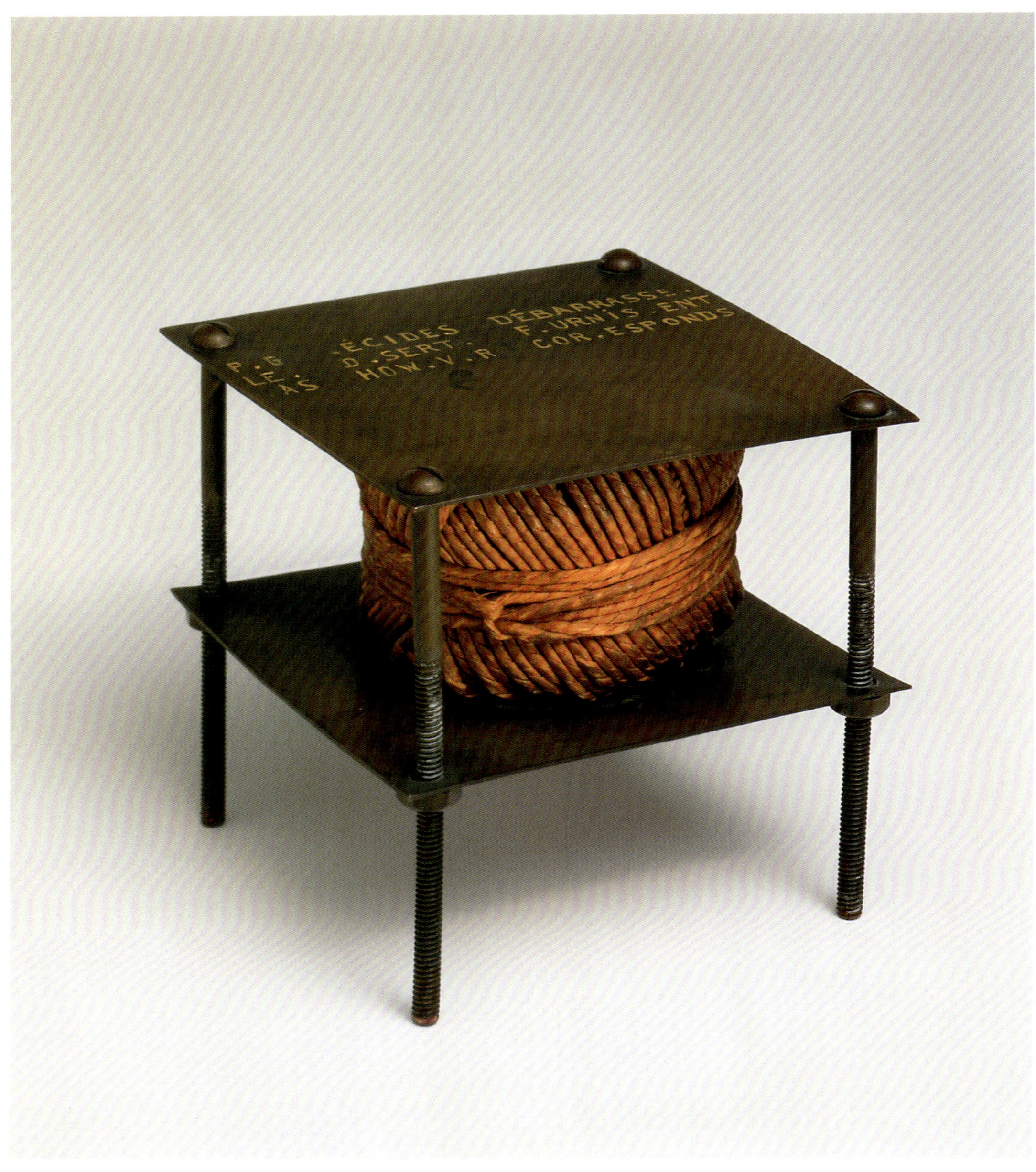

3 ***Apolinère Enameled*** 1917
Philadelphia Museum of Art.
The Louise and Walter Arensberg Collection

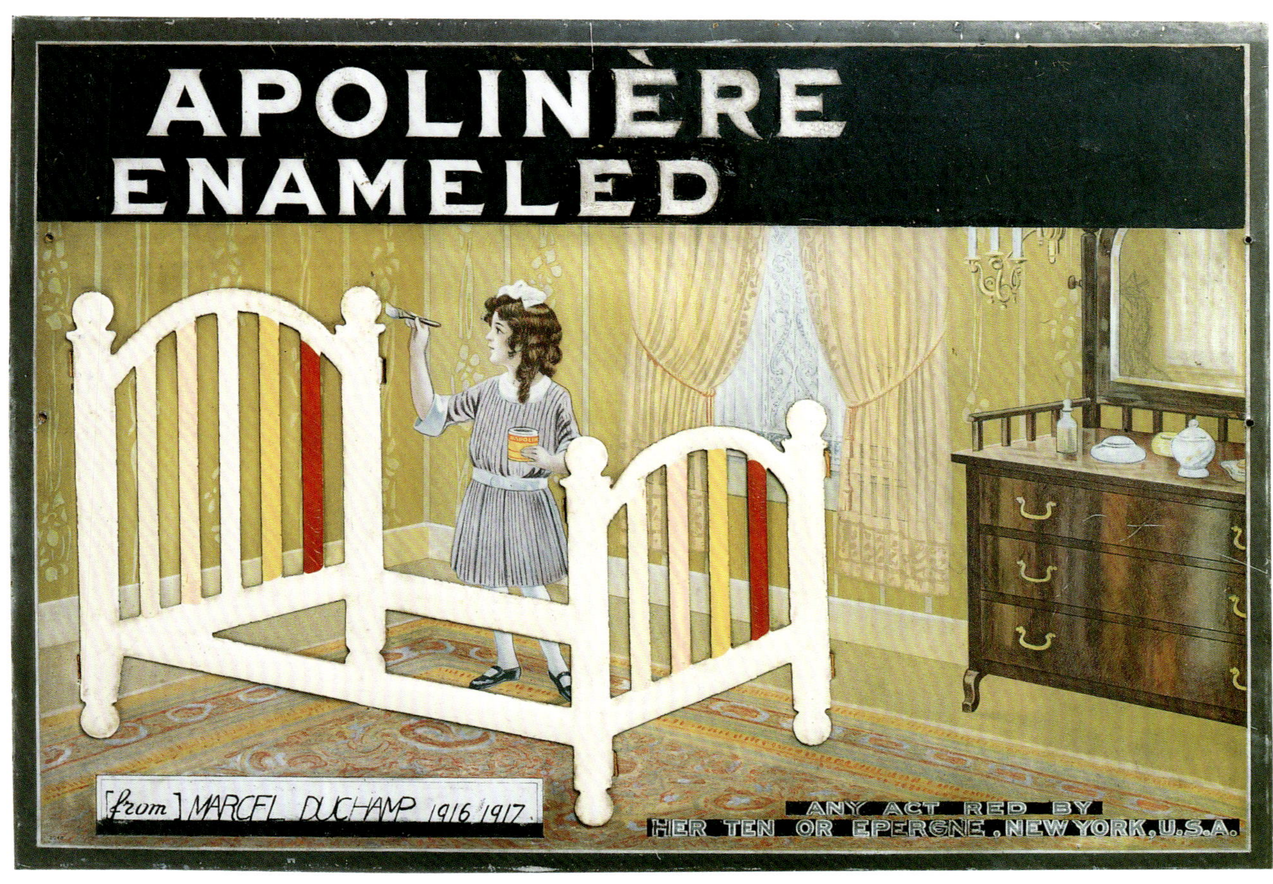

4 ***Air de Paris [50cc of Paris Air]*** 1919
Philadelphia Museum of Art.
The Louise and Walter Arensberg Collection

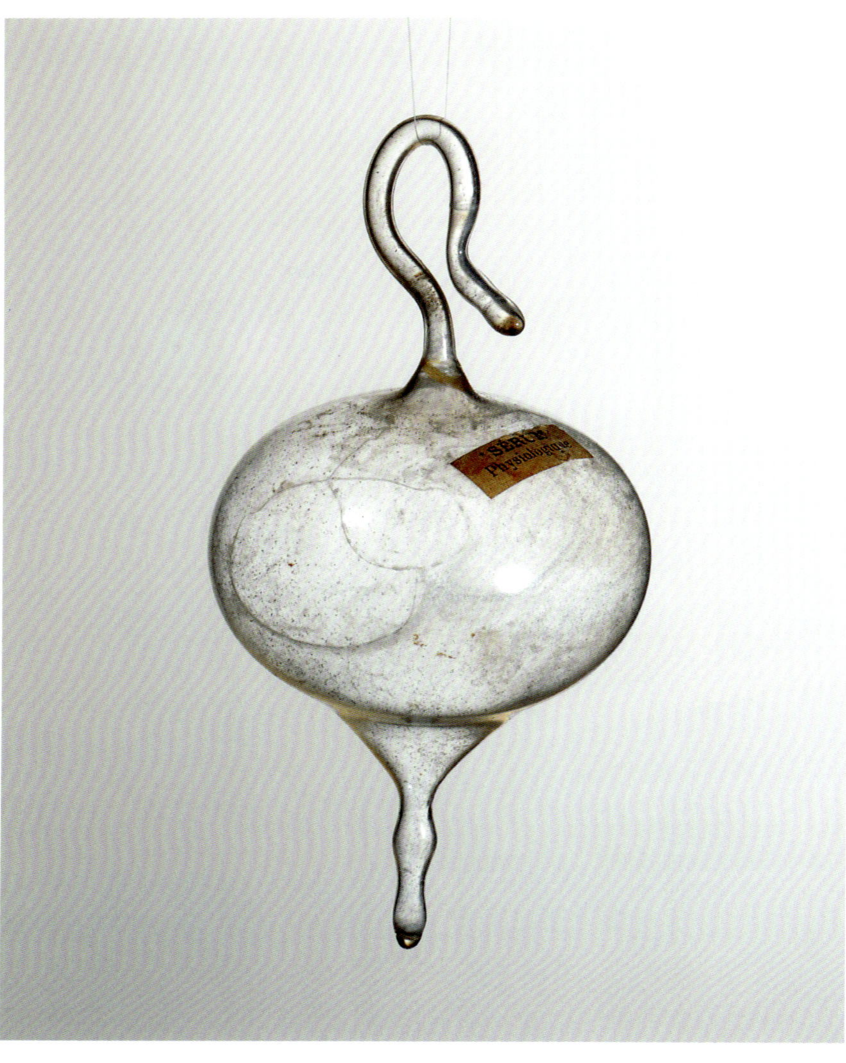

5 ***L.H.O.O.Q.*** 1919
Private collection

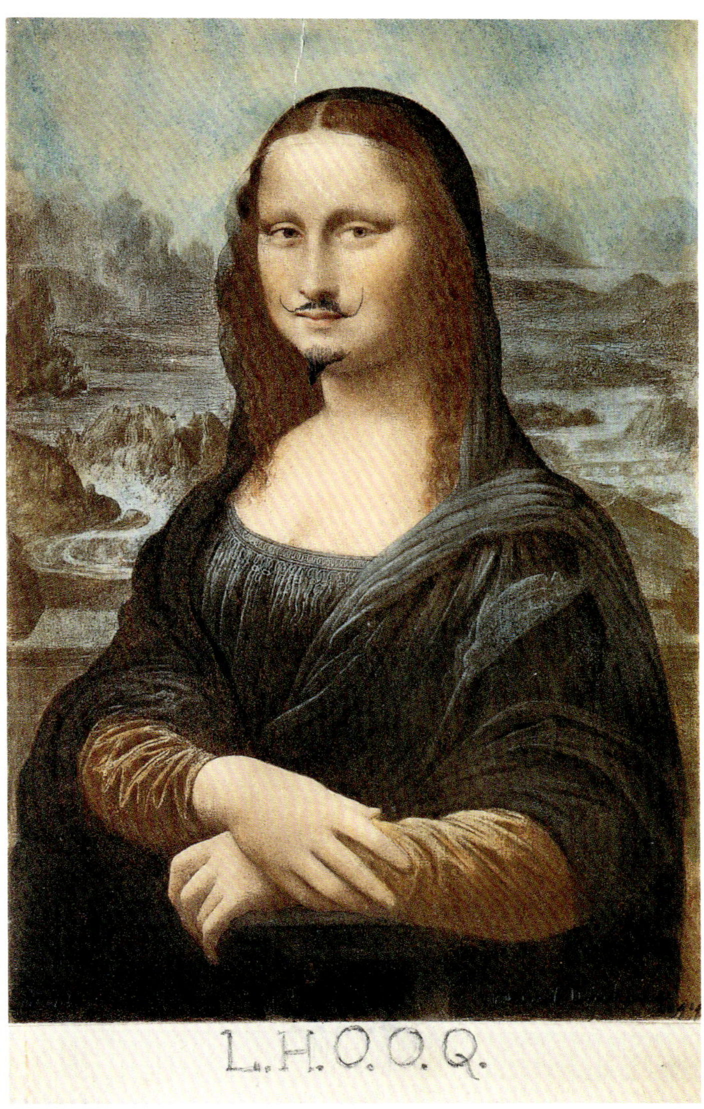

6 ***L.H.O.O.Q.*** 1930
French Communist Party

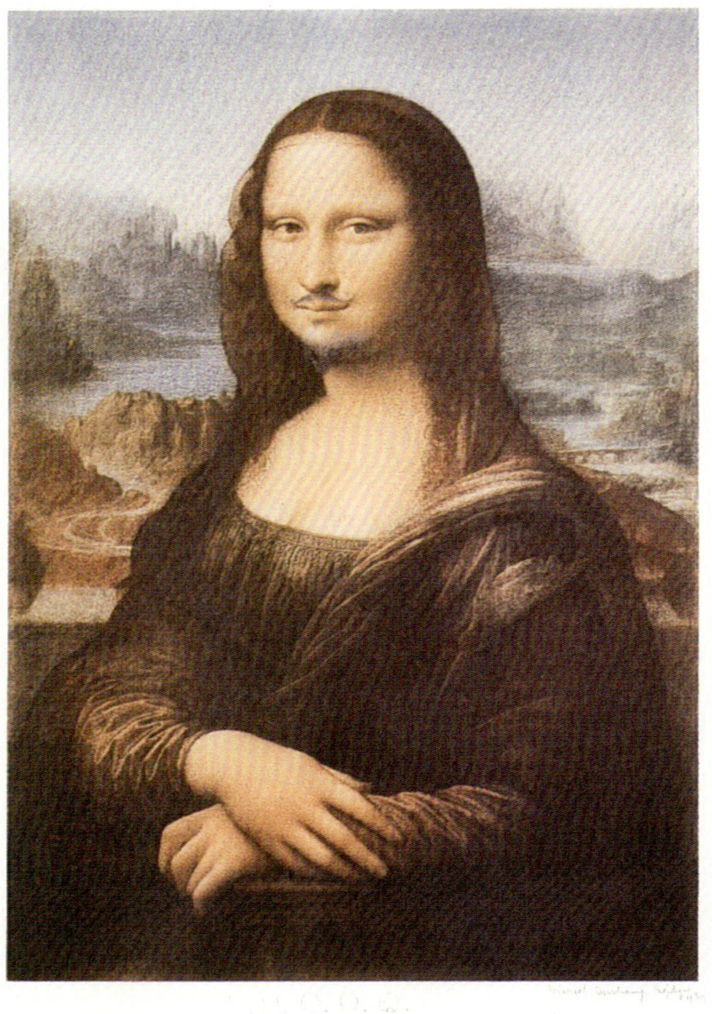

7 ***L.H.O.O.Q.: Mustache and Beard*** 1941
Collection of Virginia Green, New York

8 ***L.H.O.O.Q. rasée [L.H.O.O.Q. shaved]*** 1965
Collection of Alice Saligman, New York

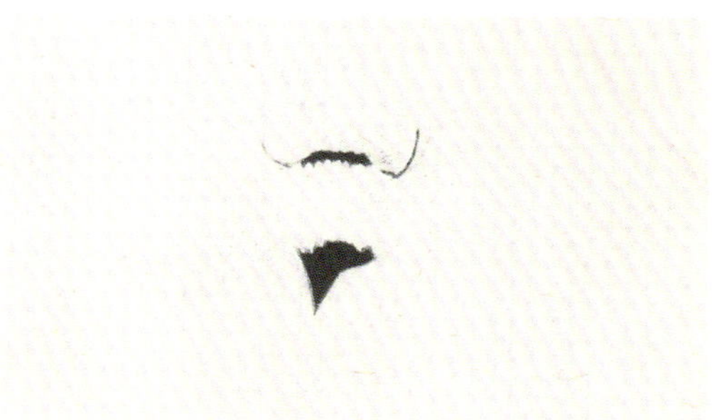

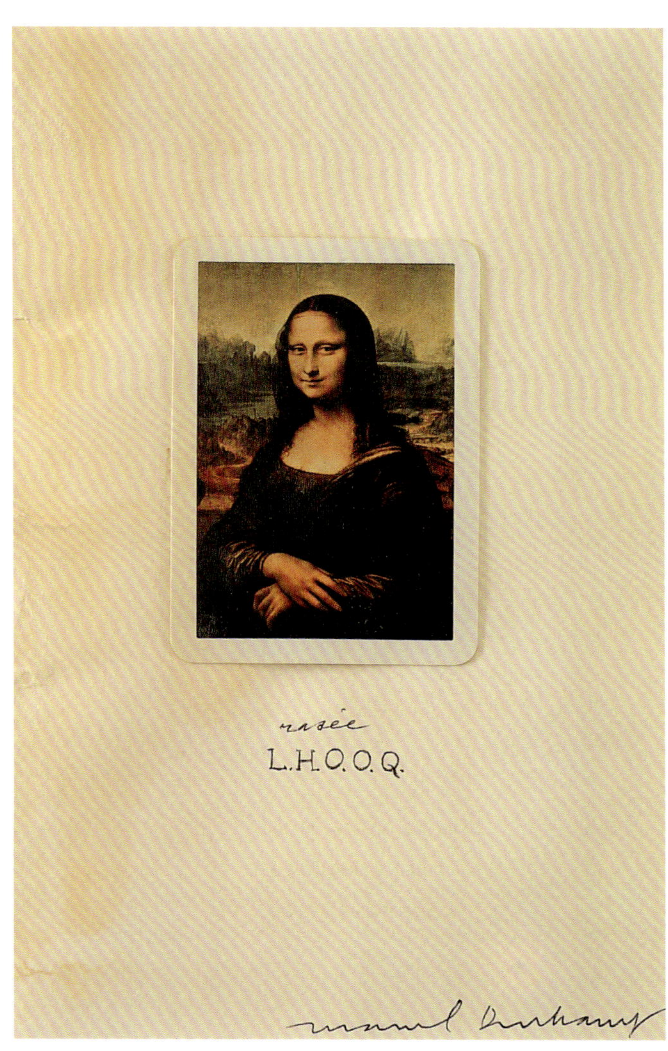

9 ***Why Not Sneeze Rose Sélavy?*** 1921
Philadelphia Museum of Art.
The Louise and Walter Arensberg Collection

10 ***Fresh Widow*** 1920/3rd version, 1964
Staatliches Museum Schwerin

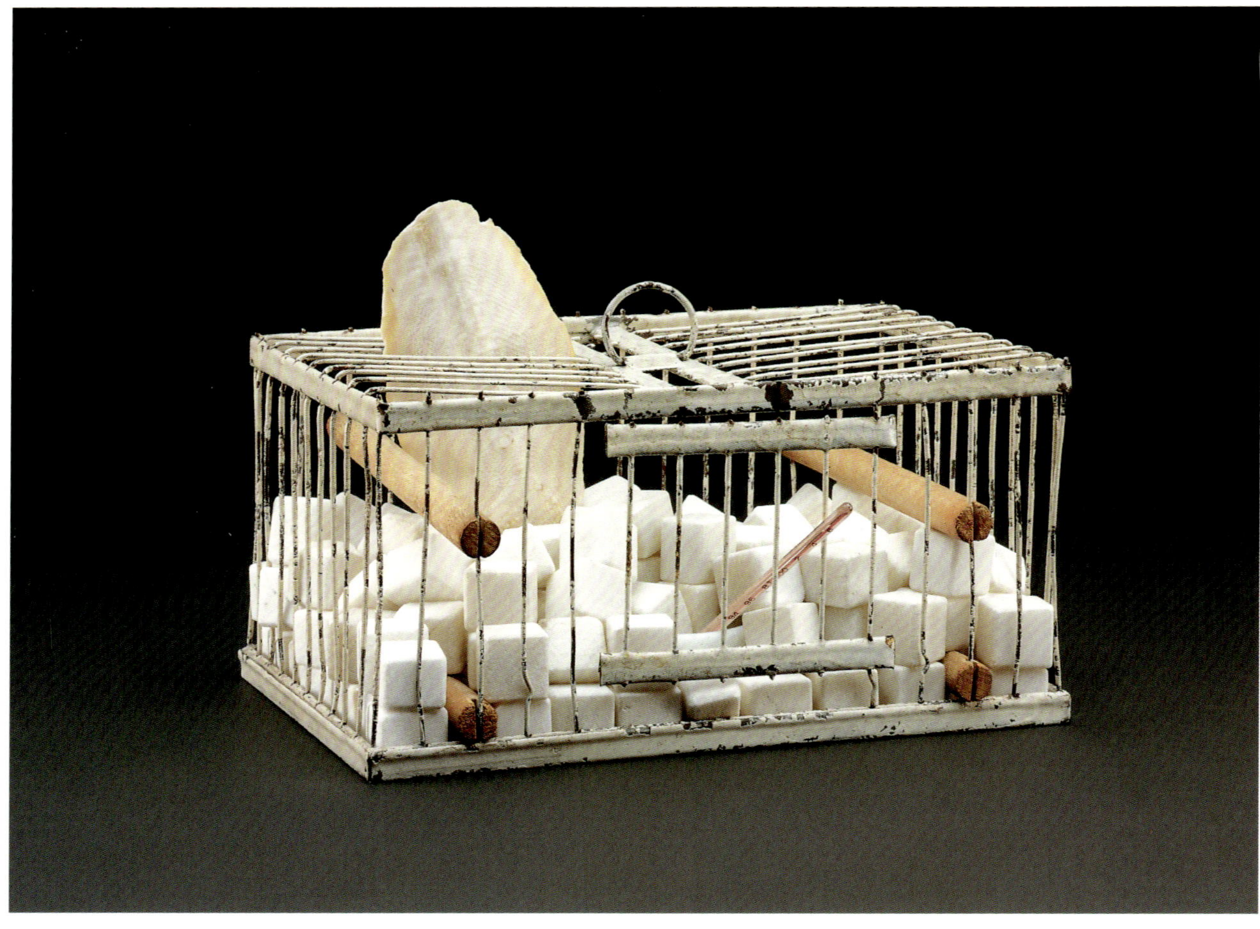

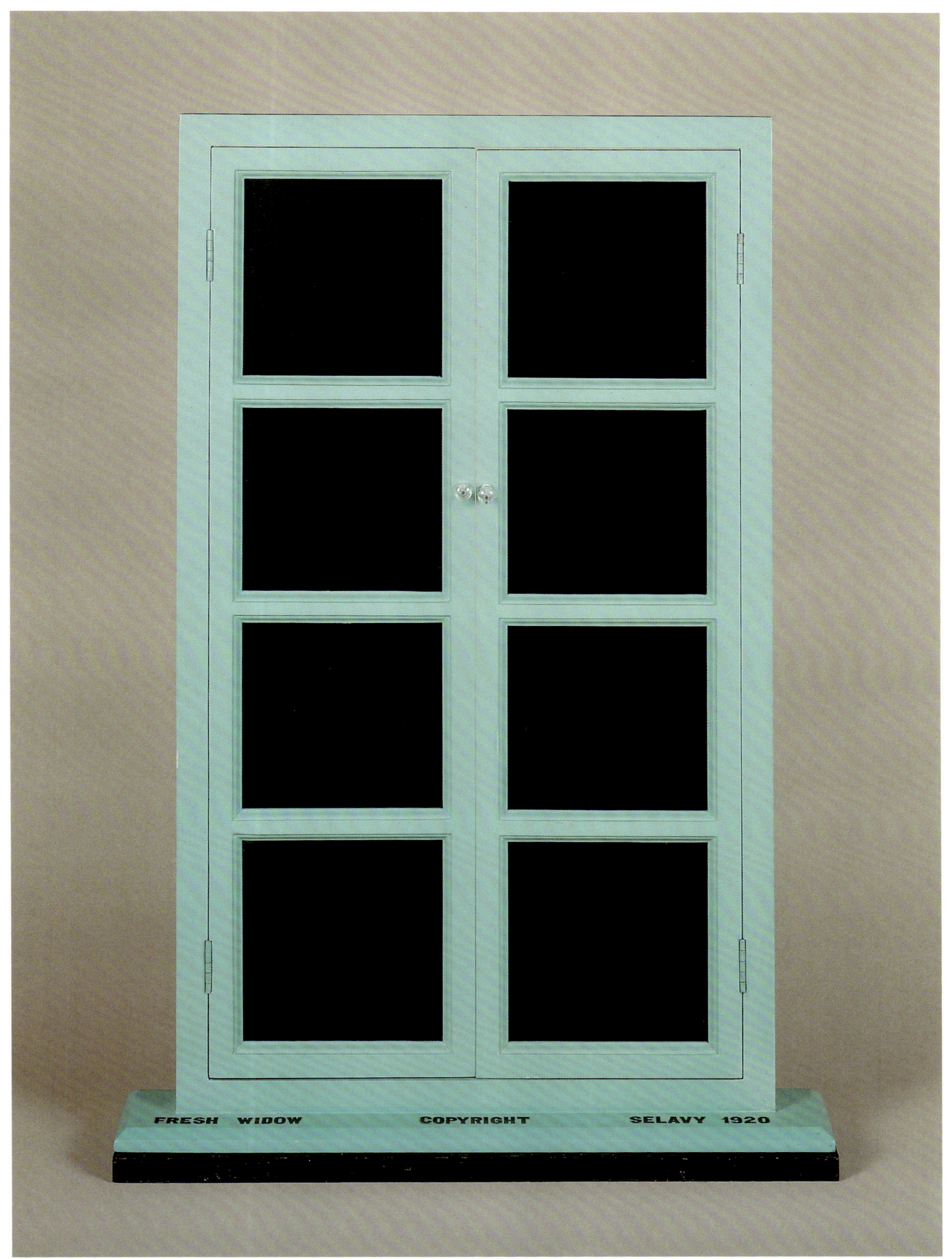
FRESH WIDOW COPYRIGHT SELAVY 1920

11 ***La bagarre d'Austerlitz [The Brawl at Austerlitz]*** 1936
From the *Boîte* edition
Private collection

12 ***La bagarre d'Austerlitz [The Brawl at Austerlitz]*** 1921
Staatsgalerie Stuttgart

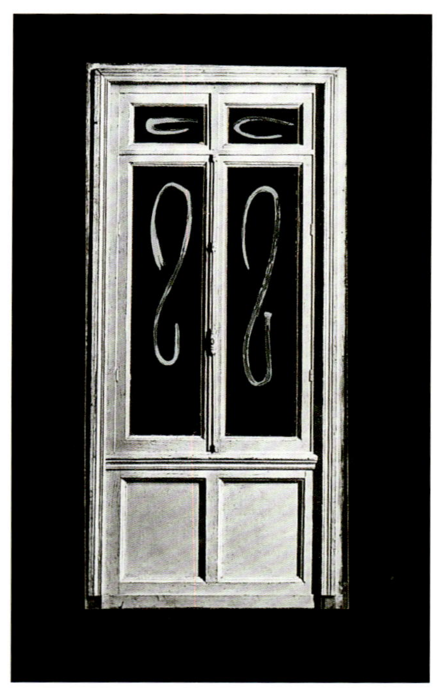

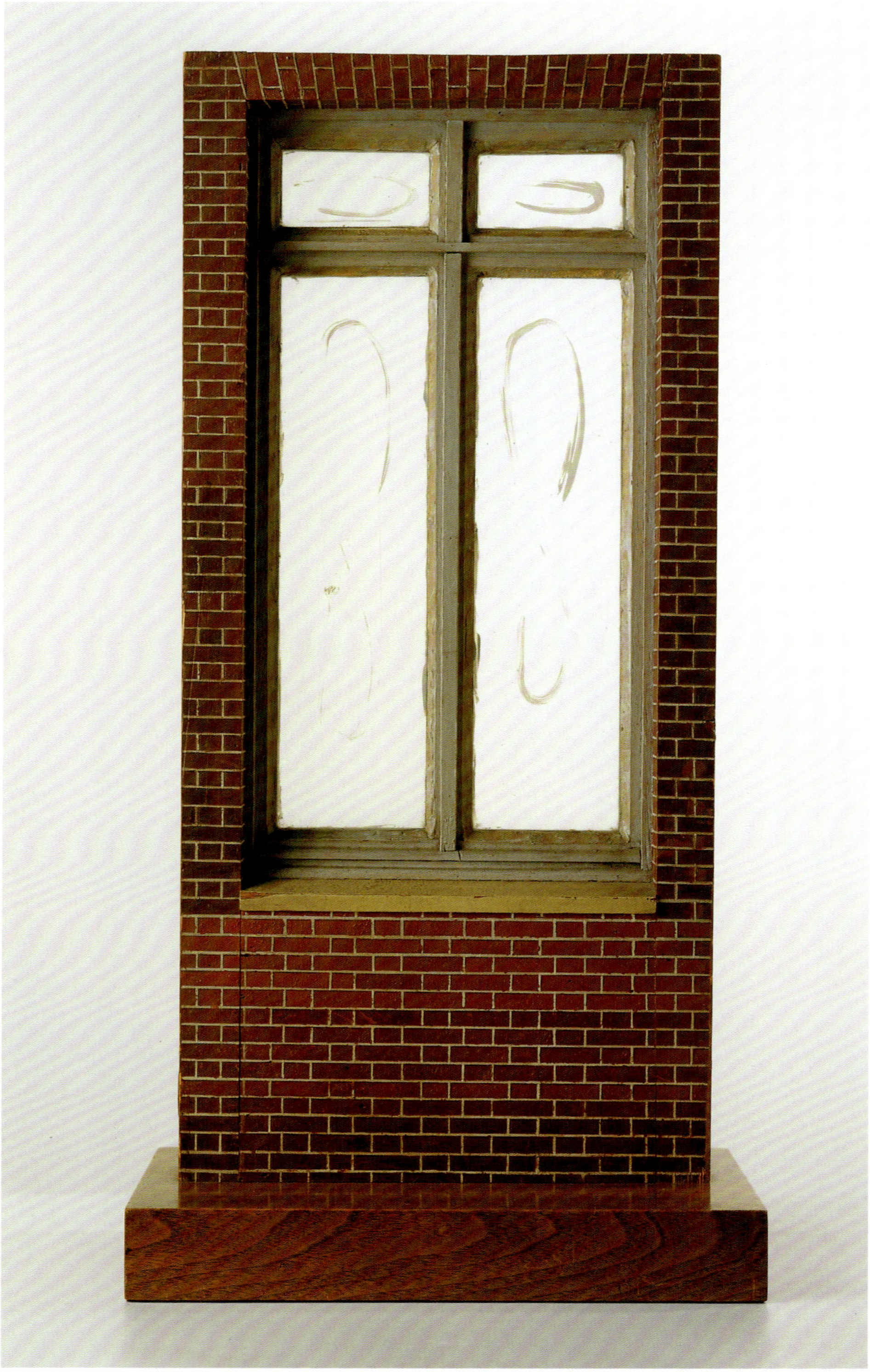

13 **Cover for *Minotaure*** 1934
Courtesy Laurence McGilvery, La Jolla, California

14 **Marcel Duchamp, Man Ray, and Marc Allégret**
Stills from *Anémic Cinéma* 1926
The Museum of Modern Art Film Library

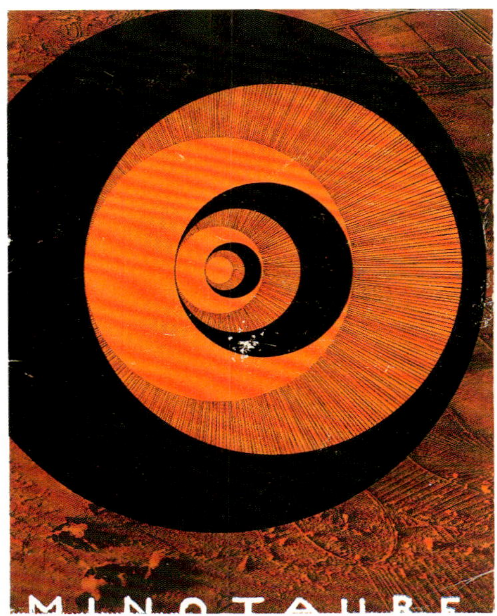

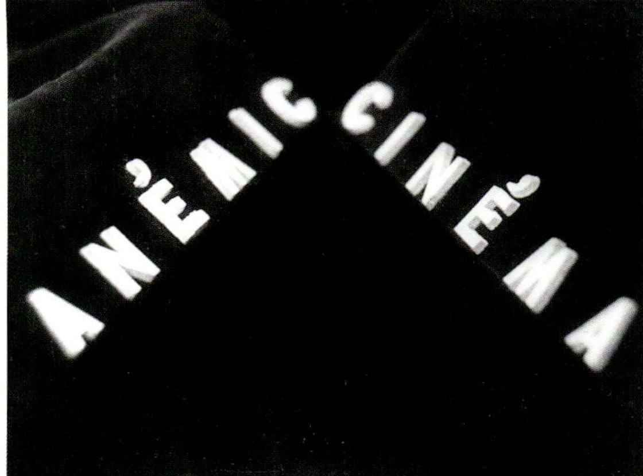

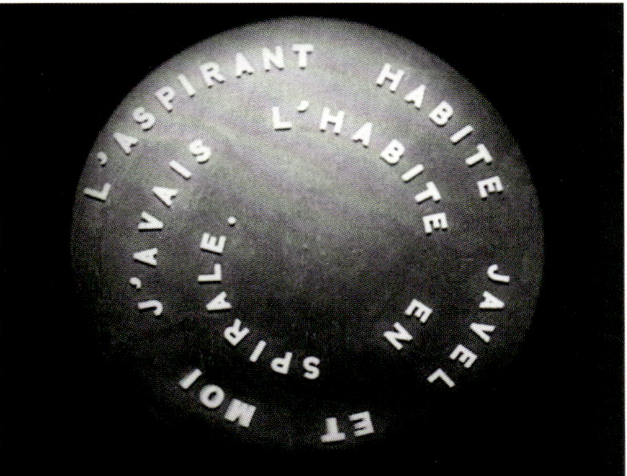

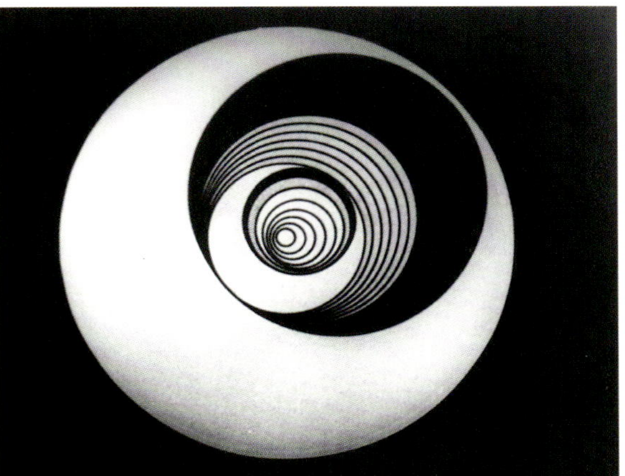

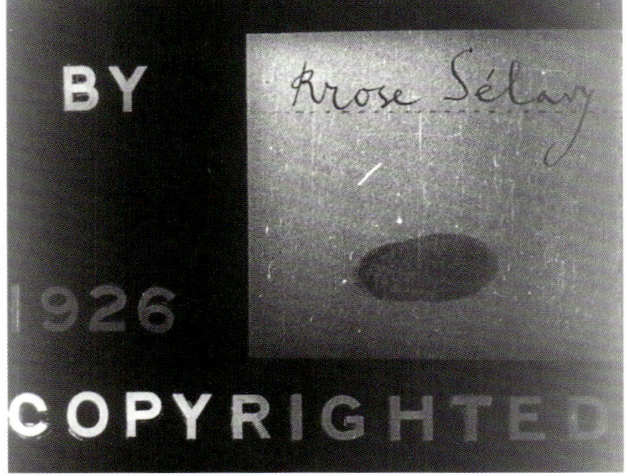

15 ***Box of 1932*** 1932
Philadelphia Museum of Art. Gift of Marion Boulton Stroud in memory of Mme. Alexina Duchamp

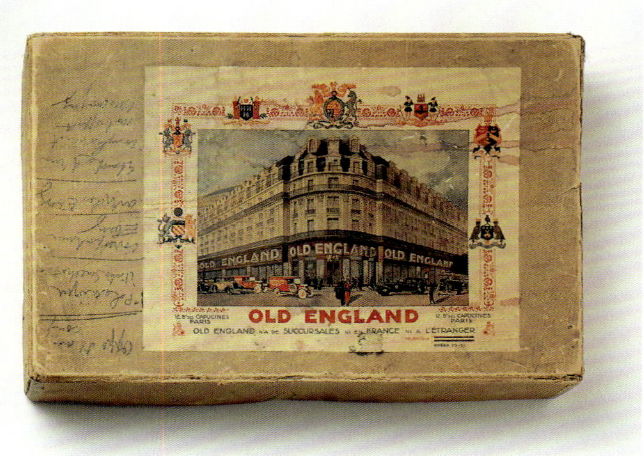

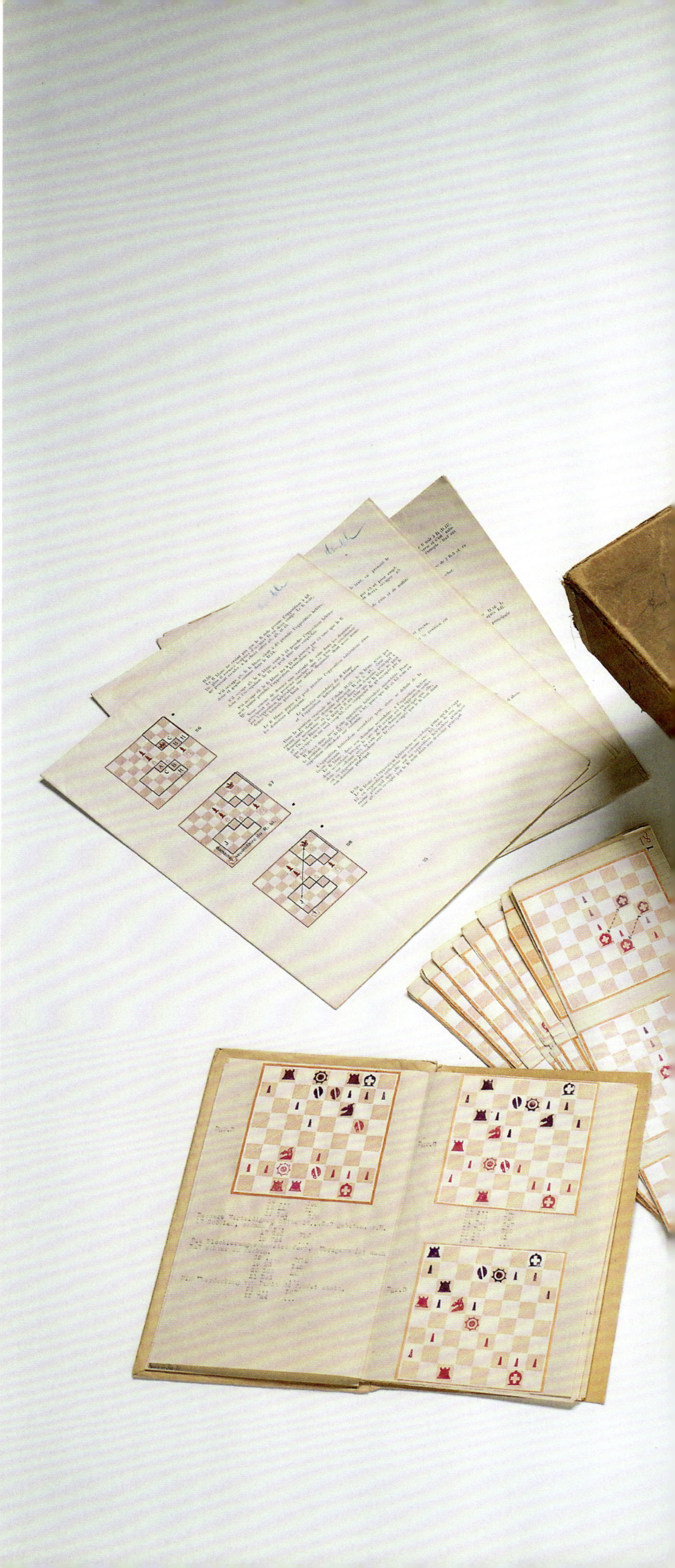

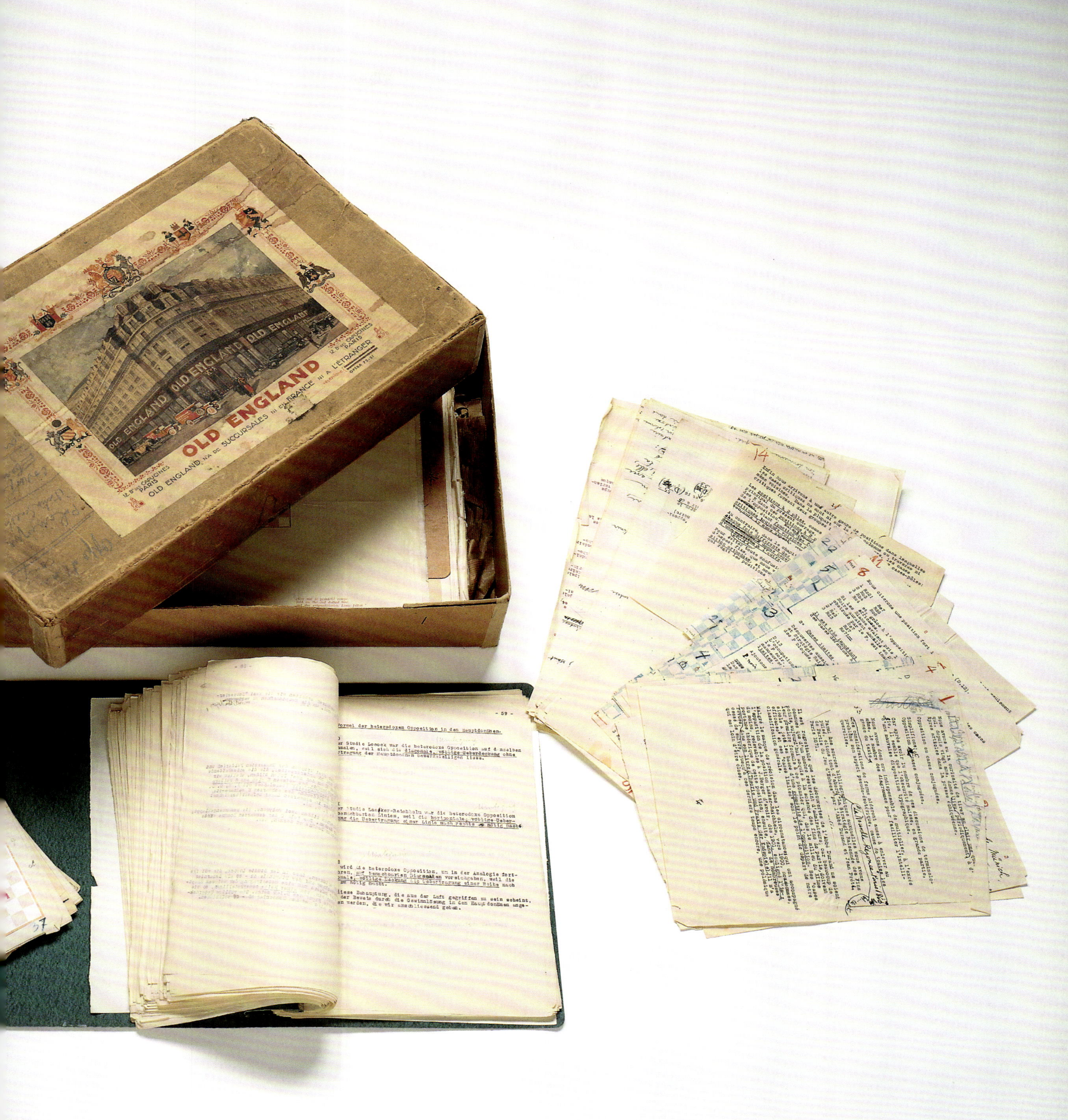
OLD ENGLAND
OLD ENGLAND N'A DE SUCCURSALES NI EN FRANCE NI A L'ETRANGER

16 ***La Mariée mise à nu par ses célibataires même*** 1934
[The Bride Stripped Bare by Her Bachelors Even] (Green Box)
Collection of Virginia Green, New York

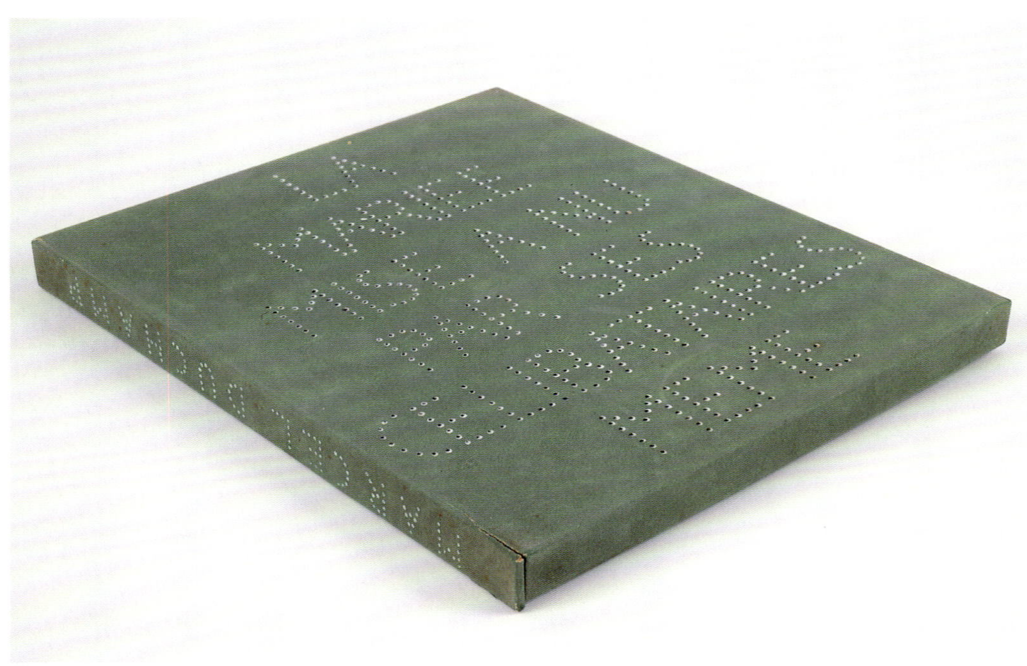

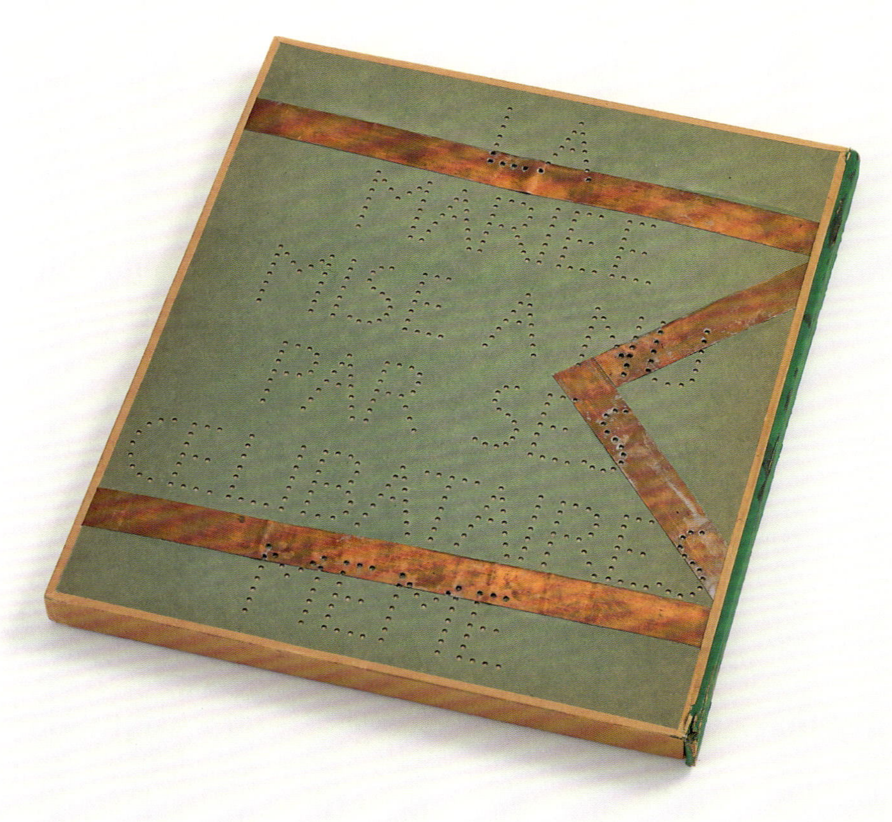

17 ***La Mariée mise à nu par ses célibataires même*** 1934
[The Bride Stripped Bare by Her Bachelors Even] (Green Box)
Deluxe edition, VI/XX
The Menil Collection, Houston
p. 128 bottom and pp. 129–31

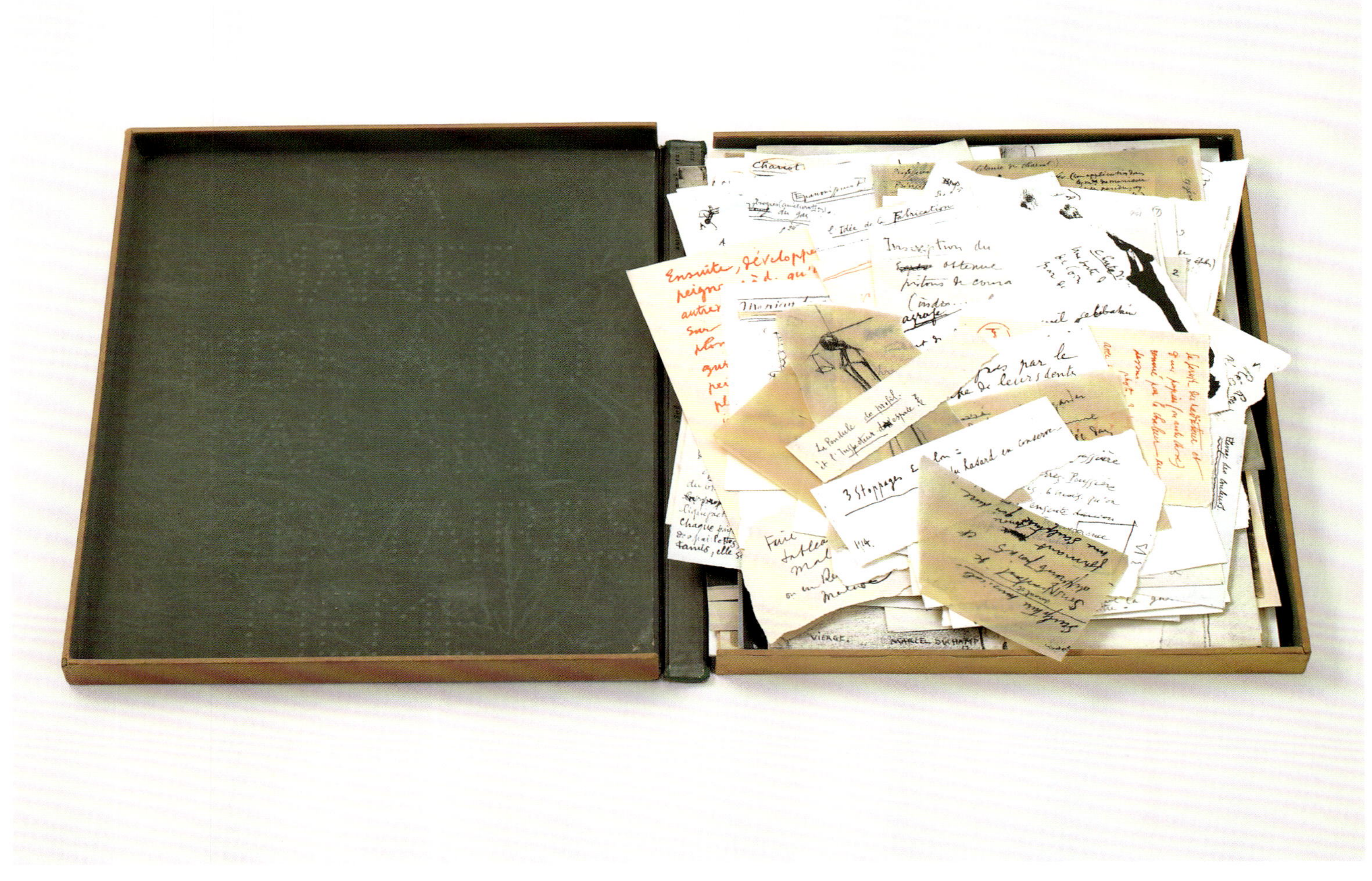

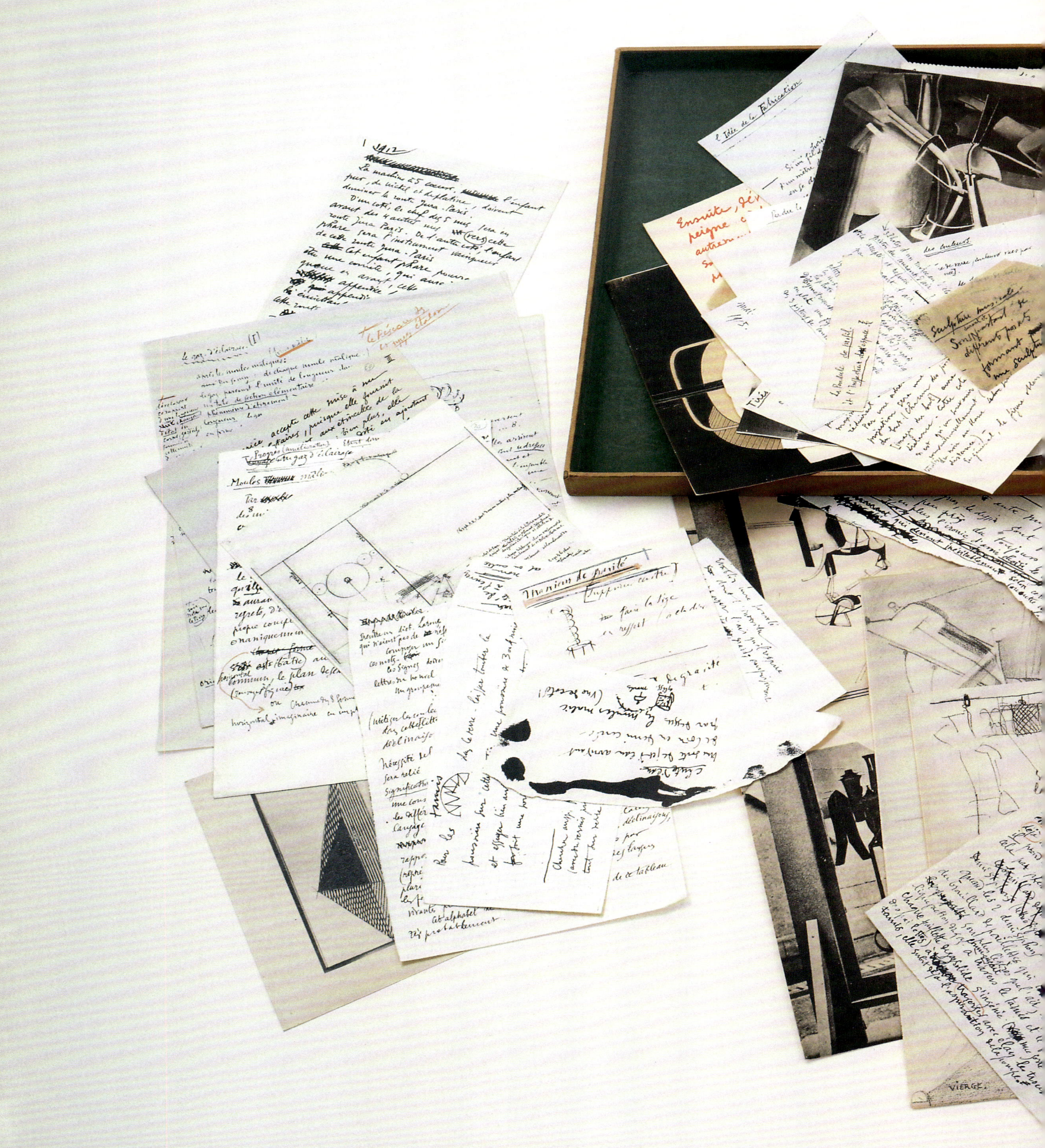
VIERGE.

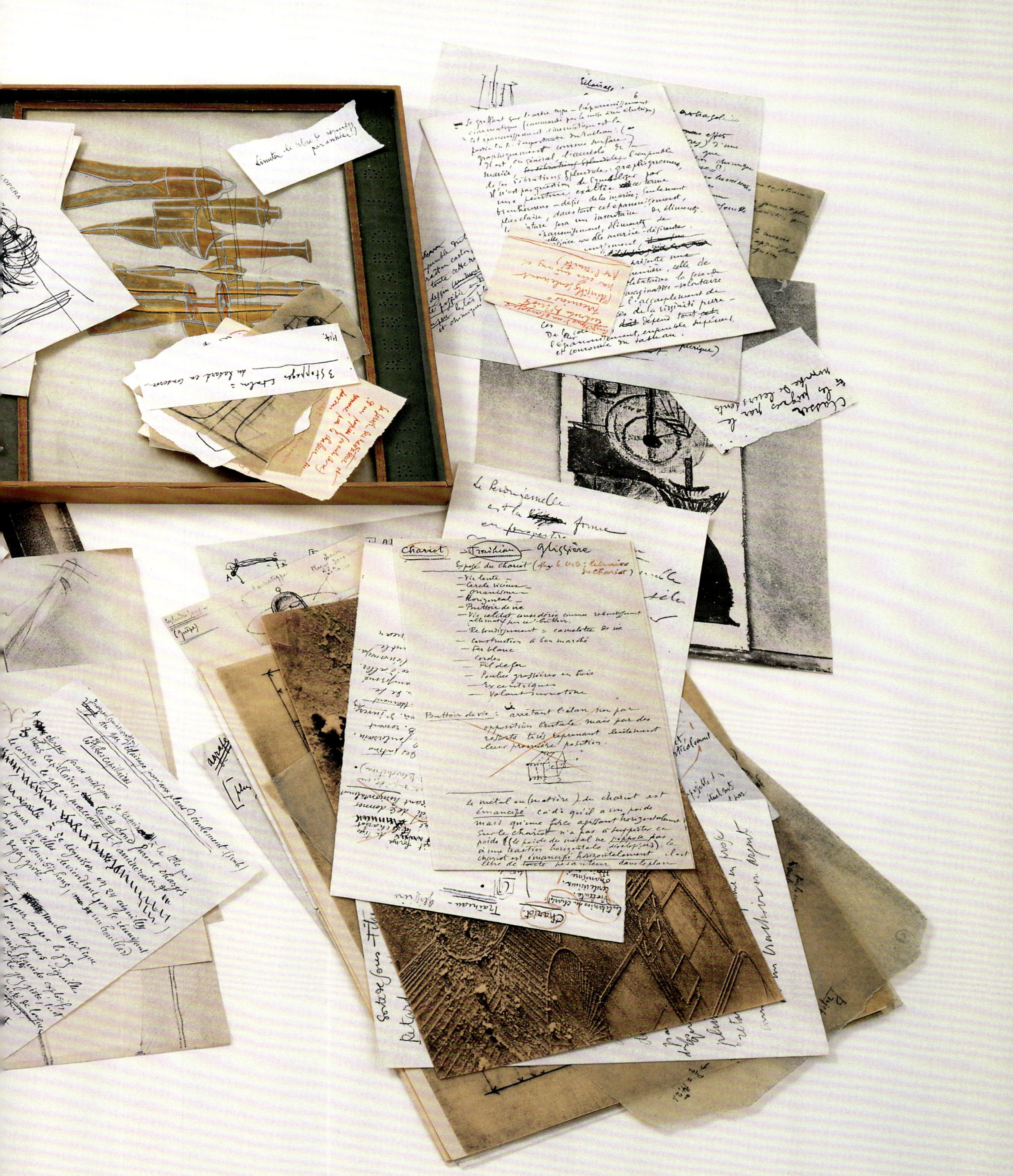
Chariot
Traîneau
glissière
Exposé du Chariot

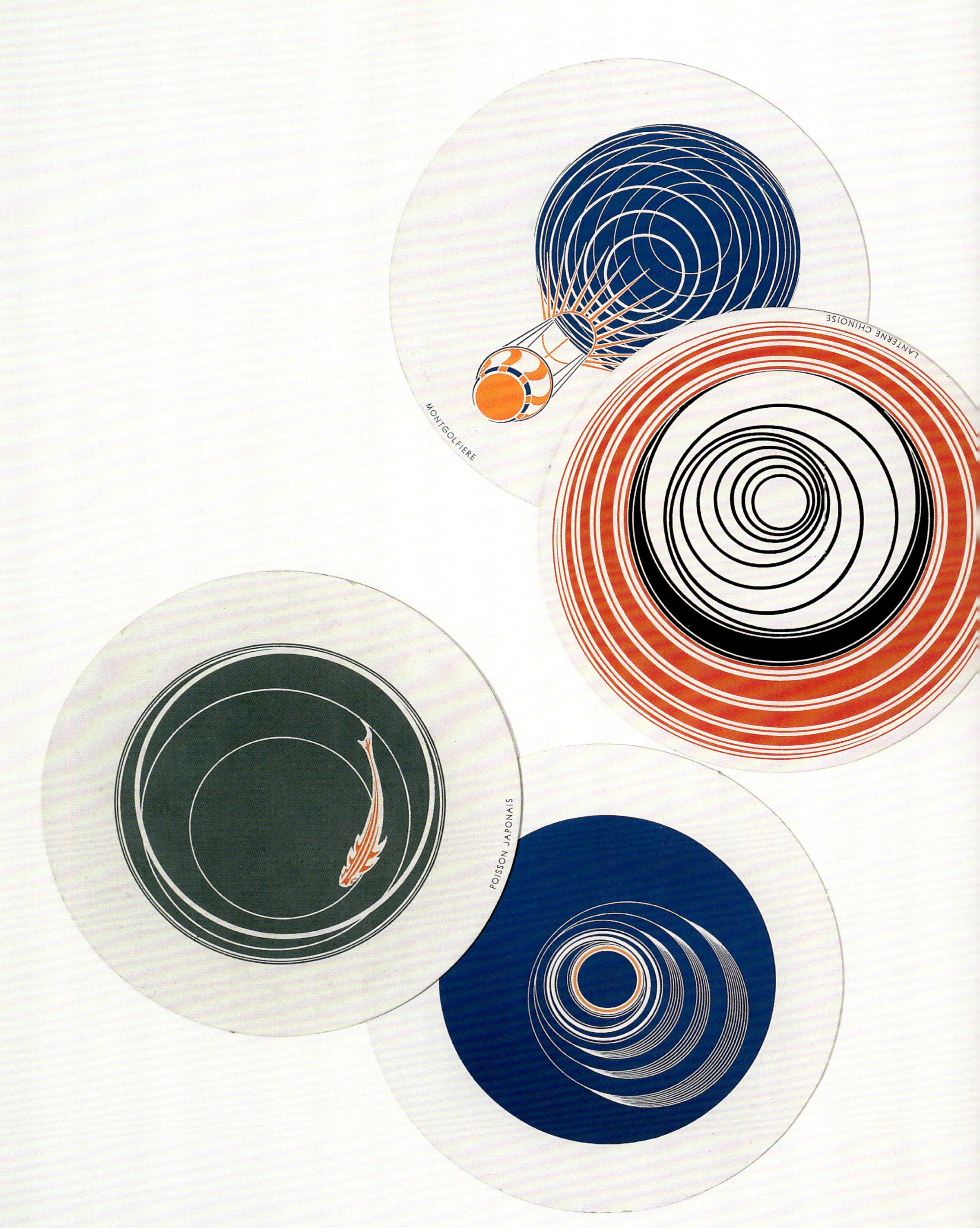
LANTERNE CHINOISE
MONTGOLFIERE
POISSON JAPONAIS

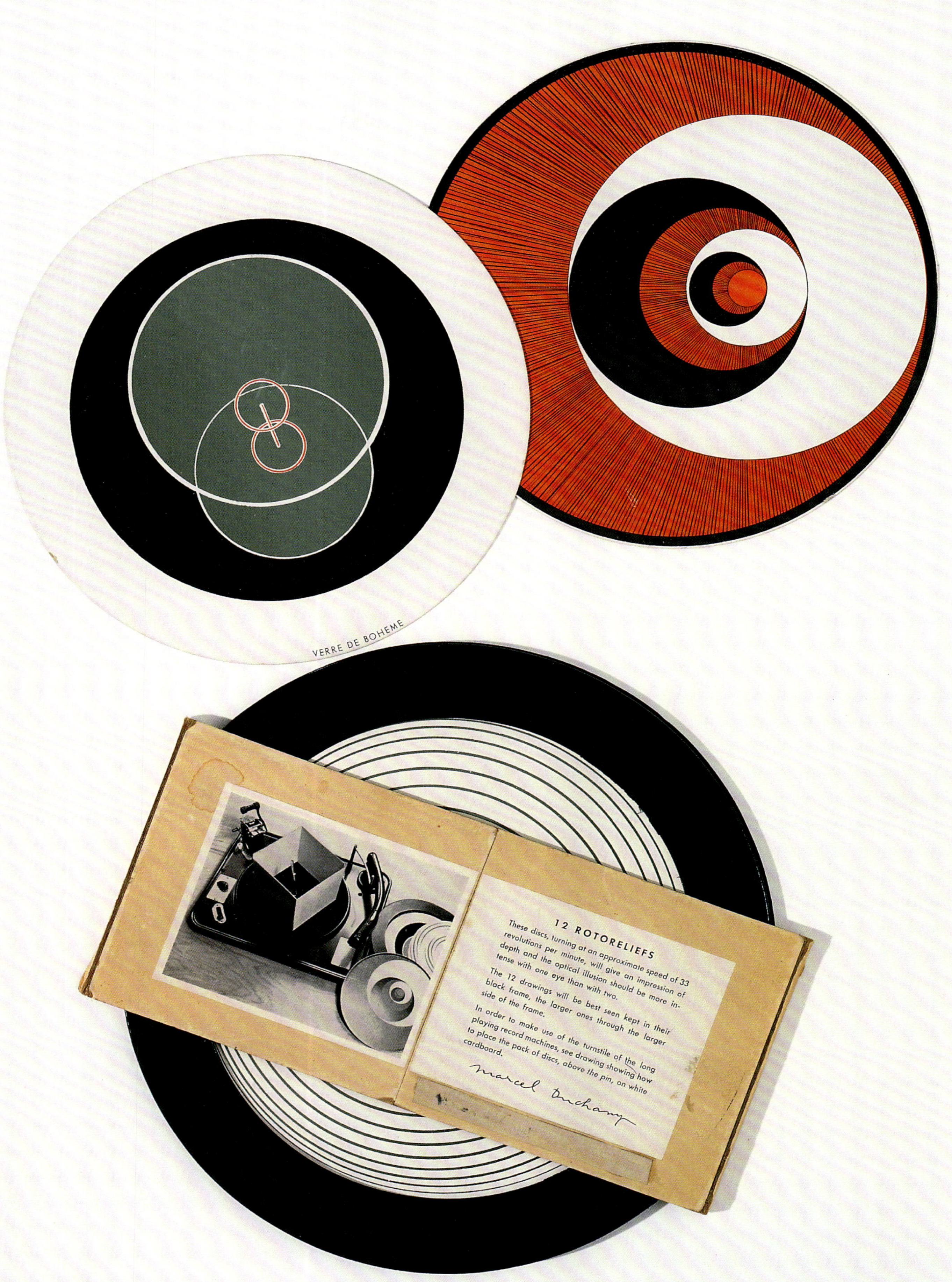
VERRE DE BOHEME
12 ROTORELIEFS
These discs, turning at an approximate speed of 33 revolutions per minute, will give an impression of depth and the optical illusion should be more intense with one eye than with two.
The 12 drawings will be best seen kept in their black frame, the larger ones through the larger side of the frame.
In order to make use of the turnstile of the long playing record machines, see drawing showing how to place the pack of discs, above the pin, on white cardboard.
marcel Duchamp

18 ***Rotorelief (disques optiques) [Rotorelief (Optical Disks)]*** 1935
Philadelphia Museum of Art.
The Louise and Walter Arensberg Collection
pp. 132–33

19 **Display folder for *Rotorelief (disques optiques)* *[Rotorelief (Optical Disks)]*** 1953
The Menil Collection, Houston
pp. 133

20 **Subscription bulletin for *de ou par Marcel Duchamp ou Rrose Sélavy* *[by or of Marcel Duchamp or Rrose Sélavy]*** 1941
Collection of Ronny Van de Velde, Antwerp, Belgium

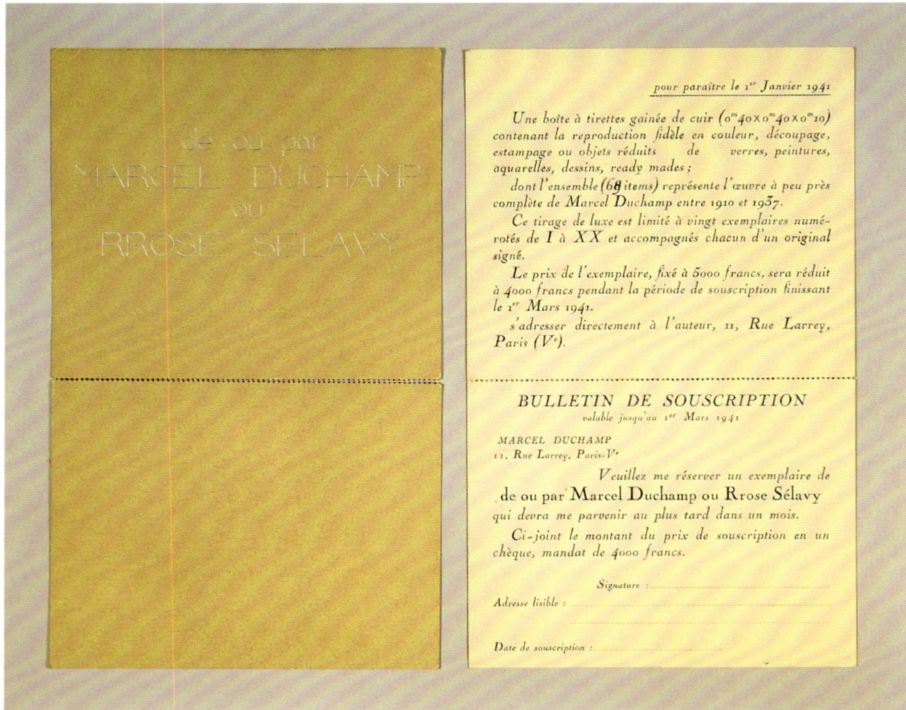
de ou par
MARCEL DUCHAMP
ou
RROSE SÉLAVY

pour paraître le 1er Janvier 1941

Une boîte à tirettes gainée de cuir (0m40×0m40×0m10) contenant la reproduction fidèle en couleur, découpage, estampage ou objets réduits de verres, peintures, aquarelles, dessins, ready mades;

dont l'ensemble (69 items) représente l'œuvre à peu près complète de Marcel Duchamp entre 1910 et 1937.

Ce tirage de luxe est limité à vingt exemplaires numérotés de I à XX et accompagnés chacun d'un original signé.

Le prix de l'exemplaire, fixé à 5000 francs, sera réduit à 4000 francs pendant la période de souscription finissant le 1er Mars 1941.

s'adresser directement à l'auteur, 11, Rue Larrey, Paris (Ve).

BULLETIN DE SOUSCRIPTION
valable jusqu'au 1er Mars 1941

MARCEL DUCHAMP
11, Rue Larrey, Paris-Ve

Veuillez me réserver un exemplaire de
de ou par Marcel Duchamp ou Rrose Sélavy
qui devra me parvenir au plus tard dans un mois.

Ci-joint le montant du prix de souscription en un chèque, mandat de 4000 francs.

Signature :
Adresse lisible :

Date de souscription :

21.1 ***de ou par Marcel Duchamp ou Rrose Sélavy*** 1935–41
[by or of Marcel Duchamp or Rrose Sélavy]
Series A, v/xx, 1942; with *Mariée [Bride]*, 1937
Collection of Jose Mugrabi

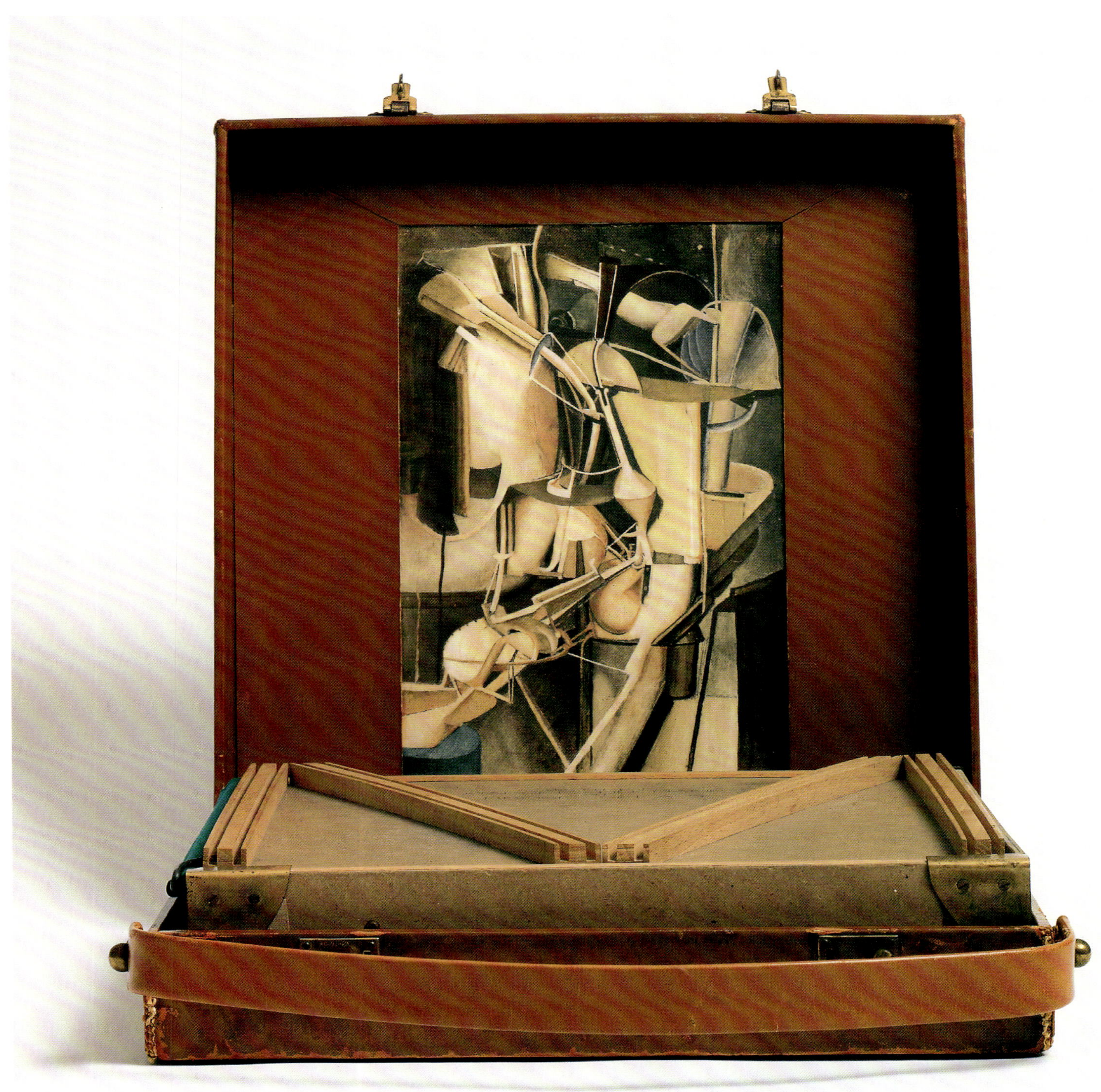

21.2 ***de ou par Marcel Duchamp ou Rrose Sélavy*** 1935–41
[by or of Marcel Duchamp or Rrose Sélavy]
Series A, v/xx, 1942
Collection of Jose Mugrabi

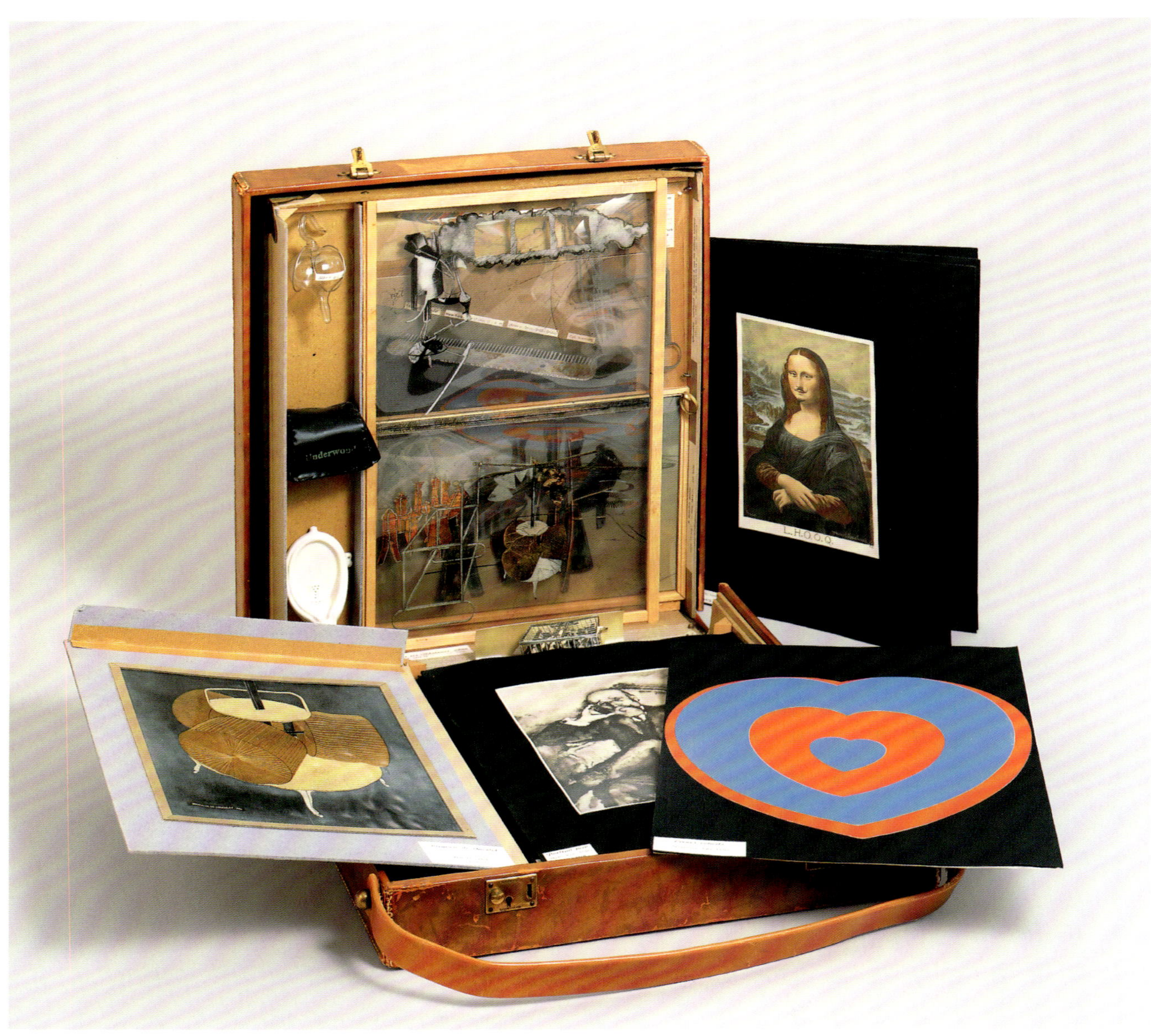

22 ***de ou par Marcel Duchamp ou Rrose Sélavy*** 1935–41
[by or of Marcel Duchamp or Rrose Sélavy]
Series A, 0/xx, 1943; with *Vierge [Virgin]*, 1938
Philadelphia Museum of Art. The Louise and Walter Arensberg Collection
below and pp. 138–39

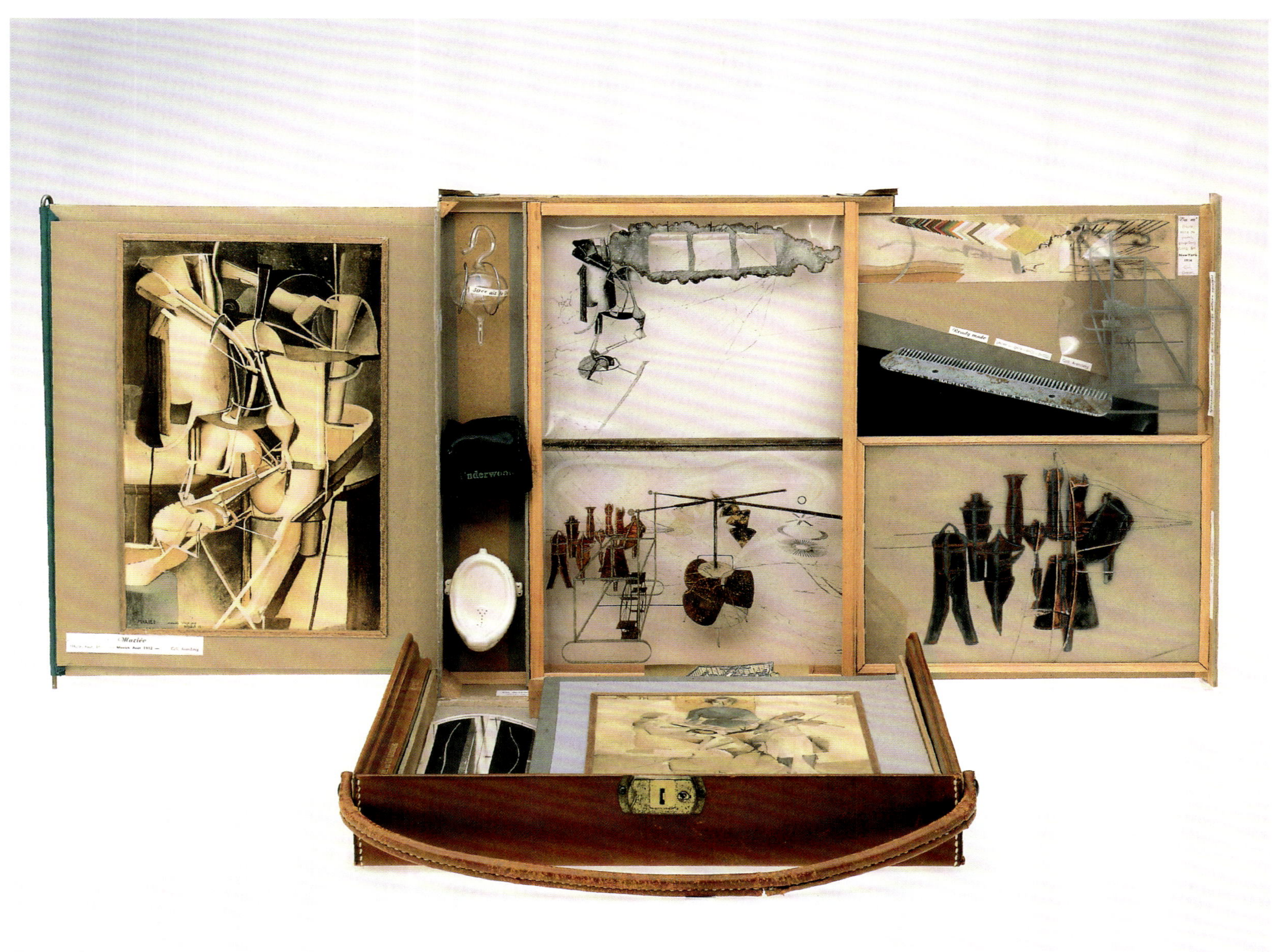

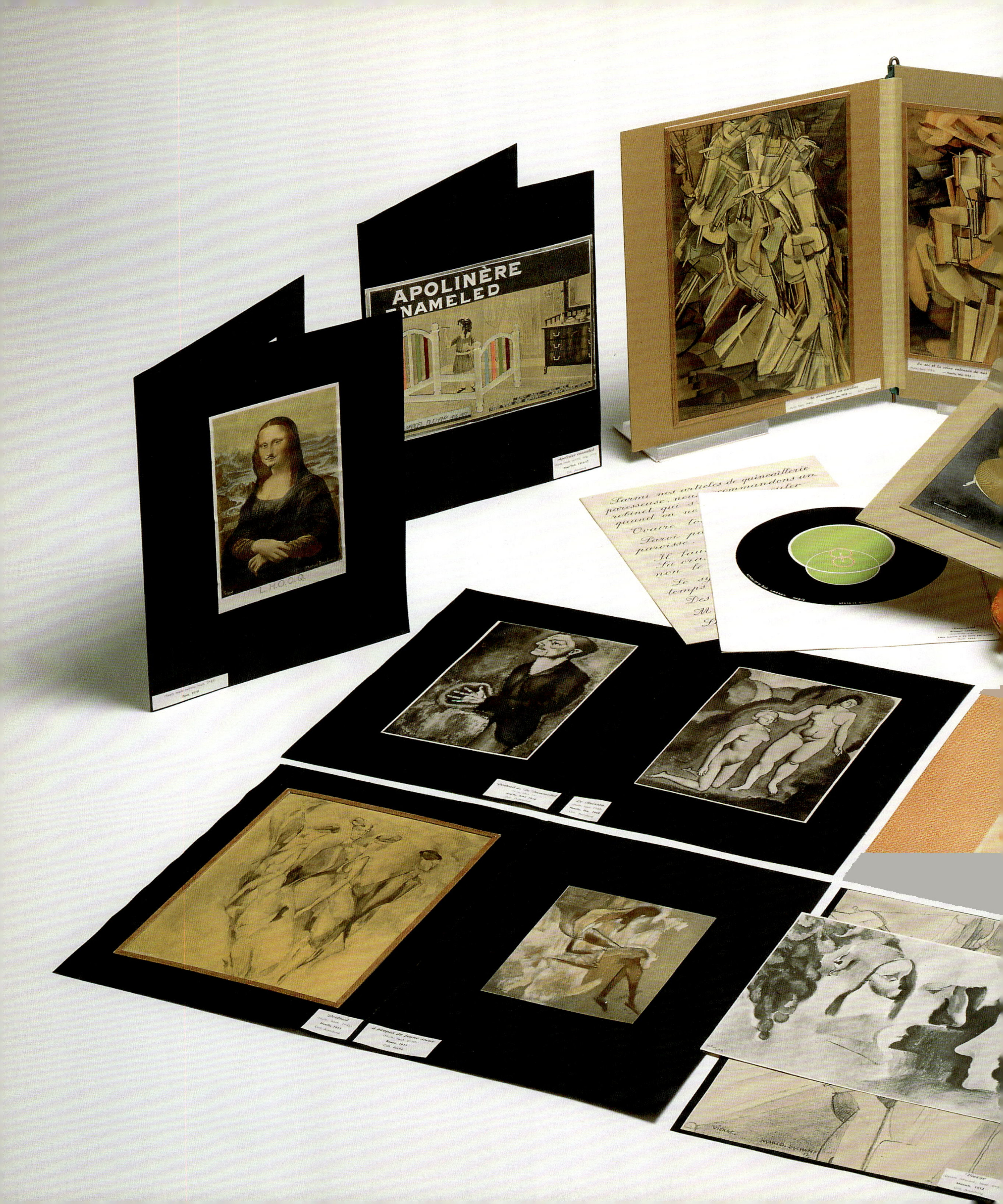
APOLINÈRE
ENAMELED
L.H.O.O.Q.

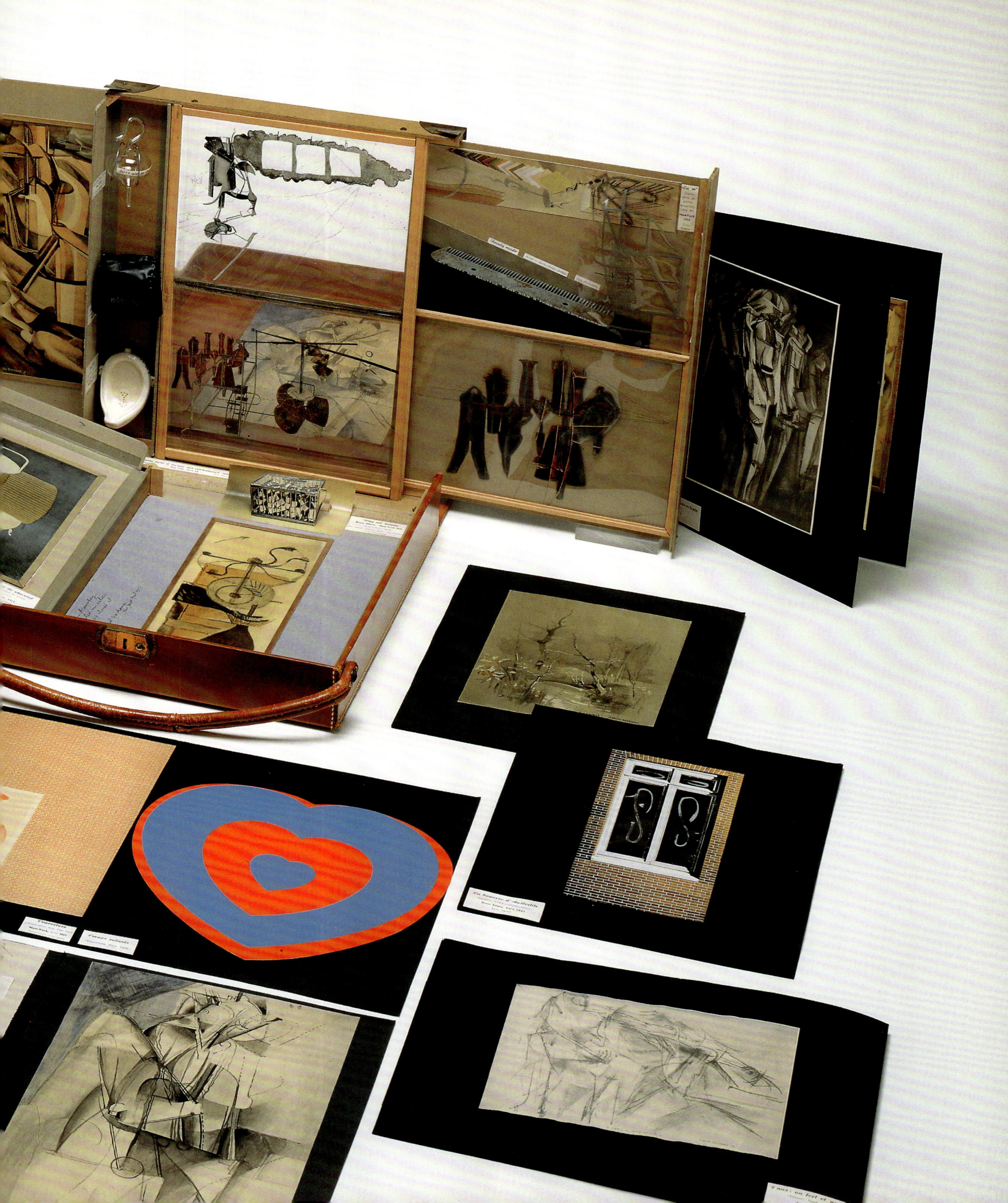

23 ***À la manière de Delvaux [In the Manner of Delvaux]*** 1942
The Israel Museum, Jerusalem. Gift of Arturo Schwarz

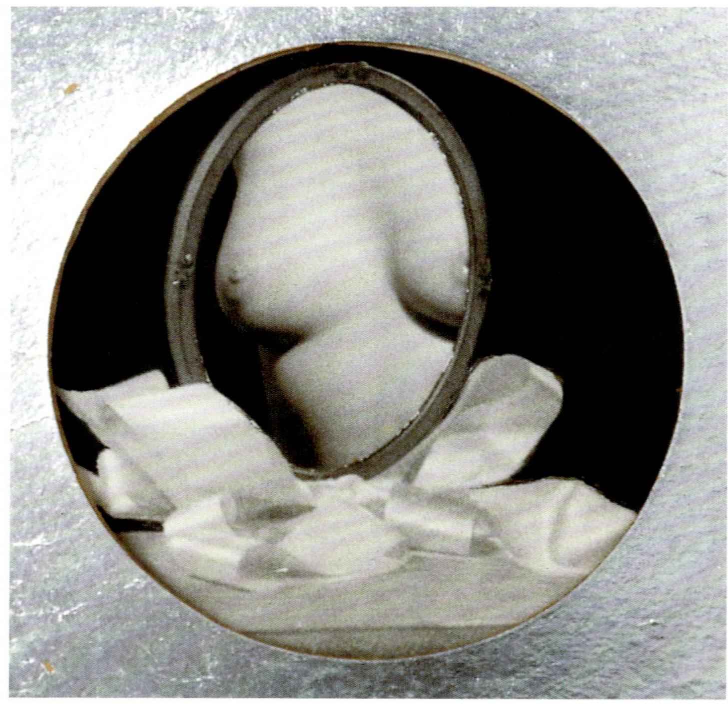

24 Cover for *First Papers of Surrealism* 1942
Philadelphia Museum of Art. Marcel Duchamp Archive, Gift of Jacqueline, Paul and Peter Matisse in memory of their mother, Alexina Duchamp

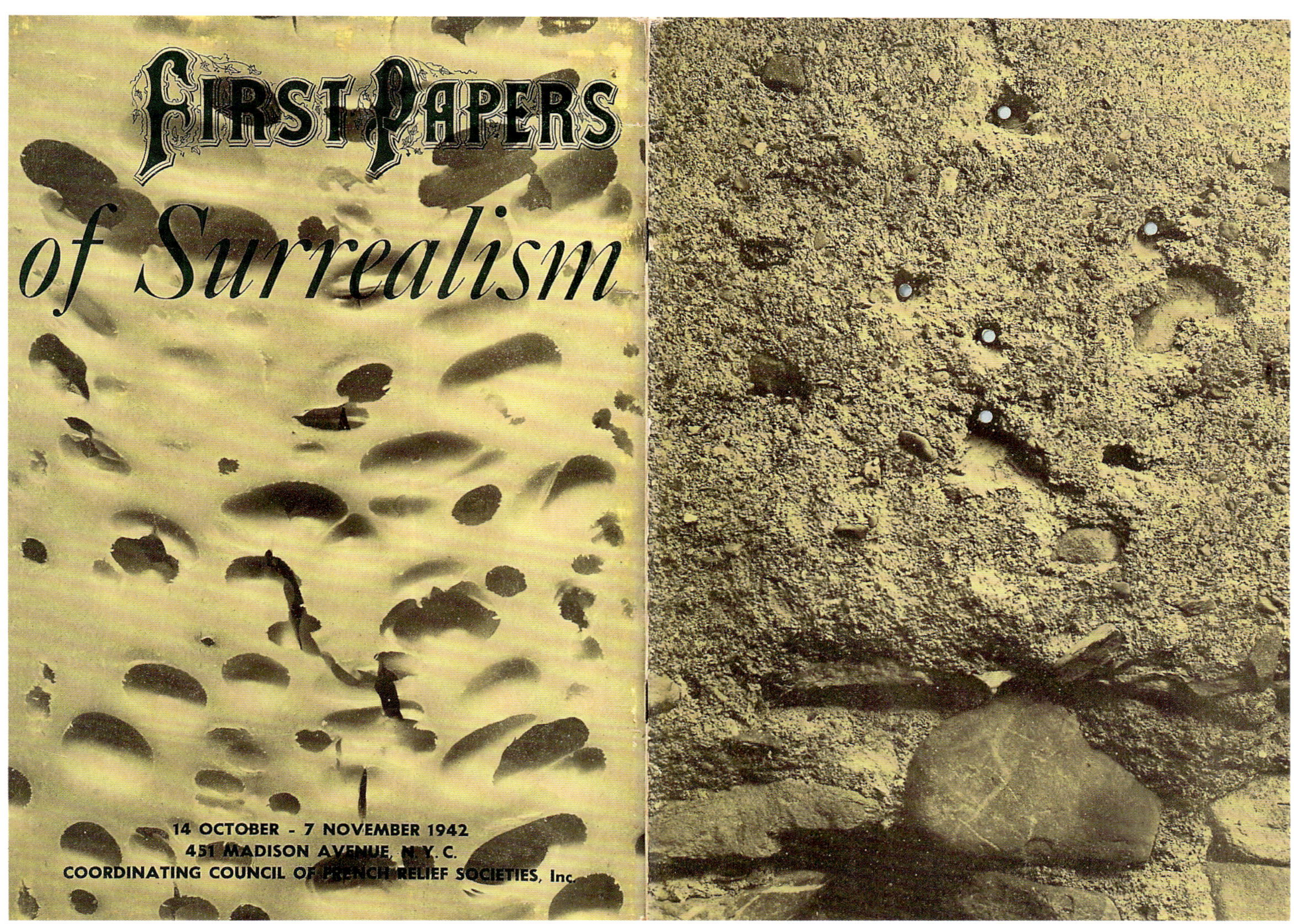

25 **Cover for *VVV Almanac for 1943*** 1943
The Menil Collection, Houston

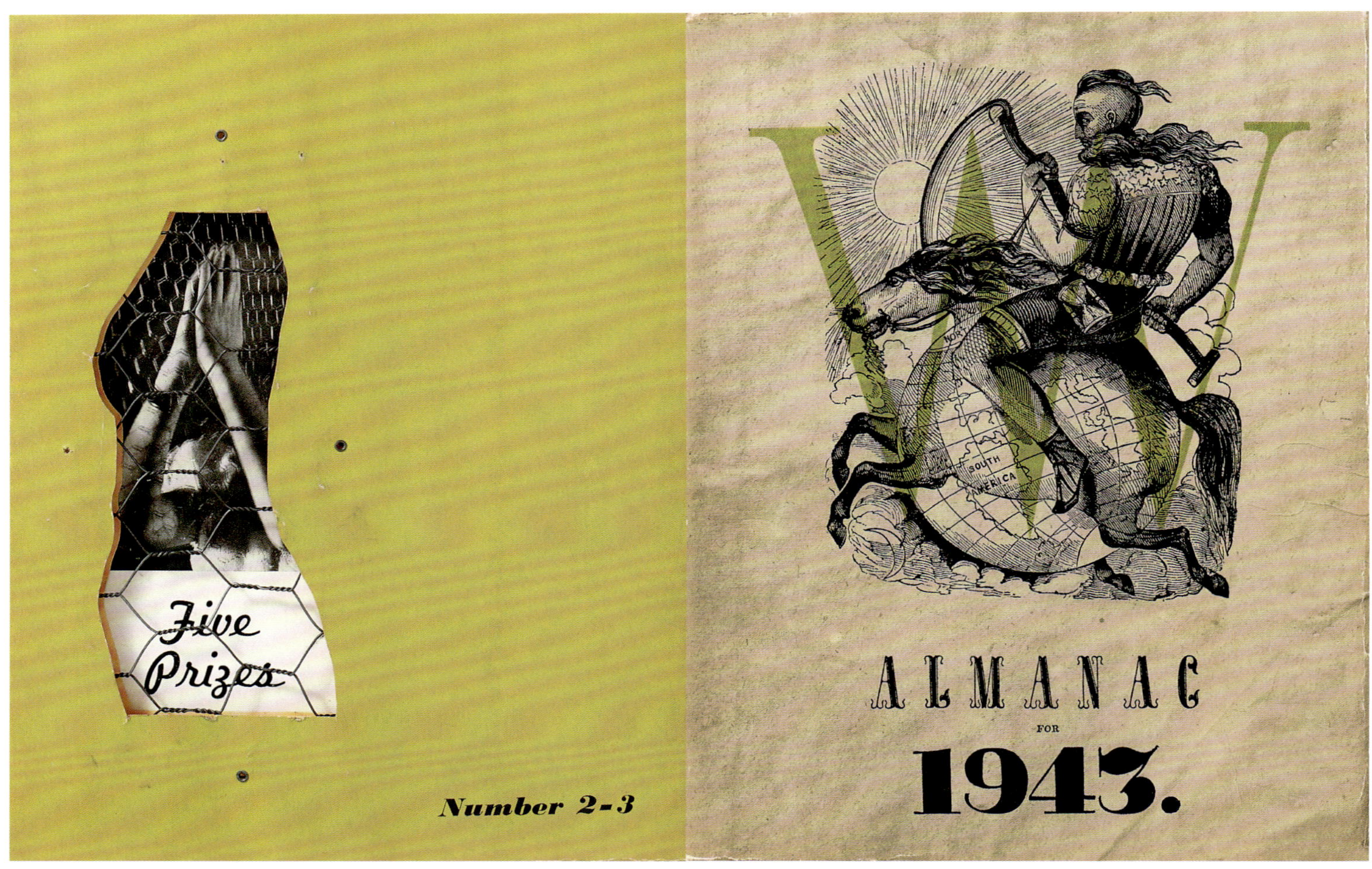

26 ***de ou par Marcel Duchamp ou Rrose Sélavy*** 1935–41
[by or of Marcel Duchamp or Rrose Sélavy]
Series A, x/xx, 1944; with *La fourchette de cavalier*, 1944
[The Knight's Fork], 1943
Mono Art Gallery, Tokyo

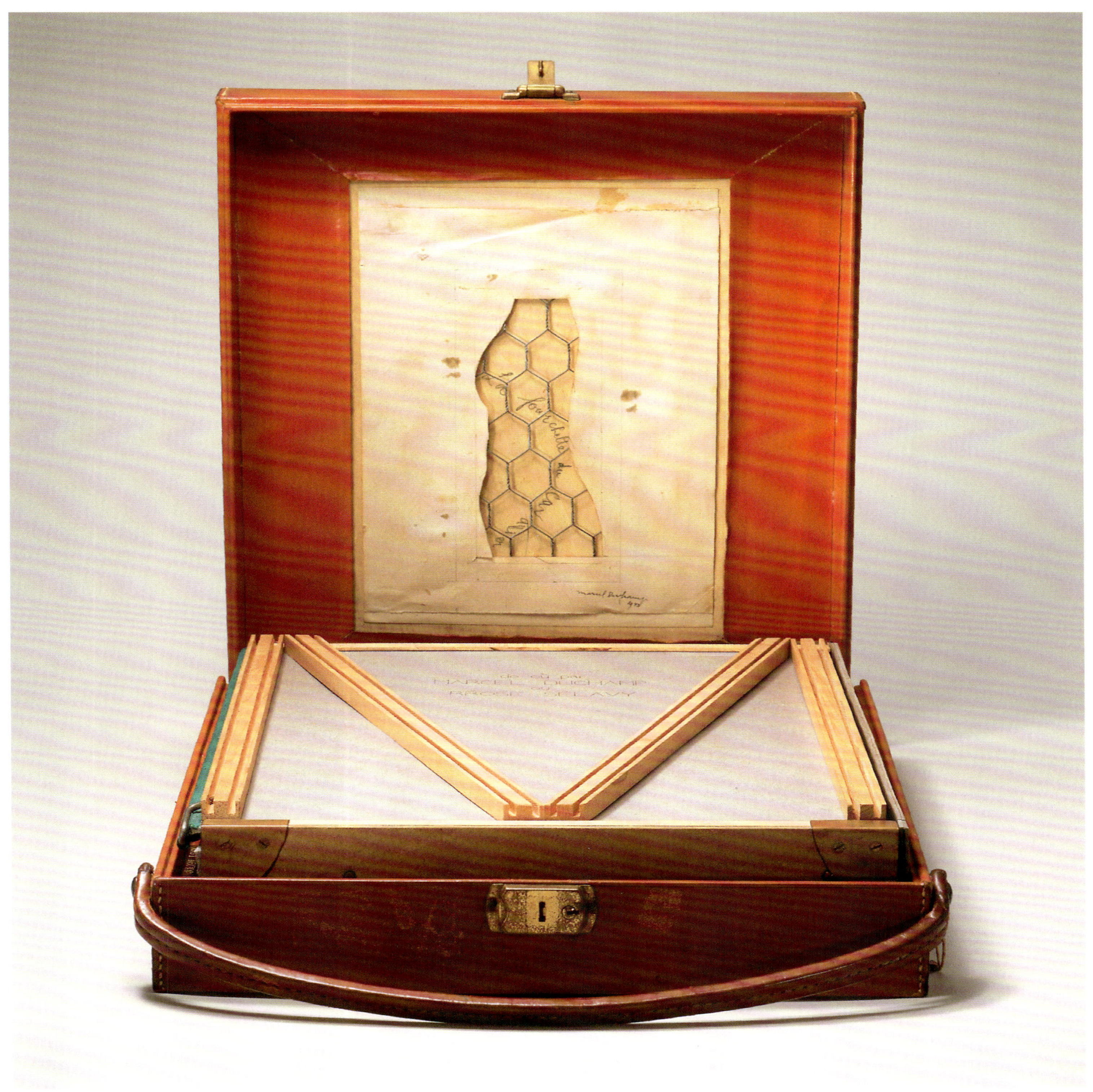

27 **Cover for *Young Cherry Trees Secured Against Hares*** 1946
The Menil Collection, Houston

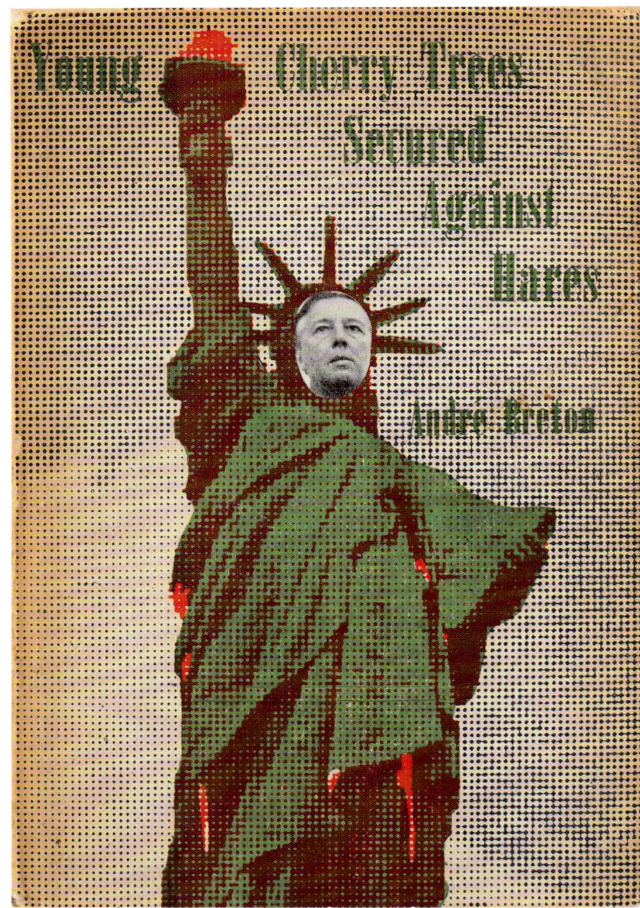

28 **Invitation for blindfold chess games during "The Imagery of Chess"** 1945
The Young-Mallin Archive, New York. The Julien Levy Papers

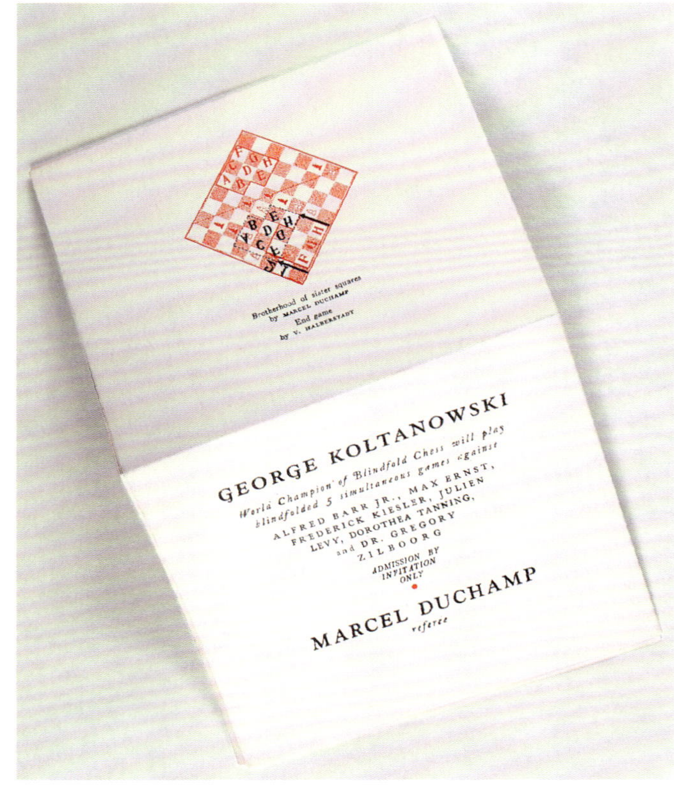

29 *de ou par Marcel Duchamp ou Rrose Sélavy* 1935–41
[by or of Marcel Duchamp or Rrose Sélavy]
Series A, XI/XX, 1944; with Untitled, 1944
Private collection

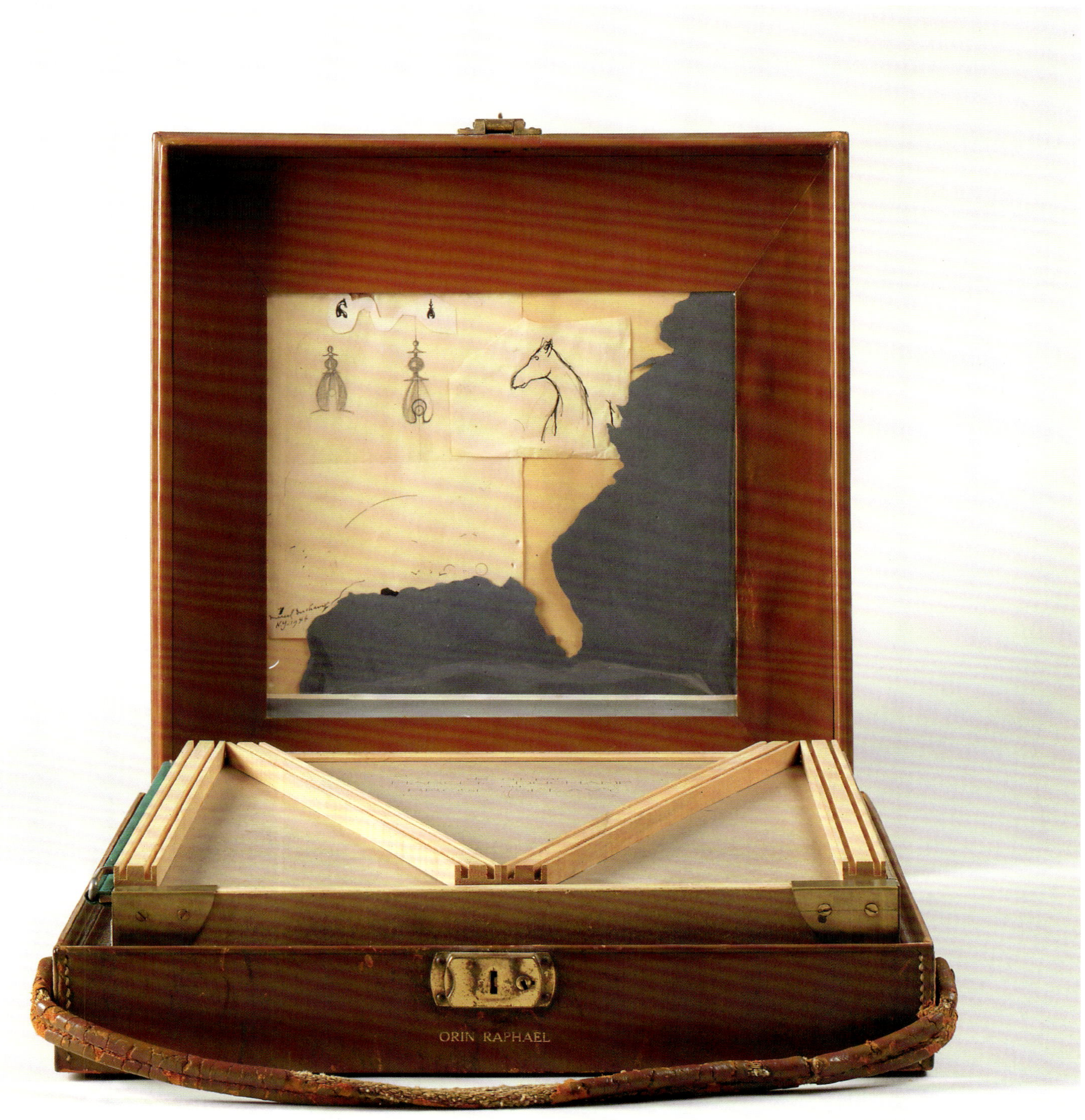

30 **Untitled *(Allégorie de genre) [Allegory of Genre]*** 1944
From Joseph Cornell, *Duchamp Dossier*, c. 1942–53 (DD 113).
Philadelphia Museum of Art. Gift of The Joseph and
Robert Cornell Memorial Foundation

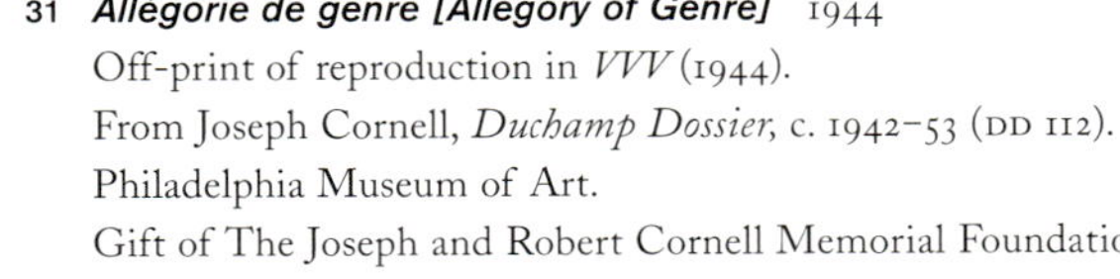

31 ***Allégorie de genre [Allegory of Genre]*** 1944
Off-print of reproduction in *VVV* (1944).
From Joseph Cornell, *Duchamp Dossier*, c. 1942–53 (DD 112).
Philadelphia Museum of Art.
Gift of The Joseph and Robert Cornell Memorial Foundation

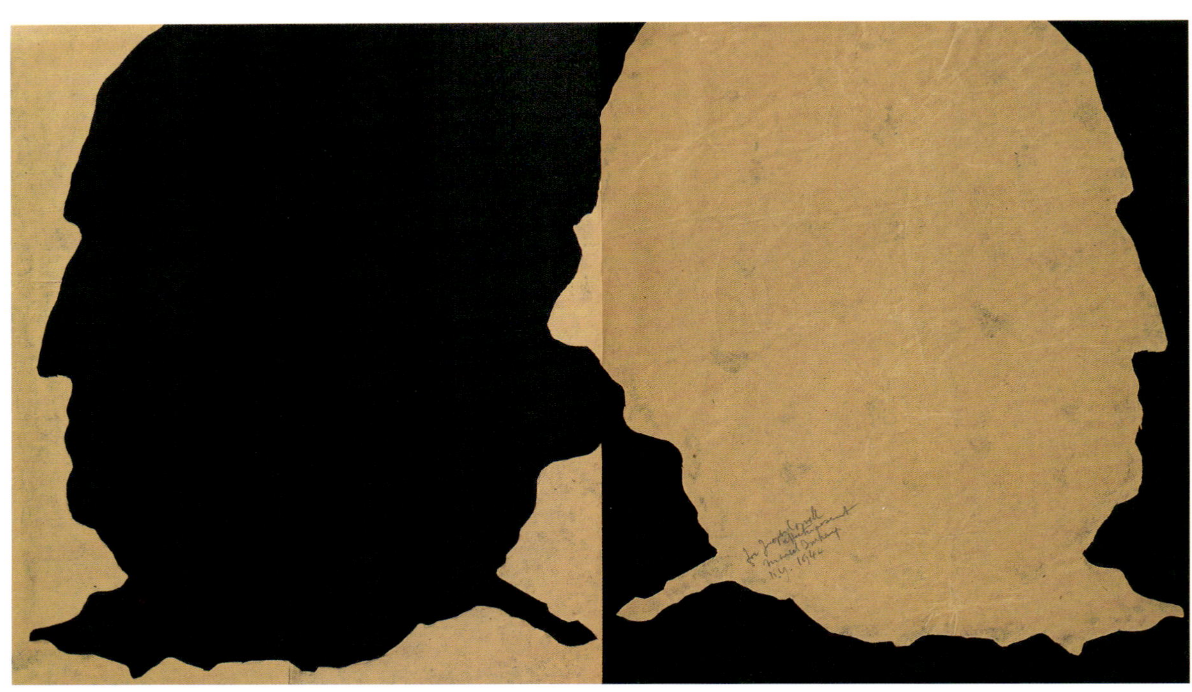

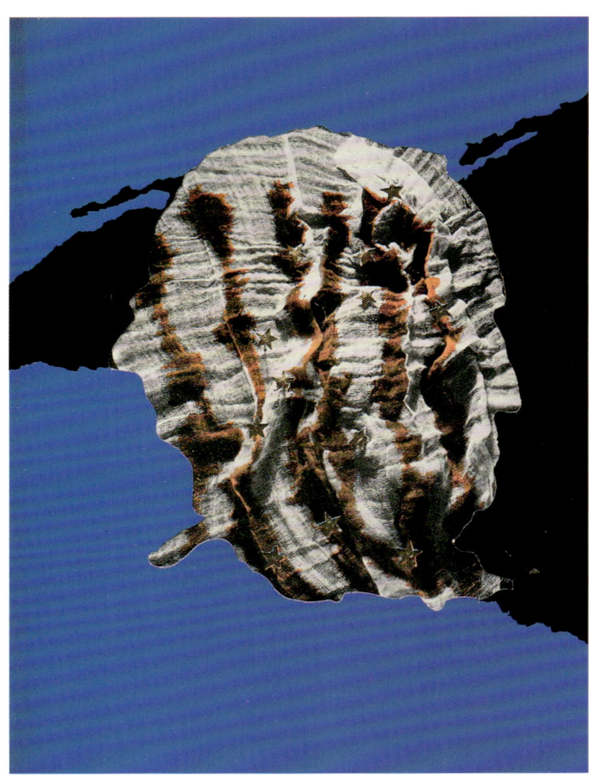

32 *Allégorie de genre [Allegory of Genre]* 1943
Musée National d'Art Moderne, Centre Georges Pompidou, Paris

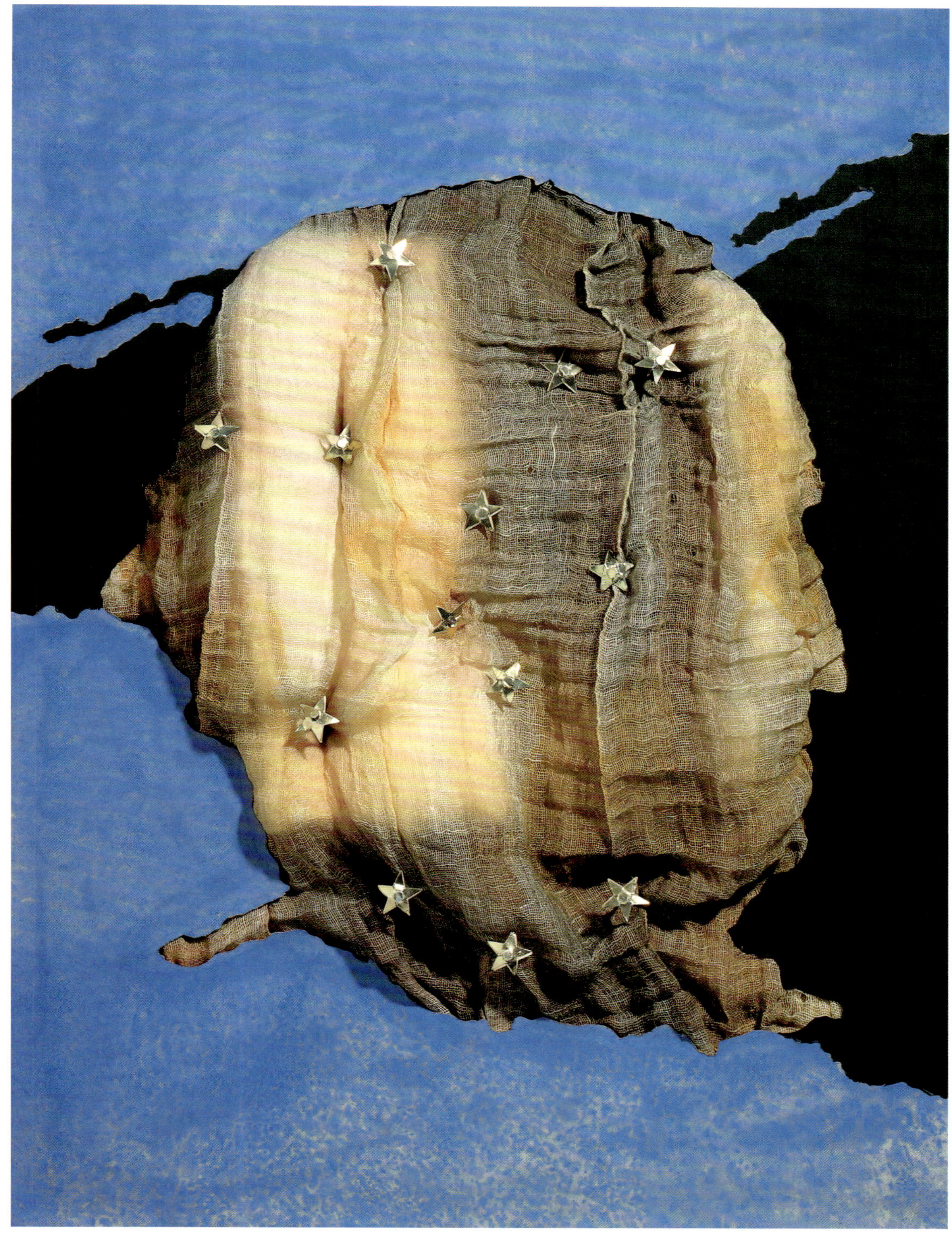

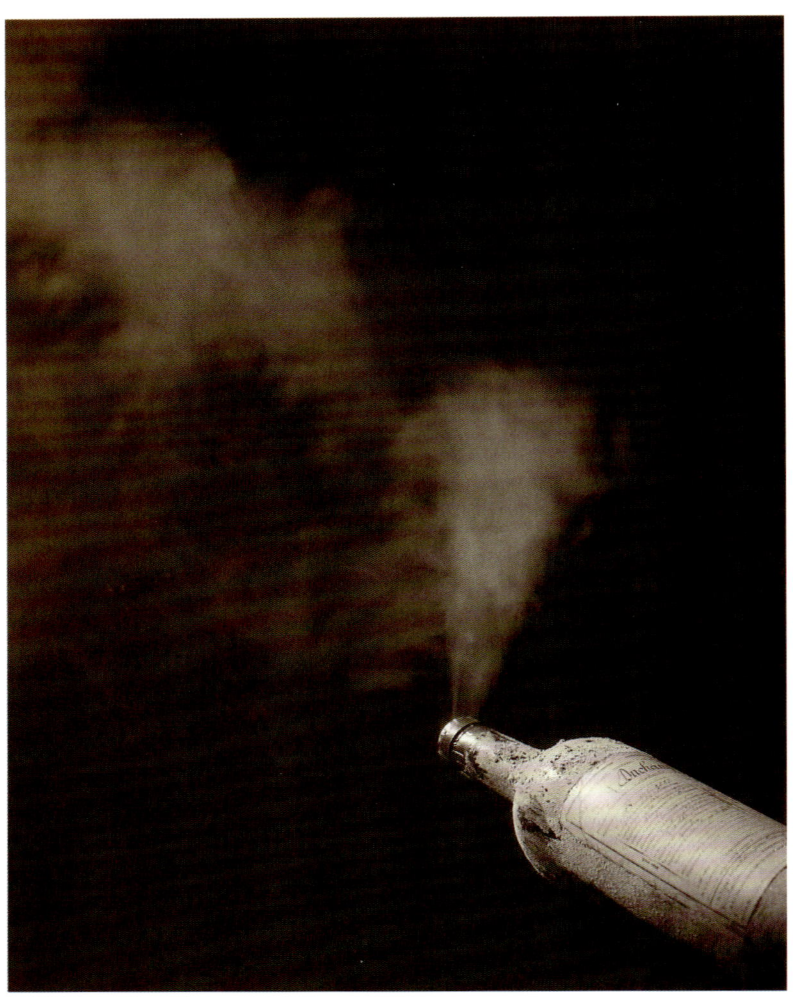

33 **Man Ray**
Untitled [setup for *View* cover] c. 1945
Philadelphia Museum of Art. Marcel Duchamp Archive, Gift of Jacqueline, Paul and Peter Matisse in memory of their mother, Alexina Duchamp

34 **Signature page and *Pharmacie [Pharmacy]* reproduction from *View*** 1945, deluxe edition
Philadelphia Museum of Art.
The Louise and Walter Arensberg Archives

35 **Cover for *View*** 1945
The Menil Collection, Houston

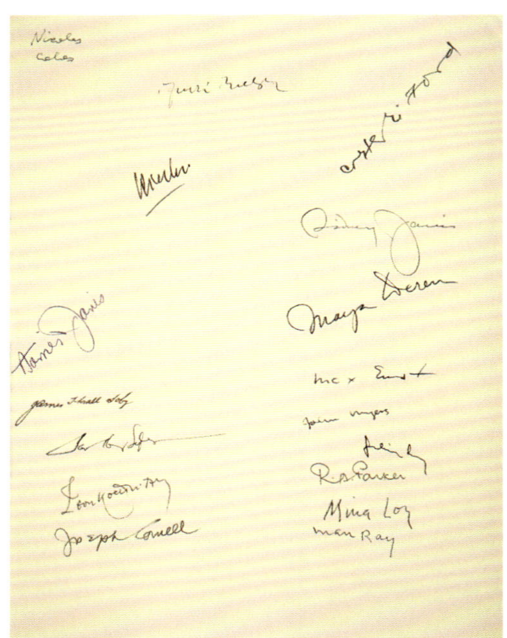

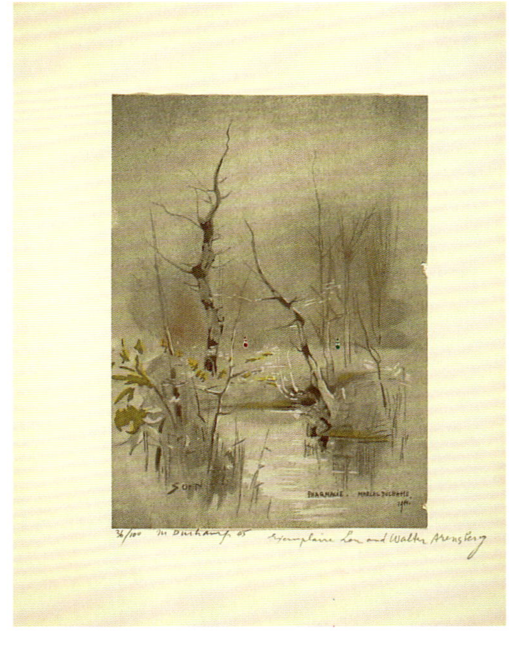

Quand
la fumée de tabac
sent aussi
de la bouche
qui l'exhale,
les deux odeurs
s'épousent par
infra-mince

marcel Duchamp

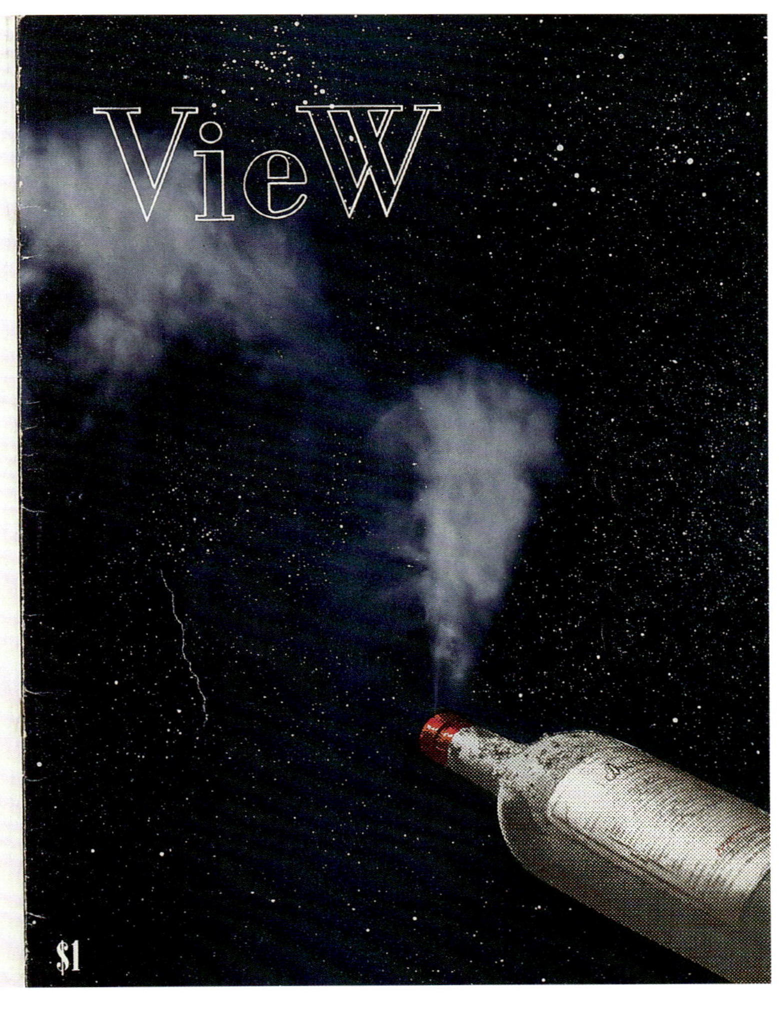

36 Study for *Étant donnés: 1° la chute d'eau / 2° le gaz d'éclairage* c. 1947
[Given: 1. The Waterfall / 2. The Illuminating Gas]
Private collection, on loan to Philadelphia Museum of Art

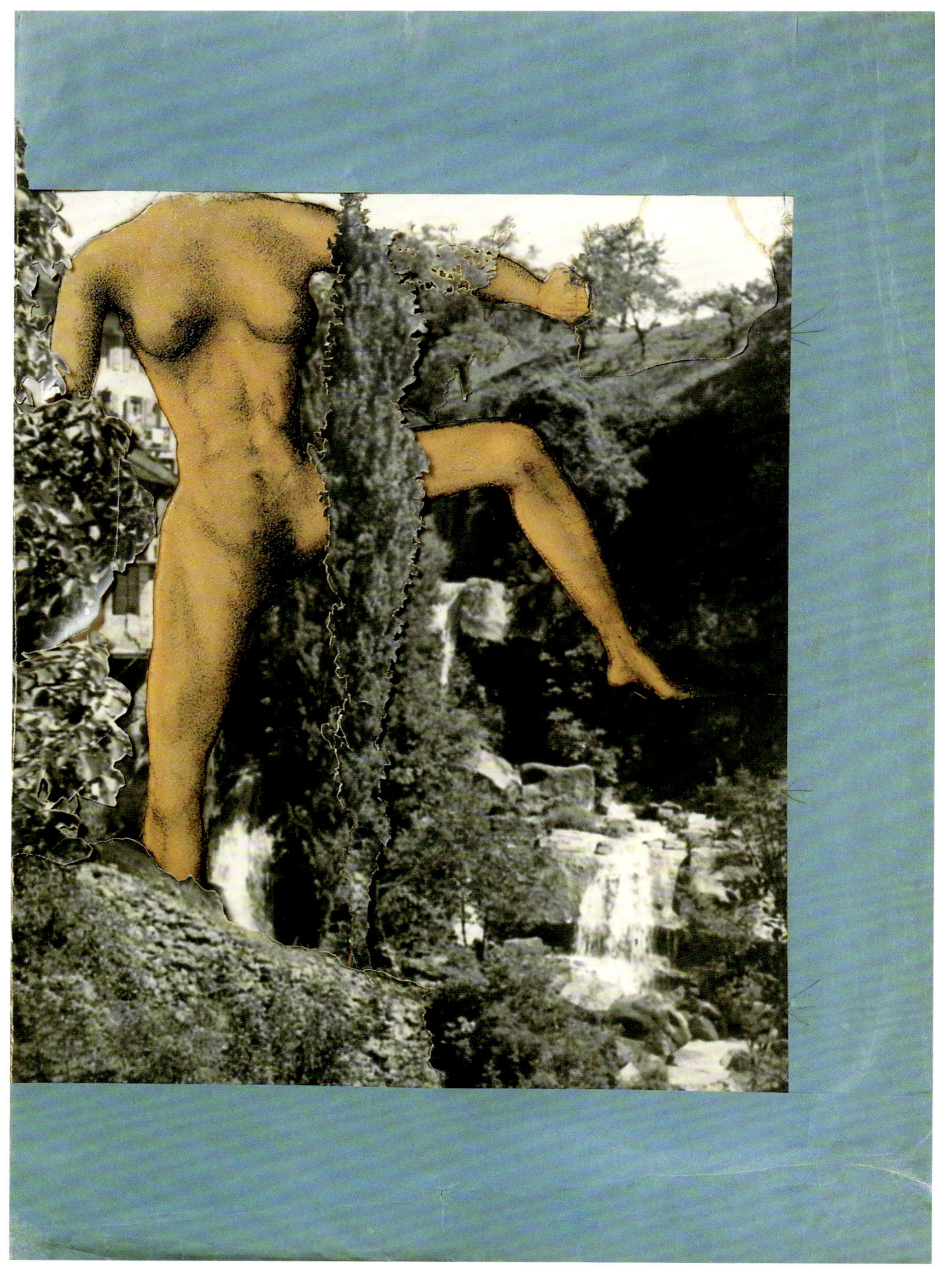

37 **Study for *Étant donnés: 1° la chute d'eau / 2° le gaz d'éclairage*** 1948–49
[Given: 1. The Waterfall / 2. The Illuminating Gas]
Moderna Museet, Stockholm

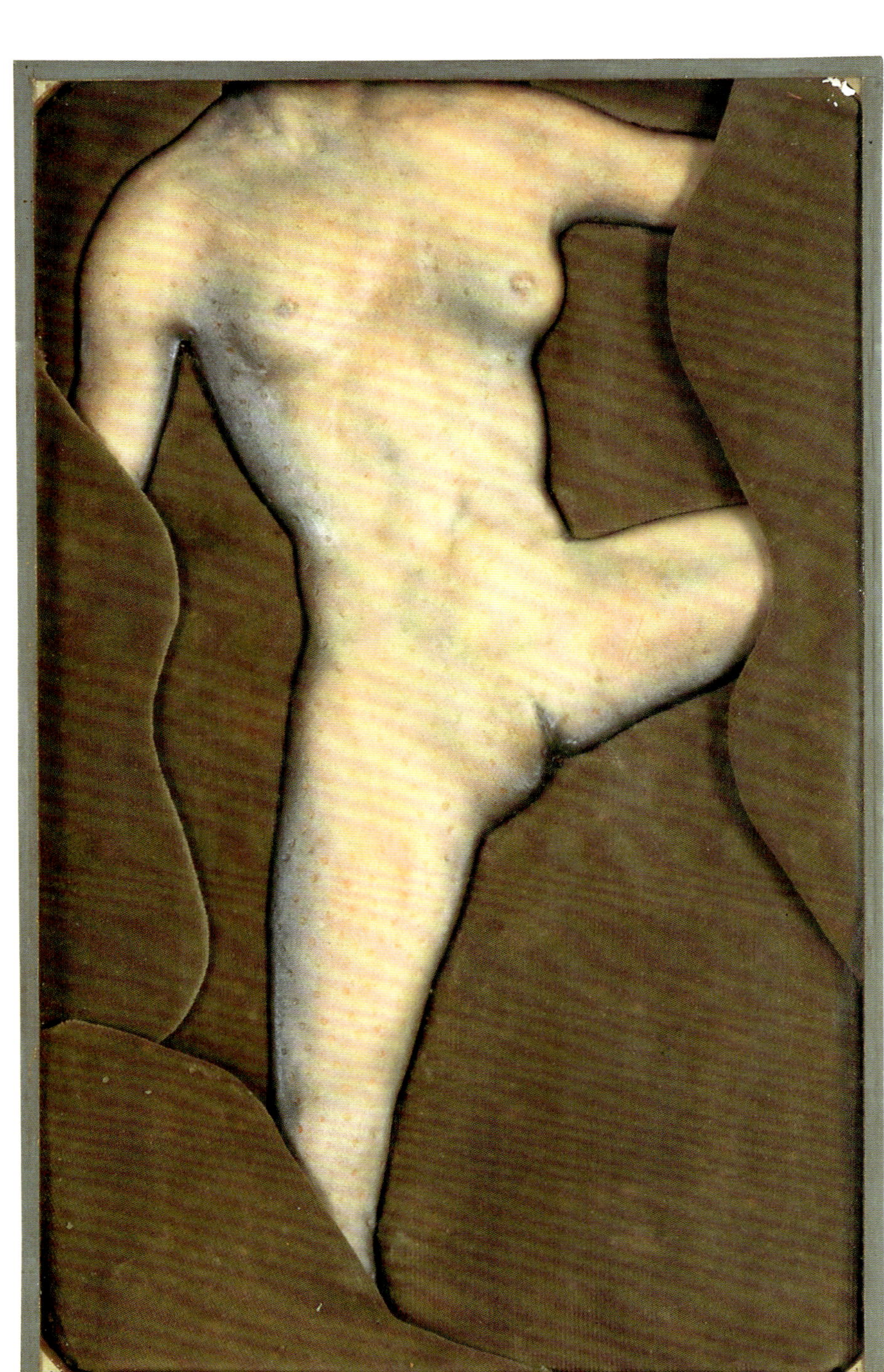

38 **Study for *Prière de toucher [Please Touch]*** 1947
Philadelphia Museum of Art. Gift of Enrico Donati

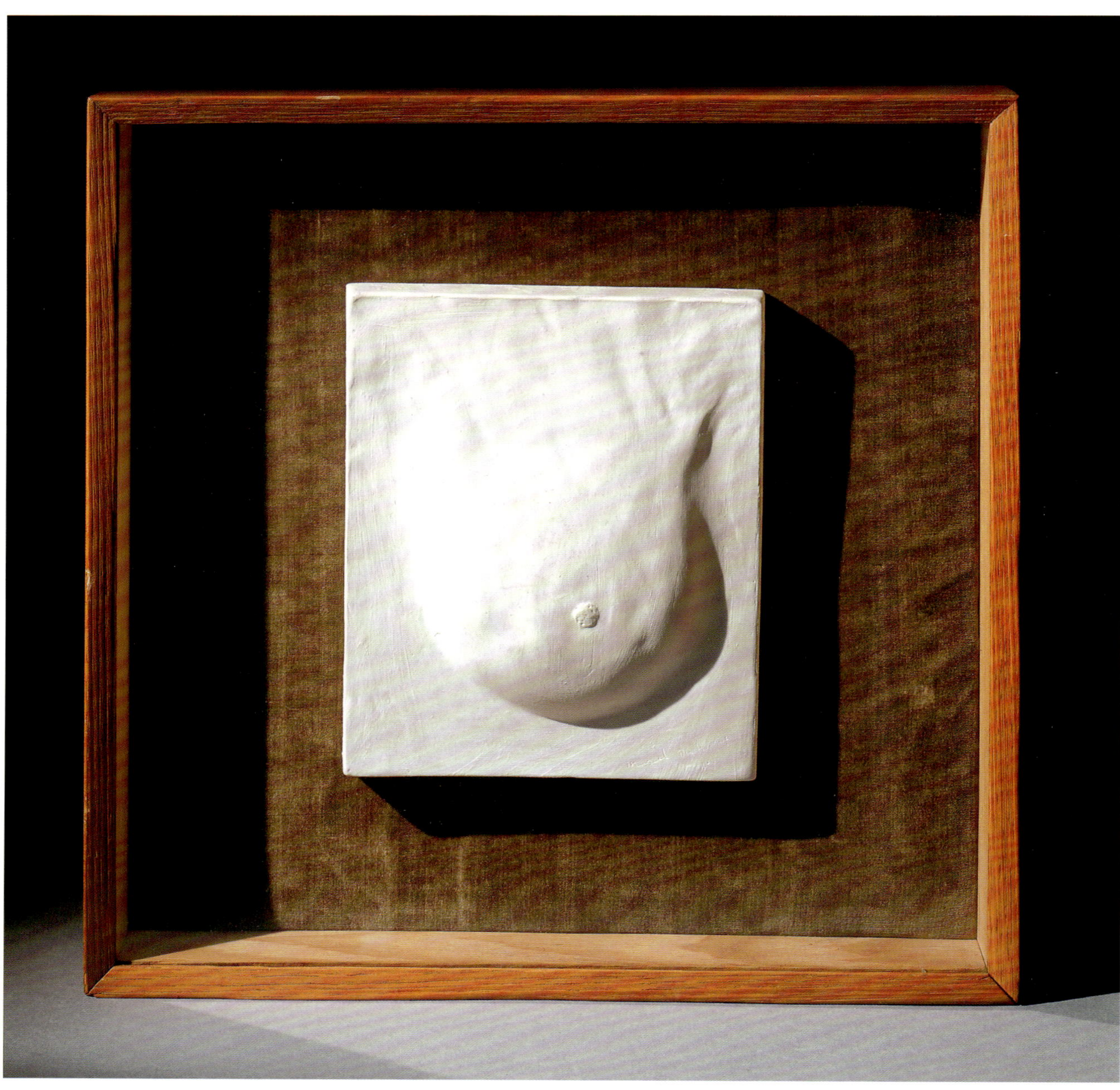

39 **Marcel Duchamp and Enrico Donati**
Cover for *Le Surréalisme en 1947* 1947
The Menil Collection, Houston

40 **Marcel Duchamp and Enrico Donati**
Cover for *Le Surréalisme en 1947* 1947, deluxe edition
Philadelphia Museum of Art. Purchased with the Gertrud A. White Memorial Fund

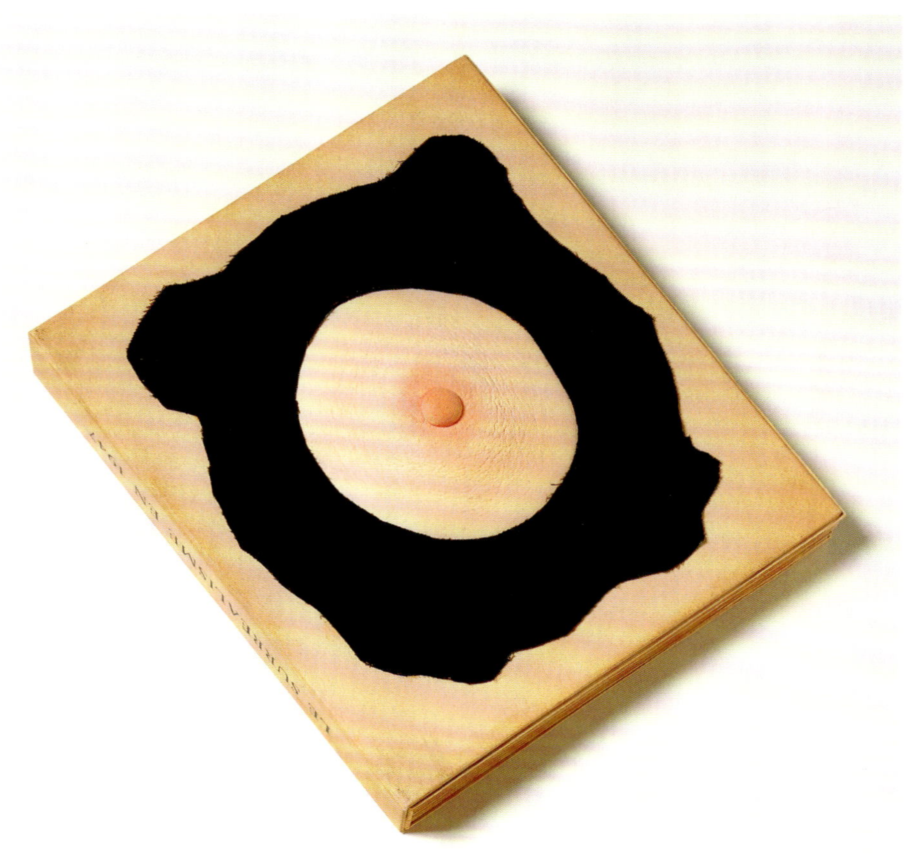

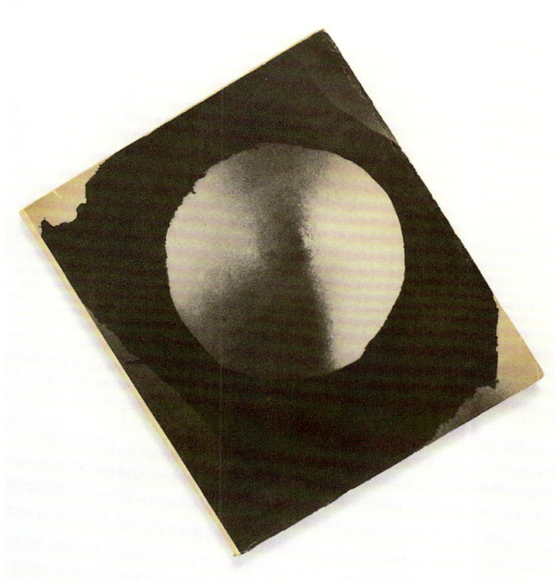

41 ***de ou par Marcel Duchamp ou Rrose Sélavy*** 1935–41
[by or of Marcel Duchamp or Rrose Sélavy]
Series A, XVIII/XX, 1949;
with *Réflection à main [Hand Reflection]*, 1948
Private collection

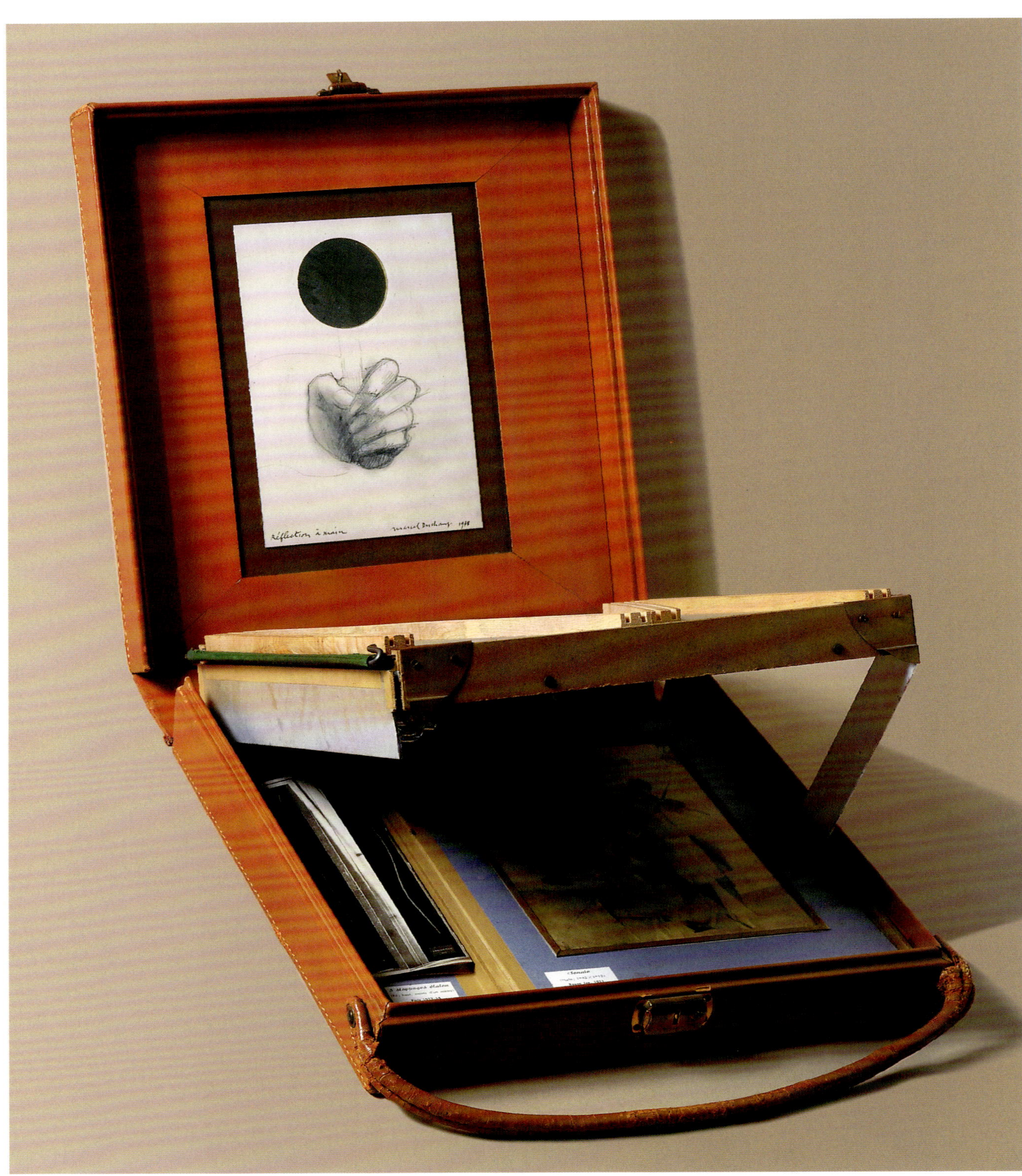

42 Untitled *(Étant donnés: 1° la chute d'eau / 2° le gaz d'éclairage)* c. 1948
[Given: 1. The Waterfall / 2. The Illuminating Gas]
Achim Moeller Fine Art, New York

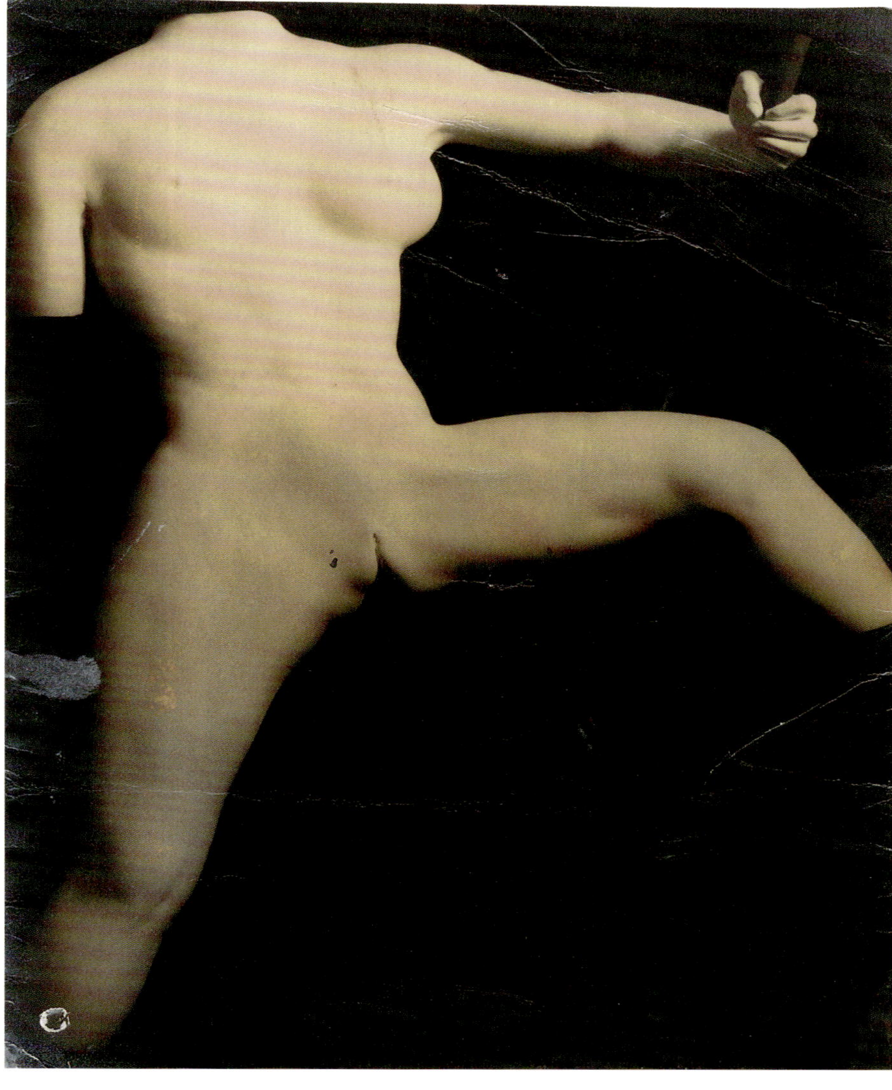

43 ***Moonlight on the Bay at Basswood*** 1953
Philadelphia Museum of Art.
Gift of Mr. Frank Brookes Hubachek

44 ***Étant donnés: 1° la chute d'eau / 2° le gaz d'éclairage*** 1946–66
***[Given: 1. The Waterfall / 2. The Illuminating Gas]*, exterior view**
Philadelphia Museum of Art. Gift of the Cassandra Foundation

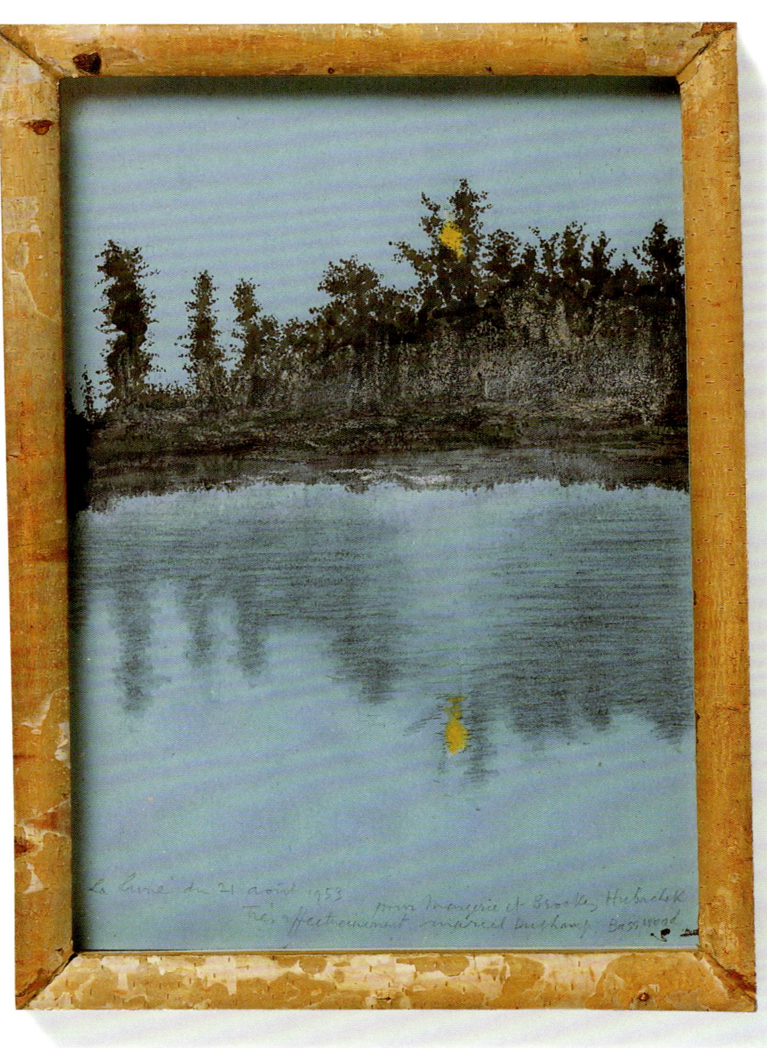

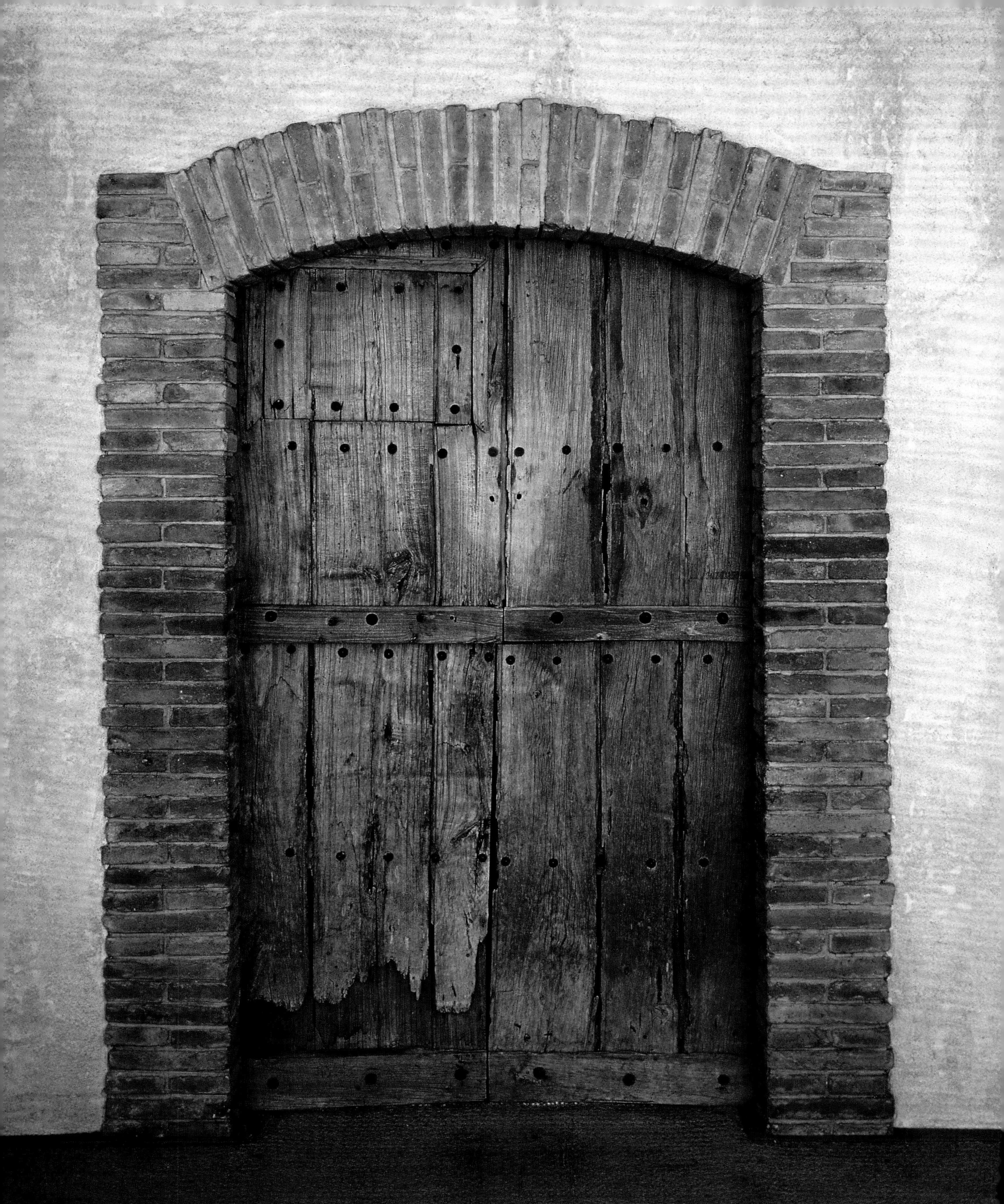

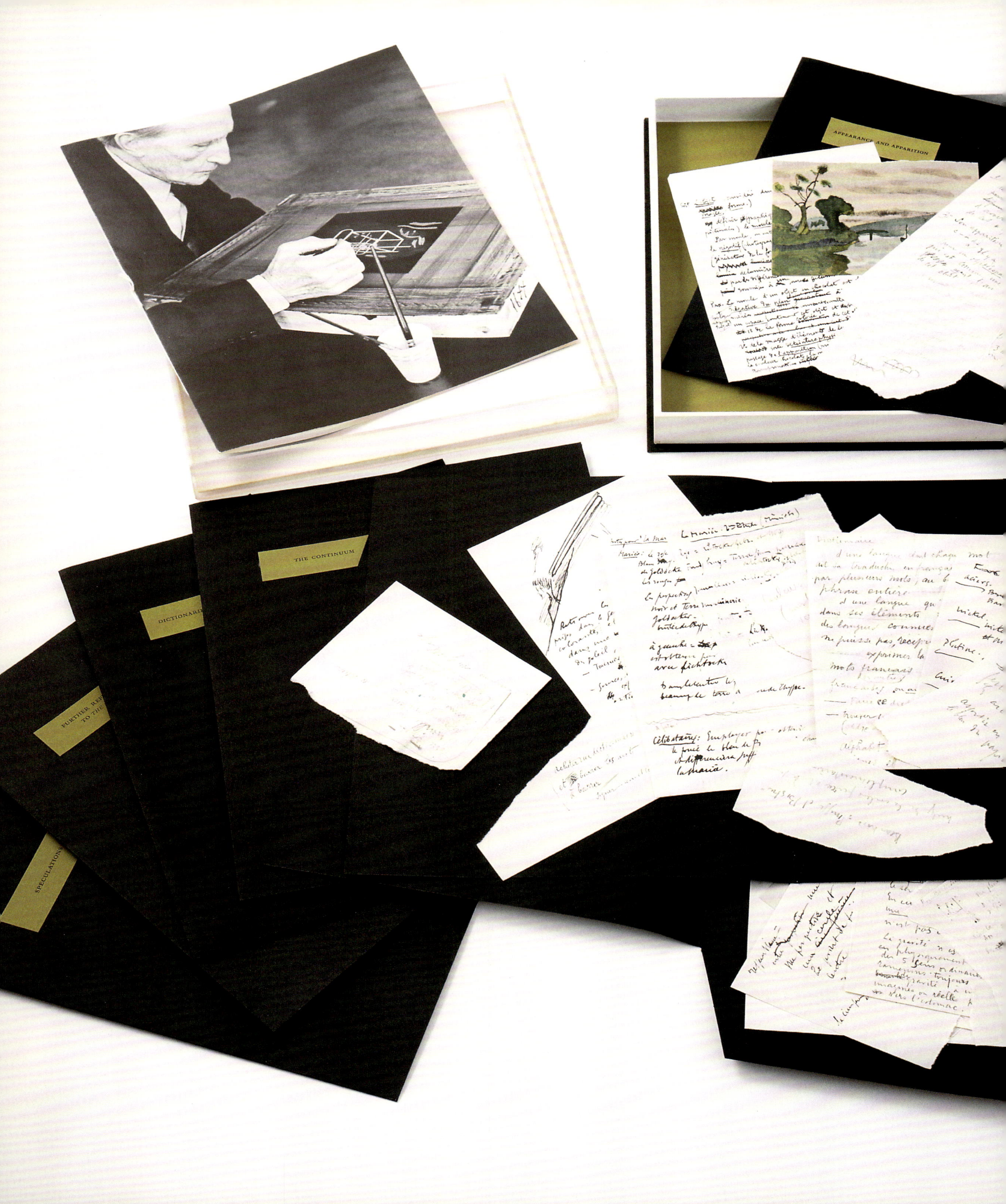

APPEARANCE AND APPARITION
THE CONTINUUM
SPECULATIONS

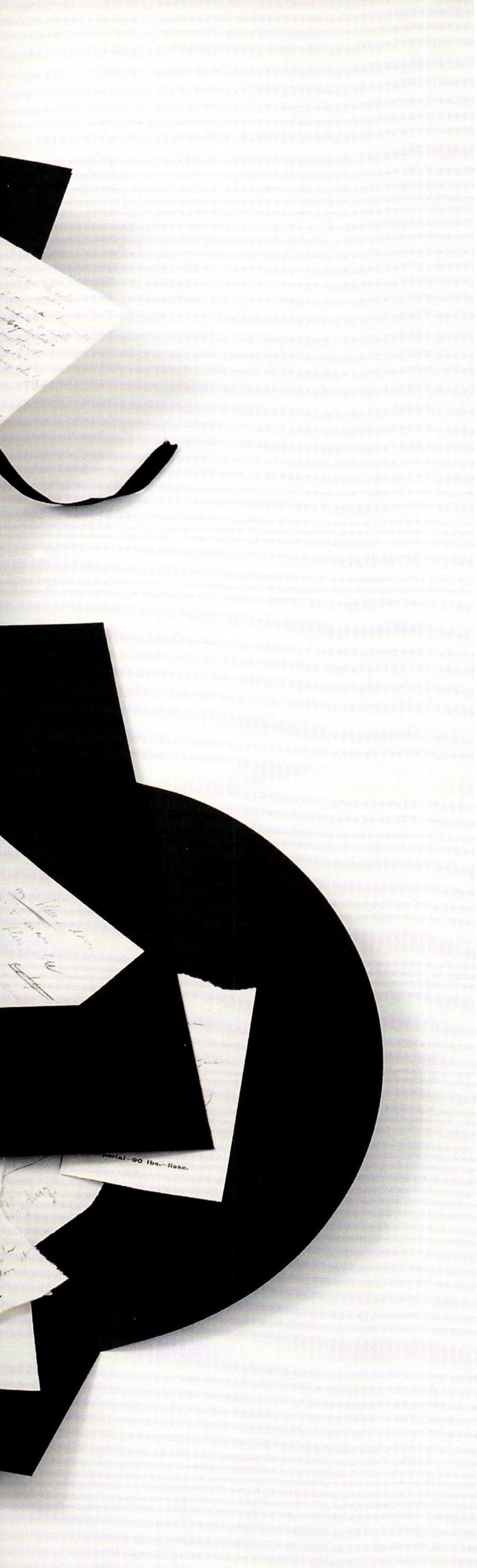

45 ***à l'infinitif [In the Infinitive] (White Box)*** 1967
The Menil Collection, Houston

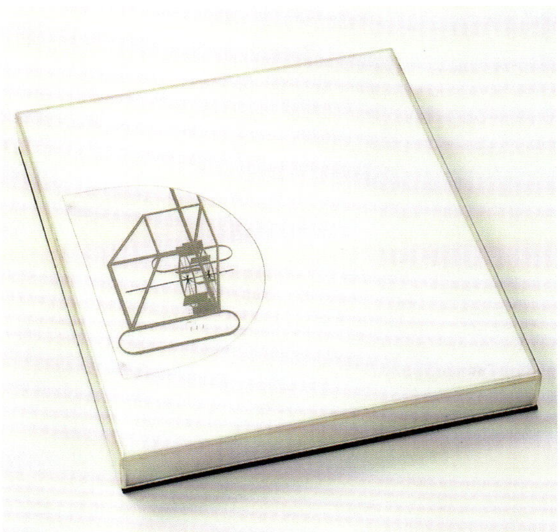

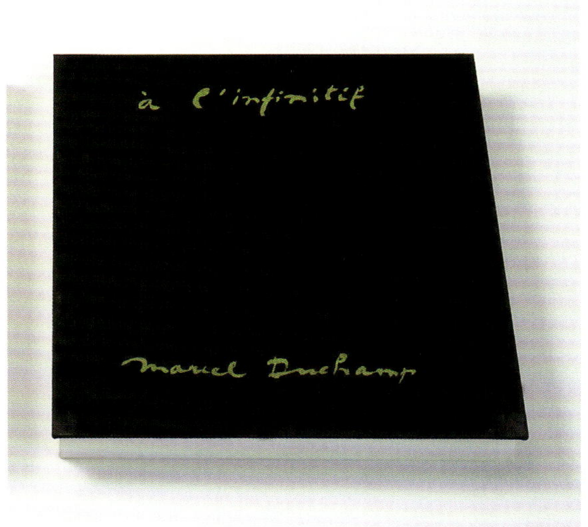

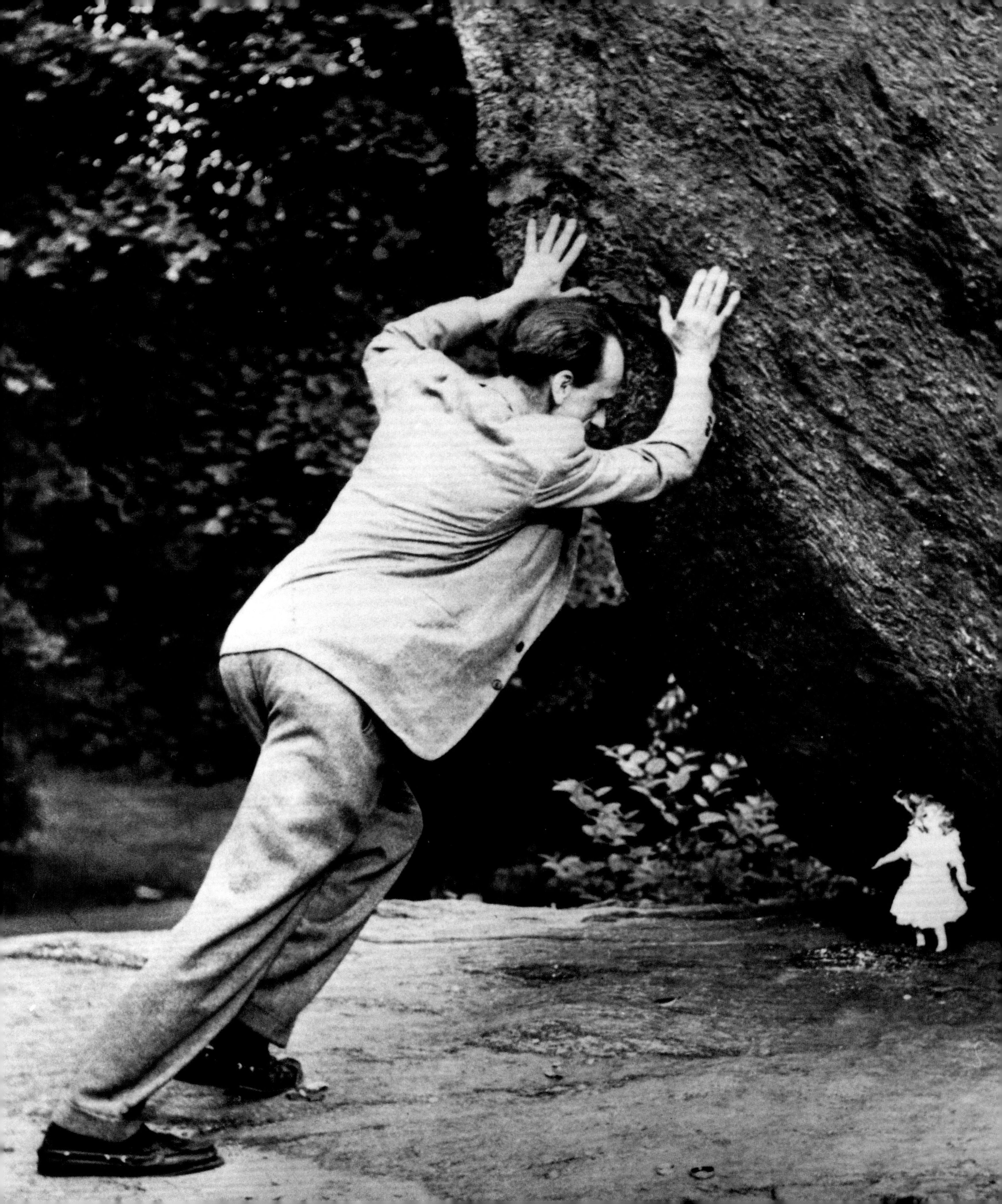

Joseph Cornell Plates

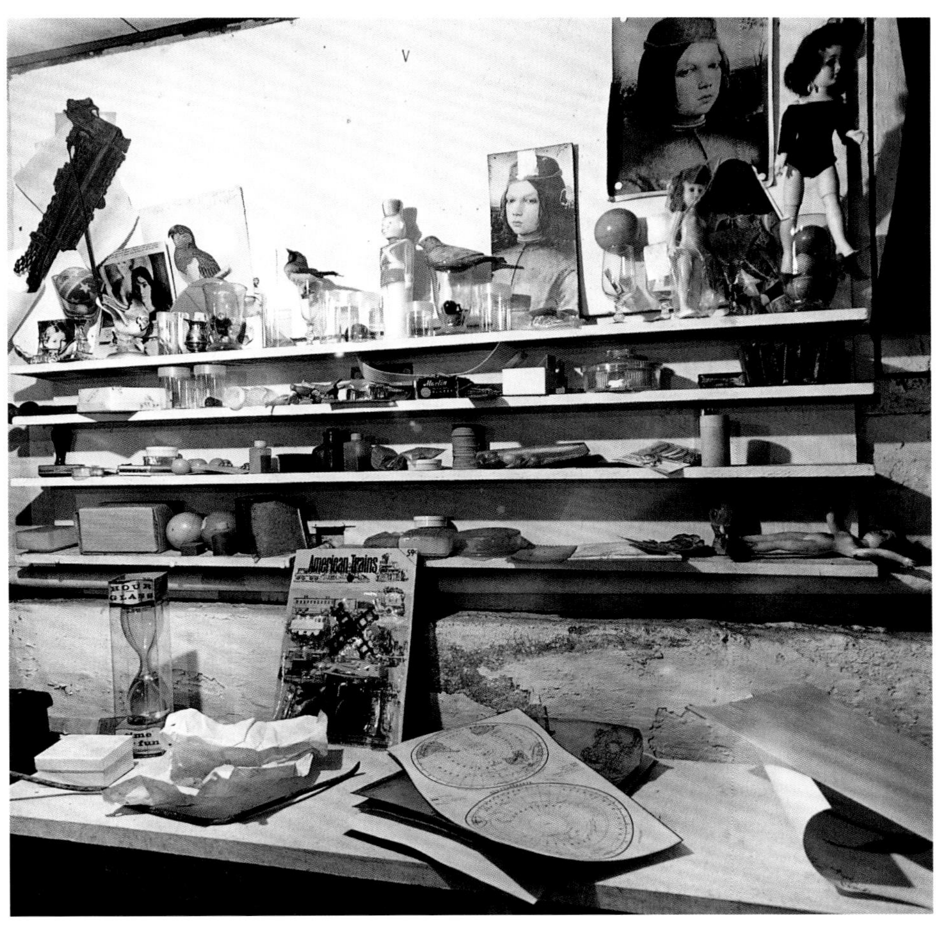

46 ***Jouet Surréaliste [Surrealist Game]*** c. 1932
National Museum of American Art, Smithsonian Institution.
Gift of Mr. and Mrs. John A. Benton

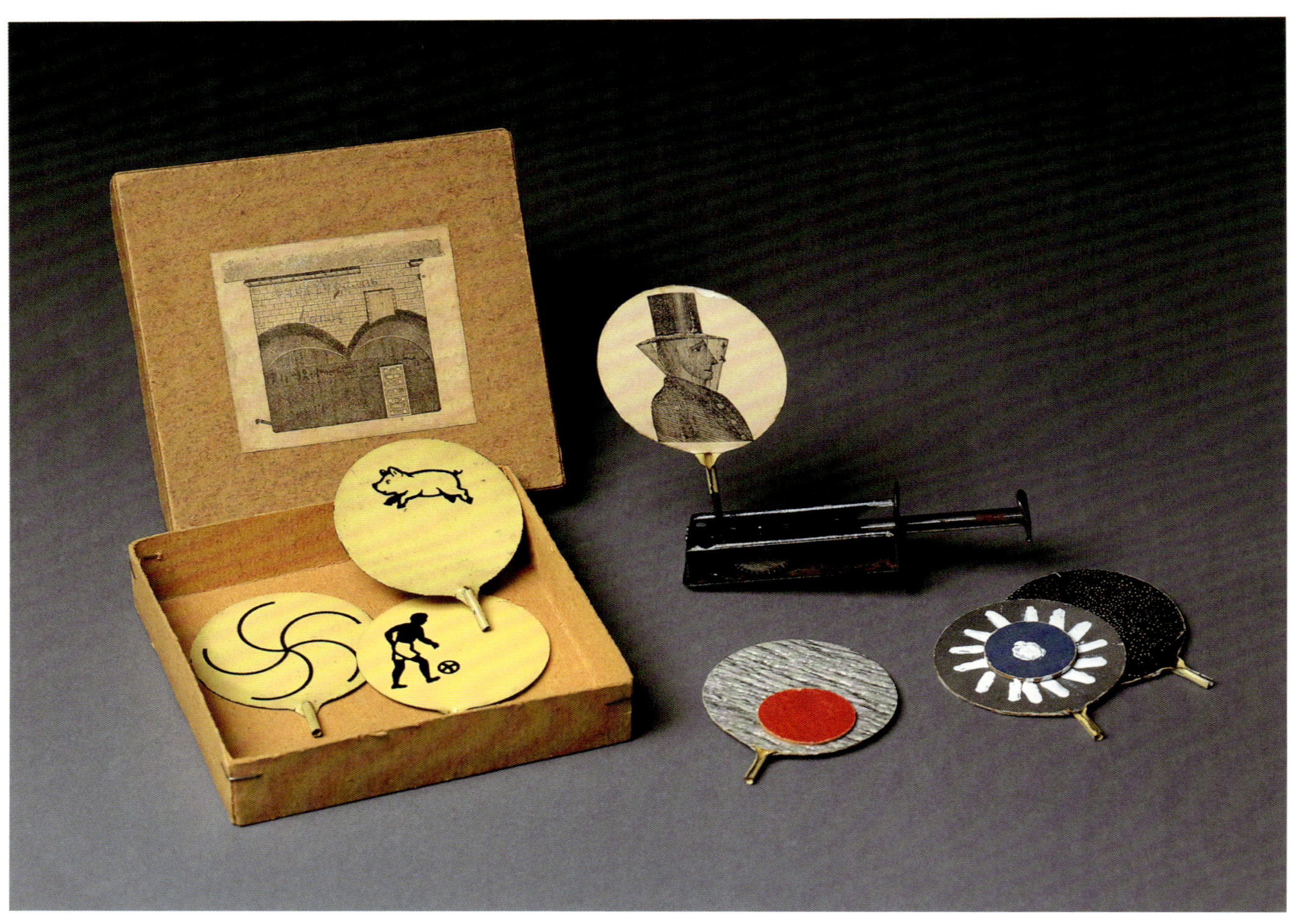

pp. 160–61

94 Cornell in Central Park, New York, June 1948. Arranged by Cornell; photograph by Ernst Beadle.

95 Cornell's studio, 3708 Utopia Parkway, Flushing, New York, 1969. Photograph by Hans Namuth.

47 ***Le Voyageur dans les Glaces [The Traveler in the Mirrors]*** c. 1932
Collection of Lindy Bergman, Chicago

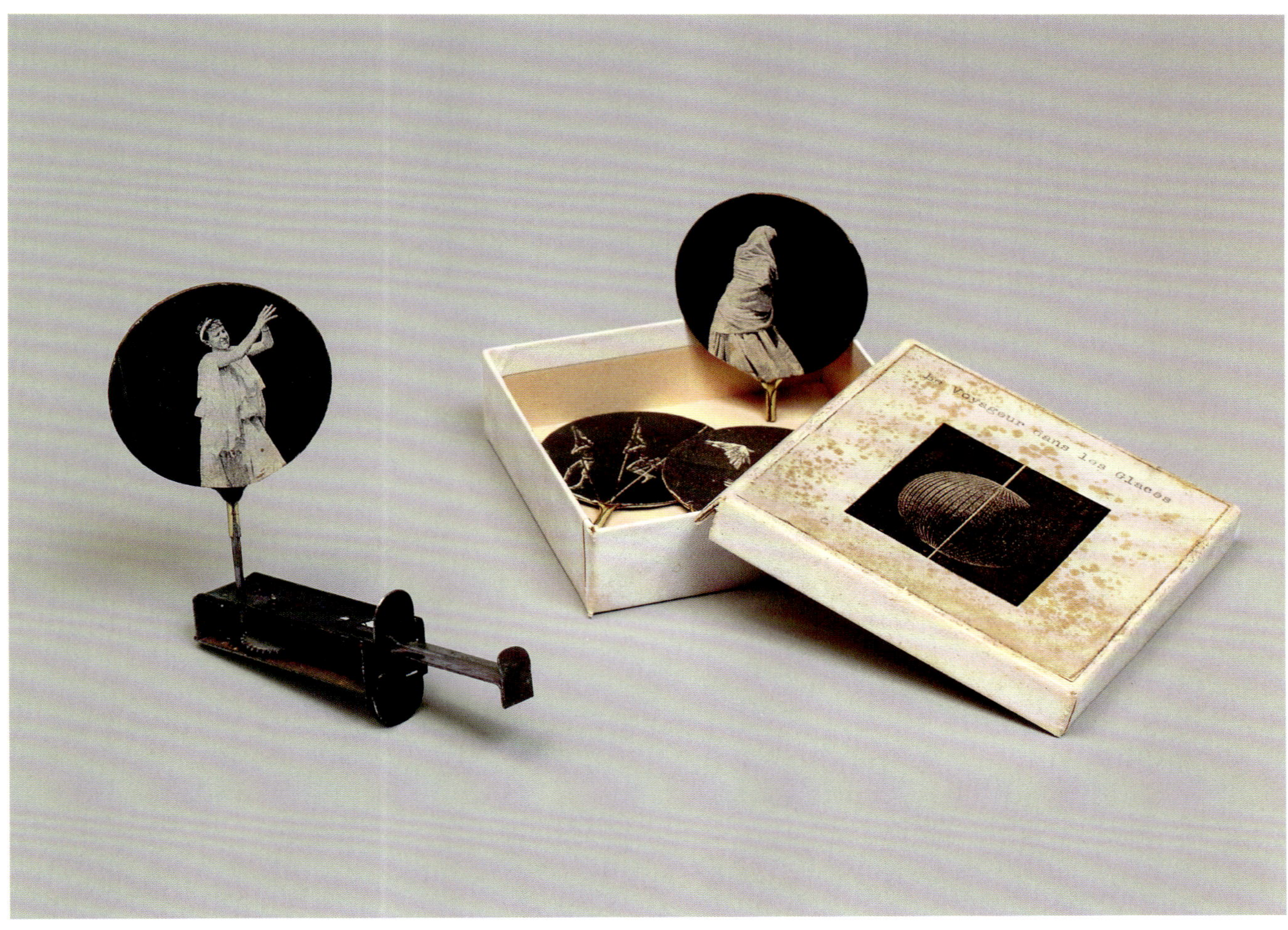

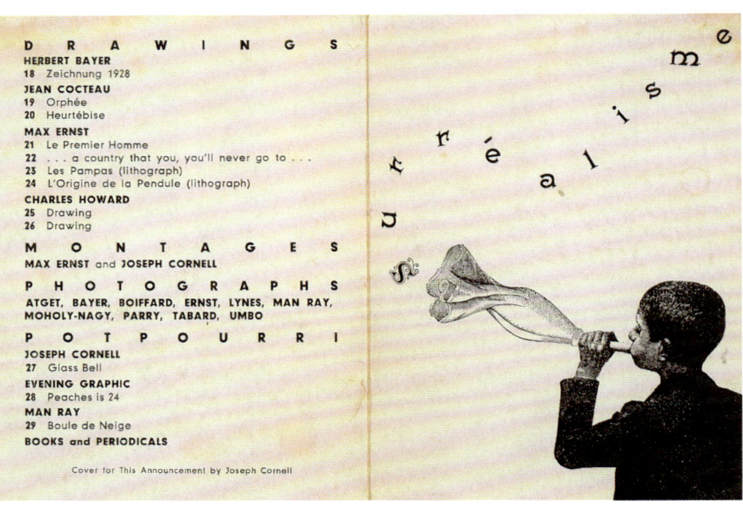

D R A W I N G S
HERBERT BAYER
18 Zeichnung 1928
JEAN COCTEAU
19 Orphée
20 Heurtébise
MAX ERNST
21 Le Premier Homme
22 . . . a country that you, you'll never go to . . .
23 Les Pampas (lithograph)
24 L'Origine de la Pendule (lithograph)
CHARLES HOWARD
25 Drawing
26 Drawing

M O N T A G E S
MAX ERNST and **JOSEPH CORNELL**

P H O T O G R A P H S
ATGET, BAYER, BOIFFARD, ERNST, LYNES, MAN RAY, MOHOLY-NAGY, PARRY, TABARD, UMBO

P O T P O U R R I
JOSEPH CORNELL
27 Glass Bell
EVENING GRAPHIC
28 Peaches is 24
MAN RAY
29 Boule de Neige
BOOKS and PERIODICALS

Cover for This Announcement by Joseph Cornell

Surréalisme

49 Exhibition announcement for "Surréalisme" 1932
Joseph Cornell Study Center, National Museum of American Art, Smithsonian Institution. Gift of Mr. and Mrs. John A. Benton

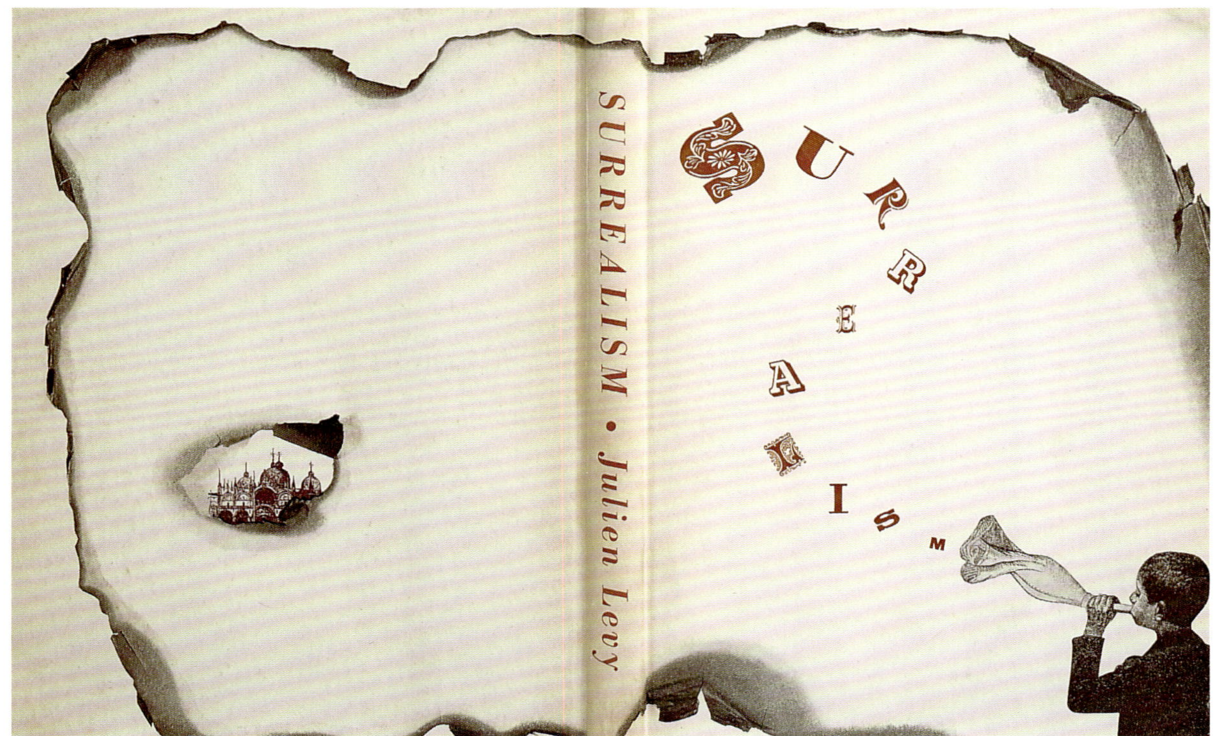

48 Cover for *Surrealism* 1936
The Menil Collection, Houston

50 ***Monsieur Phot*** 1933, no. 12
The Art Institute of Chicago. Mary Reynolds Collection

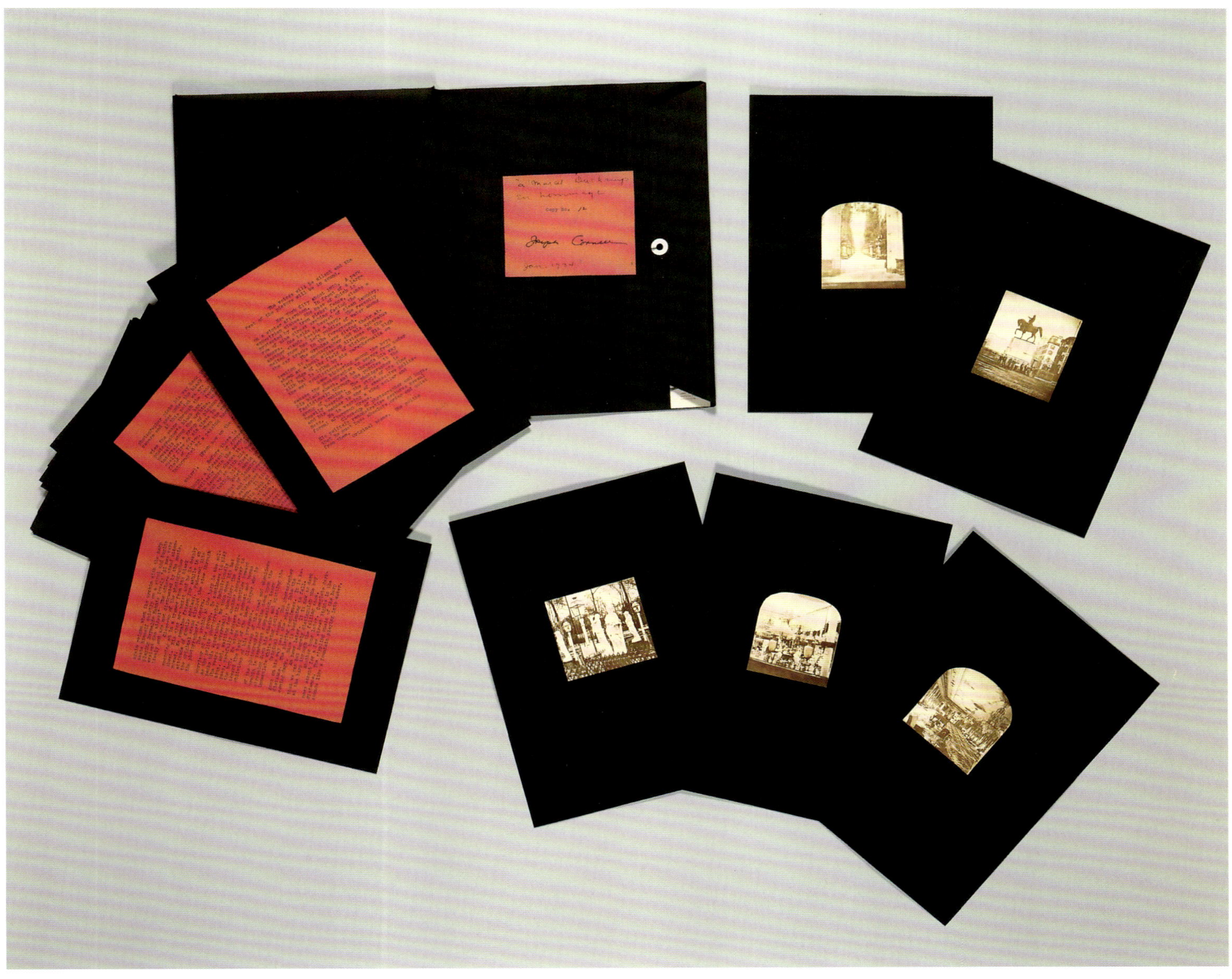

51.1–.4 Untitled Book Object *(Journal d'Agriculture Pratique et Journal de l'Agriculture)* c. 1933–mid 1940s
The Joseph and Robert Cornell Memorial Foundation
pp.166-67

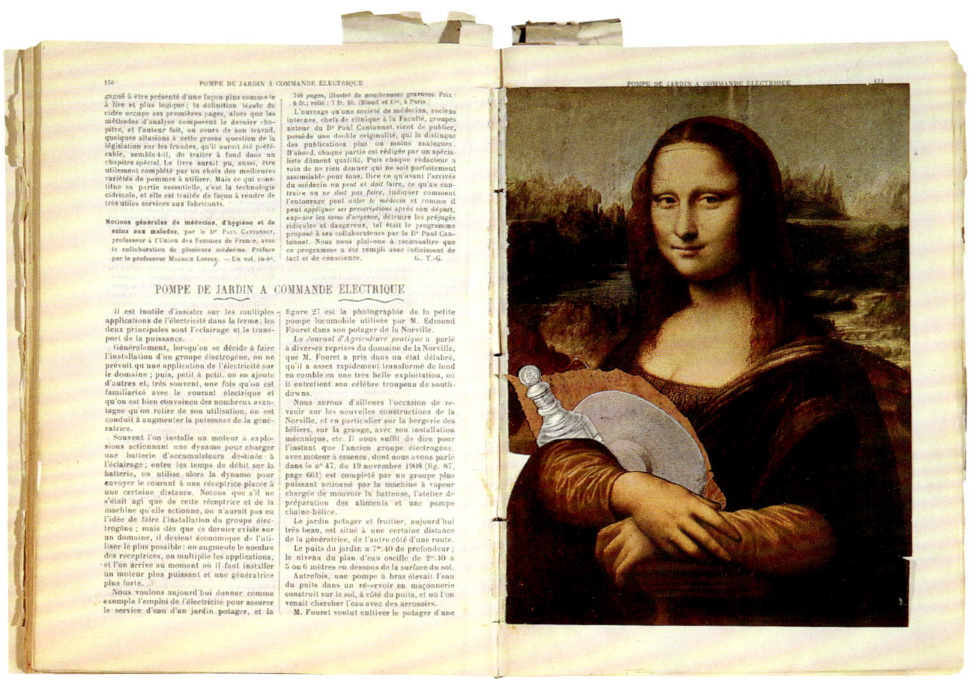

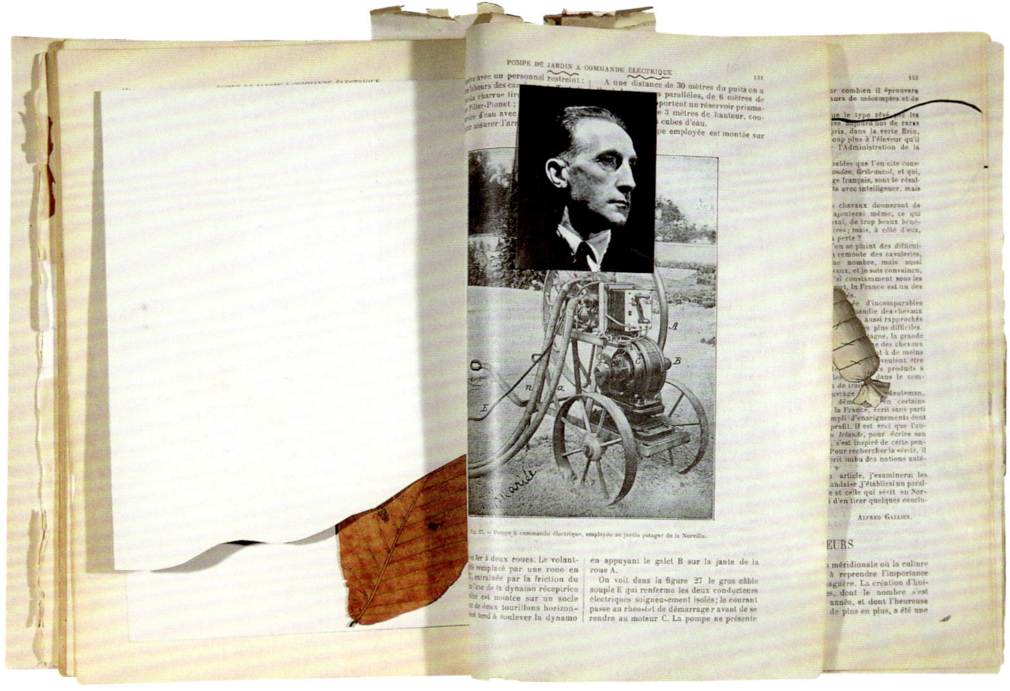

51.5 Untitled Book Object *(Journal d'Agriculture Pratique et Journal de l'Agriculture)* with loose folder c. 1933–mid 1940s
The Joseph and Robert Cornell Memorial Foundation
right

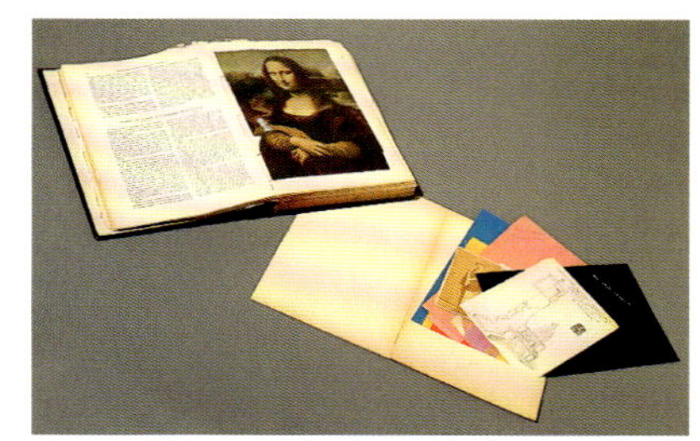

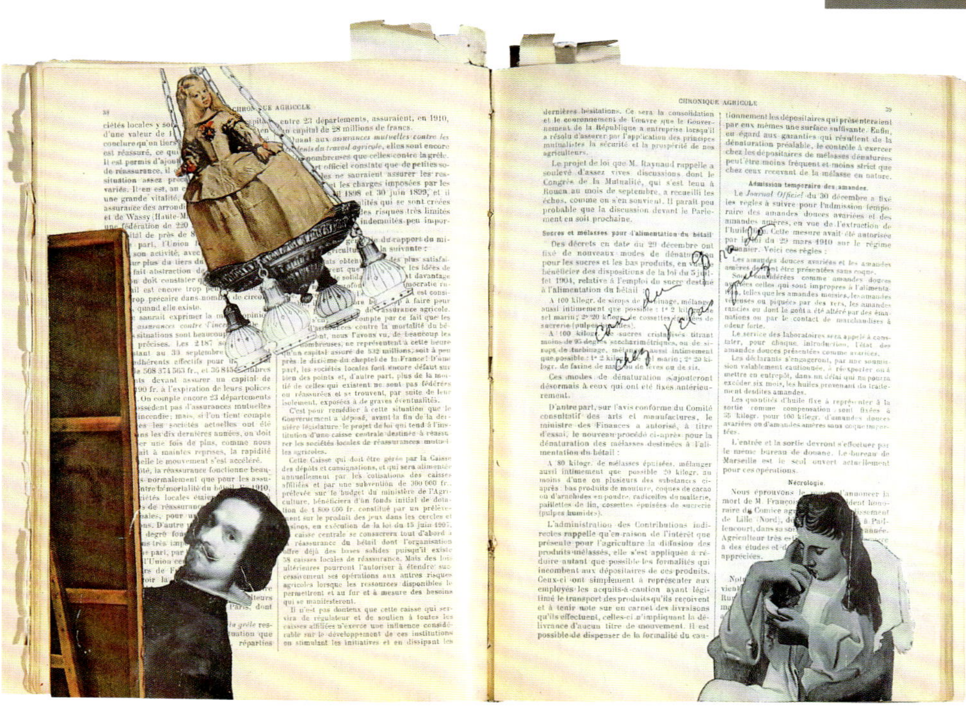

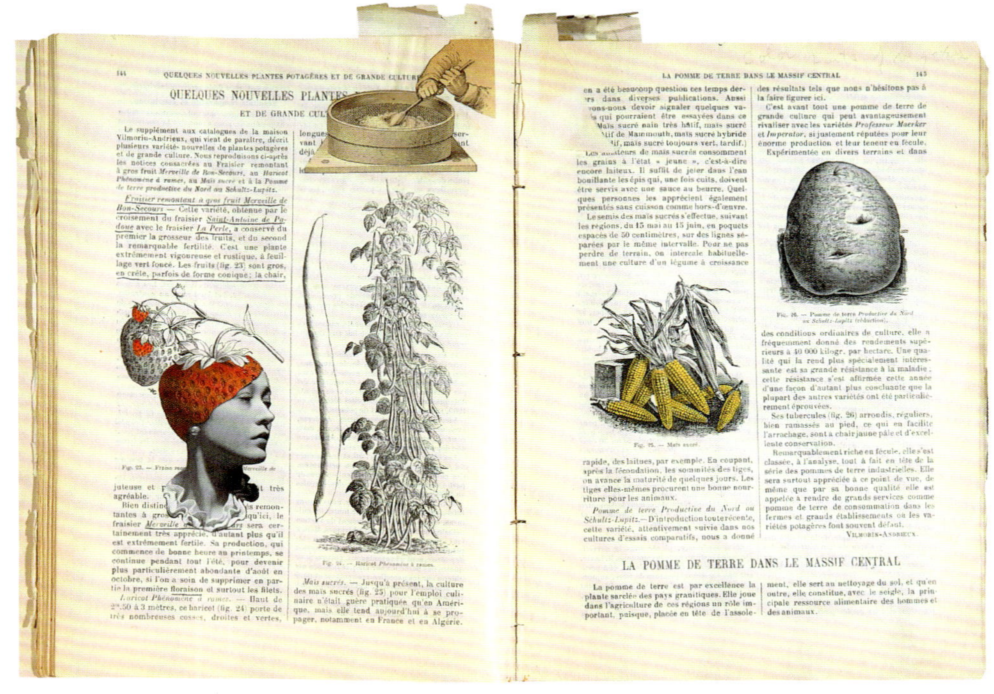

51.6–.9 Untitled Book Object ***(Journal d'Agriculture Pratique et Journal de l'Agriculture)*** c. 1933–mid 1940s
The Joseph and Robert Cornell Memorial Foundation
pp. 168–69

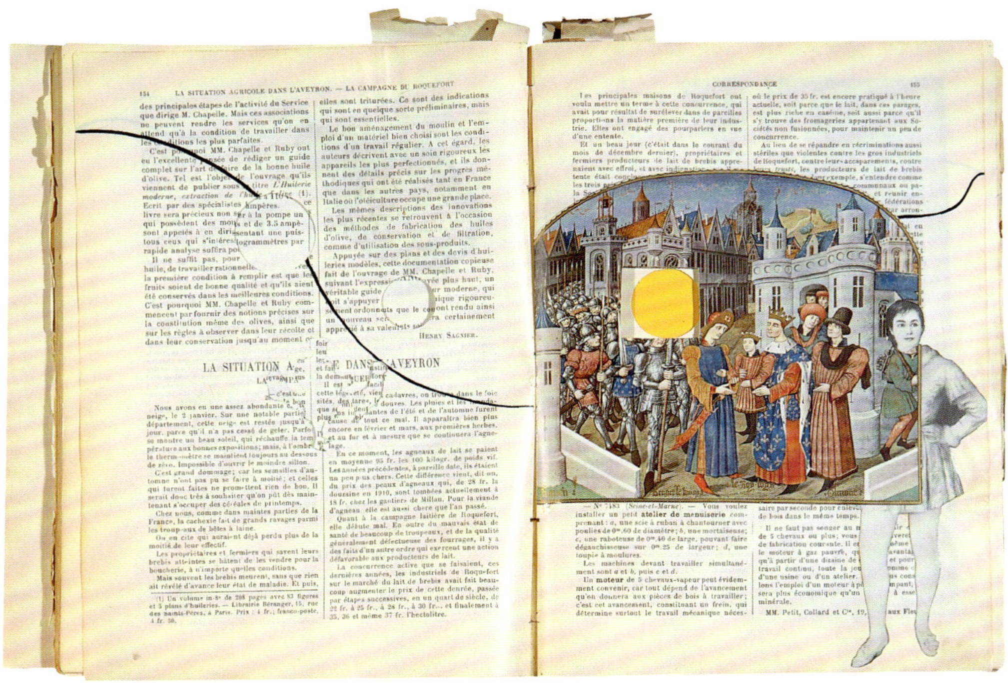

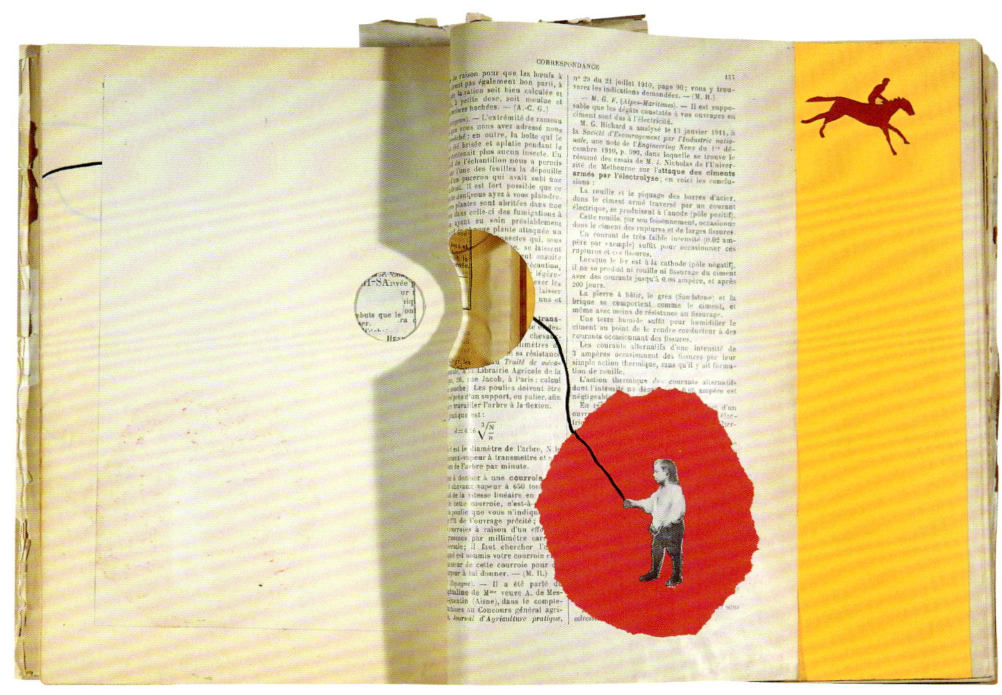

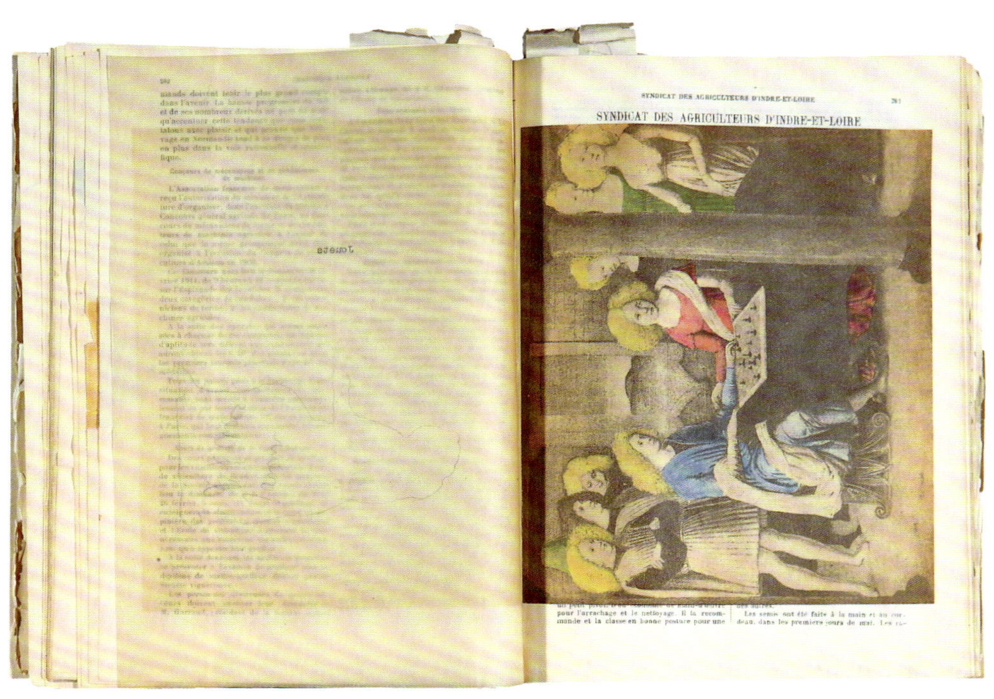
SYNDICAT DES AGRICULTEURS D'INDRE-ET-LOIRE

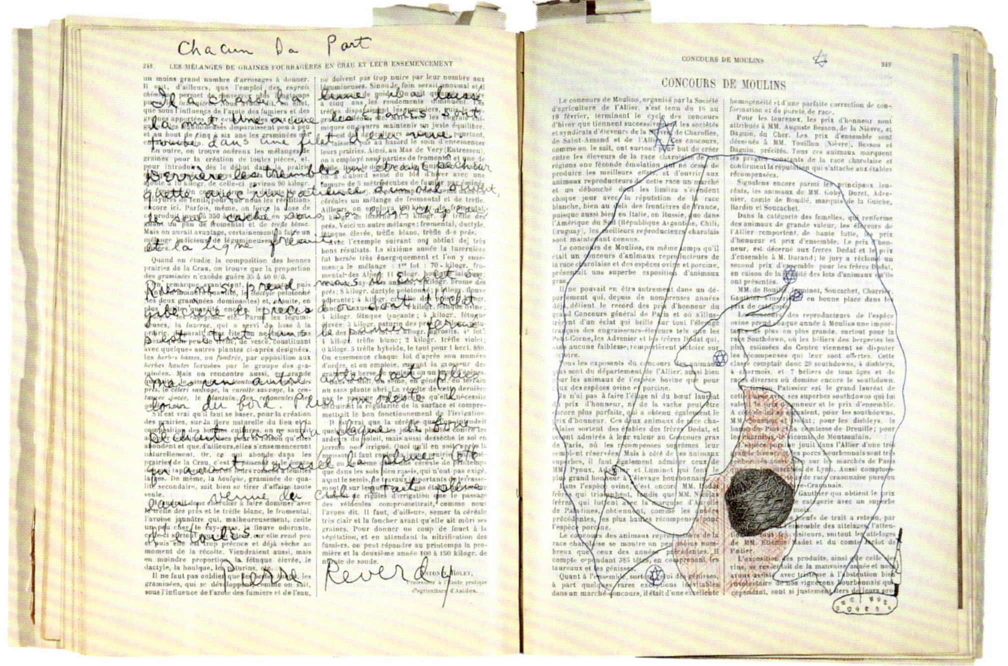
Chacun sa Part
LES MÉLANGES DE GRAINES FOURRAGÈRES EN CRAU ET LEUR ENSEMENCEMENT
CONCOURS DE MOULINS

52 ***Cabinet of Natural History (Object)*** 1934, 1936–40
Private collection

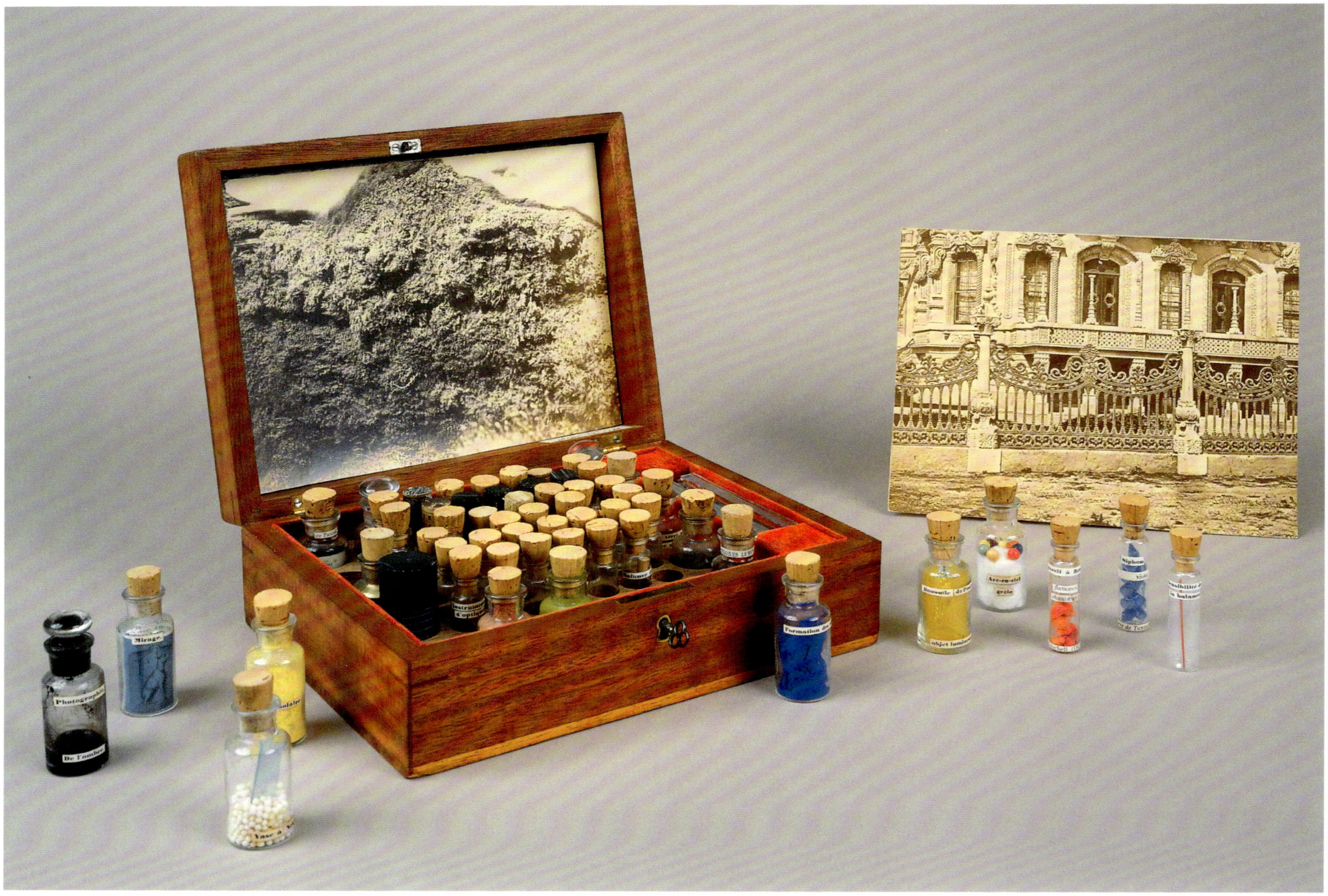

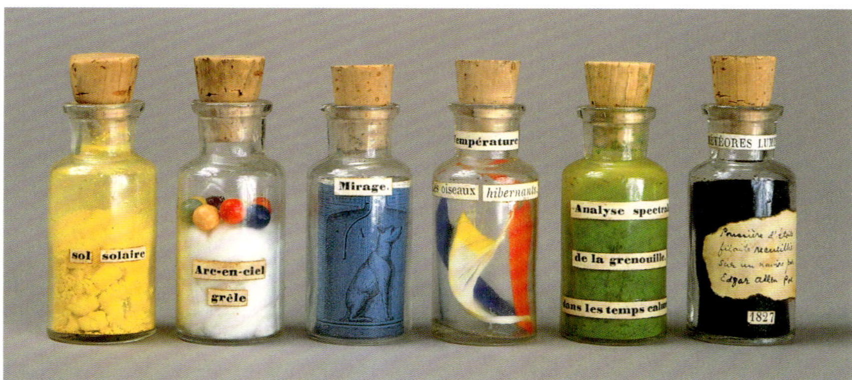

53 **Untitled (Soap Bubble Set)** c. 1936
Wadsworth Atheneum, Hartford, Connecticut.
Gift of Henry and Walter Keney

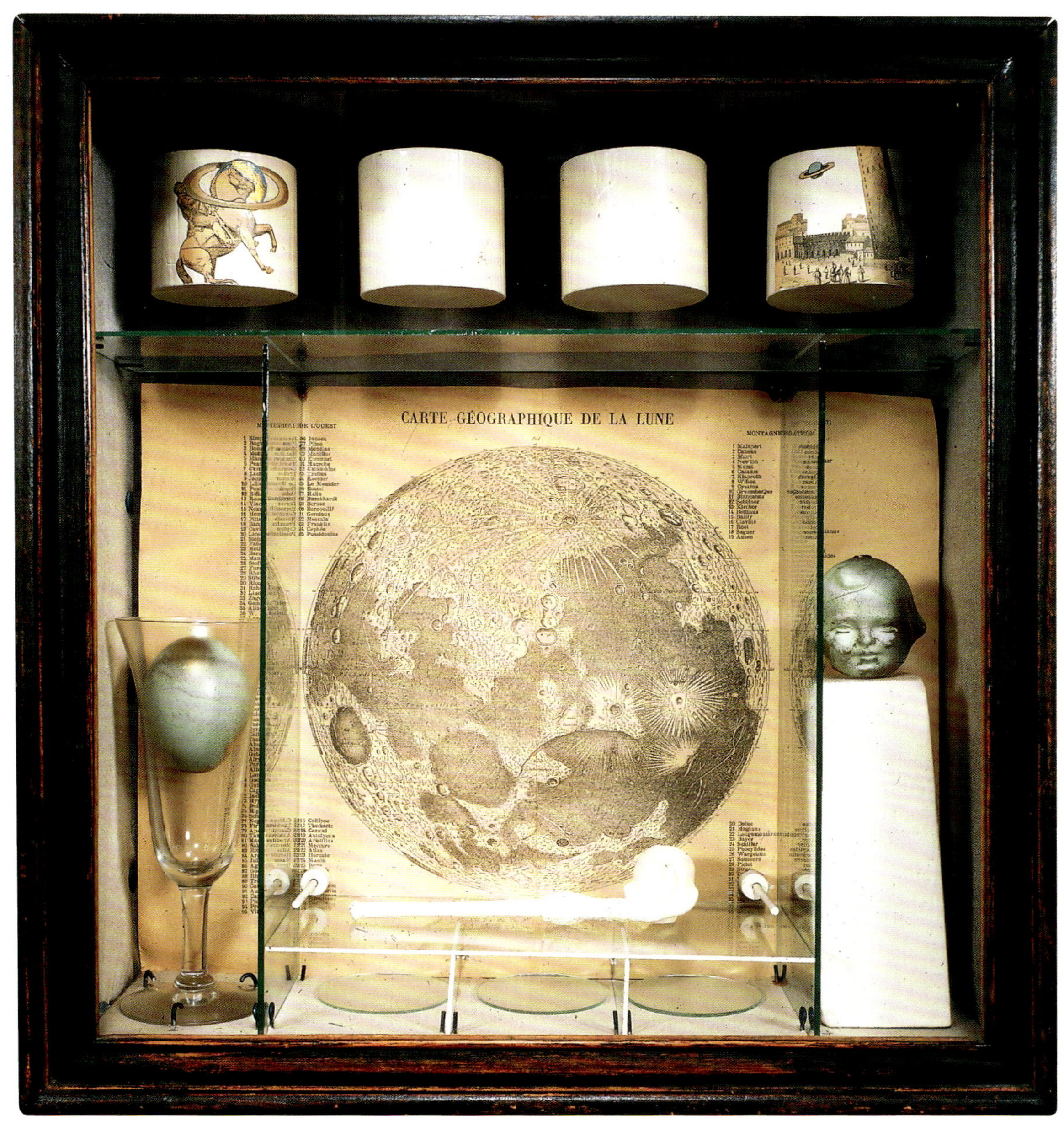

54 ***The Crystal Cage [portrait of Berenice]*** c. 1934–67
Collection of Richard L. Feigen, New York

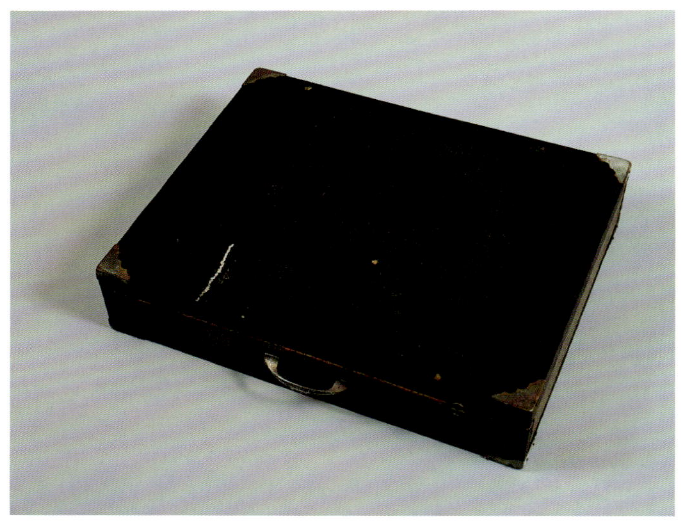

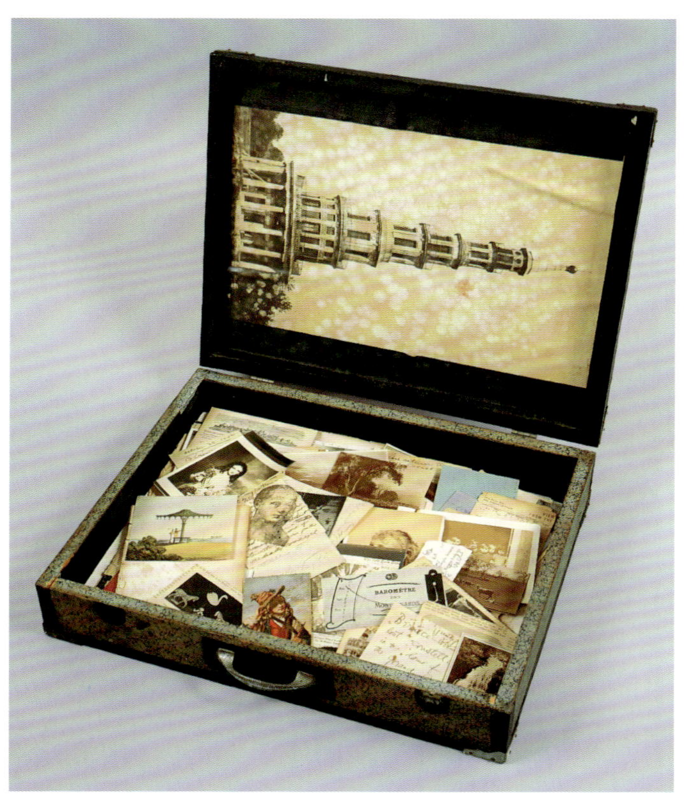

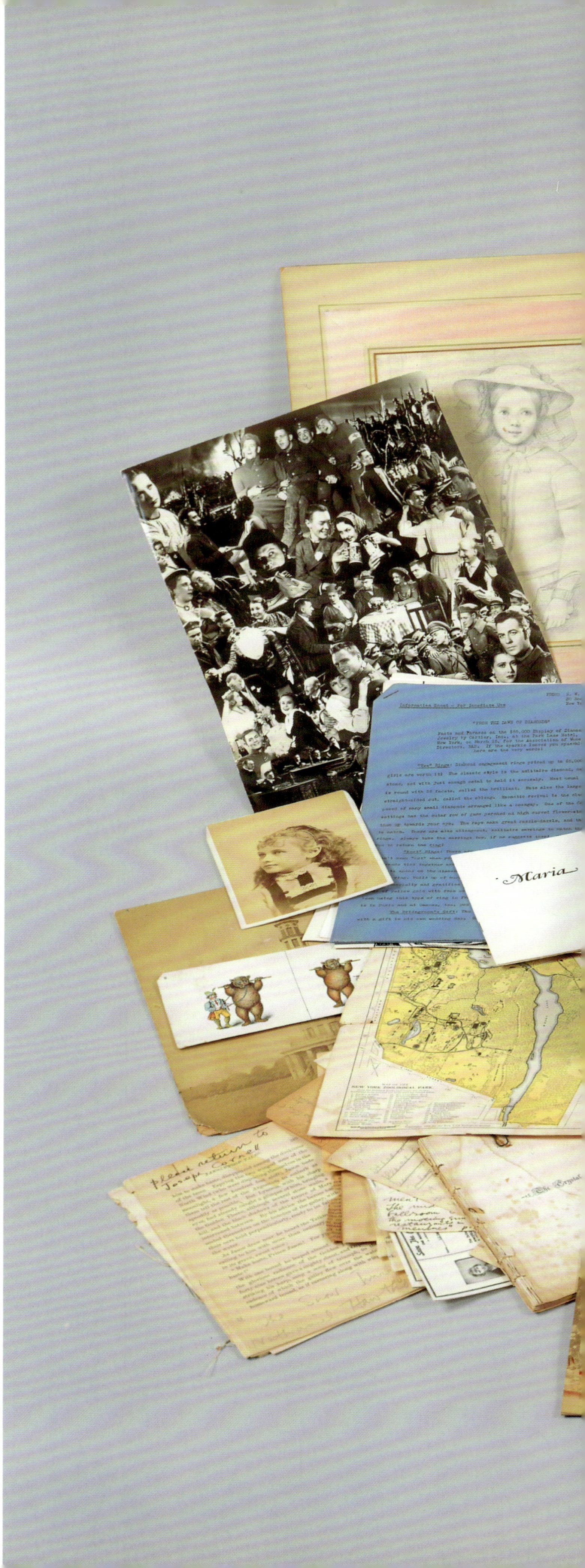

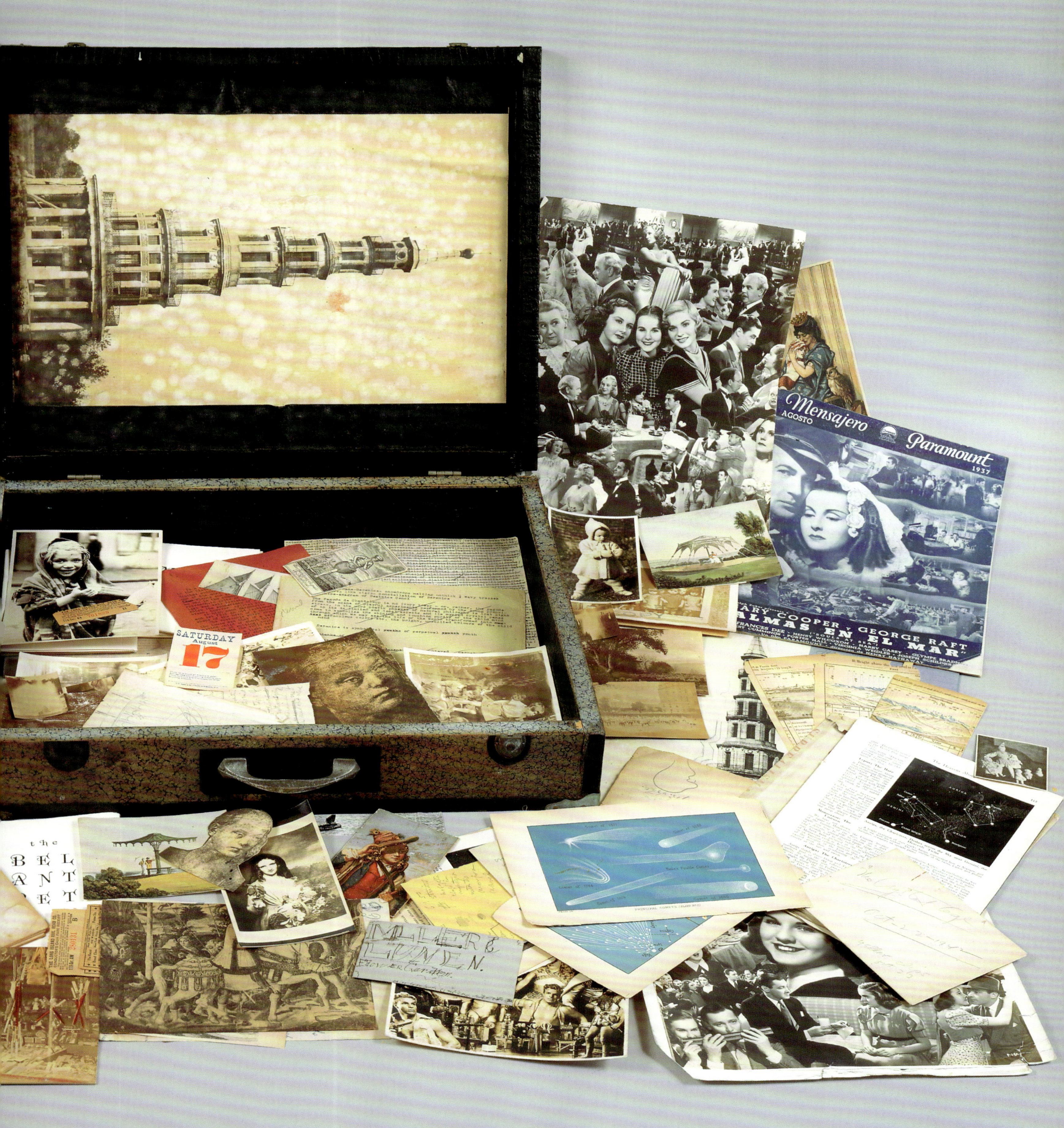
Mensajero
AGOSTO
Paramount
1937
GEORGE RAFT
ALMAS EN EL MAR
SATURDAY
August
17

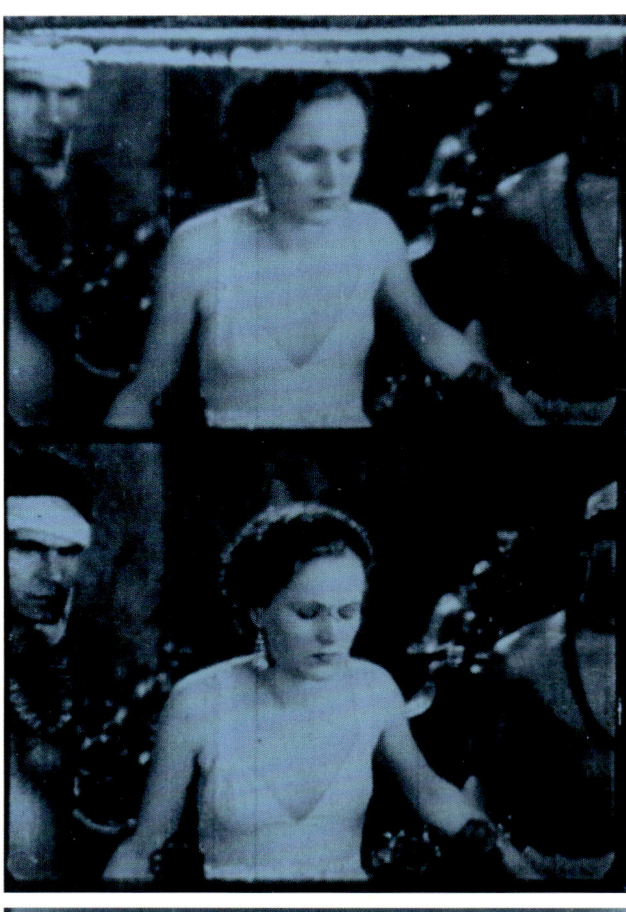

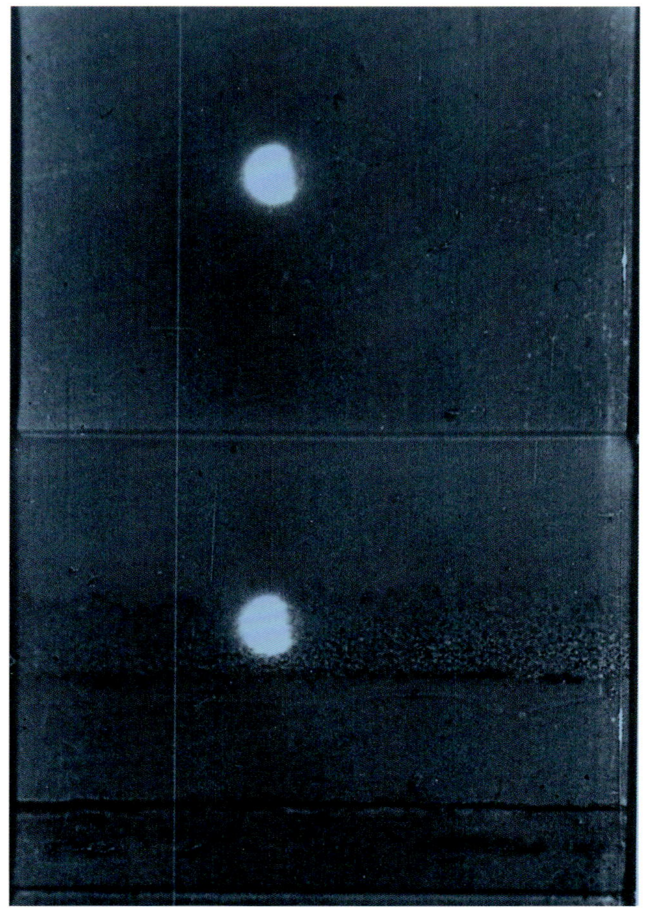

55 Stills from *Rose Hobart* c. 1936
Anthology Film Archives, New York

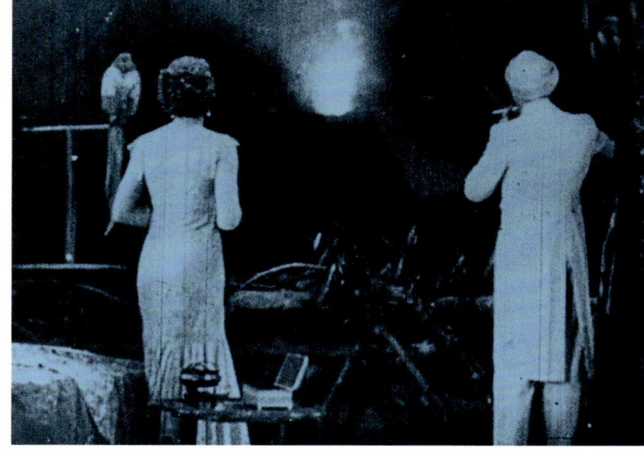

56 ***Object (Hotel Theatricals by the Grandson of Monsieur Phot Sunday Afternoons)*** 1940
Yokohama Museum of Art

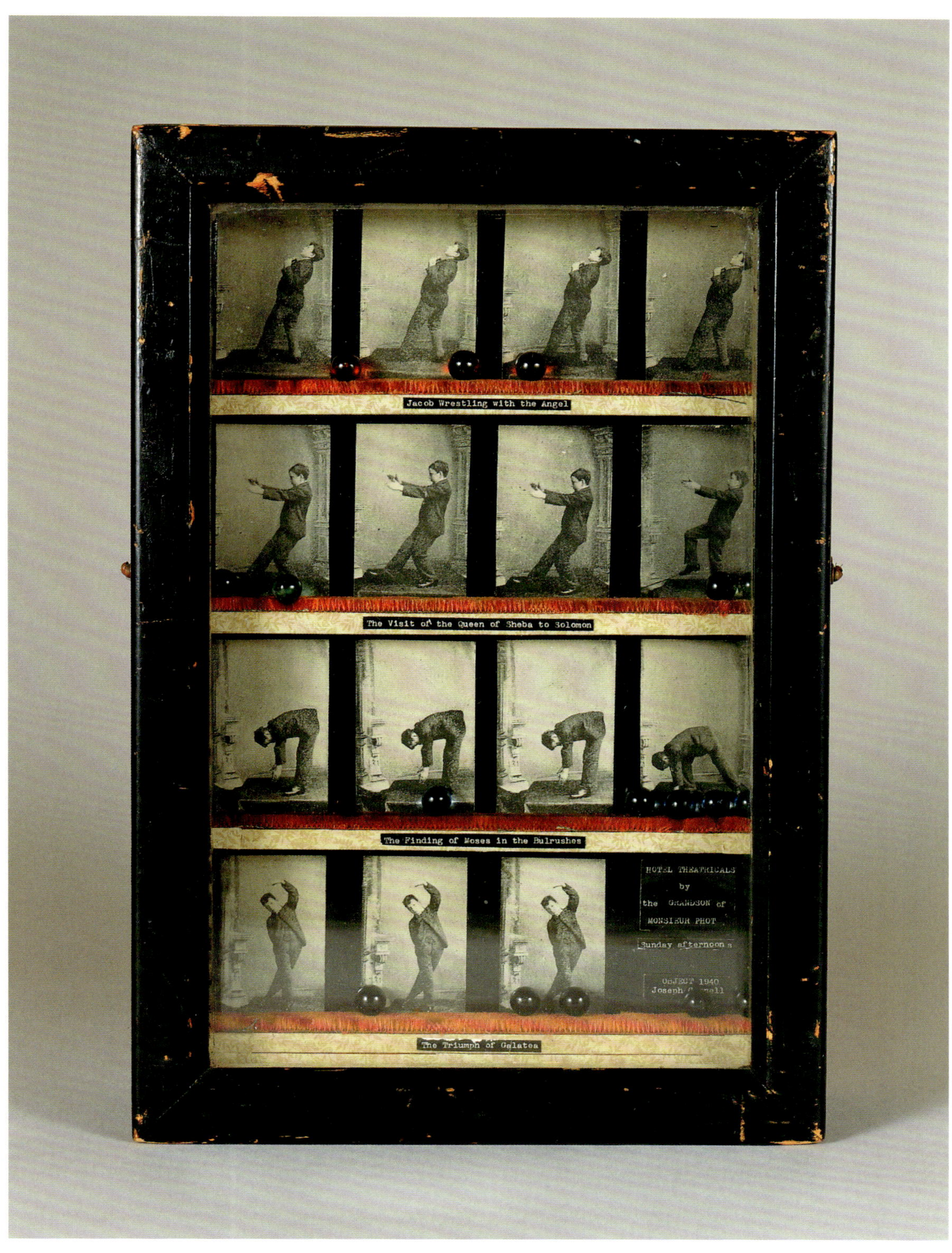

57 **Untitled [Hommage to the Romantic Ballet]** c. 1940–42
Private collection

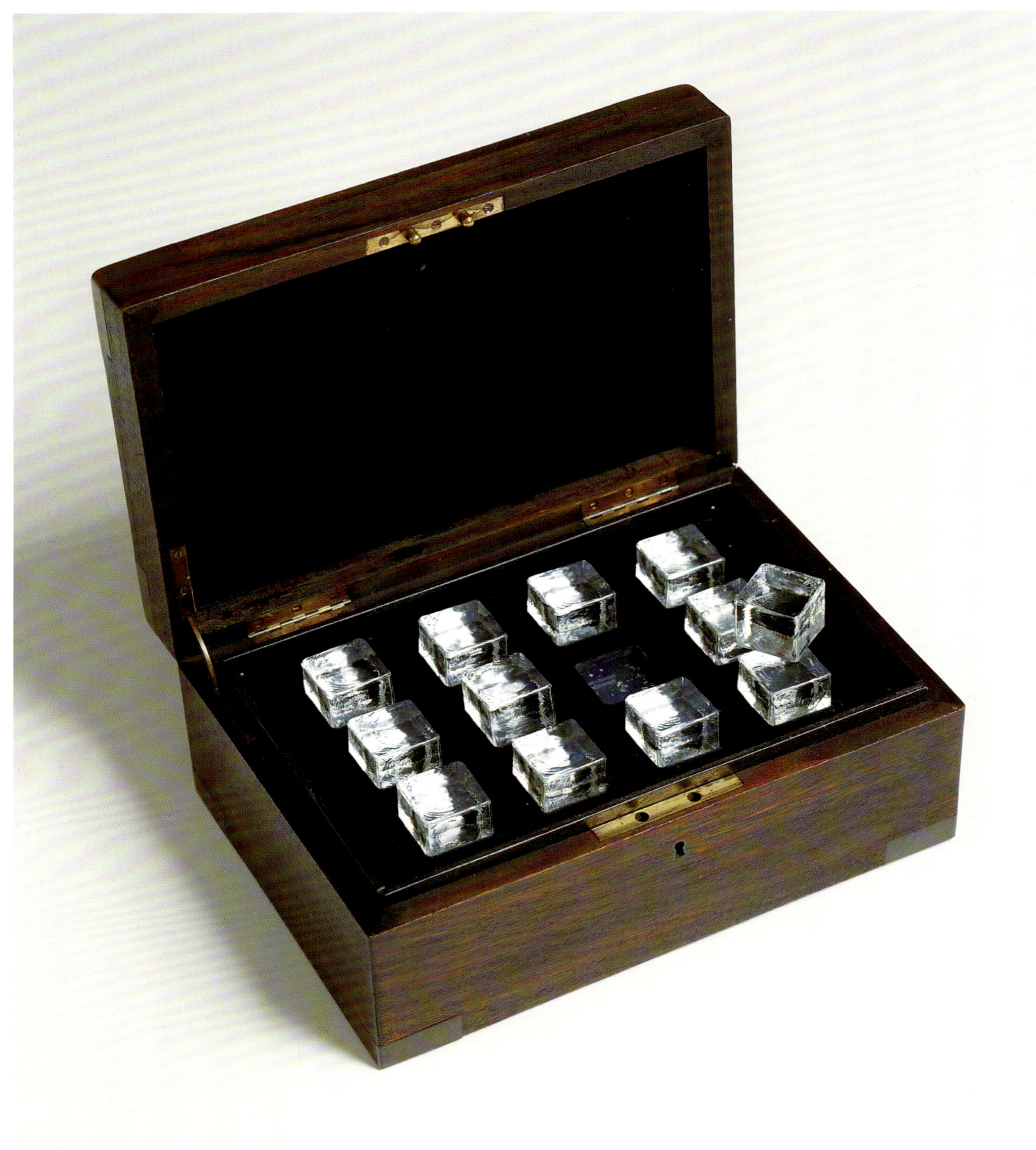

58 Untitled Object *[Mona Lisa]* c. 1940–42
The Joseph and Robert Cornell Memorial Foundation

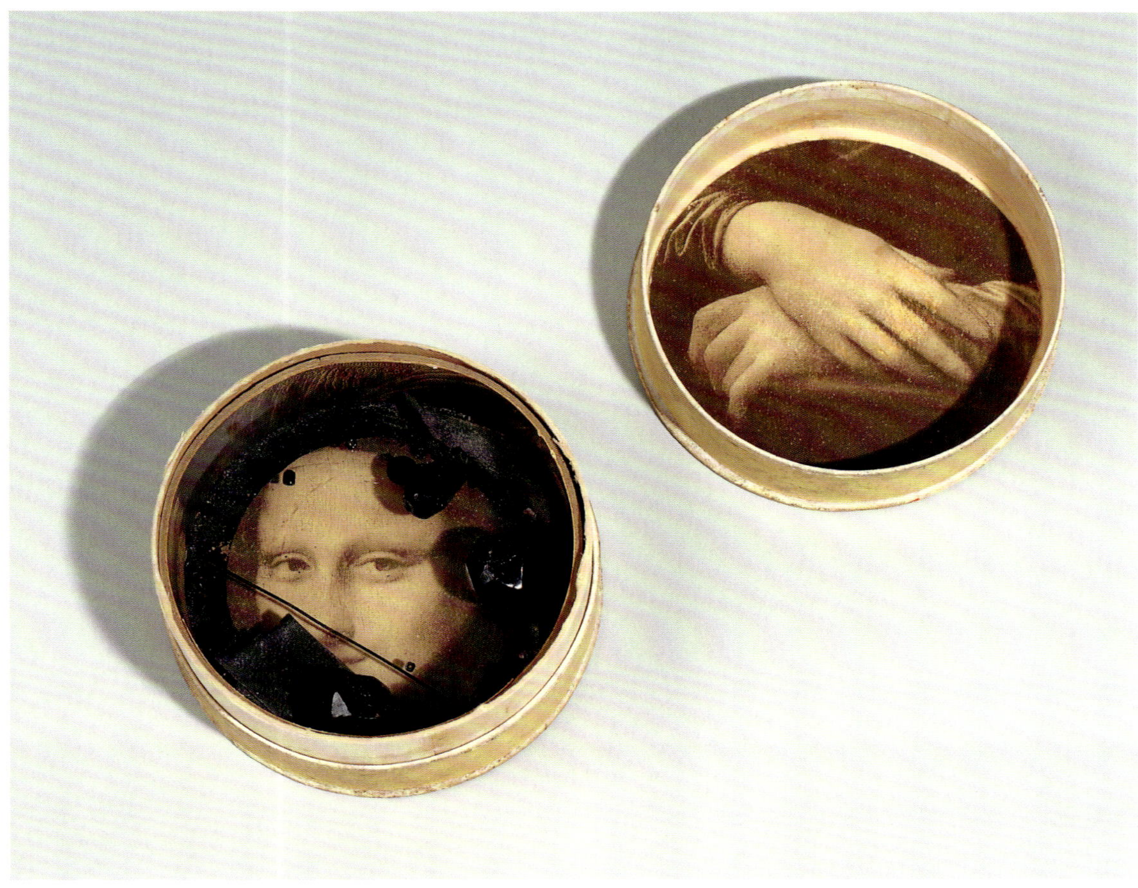

59 ***Portrait of Ondine*** c. 1940–late 1960s
National Museum of American Art, Smithsonian Institution.
Gift of The Joseph and Robert Cornell Memorial Foundation

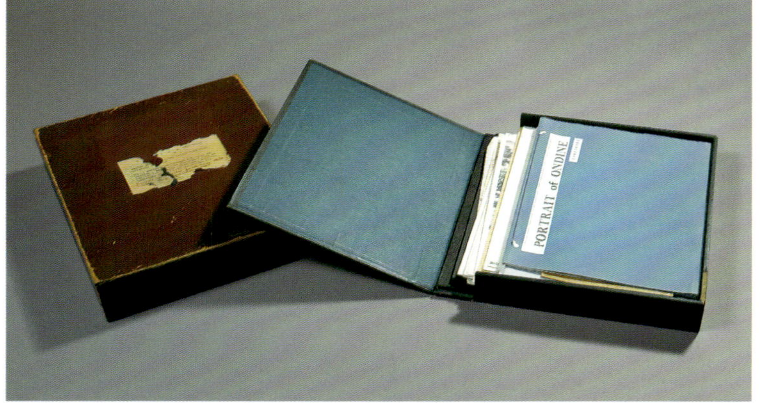

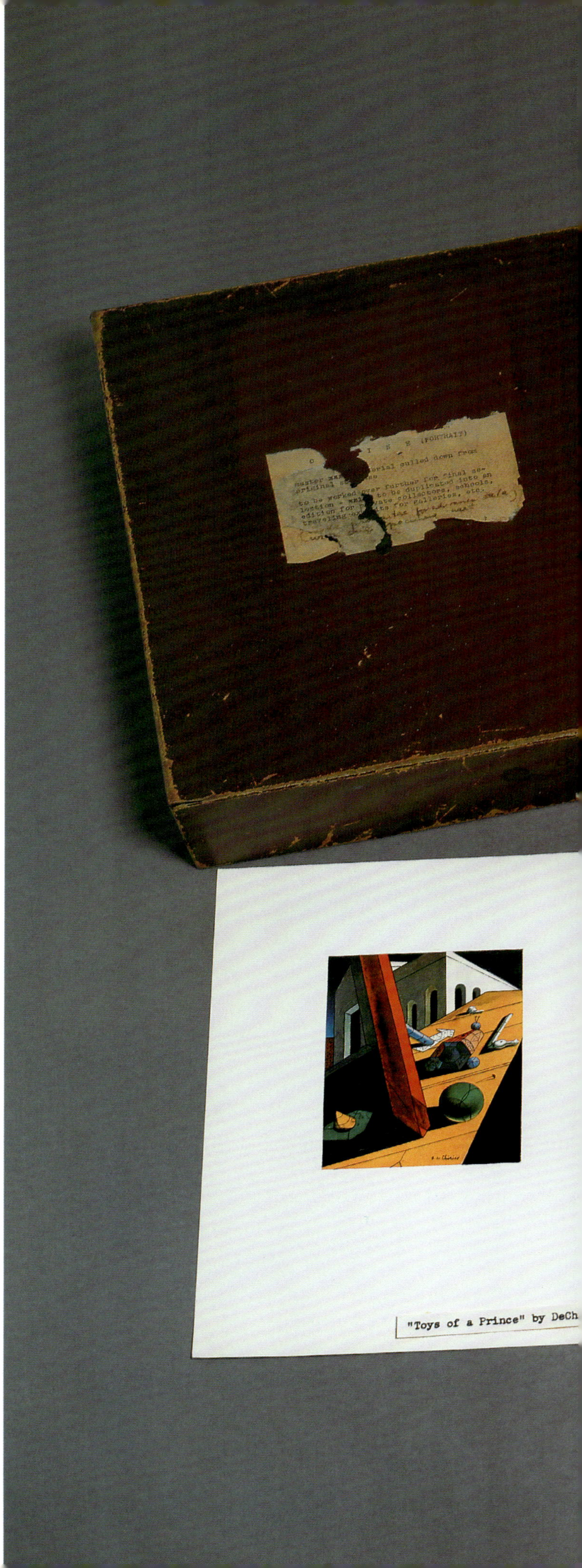

PORTRAIT of ONDINE

CONTINUED

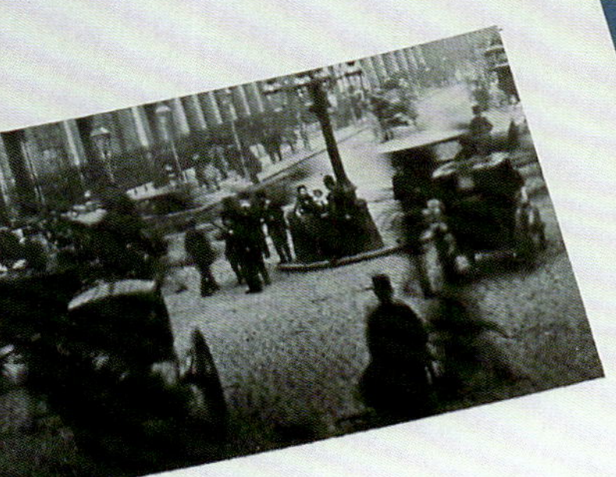

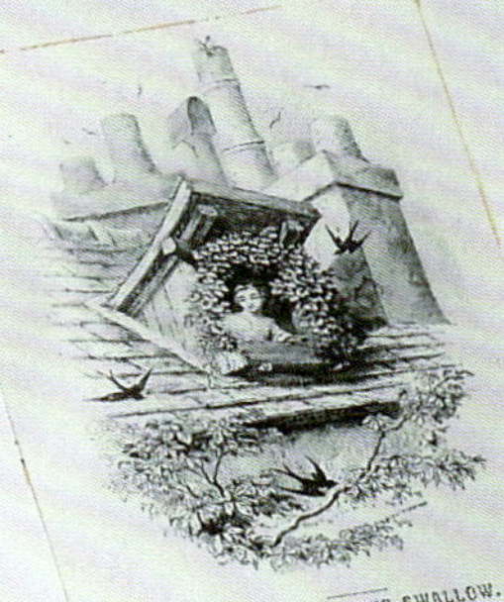

MIGRATIONS — THE SWALLOW.

BEAUTÉS DE L'OPÉRA

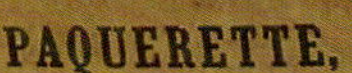

PAQUERETTE,

DE

MM. THÉOPHILE GAUTIER ET SAINT-LÉON,

Musique de M. BENOIST;

Décorations de MM. DESPLECHINS, CAMBON et THIERRY.

Représenté sur le Théâtre de l'Opéra, le 15 janvier 1851.

PRIX : 1 FRANC.

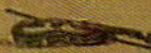

PARIS.

Mme Ve JONAS,

ÉDITEUR-LIBRAIRE DU THÉATRE DE L'OPÉRA;
PASSAGE DU GRAND-CERF, 32, ET RUE MANDAR, 4.

TRESSE, PALAIS-NATIONAL, GALERIE DE CHARTRES, 1 ET 3.

1851

" Out of the darkness, if I happen to call back the image of Fanny, up rises suddenly from a gulf of forty years a rose in June; or, if I think for an instant of the rose in June, up rises the heavenly face of Fanny. One after the other, like the antiphonies in the choral service, rise Fanny and the rose in June, then back again the rose inJune and Fanny. Then come both together, as in a chorus- roses and Fannies, Fannies and roses, without end, thick as blossoms in paradise. Then comes a venerable crocodile in a royal livery of scarlet and gold with sixteen capes; and the crocodile is driving four-in-hand from the box of the Bath Mall. And suddenly, we upon the mail are pulled up by a mighty dial, sculptured with the hours, that mingle with the heavens and the heavenly host. Then all at once we are arrived at Marlborough forest, amongst the lovely households of the roe-deer; the deer and fawns retire into the dewy thickets; the thickets are rich with roses; once again the roses call up the sweet countenance of Fanny; and she, being the granddaughter of a crocodile, awakens a dreadful host of semi-legendary animals - griffins, dragons, basilisks, sphinxes - till at length the whole vision of fighting images crowds into one towering armorial shield, a vast emblazonry of human charities and human loveliness that have perished, but quartered heraldically with unutterable and demoniac natures; whilst over all rises, as a surmounting crest, one fair female hand, with the forefinger pointing, in sweet, sorrowing admonition, upwards to heaven, where is sculptured the eternal writing which proclaims the frailty of earth and her children."

excerpt from THE ENGLISH MAIL COACH
by Thomas De Quincey

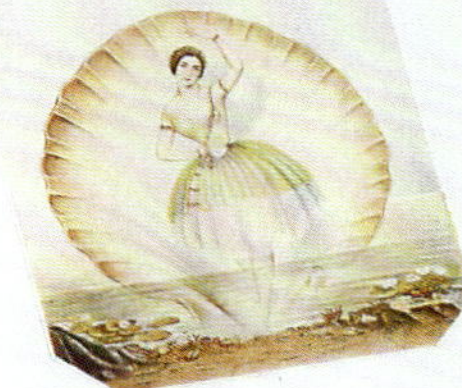

Fanny Cerrito in ONDINE

60 **Exhibition announcement for "Exhibition of Objects (Bilboquet) by Joseph Cornell"** 1939
Joseph Cornell Study Center, National Museum of American Art, Smithsonian Institution. Gift of Mr. and Mrs. John A. Benton

61 **Exhibition announcement for "Joseph Cornell: Exhibition of Objects"** 1940
Collection of Dr. and Mrs. M. Michael Eisenberg

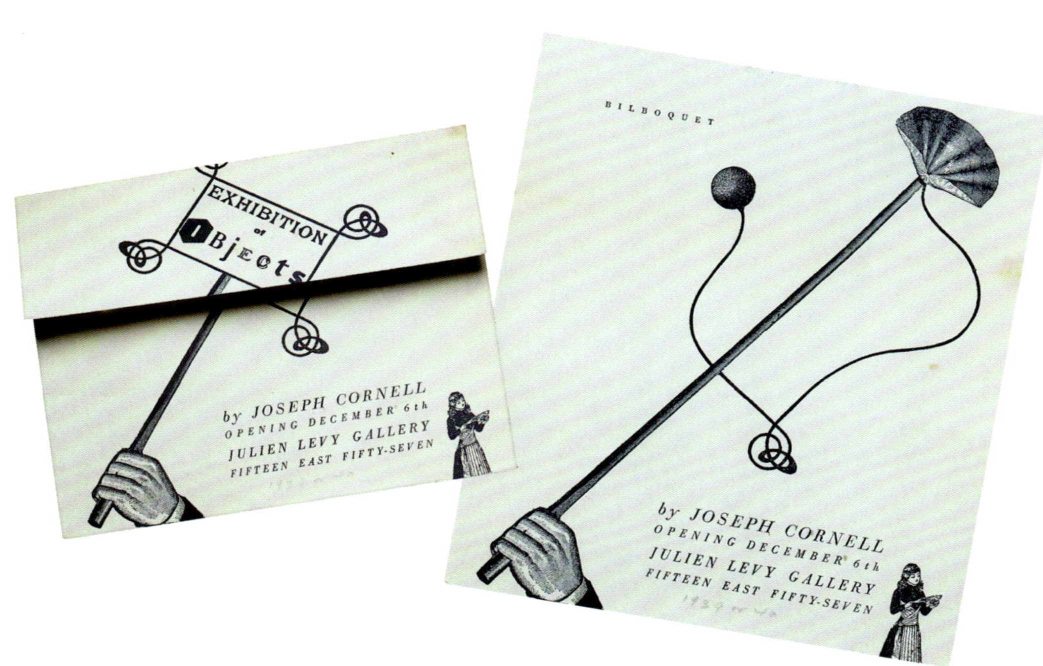

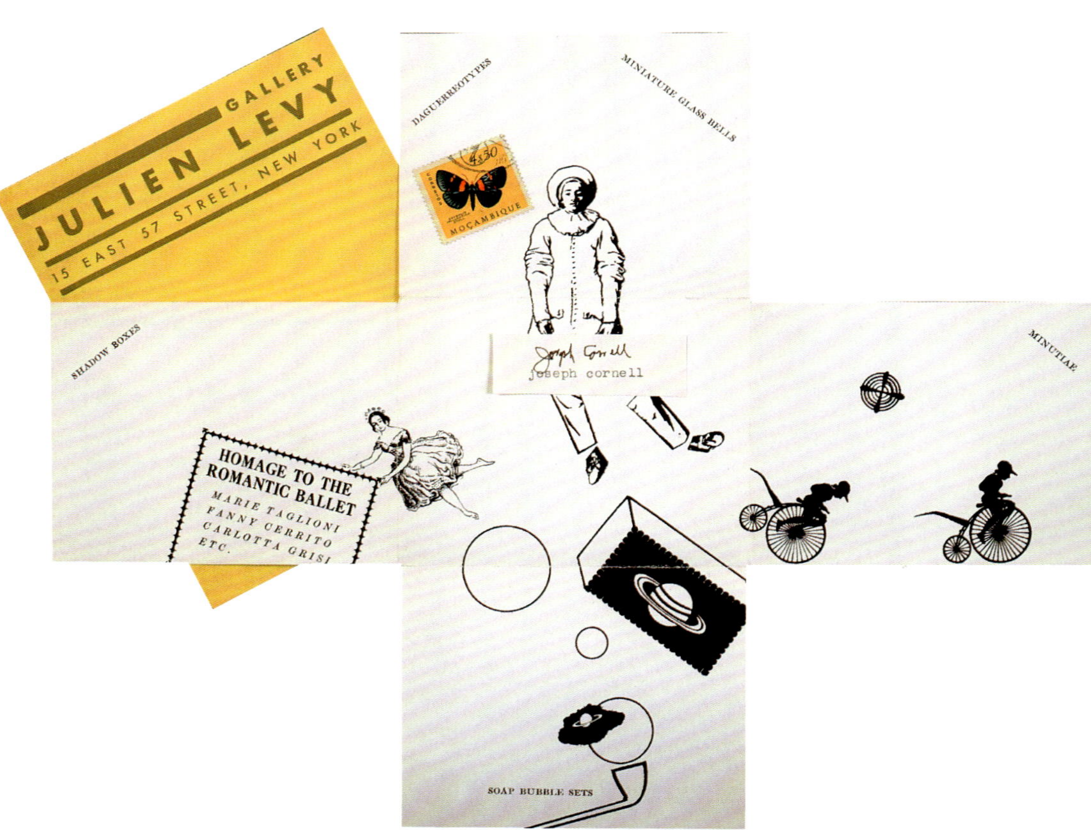

62 ***Object*** 1940
The Joseph and Robert Cornell Memorial Foundation

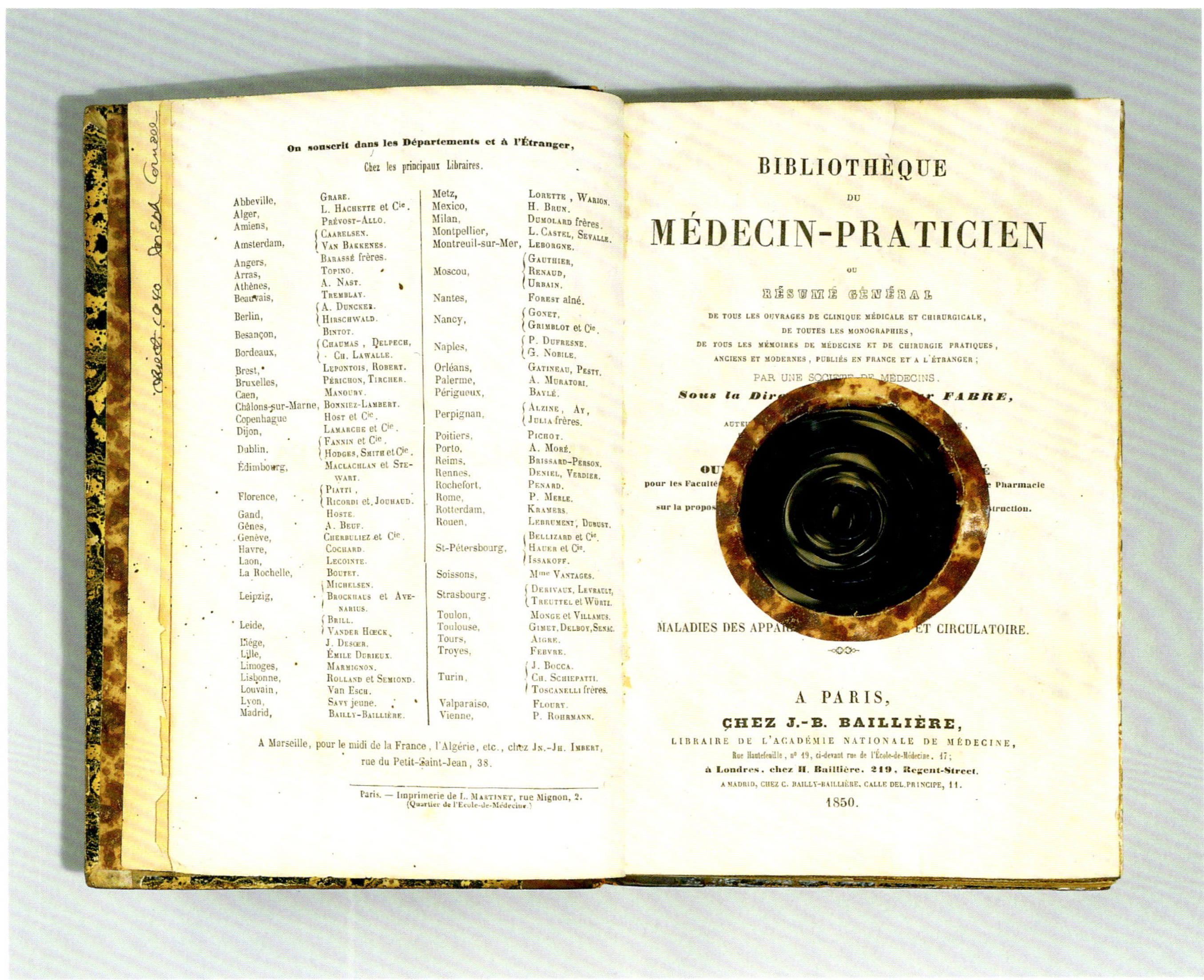

63 Joseph Cornell and unidentified photographer
Untitled (preparatory photomontage for *"Enchanted Wanderer": Excerpt from a Journey Album for Hedy Lamarr*) 1941
Joseph Cornell Study Center, National Museum of American Art, Smithsonian Institution. Gift of Mr. and Mrs. John A. Benton

64 *"Enchanted Wanderer": Excerpt from a Journey Album for Hedy Lamarr* 1941–42
Joseph Cornell Study Center, National Museum of American Art, Smithsonian Institution. Gift of Mr. and Mrs. John A. Benton

View   Page 3

"ENCHANTED WANDERER"

★ Excerpt from a Journey Album for Hedy Lamarr ★

By
JOSEPH CORNELL

Among the barren wastes of the talking films there occasionally occur passages to remind one again of the profound and suggestive power of the silent film to evoke an ideal world of beauty, to release unsuspected floods of music from the gaze of a human countenance in its prison of silver light. But aside from evanescent fragments unexpectedly encountered, how often is there created a superb and magnificent imagery such as brought to life the portraits of Falconetti in "Joan of Arc," Lillian Gish in "Broken Blossoms," Sibirskaya in "Menilmontant," and Carola Nehrer in "Dreigroschenoper?"

And so we are grateful to Hedy Lamarr, the enchanted wanderer, who again speaks the poetic and evocative language of the silent film, if only in whispers at times, beside the empty roar of the sound track. Amongst screw-ball comedy and the most superficial brand of clap-trap drama she yet manages to retain a depth and dignity that enables her to enter this world of expressive silence.

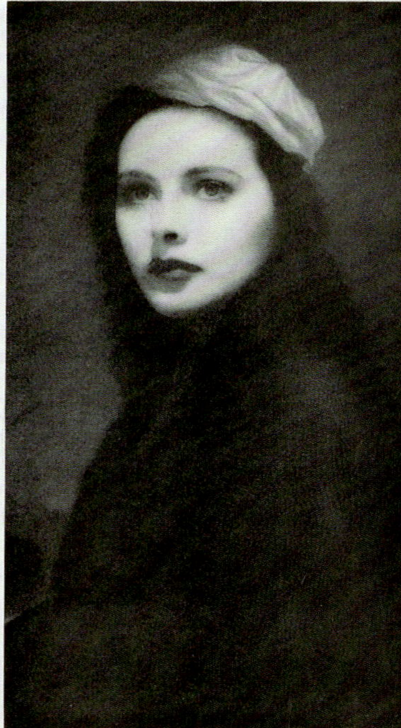

★

Who has not observed in her magnified visage qualities of a gracious humility and spirituality that with circumstance of costume, scene, or plot conspire to identify her with realms of wonder, more absorbing than the artificial ones, and where we have already been invited by the gaze that she knew as a child.

Her least successful roles will reveal something unique and intriguing — a disarming candor, a naivete, an innocence, a desire to please, touching in its sincerity. In implicit trust she would follow in whatsoever direction the least humble of her audience would desire.

*"She will walk only when not bid to, arising from her bed of nothing, her hair of time falling to the shoulder of space. If she speak, and she will only speak if not spoken to, she will have learned her words yesterday and she will forget them to-morrow, if to-morrow come, for it may not."**

(Or the contrasted and virile mood of "Comrade X" where she moves through the scenes like the wind with a storm-swept beauty fearful to behold).

* * * * * * * *

At the end of "Come Live With Me" the picture suddenly becomes luminously beautiful and imaginative with its nocturnal atmosphere and incandescence of fireflies, flashlights, and an aura of tone as rich as the silver screen can yield. Her arms and shoulders always covered, our gaze is held to her features, where her eyes glow dark against the pale skin and her earrings gleam white against the black hair. Her tenderness finds a counterpart in the summer night. In a world of shadow and subdued light she moves, clothed in a white silk robe trimmed with dark fur, against dim white walls. Through the window fireflies are seen in the distance twinkling in woods and pasture. There is a long shot (as from the ceiling) of her enfolded in white covers, her eyes glisten in the semi-darkness like the fireflies. The reclining form of Snow White was not protected more lovingly by her crystal case than the gentle fabric of light that surrounds her. A closer shot shows her against the whiteness of the pillows, while a still closer one shows an expression of ineffable tenderness as, for purposes of plot, she presses and intermittently lights a flashlight against her cheek, as though her features were revealed by slow-motion lightning.

In these scenes it is as though the camera had been presided over by so many apprentices of Caravaggio and Georges de la Tour to create for her this benevolent chiaroscuro . . . the studio props fade out and there remains a drama of light of the *tenebroso* painters . . . the thick night of Caravaggio dissolves into a tenderer, more star-lit night of the Nativity . . . she will become enveloped in the warmer shadows of Rembrandt . . . a youth of Giorgione will move through a drama evolved from the musical images of "Also Sprach Zarathustra" of Strauss, from the opening sunburst of sound through the subterranean passages into the lyrical soaring of the theme (apotheosis of compassion) and into the mystical night . . . the thunderous procession of the festival clouds of Debussy passes . . . the crusader of "Comrade X" becomes the "Man in Armor" of Carpaccio . . . in the half lights of a prison dungeon she lies broken in spirit upon her improvised bed of straw, a hand guarding her tear-stained features . . . the bitter heartbreak gives place to a radiance of expression that lights up her gloomy surroundings . . . she has carried a masculine name in one picture, worn masculine garb in another, and with her hair worn shoulder length and gentle features like those portraits of Renaissance youths she has slipped effortlessly into the role of a painter herself . . . le chasseur d'images . . . out of the fullness of the heart the eyes speak . . . are alert as the eye of the camera to ensnare the subtleties and legendary loveliness of her world. . . .

[The title of this piece is borrowed from a biography of Carl Maria von Weber who wrote in the horn quartet of the overture to "Der Freischutz" a musical signature of the Enchanted Wanderer.]

* Parker Tyler

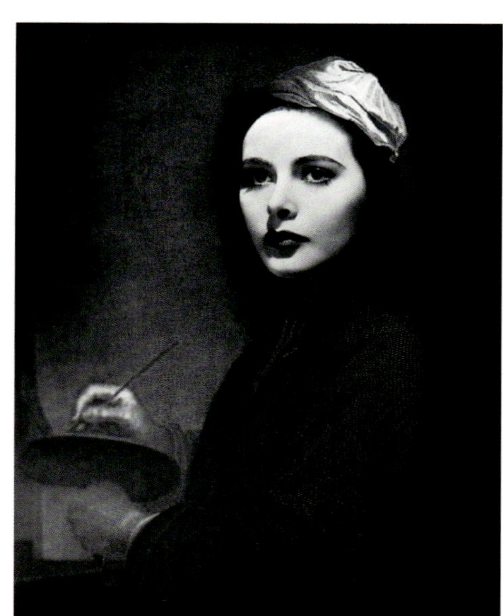

65 **Exhibition announcement for “Objects by Joseph Cornell; Marcel Duchamp: Box-Valise; Laurence Vail: Bottles”** 1942
The Young-Mallin Archive, New York. P. Guggenheim Papers

66 **Joseph Cornell with Marcel Duchamp and Yves Tanguy**
Exhibition announcement for “Through the Big End of the Opera Glass”: Marcel Duchamp, Yves Tanguy, Joseph Cornell” 1943
The Jean-Noël Herlin Archive, New York

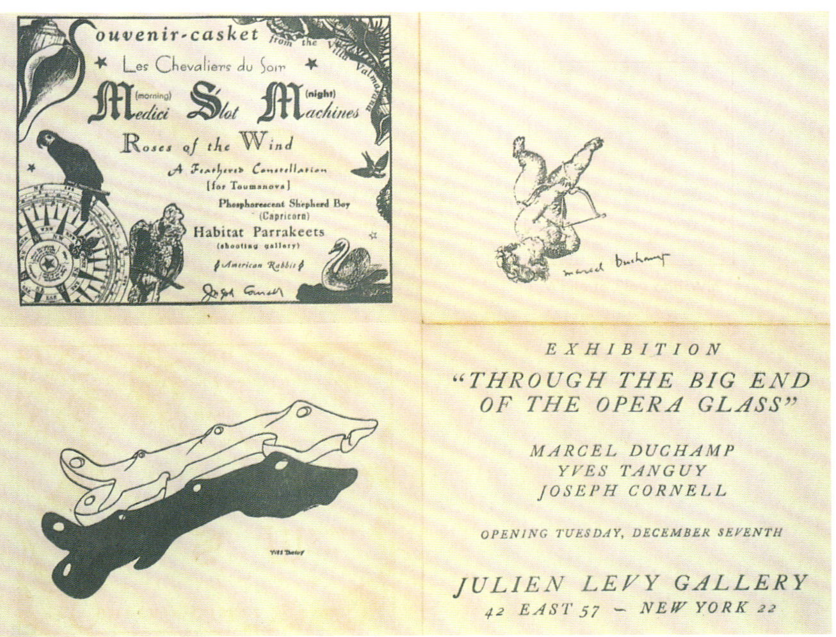

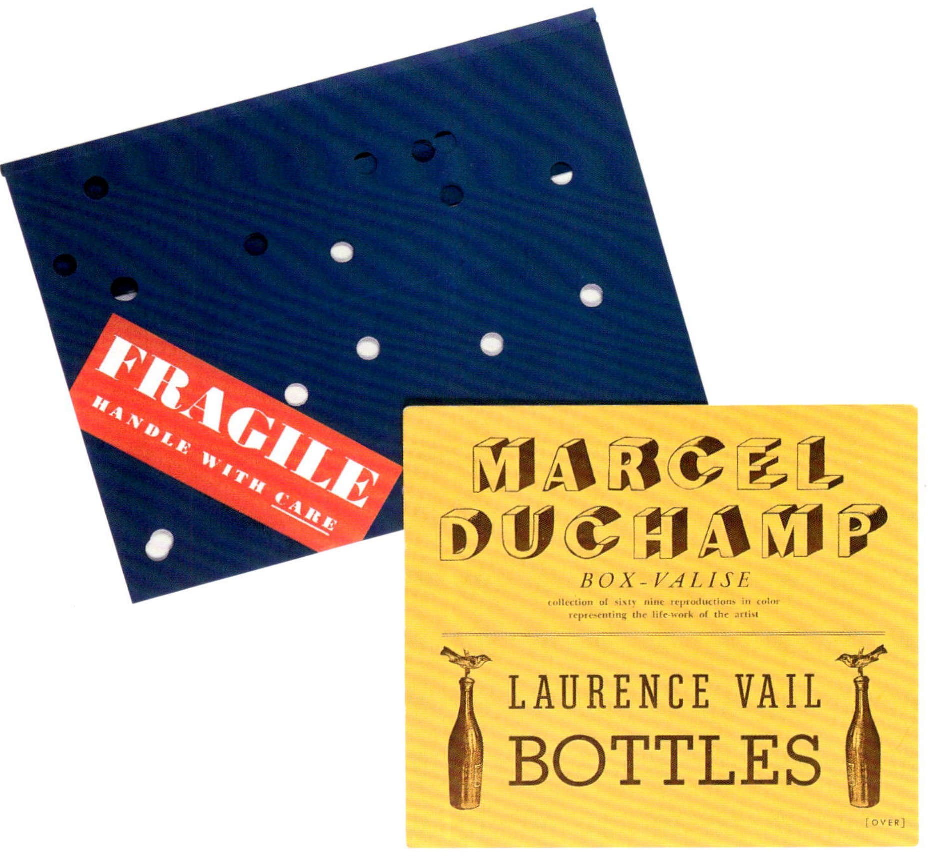

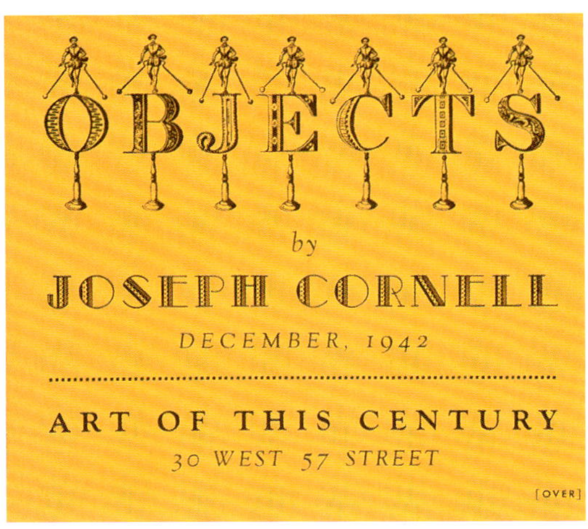

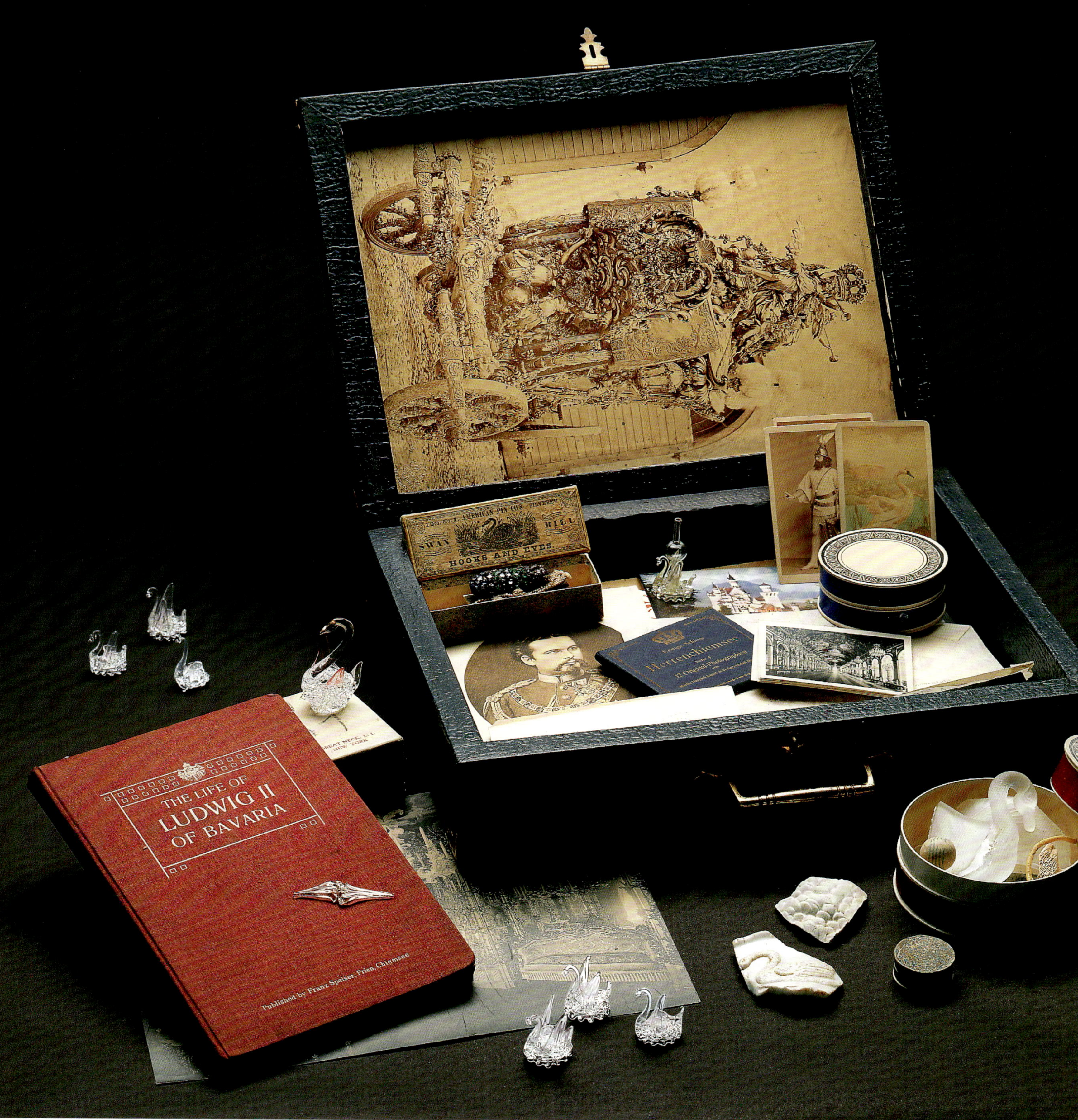
1 Gro. No. 1. AMERICAN PIN CO'S SILVERED
SWAN BILL
HOOKS AND EYES.
Herrenchiemsee
12 Original-Photographien
NEW YORK
THE LIFE OF
LUDWIG II
OF BAVARIA
Published by Franz Speiser, Prien, Chiemsee

67 Untitled (The Life of Ludwig II of Bavaria) c. 1941–52
Philadelphia Museum of Art.
Gift of The Joseph and Robert Cornell Memorial Foundation

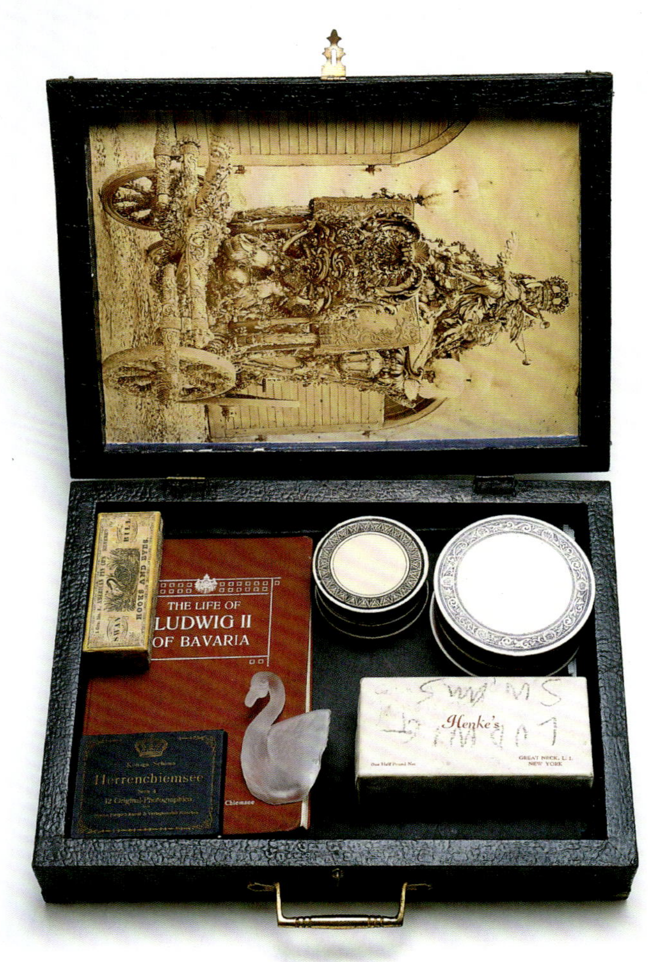

68 ***Mémoires inédits de Madame La Comtesse de G.*** c. 1942
[Unpublished Memoirs of Countess de G.]
The Joseph and Robert Cornell Memorial Foundation

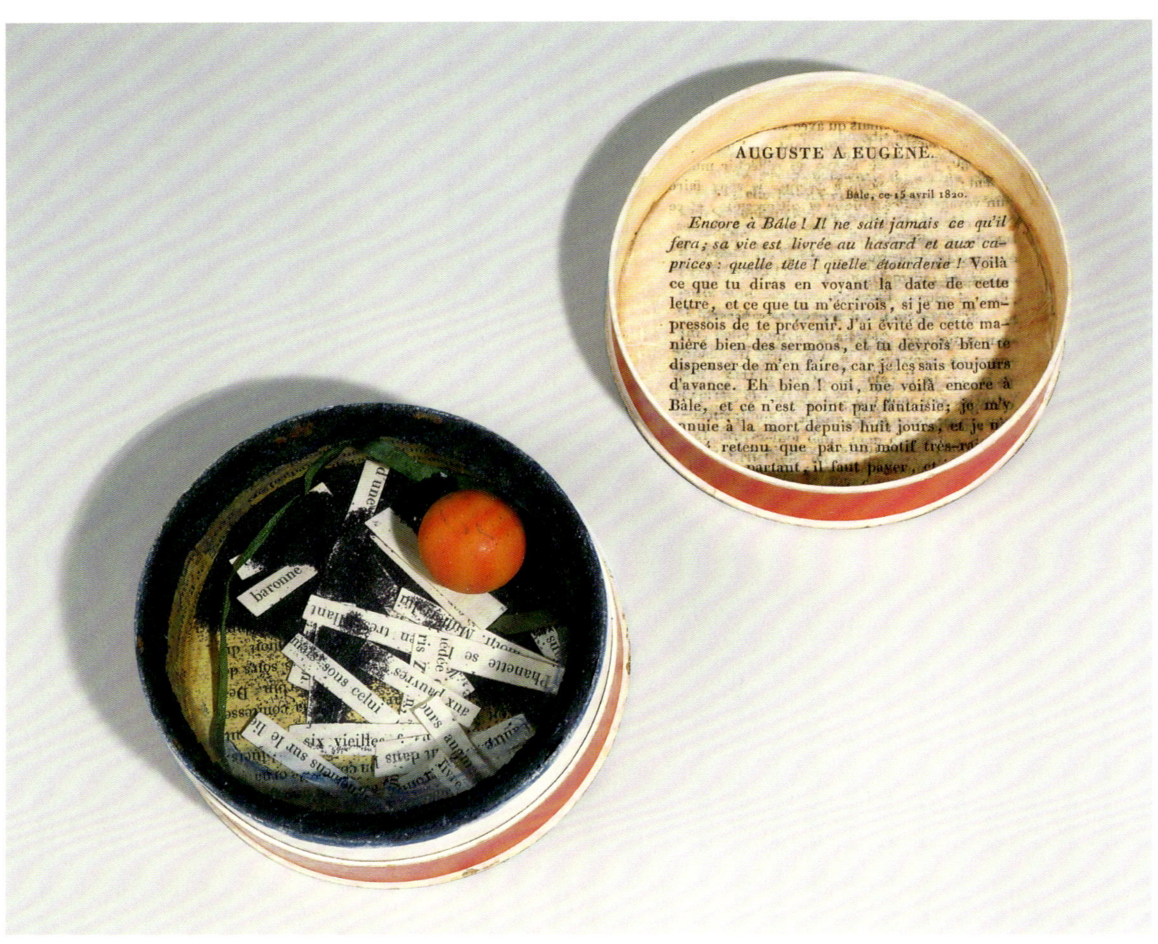

69 *Mémoires inédits de Madame de Rochejaquelein* 1943
[Unpublished Memoirs of Madame de Rochejaquelein]
San Francisco Museum of Modern Art.
Gift of Leo Castelli, Richard L. Feigen, and James Corcoran

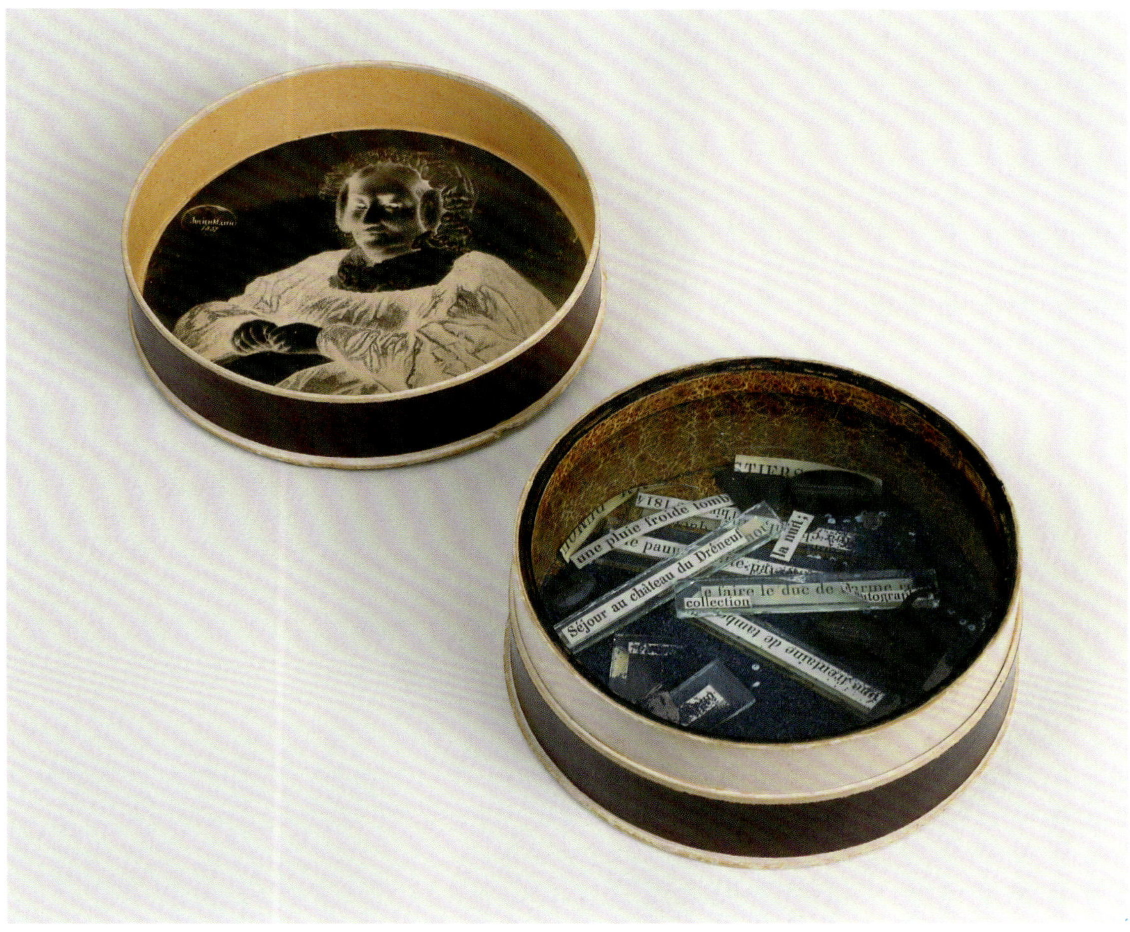

70 Untitled (Pharmacy) 1943
The Menil Collection, Houston. Gift of Alexander Iolas

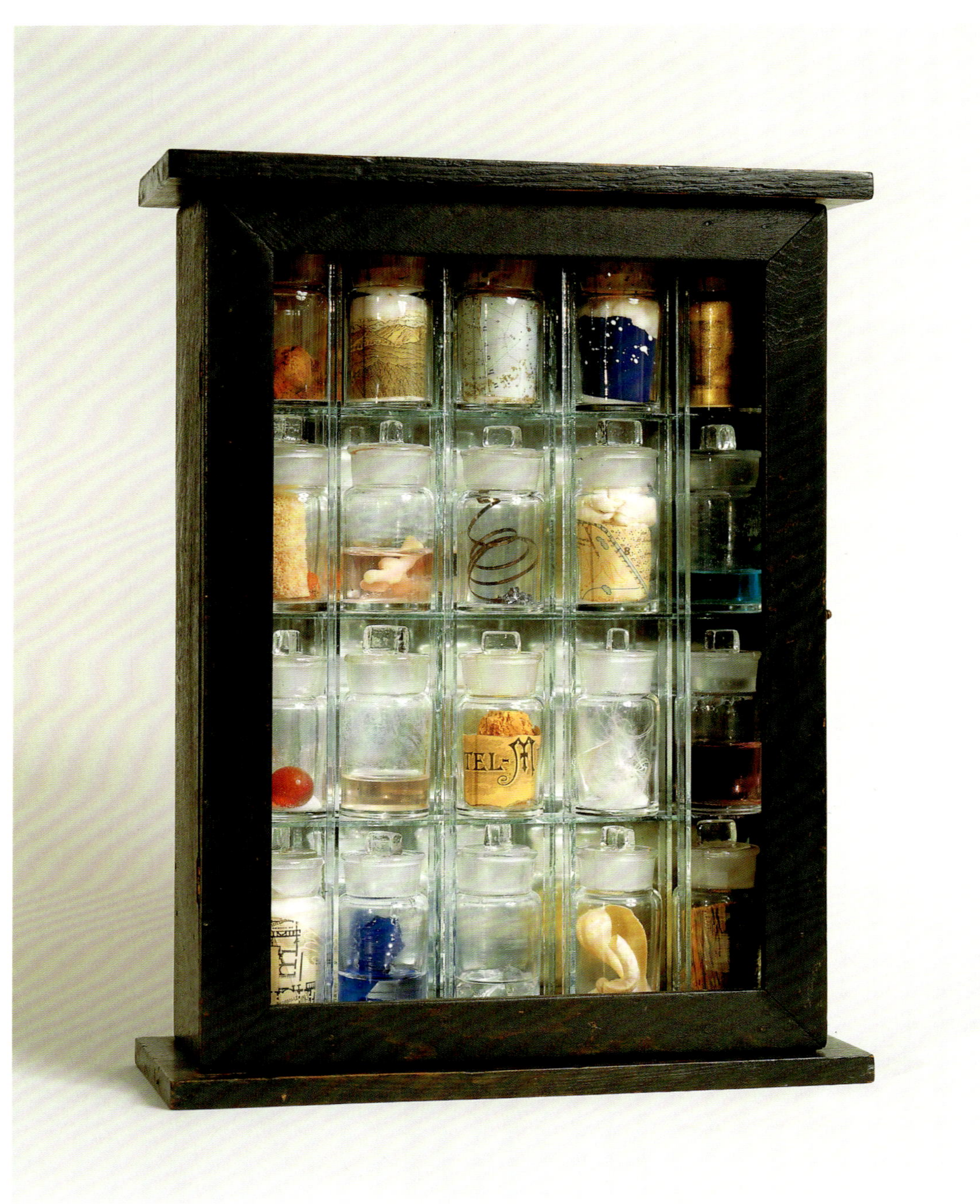

71 ***Object (Roses des Vents) [Object (Compass Roses)]*** 1942–53
The Museum of Modern Art, New York.
Mr. and Mrs. Gerald Murphy Fund

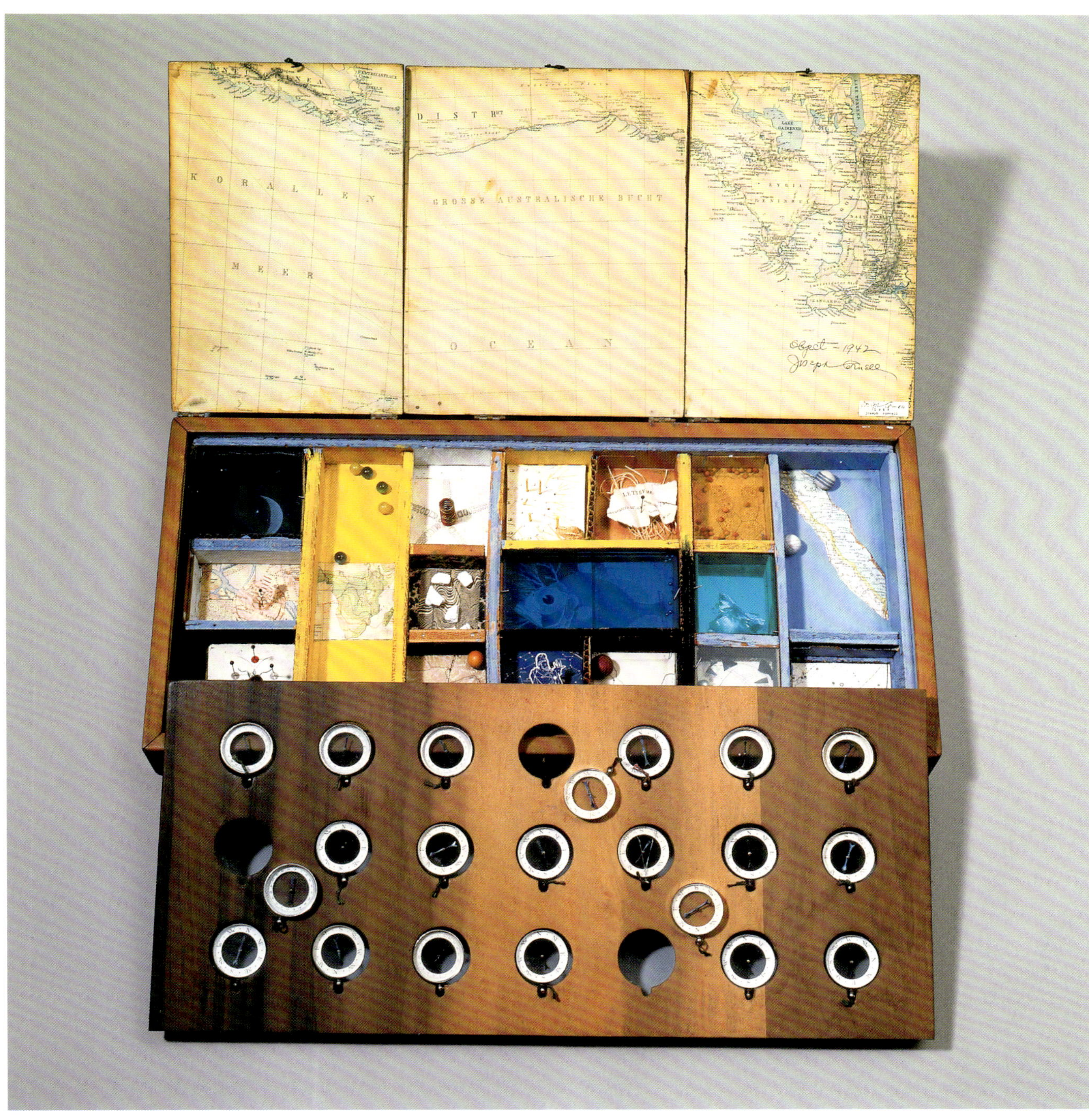

72.1 **Cover for *View* ["Americana Fantastica" issue]** 1943
The Menil Collection, Houston

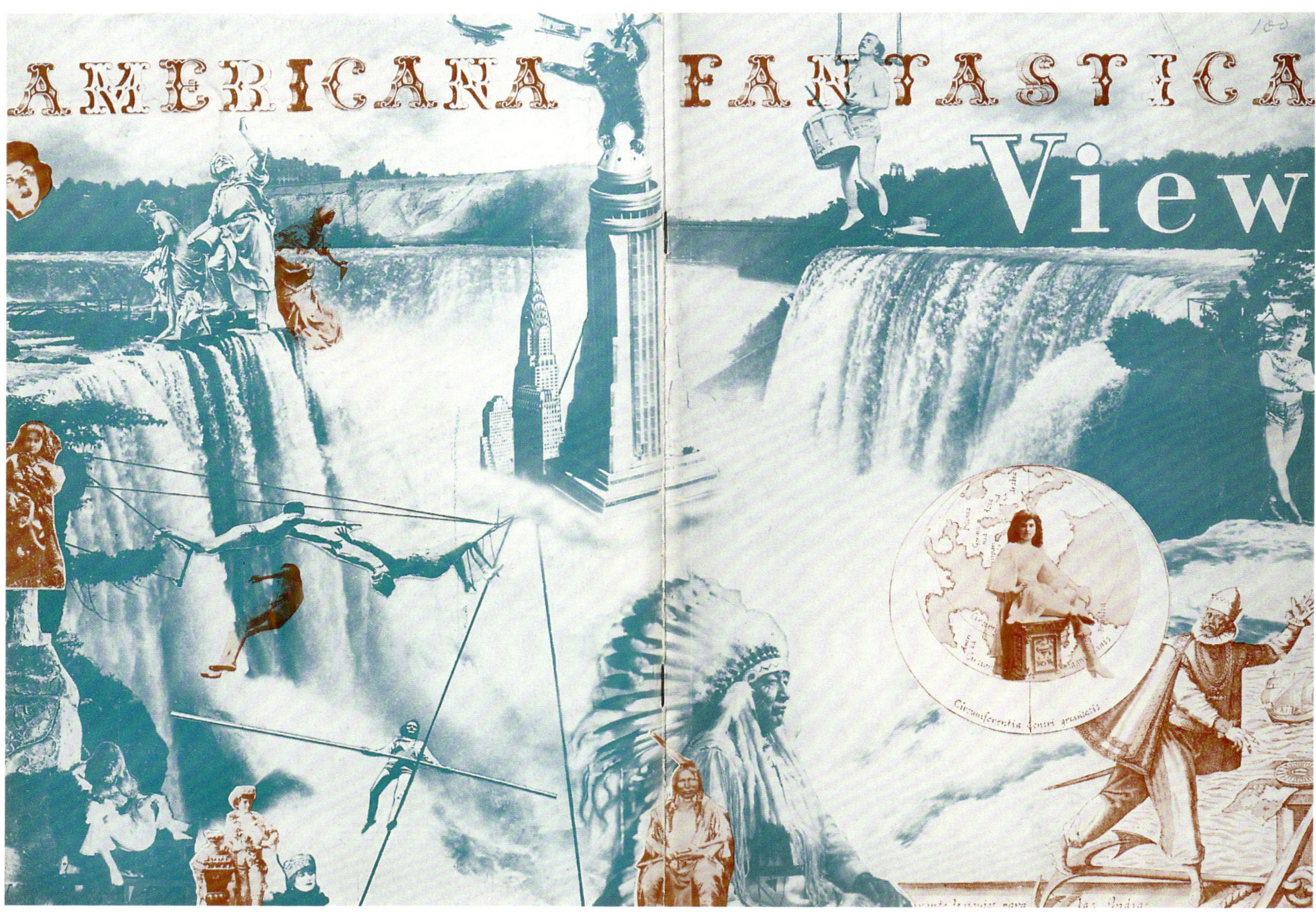

72.2 ***THE Crystal Cage [portrait of Berenice]*** **in** ***View*** **["Americana Fantastica" issue]** 1943
The Menil Collection, Houston

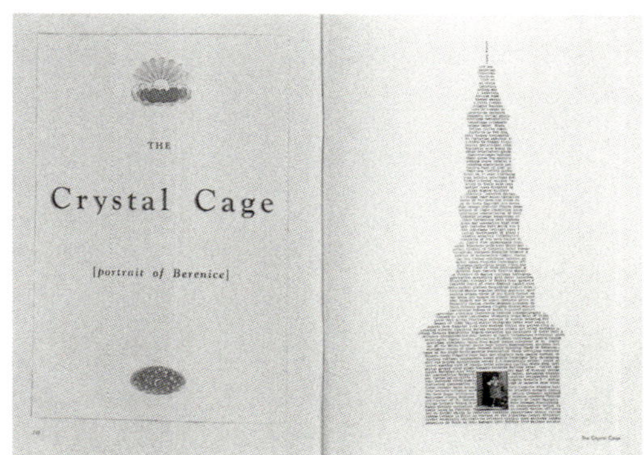
THE

Crystal Cage

[portrait of Berenice]

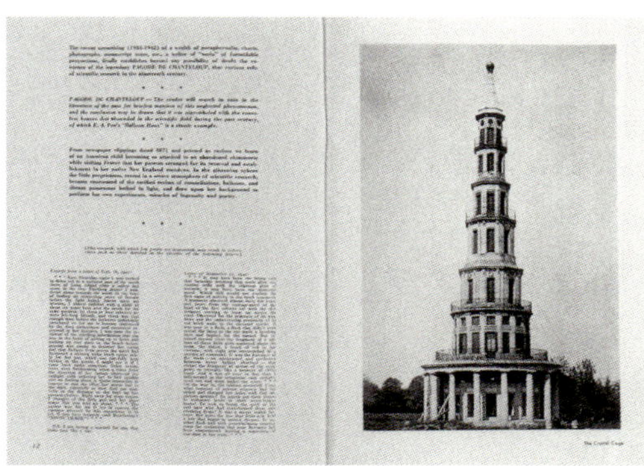

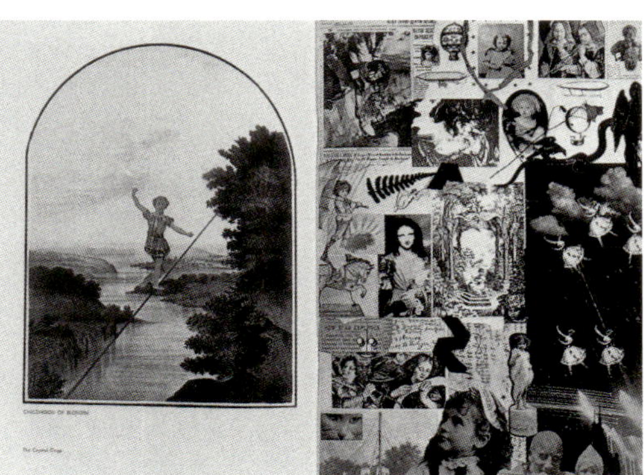

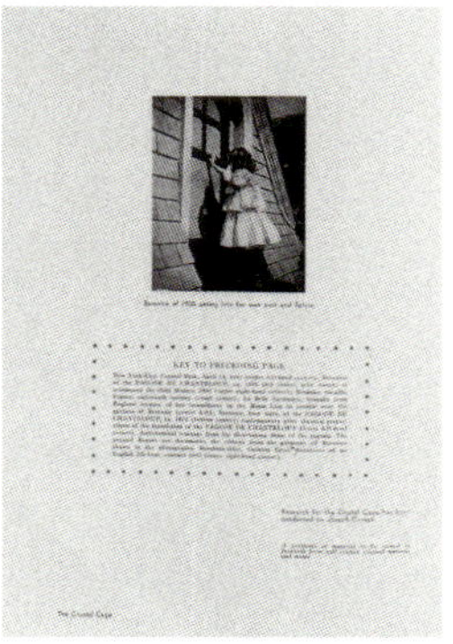

72.3 Collage from ***The Crystal Cage [portrait of Berenice]*** 1942 **reproduced in** ***View*** **["Americana Fantastica" issue]**
Collection of Richard L. Feigen, New York

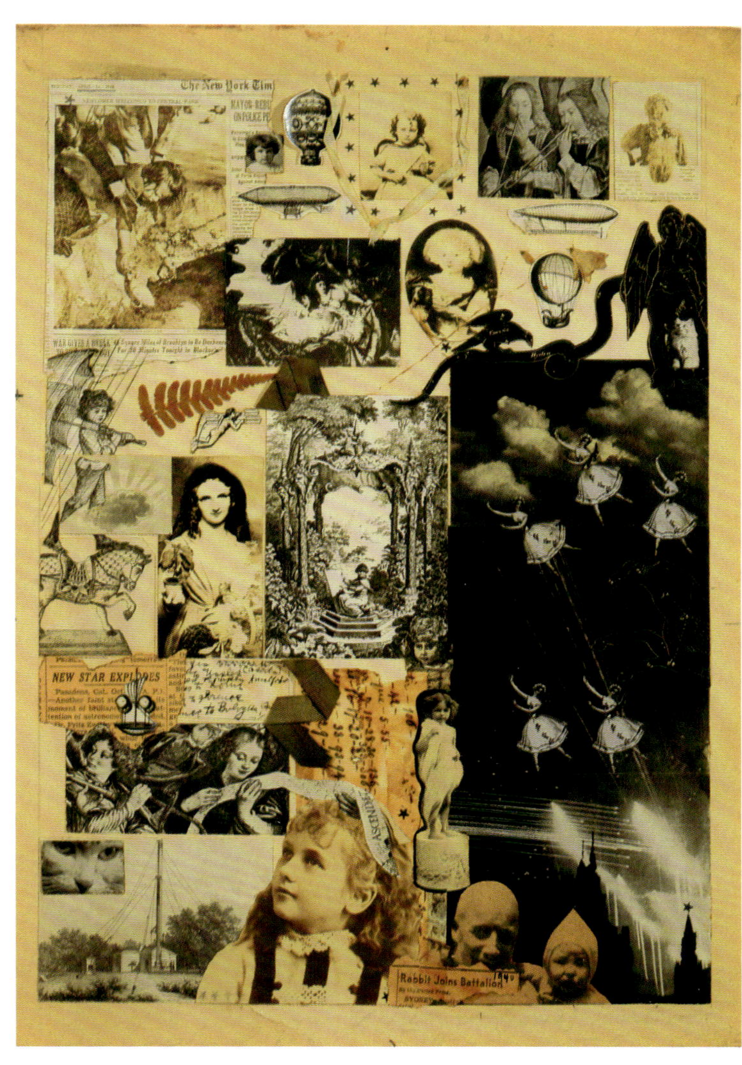

73 ***Beehive (Thimble Forest)*** 1943–48
Collection of Richard L. Feigen, New York

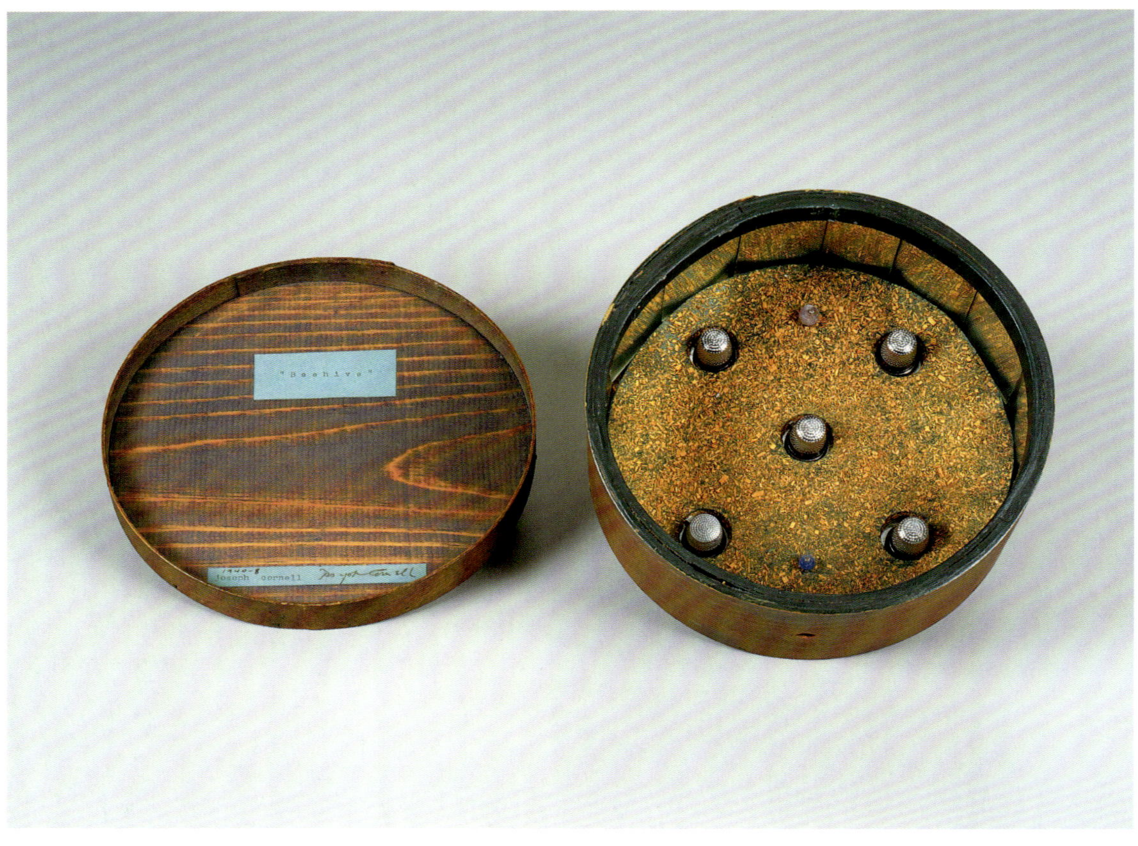

74 **Joseph Cornell and unidentified photographer**
3/4 Bird's-Eye View of 'A Watch-Case for Marcel Duchamp' 1944
Yale Collection of American Literature,
Beinecke Rare Book and Manuscript Library

75 **Joseph Cornell and unidentified photographer**
Untitled (preparatory photomontage for
***3/4 Bird's-Eye View of 'A Watch-Case for Marcel Duchamp'*)** c. 1944
Reproduced in *Arts Magazine* (December 1957): p. 26

76 ***GC 44*** c. 1944–70
Joseph Cornell Study Center, National Museum of American Art,
Smithsonian Institution. Gift of Mr. and Mrs. John A. Benton
pp. 194–95

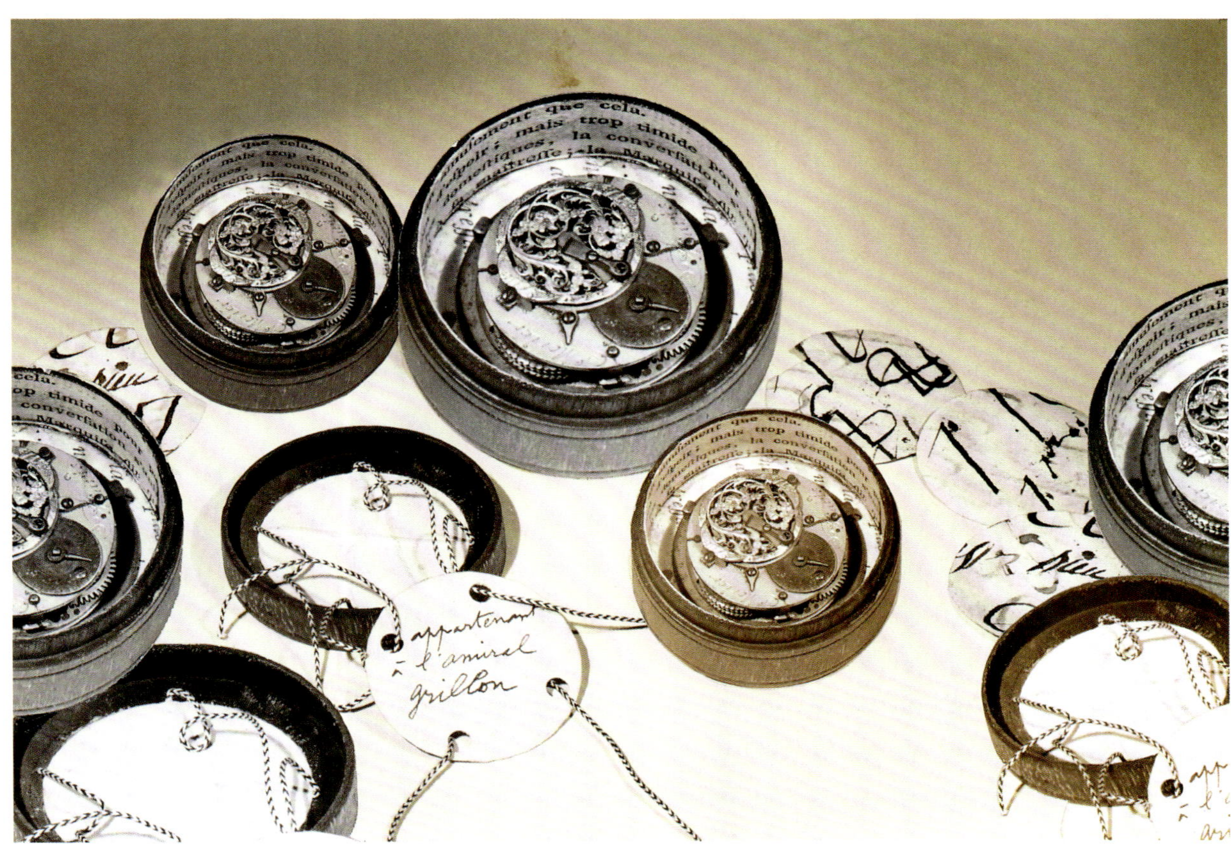

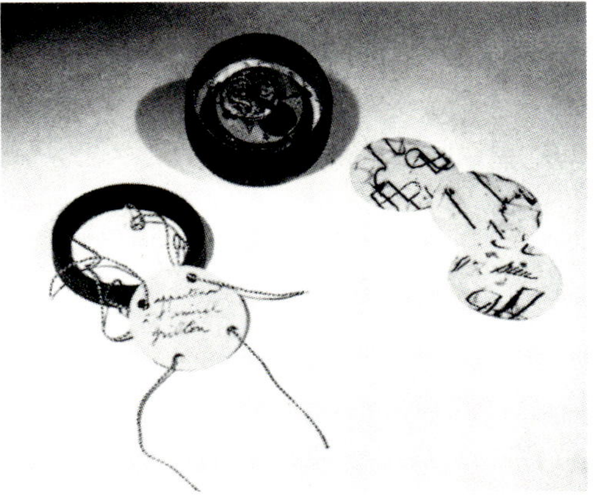

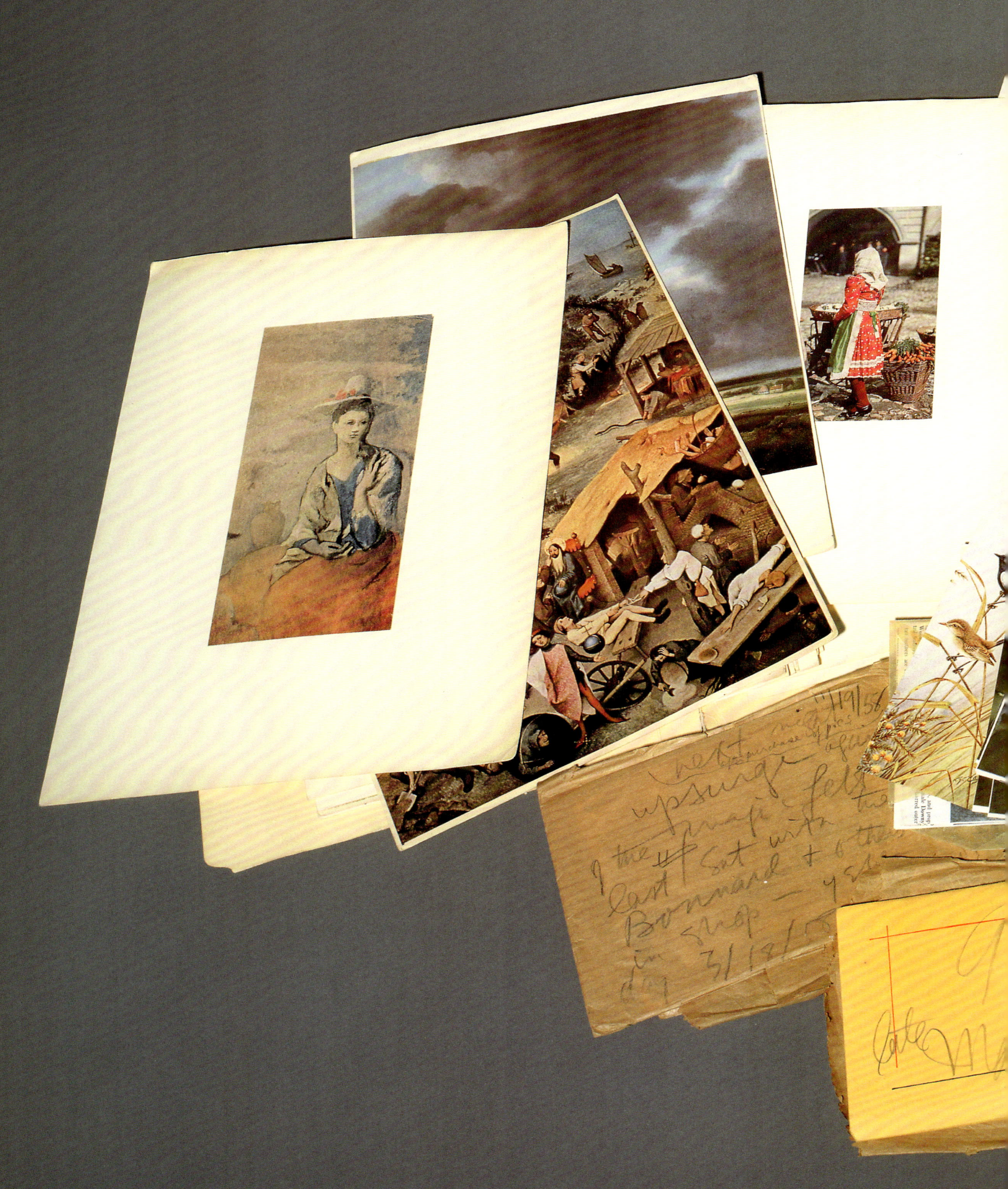

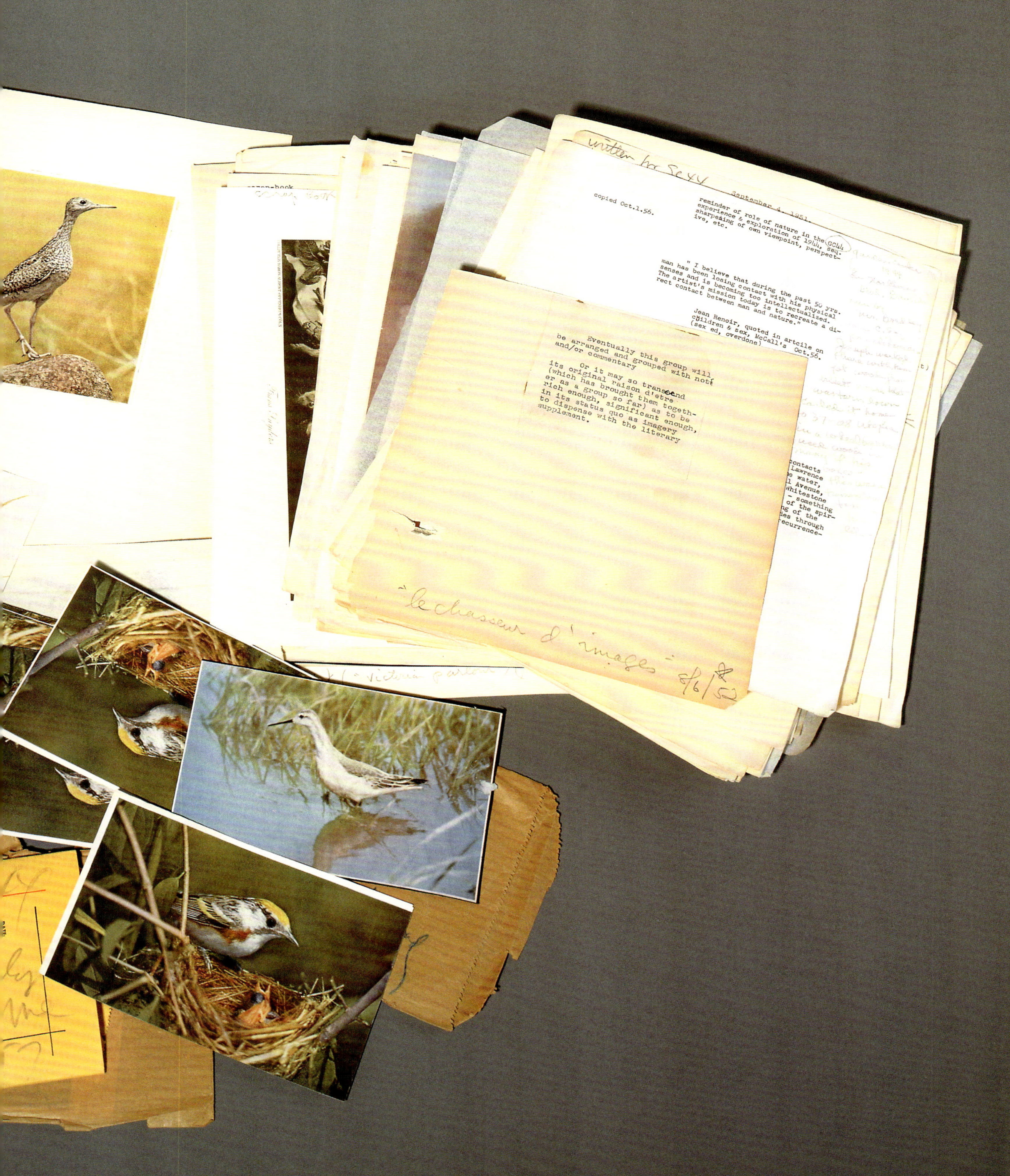
written for Sexy
September 4, 1951.
copied Oct.1.56.
reminder of role of nature in the GC44 experience & exploration of 1944, seq. sharpening of own viewpoint, perspective, etc.
" I believe that during the past 50 yrs. man has been losing contact with his physical senses and is becoming too intellectualized. The artist's mission today is to recreate a direct contact between man and nature."
Jean Renoir, quoted in artcile on children & sex, McCall's Oct.56. (sex ed, overdone)
Eventually this group will be arranged and grouped with notes and/or commentary
Or it may so transcend its original raison d'etre (which has brought them together as a group so far) as to be rich enough, significant enough, in its status quo as imagery to dispense with the literary supplement.
"le chasseur d'images" 8/6/52

77 *Palace* c. 1943
Collection of Christophe de Menil

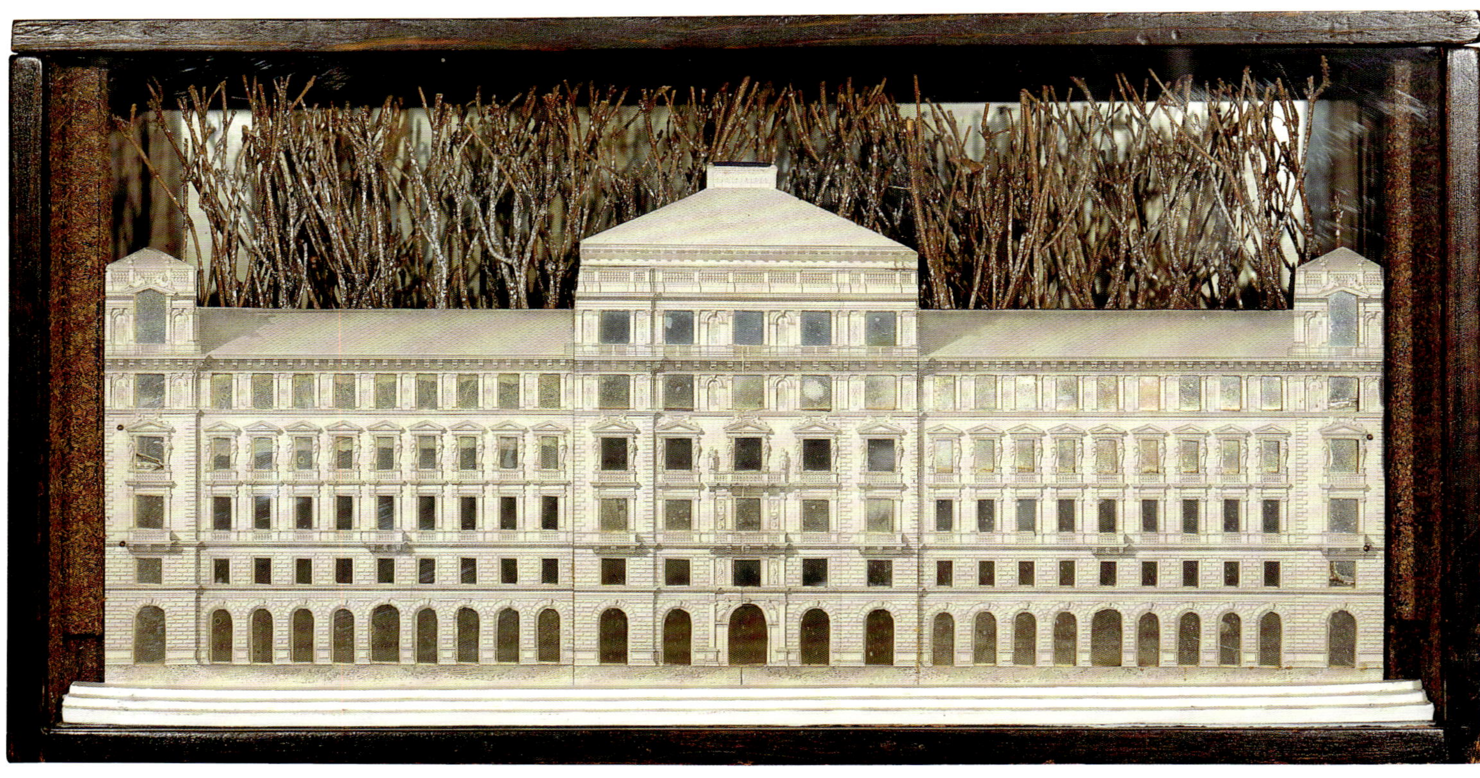

78 **Untitled (Pink Palace)** c. 1948
Collection of Mr. and Mrs. Robert Lehrman, Washington, D.C.

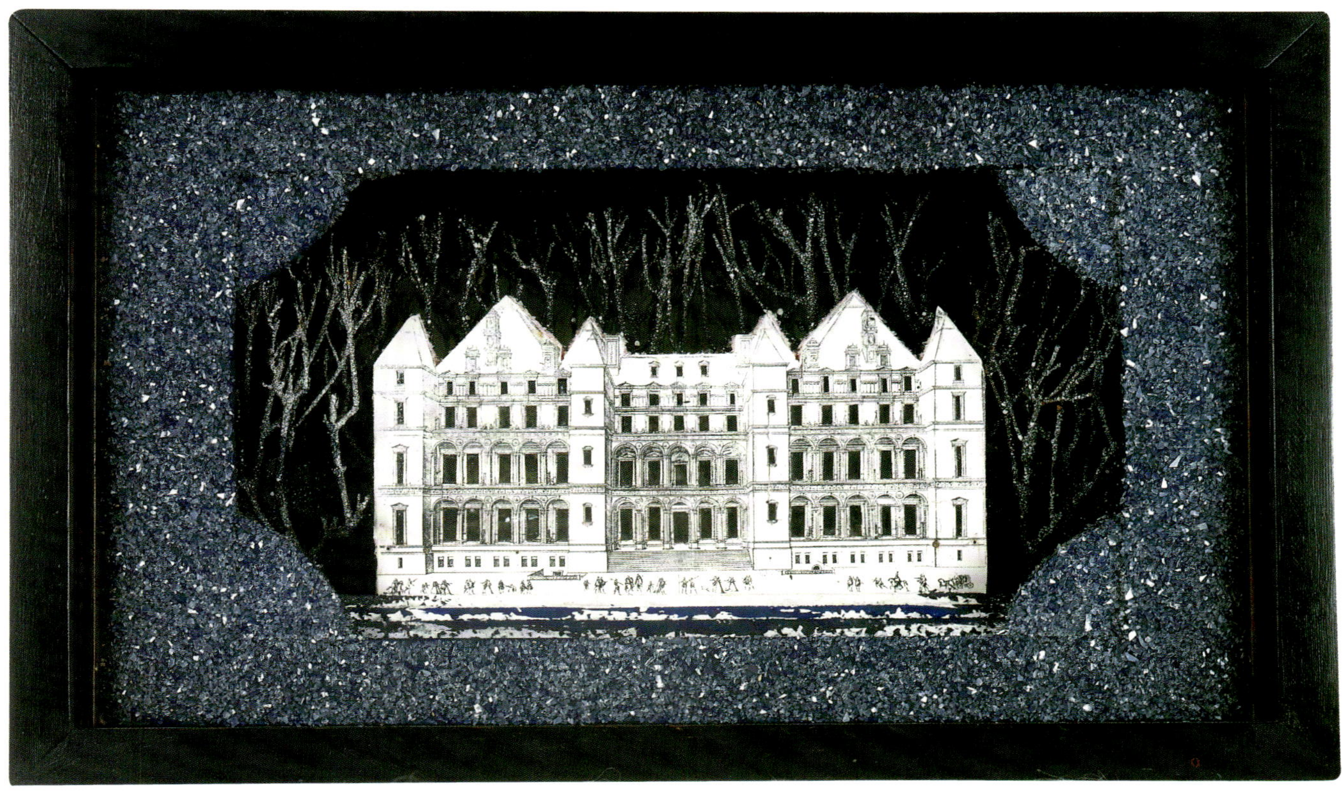

79 **Joseph Cornell and James Ogle**
Untitled (Bébé Marie) 1938
Collection of Michael Senft, New York

80 **Exhibition announcement for "Romantic Museum at the Hugo Gallery / Portraits of Women: Constructions and Arrangements by Joseph Cornell"** 1946
Joseph Cornell Study Center, National Museum of American Art, Smithsonian Institution. Gift of Mr. and Mrs. John A. Benton

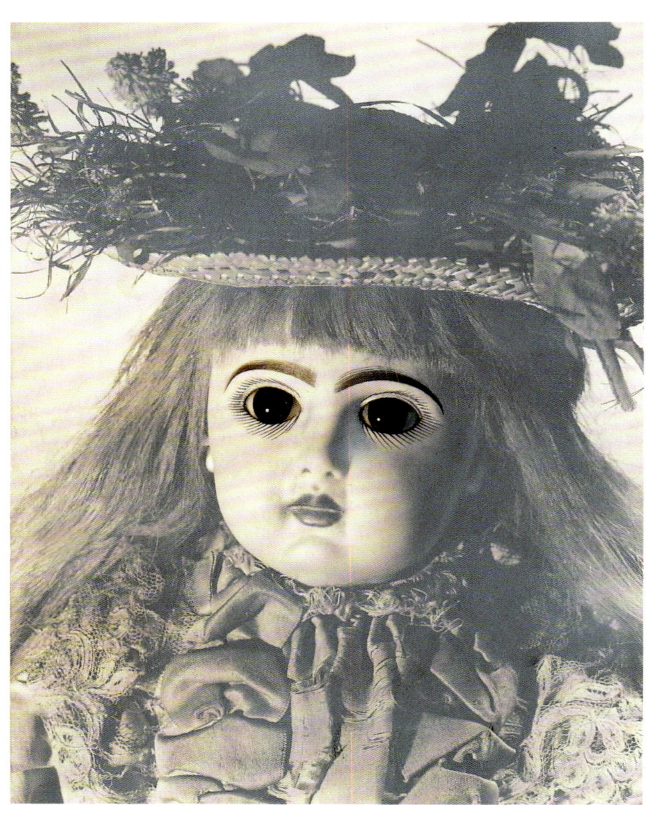

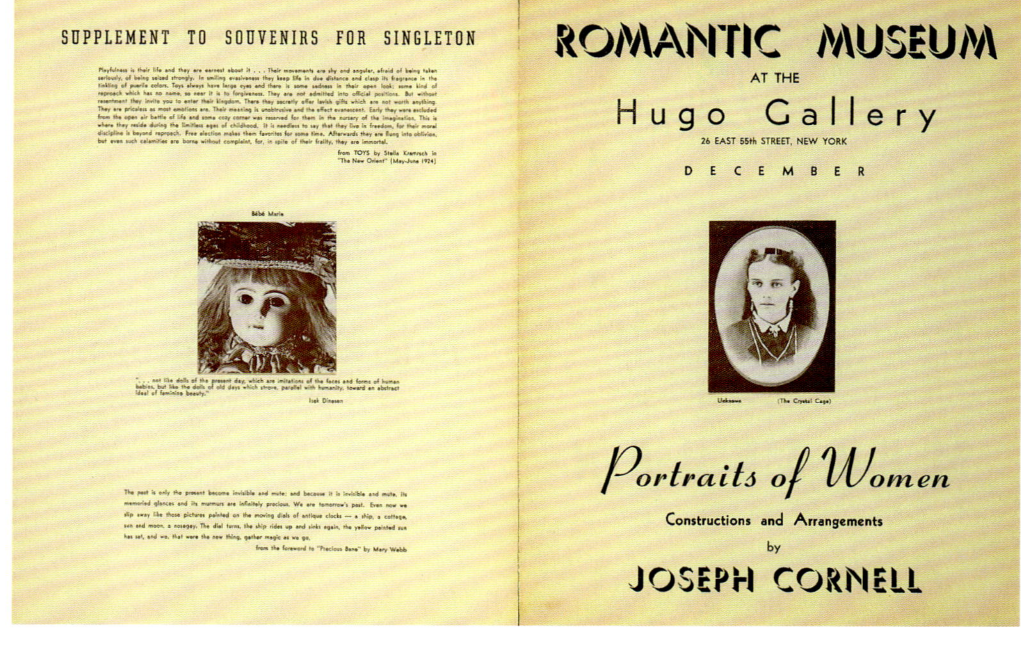

SUPPLEMENT TO SOUVENIRS FOR SINGLETON

Playfulness is their life and they are earnest about it . . . Their movements are shy and angular, afraid of being taken seriously, of being seized strongly. In smiling evasiveness they keep life in due distance and clasp its fragrance in the tinkling of puerile colors. Toys always have large eyes and there is some sadness in their open look; some kind of reproach which has no name, so near it is to forgiveness. They are not admitted into official positions. But without resentment they invite you to enter their kingdom. There they secretly offer lavish gifts which are not worth anything. They are priceless as most emotions are. Their meaning is unobtrusive and the effect evanescent. Early they were excluded from the open air battle of life and some cozy corner was reserved for them in the nursery of the imagination. This is where they reside during the limitless ages of childhood. It is needless to say that they live in freedom, for their moral discipline is beyond reproach. Free election makes them favorites for some time. Afterwards they are flung into oblivion, but even such calamities are borne without complaint, for, in spite of their frailty, they are immortal.

from TOYS by Stella Kramrisch in "The New Orient" (May-June 1924)

Bébé Marie

". . . not like dolls of the present day, which are imitations of the faces and forms of human babies, but like the dolls of old days which strove, parallel with humanity, toward an abstract ideal of feminine beauty."

Isak Dinesen

The past is only the present become invisible and mute: and because it is invisible and mute, its memoried glances and its murmurs are infinitely precious. We are tomorrow's past. Even now we slip away like those pictures painted on the moving dials of antique clocks — a ship, a cottage, sun and moon, a nosegay. The dial turns, the ship rides up and sinks again, the yellow painted sun has set, and we, that were the new thing, gather magic as we go.

from the foreword to "Precious Bane" by Mary Webb

ROMANTIC MUSEUM

AT THE

Hugo Gallery

26 EAST 55th STREET, NEW YORK

D E C E M B E R

Unknown (The Crystal Cage)

Portraits of Women

Constructions and Arrangements

by

JOSEPH CORNELL

81 **Untitled (Bébé Marie)** c. 1943
The Museum of Modern Art, New York.
Acquired through the Lillie P. Bliss Bequest

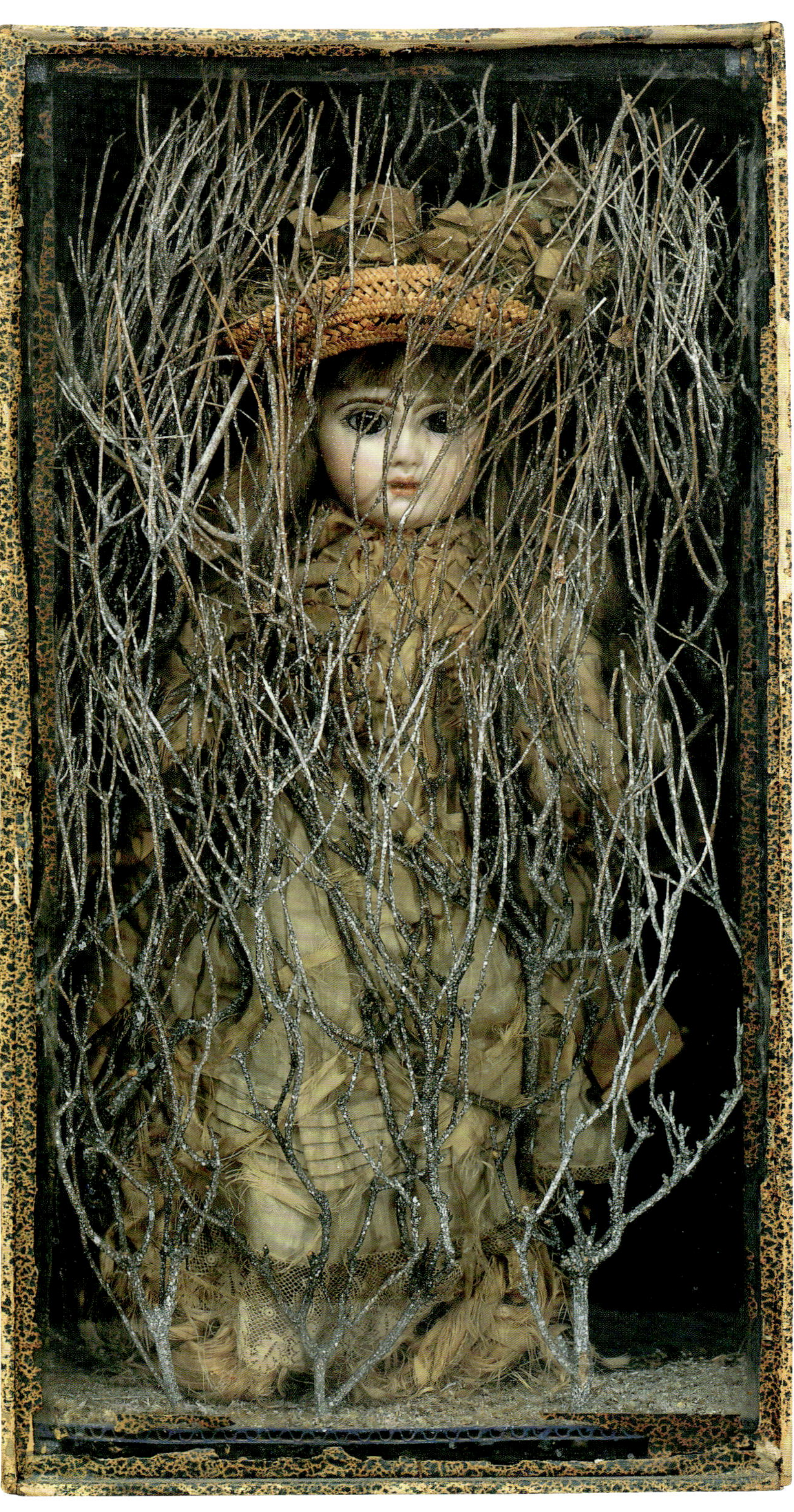

82 ***Habitat Group for a Shooting Gallery*** 1943
Des Moines Art Center, Iowa. Purchased with funds from the Coffin Fine Arts Trust; Nathan Emory Coffin Collection

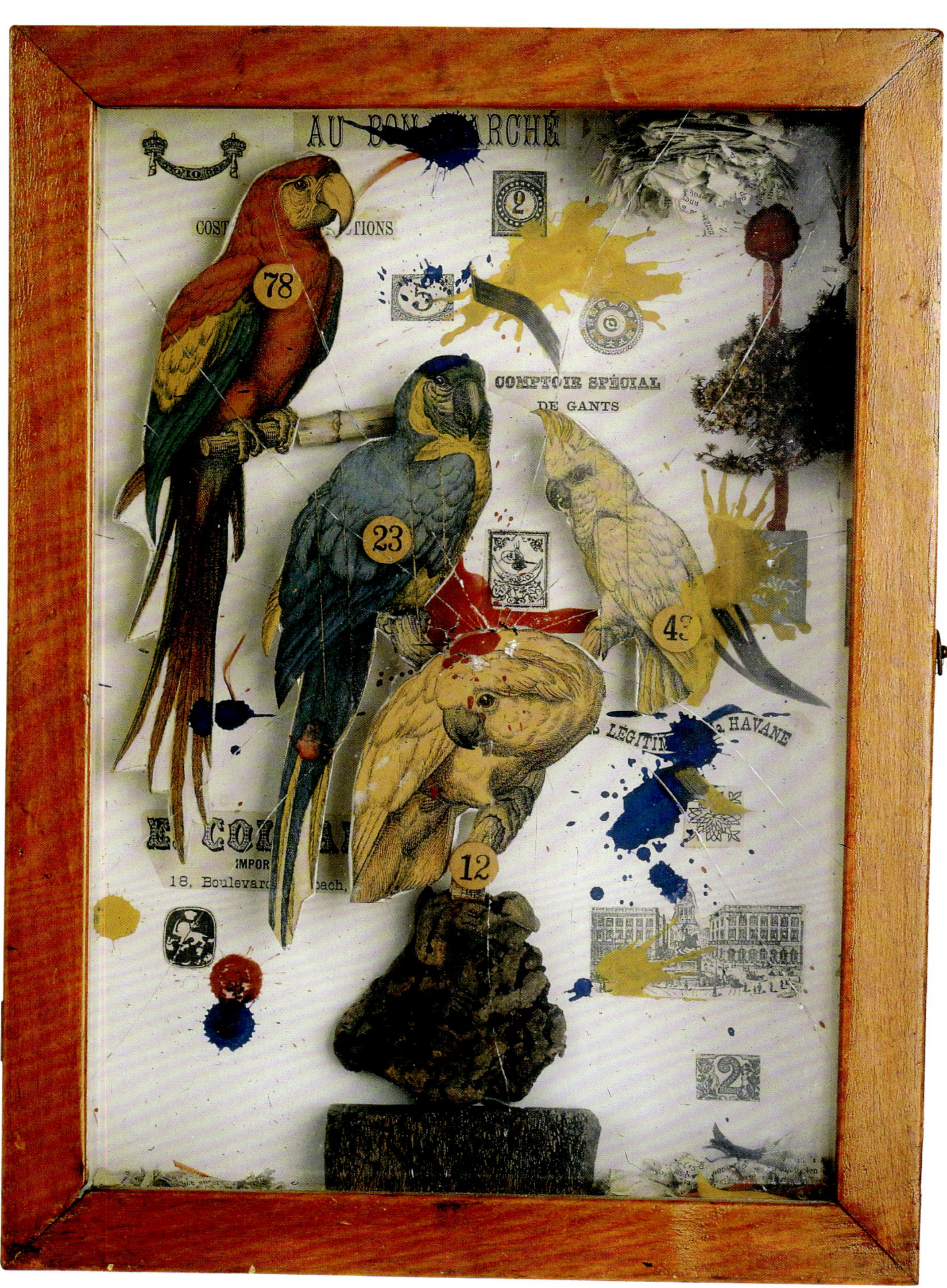

83 Untitled (The Hotel Eden) c. 1945
National Gallery of Canada, Ottawa

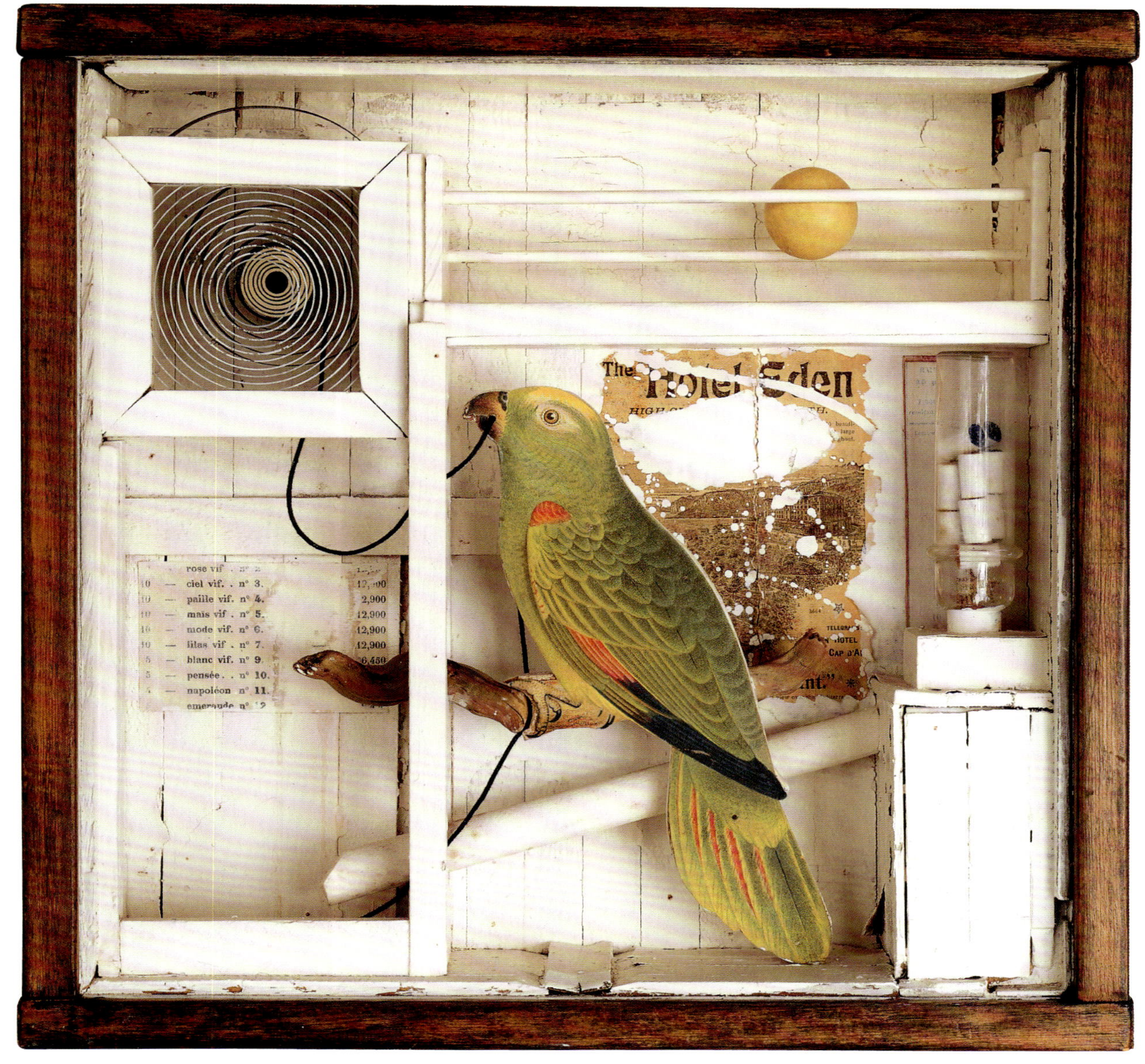

84 ***Petit musée [Small Museum]*** 1947
Private collection

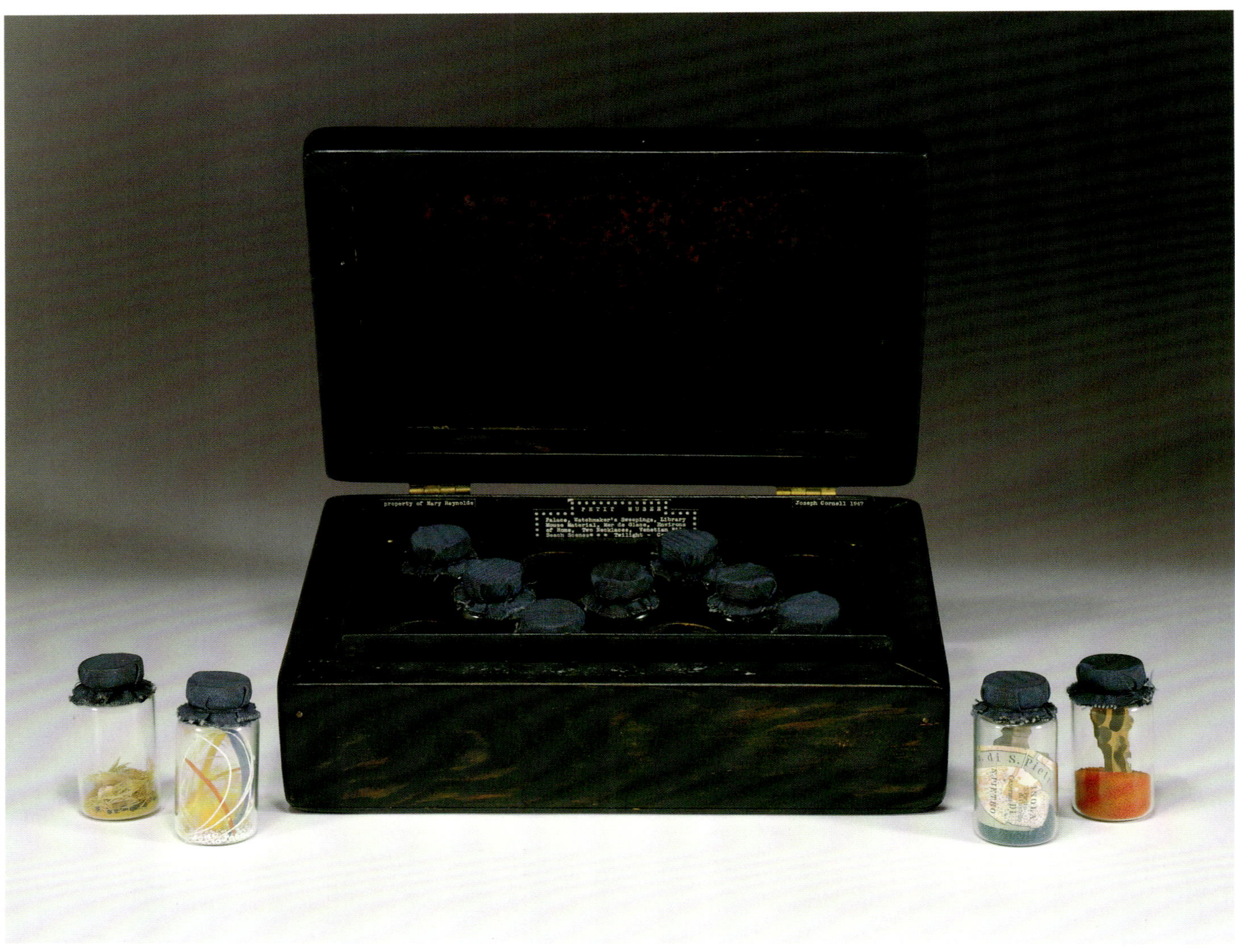

85 ***Museum*** c. 1944–48
The Menil Collection, Houston. Bequest of Jermayne MacAgy

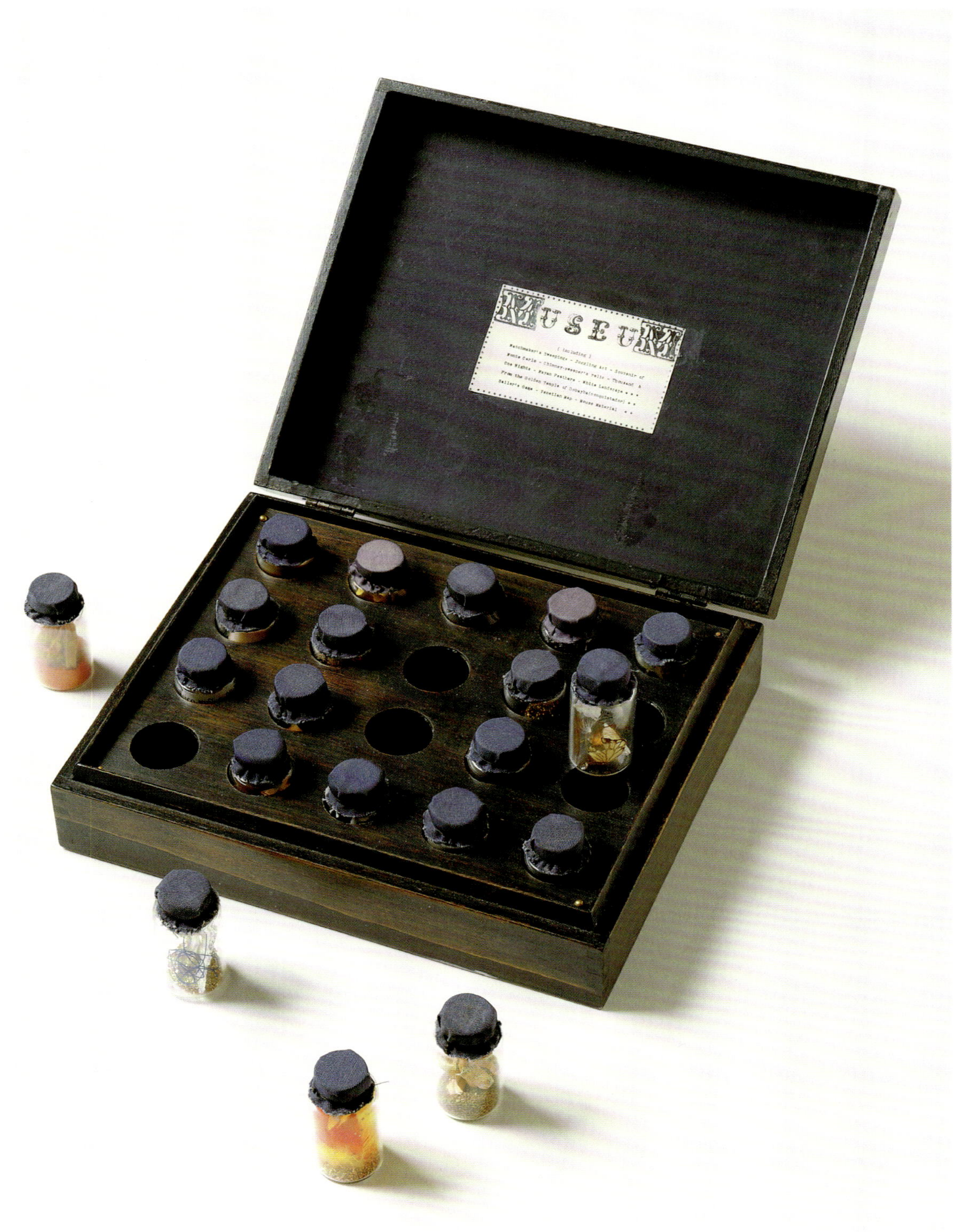

86 **Untitled** ***(Penny Arcade Portrait of Lauren Bacall)*** 1945–46
Collection of Lindy Bergman, Chicago
bottom

87 ***Penny Arcade Portrait of Lauren Bacall***
(Working Model Based Upon "To Have and Have Not") c. 1945–70
Collection of Lindy Bergman, Chicago

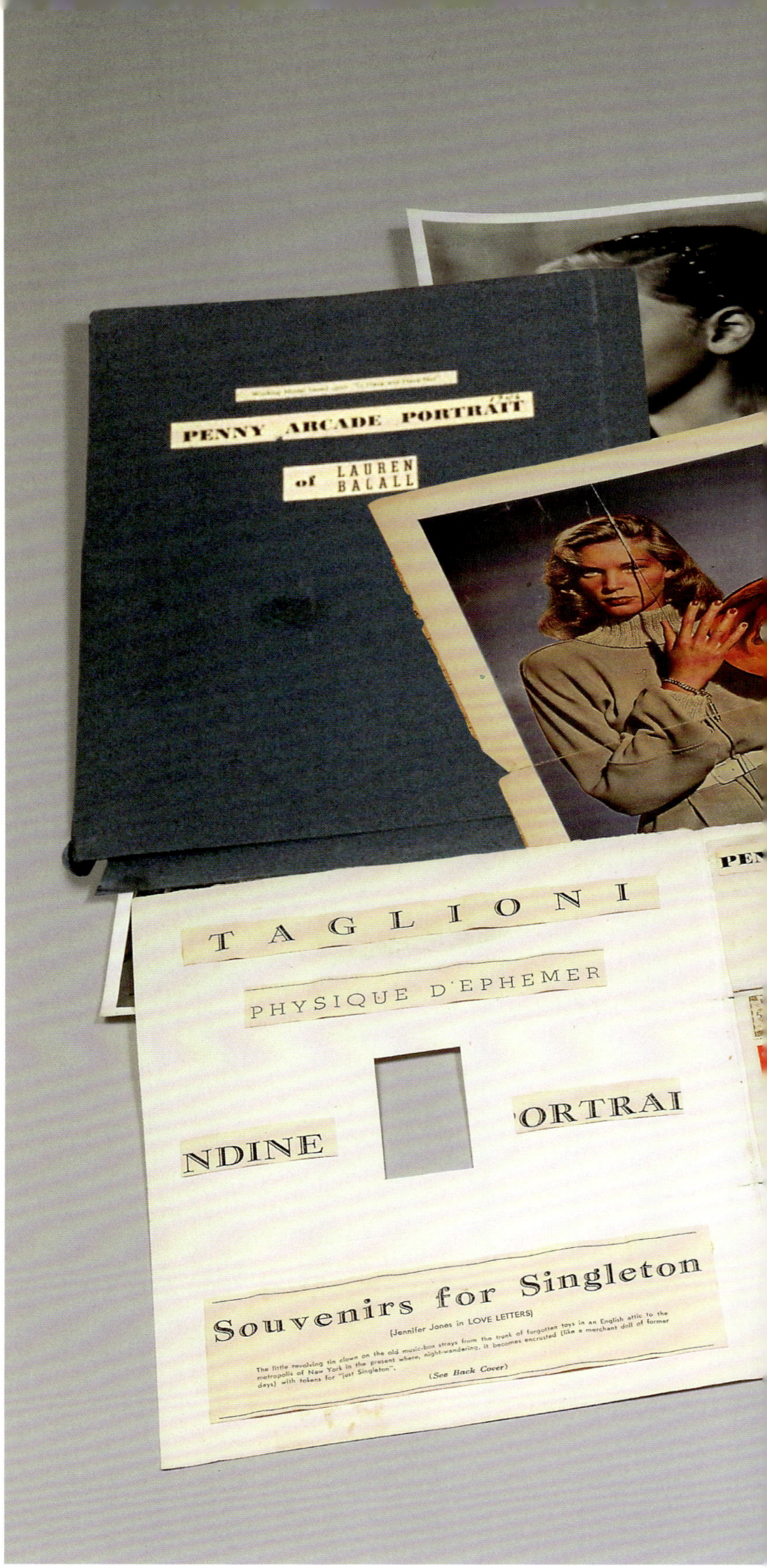

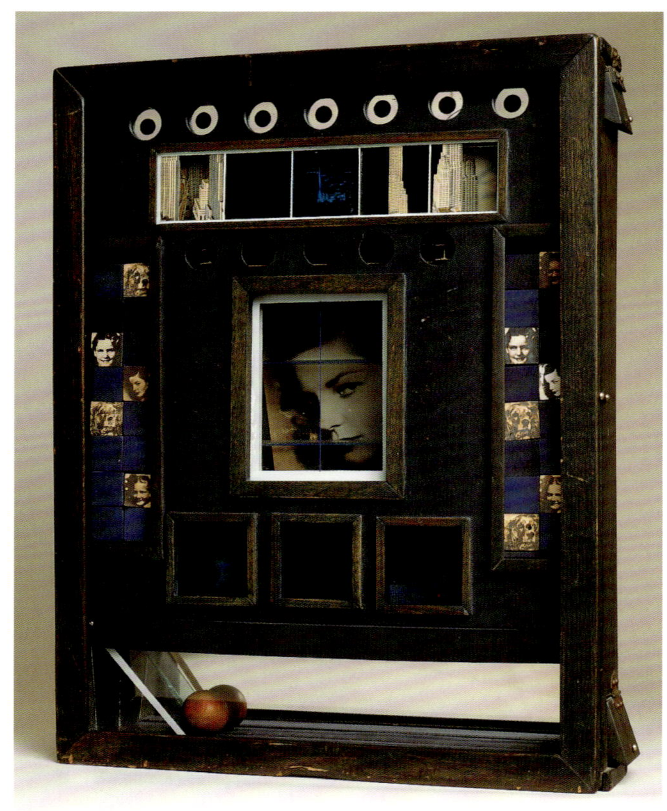

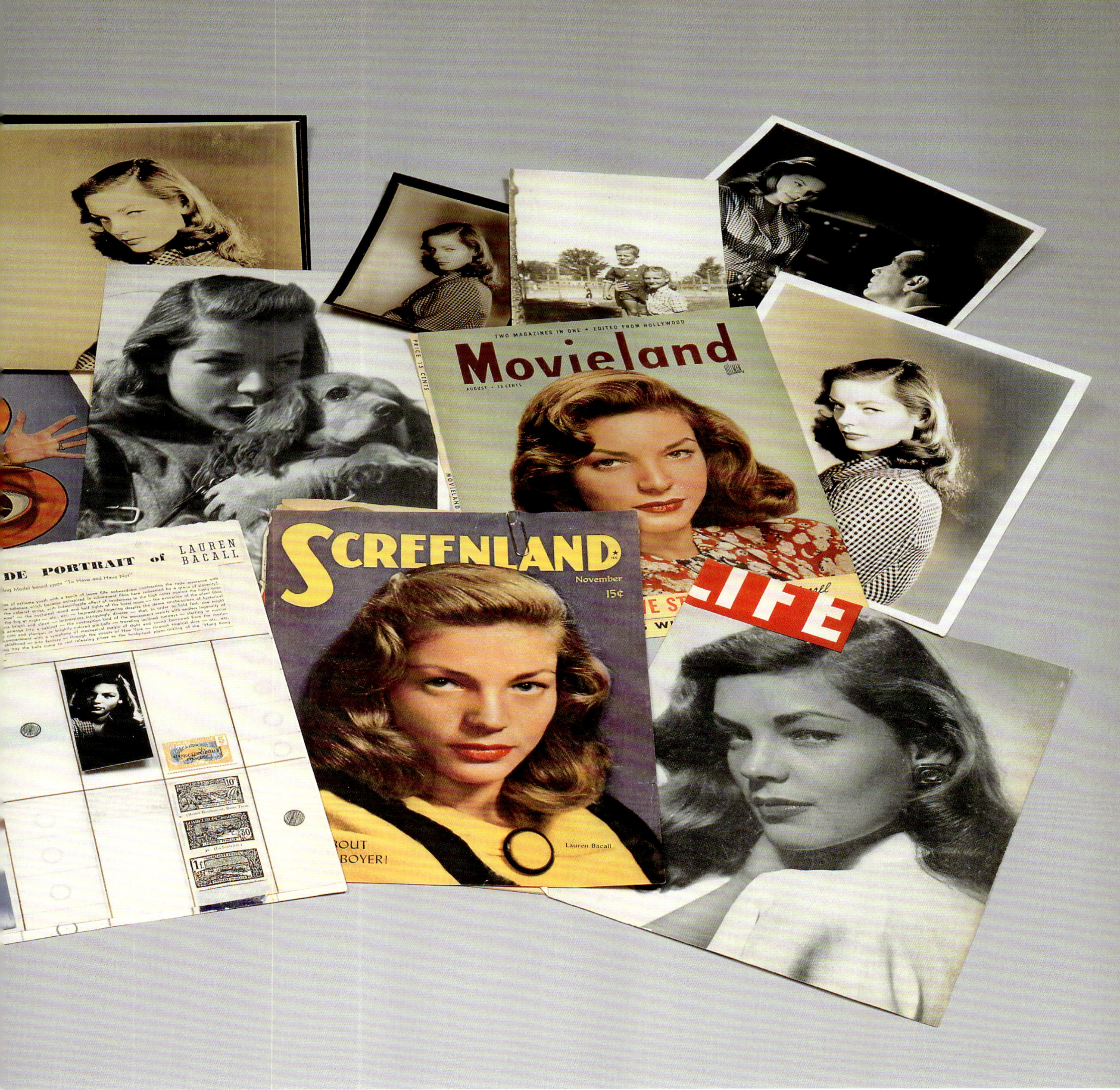
TWO MAGAZINES IN ONE • EDITED FROM HOLLYWOOD
Movieland
AUGUST • 15 CENTS
PRICE 15 CENTS
PORTRAIT of
LAUREN
BACALL
SCREENLAND
November
15¢
Lauren Bacall
LIFE

88 Untitled (Sand Box) c. 1944
The Art Institute of Chicago. Gift of Frank B. Hubachek

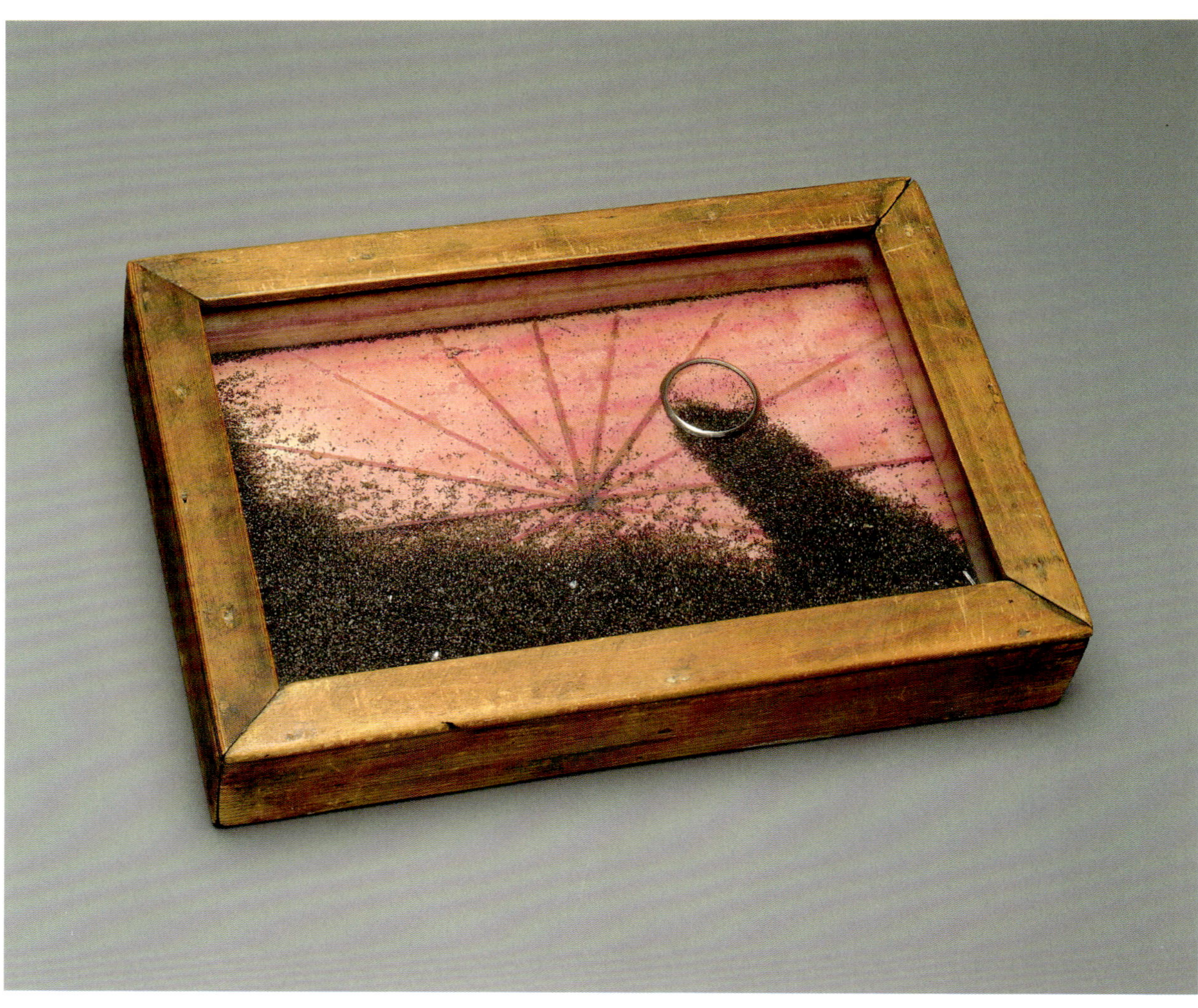

89 **Untitled (Sand Fountain)** c. 1958
Collection of Jacqueline Matisse

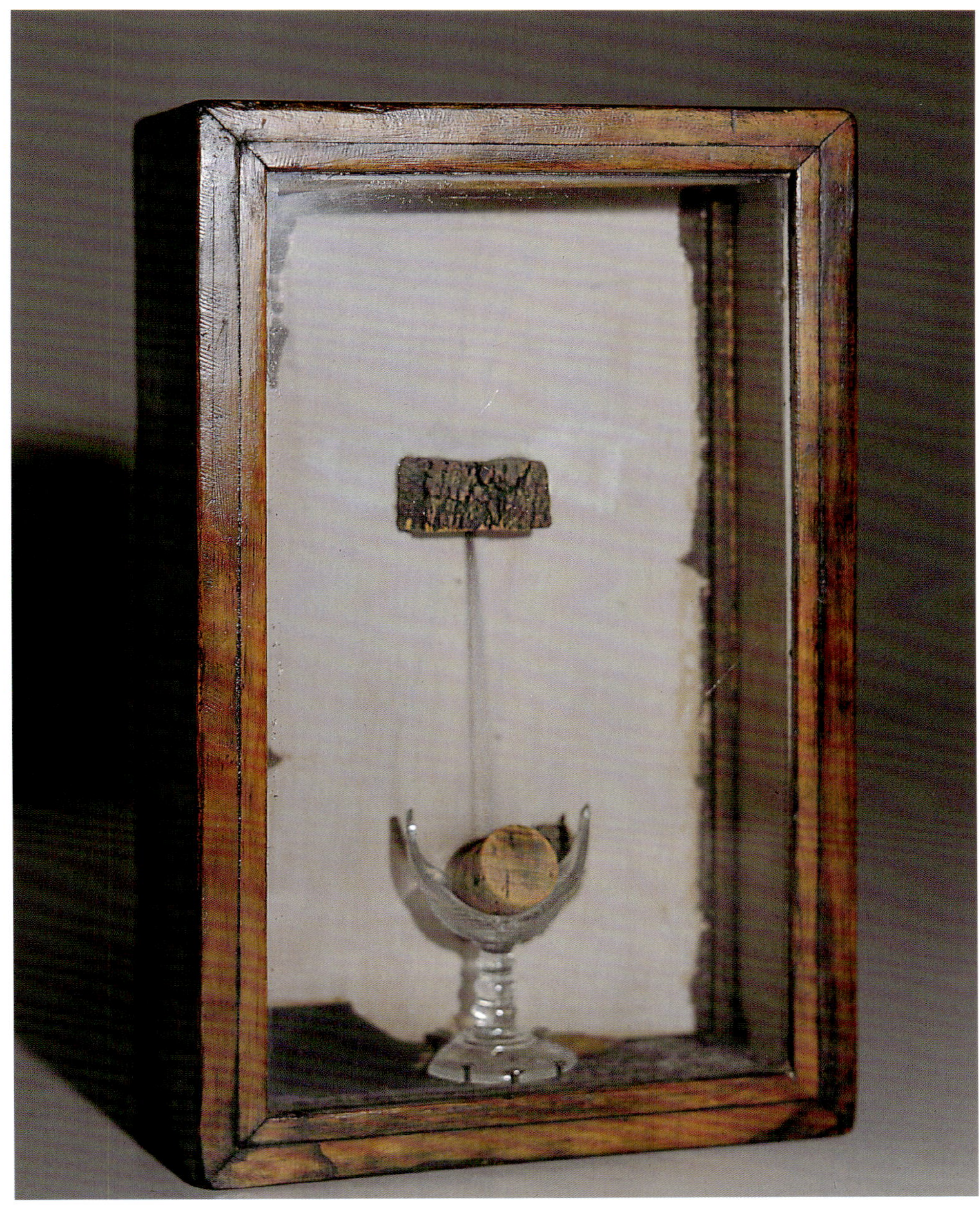

90 Untitled [Window Facade] c. 1950–52
The Menil Collection, Houston

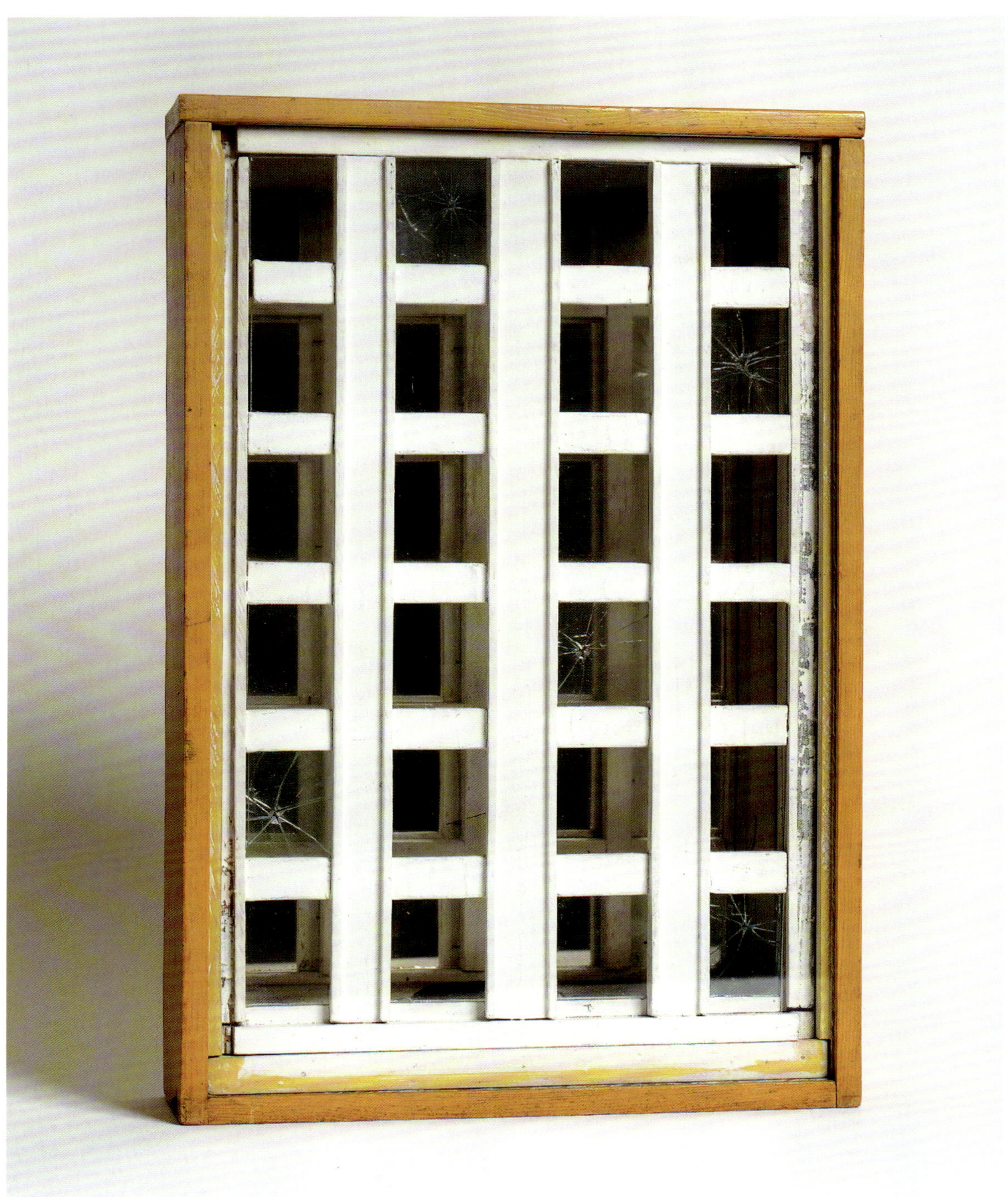

91 **Untitled (Rattle and Music Box)** c. 1955
The Menil Collection, Houston. Bequest of Jermayne MacAgy

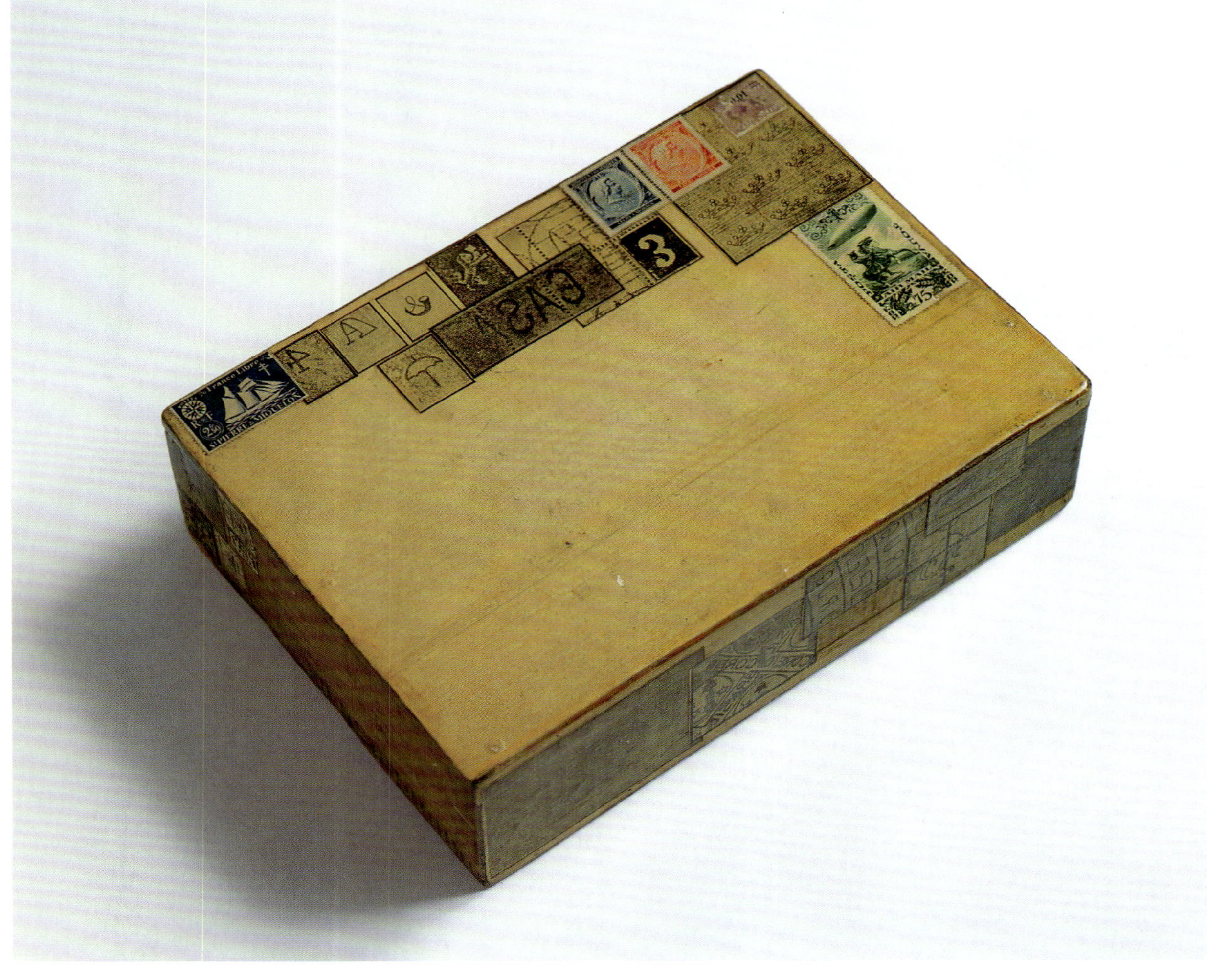

92 **Untitled [Owl Habitat]** 1946
Collection of Arno Schefler

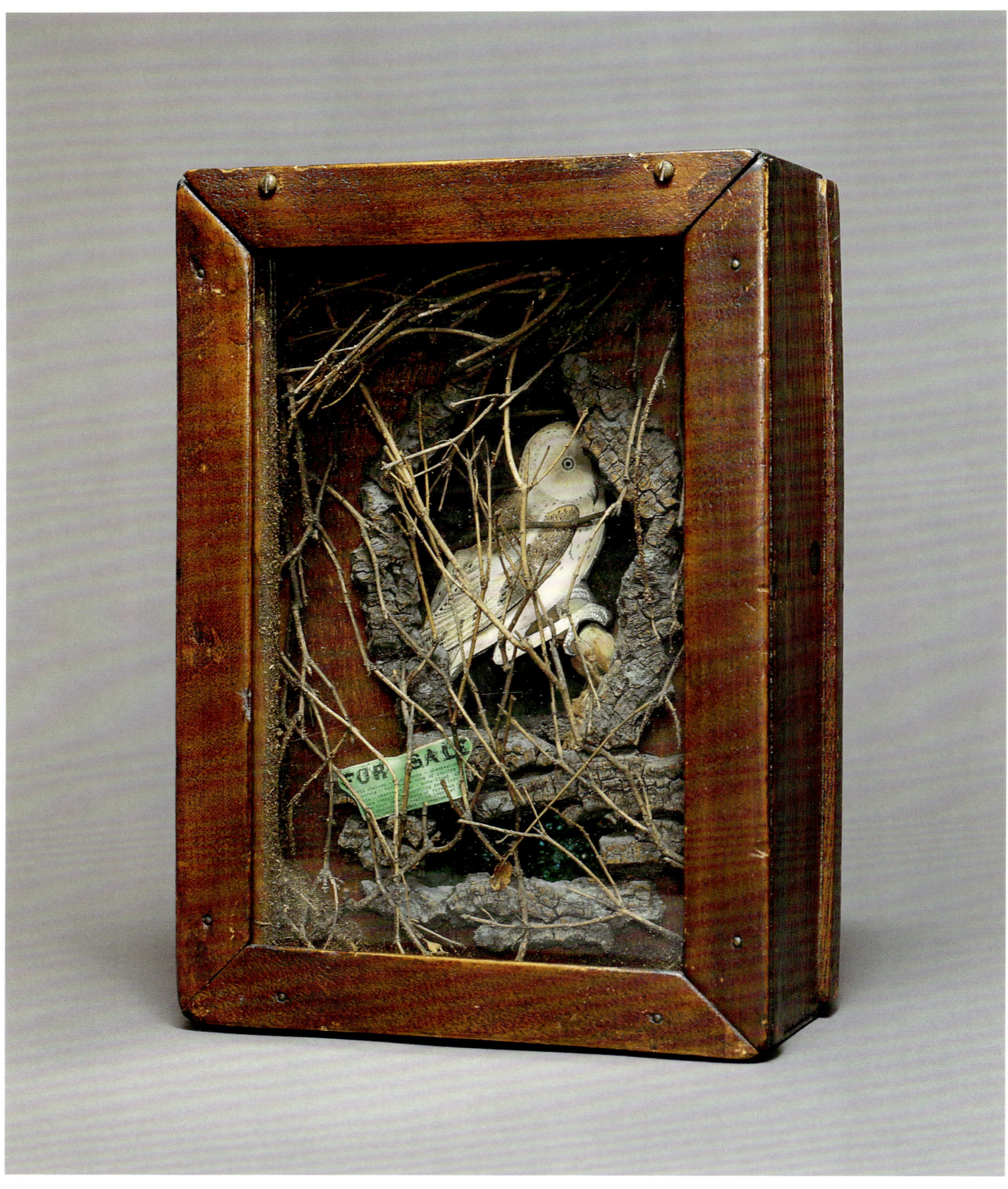

93 ***Neptun au Lac [Neptune at the Lake]*** c. 1953
The Joseph and Robert Cornell Memorial Foundation

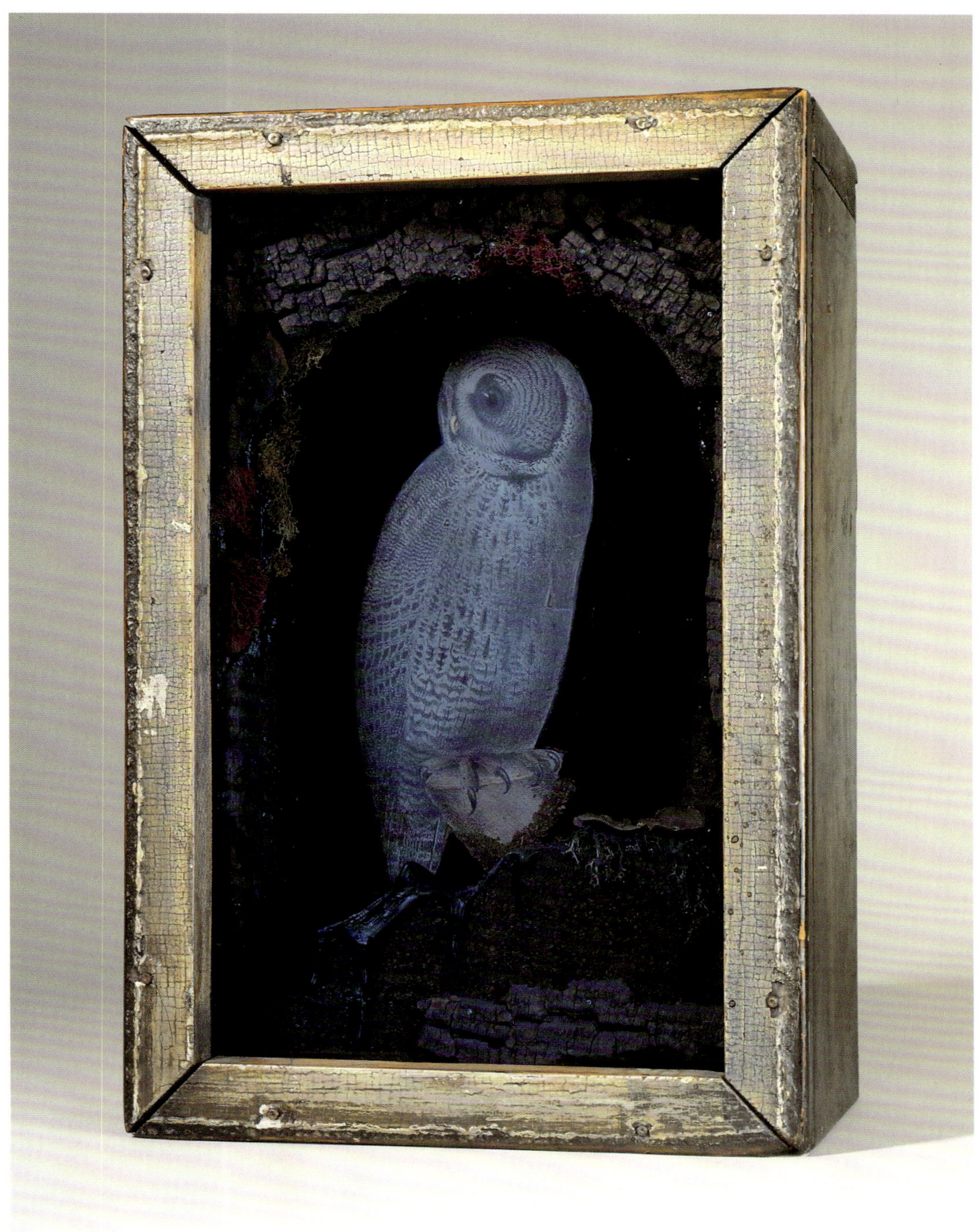

94 **Untitled (Renée Jeanmarie in *la belle au bois dormant*)** 1949
[Sleeping Beauty]
Private collection

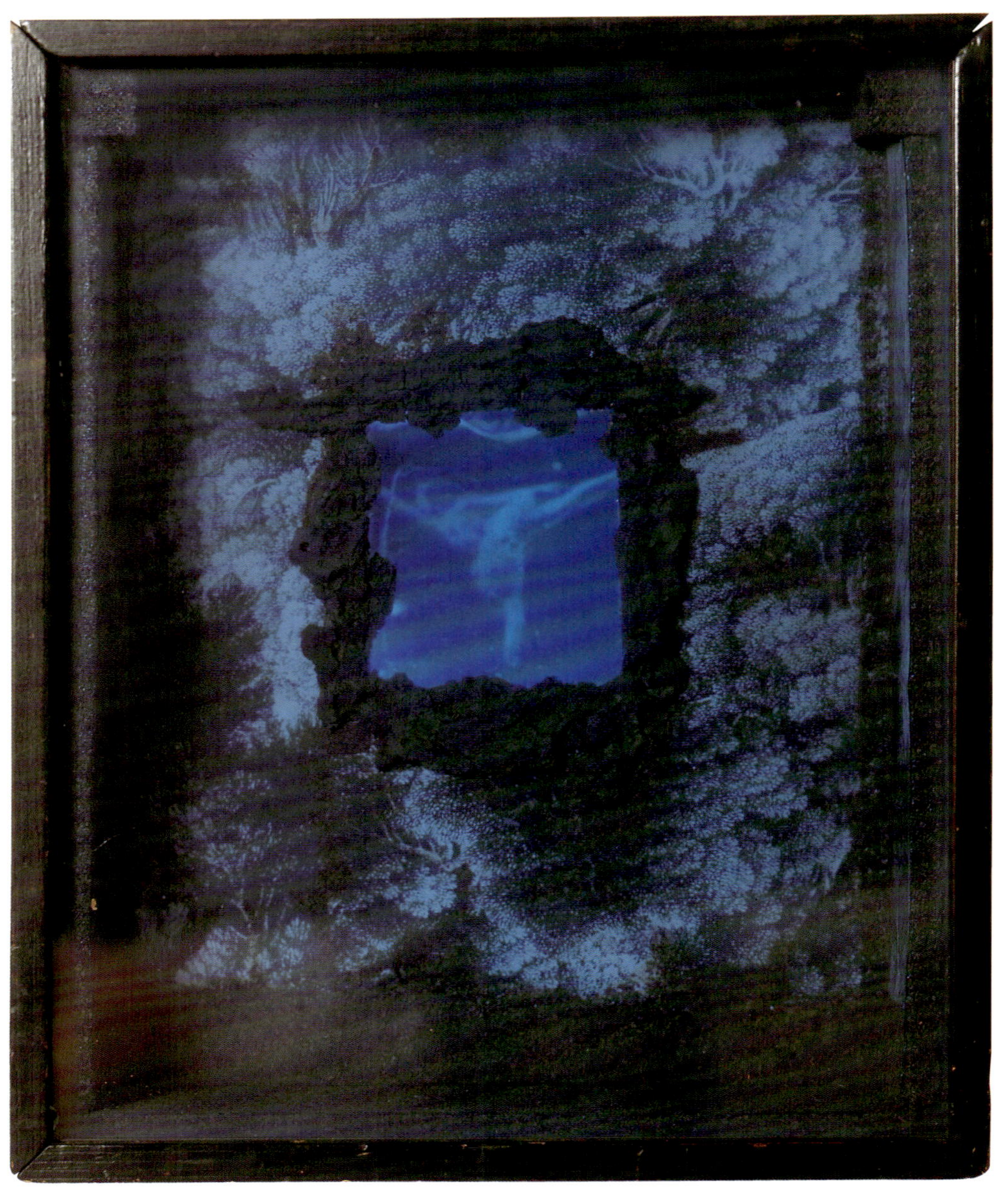

95 **Untitled [Sequestered Bower]** c. early 1950s–early 1960s
The Art Institute of Chicago. The Lindy and Edwin Bergman Joseph Cornell Collection

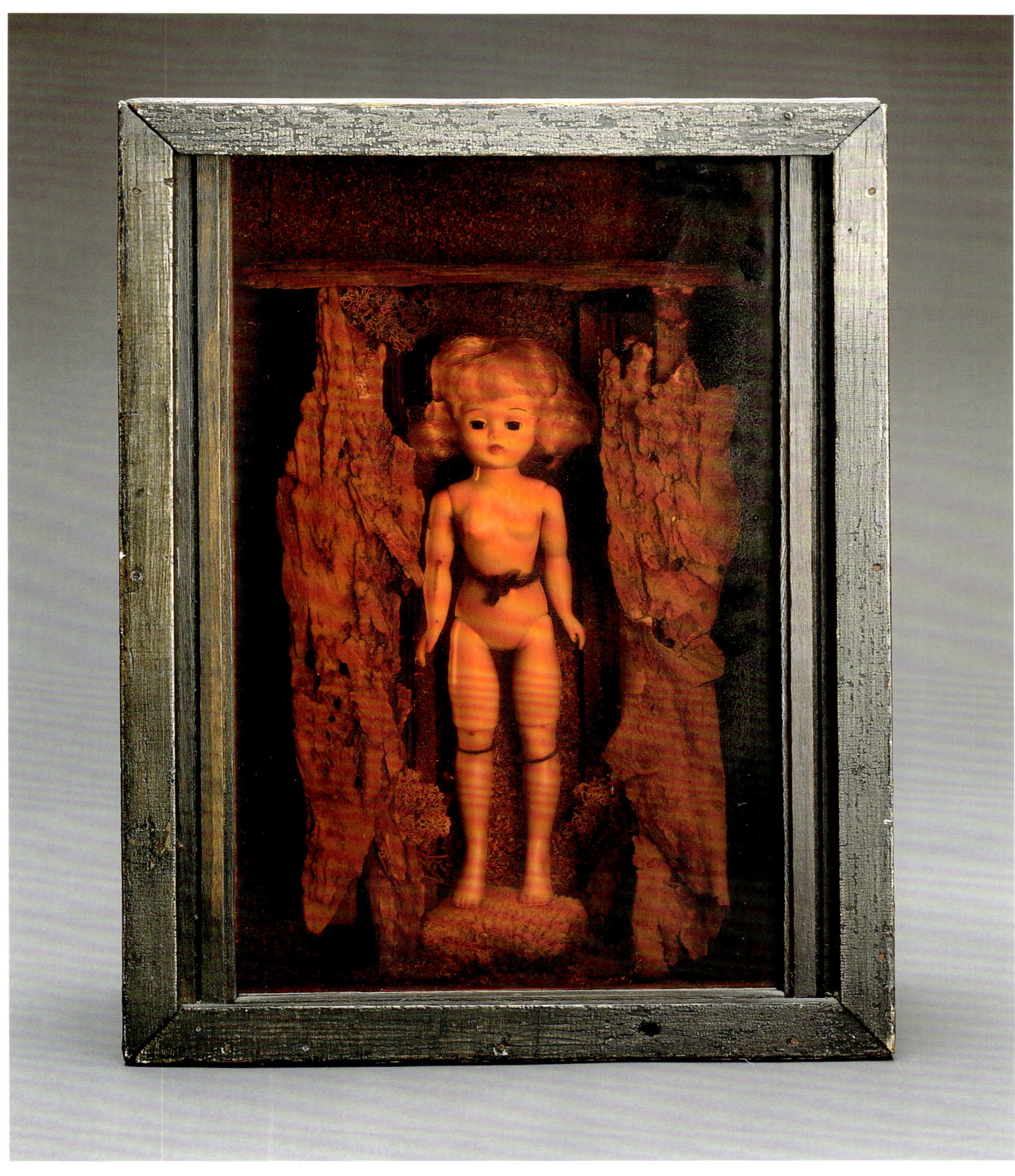

96 **Untitled [Landscape with Reclining Nude and Castle]** late 1950s
Private collection, courtesy PaceWildenstein, New York

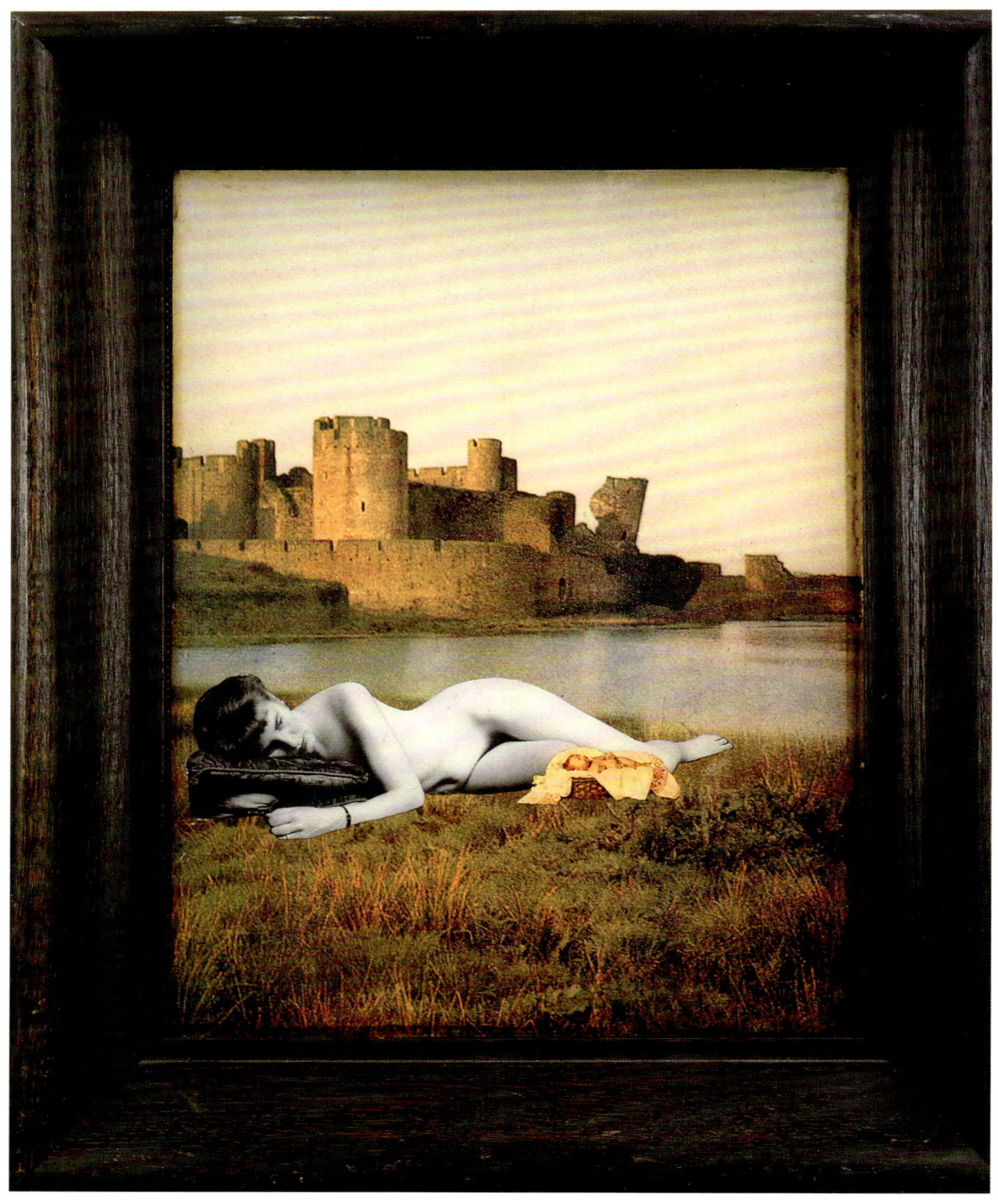

97 **Untitled (Mélisande)** c. early 1950s–early 1960s
Private collection

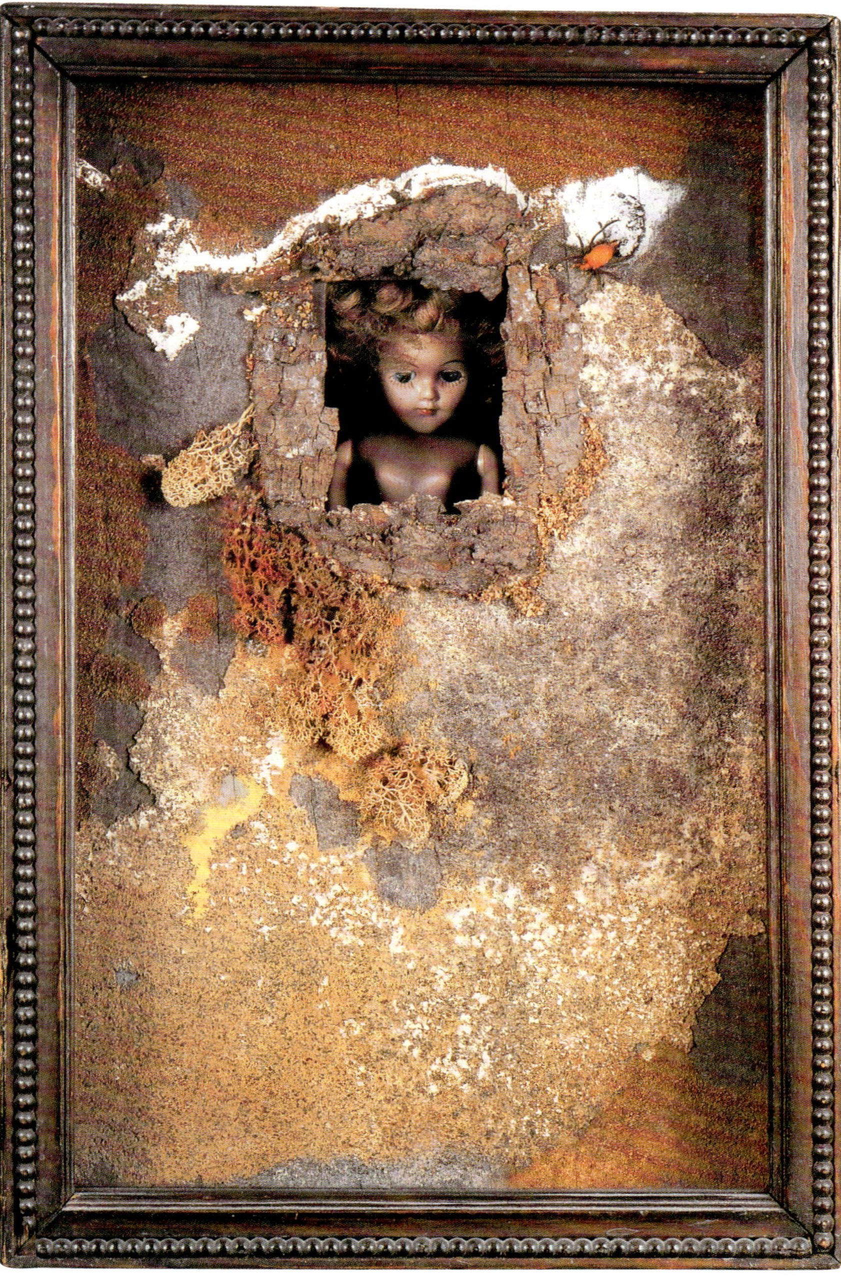

98 **Untitled [Doll Habitat]** c. early 1950s–1965
Collection of Janice and Mickey Cartin

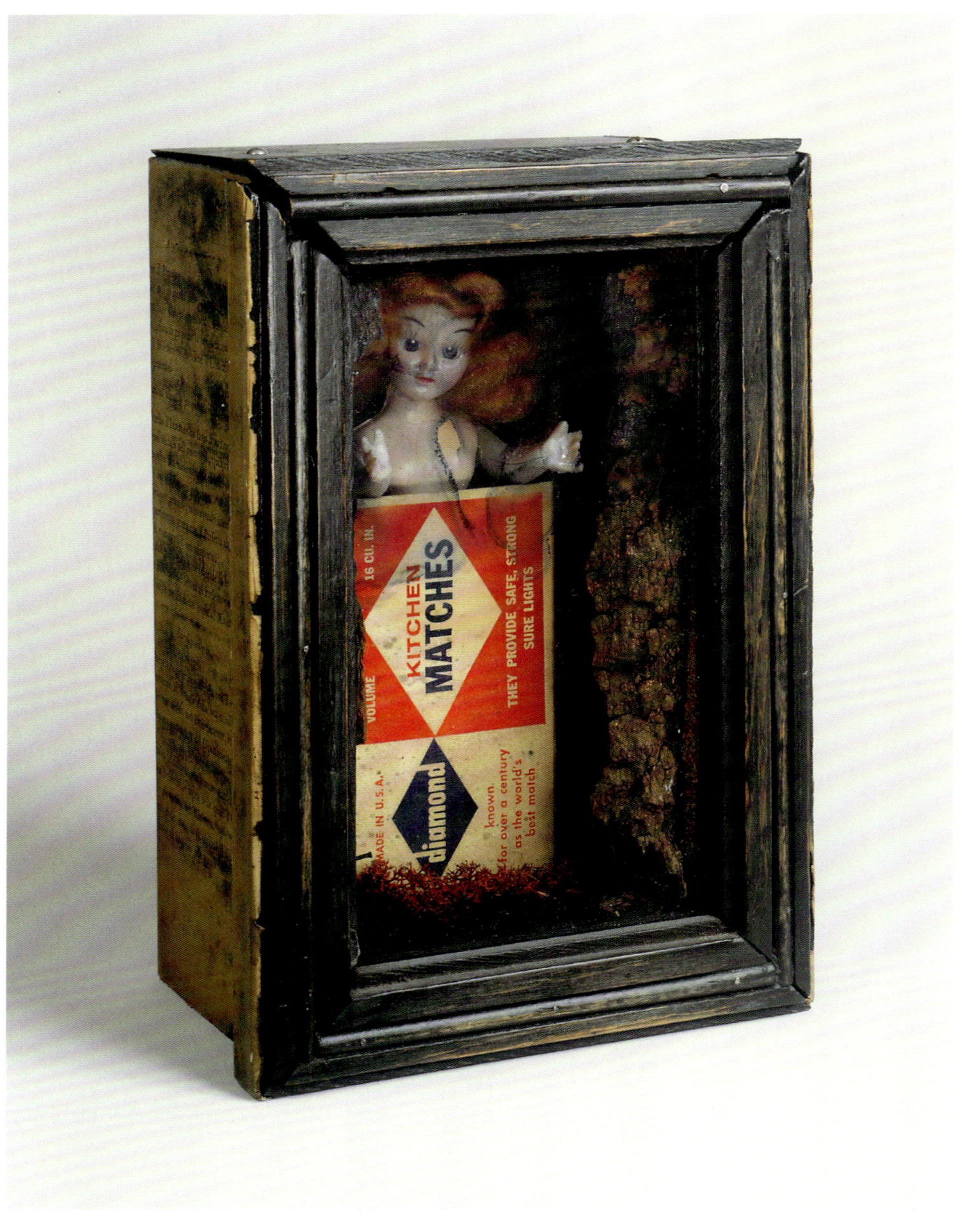

99 *Sorrows of Young Werther* c. 1966
Hirshhorn Museum and Sculpture Garden, Smithsonian Institution. Gift of Joseph H. Hirshhorn

100.1 **"Medici Slot Machine" shoe box of working materials** c. 1940s–1950s
Joseph Cornell Study Center, National Museum of American Art, Smithsonian Institution. Gift of The Joseph and Robert Cornell Memorial Foundation

100.2 **"Medici Slot Machine" source material files** c. late 1930s–1966
Joseph Cornell Study Center, National Museum of American Art, Smithsonian Institution. Gift of Mr. and Mrs. John A. Benton
pp. 218–219

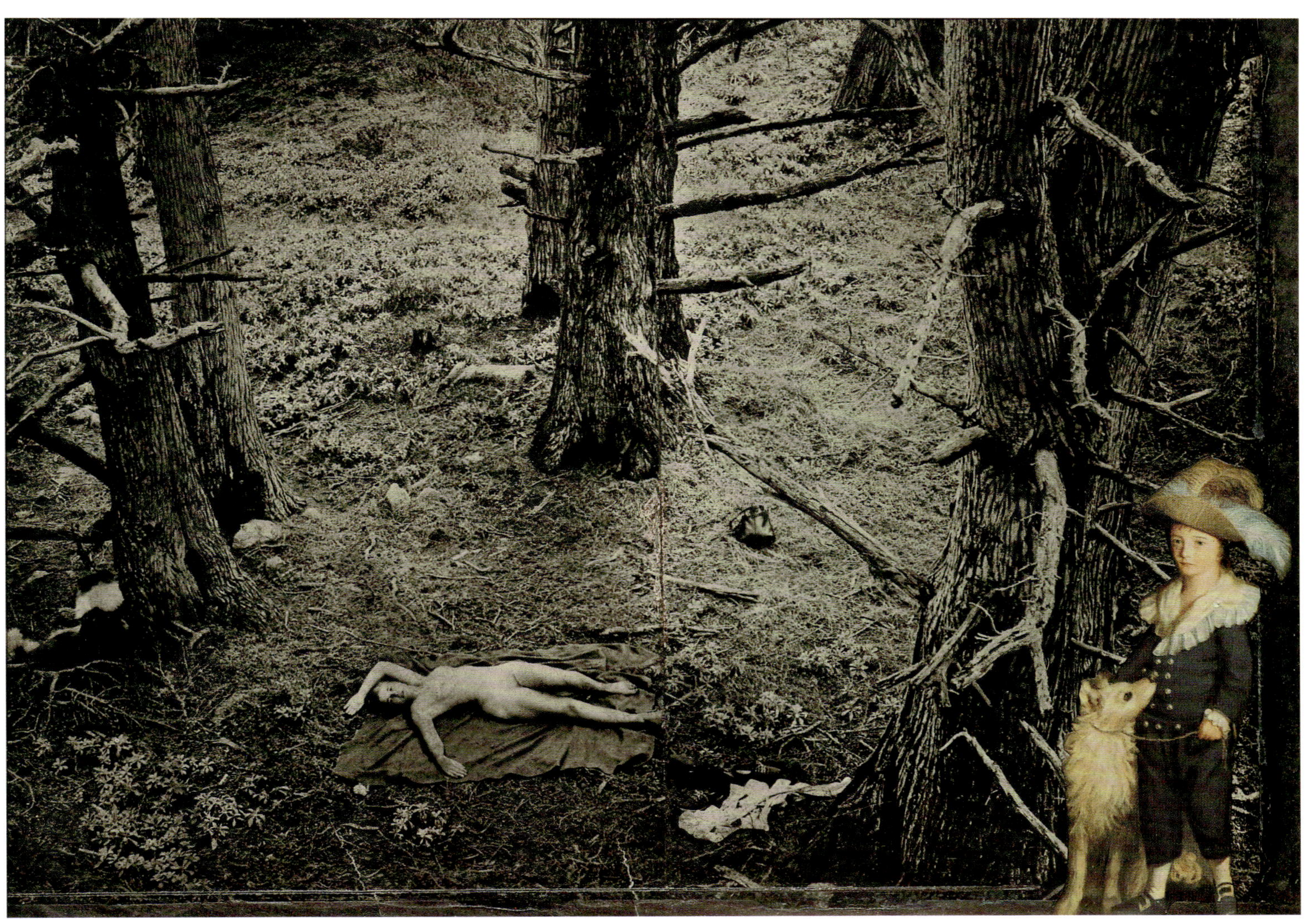

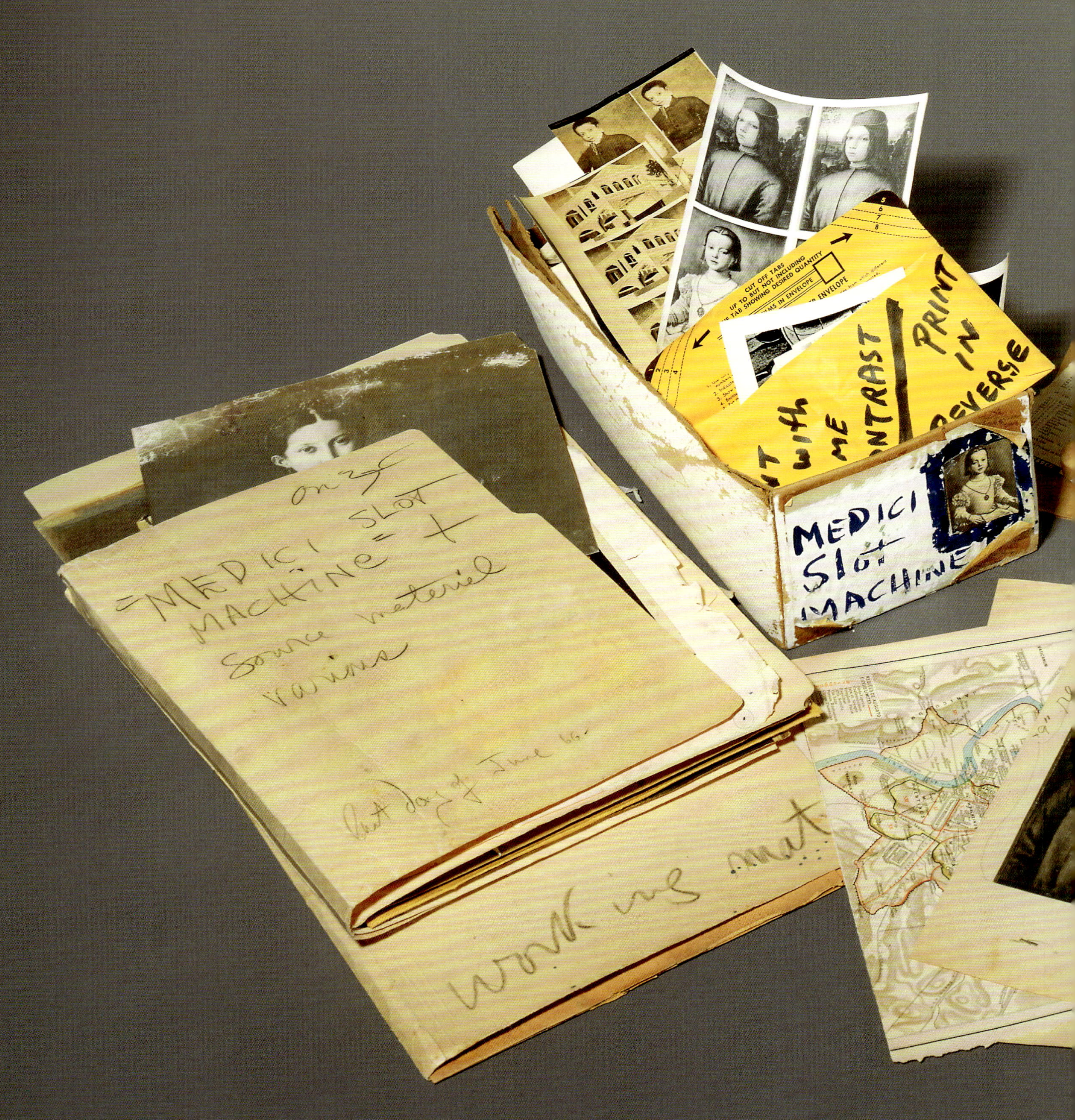
MEDICI SLOT MACHINE
Source material various
PRINT IN REVERSE
MEDICI Slot MACHINE

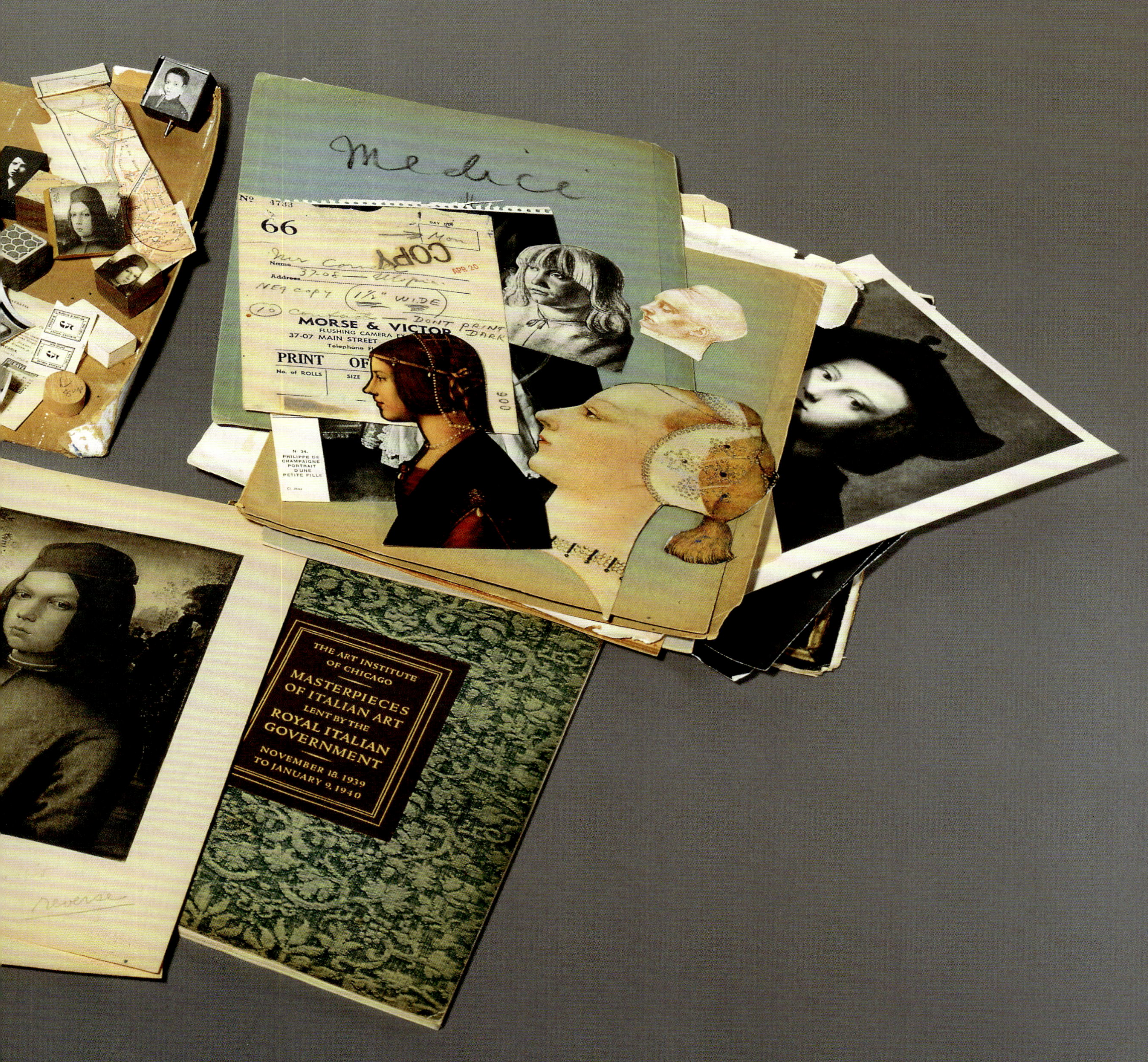
Medici
66
COPY
MORSE & VICTOR
37-07 MAIN STREET
PRINT
THE ART INSTITUTE
OF CHICAGO
MASTERPIECES
OF ITALIAN ART
LENT BY THE
ROYAL ITALIAN
GOVERNMENT
NOVEMBER 18, 1939
TO JANUARY 9, 1940
reverse

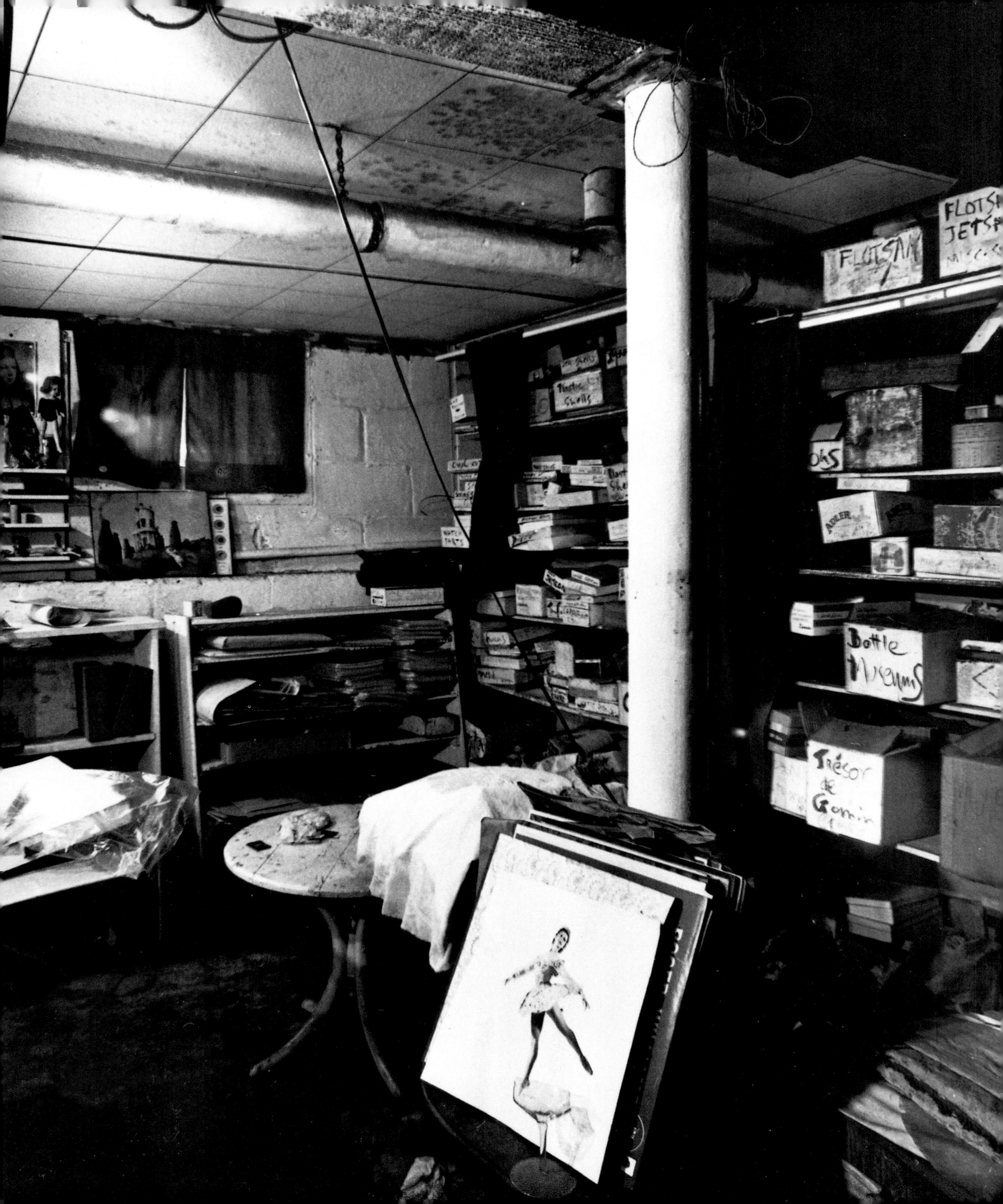
FLOTSAM
ADLER
Bottle Museums

Joseph Cornell's Explorations: Art on File

LYNDA ROSCOE HARTIGAN

The poet, they say, borrows nothing that is foreign or unfamiliar to himself. He takes back what was his to begin with—those things, precisely, in which he recognizes himself.
—Wallace Fowlie[1]

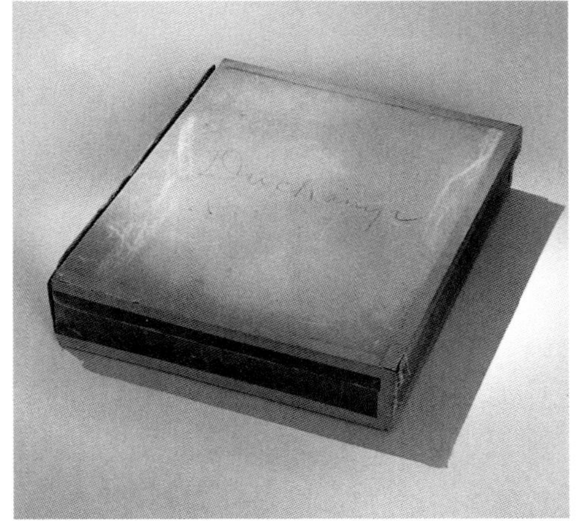

With its old-fashioned implications of propriety and humility, the word *gratitude* might seem like an odd point of reference for the notes, ephemera, and artworks that Joseph Cornell placed in a cardboard container simply labeled *Duchamp* (fig. 97; DD 0). Yet, sources as diverse as anonymous faces in a crowd and passages by Marcel Proust had provided Cornell with countless moments of inspiration, often recorded "in gratitude" in his diaries.[2] Marcel Duchamp's public use of the word *gratitude* was more selective, limited to a characteristically piquant observation: "When an unknown artist brings me something *new*, I all but burst with gratitude."[3] Between December 1933 and January 1934, Cornell gave a photograph and a copy of his first film scenario, *Monsieur Phot* (pl. 50), to Duchamp, who reciprocated later in January with an autographed magazine reproduction of *La Mariée mise à nu par ses célibataires, même [The Bride Stripped Bare by Her Bachelors, Even] (Large Glass)* (1915–23; DD 108). This initial exchange of materials between the two artists sparked a relationship that may forever tantalize us with possibilities, among them the element of gratitude.

Cornell's "explorations," which include the cardboard container inscribed *Duchamp*, are still a little known aspect of his work. Loosely assembled in everything from paper bags to handmade "suitcases," they are fascinating precisely because they are not the glass-paned, exquisitely crafted box constructions for which he has been so celebrated. In the elaborate lexicon of terms that Cornell applied to his archival and creative activities, what is his assembly of materials devoted to Duchamp—*document*, *case study*, *scrapbook*, *dossier*, *exploration*, or *imaginary portrait*? Was he storing or arranging, preserving or preparing? The challenge lies in positioning this project along Cornell's sliding scale between minutiae and art and between private and public intention.

What's in a Box? Just mentioning Cornell's "explorations," however, introduces an essential irony: poetic containment and contained poetry were his consummate specialties, yet he spent the better part of his career chafing under the "limitations of the box format."[4] Admiring Mozart and Emily Dickinson for their "genius" in navigating small forms, Cornell lamented his inability to follow suit. A variety of factors contributed to this frustration. Highly self-critical, he never quite shook the insecurity that he felt in the absence of higher formal education and art training. Moreover, according to his beliefs

96 Cornell's studio, 3708 Utopia Parkway, Flushing, New York, 1969. Photograph by Hans Namuth.

97 Cornell, *Duchamp Dossier*, c. 1942–53 (DD 0). Philadelphia Museum of Art. Gift of The Joseph and Robert Cornell Memorial Foundation.

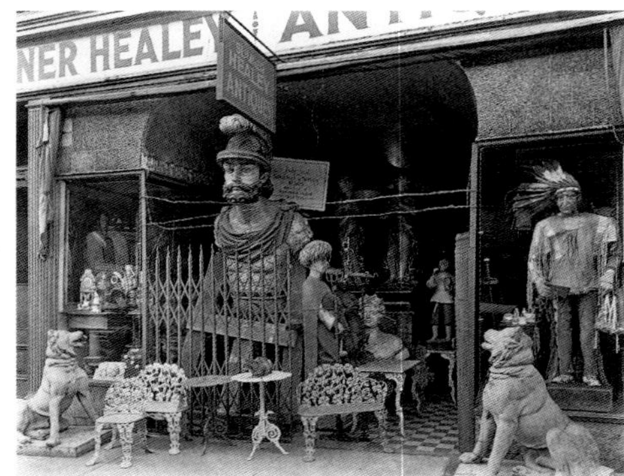

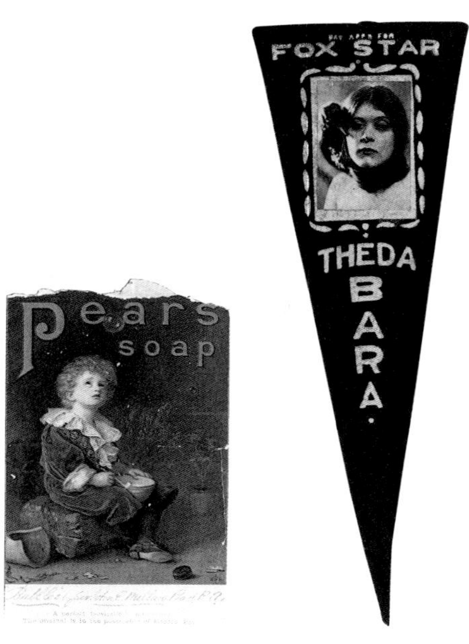

98 ***Sumner Healy Antique Shop, 942 Third Avenue,*** New York, October 6, 1936. Photograph by Berenice Abbott, Federal Arts Project, "Changing New York." Berenice Abbott/Commerce Graphics Ltd, Inc.

99, 100 **Late nineteenth- and early twentieth-century advertising ephemera from Cornell's collection.** Joseph Cornell Study Center, Natl. Museum of American Art, Smithsonian. Gift of Mr. and Mrs. John A. Benton.

as a Christian Scientist, talent was a reflection of the "one Creator, God," and did not originate with the individual. It is not surprising, then, that the themes of modesty and selflessness recur in his writings. These tendencies frequently distorted his assessment of his own intelligence, which was not just adventuresome but also surgically deft in manipulating ideas, images, and materials.

". . . cumbersomeness, immobility, loss of lustre having passed into collectors' hands . . ."—this was another variation on Cornell's tune of frustration with his box constructions.[5] The phrase "loss of lustre" suggests the sadness many artists experience as works leave the studio's private world, terminating not just the maker's control but the stimulation of tinkering and change. The act of finishing is frequently difficult, even elusive, for such artists. Less understandable at first glance is Cornell's use of the words *cumbersomeness* and *immobility* to describe his lyrical, certainly portable boxes. Again, we encounter an irony, this time one that reflects the complex relationship between his materials and his processes.

During the 1920s, Cornell discovered the joy of browsing through all manner of things and places, out and about in Manhattan. Too young for his job as a salesman and for his role as the family breadwinner, he followed his instinct for self-preservation into bookstores, libraries, theaters, galleries, penny arcades, secondhand stores (fig. 98), and the Christian Science Church. The intense solace and relief that Cornell experienced during this period would remain palpable even in recollections written in the late 1960s. Although not yet an artist, the young browser did not come away empty-handed. Mementos of favorite pastimes—posters from silent movies and Metropolitan Opera librettos—were carried home, while images of shop windows, street life, and art reproductions registered in a memory that merits the description *prodigious* (figs. 99 and 100). A quickly confident familiarity with the city also triggered Cornell's uncanny knack for finding things on a shoestring budget. Among his acquisitions that can be dated to the 1920s with certainty are a 1923 edition of *Lettres d'Odilon Redon, 1878–1916*, a Peggy Bacon drawing from a Whitney Studio Club auction, and the first copies in his eventually complete run of *Camera Work*.[6] Once a mediocre student at the prestigious Phillips Academy, Cornell found in New York the resources for an education without walls that pointed the way to his adventures in the arts.

The classic profile of a collector includes not just a compulsive or obsessive nature but also a sense of purpose, an attachment to the objects of desire, an appreciation of arranging, and a strong urge to share, whether to egotistical or unselfish ends. In Cornell's case, collecting inspired creative experimentation with his materials; his first documented artworks are dated 1931. Soon both activities would necessitate organizing his collection for its use as source materials and art supplies.

At Cornell's death in 1972, some three thousand books and magazines, hundreds of record albums, thousands of pieces of paper comprising his diaries and correspondence, and truly uncountable numbers of two- and three-dimensional ephemera all coexisted in his modest house—from cellar studio to attic, on shelves and table tops, along the floors and stairs (fig. 96).[7] Living and working in the midst of such a staggering volume and diversity of materials, Cornell experienced "transcendent moments" and "spells of inertia—maddening" as he juggled the multiple pursuits of artist, collector, and resident archivist responsible for sorting and maintaining it all.

This was an artist for whom browsing, collecting, and sifting were, at heart, experiences to be savored and lingered over for equal measures of stimulation and reverie (fig. 101).

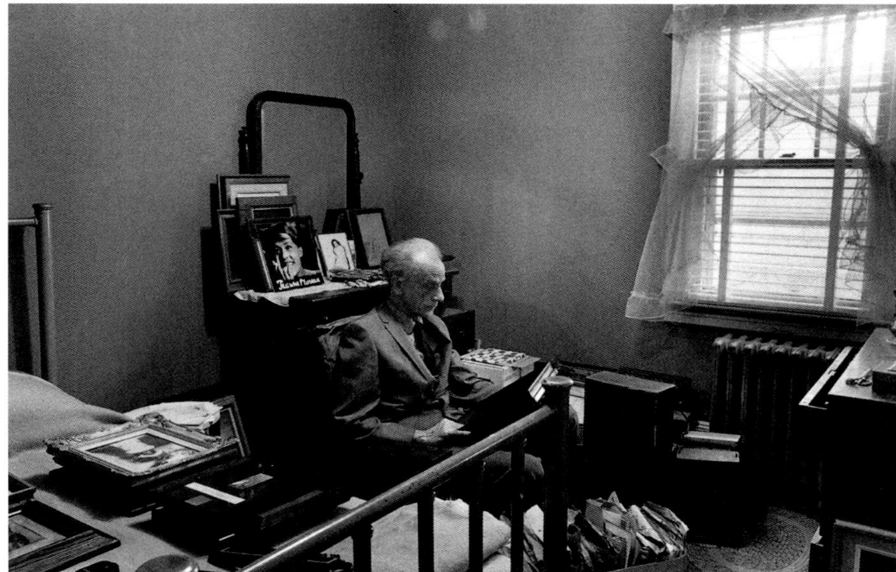

This was also an artist who lived to capture the "fleeting impressions" and "spontaneous unfoldment" of images and who frequently worked in "an automatic or semi-automatic state," especially when beginning a series of boxes or collages.[8] Conversely, Cornell relished handwork and took the acts of cutting, sanding, staining, painting, and pasting to elaborate levels in crafting his boxes and collages (fig. 102). Although this combination of activities was critical to how and what he created, they consumed enormous amounts of time and often led to detours or obstacles. Not unexpectedly, Cornell both resented and valued time's role in his art. As suggested by the title "Time Transfixed," which he borrowed from René Magritte for a collage series in the mid 1960s, Cornell longed for a way to collapse inspiration and execution into one moment, or at least into the shortest arc of time possible.[9] On the other hand, he recognized passing time's tonic effect on his work and welcomed the "spirit of renewal" that would transform ideas or works once set aside. Well aware of these conflicting concerns, Cornell often wondered how he could truly distill his ideas within the framework of a box. For someone who associated even the literal "sweepings" from his studio floor with "all the rich cross-currents ramifications etc. that go into the boxes but which are not apparent (I feel at least) in the final result," words like *cumbersomeness* and *immobility* could readily loom in his perception of the box format.[10]

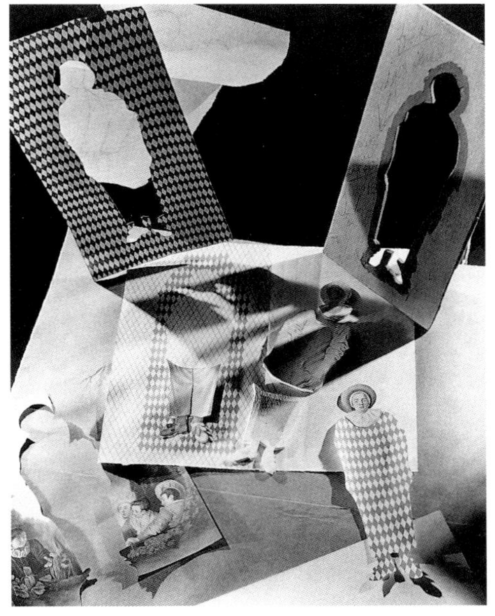

What's in a File? If all of this sounds more negative than not, frustration must nonetheless be recognized as a powerful motivational force in Cornell's work. He may have seesawed between dry spells and intense periods of activity, but he did not stop making boxes, even in the final year of his life.[11] Persistent in his search for "freer possibilities," however, he also developed a complement of works in other media and formats. His dozen or so experimental films and hundreds of collages are the conspicuous examples. Far less conspicuous are his "explorations," a small group of projects with considerable implications.

Anyone who wades into Cornell's papers and source materials quickly discovers a thicket of terms with interchangeable, multiple, or specific connotations. His use of the word *exploration* is particularly rich. He favored *exploration* and *voyaging* as synonymous descriptions of creativity, the pursuit of knowledge, and life itself. Allusions to a series of

101 **Cornell in an upstairs bedroom,** 3708 Utopia Parkway, Flushing, New York, 1972. Photograph by Duane Michals.

102 **Cornell's arrangement of materials after Watteau's *Portrait of Gilles*, c. 1938, prior to constructing *A Dressing Room for Gille*, 1939.** Vintage gelatin silver print, 10 x 8 in. Photograph by James Ogle.

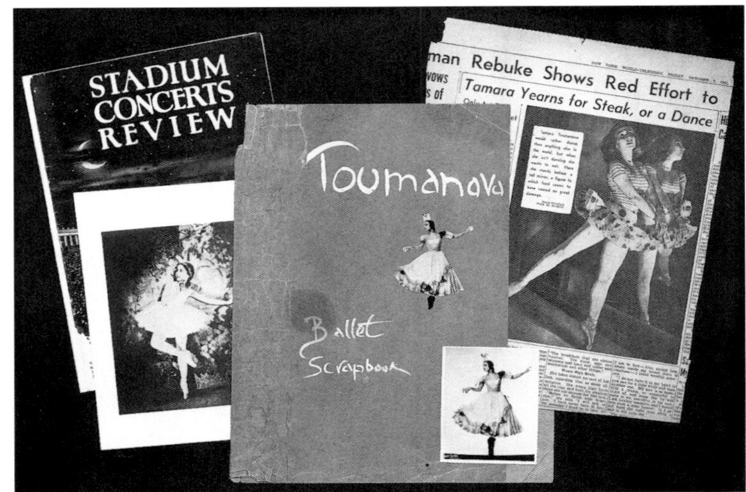

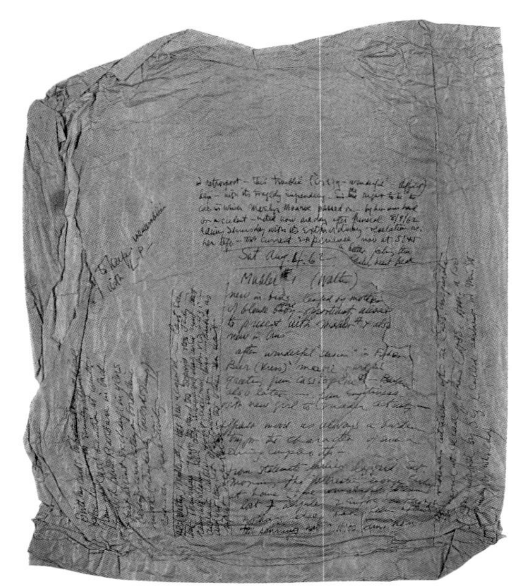

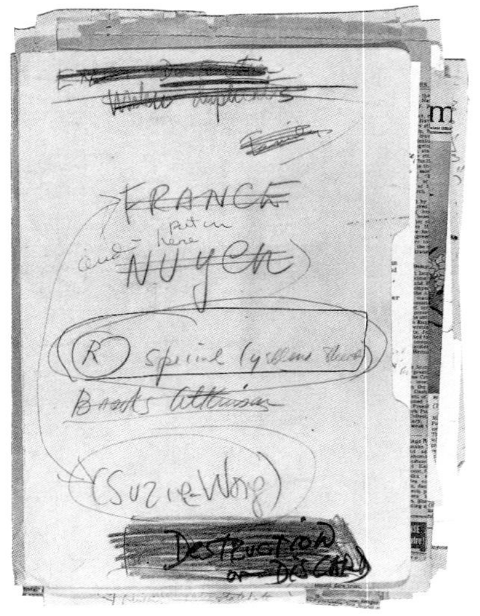

103 Cornell, paper bag with notes for "Marilyn Monroe" file, 1962–71. Joseph Cornell Study Center, Natl. Museum of American Art, Smithsonian. Gift of Mrs. Helen Batcheller.

104 Cornell, *Toumanova Ballet Scrapbook*, c. 1941. Dossier, 1/2 x 9 3/4 x 11 3/4 in. Joseph Cornell Study Center, Natl. Museum of American Art, Smithsonian. Gift of Mr. and Mrs. John A. Benton.

105 Cornell, *Suzie Wong (France Nuyen) Dossier*, c. 1958–71. Dossier, 2 x 8 x 11 in. Collection of Carolyn Farb, Houston.

boxes or collages as an "exploration" conveyed his sense of a common thread or touchstone uniting each. For pragmatic or archival purposes, he usually referred to his hundreds of subject and image files as just that—files—but he also used the terms *documents, dossiers, portfolios, scrapbooks*, and, yes, *explorations*.

Between 1926 and 1930, Cornell had kept a three-ring binder of clippings about art, literature, music, philosophy, and religion, drawn primarily from the "Home Forum" page of *The Christian Science Monitor*.[12] Filled with these didactic and evocative excerpts mounted on inexpensive notebook paper, the binder suggests the preoccupation of a Victorian schoolboy. Once he became an artist, Cornell began using similar binders to keep some of his files, especially those of favorite newspaper clippings, as well as illustration-board portfolios to protect oversize items like prints and photographs. Most of the filed materials, however, occupied traditional manila folders, legal-size envelopes, or those large, squarish, thin brown paper bags once favored by music stores and five-and-dimes like Woolworth's. In the interest of efficiency, the folders, envelopes, and bags provided ample surface for labeling and notation in addition to storage space (figs. 103 and 105). Whether devoted to people (particular ballerinas, actresses, writers, musicians, etc.) (fig. 104) or a topic ("Medici Slot Machine," "Falling Star Overflow," "Nostalgia of the Sea," and so on), the contents of a file were usually a helter-skelter affair. Maintaining an internal sequence was simply not a concern, especially when items tended to come and go—into artworks, magazine layouts, other files, other hands, even the trash. In Cornell's files, the vintage and the contemporary mingled freely in the form of photographs, Photostats, lithographs, engravings, postcards, excerpts from books, newspapers, and magazines, and notes—often lots of notes—on everything from envelope flaps to typing paper.

By whatever name, these paper-rich files complemented what Cornell called his "spare parts department."[13] Also stored in the basement studio were all manner of salvaged commercial containers—especially shoe boxes, cookie tins, stationery boxes, and packing cartons—their original identity often lost under coats of whitewash, penciled and painted inscriptions, and even pasted images to facilitate identification. Crammed into these containers were traditional art supplies as well as a breathtaking array of objects,

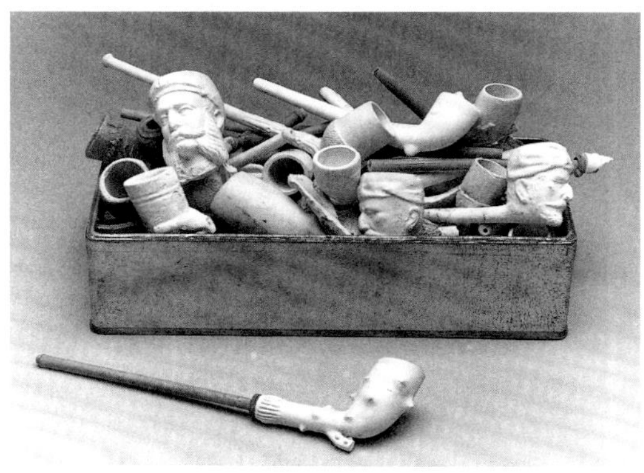

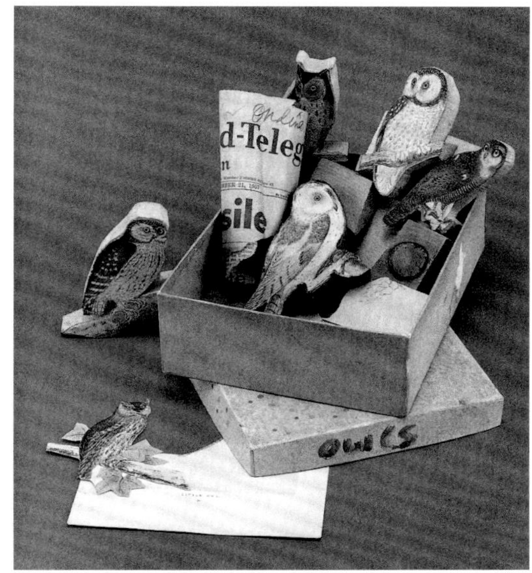

usually stored by type. Many, like the clay pipes and wineglasses, were "found" or "store-bought" (fig. 106). Cornell also prefabricated elements in bulk for his boxes, like mounted silhouettes of birds (fig. 107). With these files and cartons of materials on hand for both practical use and inspiration, the possibilities were endless, particularly for someone who described his studio as a "laboratory" and "experimental workshop."[14]

Inevitably, some of these materials took on an artistic life of their own rather than being assimilated into boxes and collages or simply lying fallow, waiting to be used. By 1940, Cornell had devised an alternative approach that freed him from the time-consuming tasks of building and hand-finishing his elaborate boxes and also offered the tantalizing prospect of keeping the "cross-currents" in flux. To describe this new approach— gathering together loosely arranged, primarily two-dimensional materials to express a central poetic idea—he chose the term *exploration*. Cornell usually housed these projects in folders, slipcases, or small suitcases that recalled old-fashioned portable artist's kits (fig. 108). He hoped eventually to produce his "explorations" as editions, publications, and even exhibitions. Soon, however, words like *dossier*, *case study*, and *scrapbook* began scuttling back and forth between the archival and creative realms of his vocabulary to augment *exploration* as synonyms for these projects. But while he inflected each "exploration" with different shades of meaning depending on which synonym he chose, his love of equivalents is the larger point.

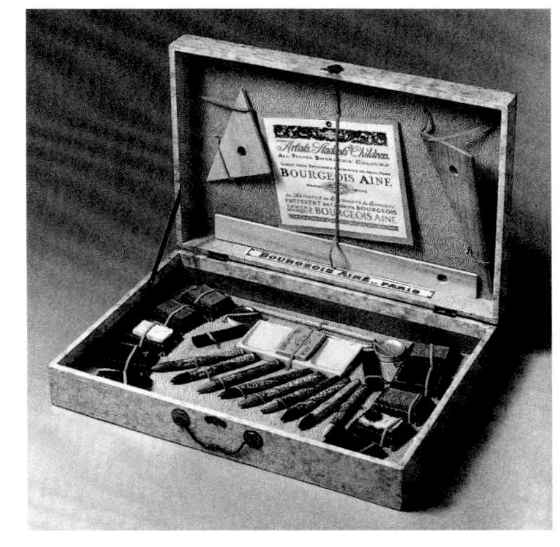

This taxonomic sketch facilitates rummaging through several examples of the two dozen or so projects that Cornell called "explorations."[15] It is impossible, however, to determine which "exploration" he considered his first. Dating these projects, in fact, is a challenge. Did each begin when Cornell started collecting the material, or when his priority for the material shifted from file fodder to project, or when he chose the kind of container he considered appropriate for either storage or presentation purposes? And how much time should the dates of an "exploration" encompass, especially since his start-and-stop revisions often stretched over several decades?[16]

"Did I tell you or Charles or Parker that Fanny Cerrito now reposes in a suitcase?" So Cornell wrote to his friend the Russian émigré painter and designer Pavel Tchelitchew on October 21, 1941.[17] Between December 1939 and March 1940, Cornell had regularly visited

106 Tin of clay pipes. Joseph Cornell Study Center, Natl. Museum of American Art, Smithsonian. Gift of Mr. and Mrs. John A. Benton.

107 Stationery box with owl cutouts. Joseph Cornell Study Center, Natl. Museum of American Art, Smithsonian. Gift of The Joseph and Robert Cornell Memorial Foundation.

108 Artist's kit, "Couleurs sans danger." Bourgeois Ainé, Paris, twentieth century. Joseph Cornell Study Center, Natl. Museum of American Art, Smithsonian. Gift of Mr. and Mrs. John A. Benton.

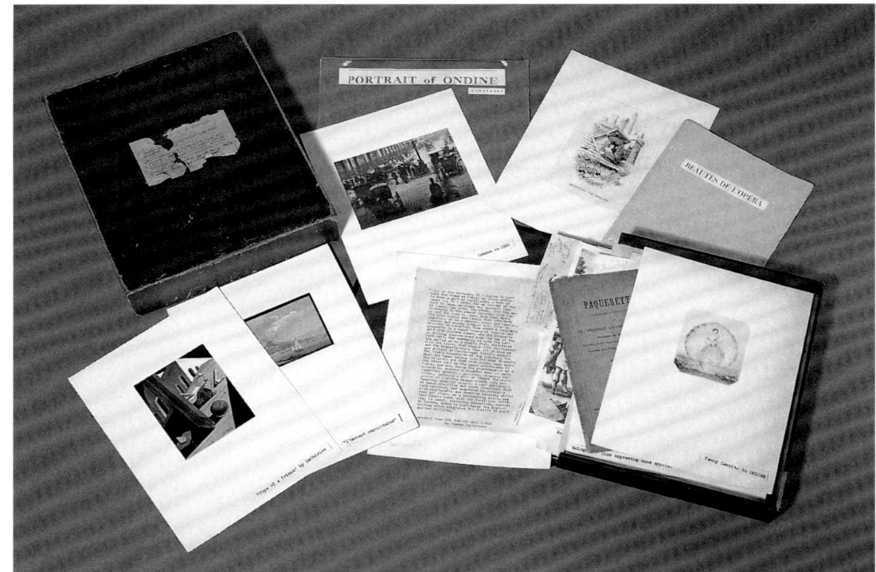

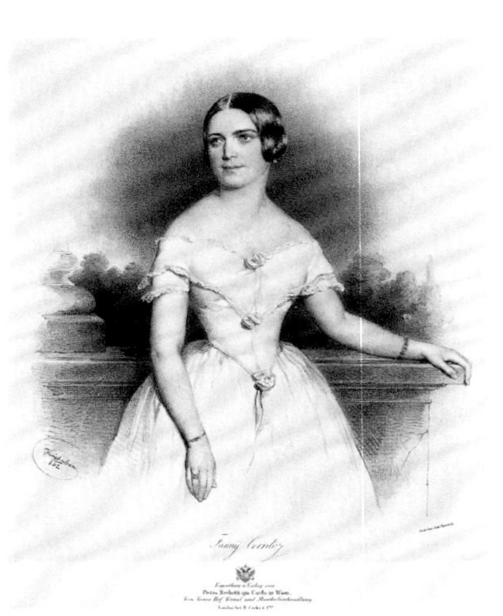

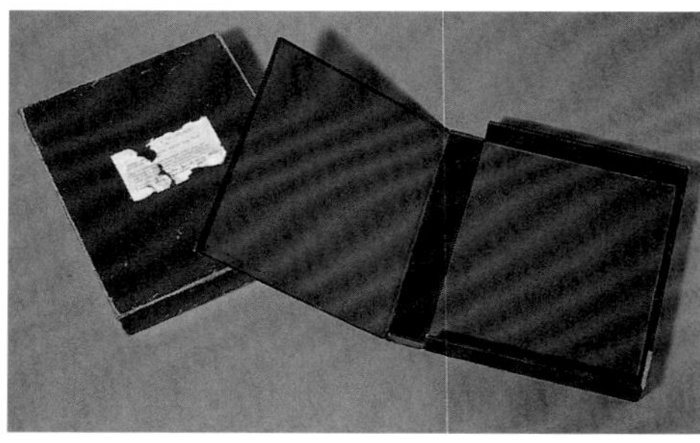

109 Cornell, *Portrait of Ondine*, c. 1940–late 1960s. Dossier, 2 1/2 x 10 3/4 x 12 3/4 in. Natl. Museum of American Art, Smithsonian. Gift of The Joseph and Robert Cornell Memorial Foundation.

110 Josef Kriehuber after Johannes Höfelich, *Fanny Cerrito*, 1842. Lithograph and chine-collé, 12 3/4 x 11 in., image. Joseph Cornell Study Center, Natl. Museum of American Art, Smithsonian. Gift of Mr. and Mrs. John A. Benton.

111 Cornell, paperboard slipcase and lid for *Portrait of Ondine*, c. 1940–late 1960s.

The Museum of Modern Art's newly opened Dance Archives, which had ignited his interest in the Romantic ballet.[18] Intuitively understanding the evanescent nature of dance, he began to assemble his own dance archives as well as a large group of boxes and collages to celebrate historical and contemporary ballerinas. In the summer of 1940, he "met" the Romantic ballerina Fanny Cerrito from Naples (1817–1909) while browsing in a Fourth Avenue bookstall, where he unearthed a rare example of Josef Kriehuber's 1842 souvenir lithograph of Cerrito, famous for dancing the role of the water nymph in the ballet *Ondine* (fig. 110). During two separate but particularly receptive reveries not long after, he caught sight of the ballerina in the window of a Manhattan building and while riding a train to Long Island. These events inspired Cornell's *Portrait of Ondine* (c. 1940–late 1960s), an "exploration" that went well beyond the boxes and collages also dedicated to Cerrito (pl. 59; fig. 109).[19]

Conceived in a bookstall, *Portrait of Ondine* began as an album, moved into a suitcase, made a public appearance in a shadow box, and wound up (but did not end) in the lidded paperboard slipcase that we encounter today (fig. 111).[20] The project, however, remained true to its goal as an "imaginary portrait" and "unauthorized biography," allusions to the poetic license that Cornell granted himself and his audience in reviving "Mlle. Cerrito."[21] Images mounted on white paperboard sheets, in the tradition of album pages as well as bookplates, formed the principal core of the "exploration," even as its housing changed and its contents expanded and contracted. Excerpts from nineteenth-century books (sometimes bound, sometimes loose), nineteenth-century watercolors of Naples, Kodachrome postcards of New York, European maps, a Cerrito autograph, and drafts of explanatory notes typically supplemented the plates. In the heat of the project's early production, between 1940 and 1942, Cornell apparently intended to augment the visual elements with a written text. The numerous drafts in his papers and his laments about the task in letters to friends, however, make clear that this component of *Portrait of Ondine* was destined to languish.[22]

Cornell's elliptical tendencies aside, he endowed the assembly of materials with a sense of direction by choosing a "key picture," a photographic reproduction of the Kriehuber lithograph.[23] The subject thus identified, the plates move from the documentary to the imaginative in their labeled references to Stendahl, Hans Christian Andersen, New York's

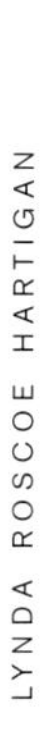

skyscrapers, Bologna's architecture, the paintings of Giorgio de Chirico, and other topics in no particular order. To those who prefer the linear or who are unschooled in the finer points of everything from Cerrito's biography to all of art history, the contents will certainly appear disconnected or haphazard. On one level, it is helpful to know that the image labeled "Migrations–The Swallow" refers to Andersen's description of Cerrito's dancing: "It was a swallow in flight in the dance, a sport of Psyche" (fig. 112).[24] On the other hand, such specific knowledge is absolutely unnecessary as long as one is open to enjoying a "bouquet of the past and the present."[25] The intent and process are highly associative, and the work invites us to join the artist in experiencing the materials gathered and offered in the spirit of "image making akin to poetry."[26]

This spirit unites all of the "explorations," yet each has its own character. *The Crystal Cage [portrait of Berenice]* (pl. 54), for example, is decidedly literary, a piece of visual fiction for which Cornell invented a short story featuring Berenice, an imaginary heroine. The story begins:

> The recent unearthing (1934–1942) of a wealth of paraphernalia, charts, photographs, manuscript notes, etc., a welter of "varia" of formidable proportions, finally establishes beyond any possibility of doubt the existence of the legendary PAGODE DE CHANTELOUP, that curious relic of scientific research in the nineteenth century.[27]

The person responsible for unearthing the "varia" was, of course, Cornell himself. Much of the dated material in the suitcase version of *The Crystal Cage* falls within the years 1936 and 1942, but the contents do not correspond directly to the description given. In the literal sense, "paraphernalia" and "charts" are nowhere to be found in the handmade wood case, complete with papered exterior and a brass handle. The most prominent item is a large untitled collage (pl. 72.3) that Cornell made in 1942 in a style reminiscent of both Victorian scrapbook pages (fig. 113) and the montage technique then favored by publicists in the film industry. The collage, however, almost gets lost in the "welter" of photographs, reproductions, and clippings pertaining to the arts, children's activities, historical sites, and scientific phenomena. Lining the lid is a photographic reproduction of the Pagode de Chanteloup, an eighteenth-century folly that did exist, and still does, in the Loire Valley of France.

But to return to Cornell's story, in 1871 the young Berenice formed such a strong attachment to the Pagode de Chanteloup that her parents moved it, like heaven and earth, from France to their home in New England. In the tower, Berenice performed ingenious experiments inspired by the sights and sounds of the visible world. The materials gathered in *The Crystal Cage* are thus intended to substantiate these fantastic events and the girl's "marvels of ingenuity and poetry."[28] Cornell's heroine is the child of all times and places whose adventuresome curiosity leads to creativity and knowledge (fig. 116).

Very rough drafts of the brief text appear in the encased version of *The Crystal Cage* (fig. 115) as well as in two separate source material files, "Crystal Cage" and "Towers."[29] For a cleaner, edited version, one must turn to the pages of the avant-garde magazine *View* in its "Americana Fantastica" issue of January 1943. Cornell designed the issue's covers and contributed a variety of designs throughout, including a seven-page layout, *THE Crystal Cage [portrait of Berenice]* (pl. 72). The layout is composed of text, illustrations, a typographic "folly" emulating the Pagode de Chanteloup's silhouette (fig. 114), and a full-page

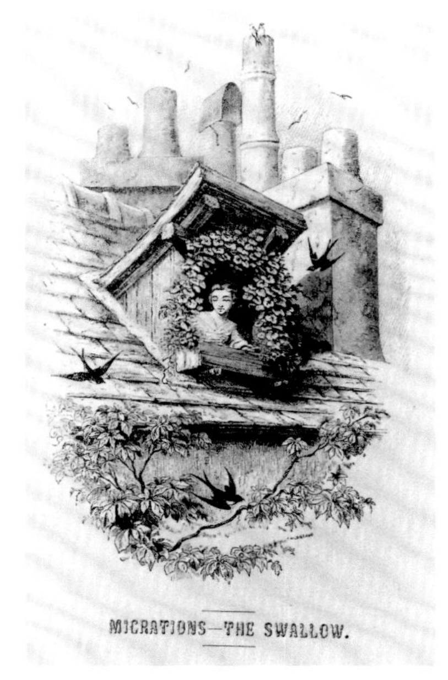

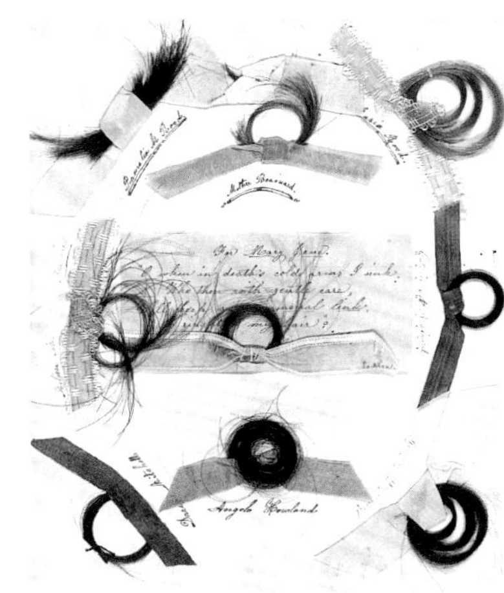

112 Cornell, mounted plate of "Migrations–The Swallow," from *Portrait of Ondine*, c. 1940–late 1960s.

113 Page of hair wreaths from Mary E. Brainard's personal album, *Flower Tokens*, 1852–56. Collection of Mrs. John A. Benton.

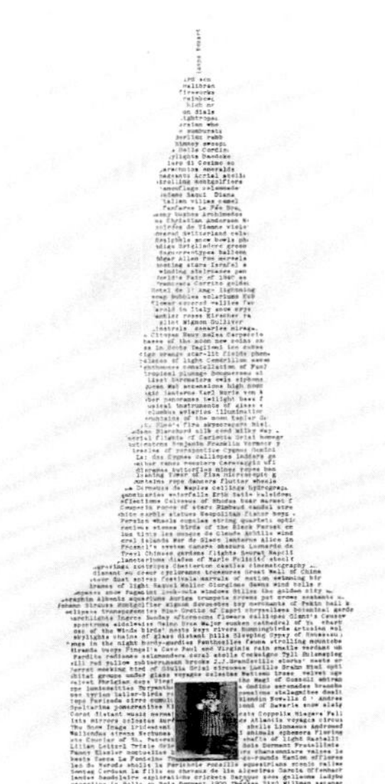

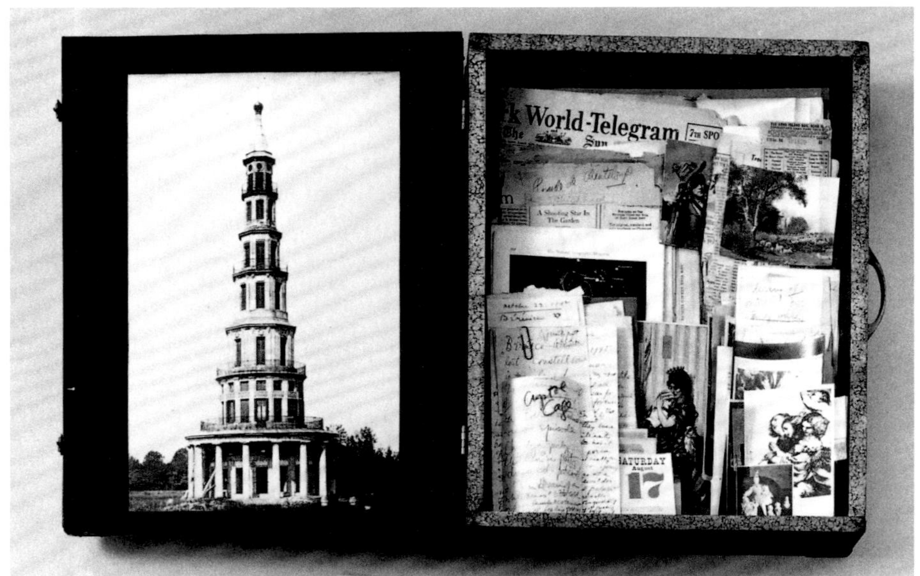

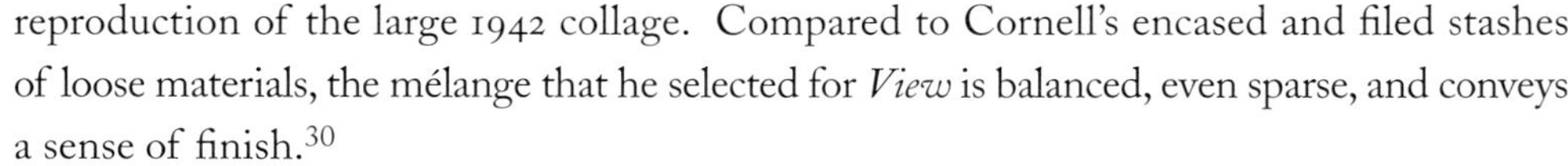
reproduction of the large 1942 collage. Compared to Cornell's encased and filed stashes of loose materials, the mélange that he selected for *View* is balanced, even sparse, and conveys a sense of finish.[30]

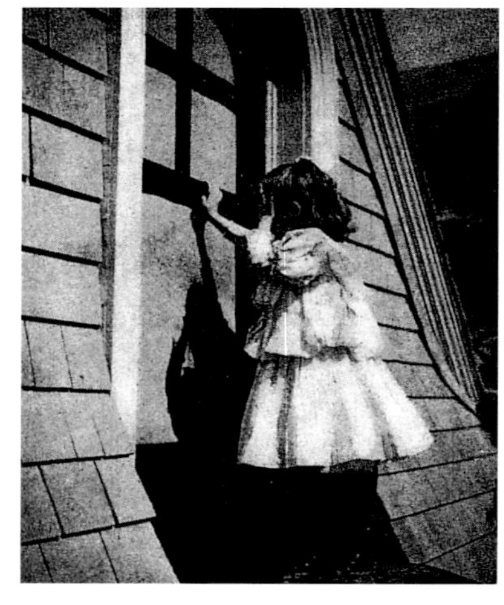

Writing to poet Marianne Moore two months after *THE Crystal Cage* appeared in print, Cornell observed that "I had felt the whole thing was much too subtle and complex to attempt in the comparatively limited space of a magazine, and without your appreciative words, I would continue to think of the [Berenice project] as futile."[31] Subtlety is the crux of successful sleight-of-hand, or sleight-of-word in the instance of the multipart *Crystal Cage*. Cornell's references to the years 1934 to 1942 in the project's text suggest that it was well under way before the editors of *View* solicited his contribution, and his letter to Moore confirms the published layout as part of a larger whole. He wrote the flurry of notes and drafts found in the suitcase version, however, primarily over the nine months preceding the layout's publication in *View*. Further, Cornell clearly entertained both "Pagode de Chanteloup" and "Crystal Cage" as titles before settling on the latter. Had the project already taken on its character of a fictional story through the gathering of specific materials since 1934? Or did he cull material from diverse files to compose the project as a story for publication and then encase it all for ongoing revision and consultation?

These questions arise because the project's origin is nebulous. Although Cornell was very inconsistent about recording information pertaining to his boxes, he credited most of the "explorations" to a specific momentous event, which he wrote about over time—in his diaries, in correspondence, and usually in notes incorporated into each "exploration." That *The Crystal Cage* seems to lack a singular moment of inspiration is striking. Many of the "explorations," however, also center on an individual, whether actual or invented. In this instance, Cornell's "Berenice" is a metaphorical composite:

> . . . these Berenices encountered all and always unexpectedly seen for a few moments and then gone forever—on subways, in a city crowd, that is the crux perhaps if they were seen too often—familiarity breeds contempt—this habit of read[ing] so much into a person on first sight especially an appealing child or young girl. . . .[32]

114 Cornell, typographic rendering of the Pagode de Chanteloup, from *THE Crystal Cage [portrait of Berenice], View* (January 1943): p. 11.

115 Cornell, *The Crystal Cage [portrait of Berenice]*, c. 1934–67. Dossier, 4 3/8 x 15 5/8 x 19 7/8 in. Collection of Richard L. Feigen, New York.

116 Cornell, "Berenice of 1900 gazing into her own past and present," detail, from *THE Crystal Cage [portrait of Berenice], View* (January 1943): p. 16.

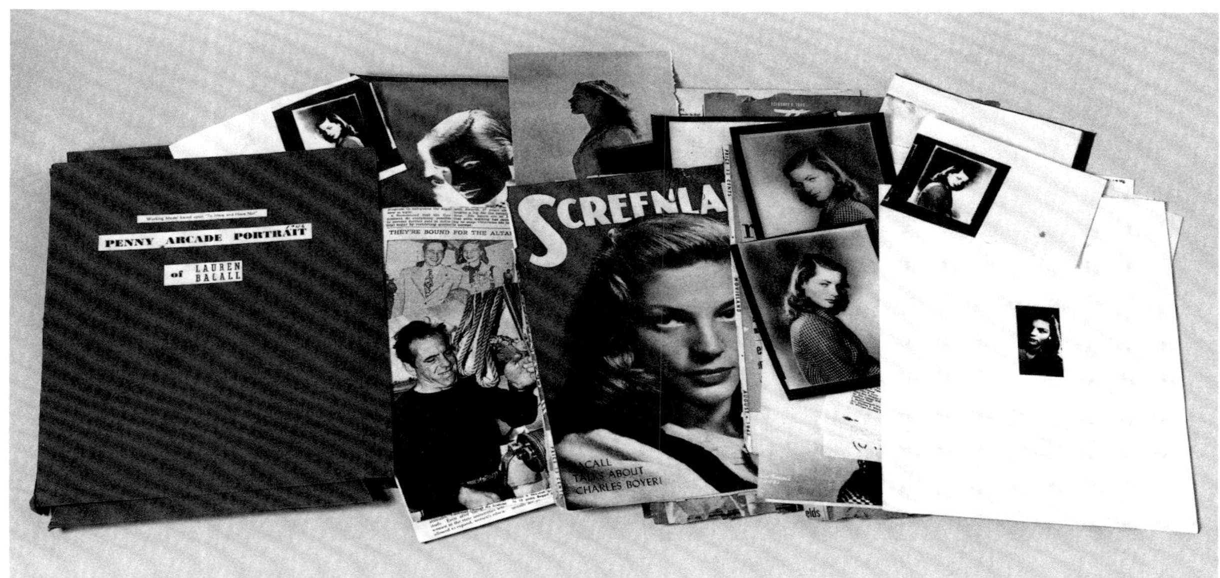

In keeping with his interest in repeated sightings, Cornell's proposal for *Paris Exhibition of 1900 (Seen Through the Eyes of Berenice)* in the mid 1940s adds to the sense that an "exploration" could inspire variants in a manner comparable to the serial character of his boxes and collages.[33] The prospect of Berenice's Parisian adventure also confirms his need to keep the visionary nature of childhood close at hand.

Working on his "imaginary portrait" of the actress Lauren Bacall during the mid 1940s, Cornell observed: "The Portrait became wonderfully 'alive' and even a soiled piece of newspaper with an account of the Danish underground in the War seemed to 'belong' [somehow indispensably to this scrap-album material accompanying it.]"[34] Over the course of 1945, Cornell saw Bacall's first film, *To Have and Have Not* (1944), six times. He began accumulating biographical material, photographs of Bacall as a fashion model, and Hollywood publicity shots with the help of his contacts at *Vogue* and *Harper's Bazaar*. By August 1945, he was busy working on a box construction, Untitled *(Penny Arcade Portrait of Lauren Bacall)* (pl. 86), having resolved that "in order to hold fast (impressions intriguingly diverse), one might assemble, assort, and arrange into a cabinet, the contraption kind of the amusement resorts with endless ingenuity of effect."[35] By December 1946, the box was finished, as was the heavyweight paper folder that he had made to house his collection of Bacall photographs, movie magazine excerpts, and copious notes (pl. 87; fig. 117). Within Cornell's entire body of work, this box and its companion "scrap-album material" enjoy a singular partnership.

Hands down, the box is the handsome member of the pair, with its smooth, gleaming wood exterior, alluring photograph of Bacall, veils of blue glass, and well-orchestrated design. It is, moreover, a masterful synthesis of three of the artist's interests: the penny arcade, the actress herself, and the history of film. From the atmosphere and games of New York's penny arcades, Cornell had derived one of the principal symbols for his childhood memories. He was fascinated by Bacall's sultry screen persona, but he also sensed that the decade's new siren was quite different in real life and focused on this dichotomy once he realized that the nineteen-year-old actress struggled with it herself. References to film—those early peephole picture machines in penny arcades (fig. 118), the blue-tinted

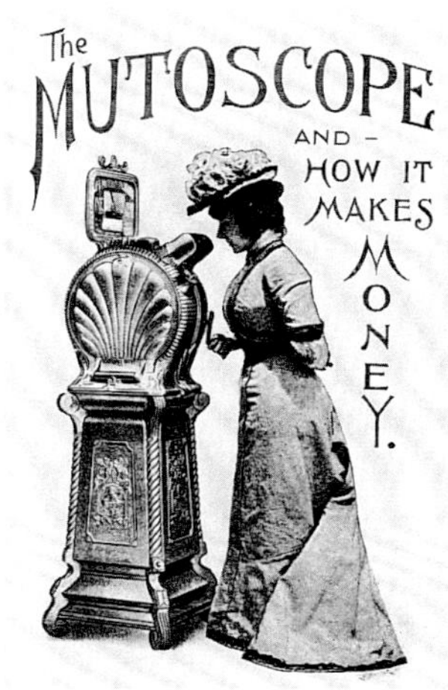

117 Cornell, *Penny Arcade Portrait of Lauren Bacall (Working Model Based Upon "To Have and Have Not")*, c. 1945–70. Dossier, 3/4 x 8 3/4 x 12 in. Collection of Lindy Bergman, Chicago.

118 Advertisement for The Mutoscope, a moving picture machine invented in 1895. Private collection.

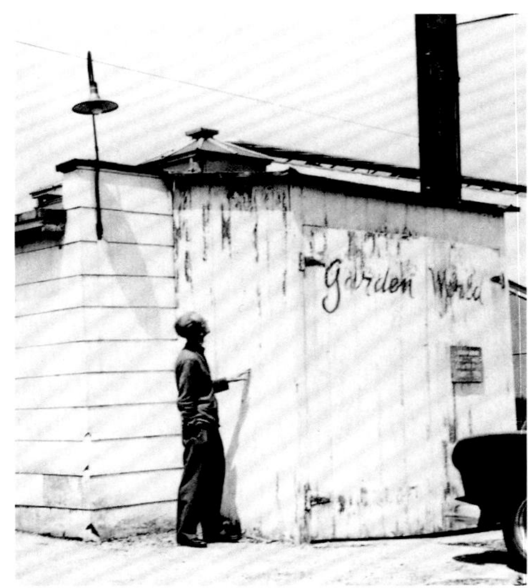

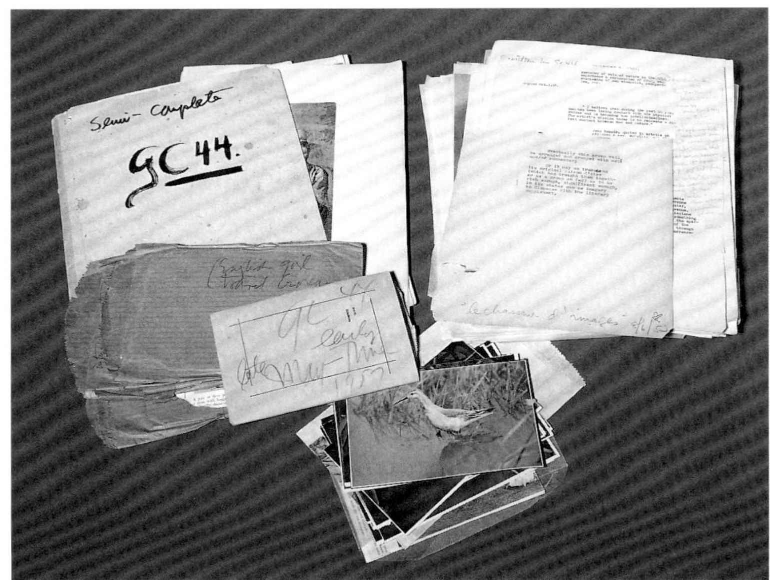

silent movies, and the glamorous stars of the silver screen—abound in the work's structure and spirit, informed by Cornell's knowledgeable appreciation of the medium.

With blue covers echoing the box's color scheme, the companion folder is nondescript in appearance. Yet it, too, is an intriguing synthesis of allusions. Its hand-creased, unpretentious design has the charm of a schoolboy's report or a fan's scrapbook. The cover's primary label, which names Bacall, as well as the pictures and notes inside suggest something official, along the lines of a publicist's dossier. The folder also evokes a film scenario or script, courtesy of its label *Working Model Based upon "To Have and Have Not."*

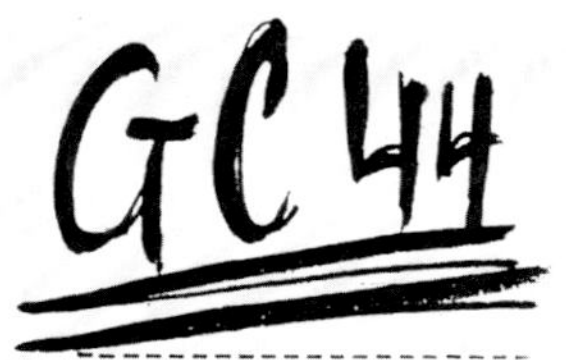
GC 44

journey album
journal album
esperanto of imagery
keepsake
repository
romantic museum
childhood regained
tower of visions
heritage
center of a labyrinth
sanctuary
diary
a "method" ~~for the reader~~

Cornell's most focused "exploration" lives up to the promise of these multiple associations. As appealing to us today as it was to him then, this mini-survey of Bacall's photographs and press coverage provides an enlightening glimpse of the ambitious publicity campaign that heralded her debut. Contrary to his usual approach in a dossier or "exploration," however, Cornell did not amass multiple copies of images but instead kept to a minimum items that seem more tangential. Typed sheets headed "personal notes," "revised notes," "technique," "general working notes," and "note of gratitude" provide his clearest written exposition of the origin and evolution of a specific box. These notes amply fulfill the dossier's stated function as a "working model."

Ironically, while the folder is dated 1946 and bears the title *Penny Arcade Portrait of Lauren Bacall (Working Model Based upon "To Have and Have Not")*, the box itself is undated and untitled. And although he based the box on his Medici Slot Machine series, Cornell stepped away from his usual practice and made neither variants nor other types of work dedicated to Bacall. His additions and revisions to the folder's contents were relatively minimal once the box had been completed.[36] No other box construction can claim such a dossier, cogently documentary yet richly associative in its own right. And no other "exploration" evolved so closely in tandem with a single box. The pair, then, are pendants in subject and moment.

If the dossier *Penny Arcade Portrait of Lauren Bacall* is the artist's most disciplined, then the voluminous "exploration" *GC 44* (pl. 76; fig. 120) is his most ambitious. Cornell worked at the Garden Center, a large nursery in Bayside, New York, from spring to winter

119 Cornell at Garden World, Bayside, New York, 1957, from *GC 44*, c. 1944–70. Joseph Cornell Study Center, Natl. Museum of American Art, Smithsonian. Gift of Mr. and Mrs. John A. Benton.

120 Cornell, *GC 44*, c. 1944–70. Dossier, 3½ x 9½ x 11 in. Joseph Cornell Study Center, Natl. Museum of American Art, Smithsonian. Gift of Mr. and Mrs. John A. Benton.

121 Cornell, undated sheet of working notes, detail, from "GC 44" file, c. 1944–70. Joseph Cornell Papers, Archives of American Art, Smithsonian.

1944 (fig. 119). The nursery's Arcadian atmosphere, combined with an avalanche of impressions and dreams inspired by his bicycle rides along streets, through meadows, and by the water, precipitated this autobiographical "exploration."

Like an antenna, Cornell seemed to quiver with the receipt of rapid and frequent signals from diverse directions. Nowhere is this more evident than in his struggles to shape *GC 44* as an intimate "journal album."[37] Its theme was his abiding love of the "ethereal magic of simplicity in the commonest aspects of Nature," expressed in observations like "the expansiveness of the heavens, the song of nature throughout the night, the breezes, the fragrances of the grasses,—like a great breathing, deep, harmonious, elemental, cosmic."[38] Under this umbrella theme, he hoped to capture the revelatory beauty he had experienced during the summer of 1944.

The sheaves of materials that remain in *GC 44* reveal the enormity of the challenge Cornell had set for himself in conceiving the project's multivalent character: "journey album, journal album, esperanto of imagery, keepsake, repository, romantic museum, childhood regained, tower of visions, heritage, center of a labyrinth, sanctuary, diary, a 'method' [for the reader]," all in one (fig. 121).[39] Cornell considered Alain-Fournier's novel *Le Grand Meaulnes [The Wanderer]* (1912), which he had first read in translation in 1942, as the "key" to compiling the project.[40] The themes of this popular novel were nostalgia, escapism, the child's world of innocence and purity, and the intermingling of dream and reality, all concepts for which Cornell had great affinities. Comparing the novel's "air of expectancy" to that of a mystery or detective story, he attributed a fair degree of that aura to Fournier's use of evocative chapter titles.

Cornell apparently had all this in mind when he conceived *GC 44* in the form of "an adventure or mystery novel," albeit minus the genre's sensational elements. Clearly, he regarded the summer of 1944 as an adventure. Experiences as diverse as sighting a sign on a moving truck or dreaming about riding his bicycle to Buffalo had coalesced into "an apocalyptic realm of shining beauty" visible in unexpected yet everyday circumstances. From these revelatory incidents, Cornell culled seven associative themes for the "exploration's" chapterlike sections: "The Old Farm," "Festival of Nature," "Rue Bicherie (for D.T.)," "The Floral Still-Life," "The Little Dancer," "The House on the Hill," and "Americana."[41] He planned a group of portfolios, each with a title page identifying its theme (fig. 122), an array of evocative mounted plates, and an expository written supplement.

Poring through magazines (especially art periodicals), newspapers, and photographs, Cornell gathered all manner of picturesque images—from medieval illuminated manuscripts to a photojournalist's essay on English dairy farms—as visual equivalents of each section's theme. In language that many contemporary artists would appreciate, he noted that "the process of 'appropriating' has been employed: a still-life of Morandi, the Kodachrome of the upland plover, the Chinese Autumn panel of the Sung epoch, etc."[42] He mounted many of the images on album-size sheets of heavy white watercolor paper. He also typed title pages for each thematic section, searched his diaries for relevant notations, and drafted still others. His intended order for the plates within a given portfolio is virtually impossible to determine, as is any sequence he may have intended for the portfolios as a group. One of his notes, however, suggests that while Cornell wanted to provide a sense of direction, he also hoped that viewers would feel free to make choices: "aspect of leaving plates clean mounted supplying 'experiences' via sets of numbers (of the pages, to

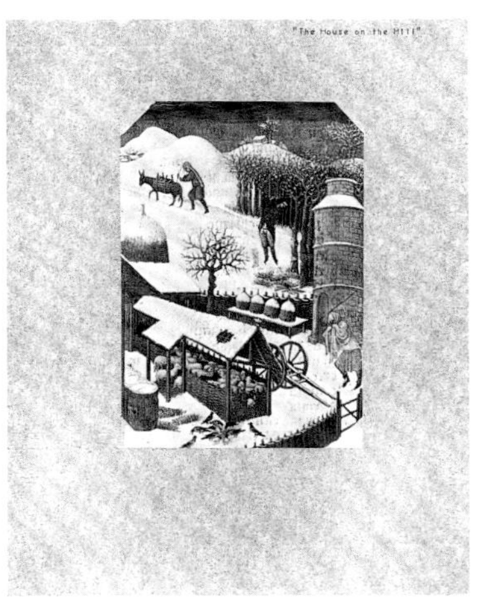

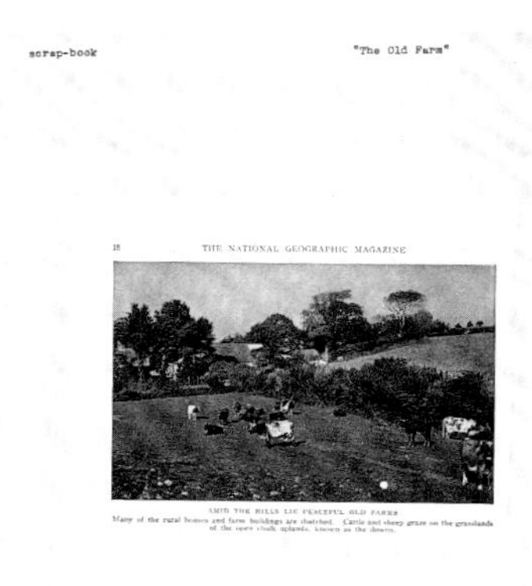

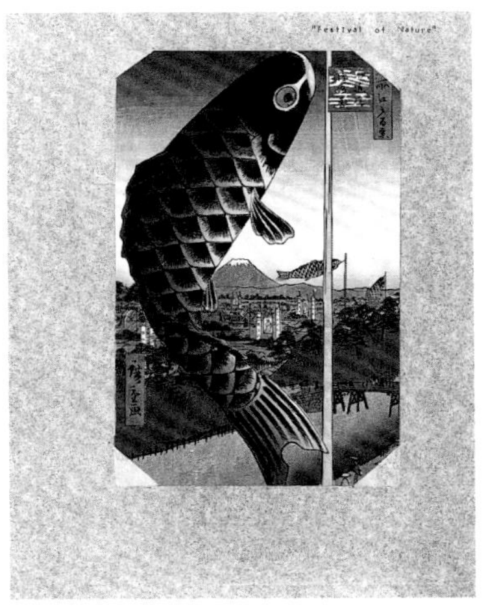

122 **Cornell, mounted chapter title pages, "The House on the Hill," "The Old Farm," and "Festival of Nature," from *GC 44*, c. 1944–70.** Joseph Cornell Study Center, Natl. Museum of American Art, Smithsonian. Gift of Mr. and Mrs. John A. Benton.

be looked at in a given order) the reader is thus left to 'enter' the 'House on the Hill' via the plates of his own choosing."[43] This approach echoes that of Stéphane Mallarmé, one of Cornell's greatest sources of inspiration, and tellingly, the *GC 44* materials include a newspaper article "What a Poet Knows," which opens with the statement, "Yeats was fond of quoting Mallarmé: 'A poem is a mystery for which the reader must seek the key.'"[44]

By the early 1950s, however, Cornell himself appeared to have lost the key, for *GC 44* had become a source of immense frustration. Sifted, reviewed, tended to, or set aside—nothing seemed to yield a satisfactory portfolio, let alone a full set of "illustrated chapters" complete with text. As late as 1970, laments of faded inspiration and confusion about his intentions alternated with exhilarating moments of renewal or relief from feeling guilty about the project's lack of resolution. But even in the genuinely casual state in which Cornell left it, the mounted plates are sufficient in number and variety to suggest an album, traditionally a sampling rather than a catalogue. His fragmentary but extensive notes are the stuff of a diaristic journal, and the outline of an adventure or a mystery is there for anyone curious enough to enter the "exploration" in the spirit of the mysterious chateau that is the leitmotif of Fournier's novel.[45]

Fond of the word *apotheosis*, Cornell would be surprised to know that *GC 44* could be considered just that in his family of "explorations." Expanding in *GC 44* upon the album-style mounting of *Portrait of Ondine*, he also shifted from using one "key picture" with its "Mallarméan nuance" to endowing many key pictures with multiple possibilities.[46] His attempts to create an adventure mingling reality and fantasy in the encased and published versions of *The Crystal Cage* echo in the larger ambitions of multiple visual chapters within *GC 44*'s composite of adventures and impressions. His hopes that "G.C. 44 realized successfully can become a 'method' for crystallizing experiences . . . in a communicable form" and that "discipline will also be acquired against the habit of too much piling up" did not materialize in the project itself, yet the desire for discipline bore obvious fruits in the leaner dossier *Penny Arcade Portrait of Lauren Bacall*.[47]

Given that Cornell found the discipline and "crystallization" of his boxes confining, it is ironic that he yearned for these very qualities to harness the open-ended, elusive "exploration" *GC 44*. Marked "semi-complete," the project is Cornell's fullest expression of the possibilities inherent in not finishing. A lengthy observation written in 1952 summarizes how he came to terms with this:

> also early morning (while ironing) . . . the dormant periods of works in progress like PORTRAIT OF ONDINE, etc. CRYSTAL CAGE, THE FLORAL STILL LIFE, the aspect of what might have come about in the way of development, the "compounded interest," "crystallization." But at the same time nothing could have been more complete than the summer experiences of 1951 transcending (especially at river's edge L.I.City—across from the skyline)—thoughts while pressing—one cannot leave a hot iron plugged in & forget about it like the projects—however, a more relaxed attitude antidoting this startling idea,—the sense of continuity (and the experiences such as just mentioned) as vs. winding up once & for all.—Another thought as of 3/19/52.—Can the ecstacy [sic] of the original GC44 expers. ever be done justice to—if not then the consideration of looking upon this compilation as a "phenomenon," an absorbing residue for which to be grateful even if the intensity of the original exps. cannot be recaptured & presented with the original full flavor & context.[48]

What's in a Name? Cornell's "explorations" were a constellation of works in various states of readiness, always to be continued. Only his death finally determined their state as unfinished. Although they provided territory for his intense tending and contemplation, examples like *Portrait of Ondine* and *The Crystal Cage* were not so private or unresolved that he considered an audience for the works irrelevant. In fact, an audience is precisely what he wanted. Having credited his origins as an artist to "the exploring that became creative," Cornell believed in art's potential for communication and education in a distinctly imaginative rather than didactic fashion.[49] The phrase "imaginative picture research," which recurs in notes pertaining to many of the "explorations," is not just an allusion to their associative method or to his lengthy career as a free-lance picture researcher, which began in the mid 1930s with assignments from fashion photographer Cecil Beaton, film critic Gilbert Seldes, and American fashion and popular home magazines (figs. 123 and 124). No, it is something of a mission statement for this inherently idealistic artist. Cornell hoped that encounters with his "explorations" especially would encourage others to pursue beauty and knowledge in the "warp and woof of daily life," just as he had. Friends, strangers, artists, working-class people—"readers," as he considered them all—would have direct access to the projects, browsing through them as if through a Victorian album, a bookstall, or even a secondhand store.

Cornell, however, had no intention of leaving those encounters completely to chance. The label on the lidded slipcase of *Portrait of Ondine* outlines his plans: "master material culled down from original suitcase to be worked over further for final selection—to be duplicated into an edition for private collectors, schools, traveling exhibits for galleries, etc. (make prospectus for advance sale with original specimen sheet)."[50] Comparable statements, also focusing on the prospect of editions and exhibitions, accompany *The Crystal Cage* in its encased and published versions and even the sprawling *GC 44*.

Although the language in *Portrait of Ondine*'s label shares similarities with that of Duchamp's four boxed editions, Cornell's editorial phrases "to be worked over further" and "to be duplicated" also hint at an important difference between the two men's sensibilities. Duchamp pursued his plans for any number of artworks and editions over long periods of time with a single-mindedness that reflected the strategy-oriented thinking of a chess player. Cornell persisted erratically in revising most of his "explorations," but a systematic means of producing them in editions eluded him, in part because he resisted the finality inherent in editing and duplicating the contents. The lengthy list of Cornell's pictorial designs published in the specialized periodicals *View* and *Dance Index*, as well as in commercial magazines such as *Vogue*, during the 1940s belies the degree to which editors and art directors lamented his legendary perfectionism and phobic disregard of deadlines.[51]

Publishing, however, was the only means by which Cornell produced multiples and limited editions of some projects. His pictorial essays in *View*—*"Enchanted Wanderer": Excerpt from a Journey Album for Hedy Lamarr* (pl. 64) and THE *Crystal Cage*—as well as the three thematic issues that he contributed to *Dance Index* between 1945 and 1947 can be considered multiples. Cornell's first film scenario, *Monsieur Phot,* could be described as both a multiple and a limited edition, based on the twenty numbered copies he typed and assembled within heavy black paper folio covers. He also privately printed the pamphlets *Maria* (1954) and *the* BEL CANTO PET (1955) as editions, drawing on materials he had started to gather in the mid 1930s on the nineteenth-century opera divas Maria Malibran

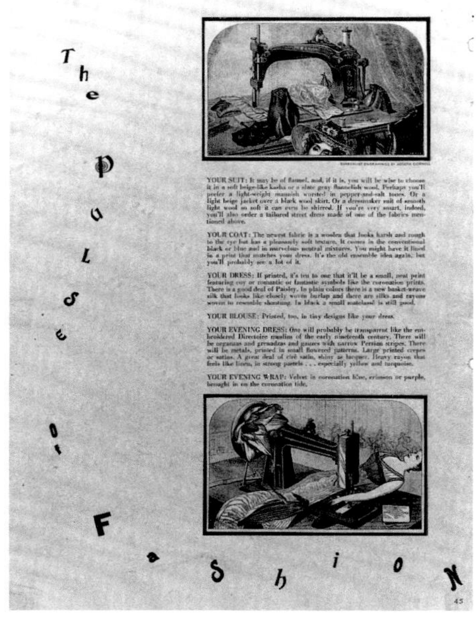
The Pulse of Fashion

YOUR SUIT: It may be of flannel, and, if it is, you will be wise to choose it in a soft beige-like kasha or a slate gray flannelish wool. Perhaps you'll prefer a light-weight mannish worsted in pepper-and-salt tones. Or a light beige jacket over a black wool skirt. Or a dressmaker suit of smooth light wool so soft it can even be shirred. If you're very smart, indeed, you'll also order a tailored street dress made of one of the fabrics mentioned above.

YOUR COAT: The newest fabric is a woolen that looks harsh and rough to the eye but has a pleasantly soft texture. It comes in the conventional black or blue and in marvelous neutral mixtures. You might have it lined in a print that matches your dress. It's the old ensemble idea again, but you'll probably see a lot of it.

YOUR DRESS: If printed, it's ten to one that it'll be a small, neat print featuring coy or romantic or fantastic symbols like the coronation prints. There is a good deal of Paisley. In plain colors there is a new basket-weave silk that looks like closely woven burlap and there are silks and rayons woven to resemble shantung. In black a small matelassé is still good.

YOUR BLOUSE: Printed, too, in tiny designs like your dress.

YOUR EVENING DRESS: One will probably be transparent like the embroidered Directoire muslins of the early nineteenth century. There will be organzas and grenadines and gauzes with narrow Persian stripes. There will be metals, printed in small flowered patterns. Large printed crepes or satins. A great deal of ciré satin, shiny as lacquer. Heavy rayon that feels like linen, in strong pastels . . . especially yellow and turquoise.

YOUR EVENING WRAP: Velvet in coronation blue, crimson or purple, brought in on the coronation tide.

43

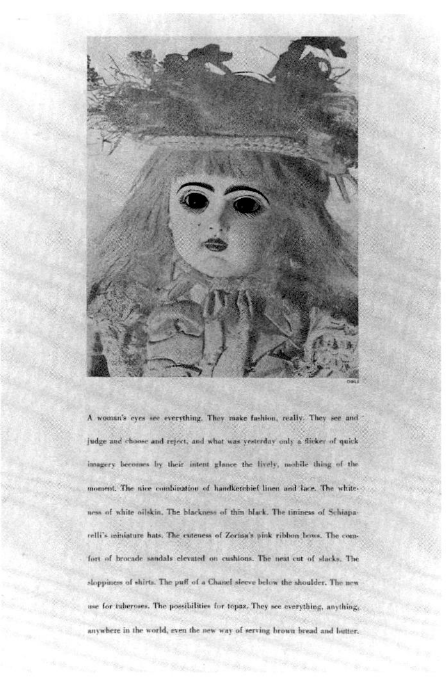
A woman's eyes see everything. They make fashion, really. They see and judge and choose and reject, and what was yesterday only a flicker of quick imagery becomes by their intent glance the lively, mobile thing of the moment. The nice combination of handkerchief linen and lace. The whiteness of white oilskin. The blackness of thin black. The tininess of Schiaparelli's miniature hats. The cuteness of Zorina's pink ribbon bows. The comfort of brocade sandals elevated on cushions. The neat cut of slacks. The sloppiness of shirts. The puff of a Chanel sleeve below the shoulder. The new use for tuberoses. The possibilities for topaz. They see everything, anything, anywhere in the world, even the new way of serving brown bread and butter.

123 "The Pulse of Fashion" featuring two untitled collages by Cornell, *Harper's Bazaar* (February 1937): p. 43. Joseph Cornell Study Center, Natl. Museum of American Art, Smithsonian. Gift of Mr. and Mrs. John A. Benton.

124 "A Woman's Eyes" featuring photograph of Victorian doll "Bébé Marie," *Harper's Bazaar* (July 1938): p. 23. Arranged by Joseph Cornell; photograph by James Ogle. Joseph Cornell Study Center, Natl. Museum of American Art, Smithsonian. Gift of Mr. and Mrs. John A. Benton.

and Julia Grisi, respectively. He alluded to plans for album-style "explorations" comparable to *Portrait of Ondine* during the 1940s, but the pamphlets *Maria* and *the* BEL CANTO PET are each no bigger than five by seven inches, designed as "bouquets" of excerpted texts, tipped-in reproductions, interleafed tissue paper, and pasted cutouts. He inscribed individual examples, housed in matching envelopes, and distributed them to friends as gifts.[52]

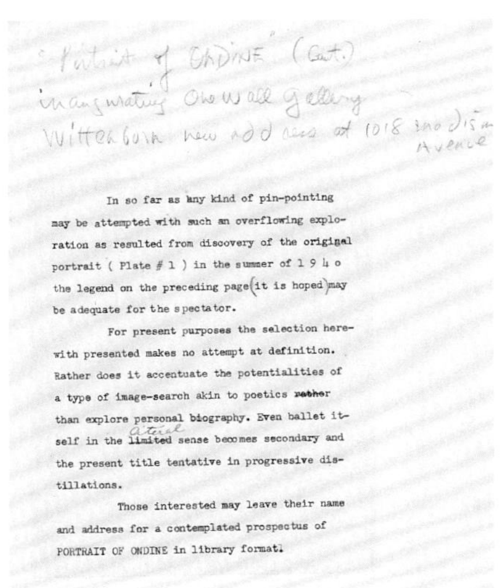
In so far as any kind of pin-pointing may be attempted with such an overflowing exploration as resulted from discovery of the original portrait (Plate # 1) in the summer of 1 9 4 o the legend on the preceding page (it is hoped) may be adequate for the spectator.

For present purposes the selection herewith presented makes no attempt at definition. Rather does it accentuate the potentialities of a type of image-search akin to poetics rather than explore personal biography. Even ballet itself in the limited sense becomes secondary and the present title tentative in progressive distillations.

Those interested may leave their name and address for a contemplated prospectus of PORTRAIT OF ONDINE in library format!

Cornell attained the closest approximation to a master set for a boxed edition of his "explorations" in *Portrait of Ondine*. The slipcased container is small and sturdy, more amenable to transport by hand or mail, as well as to accommodation on shelves and tables, than the larger handmade suitcases he initially favored. The case contains twenty-six mounted and labeled plates and Cornell's mockups for two slim pamphlets. One, "PORTRAIT OF ONDINE CONTINUED," features a reproduction of the inspirational Kriehuber lithograph of Cerrito, a statement of purpose, and a teaser: "Those interested may leave their name and address for a contemplated prospectus of PORTRAIT OF ONDINE in library format"[53] (fig. 125). The other, "Beautés de l'Opéra," offers the chapter "Ondine" excerpted from the album *Les Beautés de l'Opéra* (1844–45) by Théophile Gautier, Jules Janin, and Philarête Chasles. A vintage pamphlet devoted to *Pâquerette*, another ballet associated with Cerrito, is the principal item among the sundry loose materials.

The teaser to "those interested" apparently did not attract a waiting list of clients, and one wonders about the complex interplay of Cornell's reluctance to finish, a temperament unsuited to salesmanship, let alone self-promotion, and the tenor of the times when even Duchamp had difficulty selling his boxed editions. In 1956, the price that Cornell had in mind when he offered *Portrait of Ondine* to the trend-setting museum director Jermayne MacAgy, though, was reasonable: "tentative price for double set of plates, approx. 50–100/$100–150."[54]

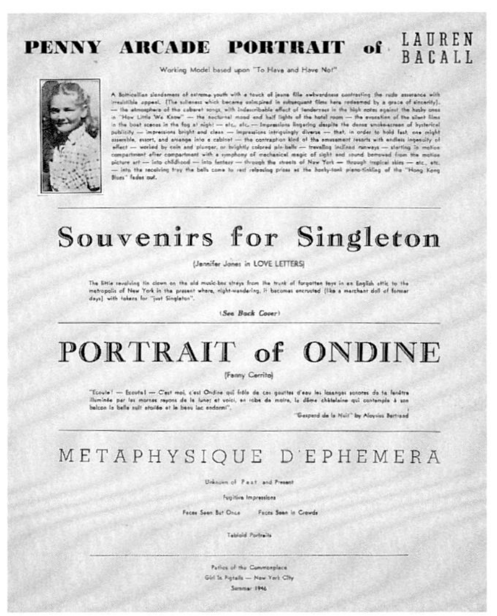
PENNY ARCADE PORTRAIT of LAUREN BACALL

Working Model based upon "To Have and Have Not"

Souvenirs for Singleton

(Jennifer Jones in LOVE LETTERS)

(See Back Cover)

PORTRAIT of ONDINE

(Fanny Cerrito)

"Gaspard de la Nuit" by Aloysius Bertrand

METAPHYSIQUE D'EPHEMERA

Unknown of Past and Present

Fugitive Impressions

Faces Seen But Once Faces Seen in Crowds

Tabloid Portraits

Pathos of the Commonplace

Girl in Pigtails — New York City

Summer 1946

From the outset of his career, Cornell never lacked for exhibition opportunities in prestigious museums and avant-garde galleries, yet his desire to exhibit his "explorations" met with only mild success during his lifetime. The most notable occasion was the presentation of "Romantic Museum at the Hugo Gallery/Portraits of Women: Constructions and Arrangements by Joseph Cornell" in New York during December 1946. Sadly, both eyewitness accounts and installation photographs are lacking for this show, which included *Portrait of Ondine*, *The Crystal Cage*, Untitled *(Penny Arcade Portrait of Lauren Bacall)*, and the last's companion dossier. Although the elaborate announcement (pl. 80; fig. 126) that Cornell designed for the event conveys the sense of a bevy of objects and documentary materials gathered in celebratory fashion, it provides few hints of the installation itself, which he also arranged.

Just a year earlier, *Portrait of Ondine* had made its debut in the Auditorium Gallery at The Museum of Modern Art in New York, and the museum's press release provides some insight into what visitors to the Hugo Gallery might have encountered on an expanded scale:

> The exhibition . . . is an extremely small one—so small that the entire display is contained within a large shadow box. . . . Specifically, the imaginative portrait consists of prints, books, music covers, colored fashion plates, rare original photographs, coins, fragments of materials, etc. and explanatory labels and appropriate quotations.[55]

125 Cornell's statement of purpose for "Portrait of Ondine" exhibition (November 1–15, 1956), Wittenborn Bookstore, 1018 Madison Avenue, New York, from *Portrait of Ondine*, c. 1940–late 1960s.

126 Cornell, announcement for "Romantic Museum at the Hugo Gallery/Portraits of Women: Constructions and Arrangements by Joseph Cornell" (December 3, 1946), Hugo Gallery, 26 East 55th Street, New York, right inside panel of exhibition folio.

More hints of Cornell's design aesthetic for the "Romantic Museum" exhibition can be extrapolated from his undated proposal [c. 1955] for another installation: "SCRAP-BOOK OF SWITZERLAND (presented as a sideshow or fair booth) or exhibition" with "memorabilia, orig. photos prints etc. Baedeckers"[56] (fig. 127). Although never realized, the proposal suggests a three-dimensional, multisensory "exploration," complete with a series of booths à la Coney Island, plans for seating, music, and poetry readings, with "The black of mounting paper and curtains always borne in mind to set off the material."[57] Cornell's aspirations for his "explorations" as installations reveal not just an imaginative alternative for experiencing his projects and collections but also his love of props and atmospheric display as theater.

Despite Cornell's intense interest in using his "explorations" as a means of reaching the public, the projects themselves also speak to private, contemplative moments, whether for the artist or the viewer/reader. They are the creation of a man who valued his privacy and did not feel the need to reveal all, especially when it came to his art. It is this sense of the personal and the private that envelops his *Duchamp Dossier*.[58]

On July 31, 1942, Cornell received Duchamp at his house on Utopia Parkway; his guest had emigrated from wartime France to New York in late June. Having shared a modest lunch, they spent the afternoon looking at an example of Duchamp's *Boîte-en-valise [Box-in-a-Valise]* (1935–41)—"a case of his life's work," as Cornell's brother, Robert, described it.[59] Word of the two artists' friendship and Cornell's participation in assembling examples of the *Boîte* edition would spread, fade away, and inevitably resurface. How fitting, then, that the container Cornell used for his *Duchamp Dossier* resembles a *Boîte* or incorporates its structural elements.[60]

Shortly after Duchamp's death on October 2, 1968, Cornell struggled to draft a condolence note to the artist's widow, Teeny. He cited their first brief encounter in December 1933 at Brummer Gallery, where Duchamp had organized an exhibition of Constantin Brancusi's sculpture.[61] Unemployed because of the Depression, Cornell had begun making and exhibiting his objects two or so years earlier and was about to celebrate his thirtieth birthday. In his condolence note, he recalled "the piquant flavor of contact with a unique personality. Rare, rare qualities . . . I feel my debt is real & great."[62] Six months after Duchamp's death, Cornell's investigation of the word *salamandre* revived a wistful memory that affords another glimpse into the nature of their relationship: "the salamandre was a kind of old fashioned stove—too late—how one would like to quiz Marcel Duchamp on this—his courtly 'coming up smiling' on so many subjects. . . ."[63] Both of these recorded memories resonate with all that Cornell often wrote in his diaries and correspondence about "the transformation of persons, places & objects etc. in the exaltation of experience—nec[essity] of the realization of the mental nature of this—the significance of its spiritual nature—the importance of recapturing its meaning in its context & full flavor."[64]

The *Duchamp Dossier* contains ample evidence of Cornell's efforts to recapture a relationship based on mutual admiration and affection. Like the lithograph that inspired *Portrait of Ondine*, the autographed reproduction of the *Large Glass* is the "key picture," the token of that first meeting between strangers. It is highly likely, however, that Cornell was already aware of the older artist's work. Those bookstalls and bookstores that he frequented on the Lower East Side during the 1920s handled not just secondhand material but the latest publications about French art and culture, as well as New York's avant-garde "little" magazines. In his diaries during the 1960s, Cornell recorded his memories of the

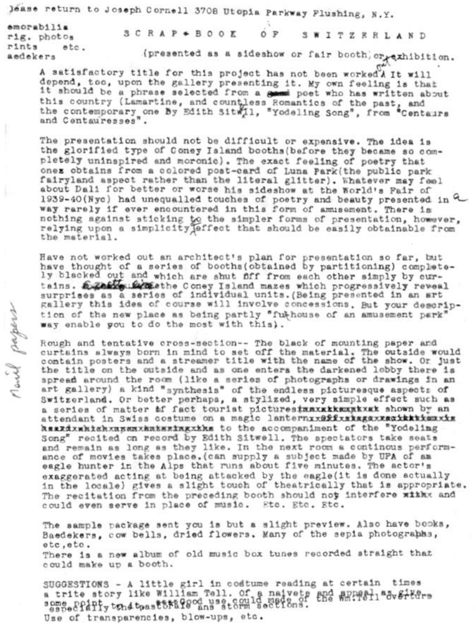

Please return to Joseph Cornell 3708 Utopia Parkway Flushing, N.Y.

memorabilia
orig. photos
prints etc.
Baedekers

S C R A P - B O O K O F S W I T Z E R L A N D

(presented as a sideshow or fair booth) or exhibition.

A satisfactory title for this project has not been worked out. It will depend, too, upon the gallery presenting it. My own feeling is that it should be a phrase selected from a poet who has written about this country (Lamartine, and countless Romantics of the past, and the contemporary one by Edith Sitwell, "Yodeling Song", from "Centaurs and Centauresses".

The presentation should not be difficult or expensive. The idea is the glorified type of Coney Island booths(before they became so completely uninspired and moronic). The exact feeling of poetry that ones obtains from a colored post-card of Luna Park(the public park fairyland aspect rather than the literal glitter). Whatever may feel about Dali for better or worse his sideshow at the World's Fair of 1939-40(Nyc) had unequalled touches of poetry and beauty presented in a way rarely if ever encountered in this form of amusement. There is nothing against sticking to the simpler forms of presentation, however, relying upon a simplicity effect that should be easily obtainable from the material.

Have not worked out an architect's plan for presentation so far, but have thought of a series of booths(obtained by partitioning) completely blacked out and which are shut off from each other simply by curtains. ... the Coney Island mazes which progressively reveal surprises as a series of individual units.(Being presented in an art gallery this idea of course will involve concessions. But your description of the new place as being partly "funhouse of an amusement park" may enable you to do the most with this).

Rough and tentative cross-section-- The black of mounting paper and curtains always born in mind to set off the material. The outside would contain posters and a streamer title with the name of the show. Or just the title on the outside and as one enters the darkened lobby there is spread around the room (like a series of photographs or drawings in an art gallery) a kind "synthesis" of the endless picturesque aspects of Switzerland. Or better perhaps, a stylized, very simple effect such as a series of matter of fact tourist pictures shown by an attendant in Swiss costume on a magic lantern to the accompaniment of the "Yodeling Song" recited on record by Edith Sitwell. The spectators take seats and remain as long as they like. In the next room a continous performance of movies takes place.(can supply a subject made by UPA of an eagle hunter in the Alps that runs about five minutes. The actor's exaggerated acting at being attacked by the eagle(it is done actually in the locale) gives a slight touch of theatrically that is appropriate. The recitation from the preceding booth should not interfere and could even serve in place of music. Etc. Etc. Etc.

The sample package sent you is but a slight preview. Also have books, Baedekers, cow bells, dried flowers. Many of the sepia photographs, etc,etc.
There is a new album of old music box tunes recorded straight that could make up a booth.

SUGGESTIONS - A little girl in costume reading at certain times a trite story like William Tell. Of a naivete and appeal as give some point to it. Good use could made of the Wm.Tell overture especially the pastorale ans storm sections.
Use of transparencies, blow-ups, etc.

Menil papers

127 Cornell's exhibition proposal "SCRAP-BOOK OF SWITZERLAND," **undated [c. 1955].** The Menil Collection Archives, Houston.

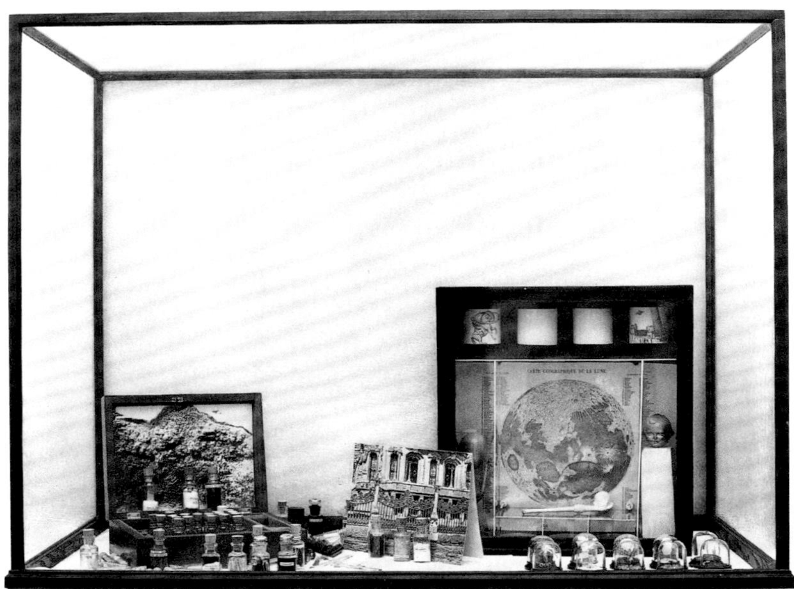

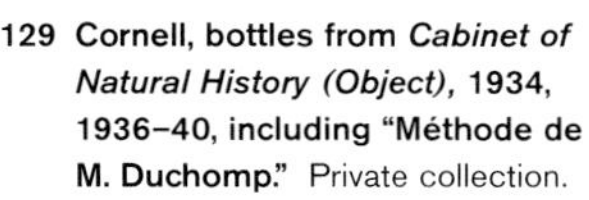

128 Cornell, *Cabinet of Natural History (Object)*, 1934, 1936–40, at left in Cornell's "Elements of Natural Philosophy and Soap Bubble Set" installation, "Fantastic Art, Dada, Surrealism" (December 9, 1936–January 17, 1937), The Museum of Modern Art, New York. Photograph by Soichi Sunami.

129 Cornell, bottles from *Cabinet of Natural History (Object)*, 1934, 1936–40, including "Méthode de M. Duchomp." Private collection.

1920s, noting regularly his hunger for information about modern French art, literature, and music. At the same time, the young man had also started visiting the Brooklyn Museum. One wonders, of course, whether he saw the museum's 1926 exhibition of the Société Anonyme's collection of modern art that included the *Large Glass*, pictured in the 1927 *Art News* reproduction that he received from Duchamp in January 1934.

Because the materials in the *Duchamp Dossier* date primarily from the years during which the two men had regular contact in New York, between 1942 and 1953, it seems likely that Cornell's accumulation of "Duchampiana" did not coalesce as a project until a decade after their initial contact in 1933. Instead, he first registered his very high regard for Duchamp as an artist in two key works made during the 1930s.

Originally an antique portable apothecary chest, *Cabinet of Natural History (Object)* bears the dates 1934 and 1936–40 (pl. 52).[65] It is a stunningly complex work for so newly emerged an artist, and the box received recognition very quickly: Alfred Barr included it in the historic exhibition "Fantastic Art, Dada, Surrealism" at The Museum of Modern Art in 1936 (fig. 128). The contents and labels of the fifty-five glass bottles and vials featured in the box provide a survey of natural phenomena—from magnetism to the polarization of light—that establishes Cornell's singular interest in science as a means of understanding existence and even creativity. Shunning the theoretical, he preferred the term "Natural Philosophy," in vogue in American and European circles until around 1860 to describe natural and manmade wonders as a synthesis of religious, aesthetic, and scientific theories. Named in the bottles' labels is a cast of characters composed primarily of innovative scientists from the seventeenth to the nineteenth centuries, Blaise Pascal, Sir Isaac Newton, and Sir John Frederick William Herschel among them. One writer—Edgar Allan Poe, who loved scientific hoaxes—and one artist—Duchamp, who transformed the quasi-scientific into an art—also make an appearance. *Méthode de M. Duchomp* is the label for a bottle filled with fairly jagged strips of clear glass (fig. 129).[66] Even a superficial reading of Cornell's deliberately altered spelling of the name suggests his understanding of the manner in which Duchamp's Cubist paintings, readymades, and the *Large Glass* had chewed up perceptions of modern art.

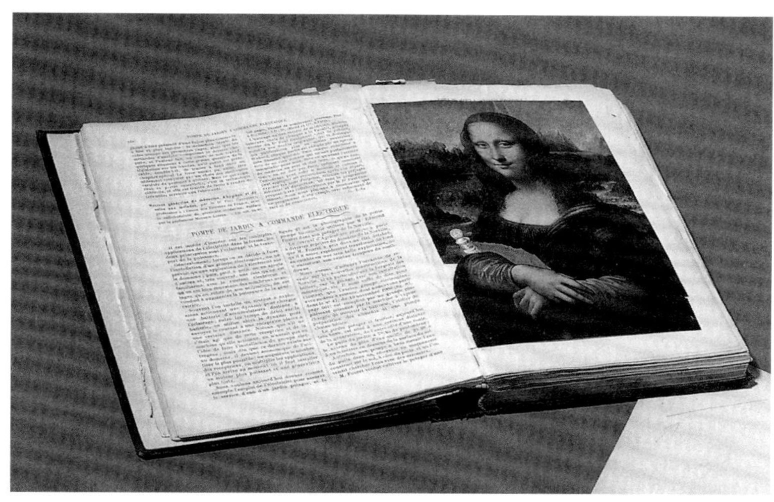

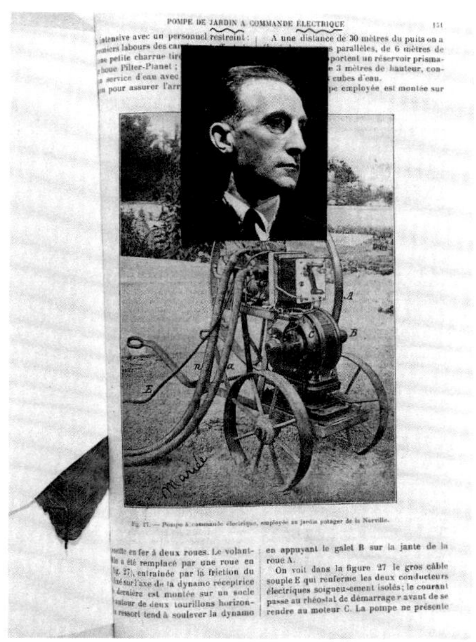

130 Cornell, collage overlay of *Mona Lisa* from **Untitled Book Object** ***(Journal d'Agriculture Pratique et Journal de l'Agriculture)*, c. 1933–mid 1940s.** The Joseph and Robert Cornell Memorial Foundation.

131 **Cornell, Duchamp collage on page "*Pompe de Jardin A Commande Électrique*," beneath *Mona Lisa* overlay, from Untitled Book Object *(Journal d'Agriculture Pratique et Journal de l'Agriculture)*, c. 1933–mid 1940s.** The Joseph and Robert Cornell Memorial Foundation.

The second work is a "book object," the armature for which Cornell chose the twenty-second volume of *Journal d'Agriculture Pratique et Journal de l'Agriculture* (1911).[67] He transformed the book with an extensive array of collages, inserts, inked designs, cutouts, overlays, and sequential effects (pl. 51). He also kept a companion folder of small collages tucked inside the altered book's rear cover, where the dates 1935 and 1938 appear in inscriptions, though this book object may have occupied Cornell from as early as 1933 and as late as the 1940s.[68] This time Duchamp appears in a company dominated by artists such as the illuminator of manuscripts for Le Duc de Berry, Diego Velasquez, Jean-Baptiste-Camille Corot, Édouard Manet, and Pablo Picasso, whose works are "quoted" as details from reproductions. Quickly paging through this feast for the eyes and mind is not possible, if only because the old volume is in delicate condition. Yet the sense of a "moving picture" book is inescapable as impressions of the images go by, top to bottom, across page spreads, and through apertures, front to back.

About a third of the way through, the *Mona Lisa* and Duchamp make a joint appearance. Tipped in, the silhouetted color reproduction of the *Mona Lisa* is slit to cradle a dried leaf and cutouts of French perfume bottles and a woman's straw hat in her arms (fig. 130). Cornell's salute to Duchamp's rectified readymade *L.H.O.O.Q.* (pl. 5) emphasizes the feminine and pastoral, while his choice of perfume bottles evokes *Belle Haleine, Eau de Voilette [Beautiful Breath, Veil Water]* (1921), the title for both a collaborative photomontage by Duchamp and Man Ray and one of Duchamp's assisted readymades featuring his alter ego Rrose Sélavy. Lifting the reproduction of the *Mona Lisa* reveals a head-shot detail of Lusha Nelson's 1934 photograph of Duchamp for *Vanity Fair* superimposed on an illustration of a "*Pompe de Jardin A Commande Électrique* [Electrically Operated Garden Pump]" (fig. 131). Cornell also inscribed *Mariée* in the lower left corner of the composition, reinforcing his imaginary portrait's allusions to the *Large Glass* in a French book about practical agriculture—the inverse, it would seem, to the occupation of "dust breeder" that Duchamp claimed for himself.

The French artist's next appearance in the book is more oblique. An inscription that accompanies the three-page section "*Fâ~~u~~cheuse Automobile* [Irritating or Troublesome

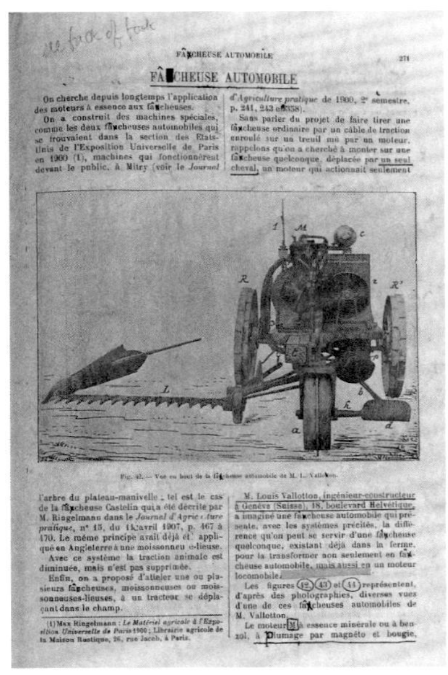

FÂCHEUSE AUTOMOBILE 271

FÂCHEUSE AUTOMOBILE

On cherche depuis longtemps l'application des moteurs à essence aux fâcheuses.

On a construit des machines spéciales, comme les deux fâcheuses automobiles qui se trouvaient dans la section des États-Unis de l'Exposition Universelle de Paris en 1900 (1), machines qui fonctionnèrent devant le public, à Mitry (voir le *Journal d'Agriculture pratique* de 1900, 2e semestre, p. 241, 243 et 358).

Sans parler du projet de faire tirer une fâcheuse ordinaire par un câble de traction enroulé sur un treuil mû par un moteur, rappelons qu'on a cherché à monter sur une fâcheuse quelconque, déplacée par un seul cheval, un moteur qui actionnait seulement l'arbre du plateau-manivelle ; tel est le cas de la fâcheuse Castelin qui a été décrite par M. Ringelmann dans le *Journal d'Agriculture pratique*, n° 15, du 11 avril 1907, p. 467 à 470. Le même principe avait déjà été appliqué en Angleterre à une moissonneuse-lieuse.

Avec ce système la traction animale est diminuée, mais n'est pas supprimée.

Enfin, on a proposé d'atteler une ou plusieurs fâcheuses, moissonneuses ou moissonneuses-lieuses, à un tracteur se déplaçant dans le champ.

Fig. 42. — Vue en bout de la fâcheuse automobile de M. L. Vallotton.

M. Louis Vallotton, ingénieur-constructeur à Genève (Suisse), 18, boulevard Helvétique, a imaginé une fâcheuse automobile qui présente, avec les systèmes précités, la différence qu'on peut se servir d'une fâcheuse quelconque, existant déjà dans la ferme, pour la transformer non seulement en fâcheuse automobile, mais aussi en un moteur locomobile.

Les figures 42, 43 et 44 représentent, d'après des photographies, diverses vues d'une de ces fâcheuses automobiles de M. Vallotton.

Le moteur M à essence minérale ou à benzol, à allumage par magnéto et bougie,

(1) Max Ringelmann : *Le Matériel agricole à l'Exposition Universelle de Paris 1900* ; Librairie agricole de la Maison Rustique, 26, rue Jacob, à Paris.

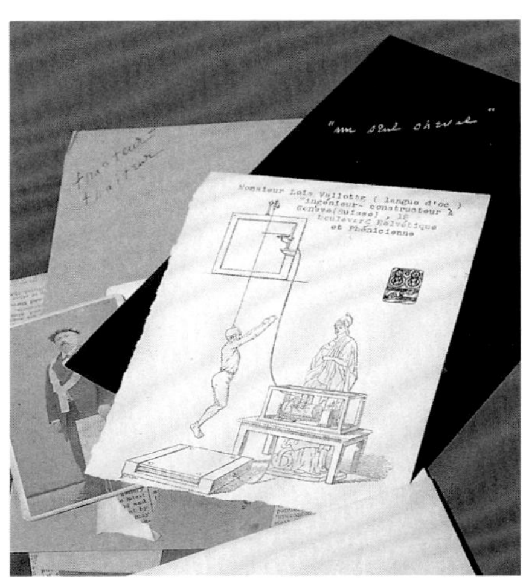

Automobile]" (fig. 132) refers readers to the back of the book and presumably to the folder inscribed *dédié à M.D.* (fig. 133). Both the section and the collages in the folder feature "M. Louis Vallotton, *ingénieur-constructeur* [engineer and builder]" of Geneva who had invented a vehicle capable of transforming itself.[69] Depending on how one reads the French phrase "*pour le déplacement de faible charges*," the vehicle had the capacities of a tractor for moving light loads or could transform positive/negative charges of photoelectricity. The principal collage in the folder depicts a helmeted man attached by long wires to a machine. It is tempting to see in M. Vallotton, *ingénieur-constructeur*, Cornell's new friend Duchamp, the artist as transformer.

Add to these multiple references a tipped-in, hand-colored reproduction of a medieval representation of a chess game, complete with a tissue overlay marked *Jouets/Jouer d'échecs [Games/Playing Chess or Chess Player]*, and one can readily begin to think of the book as an homage to Duchamp.[70] It is, and yet it is more. Inserted immediately after the volume's title page is the dedication page from another book, *Astronomie Populaire: Description Générale du Ciel [Popular Astronomy: General Description of the Heavens]* (1880). The dedication reads: "*Aux Génies Immortels de Copernic, Galilée, Képler, Newton Qui Ont Ouvert à l'Humanité Les Routes de L'Infini* [To the Immortal Geniuses . . . Who Opened to Humanity the Pathways of the Infinite]." Like *Cabinet of Natural History*, this book object demonstrates Cornell's evolving pantheon of innovative minds. Two decades later, Duchamp would return the compliment, writing in a memo, "Personally I consider him [Cornell] one among the best American artists of today."[71]

Both *Cabinet of Natural History* and this untitled book object provocatively trace the arc of time that transpired between Cornell's initial impressions of Duchamp as "a unique personality" in 1933 and his decision to encase "the flotsam and jetsam" of their relationship after Duchamp's return to New York in 1942. Cornell enjoyed using the phrase "flotsam and jetsam," for it fit all manner of discarded things that he saved, from scraps of paper and metal picked up from the streets to the "mouse matter" and dust swept up from the cellar studio floor.

The *Duchamp Dossier* is Cornell's harvest of discards gleaned from his regular encounters with Duchamp into the early 1950s (fig. 134). How else should we consider this genuinely scruffy array of Duchamp's crumpled laundry tickets, torn fragments of bags and envelopes, opened sugar wrappers, and the like? Since 1940, Cornell had subscribed to ballet historian Cyril Beaumont's assertion that "every shred" related to the Romantic ballerina Marie Taglioni should be preserved because of her significance and life's fleeting nature (fig. 135).[72] Retaining flotsam and jetsam as "Duchampiana" not only echoed Beaumont's belief but prefigured the swell of interest that all manner of Duchamp-related material has elicited among subsequent generations of scholars and aficionados.

The *Duchamp Dossier* is also the repository of legitimate documents and gifts. Gallery announcements recall their history of exhibiting together. The warm letters that Cornell received from Duchamp's great love Mary Reynolds afford tantalizing glimpses of both artists through her eyes. Telegrams and short notes from Duchamp provide the principal evidence of the two men's relationship. The same can be said for the gifts from Duchamp: the formal autographed image of the *Large Glass*, the small readymades he most likely presented to Cornell on an impromptu basis, and the handful of components associated with the *Boîte* edition.

132 Cornell, first page of section "*Fâucheuse Automobile*" from Untitled Book Object *(Journal d'Agriculture Pratique et Journal de l'Agriculture)*, c. 1933–mid 1940s. The Joseph and Robert Cornell Memorial Foundation.

133 Cornell, folder of collages included in Untitled Book Object *(Journal d'Agriculture Pratique et Journal de l'Agriculture)*, c. 1933–mid 1940s. Folder, 10¼ x 6⅞ in. The Joseph and Robert Cornell Memorial Foundation.

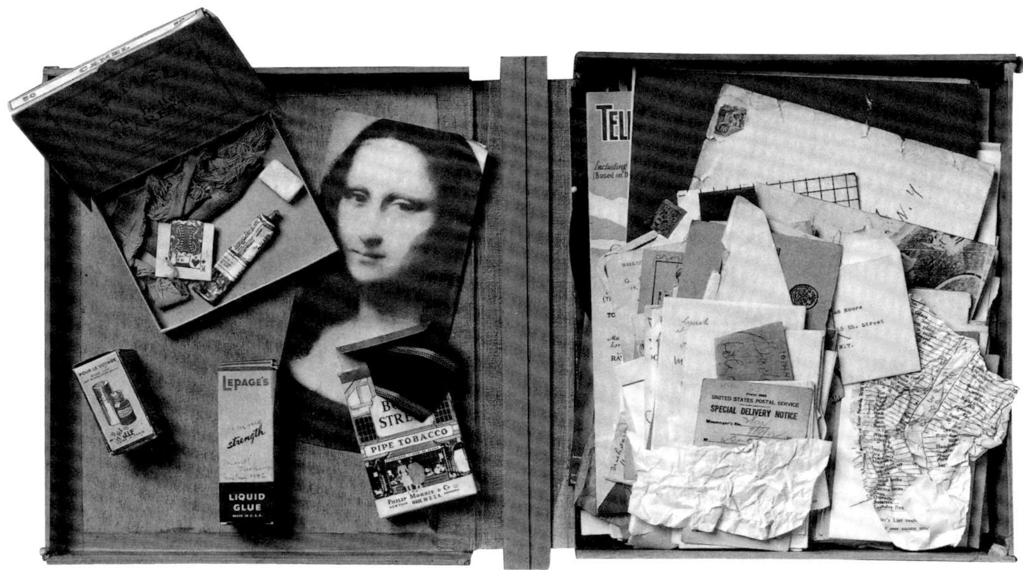

Whether in a state of exhilaration or frustration, Cornell often recorded his thoughts about a project and kept his friends informed, sometimes lending "explorations" for their comment or perusal. Occasionally, he even confided to particular friends that their "file" was in progress. But in the instance of the *Duchamp Dossier*, the record as Cornell left it is truly silent, perhaps in deference to the two artists' shared appreciation of privacy as a creative environment. While it is not difficult to consider the project an "unauthorized biography" in the tradition of many of Cornell's "explorations" and dossiers, there is simply no hint of preparing this example for the public circumstances of an edition, an installation, or a publication. And we don't know—perhaps don't need to know—whether Duchamp understood that he was the subject of a dossier or whether he contributed deliberately to his file. He was certainly aware of Cornell's collections, commenting on his "passion for collecting old prints and books with no special art value but which have a curious relationship with some past event or the biography of some important figure of the past."[73] One inevitably wonders how the death of his friend and early mentor affected not just Cornell's perception of the *Duchamp Dossier* but his subsequent interaction with its contents.

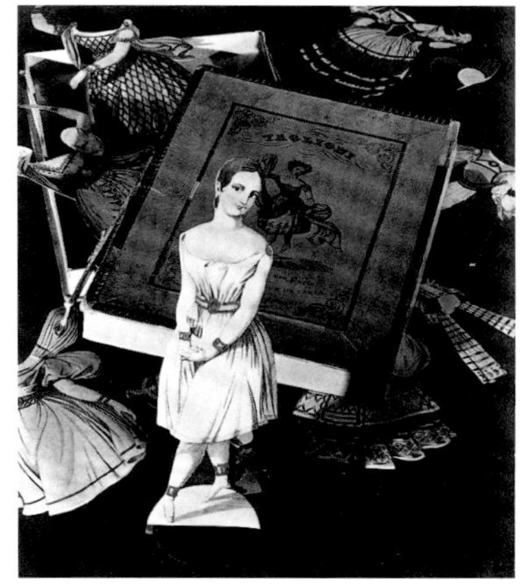

In the fall of 1972, just months before his own death, Cornell contemplated whether "the Utopia house might become a home museum and/or experimental workshop."[74] Here would be the richest "exploration" of all, a "Crystal Cage" of a house full of sample projects and source materials literally available to anyone. He envisioned visitors, especially young people, receptive to browsing, research, experimentation, and even appropriation as their passports to knowledge and creativity (fig. 137). Decades before, Cornell had come to terms with his own acts of appropriation from diverse literary and artistic sources, learning from his friend the poet and artist Mina Loy about "borrower's rights. . . . A contemporary brain weilding [sic] a prior brain as a more potent implement than a paintbrush."[75] His eagerness to share the lesson of imaginative transformation is evident in his aspirations for a "home museum."

Although never realized, Cornell's concept also echoes his description of *GC 44* as "a museum without walls" in 1950,[76] as well as his designation of both box constructions and "explorations" as "*musées de poches* [pocket museums]." Here, of course, his language

134 Cornell, *Duchamp Dossier*, c. 1942–53. Philadelphia Museum of Art. Gift of The Joseph and Robert Cornell Memorial Foundation.

135 Nineteenth-century paper dolls of Marie Taglioni, possibly arranged by Cornell, c. 1940. Vintage gelatin-silver print, 5⁵/₈ x 4⁵/₈ in. Joseph Cornell Study Center, Natl. Museum of American Art, Smithsonian. Gift of Mr. and Mrs. John A. Benton.

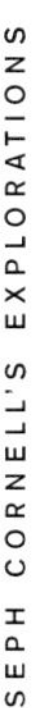

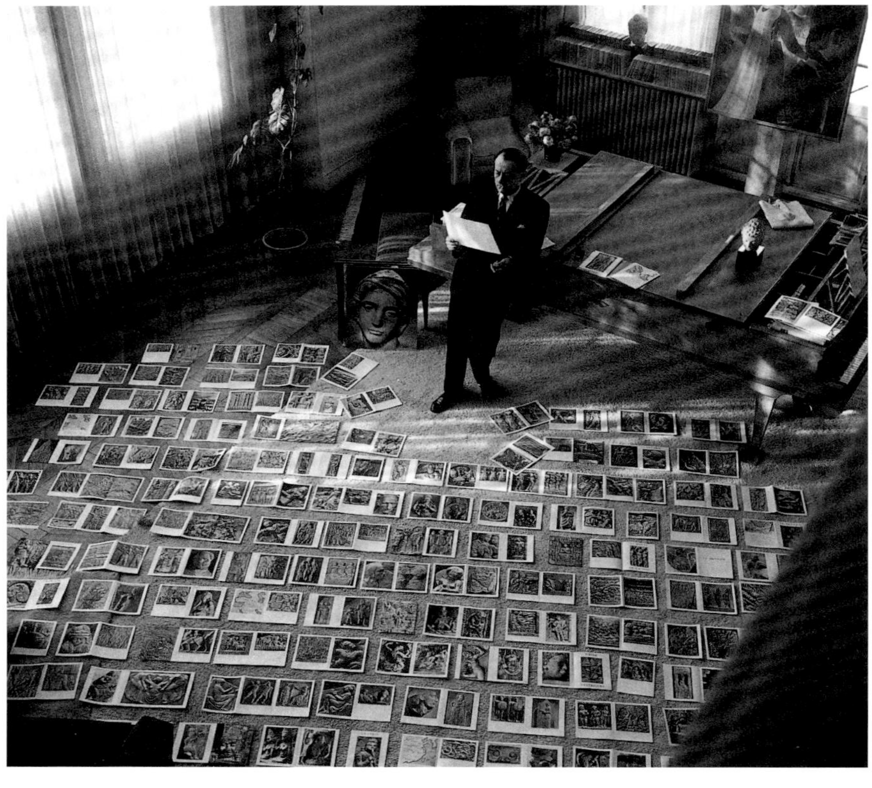

and concepts intersect most closely with those of Duchamp's *Boîte* edition as a portable museum. Yet the phrase "museum without walls" introduces an intriguing instance of "borrower's rights," not just for Cornell, the freelance picture researcher, but also for Duchamp, the one-time librarian. In 1922, André Malraux, later to distinguish himself as an influential French Minister of Culture, had begun developing his thoughts about art as an assembly of meaning informed by different voices across time and place. Focusing on the photographic reproduction's potential for expanding the horizon of art and archives, Malraux's ideas gained currency even before the publication of his two influential books, *Le musée imaginaire [The Museum without Walls]* in 1947 and the expanded study *Les voix du silence [Voices of Silence]* four years later (fig. 136). Whether by coincidence or design, Cornell and Duchamp explored reproducing, transforming, and distributing images under the rubric of the "museum" contemporaneously with Malraux's philosophy of culture.[77] Linking their art in boxes and dossiers to their time, these concerns also positioned Cornell and Duchamp as "prior brains" for the many artists drawn more recently to images as information and information as art.

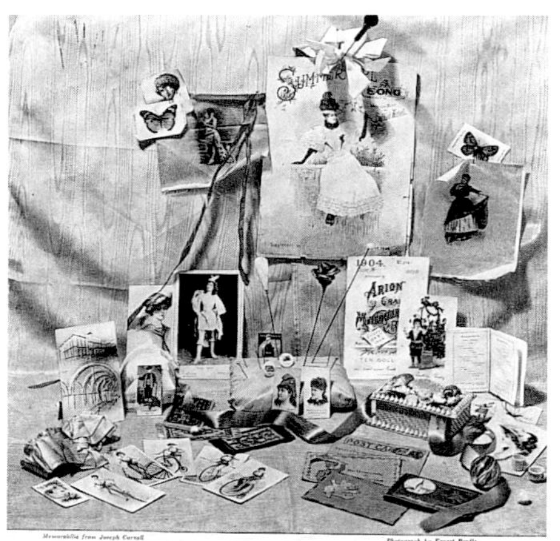

Memorabilia from Joseph Cornell

Photograph by Ernest Beadle

What did you collect?

★

BY FRANK SULLIVAN

A gentleman of my acquaintance, who is in the fourth grade, started a train of recollection in me not so long ago by asking if I would save for him the lump-sugar envelopes used by many hotels, dining cars, night clubs, and other eating places. These frills disappeared during the war, shortly after lamb chops were stripped of their paper rompers, but my friend says they have returned. He is collecting them.

I had not heard of that item. I have come to know the predatory glitter that comes into a boy's eye when he sees a match cover not in his collection, and long since learned to save for a young collector the stamps from (Continued on page 104)

GOOD HOUSEKEEPING JULY 1948

33

complete illustration and arrangement by Joseph Cornell

136 André Malraux selecting photographs for *Le musée imaginaire [The Museum without Walls]*, Paris, c. 1947.

137 Memorabilia featured in "What did you collect?" *Good Housekeeping* (July 1948): p. 33. Arranged by Cornell; photograph by Ernest Beadle.

Notes

I would like to dedicate this essay to Janna Leepson, whose years of devoted volunteer work at the Joseph Cornell Study Center has so enriched the use of its resources.

1. Wallace Fowlie, *Age of Surrealism* (1950; reprint, Bloomington, Ind.: Indiana University Press, 1960), p. 201. Fowlie's book includes an epilogue that summarizes his key points, among them the Surrealists' contribution to the theory of poetics. The quotation cited here continues: "This is why the surrealists claim that the poet feels in himself all of universal life. They speak constantly of the state of poetry (*état poétique*) as something that is lived and thought of as an interrogation, as a quasi-discovery. The poet changes life and the world, and he transforms man." Cornell owned this 1960 reprint of Fowlie's book.

2. Particular phrases or words that Cornell used frequently appear in quotes throughout the essay. His diaries and correspondence should be considered the general source.

3. Marcel Duchamp, quoted in H. P. Roché, "Souvenirs of Marcel Duchamp," in *Marcel Duchamp*, edited by Robert Lebel (New York: Paragaraphic Books, 1967), p. 85.

4. Betty Freeman, notes on Joseph Cornell, 13 January 1966, p. 1. I am grateful to Mrs. Freeman for sharing her notes.

5. Joseph Cornell, diary entry, 20 August 1951, Joseph Cornell Papers, Archives of American Art, Smithsonian Institution, Washington, D.C., microfilm 1059: 338.

6. The Redon volume is in the collection of the Joseph Cornell Study Center, National Museum of American Art, Smithsonian Institution, Washington, D.C. The location of the Peggy Bacon drawing is unknown. According to his sister Mrs. John A. (Elizabeth) Benton, Cornell retained his complete run of *Camera Work* until his death, after which it was sold.

7. According to numerous people who visited Cornell's house regularly from the 1940s forward, the massive presence of his materials was evident throughout the house for decades. After Cornell's death in 1972, his sister Mrs. John A. (Elizabeth) Benton inherited his personal and studio effects, while his artworks became the responsibility of his estate executors, attorney Richard Ader and architectural historian Wayne Andrews, also a longtime friend of the artist. After a period of review by the executors in 1973 and at Andrews' urging, Mrs. Benton began lending Cornell's diaries, correspondence, and a selection of his source materials to the Archives of American Art, Smithsonian Institution, Washington, D.C., for microfilming. She began donating these materials to the Archives of American Art in 1977. In 1973, Walter Hopps, curator, and Joshua Taylor, director, National Museum of American Art, Smithsonian Institution, Washington, D.C., had preliminary discussions about establishing a study center devoted to the artist. In 1978, Mr. and Mrs. John A. Benton gave the bulk of Cornell's source materials and library, as well as a small group of finished and unfinished examples of Cornell's boxes and collages, to the National Museum of American Art to create the Joseph Cornell Study Center. The Center's collection has grown subsequently with additional gifts of source materials and artworks from the artist's sister Helen Jagger, his niece Helen Batcheller, The Joseph and Robert Cornell Memorial Foundation, and private donors.

8. Frances Pernas, letter to author, 24 April 1977.

9. Cornell, however, created this series of collages as a memorial to his brother, Robert, who died in 1965. Not only do the collages take their title from René Magritte's 1938 painting, but they also feature a reproduction of the painting as their central image.

10. Diary entry, 15 April 1946, Cornell Papers, AAA, 1059:8.

11. Based on the number of dated or otherwise documented examples, Cornell made boxes until the year of his death. The persistent belief that Cornell drastically reduced his output of boxes during the 1950s and 1960s requires revision.

12. I did not have the privilege or pleasure of examining Cornell's source materials *in situ*. These observations and characterizations are derived from my stewardship of the materials as the founding curator of the Joseph Cornell Study Center since 1978.

13. Family members and a number of Cornell's assistants have identified this phrase as his in interviews with the author. The phrase itself does not appear verbatim in Cornell's papers.

14. See diary entry, 5 May 1948, Cornell Papers, AAA, 1059:121, for a sample characterization of the studio.

15. In suggesting this number as a working estimate, I have tried to distinguish between files that Cornell used as working resources and files that he treated as artworks in progress.

16. Currently, my efforts to date Cornell's "explorations" take into consideration the broadest possible time frame to encompass the accumulation of materials prior to his choice of a container as well as the ongoing revisions characteristic of most of them.

17. Joseph Cornell to Pavel Tchelitchew, 21 October 1941, Parker Tyler Papers, Harry Ransom Humanities Research Center, The University of Texas at Austin.

18. Donald Windham, "Comment," *Dance Index* 3, nos. 7/8 (July/August 1944): p. 103, and Joseph Cornell to Parker Tyler, 14 March 1940, Tyler Papers.

19. The Joseph Cornell Study Center's collection includes the inspirational Kriehuber lithograph of Cerrito. For a useful discussion of Cornell's interest in Fanny Cerrito and *Portrait of Ondine*, see Sandra Leonard Starr, *Joseph Cornell and The Ballet* (New York: Castelli, Feigen, Corcoran, 1983), pp. 19–35.

20. These stages are inferred from references to the work in Cornell's papers and from a November 1945 press release from The Museum of Modern Art, New York. Annotated materials in *Portrait of Ondine* suggest that Cornell housed the "exploration" in a slipcase after its exhibition at the One-Wall Gallery of Wittenborn Bookstore, 1018 Madison Avenue, New York, in 1956.

21. These phrases appear in the pamphlet "PORTRAIT OF ONDINE CONTINUED" in the "exploration" itself, recurring as well in Cornell's diary notes about the project.

22. Laments about the difficulties of drafting the project's literary supplement are particularly evident in Cornell's correspondence with Tyler and Tchelitchew during the early 1940s.

23. Harry Roseman's 1970 photograph of a discarded suitcase-style box in Cornell's garage may document an early housing for *Portrait of Ondine*, its lid interior bearing a photomechanical reduction of the Kriehuber lithograph (see fig. 3). In the slipcase that housed *Portrait of Ondine* at the time of Cornell's death, a much smaller reproduction of the Kriehuber lithograph, mounted on heavy white paper, is the opening image of the pamphlet "PORTRAIT OF ONDINE CONTINUED."

24. Starr, *Joseph Cornell and the Ballet*, p. 27.

25. Diary entry, 16 June 1951, Cornell Papers, AAA, 1059:324. In a letter to Marianne Moore, Cornell referred to *Portrait of Ondine* as a "little album-chest that will exhale a 'romantic vapor,' in the words of Marcel Duchamp, spoken as an unconscious contribution to it." Joseph Cornell to Marianne Moore, 21 June 1944, Marianne Moore Archives, Rosenbach Museum and Library, Philadelphia.

26. This phrase appears in Cornell's statement in the pamphlet "PORTRAIT of ONDINE CONTINUED" and in numerous drafts of the statement in his papers.

27. Joseph Cornell published a version of this work as *THE Crystal Cage [portrait of Berenice]* in *View*, series 2, no. 4 (January 1943); the quotation is from p. 12. Useful discussions of this "exploration" include John Bernard Myers, "Cornell: The Enchanted Wanderer," *Art in America* 61, no. 5 (September–October 1973): pp. 76–81; Helen H. Haroutunian, "Joseph Cornell in 'View,'" *Arts Magazine* 55, no. 7 (March 1981): pp. 101–108; and Sandra Leonard Starr, *THE Crystal Cage [portrait of Berenice]* (Tokyo: Gatoda Gallery, 1987).

28. Ibid.

29. These two source material files can be found in Cornell's papers in the Archives of American Art.

30. The encased version of *The Crystal Cage* includes a rectangular page-size design of names and words rather than the towerlike typographic "folly" that Cornell published in *View*, suggesting the degree to which he made changes specifically for the publication.

31. Joseph Cornell to Marianne Moore, 23 March 1943, Moore Archives.

32. This passage appears in a note titled "Métaphysique d'ephemera," dated August 25, 1945, in the "exploration" itself. The encased materials also include a variety of published references to the star cluster *Coma Berenices*, suggesting another source for his use of the name.

33. Joseph Cornell, note, "Paris Exhibition of 1900/(through the eyes of Berenice)," 7 April 1945, Cornell Papers, AAA, "Crystal Cage" file, box 1.

34. Joseph Cornell, "note of gratitude," 2 May 1945, in the dossier *Penny Arcade Portrait of Lauren Bacall (Working Model Based upon "To Have and Have Not")*.

35. Joseph Cornell, statement in exhibition announcement for "Romantic Museum at the Hugo Gallery/Portraits of Women: Constructions and Arrangements by Joseph Cornell," December 1946, Joseph Cornell Study Center.

36. The contents of this dossier include Cornell's unfinished designs for a variation on the "Romantic Museum" exhibition announcement in 1948 and notes dated 1970, suggesting that he revisited the materials intermittently.

37. Joseph Cornell, undated sheet of working notes and list, Cornell Papers, AAA, "GC 44" file, 1072:123. The working materials and notes comprising *GC 44* are divided between the Joseph Cornell Study Center (primarily the mounted plates and title pages plus some notes and cutting materials) and Cornell's papers in the Archives of American Art (primarily notes). I wish to acknowledge the help of Harvey Overton and Joanna R. Roche in sorting through this material. Roche's dissertation "Joseph Cornell and the Making of Memory" (University of California, Los Angeles, 1998) includes a chapter on *GC 44*.

38. Diary entry, 26–27 September 1951, Cornell Papers, AAA, 1059:356, and diary entry, 21–22 September 1951, Cornell Papers, AAA, 1059:352.

39. Joseph Cornell, undated sheet of working notes and list, Cornell Papers, AAA, "GC 44" file, 1072:161.

40. Ibid.

41. These titles appear on typed sheets in the "semi-complete GC 44" file in the Joseph Cornell Study Center collection. "D.T." is Dorothea Tanning, with whom Cornell enjoyed a fruitful correspondence and genuine friendship during this period.

42. Joseph Cornell, note, 4 September 1951, Joseph Cornell Study Center, "semi-complete GC 44" file.

43. Joseph Cornell, note, 3 August 1951, Cornell Papers, AAA, "GC 44" file, 1072:464.\

44. Joseph Cornell, note, undated, Cornell Papers, AAA, 1072:379.

45. References to this novel begin to appear in Cornell's papers and correspondence c. 1942. He recommended the book to many friends and acknowledged that it had affected the evolution of his Palace series of boxes during the early 1940s.

46. Joseph Cornell, note, 6 March 1967, Joseph Cornell Study Center, "semi-complete GC 44" file. He cites *Portrait of Ondine* in this note and elsewhere in his papers as the model for his plans to develop a "museum format" for exhibiting *GC 44*.

47. Joseph Cornell, "Random Notes p. 2," undated, Cornell Papers, AAA, "GC 44" file, 1072:125.

48. Diary entry, 20 March 1952, Cornell Papers, AAA, 1072:475.

49. Diary entry, 4 February 1947, Cornell Papers, AAA, 1076:3.

50. Joseph Cornell, *Portrait of Ondine*, National Museum of American Art, gift of The Joseph and Robert Cornell Memorial Foundation.

51. Donald Windham as editor of *Dance Index*, Charles Henri Ford as editor of *View*, and Alexander Liberman as art director for *Condé Nast* publications, interviews with author, New York, N.Y., 1979.

52. Cornell published *Maria* in the name of Salamander Editions and *the BEL CANTO PET* in the name of Silver Swan Editions. In a letter to Parker Tyler in 1940, Cornell noted that discussions with Tyler had encouraged him to think about "a limited, subscribed edition." Although the subject of the edition is not stipulated, the letter's date suggests *Portrait of Ondine* as a likely candidate. Joseph Cornell to Parker Tyler, 6 October 1940, Tyler Papers.

53. Pamphlet "PORTRAIT of ONDINE CONTINUED" in *Portrait of Ondine*, Joseph Cornell Study Center.

54. Joseph Cornell to Jermayne MacAgy, 8 April 1956, Jermayne MacAgy Papers, The Menil Collection, Houston.

55. Press release, "Museum of Modern Art Announces Opening of Two Small Exhibitions in Auditorium Gallery," 26 November 1945, The Museum of Modern Art, New York. The exhibition was presented between November 28, 1945, and February 17, 1946.

56. Joseph Cornell to Jermayne MacAgy, undated proposal "SCRAP-BOOK OF SWITZERLAND," [c. 1955], The Menil Collection Archives, Houston. Cornell became friendly with Jermayne and Douglas MacAgy in 1944. Jermayne was known for her innovative topics and installation designs for exhibitions in California and Texas museums between 1941 and 1964.

57. Ibid.

58. In 1970, Cornell noted his desire to write his memoirs, including writing about Duchamp "in a warm way." Joseph Cornell, quoted in *Peggy Guggenheim and Her Friends*, edited by Virginia M. Dortch (Milan: Berenice, 1994), p. 97.

59. Robert Cornell, diary entry, 31 July 1942, courtesy Mrs. John A. Benton.

60. In March 1980, Teeny Duchamp said that Cornell had shown her in his attic during a visit around 1970 "the suitcase where he'd dump things about Marcel. A box for a valise that Marcel had rejected." Teeny Duchamp, interview with author, Joseph Cornell Study Center, 12 March 1980. In April 1981, Teeny Duchamp said that Cornell had shown only her the *Duchamp Dossier* in his attic during a visit that she, Duchamp, and an unidentified couple made to Utopia Parkway in the late 1960s. Walter Hopps, interview with author, Washington, D.C., 27 April 1981. In 1970, Cornell said that "I have a mock *Valise* that Duchamp gave me." Joseph Cornell, quoted in *Peggy Guggenheim and Her Friends,* p. 97. See *Duchamp Dossier* Inventory (DD 0) for discussion on the container's origins. Additional research is required to identify the extent of Duchamp's awareness of the project.

61. Cornell's papers in the Archives of American Art include the announcement for the Brancusi exhibition that Duchamp had organized for Brummer Gallery in 1926. Whether Cornell saw this earlier Brancusi show is unknown at this time.

62. Diary entry, 8 October 1968, Cornell Papers, AAA, 1056:679.

63. Diary entry, 27 April 1969, Cornell Papers, AAA, 1063:864. Cornell had received a visit from Teeny Duchamp that same day.

64. Joseph Cornell, note on envelope postmarked 7 December 1940, Cornell Papers, AAA, 1059:172. The language in this note strongly reflects Cornell's awareness of Mary Baker Eddy's writings about the idea of objects and physical reality as having a "mental" or "spiritual" nature.

65. I would like to acknowledge Anne-Louise Marquis' research on *Cabinet of Natural History* during her tenure as a research assistant in the Joseph Cornell Study Center. The association of Edgar Allan Poe's name with the phrase *MÉTÉORES LUMINEUX [Luminous Meteors]* on the label of one of the bottles prefigures Cornell's layout for *Spent Meteor: Night of Feb. 10, 1843 (For E. A. Poe)* (photograph, c. 1938), which appeared as a photograph in the "Americana Fantastica" issue of *View* (January 1943): p. 21.

66. Cornell joined two separate typeset strips of paper, *Méthode de M. Duch* and *omp,* to alter the spelling of Duchamp's name.

67. Tome 22 is imprinted on the book's spine. The title page, which Cornell apparently inserted as a substitute or replacement, cites Tome 21 and the date 1911. I would like to acknowledge Libby Karlinger's excellent cataloguing of the book object and Micaela Mendelsohn's tireless assistance in providing translations and other feats of research during the course of preparing this essay.

68. In 1933, Cornell made a series of collages inspired by Raymond Radiguet's poem "Lettres d'un Alphabet" (1919) that are similar in style to collages found in this book object. The title of Radiguet's poem, published in 1925, also appears in inscriptions, suggesting that Cornell began transforming the book as early as 1933.

69. Throughout the three-page spread, Cornell inked out the letter *u* in the word *faucheuse* (mowing machine) and added the circumflex to create the word *fâcheuse* (irritating or troublesome). M. Louis Vallotton was a Swiss engineer who presented his invention at the Paris Exposition in 1900, according to the book's text.

70. The French expression for playing chess is *jouer aux échecs.* The French expression for chess player is *joueur d'échecs*, and it is possible that Cornell misspelled the word *joueur* as *jouer*. The handwritten inscription occurs within the penciled outline of a chess player.

71. Marcel Duchamp, "Memorandum regarding Joseph Cornell," 9 July 1951, photocopy in Mary Reynolds Collection, Ryerson Library, The Art Institute of Chicago.

72. Diary entry, undated, Cornell Papers, AAA, 1058:225.

73. Duchamp, "Memorandum regarding Cornell," Reynolds Collection.

74. Diary entry, 3 October 1972, Cornell Papers, AAA, 1064:683.

75. Mina Loy, undated draft of "Phenomenon in American Art CORNELL," Cornell Papers, AAA, 1065:772. Loy wrote this essay shortly after she saw Cornell's "Aviary" exhibition at the Egan Gallery, New York, in December 1949.

76. Joseph Cornell, undated note, "GC 44 Garden Center 44," Cornell Papers, AAA, 1072:162.

77. André Malraux began publishing his ideas in 1935. Photographs of Malraux with books of photographic reproductions spread out in orderly fashion resonate with Cornell's descriptions of plans to mount bulletin board-style exhibitions of "explorations" in schools and other settings during the 1950s. The only known exhibition of Cornell's source materials in an educational context during his lifetime occurred in 1959 when Bennington College presented "Selected Works by Joseph Cornell: Bonitas Solstitialis and An Exploration of the Colombier."

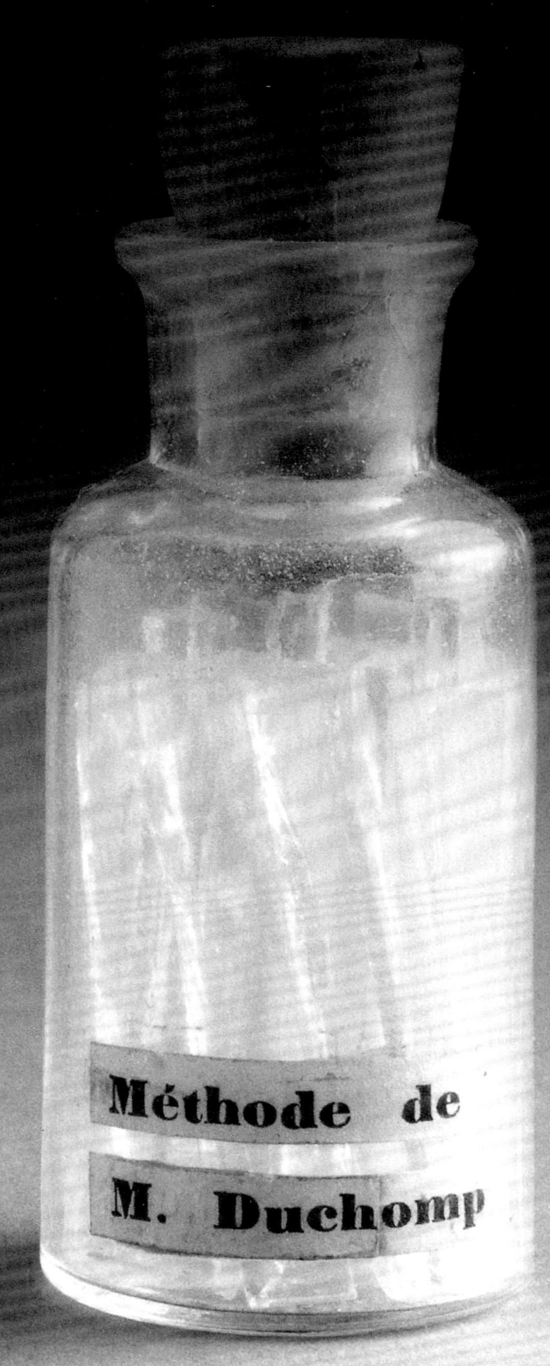
Méthode de
M. Duchomp

Ephemeral Matter: Traces of Cornell and Duchamp

DON QUAINTANCE

Delacroix's Handkerchief Soon after Marcel Duchamp's death in 1968, Joseph Cornell began recording renditions of a recurring dream in his copious diaries: "Last evening I had a vivid dream about Delacroix being alive & sounding out Marcel as to the poss.[ibility] of obtaining one of his handkerchiefs. But this meagerly betokens a great mystique. I feel D.[elacroix] to Redon to Duchamp with respect to: HOMMAGE."[1]

The dream reveals Cornell's elevation of Duchamp into an imagined French pantheon linking the Romantic master to the poetic Symbolist to the modern iconoclast. Further, its plot to obtain Eugène Delacroix's handkerchief identifies the acquisitive traits that first led Cornell to compile his "exploration" concerning Duchamp, the *Duchamp Dossier* (c. 1942–53). Cornell made a practice of collecting personal mementos from artists and performers—both living and dead—then using these objects to reconstruct his memories. For Cornell, a scrap of paper, the feathers from a tutu, or Duchamp's empty tobacco box (fig. 139) and unused pipe cleaners possessed animistic power. Compiled in dossiers, the objects became touchstones for Cornell's perception of time and reality, a phenomenon he referred to as the *metaphysiques d'ephemera* (using Gérard de Nerval's term).

On initial consideration, Duchamp's cool intellectualism and Cornell's wistful imagism appear so diametrically opposed that they mask some obvious similarities. Of course, their most famous works—the readymades and box constructions, respectively—are both based on found objects. Although their works appear stylistically divergent, certain mediums and motifs recur. And within each oeuvre special sensitivities toward the cataloguing of language and image interrelate with the two artists' allied avocations of graphic designer, archivist, and curator, demonstrating a prescient recognition of the coming information age. In its conception and in its particulars, Cornell's *Duchamp Dossier* is a fascinating embodiment of this convergence.

When Duchamp and Cornell met in 1933, each must have felt an immediate empathy. Cornell sought in Duchamp direct contact with his fantasized ideal of a European lineage; though deterred by Duchamp's pragmatism, he still must have marveled at meeting an individual who had played jackstraws with Guillaume Apollinaire and shot billiards with Juan Gris, another of Cornell's painter heroes.[2] Prizing Cornell's handling of the common object and seeing in him a semblance of the self-taught American qualities he would later admire in such artists as Morris Hirshfield,[3] Duchamp soon chose to include the gentleman from Flushing within his own circle of exhibition activities and contacts.

The two artists followed their introduction with reciprocal gifts of printed matter. Cornell presented Duchamp with an inscribed copy of his limited edition film scenario

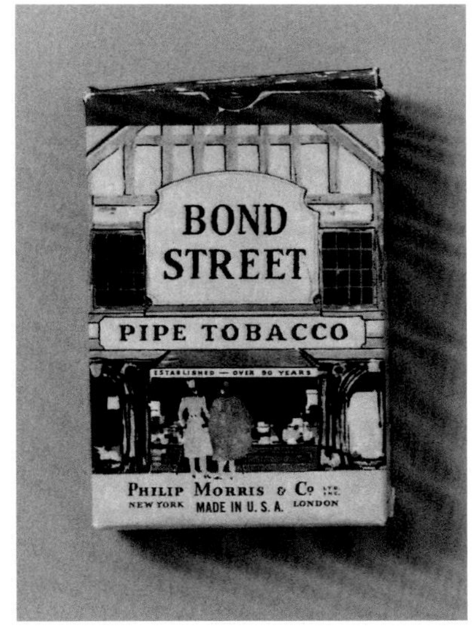

138 Cornell, "Méthode de M. Duchomp" bottle from *Cabinet of Natural History (Object)*, 1934, 1936–40. Private collection.

139 Duchamp, cardboard box [Bond Street Pipe Tobacco], December 21, 1942 (DD 1), from Cornell, *Duchamp Dossier*, c. 1942–53. Philadelphia Museum of Art. Gift of The Joseph and Robert Cornell Memorial Foundation.

Monsieur Phot (pl. 50).[4] Influenced by the disjunctive editing of Luis Buñuel's and Salvador Dalí's *Un Chien Andalou [An Andalusian Dog]* (1929) and examples from Cornell's collection of live-action stop-motion films, the filmscript links (compellingly, in relation to Duchamp's readymades) a set of preexisting halved stereopticon images (fig. 140). Duchamp gave Cornell an inscribed reproduction of an installation view of the unbroken *La Mariée mise à nu par ses célibataires, même [The Bride Stripped Bare by Her Bachelors, Even] (Large Glass)* (1915–23) photographed at the 1926 Brooklyn Museum Société Anonyme exhibition (DD 108). This exchange of an editioned artwork and a photographic memento documented the artists' first contacts: the latter became the earliest dated item in the *Duchamp Dossier*, though the collection probably did not find permanent housing until some time in the early 1940s.

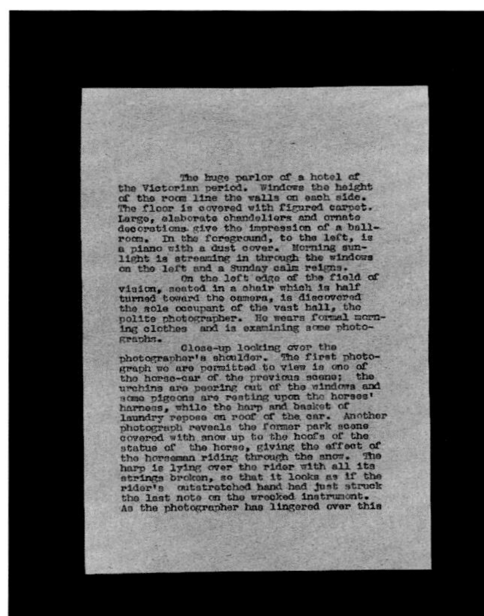

The huge parlor of a hotel of the Victorian period. Windows the height of the room line the walls on each side. The floor is covered with figured carpet. Large, elaborate chandeliers and ornate decorations give the impression of a ballroom. In the foreground, to the left, is a piano with a dust cover. Morning sunlight is streaming in through the windows on the left and a Sunday calm reigns.

On the left edge of the field of vision, seated in a chair which is half turned toward the camera, is discovered the sole occupant of the vast hall, the polite photographer. He wears formal morning clothes and is examining some photographs.

Close-up looking over the photographer's shoulder. The first photograph we are permitted to view is one of the horse-car of the previous scene; the urchins are peering out of the windows and some pigeons are resting upon the horses' harness, while the harp and basket of laundry repose on roof of the car. Another photograph reveals the former park scene covered with snow up to the hoofs of the statue of the horse, giving the effect of the horseman riding through the snow. The harp is lying over the rider with all its strings broken, so that it looks as if the rider's outstretched hand had just struck the last note on the wrecked instrument. As the photographer has lingered over this

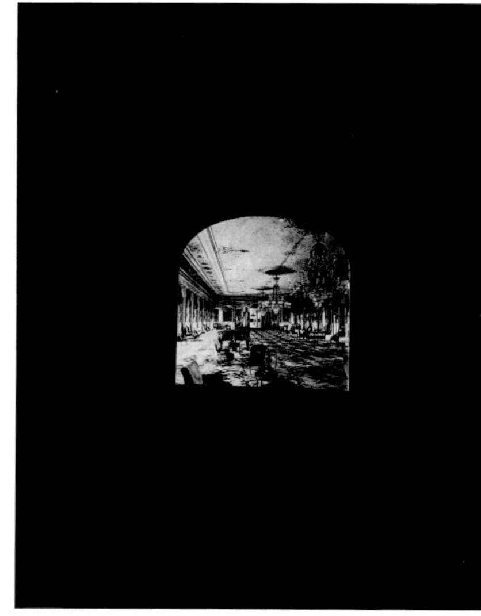

140 Cornell, mounted text and stereopticon photograph from *Monsieur Phot*, no. 5, 1933. Joseph Cornell Study Center, Natl. Museum of American Art, Smithsonian. Gift of Mr. and Mrs. John A. Benton.

Subsequent to their first meeting, Cornell received from Paris Duchamp's subscription announcement and facsimile note (DD 90) for his *La Mariée mise à nu par ses célibataires même [The Bride Stripped Bare by Her Bachelors Even] (Green Box)* (1934). Receipt of the *Green Box* mailing may have confirmed for Cornell the viability of housing his steadily proliferating files in album boxes, which also provided a workable distribution model. While Cornell was saving materials and souvenir ephemera as early as the 1920s, the migration of his ephemera into album boxes is difficult to pinpoint. Such containers are mentioned in his correspondence in 1941.[5] By 1944 Cornell had told Marianne Moore that Fanny Cerrito ["Ondine"] was "... to be boxed in a little album-chest that will exhale 'romantic vapor,' in the words of Marcel Duchamp, spoken as an unconscious contribution to it."[6]

When Duchamp escaped World War II by sailing to New York in June 1942, a portion of the components to make the portable museums of *de ou par Marcel Duchamp ou Rrose Sélavy [by or of Marcel Duchamp or Rrose Sélavy] (Boîte* edition) (1935–41) had already been shipped to Peggy Guggenheim's Manhattan townhouse. In a fortuitous convergence of time and place, Duchamp contacted Cornell to assist in the assembling of these portable units. Little is documented of the exact nature of Cornell's participation in the project. However, in the *Duchamp Dossier,* sundry remnants, notations, drawings, correspondence, and receipts related to the *Boîte* edition indicate that Cornell worked on a number of specific components and may also have helped assemble some of the complete ensembles. Cornell assisted Duchamp from sometime after July 1942 until January 1946.[7] Work on the *Boîte* edition, a concrete expression of the two artists' association, was nonetheless grounded in practicality—essentially Duchamp employed Cornell as a craftsman for the assembly process (fig. 142).

Motivated by Duchamp's example, Cornell broadened his use of the boxed portfolio format—a crucial step for several reasons. First, it tied the dossiers generically to Cornell's other, better known box constructions. Second, the volumetric format provided greater flexibility, expanding to include mismatched contents and even three-dimensional objects, while, third and conversely, it enforced at least marginal limitations on the scope of his rapidly bloating files and folders.

Handy valises for traveling art. Portable ideas. For the two artists, while the format offered an inspirational and workable format, it necessitated a patient approach to the realities of distribution. Once Duchamp and Cornell came in contact again in July 1942, their relationship soon deepened, and after receiving a cardboard album prototype resembling a *Boîte* inner box, Cornell established it as the "communicating vessel" for his *Duchamp Dossier.*[8] No other repository could have been more fitting.

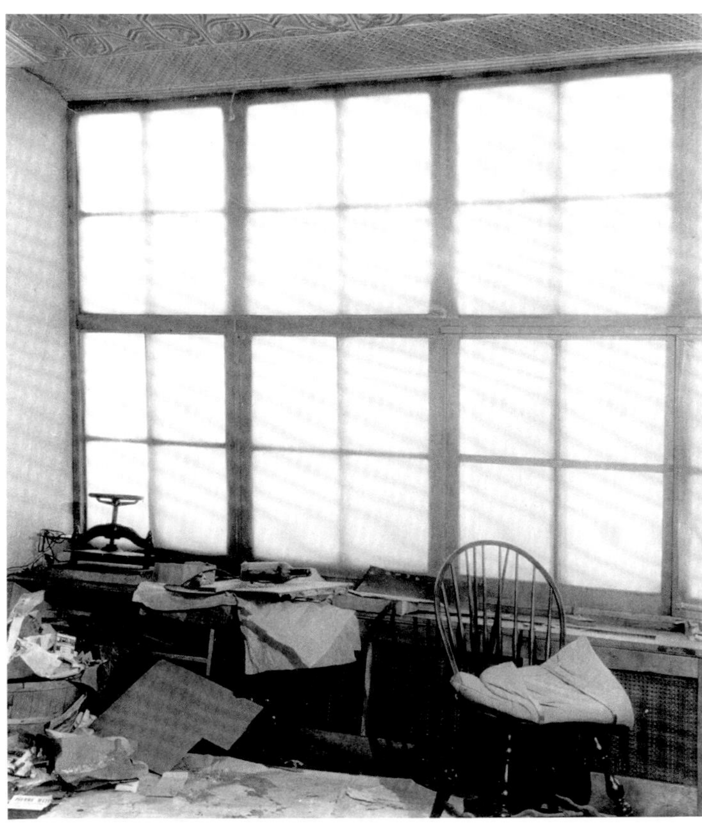

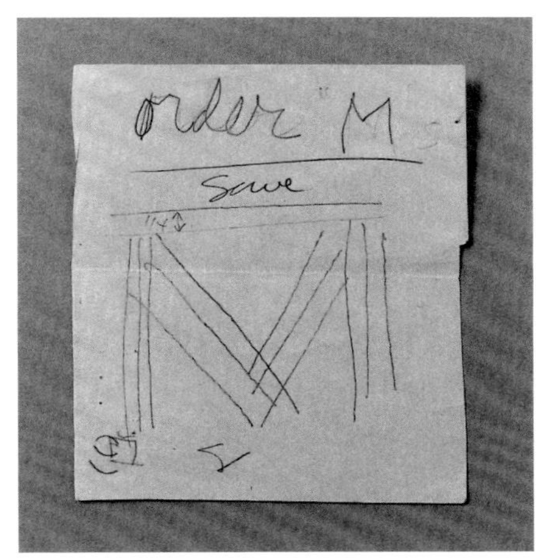

Good Housekeeping Serious consideration of the *Duchamp Dossier* is hindered by the idea that much of its contents appear to have been acquired from the trash baskets of Duchamp's residences or studio. But Cornell felt ample justification for collecting even cast-off detritus from Duchamp. For one thing, it fit an established pattern, given that Cornell believed all artifacts, no matter how lowly, possess a talismanic capacity. Duchamp himself was not immune to the use of tokens as amulets, having suggested to Tristan Tzara the manufacture of a "DADA" monogram chain whose insignia would "protect against certain diseases, against the numerous annoyances of life . . . a universal panacea, a fetish in this sense."[9] The evidence also suggests that Duchamp willingly participated in the game of retrieving his personal effects—a kind of hide-and-seek for grown-ups. Duchamp's signature or initials on much of the contents, even items clearly not intended as gifts for Cornell, is a legible admission of a silent conspiracy. The *Duchamp Dossier* provides in both its texts and its objects clear evidence of a mutually deferential and cordial camaraderie.

Modern usage has transformed the verb *to refuse* (the antonym of *to accept*) into the noun *refuse,* connoting trash. When Cornell visited Duchamp in his temporary quarters, at first Guggenheim's townhouse then Frederick Kiesler's penthouse, or dropped by Duchamp's 14th Street studio and scrutinized the typically overflowing trash baskets (fig. 141)—their contents piled high and spilling onto the floor—the colloquialism about a "circular file" (for an office trash bin) became an invitation. Cornell made the circular file's function literal as he converted Duchamp's garbage into his own source material.

As if Cornell had stumbled upon an earlier equivalent of the computer "undo" or "undelete" function key, he meticulously gleaned the tossed-off data. It was perhaps at this level of jotted-on sugar wrappers that the *Duchamp Dossier* metamorphosed, transforming

141 **Duchamp's studio,** 210 West 14th Street, New York, 1945. Photograph by Percy Rainford.

142 **Cornell, note, undated (DD 60b), relating to manufacture of wooden "M" for *Boîte* edition,** from Cornell, *Duchamp Dossier,* c. 1942–53. Philadelphia Museum of Art. Gift of The Joseph and Robert Cornell Memorial Foundation.

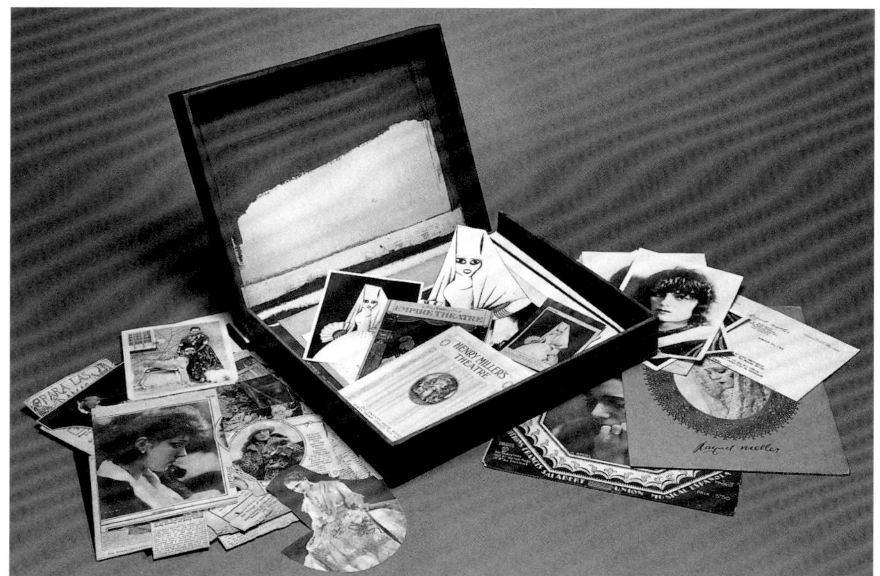

Cornell's fixation into the kind of engrossing challenge that all of his dossiers raised: an attempt to shelter the data of the commonplace and, by extension, to preserve memory. One of the rare examples within Cornell's archive that documents a living artist, the *Duchamp Dossier* by its very existence sustains the *parfum original* of the Cornell/Duchamp relationship.

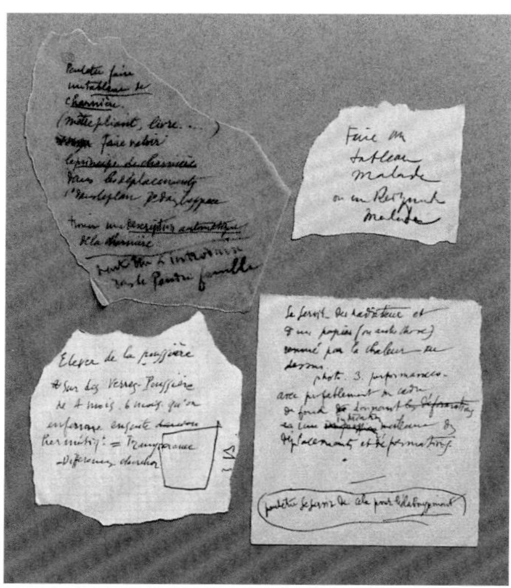

The torn and frayed remnants in the *Duchamp Dossier* are not exceptional when compared with other Cornell filing projects. Although examples such as *Portrait of Ondine* (pl. 59), Untitled *(Penny Arcade Portrait of Lauren Bacall)* (pl. 86), and *The Crystal Cage [portrait of Berenice]* (pl. 54) that evidence a more refined organization have been more frequently published and commented on, the recycled contents of other more neglected conglomerations such as *GC 44* (pl. 76) and *Raquel Meller Dossier* (c. 1940–59; fig. 143) resemble those found in the *Duchamp Dossier*. This ragged look persists even though the tossed-off material in the *Duchamp Dossier*, the pilfered (or offered) trash, is only one primary component: the box also contains conscious gifts and exchanges, remnants of the *Boîte* enterprise, handwritten correspondence, Duchamp artworks, and numerous items that Cornell added by whim or personal motive.

Even if Cornell acquired some of the Duchamp cast-offs surreptitiously, ample objectified evidence shows that Duchamp was a willing participant in the concept, if not always in the logistics, of the procurement. Further, the scraplike components of the *Duchamp Dossier* have a clear precedent in Duchamp's own facsimile note projects. He was so attached to the impromptu style of casual handwriting that he would spend innumerable hours painstakingly reproducing *with exactitude* the informality of such scribblings (fig. 144). The effect often seemed contradictory: for example, the seeming spontaneity of the hand-done inscriptions in the *Green Box* (pl. 17) disguises the complex conceptual preparation evidenced by its mechanistic foreplay and encoded messages. Duchamp exploited such paradoxes. In 1921 he hinted, albeit in a facetious context, at how the process of note-making stimulates creative thought when he designed a satirical ad for the Archie Pen Co. promoting a writing instrument that "thinks for you. To use it reveals new experiences, even to the most blasé."[10]

143 Cornell, *Raquel Meller Dossier*, c. 1940–1959. Dossier, 2 1/2 x 12 1/8 x 15 in. Joseph Cornell Study Center, Natl. Museum of American Art, Smithsonian. Gift of Mr. and Mrs. John A. Benton.

144 Duchamp, four facsimile notes from the *Green Box*, 1934.

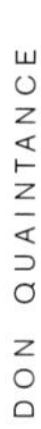

Cornell's relentless memoirs were, in a similar way, directed: though his papers were left in a somewhat chaotic state, he studiously dated the vast majority of handwritten scraps. Beginning in the mid forties, as if aware of their eventual public disposition, he personally made a valiant but hopeless effort to transcribe many handwritten entries onto typewritten pages, carefully noting the original date followed by the date of transcription. Cornell demonstrated a compulsive graphomania, an obsessive execution of handwriting, often cited as a defense mechanism for sublimating emotional responses. Duchamp, who had little regard for saving correspondence, did meticulously save his conceptual notes, despite his peregrinations, doling them out for public release in boxed batches over his lifetime.

Cornell's dossiers and Duchamp's facsimile projects are a testament to a school of note-making that found even the most rudimentary tablet unnecessary. Certainly no leather-bound journals were in evidence. Instead, both artists wrote on any scrap of paper at hand. Numerous dossier items record a back-and-forth interplay of notations and dates. Cornell especially was fond of overwriting printed materials, squeezing words into every blank space, front and back, sideways or upside down (figs. 145 and 146).

Cornell's diaries, created hand-in-glove with the archive of printed materials in his "combination library and workshop,"[11] form with them a complex matrix of language, image, and memory. Simple or linear correspondences were discouraged. Preternaturally aware of the elaborate taxonomic distinctions between his files, source materials, dossiers, and finished boxes, Cornell kept effortless track of the archival mass, noting in a letter to Charles Henri Ford: "I had a Mina Loy original to mail you . . . now I can't find it! This is a very rare occurrence for me despite ceaseless flow of ephemera, sifting, sorting, etc. . . ."[12]

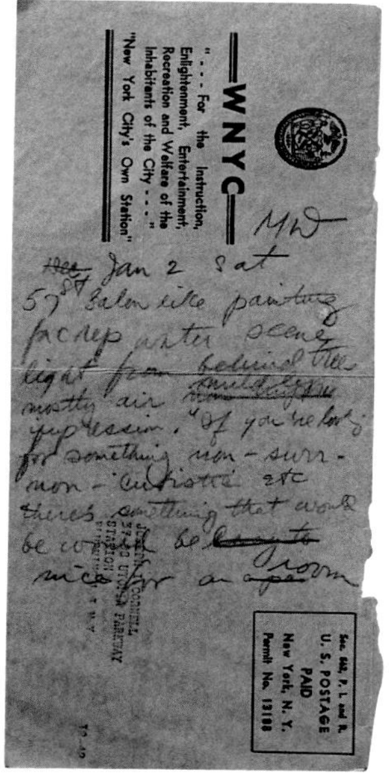

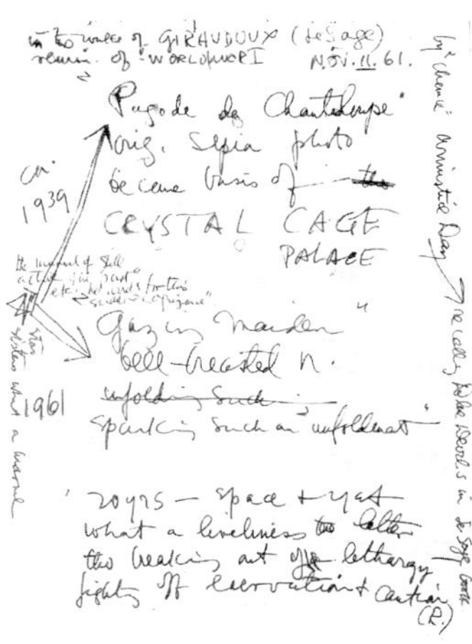

Art Supplies

The underlying theme of the *Duchamp Dossier*, relevant to the work of both artists, is the systematic elevation of the most ordinary minutiae, of reproduction and facsimile, of seemingly mundane paperwork, as valid vehicles for entering the realms of imagination and memory. Similarly, each artist used in other works certain commonplace mediums, including glass, dust, and found paper or printed material. These hardly could be more ephemeral—glass by virtue of its transparency, dust by its fugitive lowliness, and found or discarded paper by its expendability.

Both Cornell's and Duchamp's fascination with glass operated on several levels, and intact and broken glass are central motifs for each. In one of his autobiographical guises, Duchamp confessed: "Instead of being considered a painter, I would have liked on this occasion to be thought of as a *fenêtrier*! [window glazier]. . . ."[13] Combining glass with an even more evanescent medium in *Air de Paris* (pl. 4), Duchamp used a pharmicist's ampoule to isolate, identify, and display 50cc of invisible, weightless atmosphere. Cornell sometimes consciously employed shattered glass to convey the overt symbolism of heightened emotional states: for example, dislocation in *L'enfant poete (Rimbaud à dix-huit ans, Dauguerrotype Objet)* (1935) or the threat of violence in *Habitat Group for a Shooting Gallery* (pl. 82). Mirrors, colored glass, glass grids and partitions, and broken shards are often integral to his boxes. Just as Duchamp turned the accidental breaking of his magnum opus, the *Large Glass,* to his advantage by embracing its chance effects, Cornell did not object to such an occurrence. He must have indicated as much to Julien Levy, who wrote a reply complaining that "I find I can't quite agree with you that the cracked glass on the sand fountain does not interfere. It disturbs me."[14] Among the specimen bottles in Cornell's early

145 Cornell, note, January 2, 1943 (DD 31), from Cornell, *Duchamp Dossier,* c. 1942–53. Philadelphia Museum of Art. Gift of The Joseph and Robert Cornell Memorial Foundation.

146 Cornell, note, November 11, 1961. Joseph Cornell Papers, Archives of American Art, Smithsonian, 1061:286.

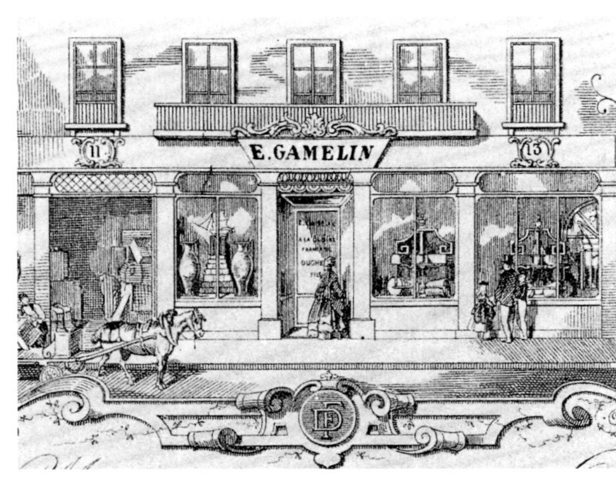

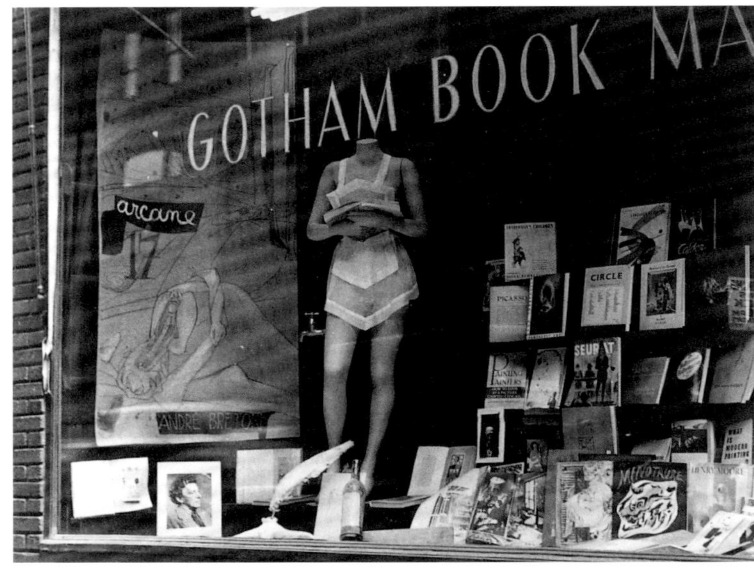

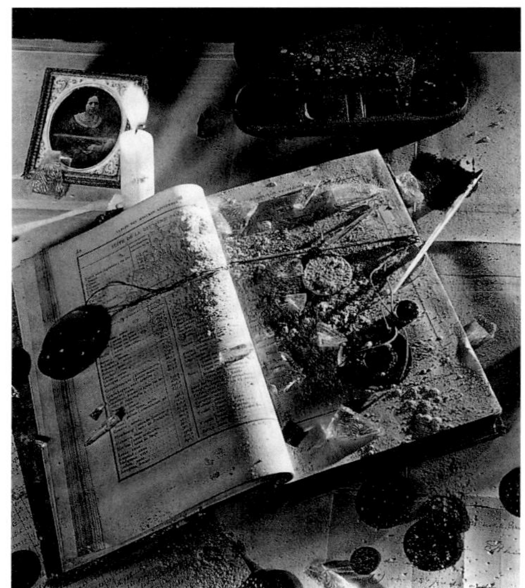

147 Engraving of E. Gamelin chocolate shop, Rouen, c. 1900.

148 Duchamp and André Breton, *Lazy Hardware*, 1945, Gotham Book Mart, 51 West 47th Street, New York, (April 1945). Photograph by Maya Deren. Philadelphia Museum of Art, Marcel Duchamp Archive.

149 Cornell's arrangement of an untitled book object, c. 1938. Vintage gelatin silver print, 10 x 8 in. Reproduced as *Spent Meteor: Night of Feb. 10, 1843 (For E. A. Poe),* in *View* (January 1943): p. 21. Photograph by James Ogle.

miniature museum case, *Cabinet of Natural Philosophy (Object)* (pl. 52), is one acknowledging his and Duchamp's mutual attraction to glazing. Bearing a misspelled label of pasted found typography, it contains jagged glass strips classified as *Méthode de M. Duchomp* (fig. 138).

In separate explanations of their work, each artist has attributed special significance to particular encounters with shop windows. Duchamp recalled the original inspiration for his *Broyeuse de chocolat [Chocolate Grinder]* paintings of 1913 and 1914—a seminal use of metamorphic imagery—as an encounter with the machine in confectioner E. Gamelin's window in Rouen (fig. 147).[15] What he had seen was "a real point of departure" for his work; "it was really a very important moment in my life."[16] Over the course of his career, he was attracted to what he described as the "coition" between the browser and the shop window's contents,[17] and among other such window installations, he created (in collaboration with André Breton) *Lazy Hardware* (fig. 148)—featuring a headless and nearly nude female mannequin with a faucet attached to her right thigh—at the Gotham Book Mart in 1945. Similarly, the chronic browser Cornell described the sight of a shop window displaying compasses as one major inspiration for his box format: "I'd scarcely gone two blocks when I came on another shop window full of boxes, . . . Halfway home on the train that night, I thought again of the compasses and the boxes. It occurred to me to put the two together."[18]

Dust is another implausible artist's material, yet both these artists were intrigued by the particles of everyday existence. After Georgia O'Keeffe visited Duchamp's New York studio in 1918, she reported, "The room looked as though it had never been swept . . . and the dust everywhere was so thick that it was hard to believe."[19] Duchamp eventually used shellac to capture some of the studio dust in the depiction of the Sieves on the horizontally situated *Large Glass*. Similar conditions persisted in his 14th Street studio in New York as Jeanne Reynal recalled in the late 1940s: "The dust lay two inches thick on the floor, with a narrow path from the front door and another leading to the bathroom. . . ."[20]

Cornell often spoke of the mundane task of cleaning up debris on his cellar floor in enthralling terms. He was so attuned to dust that he actually added some to his archive in a box labeled "Mouse Material." He cited an artistic precedent: "Musing upon Morandi—dust covering his beloved used bottles, metal utensils, etc. Agreement reached with his

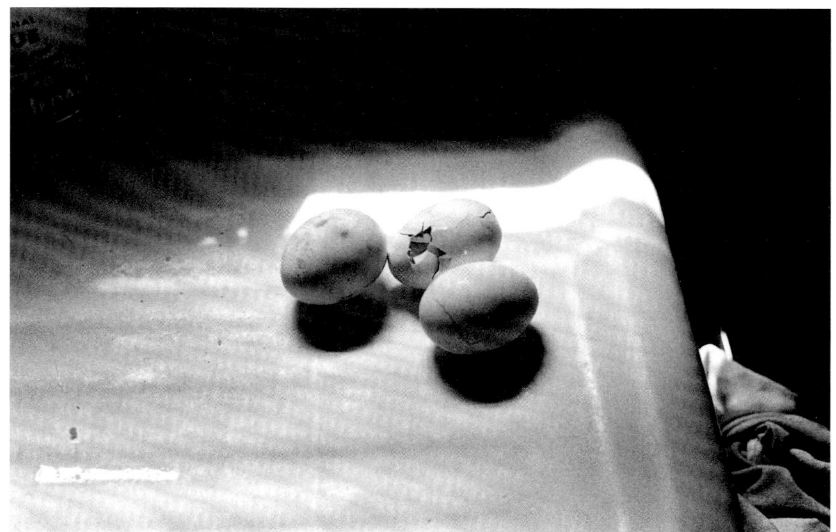

mother that she be allowed to clean up only one half of the room!"[21] In the same issue of *View* (January 1943) that first published *THE Crystal Cage*, Cornell included a photographic tableau dedicated to Edgar Allan Poe entitled *Spent Meteor: Night of Feb. 10, 1843 (for E. A. Poe)* that combined three recurrent symbols to evoke a theme of *vanitas*: a book object covered with dust and broken glass (fig. 149). While taken for granted, the gathering of dust actually marks a profound aspect of both artists' temperaments, namely a heightened awareness of natural processes. Harry Roseman's photograph taken in Cornell's garage captures this succinctly—the image of the nineteenth-century ballerina Fanny Cerrito in a decaying box is enveloped by debris, dirt, and fallen leaves (see fig. 3). For Duchamp and Cornell, dust was a benign companion.

Works by both artists convey this awareness of the physical properties of matter. Duchamp's surfaces are often intensely tactile: the marble "sugar cubes" of *Why Not Sneeze Rose Sélavy?* (pl. 9), the pitted stone or cheese close-ups on the *First Papers of Surrealism* covers (pl. 24), the plaster chin and sole, respectively, of *With My Tongue in My Cheek* and *Torture-morte [Still Torture]* (both 1959). Cornell carried this attention to physical composition even further. Many of his boxes are scattered with twigs, bark, or driftwood, trailing natural debris. He once delighted in ". . . the 'discovery' for the owl boxes in progress a particularly fine example of rotted tree. . . . Took off by the handful the wood from outer part of trunk which was in powder state."[22] Animal, bird, and owl habitats require such a setting, but the human presence in these environments is more unexpected. In Untitled *(Mélisande)* (pl. 97) the tiny doll's expression, frozen in wide-eyed innocence, seems on the verge of being swallowed by an encrustation of organic matter. After his mother's death (who would not have condoned such activity), Cornell indulged his curiosity about the subject by consciously allowing foodstuff to decay on the kitchen sink or window sill. Proving the aesthetic nature of such experiments, Cornell instructed his assistant Roseman to photograph several time-lapse sequences of rotting pears, solidifying eggs, and a piece of bread that eventually hardened (fig. 150).[23] Similarly, but with tongue in cheek, Duchamp had made his Archimboldo-like, trompe l'oeil *Sculpture-morte* (fig. 151) out of marzipan "vegetables" under assault by actual (but dead) insects.

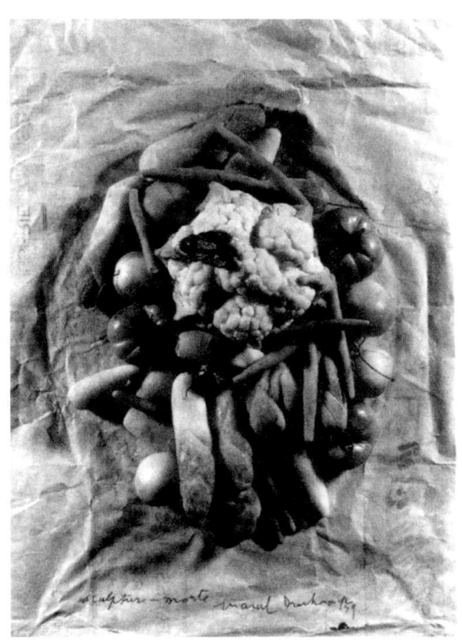

150 ***Eggs on the sink,*** 3708 Utopia Parkway, Flushing, New York, 1970. Photograph by Harry Roseman.

151 **Duchamp, *Sculpture-morte,* 1959.** Marzipan and insects on paper background, mounted on Masonite, 13¼ x 8⅞ x 2¼ in. Musée Nationale d'Art Moderne, Centre Georges Pompidou, Paris.

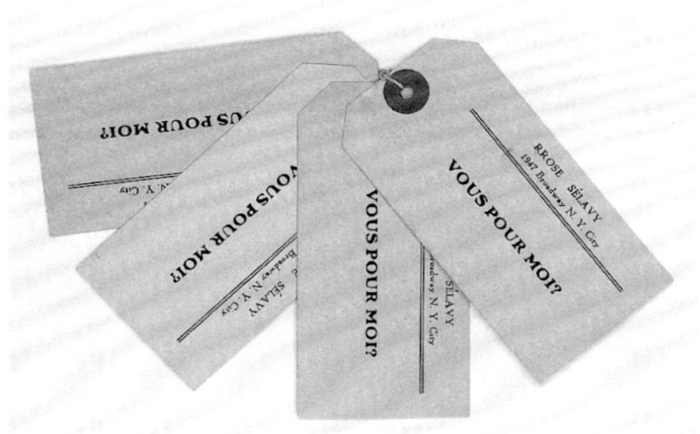

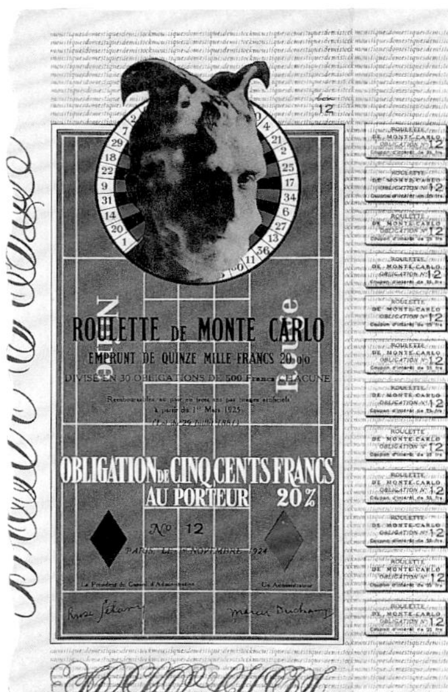

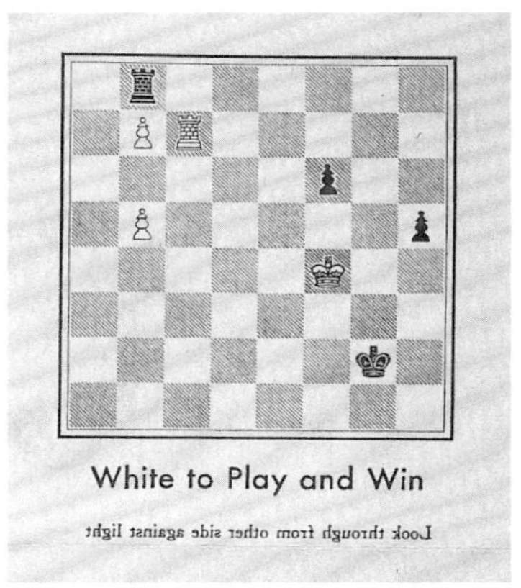

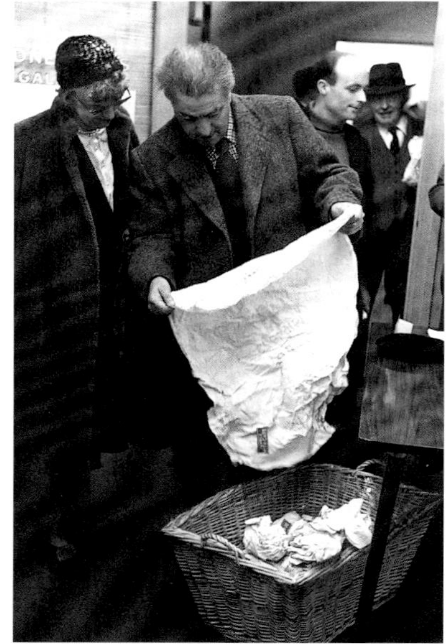

152 Duchamp, *Vous pour moi?*, 1921. Printed paper tags. Yale Collection of American Literature, Beinecke Rare Book and Manuscript Library.

153 Duchamp, *Obligations pour la Roulette de Monte-Carlo,* 1924, from the *Boîte* edition, 1938.

154 Duchamp, "White to Play and Win," detail from "'Through the Big End of the Opera Glass': Marcel Duchamp, Yves Tanguy, Joseph Cornell" exhibition announcement, Julien Levy Gallery, New York, December 7–28, 1943.

155 Edgard Varèse with crumpled catalogue for Duchamp's "DADA 1916–1923" exhibition, Sidney Janis Gallery, 15 East 57th Street, New York, 1953. Photograph by Allan Grant for *Life.*

In the artists' combined contributions to the *Duchamp Dossier*, both were intrigued by a third medium of disposables, the found or discarded paper product or fragment. Almost the entirety of the exchange detailed there is via paper products, including items more readily identified as artworks such as the "Gimme Strength" LePage's glue box (DD 67) or the double image collage of George Washington (DD 113), another version of *Allégorie de genre [Allegory of Genre]* (1943). The *Mona Lisa* variant image, inscribed *notice nose tip*, is an ordinary Louvre postcard (DD 4). Except for the occasional leather scrap, fabric fragment, or pipe cleaner, the contents are mostly flat—printed, written, or drawn, on paper or cardboard.

Many of the *Duchamp Dossier*'s contents are related to Duchamp's ongoing activity of quotidian "paperwork," confirming his enjoyment of the ephemeral gesture. Such works as the *Tzanck Cheque* (1919) and the *Obligations pour la Roulette de Monte-Carlo [Monte Carlo Bond]* (fig. 153) present elaborate artifices for exchanges of face value, in effect creating private currency. The Rrose Sélavy calling card (c. 1921) and *Vous pour moi?* luggage tags (fig. 152) explore the lowly labels of personal identification. With his designs for Ettie Stettheimer's party placecards (1918) and his contribution to the exhibition announcement for "Through the Big End of the Opera Glass" (pl. 66), Duchamp created a recto/verso printing scheme that requires the viewer to "Look through from other side against light,"[24] not only revealing the combined readable image but enforcing a closer attention to the paper medium itself (fig. 154). Duchamp mentioned these material properties in a comment to Denis de Rougemont on *inframinces* which concluded, "The cavity inside paper, between the front and back of a thin sheet. Something to study."[25] All of the aforementioned items are part of a larger constellation of everyday written records associated with Duchamp, which now should receive annotation from the contents of the *Duchamp Dossier.*

After designing the tissue-thin broadsheet/catalogue for the 1953 exhibition "DADA 1916–1923," Duchamp instructed gallery owner Sidney Janis to make crumpled-up copies available from the gallery's trash basket (fig. 155).[26] By containing such minutiae as the crumpled remnant of Duchamp's laundry bill (DD 16), the *Duchamp Dossier* provides evidence of his whimsical engagement at this very level of artifact. Through such items, Duchamp left a literal paper trail that countered Cornell's rarifications and seemingly defined the

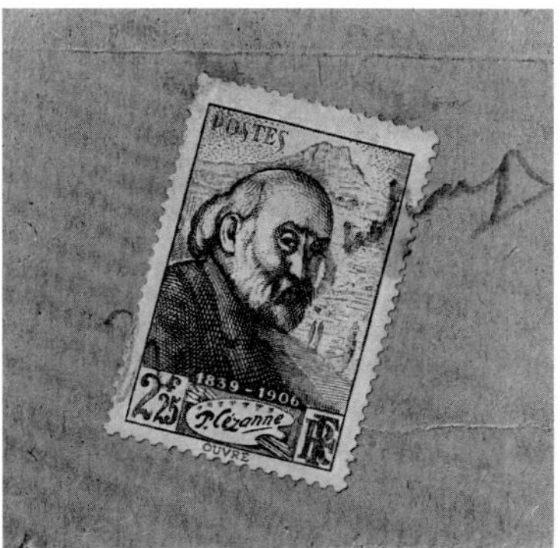

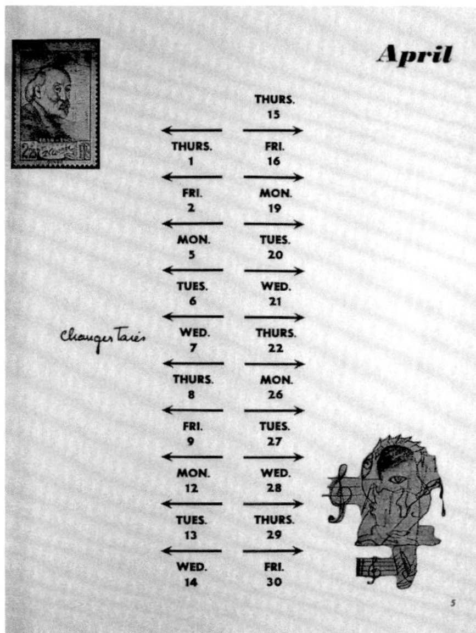

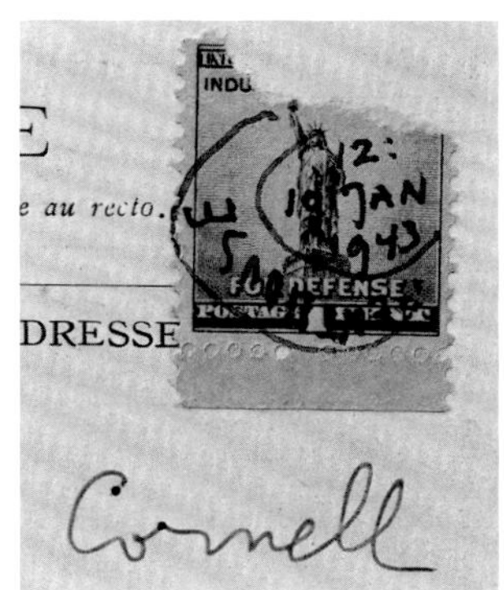

mondanités d'ephemera—an absorption no less acute but considerably more concrete.

Stamps, impressions, cancellations, receipts, signatures, dates of notation—all abound in the *Duchamp Dossier*, whether generated by Duchamp or Cornell. Like that of many American boys, Cornell's acquisitions started out with a childhood stamp collection; his sister Betty has reported that he had thousands of stamps. Stamps would remain a lifelong preoccupation for Cornell, who pasted them on boxes, collages, and intricately embellished letters and pamphlets—an alternate method of geographical voyaging from within the confines of his workshop (fig. 159). Likewise, Cornell was attuned to the semi-concealed, bureaucratic imprints distinguishing paper stocks, adding a postscript in a letter to Moore: "The enclosed blank sheet is for a lady who may appreciate exquisite 'worm-work' . . . as well as water-marks!"[27]

Duchamp, whose father was a notary and so the French embodiment of bureaucratic function, exploited notations, mechanical impressions, and (by extension) elaborately numbered editions and special off-prints as a major subtext of his working methods. Given its placement in the *Duchamp Dossier*, Duchamp's ink blotter (DD 95) surpasses random refuse and instead may signify Cornell's awareness of Duchamp's interest in the manufacturing stages of casts and transfers: residue of the *original.* The back of Duchamp's *Mona Lisa* postcard (DD 4), which was hand-delivered, not mailed, features a trompe l'oeil hand-drawn postmark over its actual U.S. Statue of Liberty stamp (fig. 158). A Paul Cézanne stamp published on the "April" calendar page of the *VVV Almanac for 1943*—which likely was contributed by Duchamp, whose handwriting is featured and who designed the covers—reappears on the Long Island Railroad conductor's receipt book cover (figs. 156 and 157; DD 98). His covert homage to Cézanne, a "retinal" painter, amusingly illustrates Duchamp's concept of how an artist may be "consecrated by posterity,"[28] even if only under a postal patron's thumb. Duchamp gave Cornell at least four different receipts that reside in the *Duchamp Dossier*, their playful spirit mimicking bureaucratic or commercial conventions.

Menus, some signed by either artist, record various lunch meetings, and napkins and empty tobacco packs are duly dated. Any signed item inevitably falls in the gray area of Duchamp studies that seeks to define the limits of his oeuvre. The attorney Joseph

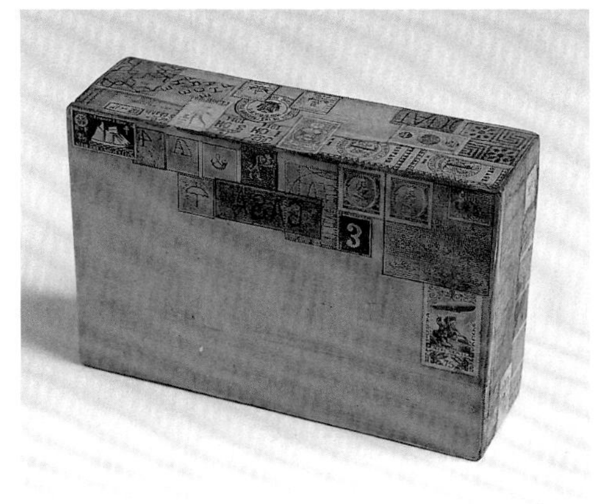

156 Duchamp, receipt [Long Island Railroad] (detail), May 3, 1943 (DD 98), from Cornell, *Duchamp Dossier,* c. 1942–53. Philadelphia Museum of Art. Gift of The Joseph and Robert Cornell Memorial Foundation.

157 Calendar page for April in *VVV Almanac for 1943* (March 1943): p. 5.

158 Duchamp, stamp and hand-drawn postmark on postcard *[Mona Lisa]* (detail), January 19, 1943 (DD 4), from Cornell, *Duchamp Dossier,* c. 1942–53. Philadelphia Museum of Art. Gift of The Joseph and Robert Cornell Memorial Foundation.

159 Cornell, Untitled (Rattle and Music Box), c. 1955. Construction, 3 1/8 x 10 1/8 x 7 1/4 in. The Menil Collection, Houston. Bequest of Jermayne MacAgy.

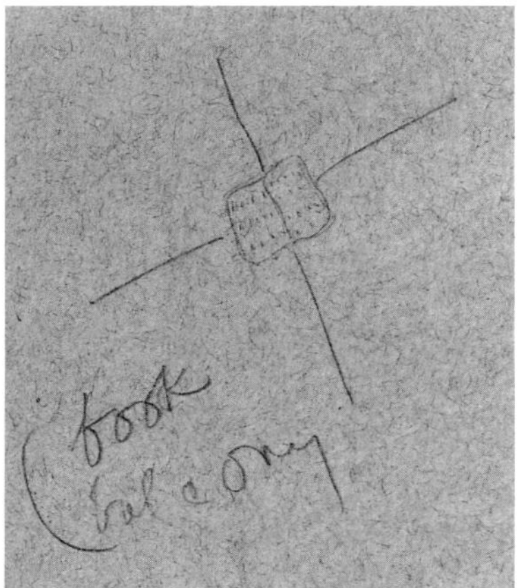

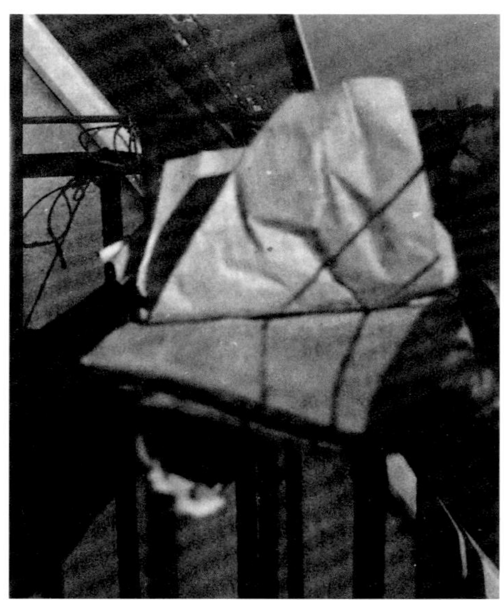

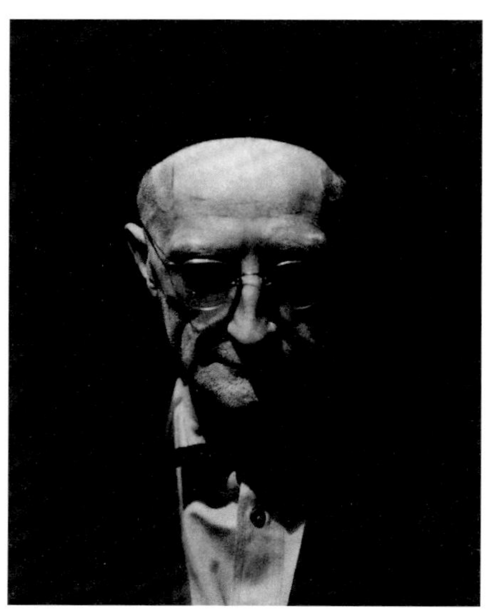

160 Sketch of *Unhappy Ready Made* on verso of magazine reproduction *[Large Glass]*, January 1934 (DD 108), from Cornell, *Duchamp Dossier*, c. 1942–53. Philadelphia Museum of Art. Gift of The Joseph and Robert Cornell Memorial Foundation.

161 *Unhappy Ready Made*, 1919 (photograph, 1920). Vintage gelatin-silver print, 4 3/8 x 2 3/4 in. Philadelphia Museum of Art. Gift of William and Virginia Camfield.

162 *Marcel Duchamp at the Age of 85*, 1945. Vintage gelatin-silver print, 7 x 4 1/2 in. Philadelphia Museum of Art, Marcel Duchamp Archive.

Solomon, Florine Stettheimer's executor, reported that in the late 1940s Duchamp was rather cavalier about autographing items from Solomon's collection of Duchamp memorabilia.[29] Referring to the *Tzanck Cheque*, Duchamp expressed a justifiable wariness about how his indulgence in such amusing transactions might be misinterpreted: "Why not, it's not a fake cheque, since it's entirely made by me! And signed! Nothing authentic! And at least it could never be taken as artistic. . . ."[30] While arguing with Robert Lebel over the inclusion of an item in the first catalogue raisonné, Duchamp lamented, "Otherwise I will send you all my daily doodles made while waiting for a telephone number."[31] In a larger sense, Duchamp consistently spoke of the spectators' role in delineating a work's value, and the excesses and mistakes intrinsic to that part of the process: ". . . it is we, posterity, who have decided that this was very good because it was painted by Cimabue or Rembrandt. Any little bit of trash by Cimabue is still very much admired."[32]

When items inside the *Duchamp Dossier* are examined, questions of their relative standing and import within Duchamp's oeuvre are rendered moot by the realization that drawing such distinctions is not only futile but also misses the point. For both Cornell and Duchamp, the methodology of their archiving defines a component primarily in the context of the whole. Presaging the art world's eventual fascination with his every jotting as he lampooned his status as an art guru within the circle of exiled European artists, Duchamp (already age 58) posed as an elderly man in a performative act at once mordant and satirical—the photograph published in *View* in 1945 is entitled *Marcel Duchamp at the Age of 85* (fig. 162). One can only imagine Duchamp's bemusement that the tantalizing bits in the *Duchamp Dossier* should now provoke such inquiry, having been hidden from scholarly discourse for the half century since they were stashed away and the quarter century since Cornell's death ended his sorting through the container's contents.

Cornell's and Duchamp's love of paper extended to a passion for books and printed matter. One of Duchamp's early conceptual works, *Ready made malheureux [Unhappy Ready Made]* (see fig. 161), connects his love of books, especially those of a scientific or technical bent, to his fascination with physical constituents. Hung from his sister's balcony and vulnerable to the erosive forces of sun, wind, and rain, a geometry textbook surrendered

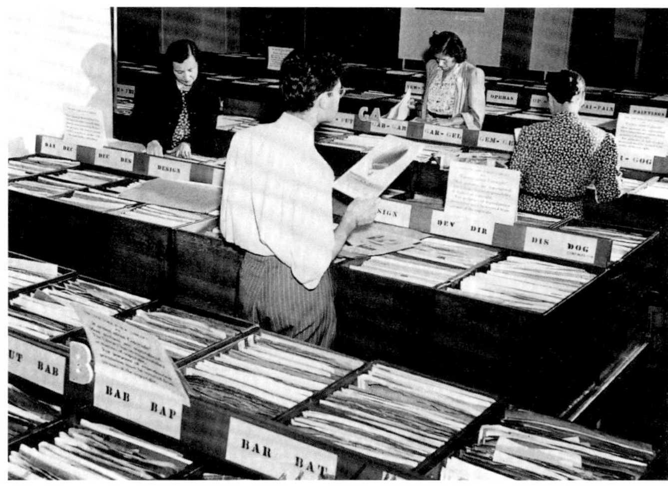

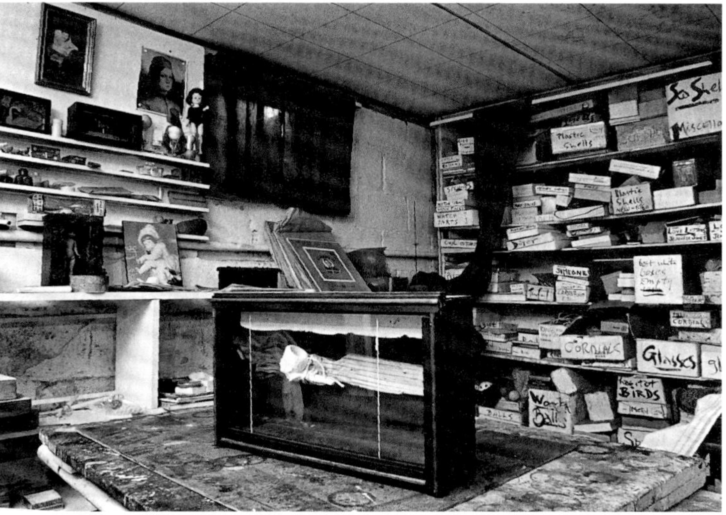

its manmade diagrams and theorems over a period of time to the processes of natural elements. A pencil drawing by Cornell of Duchamp's readymade appears on the back of the mounting for the 1933 *Large Glass* memento given to Cornell (fig. 160; DD 108).

Duchamp had worked as a librarian from 1913 to 1914 at the Bibliothèque Sainte-Geneviève in Paris and in 1915 in New York at the French Institute. Cornell was, of course, a fixture at branches of both the Flushing and New York City public libraries where he spent many afternoons in the reading rooms; his favorite haunt was the Picture Collection Room of the Main Library on 42nd Street (fig. 163). The multiple racks of pictures and clippings jammed in this vast room were officialdom's kindred version of his own archive. Cornell's obsession with books was self-acknowledged—he kept two separate files titled "Bibliomania," one for nineteenth-century and one for twentieth-century specimens.

Further, in numerous objects created from existing books, Cornell deployed a virtuosic treatment of printed matter in which the books were transformed almost *in toto* with collage elements and colorful papers, secret and see-through compartments, incisements and overlays. Such unrestrained incisions and burrowing suggest a bookworm impulse that is more than metaphorical.

Solitary Habits/ Public Archives Both artists shared a desire to do their artmaking on a closed set. Duchamp sought seclusion to foster his creativity and perfect his "indifference." His studios were remote, somewhat inhospitable, and by the 1950s his primary laboratory had become completely secret. Cornell faced more practical problems: during the years he created his seminal early boxes, he worked in his kitchen on a small table no more than about 3 x 4 feet. Not until 1941 did he manage to claim the smallish, cramped basement area of his home as his workroom. Cornell's studio was an uncontrived literalization of Duchamp's admonishment that "the great artist of tomorrow will go underground."[33] Far removed from a skylit attic or loft, the subterranean space had one small high window (fig. 164).

Within this lair, he often drifted into a semi-somnambulist state, aggravated by bouts of insomnia, work sessions that lasted until dawn, and naps and daydreams that respected

163 Picture Collection Room, New York Public Library, 42nd Street at Fifth Avenue, New York, 1955.

164 Cornell's studio, 3708 Utopia Parkway, Flushing, New York, 1969. Photograph by Hans Namuth.

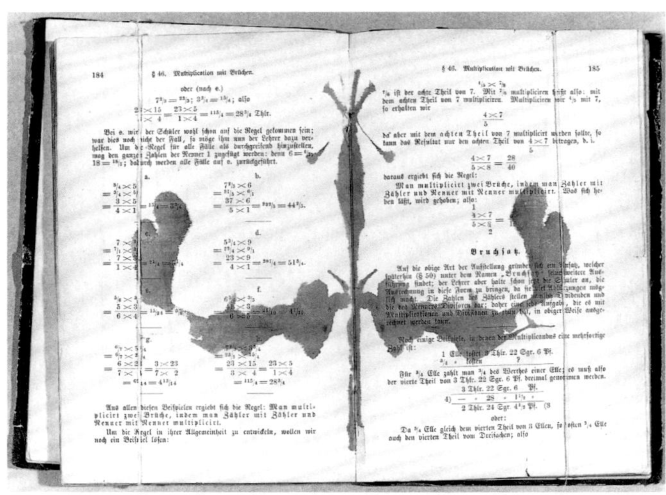

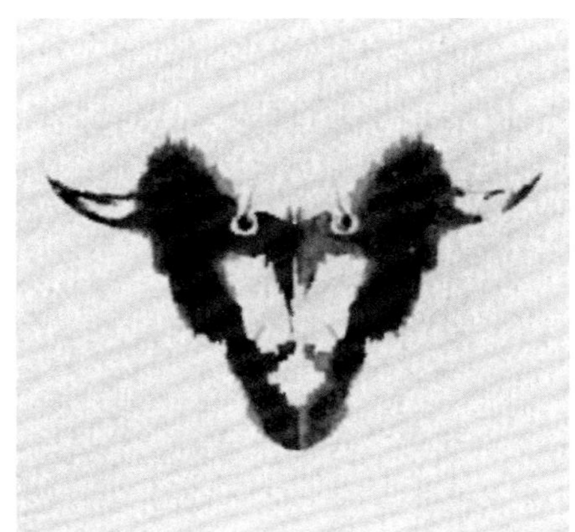

no diurnal rhythm. In 1953, citing a precedent for his associative wanderings, Cornell quoted in a letter to Mina Loy T. S. Eliot's criticism of one of her poems: "She needs the support of the image, even if only as the instantaneous point of departure. . . ."[34] In Cornell's mind, the found object or reproduced image, in alliance with linguistic, fictional, or musical inspiration, was an avenue to awareness: "Intrigued by the eidetic image—an image (experienced especially by children) which revives a previous optical impression with the clearness of hallucination."[35]

Though it is unknown whether Duchamp or Cornell is its author, an inkblot drawing in the *Duchamp Dossier* (DD 75) is a physical reminder of the associative underpinnings evident in the enterprise. As in automatic writing or frottage, the inkblot drawing generally follows Surrealist patterns of automatism: bilaterally folding the wet inked paper produces a figure governed by chance. Both artists were aware of the psychological diagnostic procedures developed by Hermann Rorschach. Cornell made hundreds of inkblot drawings he explicitly named "Rorschachs," and a Duchamp inkblot, enhanced and retouched, appears on the back cover of *Minotaure,* patently evoking a bull's head (figs. 165 and 166).[36]

The bilateral silhouette design of another key item in the *Duchamp Dossier* recalls the style of Rorschach blots: the double George Washington portrait of brown wrapping and black construction paper that is a companion to Duchamp's *Allégorie de genre*. For the *Duchamp Dossier* version (DD 113), executed in 1944, Duchamp traced either the cutout shape of the original (now in the Centre Georges Pompidou, Paris; see fig. 167) or the same cutting pattern; the dimensions and outlines coincide. The Janus-like double-portrait just fits inside the *Duchamp Dossier* box in its folded state; connecting it to its purpose of parodying nationalism, Duchamp inscribed the work to his American compatriot Cornell. Another version was published in *VVV* based on a photograph of a different gauze assemblage (fig. 168) and a die-cut map outline. A number of other works by Duchamp also are based on silhouettes, including his designs for *Chessmen* (1920), the catalogue cover for a Man Ray exhibition "Objects of My Affection" (1945), and Duchamp's *Self-Portrait in Profile* (fig. 169). Cornell had a similar attraction to silhouettes; having avidly scoured

165 Cornell, Untitled Book Object *(Anleitung zum Unterricht im Rechnen*, Berlin, 1867), c. late 1930s. Book altered with colored inks and string, 7/8 x 5 3/8 x 8 in. Natl. Museum of American Art, Smithsonian. Gift of Mr. and Mrs. John A. Benton.

166 Duchamp, inkblot drawing, 1934. *Minotaure* (Winter 1935): back cover.

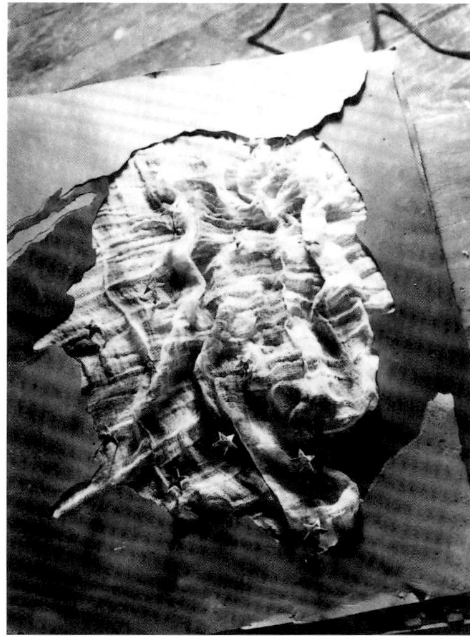

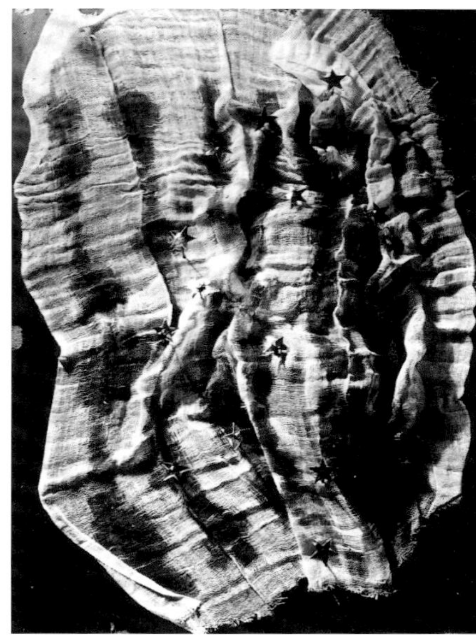

Manhattan bookstalls for them since the 1930s, he had amassed a collection that included numerous original cutouts created by Hans Christian Andersen.[37]

Though the cyclic nature of Cornell's Fourth Avenue foraging and incessant clipping of picture press images and text assured a sense of incompleteness, it also motivated many of the dossier compilations. One of Cornell's earliest significant accumulations chronicled the much-heralded 1926 arrival in New York City of the Spanish folk songstress Raquel Meller, though the cherished programs and news stories were probably not placed in their paperboard box until about 1940. Cornell, who attended one of the concerts in May 1926 with his sister Helen, embarked on a lifelong quest for memorabilia about public performers, primarily women: ballet dancers, opera divas, movie stars and starlets, and stage actresses. In 1962, Cornell alluded to Meller as an impetus that culminated in other dossiers, ". . . the context of the R-M. experience, the attitude towards the feminine muse . . . to culminate in Cerrito, Malibran, Pasta, Berenice, 'once-seens,' etc."[38]

This captivation would blossom into full-blown engagement with the cult of celebrity. Overcoming his innate reticence, Cornell eventually sought personal contact with many performers, going so far as to collect fetishistic pieces from artists, such as bits of costumes, ribbons, and ballet slippers from the ballerina Tamara Toumanova, later incorporating them into box constructions or treasuring them in dossiers. He attempted correspondence with celebrity pen pals such as Allegra Kent, Anna Moffo, Eva Marie Saint, Joan Collins, and Patty Duke, many of whom he sent gifts of collages or boxes,[39] though for the most part he received only non-responses or polite thank-yous.

Cornell tended to interpret such fixations in an Apollonian fashion, describing the object of his affection as "the feminine muse." The degree to which these infatuations carried an erotic charge is difficult to delineate, but it would be a distortion to suggest that the dossiers represent solely a veiled eroticism. Cornell was equally obsessive about dossiers on other personages or particular topics, many thematically linked—for example, Untitled *(History of Flight)* (c. 1940–65) or *Celestial Theater* (c. 1940–58). A listing of the primary source material files and dossiers in Cornell's papers fills four single-spaced typewritten pages.[40]

Still, it is fair to consider how avidly Cornell took to the chase of his muse. Cornell's

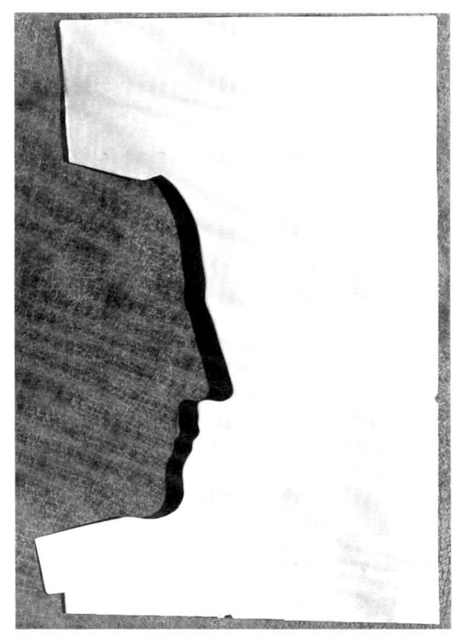

167 Preliminary state of Duchamp's *Allégorie de genre*, 1943. Vintage gelatin-silver print, $4^{3}/_{8}$ x $3^{1}/_{4}$ in. Philadelphia Museum of Art, Marcel Duchamp Archive. [Finished work, Musée Nationale d'Art Moderne, Centre Georges Pompidou, Paris].

168 Preliminary state of Duchamp's gauze assemblage for *VVV* version of *Allégorie de genre*, 1944. Vintage gelatin-silver print, 10 x 7 in. Philadelphia Museum of Art, Marcel Duchamp Archive.

169 Duchamp, metal template used to produce *Self-Portrait in Profile*, 1958 for Robert Lebel, *Sur Marcel Duchamp*, 1959.

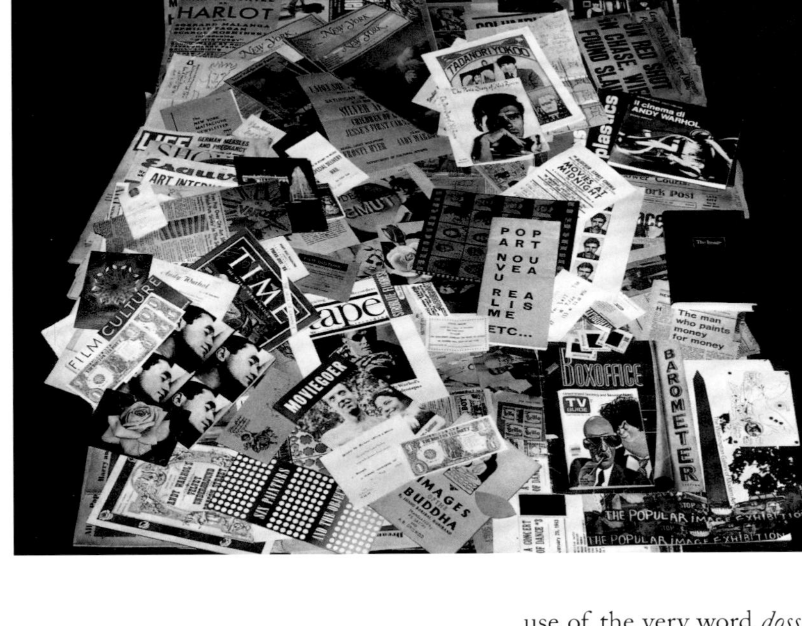

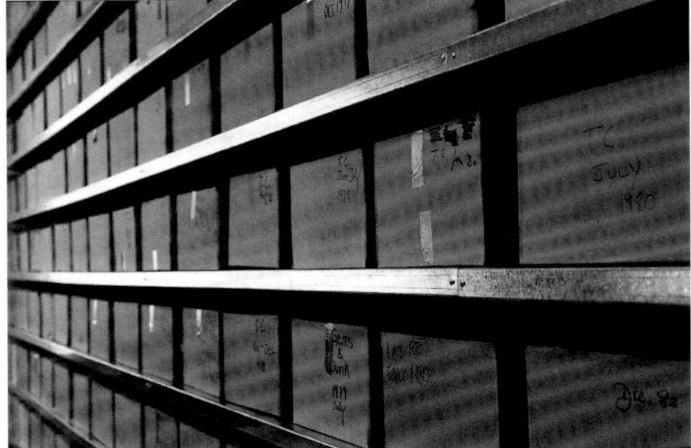

use of the very word *dossier* cannot fail to evoke its espionage origins and by implication covert activities. Further, when considering Cornell's obsessive pursuits, intimations of voyeurism, even stalking, are inescapable. For example, his file on artist Lee Bontecou, whom he knew through her dealer Leo Castelli, unmistakably chronicles an erotic preoccupation: Cornell recorded a "dream of close contact with Lee clothed in colored Khakis squatted on floor—" then recoiling, added, "nothing immodest."[41] His descriptions of their passing encounters are clearly voyeuristic: "last sighting of L.B. [Bontecou] boarding bus came along quickly—poetry—enchantment of distances—clear, graphic, beautiful image . . . what an eternity in a moment."[42]

While furtiveness played a role in many of Cornell's dossier and file projects, he was driven by a more pervasive hunting and gathering instinct. Several aspects of his dossier works anticipated Andy Warhol's practices. The Pop artist eventually became famous for his collectomania. Cornell's process of refining his dossiers was assiduous compared to Warhol's, who simply dumped the sum total of his scavenging into *Time Capsules,* differentiated only by their date of acquisition (figs. 170 and 171). Cornell, however, was consumed by an overwhelming ambition to find correlations even among such minutiae.

Archivists are primarily preservers, but an inherent aspect of their task demands selection and dumping. Sensitivity about the necessity of such deletions has engendered a variety of euphemistic terms to describe the practice of reappraisal: sampling, retention scheduling, deaccessioning, or disposition. One of Parkinson's Laws—that work expands to fill the time allotted—has its corollary in the fact that data expands to fill, then exceed, the available storage space. Simply this practical necessity, or changing modes and fashion, shifting allegiances and outright revisionism, all can cast the archivist as an arbiter and decimator of historical data. While such information may be temporarily lost, it often resurfaces amongst the ebb and flow of the overall archival fabric.

Cornell's drive to accumulate constantly forced the issue of inclusion or deletion, and as a result, he was often plagued by the lack of a finishing flourish; the dossiers could remain dormant for extended periods as he was overcome with a sense of aesthetic inertia. Following the "Romantic Museum at the Hugo Gallery / Portraits of Women: Constructions and

170 Andy Warhol, contents of a *Time Capsule*, mid 1960s. The Archives of The Andy Warhol Museum of Art, Pittsburgh.

171 Andy Warhol, storage archive for *Time Capsules*. The Archives of The Andy Warhol Museum of Art, Pittsburgh.

Arrangements by Joseph Cornell" exhibition (pl. 80), most dossiers were nearly absent from public sight until The Museum of Modern Art, New York, retrospective in 1980.[43] Throughout the same period in the 1950s and 1960s that Cornell was obsessed with his more unwieldy explorations such as *GC 44*, only *Portrait of Ondine* was publicly exhibited—at the Wittenborn Bookstore in 1956. In the gallery handout, Cornell stated, in a startling admission, that the original subject matter was becoming unfixed: "Even ballet itself in the limited sense becomes secondary and the present title tentative in progressive distillations."[44]

The subtitle of *THE Crystal Cage [portrait of Berenice]*, first published in the "Americana Fantastica" number of *View*, may have been suggested by a story by Poe, whose name is among those in the accompanying text collage. In Poe's gothic horror tale "Berenice," the monomaniacal narrator strangely echoes Cornell's difficulties with polishing off his dossiers: "To muse for long unwearied hours with my attention riveted to some frivolous device on the margin, or in the typography of a book; . . . at the conclusion of a day dream *often replete with luxury*, he [the dreamer] finds the *incitamentum* or first cause of his musings entirely vanished and forgotten."[45] This passage could describe the inevitable unravelings of Cornell's dossier projects—a compilation built on correspondences risks collapsing like a house of cards when tangential concerns overload the primary subject matter.

A painting by Gris, which Cornell cited as having "sparked" an important series of box constructions, features a particularly evocative image (fig. 172). Cornell alluded to the painting in this way: "The so-called 'Juan Gris' boxes were not worked out slavishly . . . the original inspiration was purely a human reaction to a particular painting at the Janis Gallery—a man reading a newspaper at a cafe table covered almost completely by his reading material."[46] In many ways, Cornell was that figure, a solitary man immersed, swimming for his life, in a sea of paper, printed words, and reproduced images.

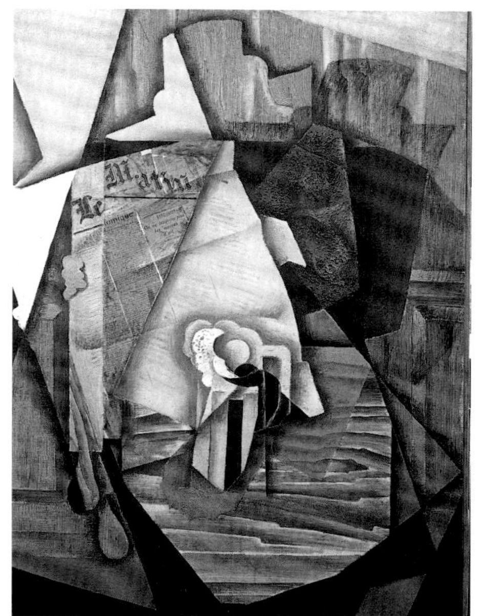

172 Juan Gris, *Figure Seated in a Cafe*, 1914. Oil on canvas, with collage, 39 x 28 1/4 in. Private collection, courtesy Acquavella Galleries, New York.

Audience Participation The *Duchamp Dossier* ideally should be displayed sitting open on a table, its contents available for sifting and contemplation by viewers. The practicalities of conservation concerns and the magnitude of the contemporary art public, however, preclude such a presentation. In some ways the two artists have succeeded all too well in their playful lifting of the discourse on ephemera.

The common, salient feature of Duchamp's boxes or valises and Cornell's dossiers is the principle of shuffling. Obviously, the portfolio album dispenses with the linear restrictions of the bound book. Beyond that indeterminacy, the prehensile nature of the artifacts moves the collection's emphasis into the tactile realm of the object. Manipulation by the hand linked to visual recognition by the eye is essentially a recapitulation of the creative process: the viewer becomes an active participant in the art-making. Before Cornell's boxes became conserved objects of the art market, the artist intended them to be held, manipulated, even played with. Duchamp's *Green Box*, *Boîte* edition, and *à l'infinitif [In the Infinitive] (White Box)* (pl. 45), now subject to white-gloved examination, originally invited casual jumbling by the viewer. In every case, initially immiscible material was expected to be freely combined. In Janis' 1944 book *Abstract & Surrealist Art in America*, Duchamp obliquely but unmistakably linked his portable museum to indeterminancy. Each represented artist was asked to explicate his or her work, and to accompany a reproduction of a *Boîte-en-valise* Duchamp provided a note from the *Green Box*: "Idea of Fabrication: If a thread (straight or horizontal) a meter long is dropped from a height of a meter onto a horizontal plane, its chance-shape gives it a new unit of length."[47]

Nowhere was the open-ended principle more crucial than in Cornell's dossiers, where the viewer was to browse, in a sense vicariously experiencing, then redirecting, Cornell's original scavenging. Yet Cornell himself was never able to "consummate" (his word) many of the dossier projects because the divisions between source material and finished artwork, between the physicality of the artifacts and the associative powers of his mind, proved too elusive.

To enter Cornell's domain when looking at his dossiers, the viewer must bring a receptive mind and lay aside certain prejudices. First, one must resist the impulse to trivialize the intent and consequence of the collection because of its physical characteristics and its "life expectancy." This obstacle also affects Duchamp's valises. Ephemera by definition is short-lived or transitory, and it is primarily the act of segregating picayune objects within a specific aggregate that bestows on them an exceptional status. Further, as with Duchamp's readymades, the distinction between high and low art is forcibly blurred, in Cornell's case by the diversity of his assembled objects: an exquisite nineteenth-century engraving may lay alongside a childlike drawing of a flower.

In addition, the viewer must look beyond the seemingly random nature of the accumulation, which can include dime-store greeting cards or reproductions of art masterworks. Cornell was advancing a concept that Robert Rauschenberg would later rediscover and define as "random order."[48] Cornell's dossiers, like Rauschenberg's combines from the mid to late 1950s, mix and match the elements of the physical world within the field of the artwork, recontextualizing perception. In a most appropriate allusion, Cornell called the *GC 44* a "tower of visions."[49] He was especially conscious of his dossiers as being distilled pinnacles of the towerlike pile that constituted his vast archive.

By contrast, Duchamp's boxed accumulations are patently cohesive, linked by an aspect of his thinking or self-reflexively to a consideration of a particular artwork (as in the *Green Box)* or of his oeuvre (as in the *Boîte* edition), where the individuality of the specific items within is subsumed to their context or relative positioning. Due to the portability and miniaturization of the ensemble, the first photograph of Duchamp with his mini-museum recalls a Fuller Brush man with a sample case, peddling his products door to door. In a letter to Jean Crotti, Duchamp made light of such self-promotion by writing, "The artists who, during their lifetimes, foist off their shoddy goods are excellent traveling salesmen, but nothing guarantees the immortality of their work. And even posterity is a terrible bitch who cheats some and reinstates others (El Greco), and reserves the right to change her mind again every 50 years."[50]

Cornell, however, carried his suitcase dossiers only on vicarious journeys, having spent the entirety of his life in or around New York City. At times he seemed swept away by secondhand emotions akin to the Stendhal syndrome experienced by nineteenth-century travelers as he swooned before visions of art and architecture viewed solely through reproduction. Duchamp offered a droll comment on Cornell's stay-at-home nature (and their dual fascination with boxed albums) when he gifted him with a Waterman ink box (DD 17) and signed his initials directly below the printed slogan referring to the ink bottle's cylindrical metal carrier: *pour le Voyage/Etui luxe [for the trip/deluxe case].*

In some respects, Cornell's fixity resonates with that of a rather obscure scientist-

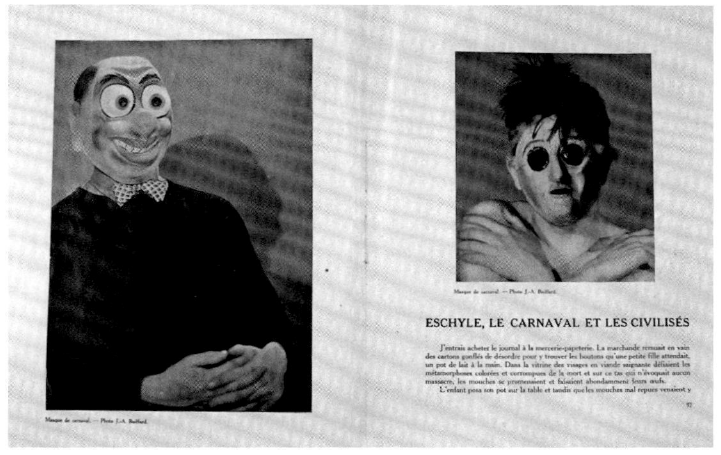

Masque de carnaval. — Photo J.-A. Boiffard.

ESCHYLE, LE CARNAVAL ET LES CIVILISÉS

J'entrais acheter le journal à la mercerie-papeterie. La marchande remuait en vain des cartons gonflés de désordre pour y trouver les boutons qu'une petite fille attendait, un pot de lait à la main. Dans la vitrine des visages en viande saignante défiaient les métamorphoses colorées et corrompues de la mort et sur ce tas qui n'évoquait aucun massacre, les mouches se promenaient et faisaient abondamment leurs œufs.

L'enfant posa son pot sur la table et tandis que les mouches mal repues venaient y

97

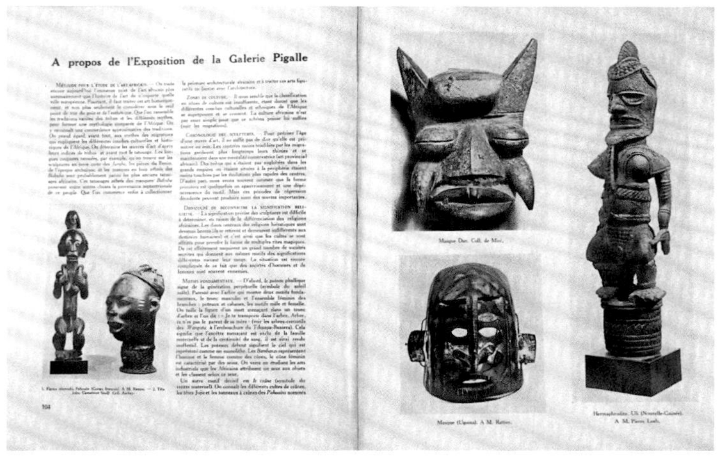

A propos de l'Exposition de la Galerie Pigalle

104

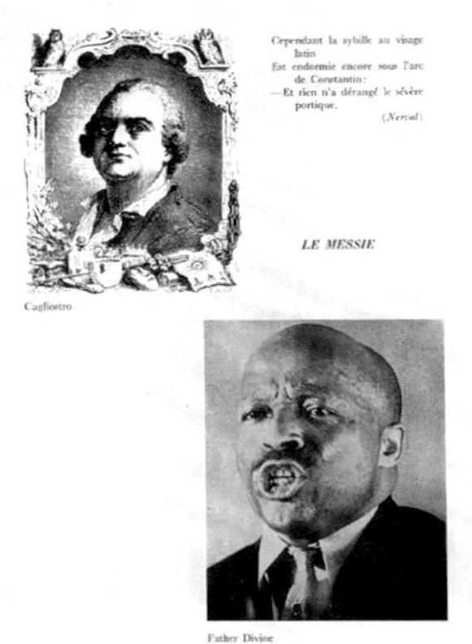

Cependant la sybille au visage latin
Est endormie encore sous l'arc de Constantin:
—Et rien n'a dérangé le sévère portique.
(*Nerval*)

LE MESSIE

Cagliostro

Father Divine

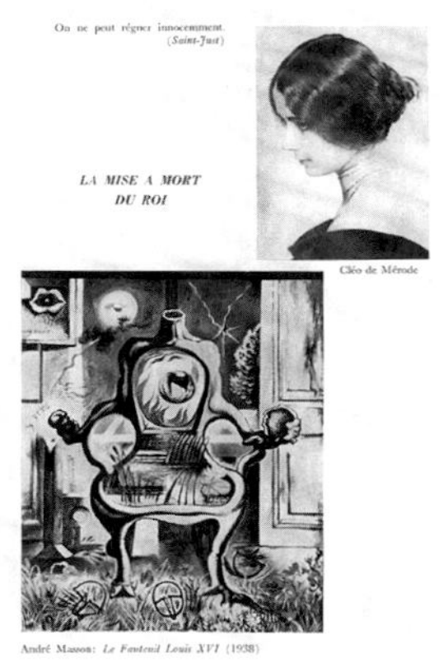

On ne peut régner innocemment.
(*Saint-Just*)

LA MISE A MORT DU ROI

Cléo de Mérode

André Masson: *Le Fauteuil Louis XVI* (1938)

engineer named David Lyle. Like Cornell, Lyle was always seeking a common thread for disparate materials. Lyle's quixotic quest, begun in 1931, to seek connections between abstract communication methods such as Morse code and the patterns of human behavior led him by 1937 to amass an archive that correlated the multiple networks of facts, events, and ideas passing through his *specific* vantage point in Paterson, New Jersey.[51] Lyle's ideas partially sparked William Carlos Williams' seminal epic poem *Paterson*.

In the *First Papers of Surrealism* catalogue, Duchamp's friend Robert Allerton Parker enthused on another renegade archivist named Charles Hoy Fort, a writer and compiler of the paranormal: "This Socrates of the Bronx . . . was primarily a collector of newspaper clippings; . . . by a craft of literary *collage* and *montage,* Fort managed to project his picture of a paradoxical and highly unpredictable universe. . . ."[52] Fort's description of himself recalls Cornell's behavioral patterns: "Sometimes I am a collector of data, and only a collector, . . . But always there is present a feeling of unexplained relations of events that I note; and it is this far-away, haunting, or often taunting, awareness, or suspicion, that keeps me piling on—."[53]

As other instances such as Lyle's and Fort's work indicate, interrelational archiving tendencies did not spring from a cultural vacuum. By the 1920s everyday life was awash in new communication modes: telephones, phonographs, radio, motion picture newsreels, and printed mass media were rapidly multiplying. Even as the information age and resultant global village entered their incubation stage, Duchamp's and Cornell's practices

173 Excerpts from two successive pictorial essays in *Documents* (Spring 1930): pp. 96–97, 104–105. "Eschyle, Le Carnaval et les Civilisés," photographs by Jacques-André Boiffard, and "A propos del' Exposition de la Galerie Pigalle"

174 Excerpt from pictorial essay by André Breton, *First Papers of Surrealism* (1942): n.p. "On the Survival of Certain Myths and on Some Other Myths In Growth or Formation"

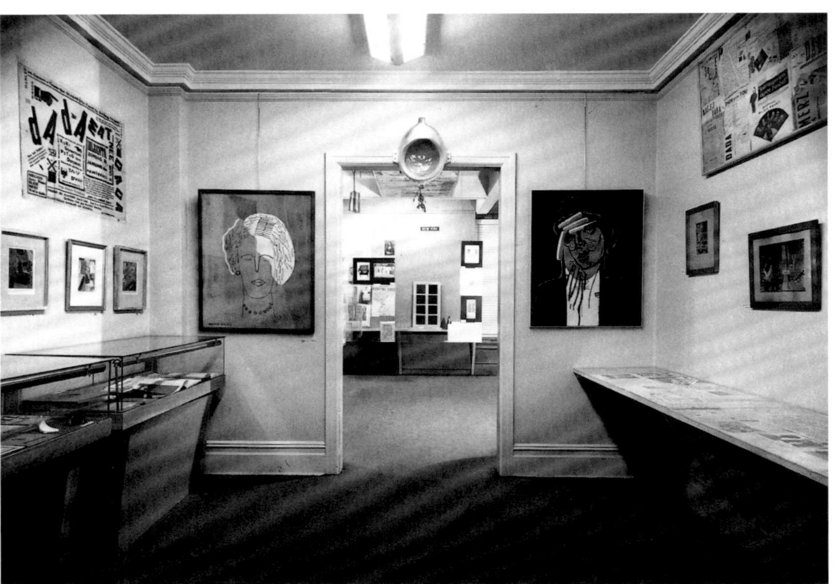

anticipated the engagement of the digital era with data retention and retrieval.

Likewise, formats dealing with classification and juxtaposition of both visual and textual material had emerged from various points in the art world fabric. From 1929 to 1930, the French journal *Documents,* with which both Duchamp and Cornell were probably familiar, was counterpoising archeological finds, serious and popular cinema, and jazz-age comic books with critiques of avant-garde art, music, and literature (fig. 173). Breton employed a similar presentation in his self-described *"Mise en scène"* pictorial published in the *First Papers of Surrealism* catalogue: the potpourri of images stretched from Hieronymus Bosch and Cléo de Mérode to Father Divine and DC Comics' Superman (fig. 174).[54] The core of juxtaposed images in these publishing projects mirrors such effects as those Cornell sought in his dossiers. Referring to *GC 44* as if seeking a universal language of pictorial elements, he called his exploration an "esperanto of imagery."[55]

While acting as archivists, both Duchamp and Cornell also were engaged in mastering and conveying information through the allied role of the curator. Despite his self-professed disengagement and a public stance dismissive of the machinations of mounting exhibitions, Duchamp was in fact a participant, instigator, or organizer of numerous exhibitions (fig. 175). It is little wonder, then, that his central public project at mid century was acting as curator of his own portable museum and that he would finally succeed by 1954 in shepherding the main body of his work into a single site, the Philadelphia Museum of Art.

Like Duchamp, Cornell often took a curatorial approach toward the exhibition of his own work—for example, at his 1932 inaugural exhibition when he collaborated with Levy on the display of his Jouets and Bell Jars, or in 1949 when he constructed a complete gridded environment for his "Aviary" exhibition at Egan Gallery (fig. 176). He carefully orchestrated the display of the "Romantic Museum at the Hugo Gallery" exhibition in 1946, the primary showing of a large selection of his dossier projects. An undated sketch by Cornell from the late 1940s (fig. 177) shows him working over or reviewing the relationships between a number of the same dossiers shown in this exhibition.[56] Possibly a contemplated layout for *Vogue,* to which Cornell was still contributing, the schematic drawing

175 Duchamp's installation of "DADA 1916–1923" (April 15–May 9, 1953), Sidney Janis Gallery, 15 East 57th Street, New York.

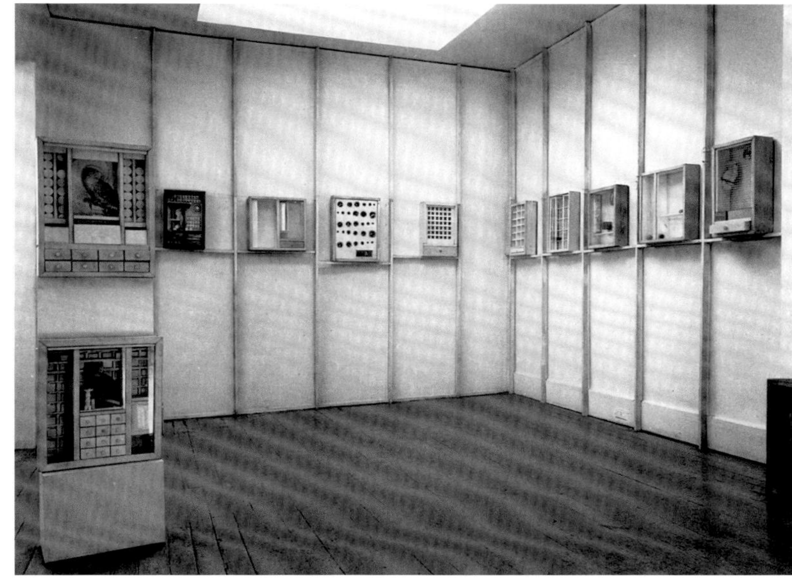

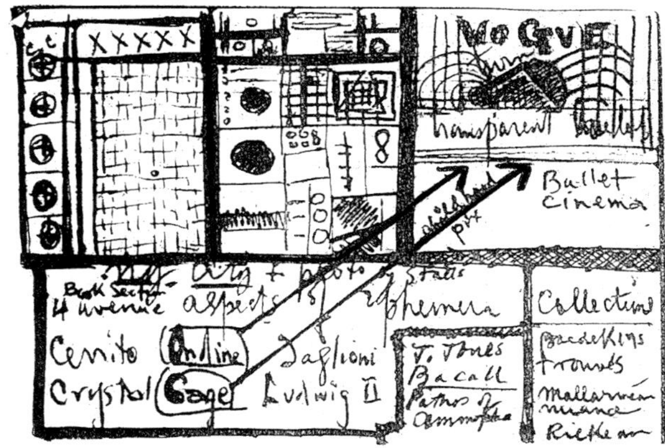

also includes, in addition to discrete dossiers, a selection of "NY City & photo stalls, Book Section / 4 Avenue, aspects of ephemera / childhood pix."

Cornell and Duchamp both courted additional public response with their graphic design projects and publications. Cornell's Flushing archive became a valuable resource for New York publishers ranging from independent small presses to *Time* magazine. His source material and design techniques not incidentally established a "look" for *View* magazine—comprising an advanced form of "clip art" (found commercial reproductions). Duchamp's inventive covers and layouts for numerous art publications were so innovative that they alone put the lie to his self-promulgated "retirement."

In March 1945, when Cornell published a visual homage to his friend in the "Duchamp" number of *View* magazine, he was elaborating on a practice that had originated in his commercial graphic arrangements for magazines like *Harpers' Bazaar* and *Good Housekeeping*. Entitled *3/4 Bird's-Eye View of 'A Watch-Case for Marcel Duchamp,'* the work began life as a pillbox object that was photographed and replicated in various sizes (pls. 74 and 75). These photographs were then used as collage elements in the final work. Like *Spent Meteor,* this is an example of a photographic arrangement mutating into an artwork destined only for publication.[57] In addition, almost every one of the few known portraits of Cornell during the 1930s and 1940s were carefully staged by the artist, including the Lee Miller pictures with the toy boat (fig. 178), Cornell with an unidentified book object (see fig. 209), and Ernst Beadle's photograph of Cornell with the imperiled doll in Central Park (see fig. 94). In such self-posed instances, Cornell's reticent temperament is personified: he is usually seen in profile or laterally, as if turning away from the camera.

As a corollary to their graphic pursuits, both artists concerned themselves with the entrepreneurial potential of their boxes and dossiers. While Duchamp patiently monitored the slow but successful distribution of his boxed accumulations in the public arena, Cornell was continually stymied, though he came up with numerous similar schemes: "In Grand Central thoughts anew about getting at the editions for various projects, ONDINE, Celestial Theatre, Gérard de Nerval, Pasta, etc., etc."[58] Later he concluded, "Explorations . . . Necessity of stating position or purpose of various projects bringing up to date,

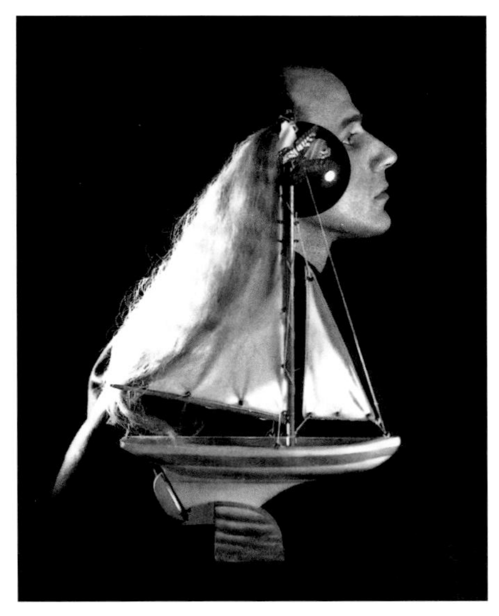

176 Cornell's installation of "Aviary by Joseph Cornell" (December 7, 1949–January 7, 1950), Egan Gallery, 63 East 57th Street, New York. Photograph by Aaron Siskind.

177 Cornell, sketch for a proposed *Vogue* layout, undated [c. 1949]. Joseph Cornell Papers, Archives of American Art, Smithsonian, 1059:170.

178 *Joseph Cornell, New York,* 1933. Vintage gelatin-silver print, 6 1/2 x 8 1/2 in. Photograph by Lee Miller. © Lee Miller Archives, Chiddingly, England.

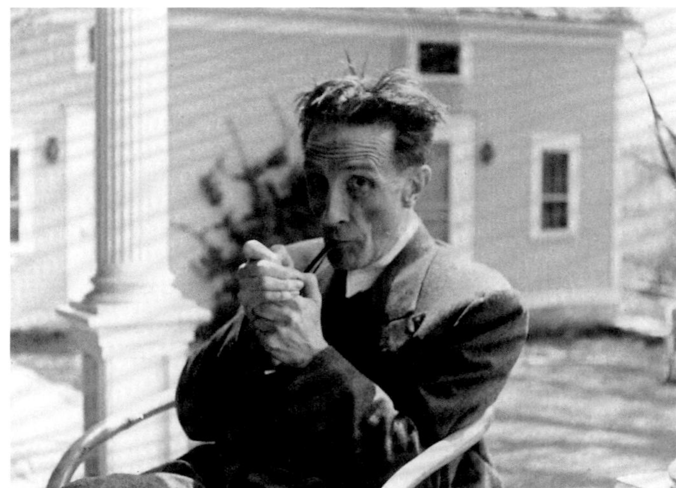

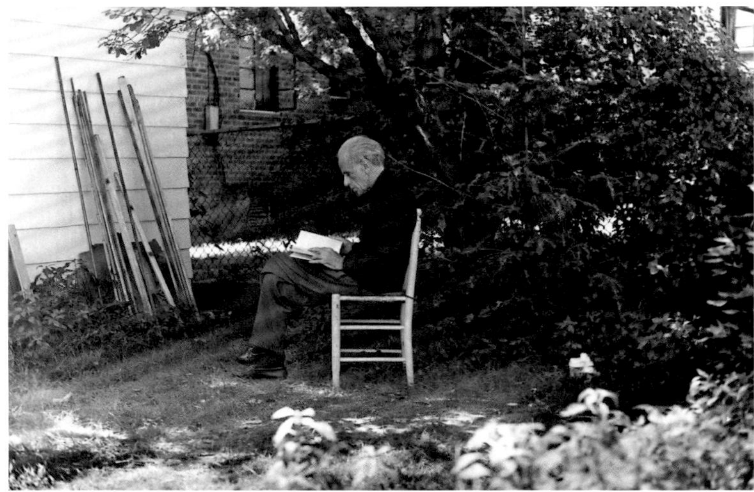

consummating, etc."[59] Once in a 1967 letter to Levy, he specifically cited Duchamp's precedent: "The format established the given subjects would fall into line— . . . it could be worked out like Duchamp's 'valise' in moderate editions."[60] Donald Windham was nonplussed when Cornell suggested that editions of a dossier on ballet dancers be sold in Woolworth's dime-stores for the edification of the masses.[61] Still, Duchamp had unsuccessfully attempted a similarly far-fetched scheme when he first exhibited and tried to sell his *Rotorelief (disques optiques)* (pl. 18) at a Paris market of household gadgets.

As late as 1967, Cornell presented Windham with the entirety of the *GC 44* dossier in hopes that he could help edit its contents or publish it in some fashion. Windham, one of Cornell's more sympathetic and indulgent collaborators, kept *GC 44* for six to eight months but was, of course, thwarted by a task that would have required him to act as the artist's surrogate.[62] Cornell probably hoped his proposal would function in a manner as productive as his collaboration on collage films with filmmaker Larry Jordan. In near desperation, Cornell approached another literary figure, seemingly in hopes of discovering workable narratives for his explorations. In 1966, Cornell told the poet John Ashbery, "I have certain dossiers capable of high potential for someone like yourself but it needs a very close rapport and empathy—they are past my own labours and have been so for a few years now."[63]

Bon Voyage While it is impossible to know when the *Duchamp Dossier* was last altered, the latest dated material within it is from 1953. Cornell is known to have remained in at least limited contact with Duchamp into the 1960s, and Teeny Duchamp became an affectionate and trusted friend. In the Cornell papers at the Archives of American Art, one finds many examples of memorabilia that at the time of Cornell's death had not found their way into the *Duchamp Dossier* mix: a *Life* magazine article on Duchamp's chess playing and an Iolas Gallery René Magritte exhibition announcement incorporating a Duchamp quote, for example.[64] The 1968 obituaries for Duchamp clipped from *Newsweek* and *Life*,[65] which now reside in Cornell's papers, would have made fitting bookends in the dossier for the 1942 *Time* article announcing Duchamp's arrival in America (DD 78).

Perhaps the primary reason for this attenuation of the collection was Cornell's feeling

179 **Duchamp at home of Yves Tanguy and Kay Sage,** Woodbury, Connecticut, May 23, 1948. Photograph by Enrico Donati. Philadelphia Museum of Art, Marcel Duchamp Archive.

180 ***Cornell Reading,*** 3708 Utopia Parkway, Flushing, New York, September 1971. Photograph by Harry Roseman.

that, unlike most of his other such projects, the *Duchamp Dossier* was in a sense a collaborative effort with a living person. That this person was Duchamp no doubt intensified the feeling of a missing and then finally lost presence. The contents of the *Duchamp Dossier* cohere around Duchamp's wartime years in America, circumscribed on one arc by his initial introduction to Cornell in the early 1930s and on the other by the closing of their period of personal interaction by the mid 1950s. For an artist like Cornell, who often experienced life most directly through his imagination, the *Duchamp Dossier* is the record of a rare and fruitful intimacy.

The contents of Cornell's and Duchamp's boxed albums evoke Breton's conception of the quotidian marvelous: "I am intimately persuaded that all one's most involuntary perceptions . . . carry within them the solution, symbolic or otherwise, of some difficulty within oneself. It is a question again, of knowing one's way about the maze. Delirium of interpretation begins only when the ill-prepared man takes fright in this *forest of indices*."[66] A fascination with the received image led both artists from a reliance on the concrete (and, in many cases, found) object to acknowledging the validity of replication or reproduction as a surrogate for the object. This argument renders the seemingly inconsequential contents of miniature museums or accumulations in hand-held dossiers crucial to current considerations of how data storage and retrieval affect the nature of perception. Today, as the information age spreads in a multilinked cybertransmission of digitally duplicated text and computer-manipulated Photoshop® nonreality obscuring any sense of an "original," it simultaneously facilitates a more profound global comprehension. With broader hindsight, Duchamp's and Cornell's rather discrete containers attain seminal status as predecessors of contemporary text and image manipulation.

The *Duchamp Dossier* offers the patient onlooker profound insights into the thought processes of both the cataloguist, Cornell, and his subject, Duchamp (figs. 179 and 180). In contemplative repose, as if surrounded by the silence of a library, the small box—a uniquely confluent record of two twentieth-century masters—bears witness to how even ephemera at the edges of recognition can expand consciousness. Among its confounding and ostensibly trivial contents can be found a between-the-scraps guidebook through the landscape of memory. In the *Duchamp Dossier*, as in their other dossier and box formats, Cornell and Duchamp have provided handy carryalls, fully packed, for such enlightening excursions.

Notes

I am indebted to Ecke Bonk, whose discussions with me over the course of our collaboration on the design of this publication sparked this essay. In addition, Susan Davidson has been a willing collaborator—offering enthusiasm, ideas, and source material. Ann Temkin provided a deft editorial hand. Lynda Roscoe Hartigan not only offered knowing guidance through the resources of the Joseph Cornell Study Center but also inestimable contributions to my understanding of Cornell's work.

1. Joseph Cornell, diary entry, 8 October 1968, Joseph Cornell Papers, Archives of American Art, Smithsonian Institution, Washington, D.C., microfilm, 1056:680. "I feel D.[elacroix] to Redon to Duchamp" was struck through in this entry. Wording of this dream appears in several variations. Another example: "Last evening I had a vivid dream about Delacroix being alive and staying in a N.Y.C. hotel. Marcel would not believe this true about N.Y.C. but was credulous when Paris was mentioned. There was this obsession to obtain a handkerchief from the Romantic painter." Cornell Papers, AAA, 1056:681.

2. "I picked up an Apollinaire item later in the day—Duchamp told me about taking a trip of a week's duration to a mountain resort and playing jackstraws every night with him." Joseph Cornell, draft of letter, 28 May 1952, Cornell Papers, AAA, 1059:496. "Duchamp studio near Renoir [Paris] played pool-like game with Gris." Joseph Cornell, diary entry, 14 October 1956, in *Joseph Cornell's Theater of the Mind: Selected Diaries, Letters, and Files,* edited by Mary Ann Caws (New York and London: Thames and Hudson, 1993), p. 219.

3. Morris Hirshfield, discovered in 1939 and championed by Sidney Janis, was included by Duchamp (in collaboration with André Breton) in the "First Papers of Surrealism" exhibition and the inaugural exhibition of Art of This Century. Duchamp noted Hirshfield's name with Max Ernst, Yves Tanguy, Joan Miró, and himself in a list written on 9 September 1942 (DD 18).

4. Duchamp's copy was no. 12 from an unknown edition number (possibly as many as twenty). The gift ended up in the possession of Mary Reynolds and resides now in her papers at the Ryerson Library, The Art Institute of Chicago, inv. no. AI 62. It is inscribed on the inside of the folio cover: *à Marcel Duchamp/ En hommage/ Copy no. 12/ Joseph Cornell/ Jan. 1934*. The text only of *Monsieur Phot* was published in Julien Levy's anthology *Surrealism* (New York: Black Sun Press, 1936), pp. 77–88.

5. Cornell informed Pavel Tchelitchew that the Fanny Cerrito materials had been placed in a suitcase. Joseph Cornell to Pavel Tchelitchew, 21 October 1941, Parker Tyler Papers, Harry Ransom Humanities Research Center, The University of Texas at Austin.

6. Joseph Cornell to Marianne Moore, 21 June 1944, in Caws, p. 104.

7. Cornell probably first saw a *Boîte-en-valise* in July 1942 when Duchamp brought an example to Utopia Parkway (Robert Cornell, diary entry, 31 July 1942, courtesy Mrs. John A. Benton). Duchamp later retrieved the leftover *Boîte* edition materials. On December 31, 1945, he wrote Cornell asking to meet for lunch on January 4, 1946, and added: ". . . Would it be asking too much to bring with you all the wood sticks and pieces we had made at one time for the boxes. I am putting some order in my affairs before leaving USA (in April)" (DD 23). The meeting at which Cornell returned the remaining materials occurred at Pappas Restaurant (DD 97). For information concerning the boxes completed during this period see the note on Cornell's assembly of the *Boîte* edition (p. 304).

8. See *Duchamp Dossier* Inventory (DD 0) for discussion concerning the container's origin.

9. Marcel Duchamp, quoted in Robert Lebel, *Marcel Duchamp* (New York: Grove Press, Inc., 1959), pp. 96–97.

10. "This brilliant caricature of a modern magazine advertisement [editor's comment]," punning on the name of the artist Archipenko, appeared as a promotion for the Société Anonyme in *The Arts* 1, no. 3 (February–March 1921): p. 64.

11. Diary entry, 2 March 1952, Cornell Papers, AAA, 1059:148.

12. Joseph Cornell to Charles Henri Ford, 6 October 1951, Charles-Henri Ford Papers, Getty Research Institute, Los Angeles, Archive #880205.

13. Marcel Duchamp referring to *Fresh Widow* (1920), quoted in Charles F. Stuckey, "Duchamp's Acephalic Symbolism," *Art in America* 65 (January/February 1977): p. 99, n. 15.

14. Julien Levy to Joseph Cornell, c. August 1959, Cornell Papers, AAA, 1055:1721.

15. The identification of the illustrated engraving of Chocolaterie E. Gamelin (c. 1900) was provided by Marie-François Rose, Bibliothèque Municipale de Rouen, Edoudard Pelay Collection, carton 25. It clearly shows two chocolate grinders at work in the shop windows. Memorandum concerning *Broyeuse de chocolat [Chocolate Grinder No. 1]* (1913), 24 April 1994, twentieth-century curatorial object files, Philadelphia Museum of Art.

16. Marcel Duchamp, quoted in James Johnson Sweeney, "Marcel Duchamp," in *Wisdom: Conversations with the Elder Wise Men of our Day,* edited by James Nelson (New York: Norton, 1958), pp. 92–93.

17. Duchamp's note reads in part, *"Pas d'entêtement, par l'absurde,: à cacher le coït à travers une glace avec un ou plusieurs objets de la devanture. La peine consiste à couper la glace et à s'en mordre les pouces dès que la possession est consommée. c.q.f.d.* [No stubbornness ad absurdum,: in hiding this coition through a sheet of glass with one or more of the objects in the shop window. The penalty consists in cutting the glass and in kicking yourself as soon as possession is consummated q.e.d.]. Richard Hamilton and Ecke Bonk, *Marcel Duchamp, in the infinitive–White Box: A Typographic Rendering* (forthcoming).

18. Joseph Cornell, quoted in David Bourdon, "Enigmatic Bachelor of Utopia Parkway," *Life* 63, no. 24 (15 December 1967): p. 63.

19. Georgia O'Keeffe, quoted in *Marcel Duchamp,* edited by Anne d'Harnoncourt and Kynaston McShine (New York: The Museum of Modern Art, 1973), pp. 213–14.

20. Jeanne Reynal, quoted in Alice Goldfarb Marquis, *Marcel Duchamp: Eros, c'est la vie, a Biography* (Troy, N.Y.: The Whitson Publishing Company, 1981), p. 278.

21. Diary entry, 19 May 1967, in Caws, p. 368.

22. Diary entry, 15 April 1946, Cornell Papers, AAA, 1059:9.

23. Harry Roseman, conversation with Susan Davidson and the author, Poughkeepsie, N.Y., 14 March 1998.

24. Mirror-printed text on recto side of the announcement for "Through the Big End of the Opera Glass" (December 7–28, 1943).

25. *"Le creux dans le papier, entre le recto et le verso d'une feuille mince . . . A étudier!"* Marcel Duchamp, quoted in Denis de Rougemont diary entry, 7 August 1945, in *Journal d'une époque (1926–1946)* (Paris: Éditions Gallimard, 1968), p. 567.

26. Described in Calvin Tomkins, *Duchamp* (New York: Henry Holt and Company, 1996), p. 378.

27. Joseph Cornell to Marianne Moore, 9 April 1944, in Caws, p. 102.

28. Marcel Duchamp speaking at "The Creative Act" symposium, American Federation of Arts, Shamrock Hilton Hotel, Houston, 5 April 1957.

29. Marquis, pp. 289, 325.

30. *"Comment donc, ce n'est pas un faux chèque, puisqu'il est entièrement fait par moi! Et signé! Rien de plus authentique! Et au moins, cela ne pouvait pas passer pour artistique. . . ."* Marcel Duchamp, quoted in Denis de Rougemont, diary entry, 6 August 1945, in *Journal d'une époque*, p. 567.

31. The item in dispute was a 1917 etching on celluloid illustrating the poem "L'Equilibre" by Francis

Picabia. "Oct 21, 1958," in *Ephemerides on and about Marcel Duchamp and Rrose Sélavy, 1887–1968,* edited by Jennifer Gough-Cooper and Jacques Caumont (Milan: Bompiana, 1993), n.p.

32. Marcel Duchamp, quoted in Pierre Cabanne, *Dialogues with Marcel Duchamp* (1971; reprint, New York: Da Capo Press, 1979), p. 69.

33. Summation of statement given at the Philadelphia Museum College of Art, 20 March 1961, quoted in Tomkins, p. 416.

34. Joseph Cornell to Mina Loy, 22 September 1953, in Caws, p. 178.

35. Diary entry, undated [1964], in Caws, p. 311.

36. *Minotaure,* series 2, no. 6 (Winter 1935): back cover.

37. Some were later published in *Dance Index* 4, no. 9 (September 1945): pp. 139, 155–59, or displayed in the "Hans Christian Andersen" exhibition in the Children's Room at the New York Public Library (April 2–June 1955).

38. Diary entry, 30 July 1962, Cornell Papers, AAA, 1061:524.

39. Kent did have a genuine friendship and lengthy correspondence with Cornell. For a clear chronicle of celebrity gifts and correspondence, see Dickran Tashjian, *Joseph Cornell: Gifts of Desire* (Miami Beach: Grassfield Press, 1992).

40. See contents summary at beginning of each microfilm reel, Cornell Papers, AAA.

41. Diary entry, 6 July 1962, Cornell Papers, AAA, 1069:654.

42. Diary entry, undated [1962], Cornell Papers, AAA, 1069:611.

43. Untitled (The Life of Ludwig II of Bavaria), c. 1941–52, was included in the Guggenheim retrospective in 1967. The same work was also included in The Museum of Modern Art retrospective along with *Penny Arcade Portrait of Lauren Bacall (Working Model Based Upon "To Have and Have Not"),* c. 1945–70 and *Portrait of Ondine,* c. 1940s–late 1960s.

44. Quoted from drafts of the gallery handout, Cornell Papers, AAA, 1074:642.

45. Edgar Allan Poe, "Berenice," in *The Short Fiction of Edgar Allan Poe,* edited by Stuart and Susan Levine (Indianapolis: Bobbs-Merril Educational Publishing, 1976), pp. 72, 73.

46. Diary entry, 16 October 1961, in Caws, p. 285. Provenance of this painting (no. 76) includes the Sidney Janis Gallery as cited in Douglas Cooper, *Juan Gris,* catalogue raisonné, vol. 1 (Paris: Bergguen, 1977), p. 126. "In 1953 Cornell had seen Gris's painting with collage, *Figure Seated in a Cafe [The Man at the Cafe]* (1914)." Lynda Roscoe Hartigan, *Joseph Cornell: An Exploration of Sources* (Washington, D.C.: National Museum of American Art, Smithsonian Institution, 1983), p. 17.

47. Originally referring to *3 stoppages étalon [3 Standard Stoppages]* (1913–14), the text was annotated: "Selected by Marcel Duchamp, 1944, from his notes on *The Bride* . . . ." Marcel Duchamp, quoted in Sidney Janis, *Abstract & Surrealist Art in America* (New York: Reynal & Hitchcock, 1944), p. 131.

48. Robert Rauschenberg outlined this principle in a photo and text collage "Random Order," *Location* 1, no. 1 (Spring 1963): pp. 27–31.

49. Draft of *GC 44* contents, undated [c. 1960s], Cornell Papers, AAA, 1072:106.

50. *"Les artistes qui, durant leur vie, ont su faire valoir leur camelotte sont d'excellents commis-voyageurs, mais rien n'est garanti pour l'immortalité de leur œuvre. Et même la postérité est une belle salope qui escamote les uns, fait renaître les autres (Le Greco), quitte d'ailleurs à changer encore d'avis tous les 50 ans."* Marcel Duchamp to Jean Crotti, 17 August 1952, quoted in *Tabu Dada: Jean Crotti & Suzanne Duchamp,* edited by William A. Camfield and Jean-Hubert Martin (Bern: Kunsthalle Bern, 1983), p. 8.

51. The description of Lyle's methods is substantially derived from Mike Weaver, *William Carlos Williams: The American Background* (London and New York: Cambridge University Press, 1971), pp. 122–27.

52. Robert Allerton Parker, "Explorers of the Pluriverse," *First Papers of Surrealism,* exhibition catalogue (New York: Coordinating Council of French Relief Societies, Inc., 1942), n.p. An obscure figure today, Fort was much admired by American writers such as Theodore Dreiser.

53. Charles Hoy Fort, *Wild Talents* (1932; reprint, New York: Dover Publications, Inc., 1974), pp. 861–62.

54. André Breton, "de la survivance de certains mythes et de quelques autres mythes en croissance ou en formation [On the Survival of Certain Myths and on Some Other Myths In Growth or Formation]," *First Papers of Surrealism,* n.p.

55. Cornell Papers, AAA, undated [1950s], 1072:106.

56. Cornell Papers, AAA, undated [1949], 1059:170.

57. When *Spent Meteor* was photographed in 1938, there were no immediate prospects for publication, and in fact it did not appear until 1943 in *View,* series 2, no. 4, January. The tableau, a collaborative effort between Cornell and photographer James Ogle, was arranged in George Platt Lynes studio (640 Madison Avenue, New York) where Ogle was an assistant. James Ogle, telephone conversation with author, 26 August 1998.

58. Diary entry, 9 December 1948, in Caws, p. 155.

59. Diary entry, 29 May 1952, in Caws, p. 177.

60. Joseph Cornell to Julien Levy, undated [draft of response to Levy letter of 2 February 1967], Cornell Papers, AAA, 1056:354.

61. Donald Windham, conversation with Susan Davidson and author, New York, N.Y., 11 March 1998.

62. Donald Windham, conversation with Susan Davidson and author, New York, N.Y., 11 March 1998, and by telephone with author, 15 May 1998.

63. Joseph Cornell to John Ashbery, 14 October 1966, in Caws, p. 344.

64. Magritte announcement, Alexander Iolas Gallery opening, Monday, March 2, 1959. Inscribed *Duchamp* by Cornell. Cornell Papers, AAA, 1058:184.

65. *Newsweek* (4 October 1968) and *Life* (11 October 1968), both in Cornell Papers, AAA, 1058:1035 and 1036, respectively.

66. André Breton, "Mad Love [*L'amour fou*]," in *What is Surrealism: Selected Writings,* edited by Franklin Rosemont (New York: Monad Press, 1978), p. 164.

pp. 268–275

181 **Grand Central Station,** 42nd Street at Park Avenue, New York, 1931.

182 **The Museum of Modern Art,** 11 West 53rd Street, New York, c. 1940.

183 ***Ads,*** New York, 1940. Photograph by Rudy Burckhardt.

184 ***Woolworth Building from West Street and Park Place,*** New York, c. 1935. Photograph by Berenice Abbott. Berenice Abbott/Commerce Graphics Ltd, Inc.

185 ***Newsstand, East 32nd Street and Third Avenue,*** New York, November 19, 1935. Photograph by Berenice Abbott, Federal Arts Project, "Changing New York." Museum of the City of New York.

186 ***Browser's Paradise,*** Fourth Avenue used bookstalls, New York, October 21, 1945. Photograph by Sidney Latham.

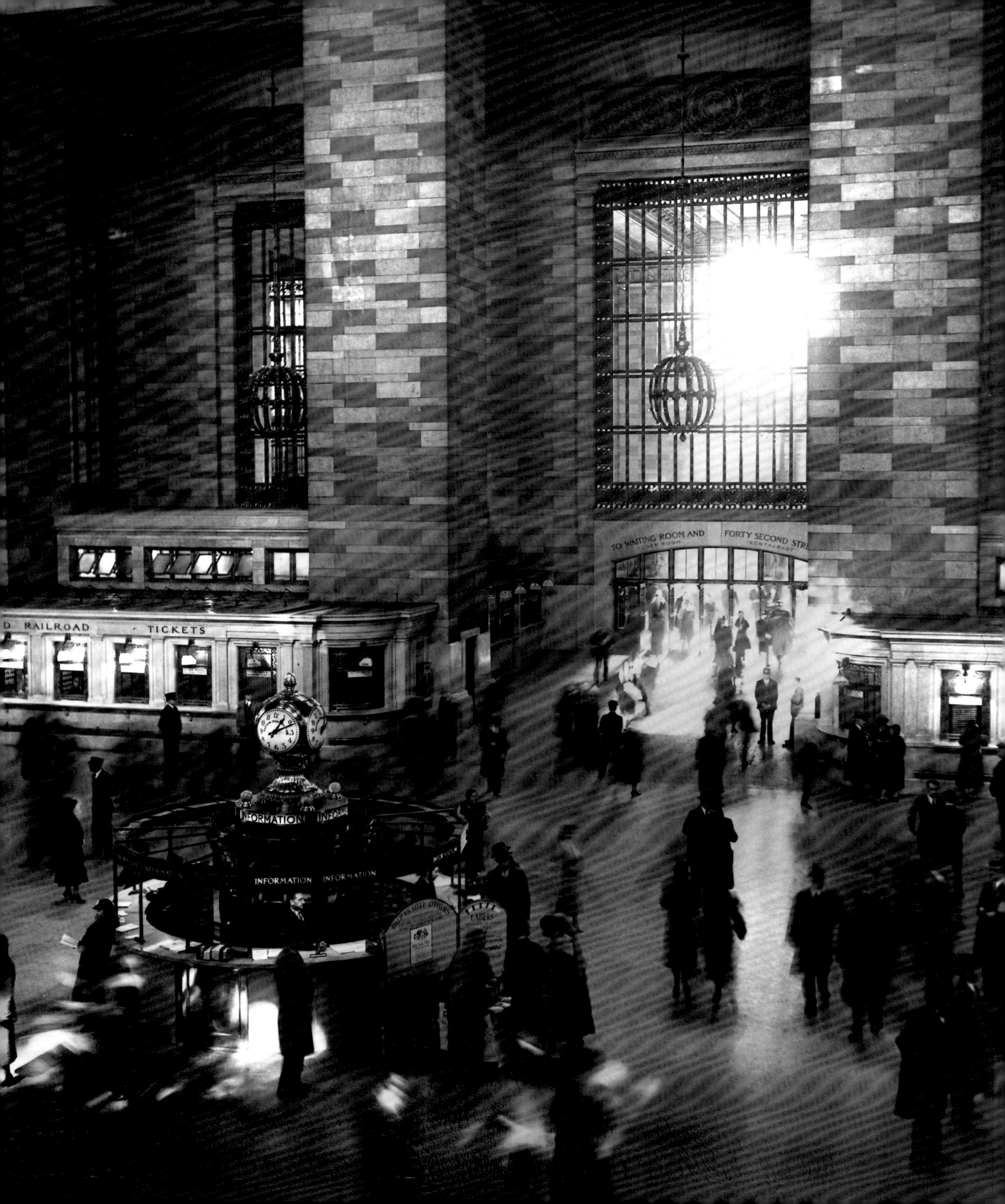
TO WAITING ROOM AND
FORTY SECOND STR
D RAILROAD
TICKETS
INFORMATION
INFORMATION
INFORMATION

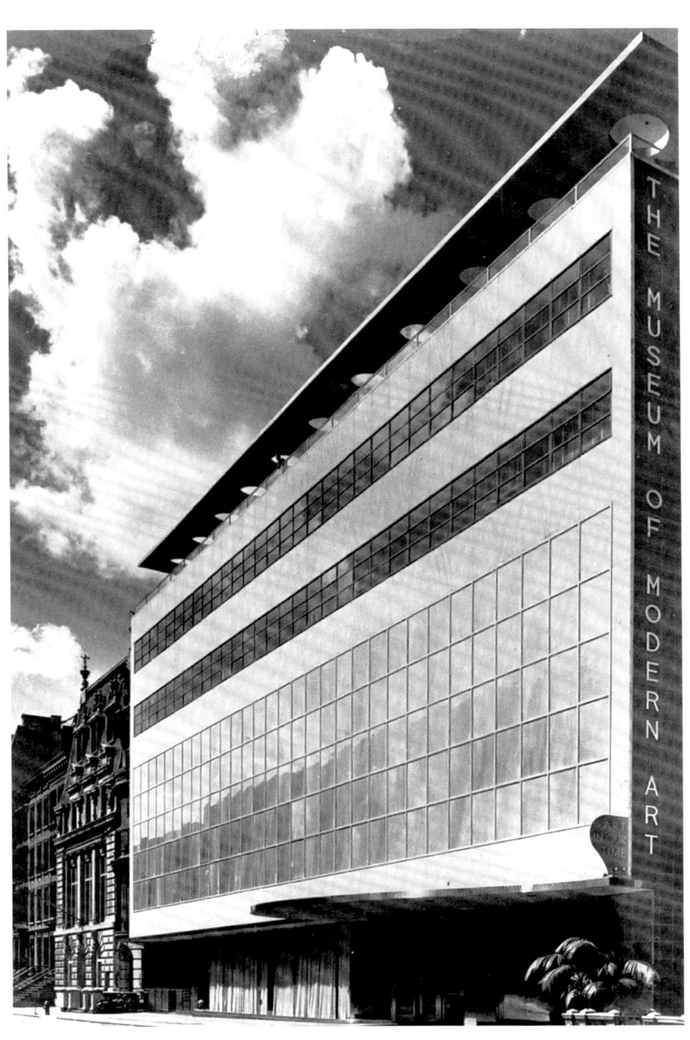
THE MUSEUM OF MODERN ART

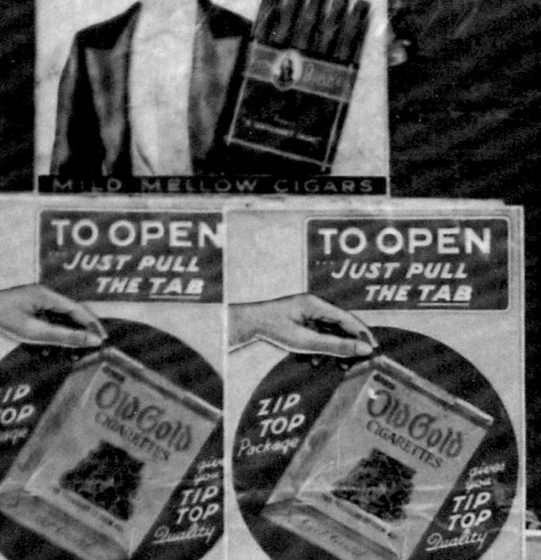
MILD MELLOW CIGARS
Howard & Shelton
in "The MODEL Minstrels"
PRESENTED BY
MODEL Tobacco
COLUMBIA BROADCASTING SYSTEM
MONDAY NIGHTS
TO OPEN
JUST PULL
THE TAB

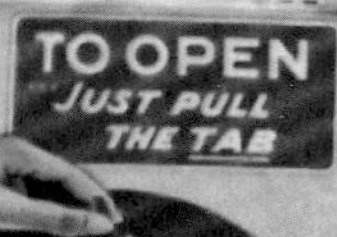
ZIP
TOP
Package

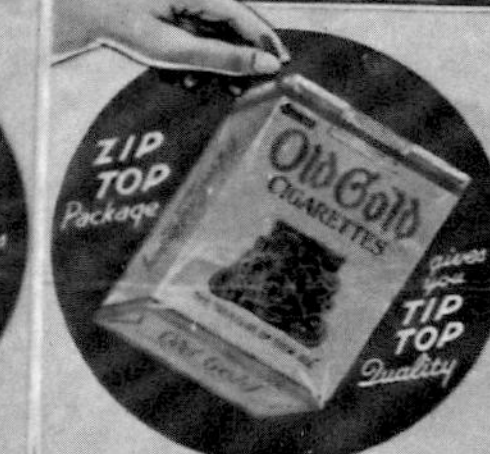
OLD GOLD
Now Double Cellophane
Opens Double Quick

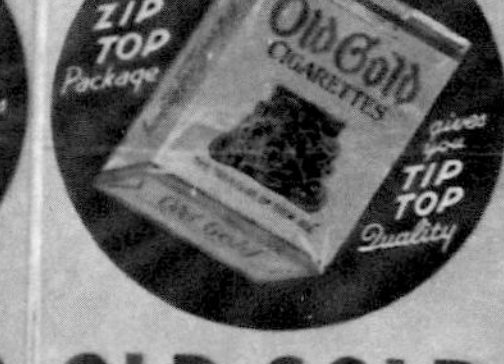
OLD GOLD
Now Double Cellophane
Opens Double Quick

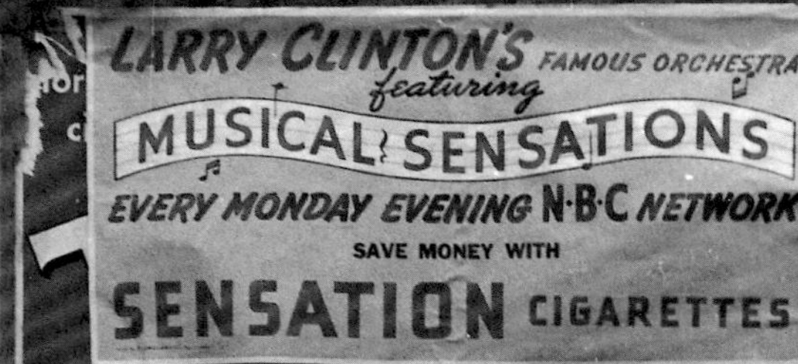
LARRY CLINTON'S FAMOUS ORCHESTRA
featuring
MUSICAL SENSATIONS
EVERY MONDAY EVENING N·B·C NETWORK
SAVE MONEY WITH
SENSATION CIGARETTES

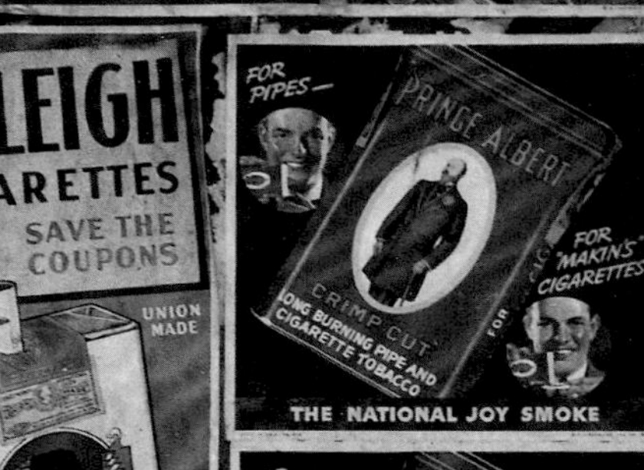
RALEIGH
CIGARETTES
SAVE THE
COUPONS
UNION
MADE
FOR PIPES—
PRINCE ALBERT
CRIMP CUT
FOR "MAKIN'S" CIGARETTES
THE NATIONAL JOY SMOKE

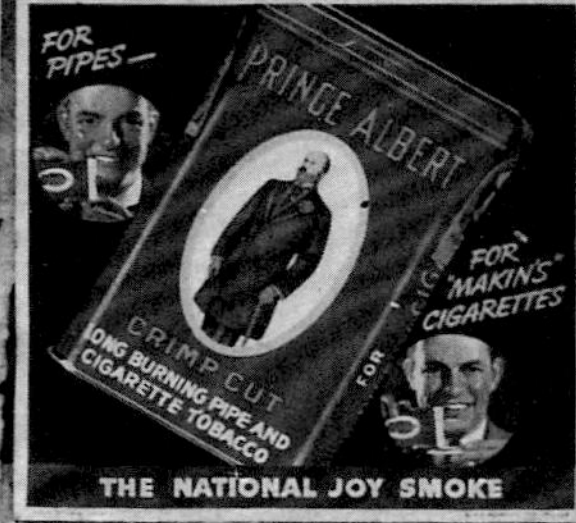
FOR PIPES—
PRINCE ALBERT
CRIMP CUT
FOR "MAKIN'S" CIGARETTES
THE NATIONAL JOY SMOKE

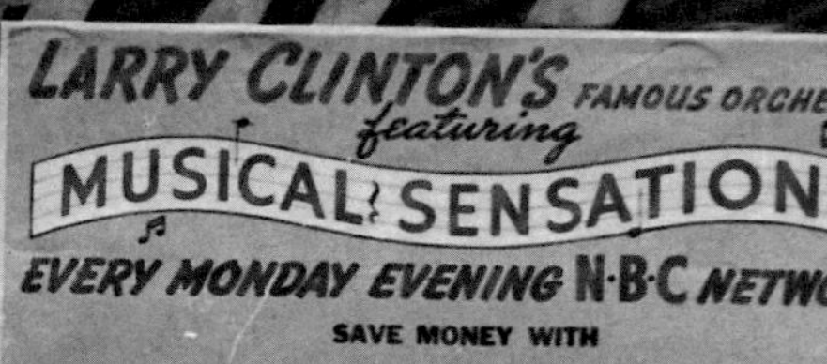
LARRY CLINTON'S
featuring
MUSICAL SENSATIONS
EVERY MONDAY EVENING N·B·C
SAVE MONEY WITH
SENSATION CIGARETTE

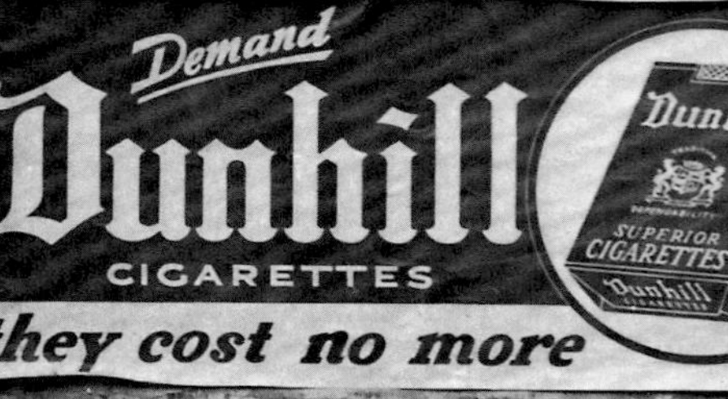
Demand
Dunhill
CIGARETTES
they cost no more

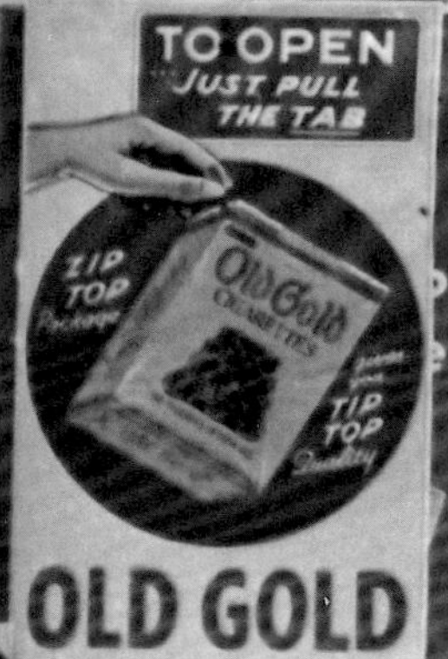
TO OPEN
JUST PULL
THE TAB
OLD GOLD
Now Double Cellophane
Opens Double Quick

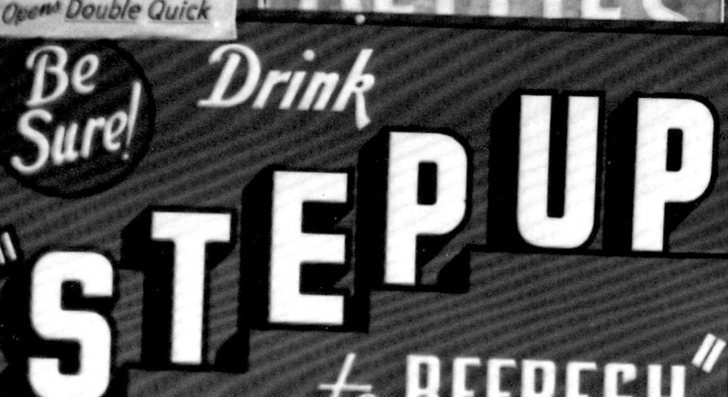
Be Sure!
Drink
"STEP UP
to REFRESH"

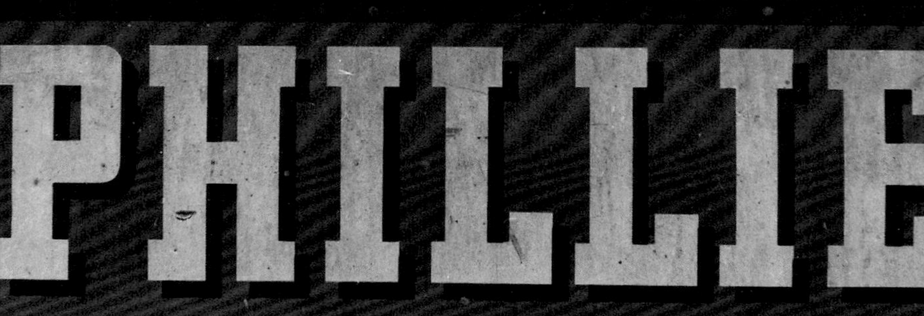
PHILLIE

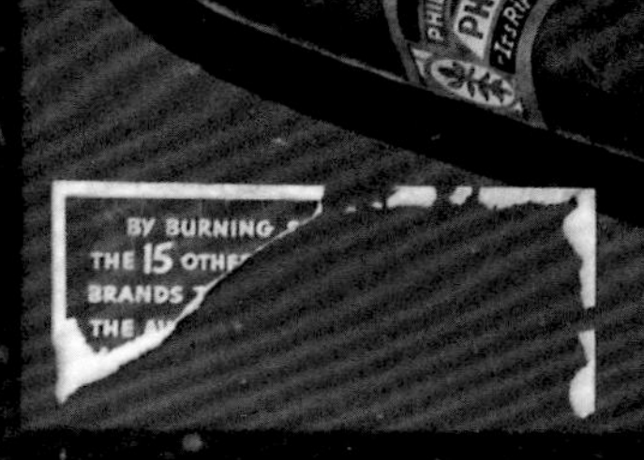
PHILLIES

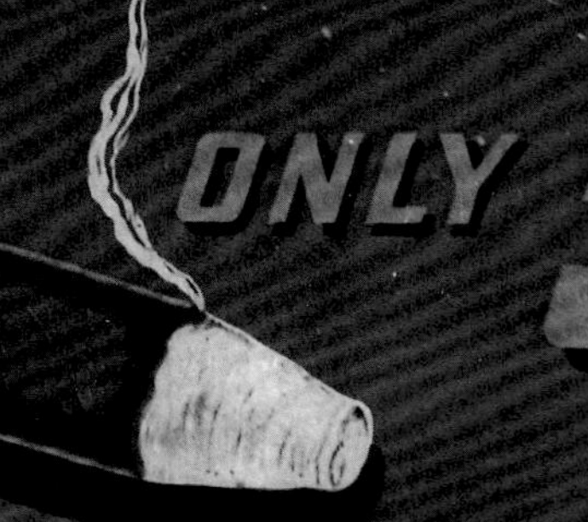
ONLY

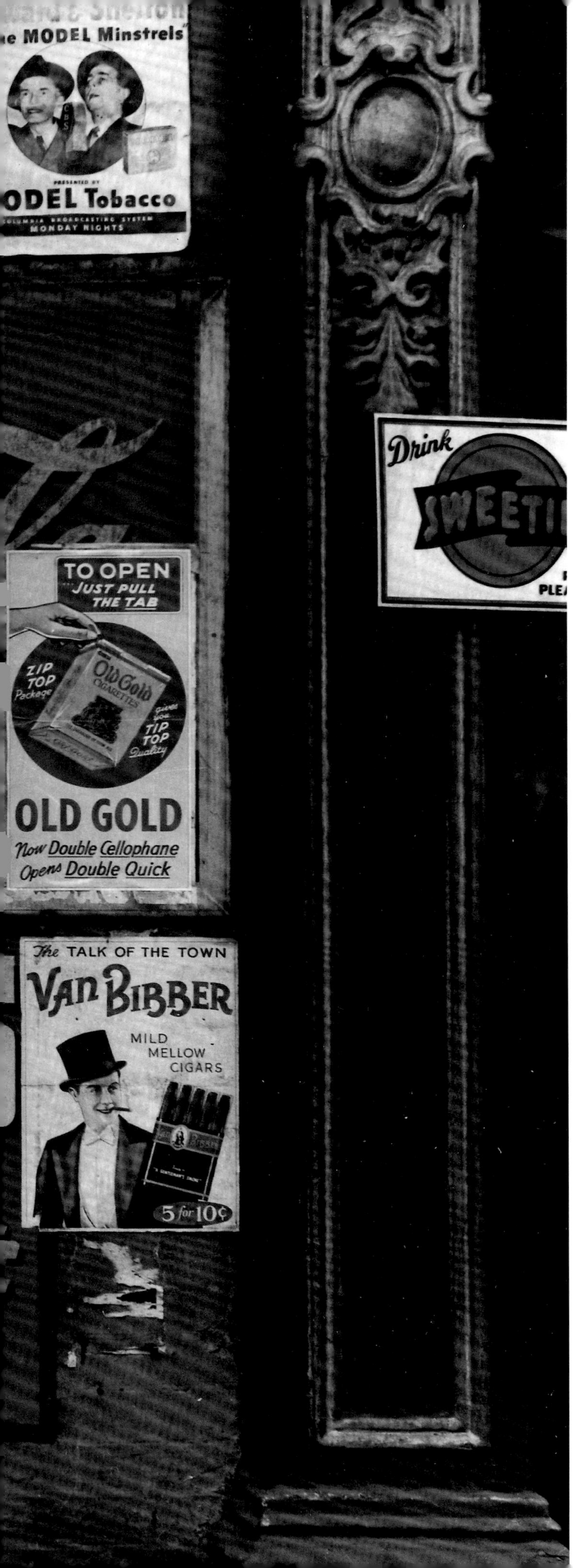

e MODEL Minstrels
PRESENTED BY
ODEL Tobacco
COLUMBIA BROADCASTING SYSTEM
MONDAY NIGHTS
Drink
SWEETI
TO OPEN
JUST PULL
THE TAB
ZIP
TOP
Package
Old Gold
CIGARETTES
gives
you
TIP
TOP
Quality
OLD GOLD
Now Double Cellophane
Opens Double Quick
The TALK OF THE TOWN
VAN BIBBER
MILD
MELLOW
CIGARS
5 for 10¢

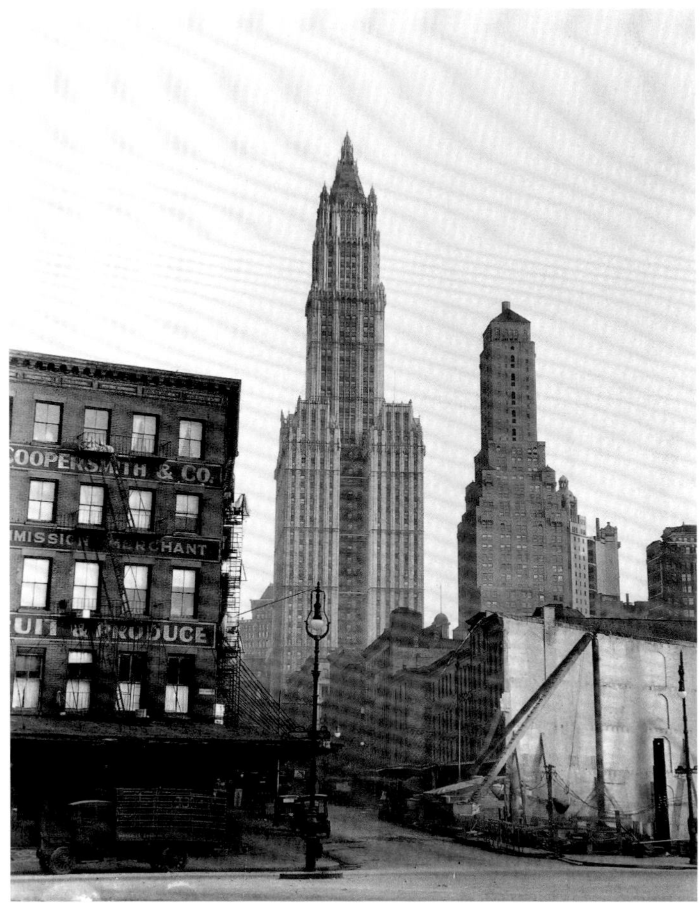
COOPERSMITH & CO.
MISSION MERCHANT
UIT & PRODUCE

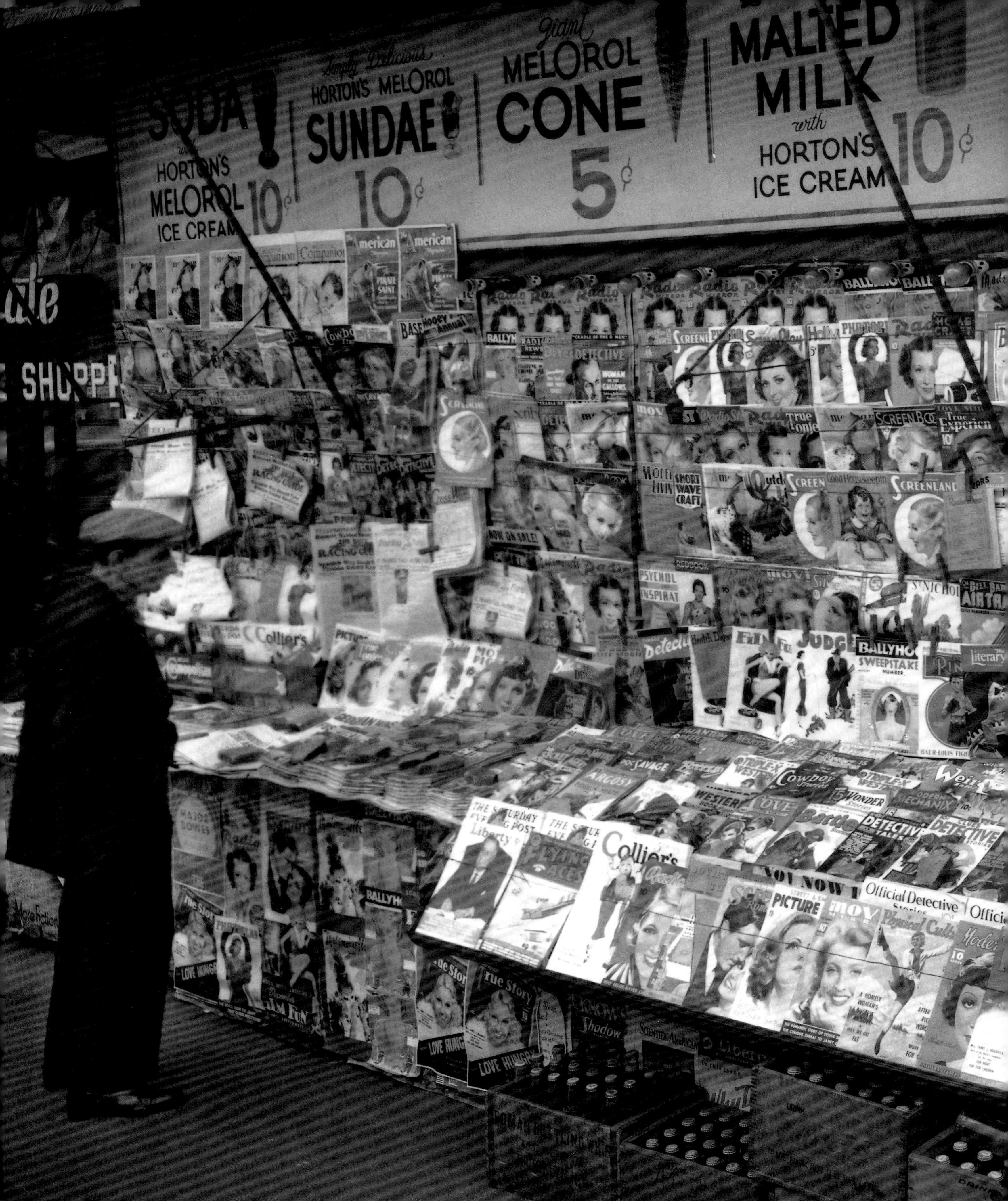

SODA
HORTON'S
MELOROL
ICE CREAM
10¢
Simply Delicious
HORTON'S MELOROL
SUNDAE
10¢
Giant
MELOROL
CONE
5¢
MALTED
MILK
with
HORTON'S
ICE CREAM
10¢
SHOPPE
The American Magazine
Companion
Radio Mirror
BALLYHOO
DETECTIVE
SCREENLAND
SHORT WAVE CRAFT
Good Housekeeping
REDBOOK
NOW ON SALE!
RACING GUIDE
Collier's
JUDGE
SWEEPSTAKE NUMBER
The Literary Digest
ARGOSY
Cowboy
WESTERN
DOC SAVAGE
MODERN MECHANIX
DETECTIVE STORIES
THE SATURDAY EVENING POST
Liberty
FLYING ACES
PICTURE
Official Detective Stories
Physical Culture
True Story
LOVE HUNGRY
Shadow
MAJOR BOWES

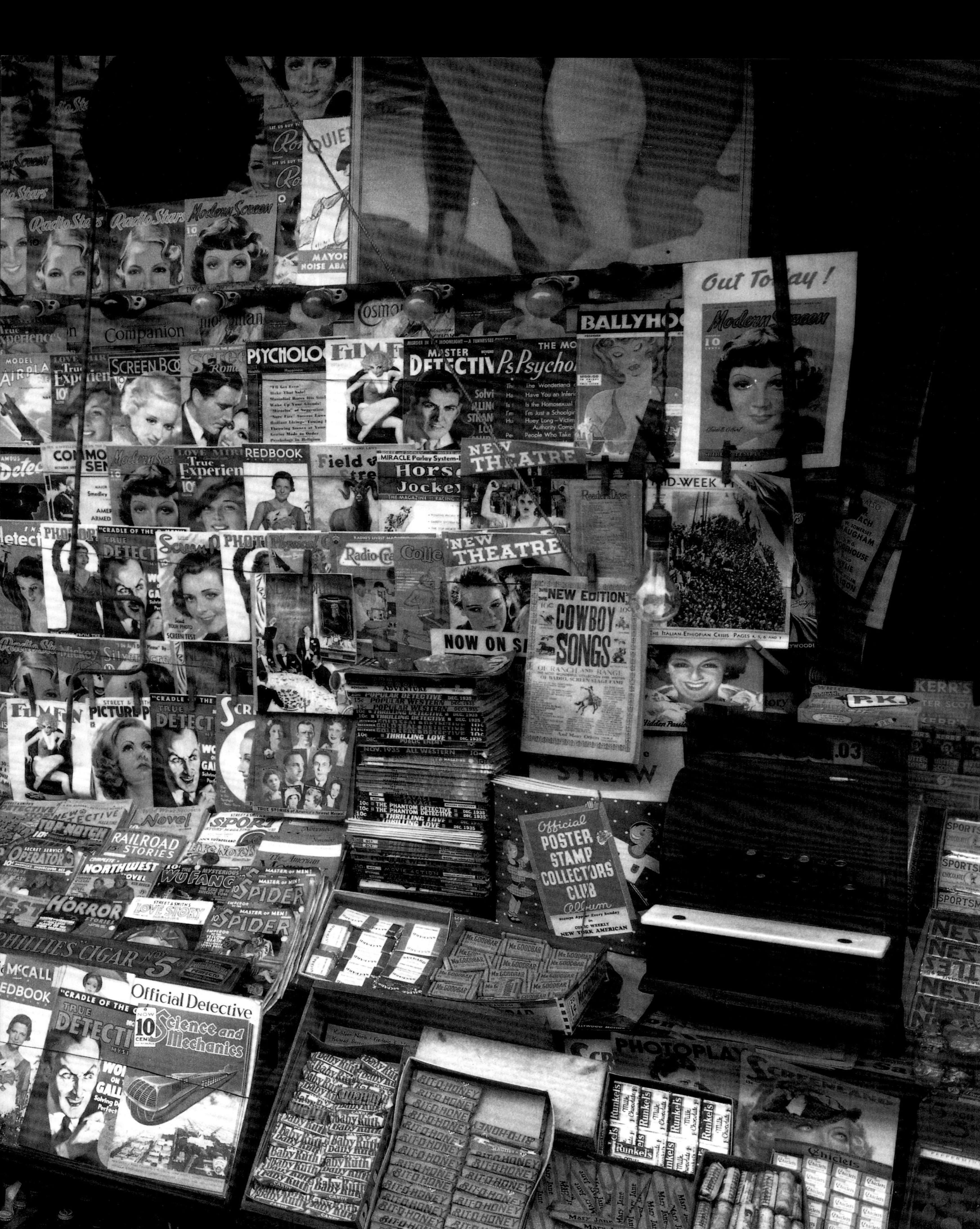

Radio Stars
Radio Stars
Modern Screen
QUIET
MAYOR
NOISE ABAT
Companion
Out Today!
Modern Screen
10 CENTS
BALLYHOO
SCREEN BOOK
PSYCHOLO
MASTER DETECTIVE
Psychology
REDBOOK
Field &
Horse and Jockey
NEW THEATRE
NEW THEATRE
MIRACLE Parlay System
TRUE DETECTIVE
"CRADLE OF THE
Radio Stars
Radio Cr
NOW ON S
NEW EDITION
COWBOY SONGS
OF RANCH AND RANGE
THE ITALIAN-ETHIOPIAN CRISIS PAGES 4, 5, 6 AND 7
ADVENTURE
POPULAR DETECTIVE
POPULAR WESTERN
THRILLING LOVE
DEC. 1935
NOV. 1935 ALL WESTERN
THE PHANTOM DETECTIVE
TRUE STORIES of America's Newest Mecca
Official POSTER STAMP COLLECTORS CLUB Album
NEW YORK AMERICAN
Novel
TOP-NOTCH
SPORT STORY
RAILROAD STORIES
SECRET SERVICE OPERATOR 5
NORTHWEST
WU FANG
MASTER OF MEN!
SPIDER
HORROR
STREET & SMITH'S LOVE STORY
SPIDER
PHILLIES CIGAR 5¢
McCALL
REDBOOK
Official Detective
NOW 10 CENTS
Science and Mechanics
TRUE DETECTIVE
Mr. GOODBAR
Baby Ruth
OH HENRY!
PHOTOPLAY
Runkel's Milk Chocolate
Chiclets
Mary Jane
SPORTSMAN
NESTLE

Marcel Duchamp/ Joseph Cornell Chronology

including *Duchamp Dossier* Citations

SUSAN DAVIDSON

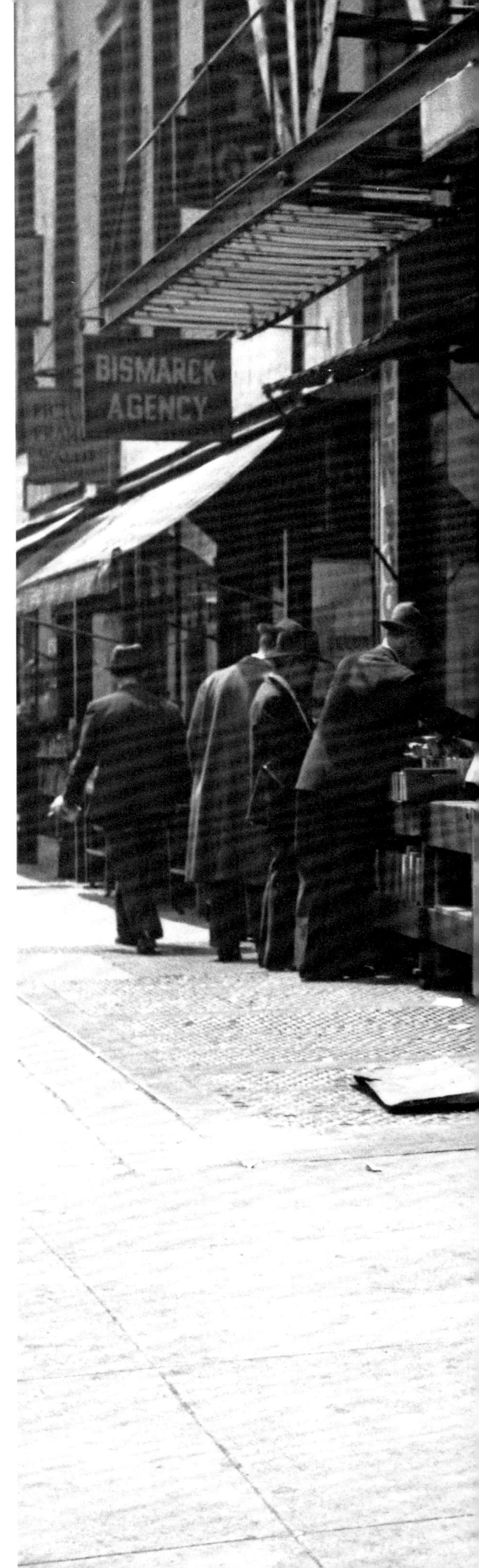

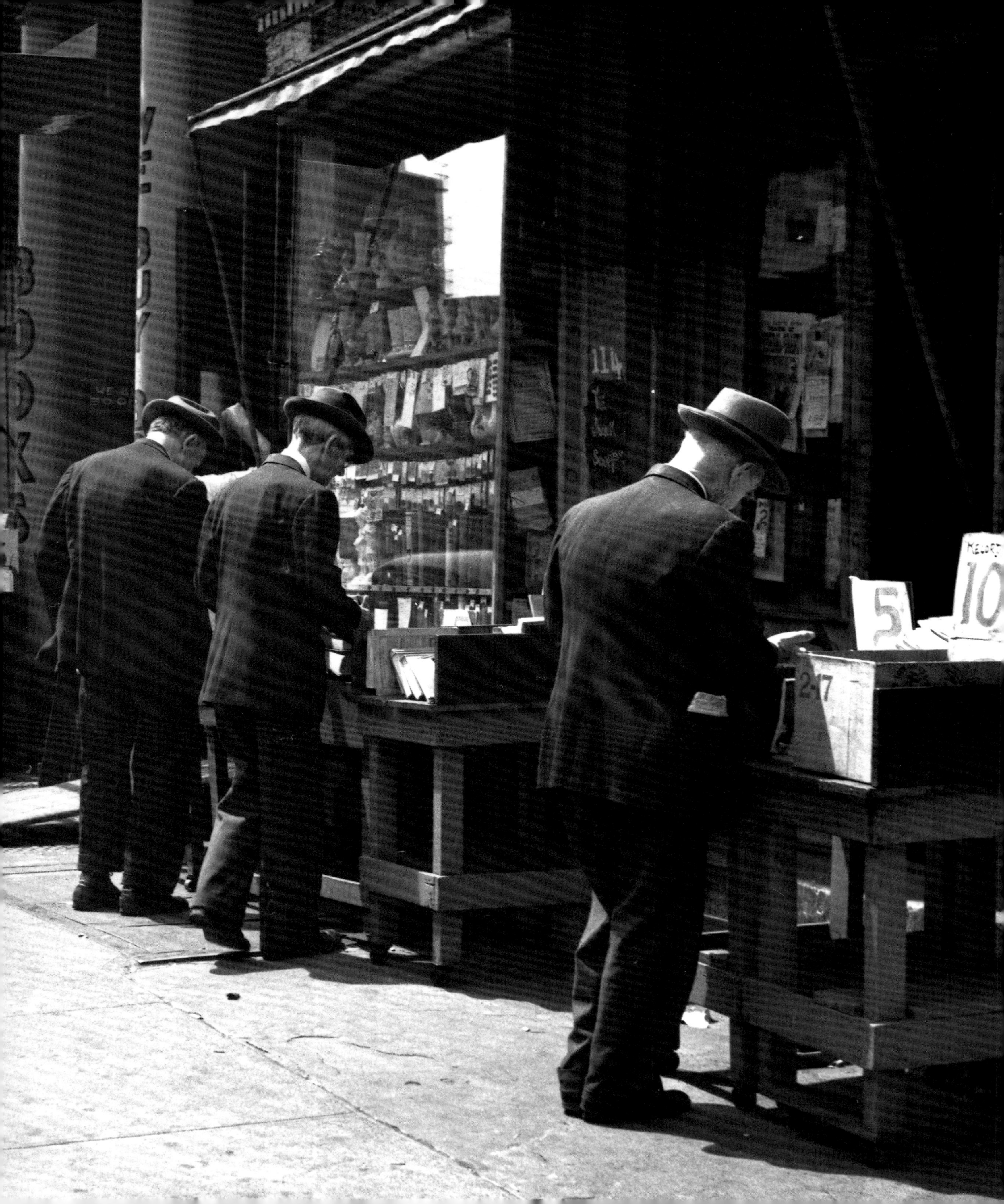
BOOKS
BUY
114
5
10
2-17

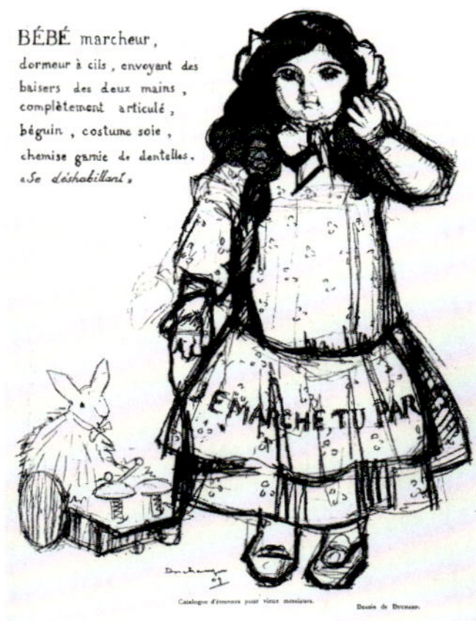

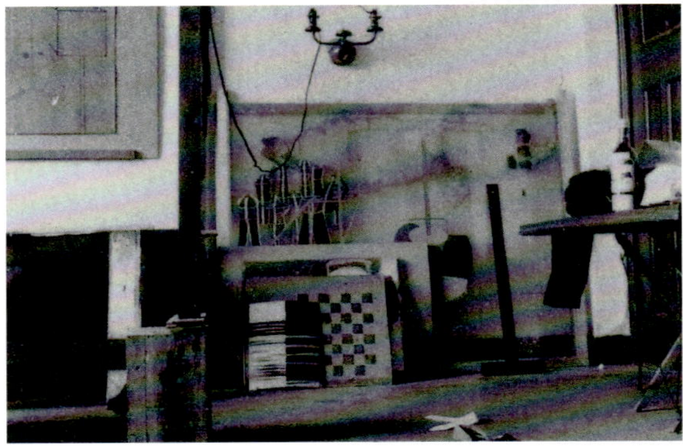

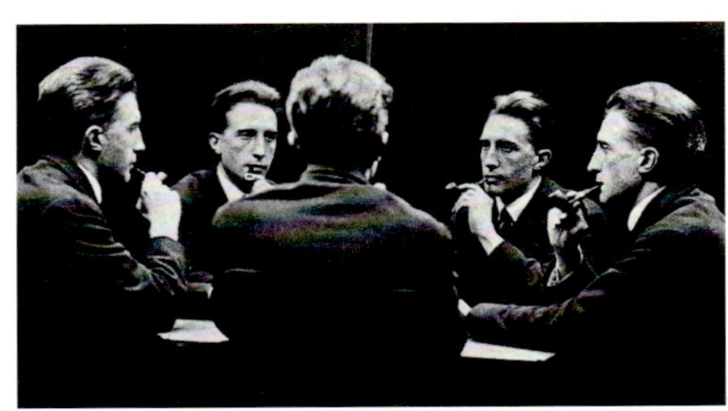

When an event cannot be dated precisely within a given year, it appears at the beginning of the year. When a date or span of dates is speculative, it appears in brackets. Unless otherwise indicated, artworks were made in the year under which they appear. Citations related to the Duchamp Dossier are indicated by dates in green ink; for example, (**August 19**).

187 **Duchamp, advertisement for *bébé marcheur*, 1909.** *Le Courrier Français* (1 January 1909): p. 5. Philadelphia Museum of Art, Marcel Duchamp Archive.

188 **Duchamp's studio,** 33 West 67th Street, New York, 1917–18. Philadelphia Museum of Art, Marcel Duchamp Archive.

189 **Portrait of Duchamp,** Broadway Photo Shop, New York, October 1917.

190 **Duchamp, *Belle Haleine, Eau de Voilette*, 1921.** Assisted readymade: Rigaud perfume bottle, 6 in., height. Private collection.

191 **Joseph Stella, *Marcel Duchamp*, c. 1920.** Silverpoint, 24¼ x 21 in. The Museum of Modern Art, New York. The Katherine S. Dreier Bequest.

192 **Cornell's yearbook photograph,** Phillips Academy, Andover, Massachusetts, 1921. Joseph Cornell Study Center, Natl. Museum of American Art, Smithsonian. Gift of Mr. and Mrs. John A. Benton.

1887

July 28 Henri-Robert-Marcel Duchamp is born in Blainville, Crevon, Normandy, to Eugène Duchamp, a notary, and Lucie Nicolle Duchamp. He is the fourth of seven children: Gaston Duchamp, later Jacques Villon (1875–1963); Raymond Duchamp, later Duchamp-Villon (1876–1918); Madeleine Duchamp (1883–1886); Suzanne Duchamp Crotti (1889–1963); Yvonne Duchamp Duvernoy (1895–1969); and Magdeleine Duchamp (1898–1979).

1903

December 24 Joseph Cornell is born in Nyack, New York, to Joseph I. Cornell, a textile salesman, and Helen Ten Broeck Storms. He is the first of four children: Elizabeth (b. 1905); Helen (b. 1906); and Robert (1910–65).

1904–1911

Having completed his baccalaureate in July 1903, Duchamp joins his elder brothers in Paris, studying at the Académie Julian from November 1904 through November 1906. From 1905 through 1910, Duchamp publishes cartoons in the French periodicals *Le Rire*, *Le Témoin*, and *Le Courrier Français*. *Le Courrier Français* (1 January 1909, p. 5) will feature an advertisement for a *bébé marcheur* [walking doll]. Beginning in 1907, Duchamp submits his paintings to the following annual exhibitions: Salon des artistes humoristes, Palais de Glace, Paris (1907 and 1908); Société des Artistes indépendants, Paris (1909, 1910, and 1911); and Salon d'Automne, Grand Palais, Paris (1908, 1909, 1910, and 1911).

1912

March Duchamp submits *Nu descendant un escalier [Nude Descending a Staircase]* to the Société des Artistes indépendants, Paris (March 20–May 16) but withdraws it when Albert Gleizes and Jean Metzinger raise objections.

July–August During a two-month stay in Munich, Duchamp paints several pictures related to, and begins notes and studies for, *La Mariée mise à nu par ses célibataires, même [The Bride Stripped Bare by Her Bachelors, Even]*, subsequently known as the *Large Glass*. He also begins to preserve notes and sketches jotted on random pieces of paper that eventually will serve as a guide to the *Large Glass* and other projects.

1913

Duchamp abandons all conventional forms of painting and drawing, with a few exceptions. In his Paris studio, he fixes a bicycle wheel on a stool *(Bicycle Wheel)*; the following year, he will purchase a commercial print of a winter landscape, adding two areas of gouache to it *(Pharmacie)*, and a bottle rack *(Bottle Rack)* from the Bazar de l'Hôtel de Ville.

February 17–March 15 Duchamp is represented at the "International Exhibition of Modern Art" (Armory Show), 69th Regiment Armory, 305 Lexington Avenue, New York, by four paintings, including *Nu descendant un escalier*, which receives national attention and makes Duchamp a well-known personality in America.

May Duchamp trains as an underlibrarian and is later engaged on a temporary basis as a librarian at the Bibliothèque Sainte-Geneviève, Paris.

1914

Duchamp produces his first boxed edition, *Box of 1914*, in an edition of five. Housed in used photographic plate boxes, it includes sixteen reproductions of notes mounted on mat board and one drawing *Avoir l'apprenti dans le soleil [To Have the Apprentice in the Sun]*.

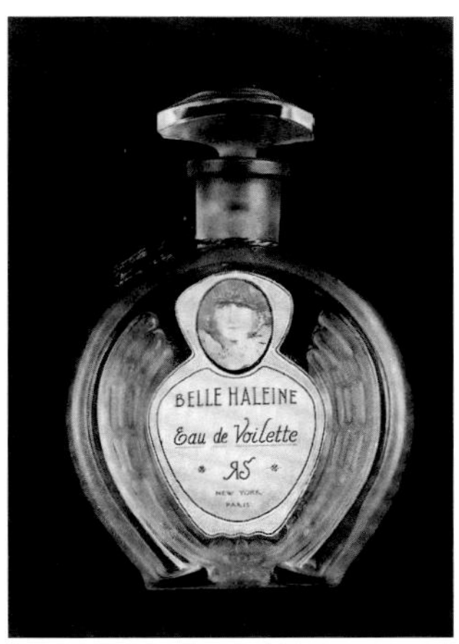

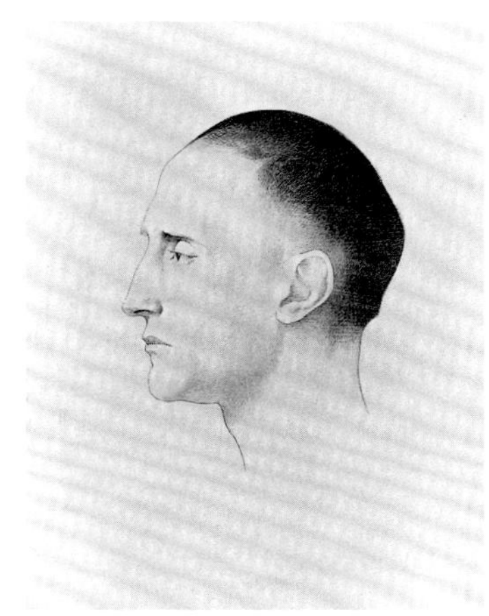

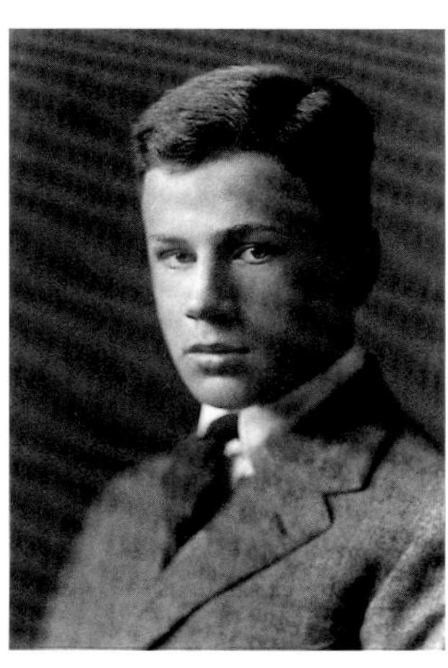

1915

June 6 After failing a medical exam for military service, Duchamp sails on the SS *Rochambeau* to New York. Arriving on June 15, he will meet Louise and Walter Arensberg through Walter Pach. They will become his most important patrons. Duchamp will meet a large circle of people in New York, including artists Joseph Stella, Man Ray, Mina Loy, and Morton Schamberg, among others.

Fall Duchamp establishes a studio in the Lincoln Arcade Building, 1947 Broadway, New York. He begins work on the upper half of the *Large Glass* and selects another manufactured object (a snow shovel for *In Advance of The Broken Arm)*, coining the term *readymade* in a letter to his sister Suzanne.

1916

Mid October Duchamp moves into a studio above the Arensberg apartment at 33 West 67th Street, New York, and embarks on the lower half of the *Large Glass*. The Arensbergs will gradually acquire ownership of the *Large Glass* in return for paying Duchamp's rent.

December Duchamp meets Henri-Pierre Roché through Florine and Ettie Stettheimer and becomes a founding member of the Society of Independent Artists, New York; he meets Katherine S. Dreier, a director and benefactor of the Society.

1917

April–June Duchamp co-edits (with Roché and Beatrice Wood) the Dada publications *The Blind Man* (nos. 1 and 2) and *Rongwrong* (unique).

April Duchamp is elected chairman of the hanging committee for the Society of Independent Artists exhibition at 20 West 31st Street, New York (April 9–May 6). He resigns from the Society when inclusion of his readymade *Fountain* (submitted under the pseudonym R. Mutt) is blocked. Alfred Stieglitz photographs *Fountain* for reproduction in *The Blind Man* (no. 2, May, p. 4).

April 29 Cornell's father dies, leaving his family in greatly reduced financial circumstances.

Fall Cornell enrolls in Phillips Academy, Andover, Massachusetts. He elects a scientific curriculum and also studies French, Spanish, and Latin.

1918

Duchamp executes *Tu m'*, a commission from Dreier for the space above her library bookcase at 135 Central Park West, New York. This will be his last major painting.

August After three years in New York, Duchamp sails on the SS *Crofton Hall* with Yvonne Chastel (the former wife of Jean Crotti) to Buenos Aires, where he will remain for nine months. Duchamp will join a chess club in Buenos Aires and play constantly, describing himself in a letter to Walter Arensberg as a "chess maniac."[1]

September The Cornell family moves to Bayside, Queens, New York.

1919

April As a wedding gift to his sister Suzanne and Crotti, Duchamp sends instructions to suspend a geometry book from their balcony, calling it *Ready made malheureux [Unhappy Readymade]*. A schematic drawing and an explanation by Cornell appear on the reverse of the cardboard mat of the *Large Glass* reproduction in the *Duchamp Dossier* (see January 1934).

June After nine months in Buenos Aires, Duchamp returns to Paris where he will remain until the end of the year. In December he will purchase a reproduction of Leonardo da Vinci's *Mona Lisa* on the rue de Rivoli, Paris; adding a moustache and goatee to her face, he will title the new work *L.H.O.O.Q.*

1920

January 6 Duchamp arrives in New York and again receives attention as the painter of *Nu descendant un escalier*. He will establish a studio at 246 West 73rd Street, New York, until July, when he will return to his former studio in the Lincoln Arcade Building.

April 29 Duchamp, Man Ray, and Dreier found the Société Anonyme, Inc.: Museum of Modern Art with offices originally at 19 East 47th Street, New York. He will serve first as chairman of the exhibition committee and thereafter as secretary for many years. Société Anonyme will remain in existence for twenty-nine years, organizing eighty-five exhibitions in a variety of locations.

1921

April Duchamp's *Belle Haleine, Eau de Voilette [Beautiful Breath, Veil Water]* appears as the cover of a unique issue of *New York Dada* (a Dada publication co-edited by Duchamp and Man Ray). Man Ray's photograph poses Duchamp in his first appearance as Rrose Sélavy, a female alter ego he conceived the preceding winter.

June Duchamp sails on the SS *France* to Paris, where he will remain until January 28, 1922.

Fall Failing to graduate from Phillips Academy, Cornell returns home and assumes the primary responsibility for his family's financial support. He becomes a traveling salesman of woolen samples for the William Whitman Company, Inc., a Boston-based textile wholesaler with offices at 25 Madison Avenue, near Madison Square in lower Manhattan. He begins scouting Manhattan for

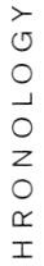

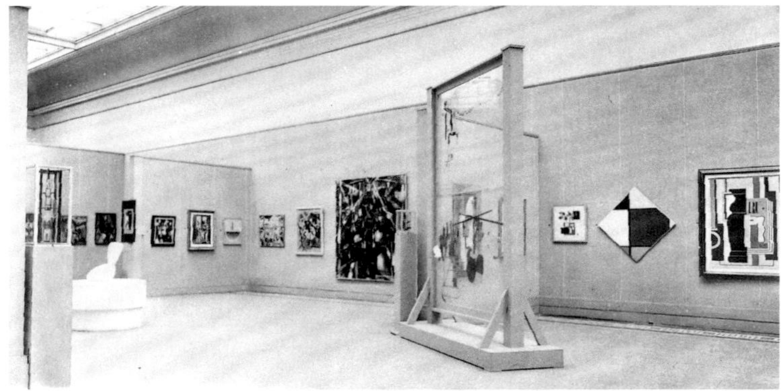

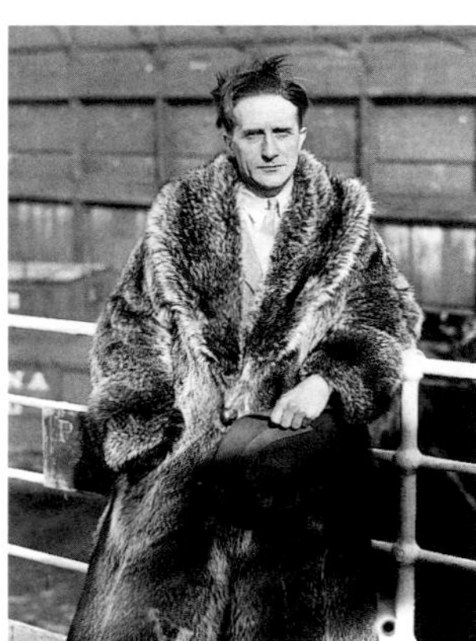

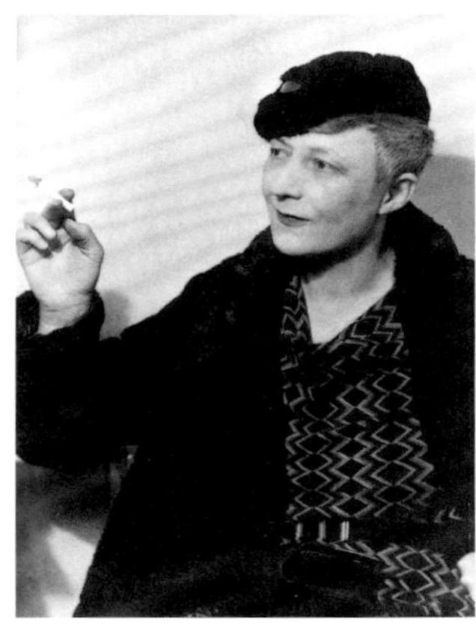

used books, photographs, records, printed reproductions, and other ephemera. Cornell also visits performance halls, museums, and prominent art galleries of his day.

1922

January 28 Duchamp sails on the SS *Aquitania* to New York. He will resume work over the next thirteen months on the *Large Glass* in the Lincoln Arcade Building; ownership of the work transfers from the Arensbergs (who moved the previous fall to Hollywood, California) to Dreier, who purchases it for $2,000.

1923

Early February Duchamp decides to sign the *Large Glass,* declaring it definitively unfinished.

February 10 Duchamp sails on the SS *Noordam* to Europe. Arriving on February 21, he will go first to Brussels for approximately four months during which he will participate in his first major chess tournament, a hobby that will rapidly become an obsession. Duchamp will remain in Europe until 1942, except for three brief visits to New York (1926–27, 1933–34, and 1936).

Mid July Duchamp returns to Paris and renews his acquaintance with Mary Reynolds, whom he first met in New York in the 1910s. Reynolds, an American widow living in Paris who will later become a renowned bookbinder, will have a relationship with Duchamp until her death in 1950.

1924

Duchamp becomes a member of the French chess team, playing with the team until 1933. He will spend the winter months each year training in Nice, followed by a steady sequence of International Team Tournaments.

1925

January 29 Duchamp's mother dies, followed by his father on February 3.

1926

As a means of support, Duchamp begins speculative purchases and sales of artworks, many on behalf of the Arensbergs.

Cornell begins clipping articles about art, music, literature, and philosophy from newspapers and magazines and compiling them scrapbook-style in binders.

January 7–30 Cornell attends the "Memorial Exhibition of Representative Works Selected from The John Quinn Collection" at the Art Center, 65 East 56th Street, New York. Quinn was a noted modern art collector who died the previous July. Cornell recalls seeing Georges Seurat's *Le Cirque* (1891, Musée d'Orsay, Paris), Henri Rousseau's *The Sleeping Gypsy* (1897, The Museum of Modern Art, New York), Pablo Picasso's *Mother and Child Seated by the Sea* (1921, The Art Institute of Chicago), and André Derain's *Window on the Park* (1912, The Museum of Modern Art, New York).

May 10 Cornell attends, with his sister Helen, the New York debut of Spanish light opera chanteuse Raquel Meller. His collection of clippings about her will provide the basis for one of his first dossiers related to a performer.

August 12 Duchamp arranges with Roché and Mrs. Charles Rumsey to buy almost thirty Constantin Brancusi sculptures from the Quinn estate before their public auction. Making these purchases along with Roché, Duchamp effectively becomes Brancusi's American agent. Duchamp also buys back three of his own paintings.

Late Summer Duchamp incorporates retinal experiments and puns into *Anémic Cinéma,* a seven-minute movie made in collaboration with Man Ray and Marc Allégret.

September Cornell becomes a Christian Scientist, joining the Mother Church in Boston and the First Church of Christ, Scientist, in Great Neck, New York.

October 13 Duchamp sails on the SS *Paris* to New York with approximately twenty Brancusi sculptures for a forthcoming exhibition he will organize at Brummer Gallery, 55 East 57th Street, New York (November 17–December 25). During the course of the exhibition, he will meet Julien Levy, a recent Harvard graduate who is interested in avant-garde photography and film.

November 19, 1926–January 1, 1927 "International Exhibition of Modern Art" is sponsored by the Société Anonyme at the Brooklyn Museum, New York, selected by Dreier with significant contributions from Duchamp. Duchamp is represented by the *Large Glass,* which will be accidentally shattered either in transit or during storage following the exhibition. Its condition will remain undiscovered until the work is removed from storage in 1931. Cornell possibly visits the exhibition.

1927

February 27 Duchamp sails on the SS *Paris* to Paris where he will rent a top-floor studio at 11 Rue Larrey. He will live there for the next sixteen years. Invited by Duchamp to travel with him, Levy goes to Paris to make a movie using Man Ray's studio and equipment, but is unable to do so. While in Paris, Levy will meet and marry Joella Loy, daughter of poet and artist Mina Loy.

June 7 To his friends' surprise, Duchamp marries Lydie Sarazin-Lavassor, the twenty-four-year-old daughter of an automotive manufacturer. The couple will divorce by January 1928.

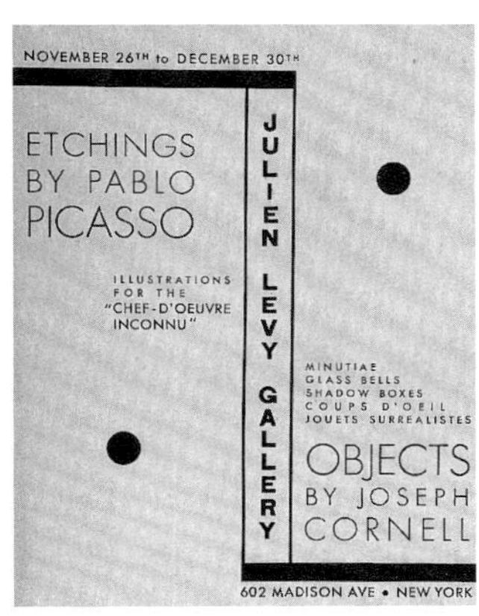

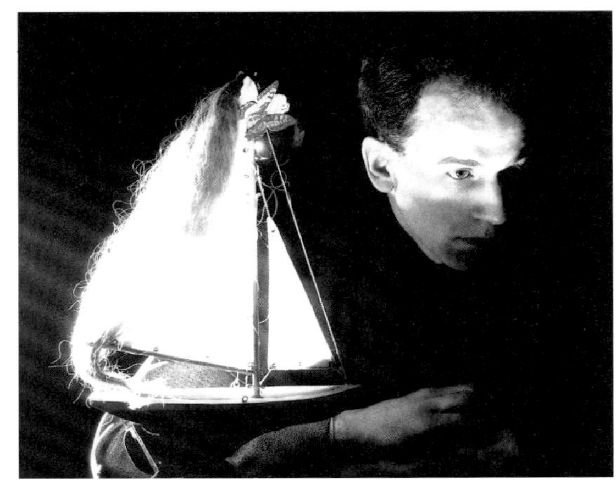

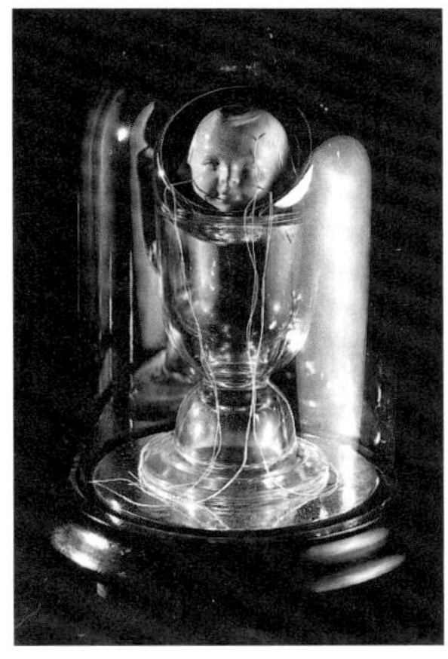

1929

May The Cornell family purchases a home in a newly constructed neighborhood at 3708 Utopia Parkway, Flushing, New York, which will remain the family residence until Cornell's death.

1931

Early in year Losing his job at Whitman's because of the Depression, Cornell begins taking a series of part-time jobs to support his family.

November Julien Levy Gallery opens at 602 Madison Avenue, New York. The gallery initially is dedicated to historical and contemporary photography, modern painting, and experimental film, but it soon will become the primary center in America for Surrealist art.

Cornell shows Levy his first "montages" (called that by the artist until the late 1940s), collages of original and reproduced black-and-white engravings and woodcuts from turn-of-the-century books, possibly inspired after Cornell saw similar work by Max Ernst at Levy's gallery. Levy becomes Cornell's dealer and friend; they will occasionally exchange photographs from their collections.

November 16 "Newer Super-Realism," organized by A. Everett "Chick" Austin, Jr., opens at the Wadsworth Atheneum, Hartford, Connecticut. This is the first exhibition of Surrealist art in America. Austin is a friend of Levy's from college, and Levy played an important role in shaping the exhibition. The exhibition includes work by Giorgio de Chirico, Salvador Dalí, Ernst, André Masson, Joan Miró, Picasso, Pierre Roy, and Leopold Survage.

1932

January 9–29 "Surréalisme," at Julien Levy Gallery, New York, is an enlargement of the Wadsworth Atheneum, Hartford, exhibition the previous fall. Levy has added American artists such as Herbert Bayer, Cornell, and Charles Howard. Cornell is represented by several montages and a large bell jar object. Cornell also designed the gallery announcement.

Early Fall Duchamp designs and co-authors with Vitaly Halberstadt *L'Opposition et les cases conjuguées sont réconciliées [Opposition and Sister Squares Are Reconciled]* (Brussels: L'Echiquier). Duchamp will assemble the manuscript, proofs, drawings, and notes related to this project in his *Box of 1932*.

November 26–December 30 "Objects by Joseph Cornell: Minutiae, Glass Bells, Shadow Boxes, Coups d'Oeil, Jouets Surréalistes" is presented in the back room of Julien Levy Gallery, New York. In the front room is "Etchings by Pablo Picasso: Illustrations for the Unknown Masterpiece."

1933

Cornell befriends Lee Miller, an American photographer who apprenticed with Man Ray in Paris before establishing herself in New York at 8 East 48th Street in October 1932. In addition to taking photographs of Cornell's artworks, Miller also makes several portraits of him.

Cornell writes *Monsieur Phot*, an illustrated film scenario about a photographer. Each of the as many as twenty numbered, handmade copies of the scenario is typed on thirteen pages of red paper, which, along with five interspersed stereopticon photographs, are mounted on black paper; all sheets are placed in a black folder. Cornell will distribute the scenario to friends over a number of years.

March Cornell attends a screening of *L'Âge d'Or [The Golden Age]* (1929) directed by Luis Buñuel with a screenplay by Dalí, New York Film Society. Later in the year, he will see *Un Chien Andalou [An Andalusian Dog]* (1929), also directed by Buñuel with a screenplay by Dalí.

193 **Duchamp's *Large Glass* installed in "International Exhibition of Modern Art"** (November 19, 1926–January 1, 1927) Société Anonyme, Brooklyn Museum, New York

194 **Duchamp on the SS *Paris*,** New York, February 27, 1927.

195 **Mary Reynolds,** Paris, c. 1930. Photograph by Man Ray. Mary Reynolds Collection, The Art Institute of Chicago.

196 **Announcement for "Objects by Joseph Cornell: Minutiae, Glass Bells, Shadow Boxes, Coups d'Oeil, Jouets Surréalistes"** (November 26–December 30, 1932), Julien Levy Gallery, New York. The Young-Mallin Archive, New York.

197 ***Joseph Cornell, New York,*** 1933. Vintage gelatin-silver print, 6½ x 8½ in. Photograph by Lee Miller. © Lee Miller Archives, Chiddingly, England.

198 ***Cornell, Bell Jar Object,*** **c. 1933.** Vintage gelatin-silver print, 6½ x 8½ in. Photograph by Lee Miller. © Lee Miller Archives, Chiddingly, England.

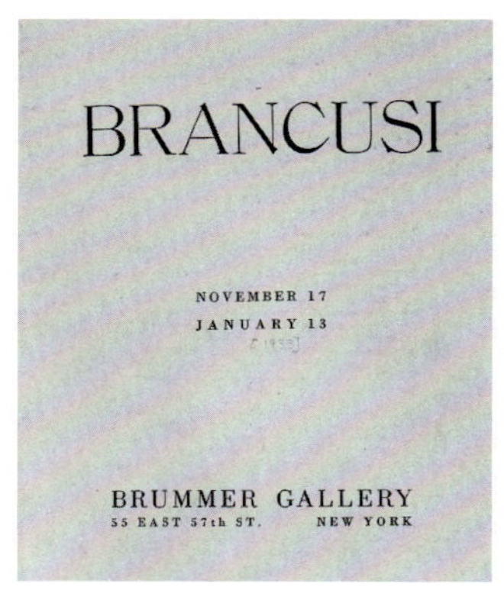
BRANCUSI

NOVEMBER 17
JANUARY 13

BRUMMER GALLERY
55 EAST 57th ST. NEW YORK

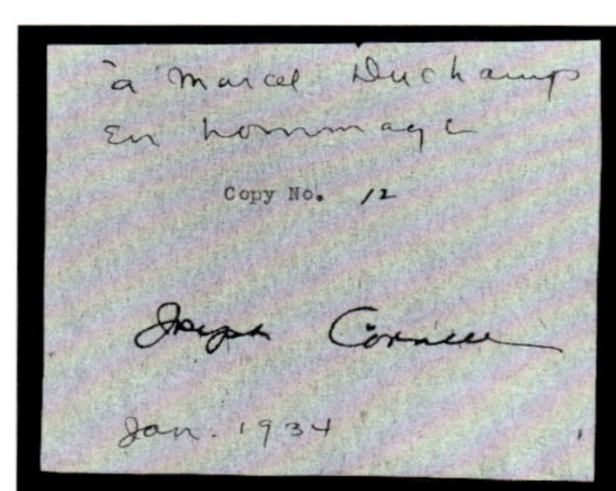

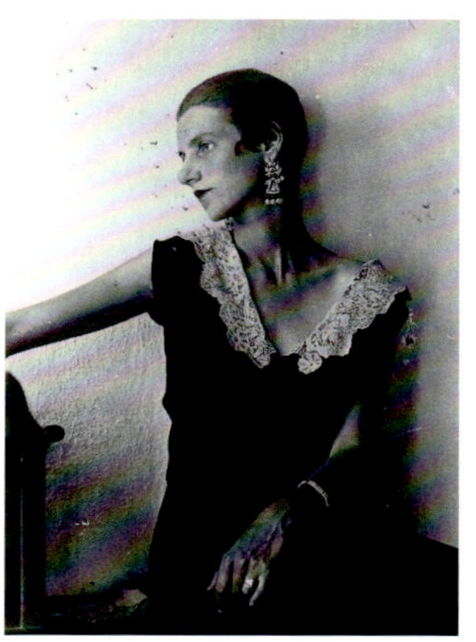

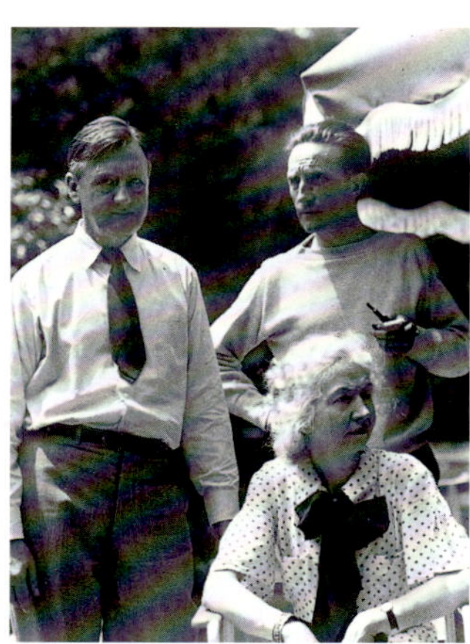

199 **Cover of checklist, Brancusi exhibition** (November 17, 1933–January 13, 1934), Brummer Gallery, New York.

200 **Cornell's dedication to Duchamp inscribed on *Monsieur Phot*, no. 12,** illustrated film scenario, January 1934. Mary Reynolds Collection, The Art Institute of Chicago.

201 **Peggy Guggenheim,** Paris, c. 1926. Photograph by Berenice Abbott. Berenice Abbott/Commerce Graphics Ltd, Inc.

202 **Walter and Louise Arensberg with Duchamp,** Arensberg residence, Hollywood, California, August 1936. Photograph by Beatrice Wood. Philadelphia Museum of Art, Marcel Duchamp Archive.

203 **Announcement for "Fantastic Art, Dada, Surrealism"** (December 9, 1936–January 17, 1937), The Museum of Modern Art, New York. Collection of Virginia Green, New York.

204 **Julien Levy,** New York, c. 1931. Photograph by Jay Leyda. The Art Institute of Chicago. Gift of Patricia and Frank Kolodny in memory of Julien Levy.

205 **Salvador Dalí, *Myself at the Age of Ten When I Was a Grasshopper Child,* 1933.** Oil on panel, 8⅝ x 6¾ in. Salvador Dali Museum, St. Petersburg, Florida.

November 9 Cornell sends Miller's photograph of one of his bell jar objects to André Breton in Paris, inscribed *A Andre Breton En Hommage Joseph Cornell November 9, 1933.*[2]

November 17, 1933–January 13, 1934 A Brancusi exhibition is presented at Brummer Gallery, New York, again organized and installed by Duchamp, who arrived in America from France on October 31 (he will return to Paris on January 20, 1934). The occasion of this exhibition is believed to be the first time that Cornell and Duchamp meet. Duchamp will write that many people come to the opening: "friends old and new, really astounded by the fish, felicitations on the arrangement—really lots of joy in the air."[3]

December Cornell presents a photograph of an unknown image to Duchamp, inscribed *A Marcel Duchamp / en amical souvenir /Joseph Cornell / Dec. 1933.*[4]

December 12, 1933–January 3, 1934 "Objects by Joseph Cornell, Posters by Toulouse-Lautrec, Watercolors by Perkins Harnley, Montages by Harry Brown" is presented at Julien Levy Gallery, New York.

1934

Cornell begins acquiring photographs and ephemera that will later be included in the "exploration" *The Crystal Cage [portrait of Berenice]* (c. 1934–67).

January Duchamp presents Cornell with the advertisement published in *Art News* (vol. 25, 14 May 1927, n.p.) for the "International Exhibition of Modern Art," Société Anonyme, Brooklyn Museum, New York, featuring the *Large Glass,* inscribed *Marcel Duchamp / for Joseph Cornell / New York Jan 1934* (DD 108).

Cornell presents copy no. 12 of his film scenario *Monsieur Phot* to Duchamp, inscribed *à Marcel Duchamp / En hommage / Joseph Cornell / Jan. 1934.*[5]

July A photograph of Duchamp by Lusha Nelson appears in "We Nominate for the Hall of Fame," *Vanity Fair* (vol. 42, no. 5, p. 22). Cornell will clip this photograph from the magazine, superimpose it onto an illustration of a "*Pompe de Jardin A Commande Électrique* [Electrically Operated Garden Pump]," inscribe it *Mariée [Bride],* and include it in his book object *Journal d'Agriculture Pratique et Journal de l'Agriculture* (c. 1933–mid 1940s).

Fall Cornell takes a job as a textile designer at Traphagen Commercial Textile Studio, 1680 Broadway, New York, remaining in their employ until 1940. Although he finds the work tedious, he nonetheless will use his free time at the New York Public Library, looking at books and periodicals and listening to music in the library's Music Room, as well as watching rehearsals at the American Ballet Theater.

September Duchamp publishes an edition of three hundred standard copies and plans an edition of twenty deluxe copies of *La Mariée mise à nu par ses célibataires même [The Bride Stripped Bare by Her Bachelors Even],* known as the *Green Box.* The portfolio contains ninety-three facsimile notes, drawings, and reproductions of original material made between 1911 and 1923 pertaining to the *Large Glass,* and one color reproduction of *9 moules mâlic [9 Malic Molds]* (1914–15). As part of an international mail solicitation, Duchamp sends his subscription bulletin with its facsimile page for the *Green Box* to Cornell. Cornell also receives (possibly on another occasion) a second facsimile page, one of which was included in each bulletin (DD 73, 90, and 107).

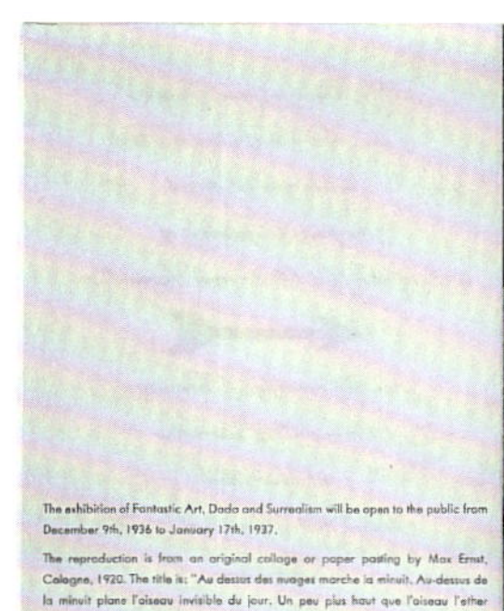

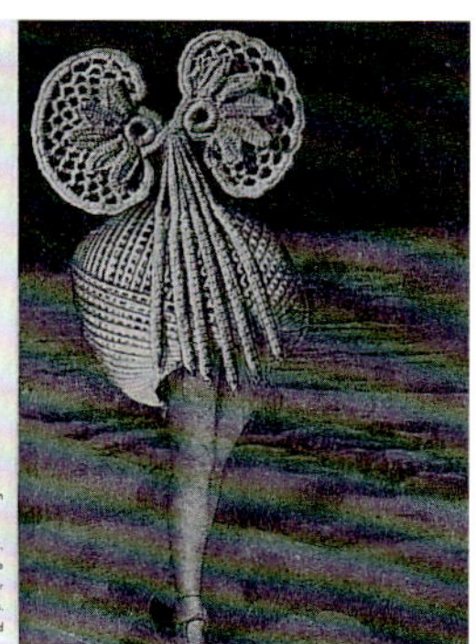

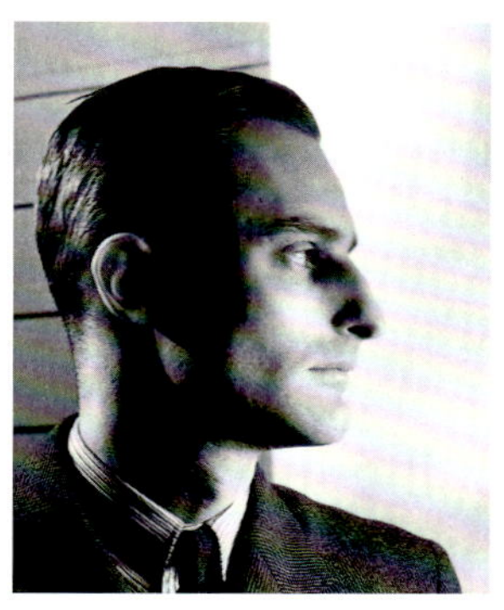

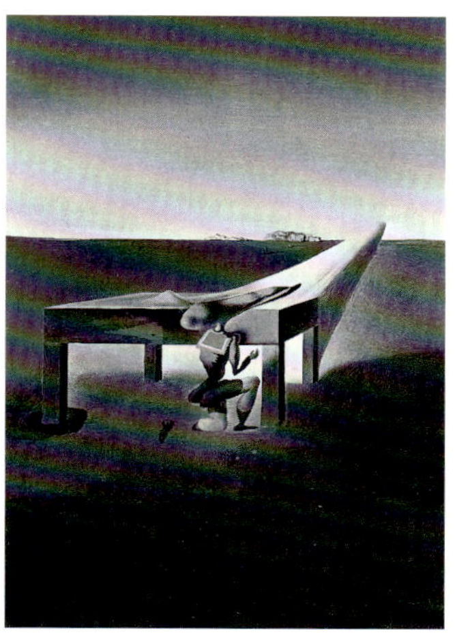

1935

March Duchamp starts collecting material and planning a special boxed *(Boite)* edition to include reproductions of all his major artworks. When completed, the edition will number twenty-four deluxe and approximately 260 standard examples. Production of the sixty-nine two-dimensional and three-dimensional facsimiles included in each example will continue until late 1940.

Summer Duchamp produces *Rotorelief (disques optiques)*—six double-sided letterpress cardboard discs—in an edition of five hundred. One set will be acquired by Cornell at an unknown date (DD 77, 79, and 109).

1936

May 2–29 In the "Exposition surréaliste d'objets," organized by Breton and presented at Galerie Charles Ratton, 14 rue Marignan, Paris, Duchamp is represented by *Bottle Rack* (1914), *Why Not Sneeze Rose Sélavy?* (1921), and *La bagarre d'Austerlitz [The Brawl at Austerlitz]* (1921).

May 20 Duchamp sails on the SS *Normandie* to New York, arriving on May 25 to undertake the two-month restoration of the *Large Glass* at Dreier's West Redding, Connecticut, home, The Haven. Upon its completion, Duchamp will install it in her library.

June 12–July 4 Duchamp is represented by *A propros de jeune soeur [Apropos of Little Sister]* (1911), *Le Roi et la Reine traversés par des nus en vitesse [The King and Queen Traversed by Swift Nudes at High Speed]* (1912), *Pharmacie [Pharmacy]* (1914), and *Rotorelief (disques optiques)* (1935) in the "International Surrealist Exhibition" at New Burlington Galleries, London.

Early August Duchamp travels by train to visit the Arensbergs in Hollywood for two weeks. While there, he will take detailed notes on the color of his artworks in the Arensbergs' collection and will arrange for Sam Little to photograph the works in black and white for reproduction in the forthcoming *Boite* edition.

Fall Levy publishes *Surrealism* (New York: The Black Sun Press) with a cover design by Cornell. The book includes a transcript of Cornell's *Monsieur Phot* scenario (pp. 77–88).

September 2 Duchamp sails from New York on the SS *Normandie*, arriving in France on September 7.

December Julien Levy Gallery, New York, presents an evening of films, including Duchamp's *Anémic Cinéma*, a selection from Cornell's film collection that he called *Goofy Newsreels*, and Cornell's first film, *Rose Hobart*. *Rose Hobart* is based on his editing of footage from George Melford's *East of Borneo* (1931) and other found footage that have been projected through a deep-blue filter. Dalí, who attends the screening, makes a scene after viewing *Rose Hobart*, claiming Cornell stole his idea for a particular effect.

December 9, 1936–January 17, 1937 "Fantastic Art, Dada, Surrealism," organized by Alfred H. Barr, Jr., is presented at The Museum of Modern Art, 11 West 53rd Street, New York. Duchamp is represented by eleven artworks in the two rooms that begin the exhibition. Cornell is represented by two boxes, *Cabinet of Natural History (Object)* (1934, 1936–40) and Untitled (Soap Bubble Set), plus ten small bell jar objects. The encased installation of these works has the title "Elements of Natural Philosophy and Soap Bubble Set." Among the components of *Cabinet of Natural History (Object)* is a glass bottle filled with glass strips and labeled *Méthode de M. Duchomp.*

1937

Cornell begins free-lance picture research for client publications by supplying photographs and ephemera from his growing collection, which will eventually number in the thousands.

Winter *Minotaure* (series 3, no. 10) reproduces Duchamp's *3 stoppages étalon [3 Standard Stoppages]* (1913–14) (p. 34), *Rendez-vous du 6 Février 1916* (p. 61), and Cornell's *Glass Bell* (c. 1932) (p. 34).

February *Harper's Bazaar* reproduces two Cornell untitled montages (both c. 1932) featuring sewing machines in the article "The Pulse of Fashion" (p. 43).

February 5–27 Duchamp's first one-person exhibition is presented by the Arts Club of Chicago, with a catalogue preface by Levy.

May Frederick Kiesler, the visionary Viennese architect, who had met Duchamp the previous year, publishes an article on Duchamp's *Large Glass* in his series "Design-Correlation" in *The Architectural Record* (no. 5, pp. 53–60) with photographs by Berenice Abbott.

Christmas In Paris, American heiress Peggy Guggenheim seeks Duchamp's advice on opening an art gallery. Guggenheim had been acquainted with Duchamp since the early 1920s, having met him through Reynolds and Laurence Vail, Guggenheim's ex-husband.

1938

January Cornell loans his Dalí painting, *Myself at the Age of Ten When I Was a Grasshopper Child* (1933, Salvador Dalí Museum, St. Petersburg, Florida), to the tour of "Fantastic Art, Dada, Surrealism." Cornell purchased the painting from Levy and later loaned it to his Dalí exhibition (November 21–December 10, 1934).

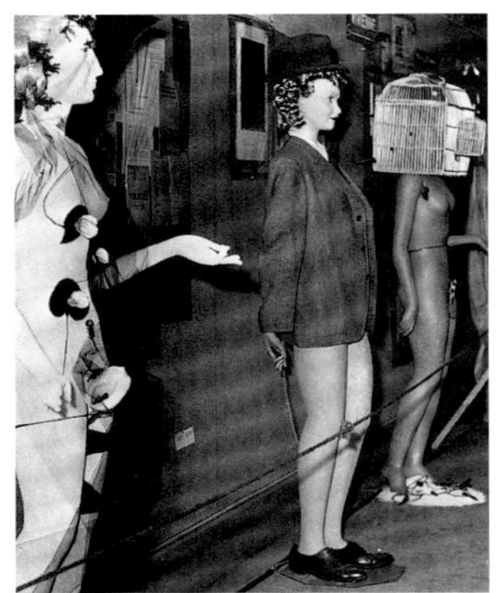

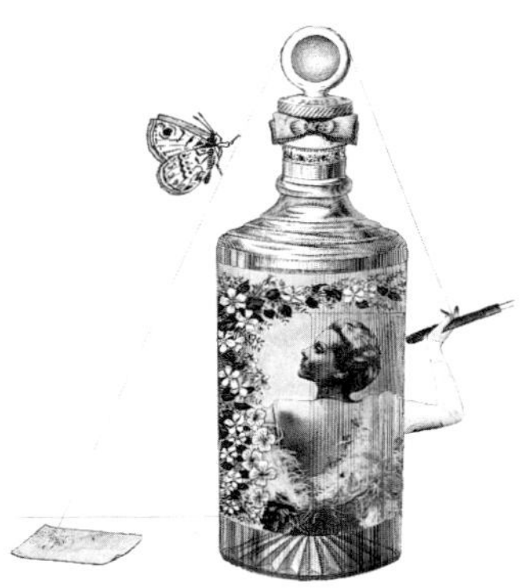

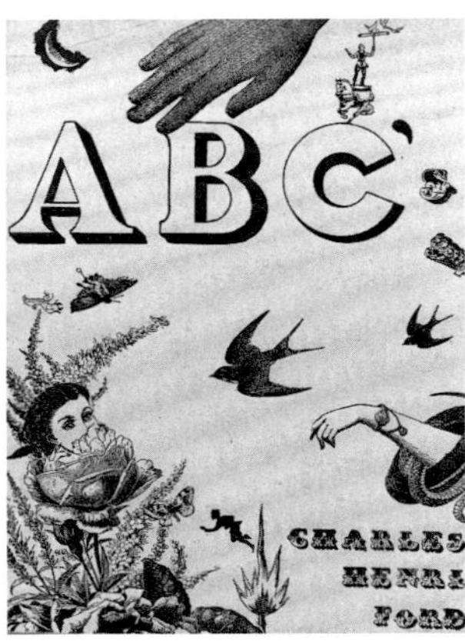

January 17–February "Exposition internationale du surréalisme," organized by Breton and Paul Eluard, installed by Duchamp, and lit by Man Ray, is presented at Galerie Beaux-Arts, 140 rue du Faubourg-Saint-Honoré, Paris. Duchamp created a forestlike bed of moss and leaves for the central hallway and hung from the ceiling 1,200 empty coal bags over a stove. Cornell is represented in the exhibition with one object supplied by Levy; *Dictionnaire abrégé du Surréalisme* (exh. cat., Paris: Galerie Beaux-Arts) reproduces nine works by Duchamp and Cornell's untitled 1932 montage of a Victorian paper doll on a sewing machine.

January 24 Guggenheim opens Guggenheim Jeune, 30 Cork Street, London. The program is predominately based on exhibitions and artists Duchamp has suggested. The gallery will present twenty-one exhibitions until its closing in June 1939.

May Austin, director of Wadsworth Atheneum, Hartford, purchases Cornell's Untitled (Soap Bubble Set) for $60, the artist's first acquisition by a museum.

[Summer] Cornell begins using his cousin's French *Bébé* doll (from the Jumeau factory, c. 1885–95) for a series of photographs and installations. He will create a box construction featuring the doll by 1943; he will use the name "Bébé Marie" for all these projects.[6]

1939

January Duchamp presents a copy of *Obligations pour la Roulette de Monte-Carlo [Monte Carlo Bond]* (1924) to The Museum of Modern Art, New York, on the occasion of the museum's tenth anniversary. This is his first work in a public collection.

Charles Henri Ford writes to Cornell, asking him to collaborate on the design of his forthcoming book of poems, *ABC's for the Children of No One, Who Grows Up to Look Like Everyone's Son* (Prairie City, Ill.: James A. Decker Press, 1940). Cornell has recently become friendly with Ford, the Russian émigré painter Pavel Tchelitchew, and the critic Parker Tyler, all of whom will play important roles in increasing awareness of Cornell's work.

Summer Cornell repeatedly visits the New York World's Fair, Flushing Meadow, New York, situated on a former dumping ground near his home. He is especially interested in the Swiss pavilion, the *Masterpieces of Art* pavilion, and Dalí's underwater fantasia, the *Dream of Venus* pavilion.

December 6–31 "Exhibition of Objects (Bilboquet) by Joseph Cornell" is presented at Julien Levy Gallery, now at 15 East 57th Street, New York, with a catalogue essay by Tyler.

1940

Late May Duchamp, Reynolds, the Crottis, Man Ray, Dalí, and his wife, Gala, leave occupied Paris for Arcachon, near Bordeaux, in the occupied zone of France. Duchamp and Reynolds will return to Paris in early September.

August Varian Fry, an American Quaker and head of the Emergency Rescue Committee, establishes Villa Air Bel, Marseilles, as a refuge for intellectuals and artists wishing to emigrate to America. Among those he assists are Breton and his wife, Jacqueline Lamba.

September The first issue of *View,* founded by Ford and Tyler, is published.

December 10 "Joseph Cornell: Exhibition of Objects" opens at Julien Levy Gallery, New York.

1941

Early in year Since leaving his job at Traphagen in Fall 1940, Cornell is now eager to work full-time as an artist, organizing the cellar of his house as his studio.

January 1 Duchamp announces via subscription bulletin his new box edition: *de ou par Marcel Duchamp ou Rrose Sélavy [by or of Marcel Duchamp or Rrose Sélavy],* known as the *Boîte [Box]* edition. The deluxe examples will sell for $200.

Late January Guggenheim purchases *Boîte-en-valise [Box-in-a-Valise]* I/XX via Roché.

May Duchamp completes and signs *Boîtes-en-valise* O/XX for Reynolds and II/XX for Georges Hugnet.

June Roché receives *Boîte-en-valise* III/XX from Duchamp.

July Duchamp prepares to emigrate to America; he moves to his sister Yvonne's house in the fishing port of Sanary (Var). A number of people, including Frank Hubachek, Jr. (Reynolds' brother), Arensberg, Dreier, Kay Boyle, Guggenheim, and Barr, work actively (at times independent of one another) to secure the appropriate papers for Duchamp to leave war-torn France.

July 14 Guggenheim—along with her soon-to-be husband, Ernst; her children, Pegeen and Sinbad; her former husband, Vail; his wife, Boyle; and Boyle's four children—arrive in New York from Lisbon. Guggenheim previously arranged for the art collection she has been assembling since 1938 to be shipped from Grenoble to New York disguised as "household goods." Included with her shipment were at least two almost completed *Boîtes-en-valise* and material for fifty more examples of the *Boîte* edition, which Duchamp had been transporting to Grenoble over the preceding months (DD 71, 89, 92, and 94).

October Duchamp and Dreier, acting as trustees of the permanent collection of the Société Anonyme, authorize its presentation to the Yale University Art Gallery, New Haven, where it will be installed permanently in January 1942.

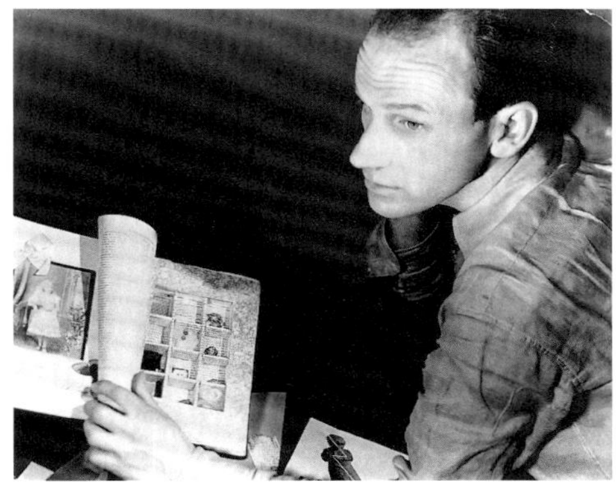

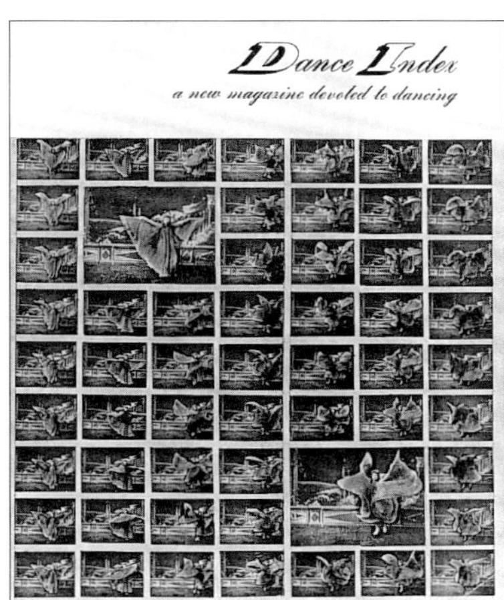

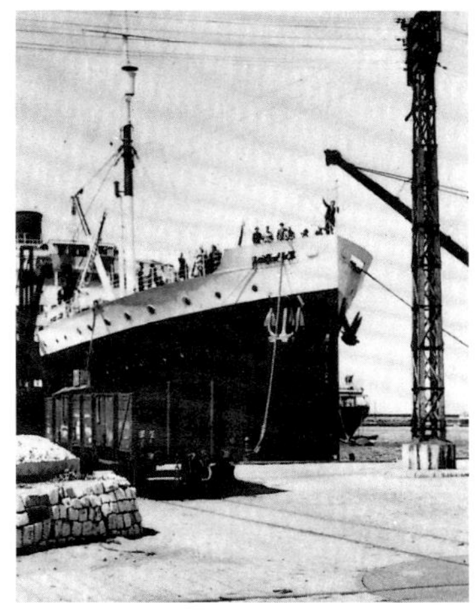

December Cornell publishes the photomontage and essay *"Enchanted Wanderer": Excerpt from a Journey Album for Hedy Lamarr* in *View* (series 1, nos. 9/10, p. 3).

1942

Early in year Cornell meets Roberto Sebastian Matta Echaurren, probably at Julien Levy Gallery, New York.

January Lincoln Kirstein founds *Dance Index* with offices at 637 Madison Avenue, New York. Donald Windham assumes the editorship when Kirstein enters the army. Windham and Cornell will develop a lifelong friendship. Cornell will design the first three covers: "Hommage à Isadora" (vol. 1, no. 1, January), "The Parker Sisters" (vol. 1, no. 2, February), and "Loïe Fuller" (vol. 1, no. 3, March).

Early March On Duchamp's advice, Guggenheim purchases from Cornell *Fortune Telling Parrot* (c. 1937–38), *Thimble Box* (1938), and *Revolving Book with Red Ball* (1934); the last two artworks will be subsequently sold or given away by Guggenheim.[7]

Before March 29 Cornell meets Robert Motherwell and his Mexican born wife, Mariá Emilia Ferreira y Moyers, through Matta. They quickly develop a close friendship that will continue until about 1949. Cornell will often send "souvenir items" to Mariá, who has the appearance of a classical ballerina.[8]

April Cornell contributes a photomontage based on sixteen of his montages from the 1930s entitled "Story without a Name–for Max Ernst" to *View* (series 2, no. 1, p. 23), an issue devoted to Ernst.

May 14 Duchamp sails on the SS *Serpa Pinto* from Marseilles (with a two-week stop in Casablanca and a one-week stop in Lisbon) to the United States. He is seen off by Victor Brauner, Jacques Hérold, and André and Henriette Gomes. As a parting gift, the Gomeses receive *Boite-en-valise* IV/XX (without its valise). Duchamp leaves slightly more than three-quarters of the materials, documents, and proofs for the *Boite* edition in France in the care of Roché.

June The first issue of *VVV* is published from offices generously provided by Bernard Reis in his CPA office at 1 East 40th Street, New York. The magazine is edited by Breton and is seen by many as his challenge to *View*. Not speaking English, Breton asked David Hare to be editor and Ernst, editorial advisor. Duchamp will join them later on the editorial board.

Cornell designs the cover "Denishawn Chart" for *Dance Index* (vol. 1, no. 6).

June 25 Duchamp arrives in New York without fanfare; he will live for one month at the home of Mr. and Mrs. Robert Allerton Parker, 1 Gracie Square, New York. Parker was one of the journalists who had interviewed Duchamp in 1915 on his first trip to America.

Late July Guggenheim invites Duchamp to stay in her townhouse, The Hale House, 440 East 51st Street, New York, while she and Ernst spend part of the summer in Provincetown, Mass. Duchamp's fellow houseguests are John and Xenia Cage.

July 28 Cornell telephones Guggenheim, and her houseguest Duchamp answers the phone. Cornell invites Duchamp to visit him on Friday.[9]

July 31 Duchamp, Cornell, and his brother, Robert, have lunch at Cornell's house. The two artists spend the afternoon looking at an example of the *Boite-en-valise*.[10] Soon after, Cornell begins assisting in the assembly of the *Boite* edition.

August 14 Cornell and Duchamp have lunch at Le Moal French Restaurant, 811 Third Avenue, New York. From the meeting Cornell retains a sugar cube, its wrapper, and a tea tag (DD 24, 30,

206 **Duchamp's *Rrose Sélavy* mannequin (center)** installed in "Exposition internationale du surréalisme," January–February 1938, Galerie Beaux-Arts, 140 rue du Faubourg-Saint-Honoré, Paris.

207 **Cornell, *Poetry of Surrealism*, c. 1935–1938, 1940.** Engravings, photomechanical reproductions, Photostats, and colored inks on paper, mounted on paperboard, 10 5/8 x 8 5/8 in. The Joseph and Robert Cornell Memorial Foundation.

208 **Cornell, cover design for Charles Henri Ford's *ABC's*,** 1940. Joseph Cornell Study Center, Natl. Museum of American Art, Smithsonian. Gift of Mr. and Mrs. John A. Benton.

209 **Cornell with Untitled Book Object, c. 1940.** Joseph Cornell Study Center, Natl. Museum of American Art, Smithsonian. Gift of Mr. and Mrs. John A. Benton.

210 **Cornell, "Loïe Fuller,"** cover design for *Dance Index* (March 1942). Joseph Cornell Study Center, Natl. Museum of American Art, Smithsonian. Gift of Mr. and Mrs. John A. Benton.

211 **Duchamp on the prow of the SS *Serpa Pinto*,** Marseilles, May 1942. Photograph by André Gomes.

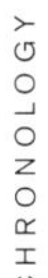

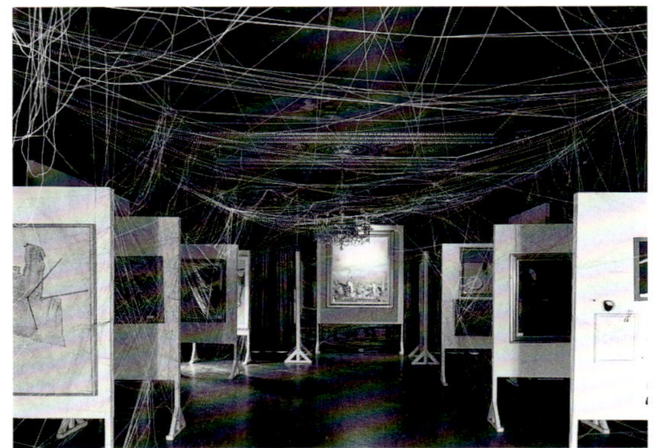

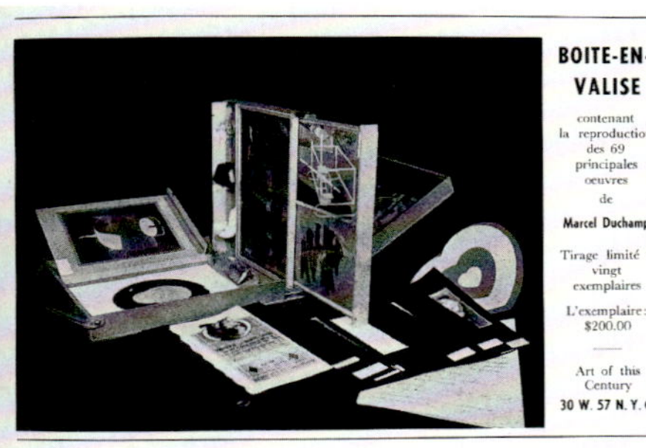

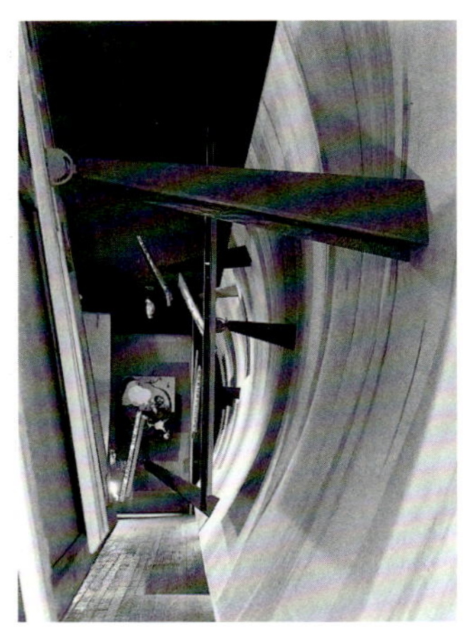

212 "First Papers of Surrealism" (October 14–November 7, 1942), Whitelaw Reid Mansion, 451 Madison Avenue, New York, installation view. Photograph by John D. Schiff. Philadelphia Museum of Art Archive.

213 Advertisement for Duchamp's *Boîte-en-Valise* in *View* (December 1944): p. 5.

214 Surrealist Gallery, detail of concave walls, Art of This Century, 30 West 57th Street, New York, 1943. Photograph by Berenice Abbott. Berenice Abbott/Commerce Graphics Ltd, Inc.

215 Duchamp and Peggy Guggenheim (background), Guggenheim's townhouse, 440 East 51st Street, New York, c. 1942. Philadelphia Museum of Art, Marcel Duchamp Archive.

216 Window display by Duchamp, André Breton, and Kurt Seligmann for Denis de Rougemont's *La Part du diable,* Brentano's, 586 Fifth Avenue, New York, February 1943.

217 Maria Martins in her studio, 471 Park Avenue, New York, 1946.

and 68c). That day Cornell also picks up the Beverly Theatre's movie schedule for the week beginning August 15 (DD 70).

August 18 Cornell and Duchamp meet. Cornell leaves with two pipe cleaners and a piece of blotting paper (DD 29 and 95). Cornell will ascribe this same date on an inkblot drawing (DD 75).

August 19 Piet Mondrian mails Duchamp a letter (DD 11).

August 21 Cornell and Duchamp have lunch at Le Moal at one p.m. (DD 29).

August 22 *Time* magazine asks Cornell to supply a photograph of Duchamp from his photo archive for a forthcoming article on Duchamp, but Cornell is unable to do so (DD 32).

August 23 Cornell and Duchamp have lunch at the Hampton Cafeteria, Madison and 59th Street, at noon (DD 5).

August 26 Cornell and Duchamp meet at Guggenheim's townhouse, and Cornell departs with a drawing related to the assembly of the *Boite* edition (DD 72).

August 30 Duchamp presents Cornell with a signed receipt for one yard of Belgian linen (DD 87).

Late August Cornell and Duchamp meet and discuss assembling *Boite-en-valise* V/XX for Reis, an accountant much involved in the New York art world and a financial backer of *VVV* (DD 71).

Late Summer Guggenheim publishes *Art of This Century: Objects–Drawings–Photographs–Paintings–Sculpture–Collages, 1910 to 1942* (New York: Art of This Century), missing the original publication date of May 15. Reproduced are Duchamp's *Jeune homme triste dans un train [Sad Young Man on a Train]* (1912) on p. 57 and *Boite-en-valise* I/XX on p. 59. Two Cornell artworks are listed—*Ball and Book* (object, 1934) and *Thimble Box* (object, 1938) on p. 149—but not reproduced.

September Duchamp completes and signs *Boites-en-valise* V/XX for Reis and VI/XX for Sidney Janis.

September 7 "Artist Descending to America," an article featuring Duchamp's arrival in America, appears in *Time* (vol. 60, no. 10, pp. 100–102) (DD 78).

September 8 Dreier sends Duchamp, via special delivery, a copy of the *Time* article (DD 38, 42, and 52).

September 9 Cornell purchases items at Bloomingdale's (DD 45 and 47).

September 29 Cornell and Duchamp meet, and Cornell leaves with a drawing of a keyhole by Duchamp (DD 8).

Early October Duchamp moves into a room with a bath offered by Kiesler and his wife, Stefi, in their penthouse at 56 Seventh Avenue, New York; he will stay there until October 1943.

October 14–November 7 "First Papers of Surrealism" is presented at Whitelaw Reid Mansion, 451 Madison Avenue, New York, organized by Duchamp and Breton and sponsored by the Coordinating Council of French Relief Societies. Duchamp's installation consists of a "mile of string," which he used to weave an intricate web from wall to wall and floor to ceiling, literally obscuring the artworks exhibited. Duchamp purchased the string (gun cotton), possibly from Samson Cordage Works, 89 Broad Street, Boston, Massachusetts (DD 25 and 48). However, another mile is required after the string catches fire from contact with the lights. Duchamp also designed the catalogue cover, a close-up of five bullet holes he made by firing a gun into Kurt Seligmann's barn in Sugar Loaf, New York; for the back cover, he used an enlarged photograph of a piece of Gruyere cheese. Each artist is represented by a "compensation portrait," a photograph of another person of their choice. Duchamp chose a Ben Shahn photograph of a Depression-era woman.

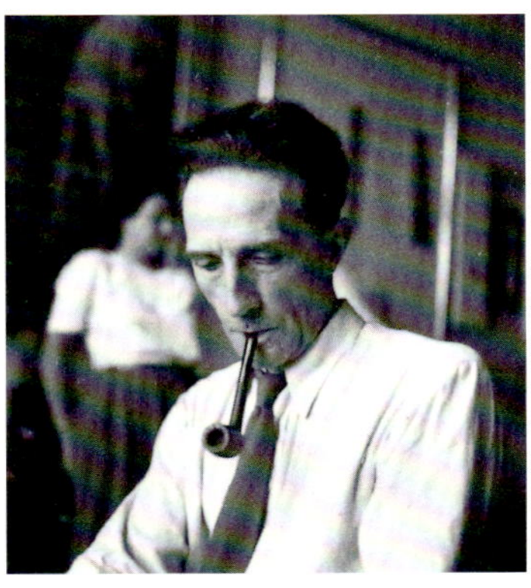

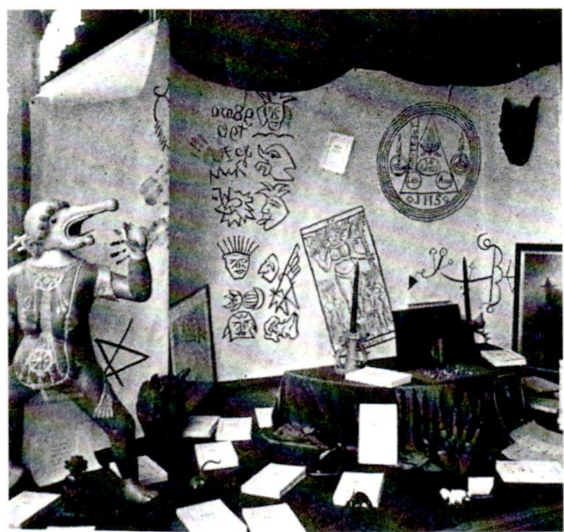

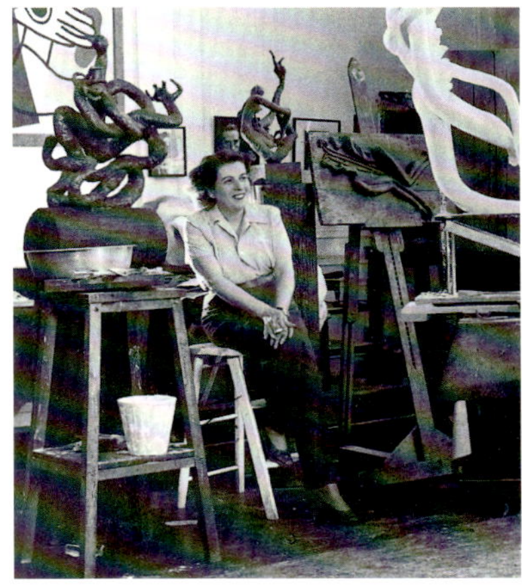

October 20 After nine months' preparation, Guggenheim's Art of This Century, 30 West 57th Street, New York, opens. Kiesler has designed four rooms for Guggenheim's permanent collection and for temporary exhibitions: the Surrealist Gallery, the Abstract Gallery, the Kinetic Gallery (which exhibits fourteen reproductions from *Boite-en-valise* I/XX seen through a small hole activated by a large wood wheel), and the Daylight/Painting Gallery.

December Duchamp completes and signs *Boites-en-valise* VII/XX for Elizabeth Paepcke and VIII/XX for James Johnson Sweeney.

December 1 Cornell and Duchamp meet. Cornell leaves with a drawing of the miniature *Fountain* used in the *Boite* edition (DD 3).

"Objects by Joseph Cornell; Marcel Duchamp: Box-Valise; Laurence Vail: Bottles" opens at Art of This Century, New York, with a preview on November 30.

December 11 Boyle sends Duchamp a letter using the stationery of her literary agent, Ann Watkins (DD 44).

December 21 Cornell visits Duchamp at the Kieslers' for about two hours in the late morning. Duchamp presents Cornell with an on-the-spot readymade of a LePage's glue box imprinted with the slogan "strength" that Duchamp amends to read "gimme strength" (DD 67). Cornell also leaves with a Bond Street Pipe Tobacco box, which he dates on the bottom (DD 1). Cornell records both items in his diary.[11]

1943

Early in year Duchamp and Dreier begin gathering materials and writing artists' biographies for a catalogue of the Société Anonyme collection to be published by Yale University Press in 1950.

Art dealer Pierre Matisse purchases an untitled Pharmacy box by Cornell, probably from Julien Levy Gallery, New York. The box will remain with his wife, Alexina "Teeny" Sattler (later Duchamp), after their divorce in 1949.

Duchamp meets Maria Martins, a sculptor professionally called Maria and the wife of the Brazilian Ambassador to the United States. Martins lives in Washington, D.C., with her husband but maintains a studio and apartment in New York at 471 Park Avenue. She will become the prime inspiration for the figure in *Étant donnés: 1° la chute d'eau / 2° le gaz d'éclairage [Given: 1. The Waterfall / 2. The Illuminating Gas]* (1946–66).

January Duchamp presents Cornell with an envelope, inscribed *New Year's intentions*, into which Cornell places several fragments of materials related to the assembly of the *Boite* edition (DD 60).

Cornell designs the cover for the "Americana Fantastica" issue of *View* (series 2, no. 4) and contributes illustrations and layouts (pp. 21, 23, and 36–38), including the pictorial essay, *THE Crystal Cage [portrait of Berenice]* (pp. 10–16).

Duchamp completes and signs *Boite-en-valise* IX/XX for The Museum of Modern Art, New York.

January 2 Cornell and Duchamp have lunch at a Horn and Hardart cafeteria (57th Street and 8th Avenue, New York) and may possibly have visited galleries on 57th Street together (DD 19 and 31).

January 6 Reynolds, who has been active in the French Resistance, arrives in New York after a perilous escape over the Pyrenees. She will take an apartment at 28 West 11th Street, New York, six blocks from Duchamp at the Kieslers'.

January 19 Cornell visits Duchamp at the Kieslers'. Duchamp gives Cornell a postcard of the *Mona Lisa,* inscribed recto *notice nose tip* (Duchamp has added a small dot of ink on her nose) and verso *Jan. 19. 1943 / Variante / Marcel Duchamp / ou Rrose Sélavy.* Cornell departs with two additional Duchamp notes (DD 4, 28, and 106).

January 22 Cornell orders milled, grooved, and mitered wood molding from Bayside Woodworking Co., 206–26 Northern Blvd., Bayside, New York, for ten M monograms to be used in the assembly of the *Boite* edition (DD 91).

January 31 Ford asks Cornell for the loan of one of his boxes and an autographed photograph to help decorate the *View* offices at 1 East 53rd Street, New York. Cornell agrees.[12]

February Duchamp completes and signs *Boite-en-valise* 0/XX for Dreier.

Vogue rejects Duchamp's collage *Allégorie de genre [Allegory of Genre]* after soliciting the design for the cover of their "Americana" issue (February 1). He receives $50 for his expenses. By March 1945, Breton will own the original artwork.

February 3 Duchamp designs (in collaboration with Breton and Seligmann) a window display for Denis de Rougemont's *La Part du diable [The Devil's Share]* (New York: Brentano) at Brentano's, 586 Fifth Avenue, New York. The display consists of a ceiling of open umbrellas hanging by their handles (Duchamp) and a collection of devil statues placed against a backdrop of diabolic emblems (painted by Seligmann).

February 8–March 13 "Retrospective exhibition of the works of Hélion" is presented at Art of This Century, New York (DD 40).

February 15 Cornell visits Duchamp at the Kieslers'. Duchamp presents Cornell with a signed and dated Encre Ideal Waterman's ink box, and Cornell departs with two Duchamp notes written on exhibition announcements and torn into multiple fragments by Duchamp before being placed in envelopes by Cornell (DD 17, 40, 49, and 51).

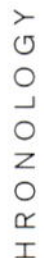

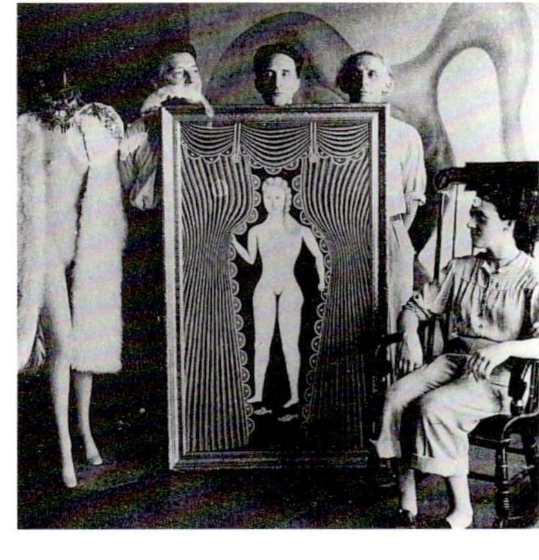

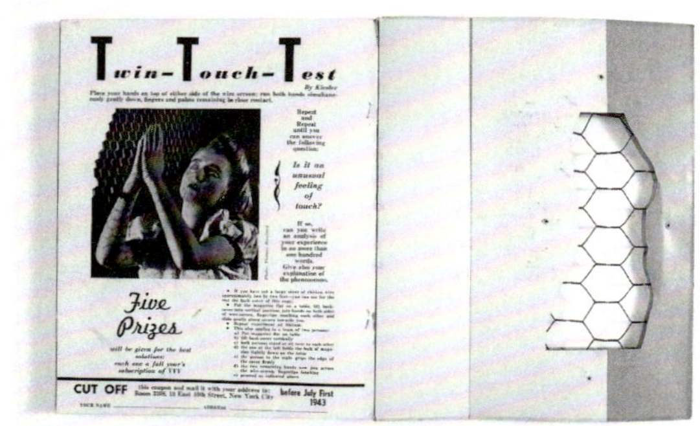

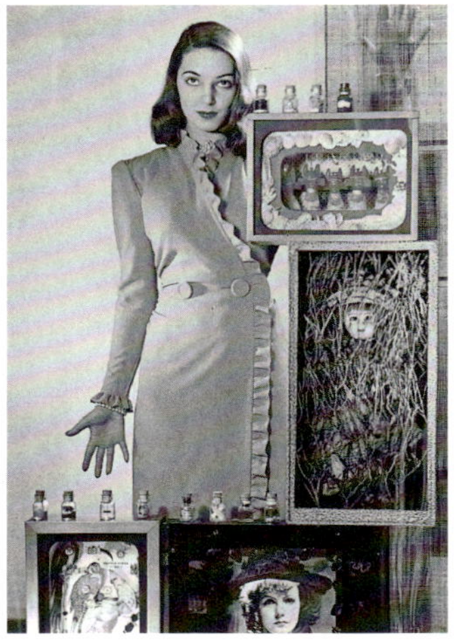

March Duchamp designs the covers for *VVV Almanac for 1943* (nos. 2–3) using an anonymous etching of an allegory of death on the front. For the back cover, Duchamp (with Kiesler's assistance) designs a die-cut of a woman's torso in profile with chicken wire inserted in the die-cut. On the last page is a photograph of Pegeen Vail demonstrating how to perform Kiesler's "Twin-Touch-Test": *Put the magazine flat on a table, lift back cover into vertical position, join hands on both sides of wire-screen finger tips touching each other and slide gently along screen towards you* (DD 40 and 51).

April Duchamp completes and signs *Boites-en-valise* 0/XX for the Arensbergs and 0/XX for Boyle.

Cornell designs the cover "Portrait of Allen Dodsworth" for *Dance Index* (vol. 2, no. 4).

As part of the war effort, Cornell begins working on the radio manufacturing assembly line of the Allied Control Company, Long Island City, New York, where he will remain until January 1944.

April 16–May 15 "Exhibition of Collage" at Art of This Century, New York, is the first American exhibition devoted to collage. It includes work by both Duchamp and Cornell.

April 19 Duchamp presents Cornell with a note inscribed *delay included* (DD 15).

May 3 Cornell delivers to Duchamp four assembled *Boites* for which Duchamp provides a receipt in the form of a collage made on the cardboard cover of a conductor's receipt tablet of the Long Island Railroad (DD 98).

June 10 Duchamp mails Cornell $20 in payment for Cornell's work on two *Boites (Boite-en-valise* IX/XX for The Museum of Modern Art, New York, and a *Boite* for Matta) and invites him to lunch with him some Sunday (DD 6).

August 15 Duchamp and Anne Matta Clark appear in Maya Deren's unfinished film *Witch's Cradle*, filmed in and around Art of This Century, outside at the Brevoort restaurant at Fifth Avenue and Eighth Street, and on the Kieslers' rooftop terrace. Duchamp is filmed playing a string game and, in later sequences, enmeshed in a web of string.

August 20 Duchamp sends a letter to Cornell asking him to assemble a standard *Boite* to be exhibited at Caresse Crosby's new gallery, 1606 20th Street, Washington, D.C. (DD 54).

August 26 At noon Cornell delivers materials related to the *Boite* edition to Duchamp (DD 36).

September 2 Duchamp writes Cornell that he is going to Washington, D.C., for a few days (see August 20 above), then to Dreier's home in Connecticut where he will supervise the removal of the *Large Glass* for its extended loan to The Museum of Modern Art, New York. He acknowledges receipt of a "Chinese letter" Cornell has sent him (DD 37).

October Reynolds moves from 28 West 11th Street, New York, to 73 Perry Street in Greenwich Village.

October 1 Duchamp moves into a fourth-floor studio at 210 West 14th Street, New York, which he will occupy for the next twenty-two years.

October 2 Cornell makes an unannounced visit to Duchamp's new 14th Street studio to find that Duchamp is not home. The studio has no telephone (DD 20).

October 9 Duchamp gives Cornell a belated receipt for the materials he delivered on August 26 (DD 66).

December 1–31 Cornell participates in the group exhibition "Natural, Insane, Surrealist Art" at Art of This Century, New York.

December 7–28 The three-person exhibition of work by Cornell, Duchamp, and Yves Tanguy, "Through the Big End of the Opera Glass," is presented at Julien Levy Gallery, now at 42 East 57th Street, New York. Based on a contemporary review of the exhibition, some of the Duchamp works shown include selections from his *Boite* edition, his "glass art," plus *L.H.O.O.Q.* and Cornell's Untitled (Bébé Marie).[13] Cornell designed the exhibition announcement with contributions from Tanguy and Duchamp (DD 14).

1944

Early in year Duchamp presents Cornell with a double-portrait collage silhouette based on his *Allégorie de genre* (DD 113).

January Duchamp completes and signs *Boite-en-valise* X/XX for Levy.

January 6 Cornell and his sister Elizabeth "Betty" Benton visit Duchamp in his 14th Street studio (DD 48).

February Janis publishes *Abstract & Surrealist Art in America* (New York: Reynal & Hitchcock). Included are reproductions of Duchamp's *Large Glass* (p. 22), *Boite-en-valise* I/XX (p. 131), and Cornell's *Medici Slot Machine* (1941; p. 106). In conjunction with the book, an exhibition, also organized by Janis, will tour five American cities from February through July. Cornell is represented by a box construction *Pipe and Cut Out* (1940) and Duchamp is represented by selections from his *Boite* edition.

March Duchamp's die-cut *Allégorie de genre* (one of three known versions) is reproduced in *VVV* (no. 4, pp. 65–66). This is the fourth and last issue of *VVV*.

Mademoiselle (vol. 18, no. 5) features four of Cornell's boxes, including Untitled (Bébé Marie), in a fashion layout photographed at Julien Levy Gallery, New York (p. 130).

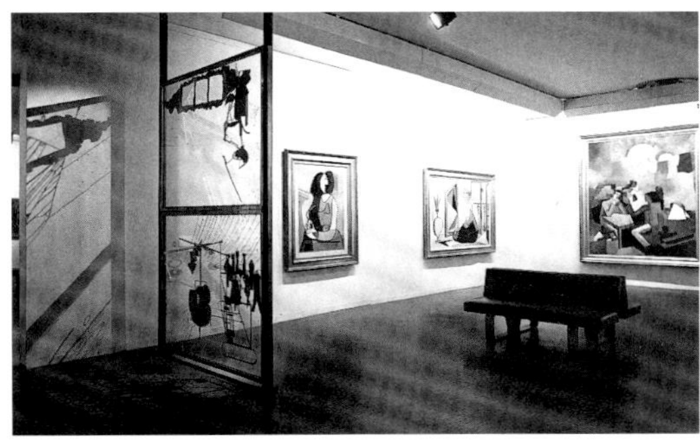

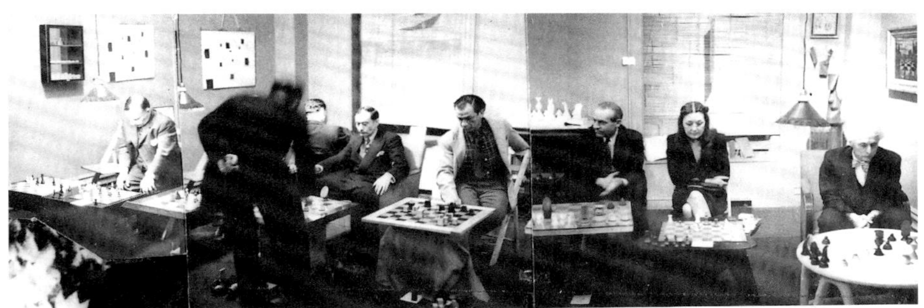

March 28–April 30 Cornell has a one-person exhibition, "Surrealist Objects," at Outlines, 222 Craft Avenue, Pittsburgh. Elizabeth Rockwell opened Outlines in October 1941 as a public gallery, library, and theater. An early multimedia alternative space, it features art exhibitions, a film and lecture series, avant-garde concerts, a lending library, gallery discussions, and classes. The gallery will close in 1947.

[Spring] Duchamp completes and signs *Boite-en-valise* XI/XX for Orin Raphael, the husband of Elizabeth Rockwell. The original artwork included is related to other versions of *Allégorie de genre.*

Spring to Winter Cornell works intermittently at the Garden Center, a large nursery on Northern Boulevard and 194th Street in Flushing, owned by a Christian Science practitioner. He begins a major "exploration," *GC 44*, centered around his love of nature.

May Dreier and Matta publish *Duchamp's Glass, La Mariée mise à nu par ses célibataires, même: An Analytical Reflection* (New York: Société Anonyme).

Reynolds moves back to 28 West 11th Street, New York.

May–September Cornell's graphic designs for *Dance Index* include the cover montages "European Dance Teachers in America" (vol. 3, nos. 4-6, May), "Le Quatuor dansé à Londres par Taglione, Charlotte Grisi, Cerrito et Fanny Elsler" (vol. 3, nos. 7/8, July), and "Three or Four Graces" (vol. 3, nos. 9/10/11, September).

May 24–October 15 Duchamp's *Large Glass* is included in the fifteenth anniversary exhibition "Art in Progress" at The Museum of Modern Art, New York. After the exhibition closes, the *Large Glass* will remain on view with the museum's permanent collection until April 1946.

October Douglas MacAgy, curator of the San Francisco Museum of Art, begins corresponding with Cornell about his film collection, and in February 1946, with his wife Jermayne (assistant director, California Palace of the Legion of Honor, San Francisco), he will begin purchasing artworks from Cornell. In 1955, John and Dominique de Menil will hire Jermayne MacAgy as the director of the Contemporary Arts Association, Houston. She will bequeath her collection, including five Cornell boxes, to The Menil Collection, Houston, upon her death in 1964.

December "Homage to the Salon D'Automne 1944 'Salon de la Liberation'" at Pierre Matisse Gallery, 41 East 57th Street, New York, includes Duchamp's *Allégorie de genre* (DD 114).

[December 9] Cornell visits Duchamp at the 14th Street studio and notes, on an envelope addressed to Duchamp, the address of Percy Rainford, a commercial photographer (DD 43).

December 12, 1944–January 31, 1945 "The Imagery of Chess: A Group Exhibition of Paintings, Sculpture, Newly Designed Chessmen, Music and Miscellany" opens at Julien Levy Gallery, New York. The exhibition, organized by Duchamp, includes chess sets designed by Breton, Alexander Calder, Ernst, Man Ray, Isamu Noguchi, and Tanguy, among others. Cornell is invited by Levy to contribute but does not participate.[14] On January 6, 1945, Duchamp will act as a referee for seven simultaneous chess games played by Levy, Kiesler, Barr, Xanti Schawinsky, Vittorio Rieti, Dorothea Tanning, and Ernst against the world champion of blindfold chess, George Koltanowski.

December 14 Reynolds writes to Cornell, addressing him as *Cher Amiral* (DD 9).

218 **André Breton, Duchamp, Max Ernst, and Leonora Carrington** with Morris Hirshfield's *Nude at the Window* (1941) in Peggy Guggenheim's townhouse, 440 East 51st Street, New York, c. 1942. Photograph by Matta. The Young-Mallin Archive, New York, A. Alpert Papers.

219 **Duchamp and Frederick Kiesler, "Twin-Touch-Test," *VVV Almanac for 1943*, (March 1943): inside back cover.**

220 **"The New You" featuring (clockwise from top) bottles from *Cléo de Merode* (1940); *A Pantry Ballet (for Jacques Offenbach* (1942); Untitled (Bébé Marie) (c. 1943); and *Legendary Portrait of Greta Garbo* (c. 1939) in *Mademoiselle,*** (March 1944): p. 130. Photograph by Leslie Gill at Julien Levy Gallery, 42 East 57th Street, New York. Joseph Cornell Study Center, Natl. Museum of American Art, Smithsonian. Gift of Mr. and Mrs. John A. Benton.

221 **Duchamp's *Large Glass* installed in "Art in Progress"** (May 24–October 15, 1944), The Museum of Modern Art, 11 West 53rd Street, New York.

222 **Duchamp (back to camera) referees seven simultaneous chess games** played by (left to right): Julien Levy (taking photograph), Frederick Kiesler, Alfred H. Barr, Jr., Xanti Schawinsky, Vittorio Rieti, Dorothea Tanning, and Max Ernst against George Koltanowski, world blindfold chess champion, at Julien Levy Gallery, 42 East 57th Street, New York, January 6, 1945. Photographs by Julien Levy; photographic assemblage by Dorothea Tanning.

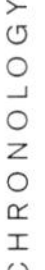

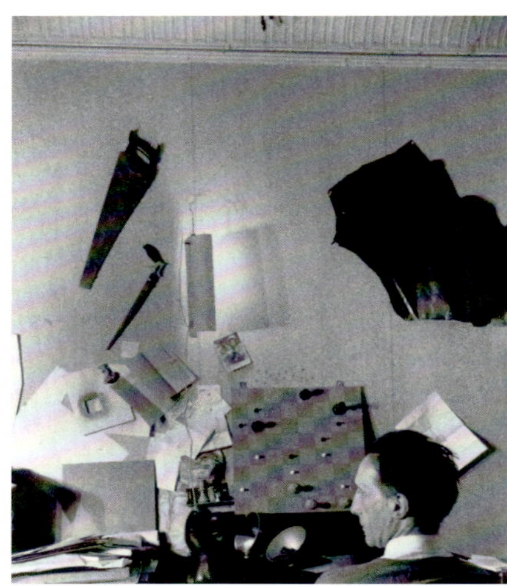

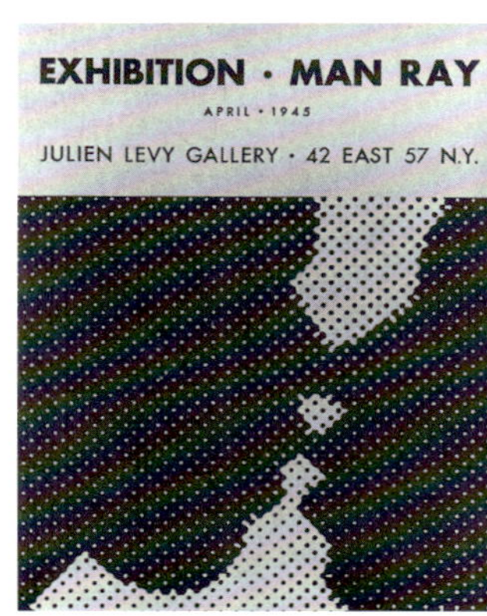

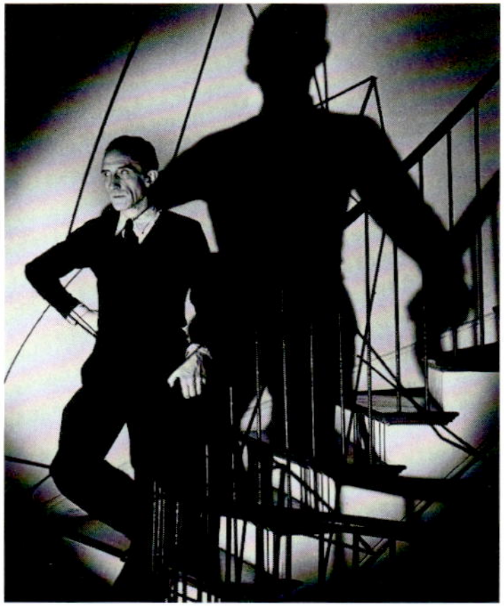

223 **Duchamp in his studio,** 210 West 14th Street, New York, 1945. Photograph by Percy Rainford.

224 **Duchamp, cover design for Man Ray's "Object of My Affection"** (April 10–30, 1945), Julien Levy Gallery, New York.

225 **Duchamp,** New York, 1946. Philadelphia Museum of Art, Marcel Duchamp Archive.

226 **Duchamp and Katherine Dreier,** The Haven, Milford, Connecticut, 1947. Philadelphia Museum of Art, Marcel Duchamp Archive.

227 **Cornell, "Clowns, Elephants and Ballerinas," cover design for *Dance Index*** (June 1946). Joseph Cornell Study Center, Natl. Museum of American Art, Smithsonian. Gift of Mr. and Mrs. John A. Benton.

228 **Window display featuring Duchamp artworks, La Hune Book Shop,** Paris, July 1946. Philadelphia Museum of Art, Marcel Duchamp Archive.

229 **Announcement for "Film Soiree: Selected Rarities from the Collection of Joseph Cornell,"** Norlyst Gallery, New York, March 2 and 16, 1947. The Young-Mallin Archive, New York.

1945

January 1 and 11 Rainford photographs Duchamp's 14th Street studio for Kiesler's contribution, "Les Larves d'Imagie d'Henri Robert Marcel Duchamp, poeme espace dédié à H(ieronymous) Duchamp," to *View* (series 5, no. 1, March, pp. 24–30).

January 15 Reynolds sends payment of $80 to Cornell for either three or four artworks: *Amiral Grillon (Watch), Mémoires inédits de Madame de Rochejaquelein*, one untitled sand tray or "Sailor's Box," and possibly a second untitled sand tray or "Sailor's Box" (DD 10).[15]

March *View* publishes an issue devoted to Duchamp, providing the first important illustrated anthology of writings on his work by numerous contributors. Cornell's *3/4 Bird's-Eye View of 'A Watch-Case for Marcel Duchamp'* is reproduced on p. 22. Cornell worked with an unidentified photographer to create the photomontage in which the inscription is in Duchamp's hand: *appartenant à l'amiral Grillon [belonging to Admiral Cricket].*

March 6 Guggenheim purchases an untitled Pharmacy box from Cornell.[16]

March 13–April 11 "European Artists in America" at the Whitney Museum of American Art, 10 West Eighth Street, New York, includes Duchamp's *Allégorie de genre*.

March 15 The editors of *View* host a cocktail party in honor of Duchamp's special issue (DD 57).

April 10–30 Duchamp designs the cover of the catalogue for the Man Ray exhibition "Objects of My Affection" at Julien Levy Gallery, New York.

April 19–26 Duchamp, Breton, and Matta design a window display for Breton's *Arcane 17* (New York: Brentano) at Brentano's, New York. The installation draws outcry from the League of Women, whose members are offended by Matta's depiction of a nude woman. The window is quickly remounted at Gotham Book Mart, 51 West 47th Street, New York. Duchamp's contribution, *Lazy Hardware,* consists of a headless female mannequin clothed in an apron with a water faucet attached to her right thigh. The wine bottle used on the cover of the Duchamp issue of *View* and a photograph of Duchamp "at the Age of 85" (with glasses) are part of the display.

April 26 Cornell receives a telegram inviting him the next day to sign, as a contributor, one hundred copies of the deluxe edition of the Duchamp issue of *View* (DD 58).

May–December Cornell's graphic designs include the cover for *Dance Index* (vol. 4, no. 5, May); the cover "Annetta Galletti, Louise Lamoureaux, Ermesilda Diana, Kate Penoyer, Joseph De Rosa" for *Dance Index* (vol. 4, nos. 6/7/8, June); the cover, a film scenario, and illustrations for "Hans Christian Andersen" for *Dance Index* (vol. 4, no. 9, September, pp. 139, 155–59); the cover "Around a Scene from Sadler Wells' 1943 Revival of The Swan Lake" for *Dance Index* (vol. 4, no. 10, October), and a Christmas card, based on a nineteenth-century astronomical engraving, for The Museum of Modern Art, New York.

June 17 Duchamp mails Cornell $3.75 with his signature on a money order receipt as a souvenir (DD 57).

Late June Reynolds returns to her home at 14 rue Hallé in Paris six weeks after VE day. She resumes her activities as a bookbinder and will serve as the Paris representative of *View* until 1947.

July *Vogue* (vol. 106, no. 1) devotes an issue to The Museum of Modern Art, New York. A color photograph by Erwin Blumenfeld of a model standing behind Duchamp's *Large Glass* appears on the cover (DD 103 and 104).

Fall Duchamp collaborates with Enrico Donati on the window display for Breton's *Le surréalisme et la peinture* (New York: Brentano, 2nd enlarged edition) at Brentano's, New York.

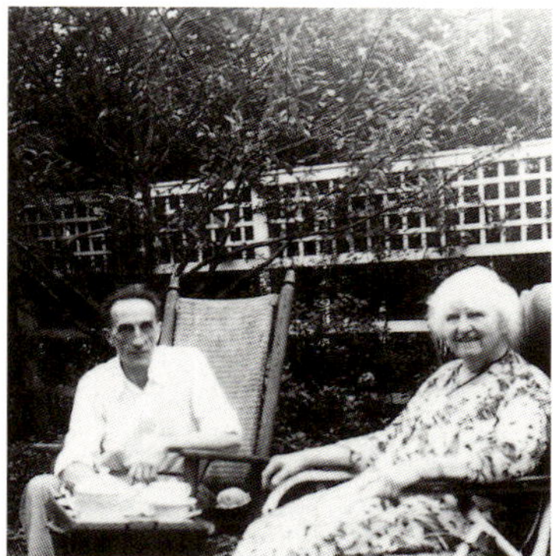

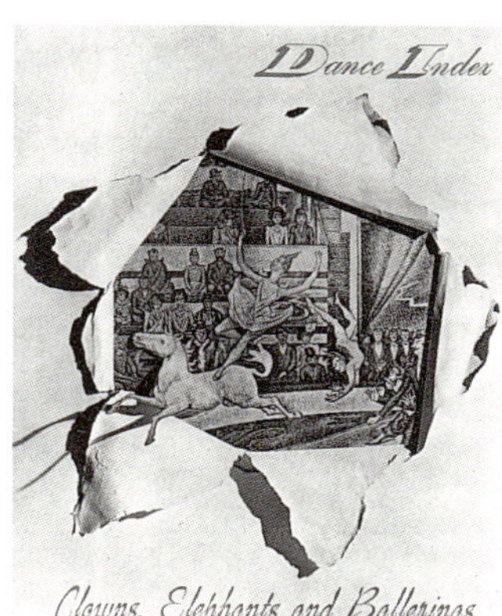

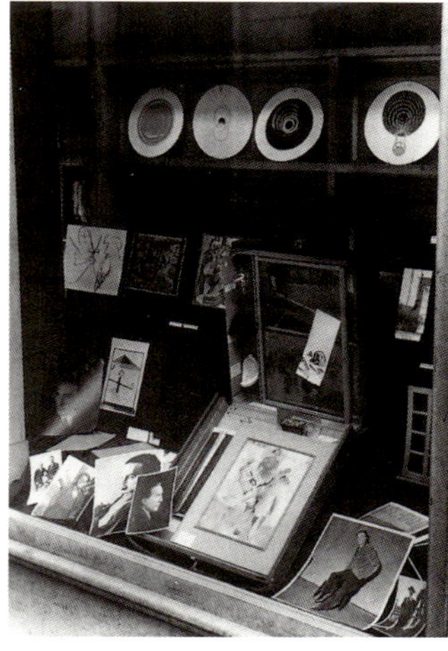

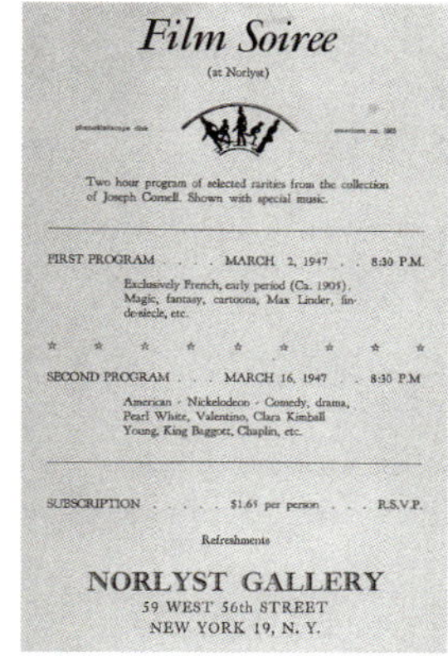

Film Soiree
(at Norlyst)

Two hour program of selected rarities from the collection of Joseph Cornell. Shown with special music.

FIRST PROGRAM . . . . MARCH 2, 1947 . . 8:30 P.M.
Exclusively French, early period (Ca. 1905). Magic, fantasy, cartoons, Max Linder, fin-de-siecle, etc.

☆ ☆ ☆ ☆ ☆ ☆ ☆ ☆ ☆

SECOND PROGRAM . . . MARCH 16, 1947 . . 8:30 P.M.
American - Nickelodeon - Comedy, drama, Pearl White, Valentino, Clara Kimball Young, King Baggott, Chaplin, etc.

SUBSCRIPTION . . . . . $1.65 per person . . . R.S.V.P.

Refreshments

NORLYST GALLERY
59 WEST 56th STREET
NEW YORK 19, N. Y.

September 12 Cornell submits an application to the John Simon Guggenheim Memorial Foundation, New York. The application includes statements of support from poet Marianne Moore, arts impresario Kirstein, and curator Monroe Wheeler of The Museum of Modern Art, New York. Cornell requests money to complete some new boxes as well as "a series of monographs presenting documents and notes on several subjects. . . . This material would be presented in individual boxed albums, or portfolios, designed to become units for exhibitions, both local and traveling. . . . There are also probabilities of publication."[17] He is not awarded the grant.

November 15 Hugo Gallery opens at 26 East 55th Street, New York, managed by Alexander Iolas with financial backing from Valentine Hugo.

November 26, 1945–February 17, 1946 Cornell has designed a special installation for his "exploration" *Portrait of Ondine* (c. 1940–late 1960s), which is presented in the Auditorium Gallery at The Museum of Modern Art, New York.

December Cornell receives a Christmas card from Reynolds (DD 41).

James Thrall Soby, assistant director, The Museum of Modern Art, New York, purchases Duchamp's *Le passage de la vierge à la mariée [The Passage from Virgin to Bride]* (1912) from Pach: Duchamp's first painting purchased by a museum.

December 31 Duchamp mails Cornell an invitation to lunch with him the following Friday. He instructs Cornell to bring "all the wood sticks and pieces we had made at one time for the boxes" because he is leaving America in April and wishes to put his affairs in order (DD 23).

1946

January 4 Cornell and Duchamp have lunch at Pappas Restaurant, 254 West 14th Street, New York (DD 97). Cornell returns the materials used in the assembly of the *Boite* edition that Duchamp requested earlier (see December 31 above). This meeting effectively ends Cornell's work on the edition. Between July 1942 and January 1946, Cornell aided in assembling as many as eleven *Boites-en-valise* (nos. V, VI, VII, VIII, IX, X, XI, XII, and three numbered zero for Dreier, Arensberg, and Boyle) and between twenty-five and thirty *Boites* (Series B).

February Charles Egan opens Egan Gallery at 63 East 57th Street, New York.

March 15 "'From the Dawn of Diamonds': An Art Exhibit which Traces the Origins of our Oldest Bridal Traditions, Created by Joseph Cornell" opens at the Park Lane Hotel, New York, for De Beers Consolidated Mines.

April Dreier moves to Laurel Manor at 130 West River Road, Milford, Connecticut. Duchamp paints the exterior of the elevator with the same floral motif as the wallpaper.

Duchamp designs the cover for Breton's new book of poems, *Young Cherry Trees Secured Against Hares* (New York: View), in which a die-cut obliterates the face of the Statue of Liberty and reveals a photographic portrait of Breton.

April 6 Duchamp completes and signs *Boite-en-valise* XII/XX for Martins.

April 30 Duchamp sends Cornell a farewell postcard (DD 33).

May 1 Reynolds writes to Cornell from Paris, thanking him for the care package that he has sent. She mentions that Duchamp is bringing with him two Cornell boxes that she had left in America (DD 80).

Duchamp sails on the SS *Brazil* to France.

Summer Duchamp completes *Boite-en-valise* XIII/XX for Matta.

June Cornell conceives and designs the cover "Clowns, Elephants and Ballerinas" for *Dance Index* (vol. 5, no. 6). He bases the cover design on Seurat's *Le Cirque* (DD 34 and 69).

Late July Duchamp and Reynolds visit Switzerland for five weeks; photographs of a small waterfall at Chexbres (near Lake Geneva) will develop into an element of the ongoing project *Étant donnés.*

December 3 "Romantic Museum at the Hugo Gallery / Portraits of Women: Constructions and Arrangements by Joseph Cornell" opens at Hugo Gallery, New York. Cornell designed an elaborate four-page brochure-style announcement for his first exhibition to feature many of his "explorations" and dossiers as well as box constructions, objects, and assorted source materials.

1947

January 13 Duchamp sails on the SS *Washington* to New York, where he will settle permanently, after arriving on January 22. He returns with some of the materials for his *Boite* edition that have been stored in France.

March 2 and 16 "Film Soiree: Selected Rarities from the Collection of Joseph Cornell" is presented at Norlyst Gallery, 59 West 56th Street, New York.

Spring The final issue (series 7, no. 3) of *View* appears.

May 5 Reynolds writes to Cornell from Rome, mentioning Cornell's lack of interest in exhibiting in the Duchamp-organized "Exposition Internationale du Surréalisme"; she also makes references to Cornell's film soirees (DD 84).

May 31 Art of This Century permanently closes. Guggenheim will move her collection to Venice, where she will settle permanently. The distribution of the *Boite* edition, which the gallery had been handling, passes now to Patricia Matta. She will

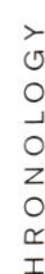

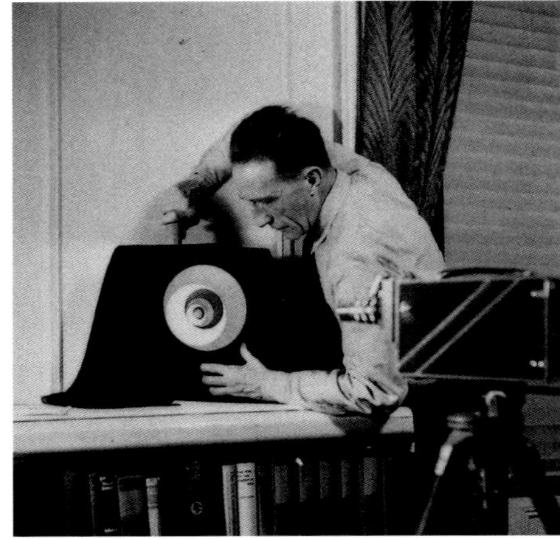

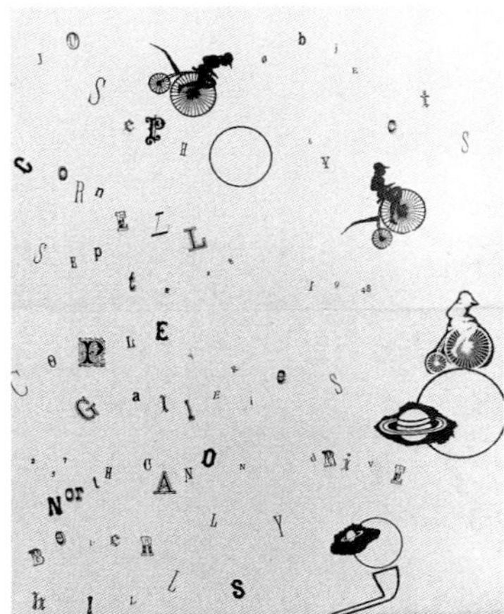

secure the services of Xenia Cage for the assembly of Series B examples of the *Boîte* edition until 1954. The remaining *Boîte* edition materials have been stored in Paris causing work on the edition to essentially stop between January 1946 and now.

July 8–October 5 "Exposition Internationale du Surréalisme," organized by Duchamp and Breton, is presented at Galerie Maeght, 13 rue de Téhéran, Paris. Duchamp is represented by two installations, both executed in absentia upon his instructions: *Le Rayon vert* and *The Juggler of Gravity*. Duchamp collaborated with Donati on the design for the catalogue, *Le Surréalisme en 1947* (Paris: Maeght Éditeur). The cover of the deluxe edition, consisting of hand-colored foam rubber "falsies" laid against black velvet, is labeled *Prière de toucher [Please Touch]*. *Allégorie de genre* is reproduced in the catalogue as pl. 36. Cornell was invited to participate, but chose not to (see May 5 above).

July 22 Reynolds writes to Cornell from Paris, thanking him for sending her the *Petit musée* box, which she had purchased from him, as well as another care package (DD 85).

September Cornell designs the cover and composes the contents and layout for the "Americana Romantic Ballet" issue of *Dance Index* (vol. 6, no. 9).

November 4 Reynolds writes to Cornell from Paris, thanking him for another care package (DD 81).

[December] Reynolds sends Cornell a late nineteenth-century multilevel cut paper tableau, identified as a Duchamp family "trophy" (DD 74).

December Duchamp completes his first known drawing relating to the nude female figure in *Étant donnés,* inscribing it to Martins: *Étant donnés: Maria, la chute d'eau et la gaz d'éclairage* (Moderna Museet, Stockholm).

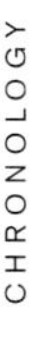

Cornell designs the layout "Make It from a Pattern for Your Dream-Child" featuring "Cindy" in five holiday wardrobe outfits for *Harper's Bazaar* (vol. 81, pp. 131–33). The photographer for the layout is Ernst Beadle, a fashion and interior photographer, who will develop a close, but short-lived friendship with Cornell.

1948

[Early in year] Duchamp completes a wax and pencil study with photographic collage (private collection) and soon after a vellum-and-gesso study for the nude figure in *Étant donnés* (Moderna Museet, Stockholm).

Duchamp completes and signs *Boîtes-en-valise* XIV/XX for Teeny Matisse, XV/XX for William Copley, and XVI/XX for John Ployardt (Copley's business partner).

January 28 Reynolds writes Cornell from Paris, thanking him for another care package (DD 82).

April Duchamp's *Rotorelief (disques optiques)* appears in the Hans Richter film *Dreams That Money Can Buy*.

Summer Martins moves to Paris, her husband's new diplomatic post.

June 1 Under Cornell's direction, Beadle photographs him in Central Park posed as if supporting a boulder that overhangs a small standing doll.

July *Good Housekeeping* (p. 33) publishes Frank Sullivan's article, "What did you collect?" accompanied by a layout of memorabilia designed by Cornell and photographed by Beadle.

August Duchamp completes and signs *Boîte-en-valise* XVII/XX for Yale University Art Gallery, New Haven.

Late September Reynolds returns to New York after spending the summer with her family on Lake Basswood, Minnesota. She stays at the Madison Square Hotel, 26th Street and Madison Avenue, writing from there to Cornell, asking to see him before she returns to Paris on October 13.[18]

September 28 "Objects by Joseph Cornell" opens at the Copley Galleries, 257 North Canon Drive, Beverly Hills, California. Cornell exhibits forty-two works from the 1930s and 1940s. Copley, a newspaper heir and later an artist (CPLY) and Ployardt, then his brother-in-law, opened the gallery earlier in the month with an exhibition of René Magritte; it will present at least five exhibitions before closing in March 1949. Copley and Ployardt met Cornell at Hugo Gallery the previous year.

December 25 Reynolds writes to Cornell from Paris, answering his questions about how to say "yours truly" in French. In her letter, she mentions the disagreement over Kiesler's inflammatory letter accusing Matta of being responsible for Arshile Gorky's suicide (DD 83).

1949

January 21 and March 4 Cornell presents an evening soiree of film and music from his collection, "Early Films from the Unique Collection of Joseph Cornell," at The Subjects of the Artist, New Art School, 35 East Eighth Street, New York. Cornell has a falling out with Motherwell, who embarrasses him by insisting he speak to the audience. Motherwell is one of the founders of the school.

April Julien Levy Gallery permanently closes.

April 8–10 Duchamp participates in a three-day session of the Western Round Table on Modern Art, organized by Douglas MacAgy (now director, California School of Fine Arts, San Francisco) and sponsored by the San Francisco Art Association. Other panelists include anthropologist Gregory Bateson; critics Kenneth Burke, Alfred Frankenstein, and Robert Goldwater; composer Darius Milhaud; museum curator Andrew Ritchie; artist Mark Tobey; and architect Frank Lloyd Wright,

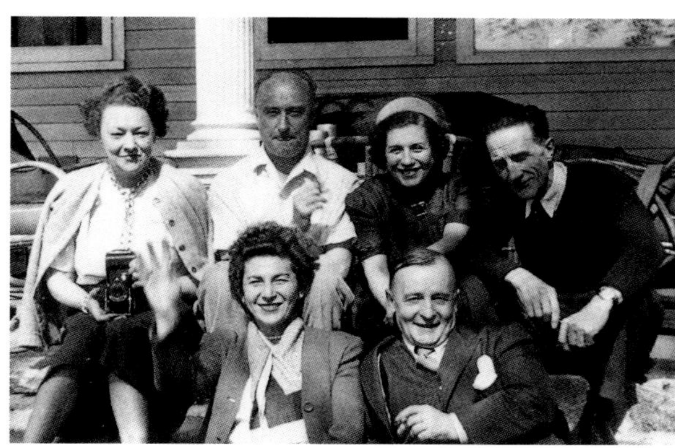

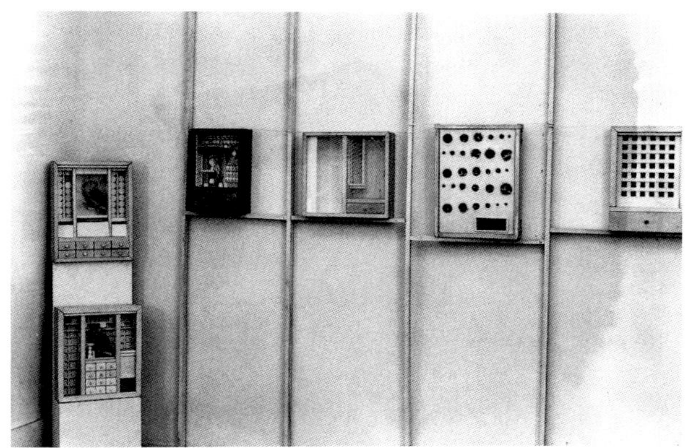

with philosopher George Boas of Johns Hopkins University as moderator.

April 12–25 After the Western Round Table symposium, Duchamp visits the Arensbergs in Hollywood.

Summer Duchamp completes and signs *Boites-en-valise* XVIII/XX for Hélène and Henri Hoppenot, XIX/XX for Marguerite Hagenbach, and XX/XX for the Stedelijk Museum, Amsterdam, thus concluding the twenty-four deluxe editions.

July 2 Cornell shows selections from his film collection at the New York studio of Beadle and his wife, Ginny.

October 20–December 18 "Twentieth Century Art from the Louise and Walter Arensberg Collection" is presented at The Art Institute of Chicago. The exhibition includes thirty Duchamp artworks. Duchamp attends the opening in lieu of the Arensbergs. The Art Institute hopes to acquire the collection and Duchamp is supportive, but the Arensbergs are ultimately unhappy with the installation and their perceived treatment.

November 14–December 5 "La Lanterne Magique du Ballet Romantique of Joseph Cornell" is presented at Hugo Gallery, New York. The exhibition is shown simultaneously with "Décors for Ballets Choreographed by Roland Petit."

December 7, 1949–January 7, 1950 "Aviary by Joseph Cornell" is installed by Cornell and presented at Egan Gallery, New York.

1950

Late April Reynolds is admitted to the American Hospital in Neuilly-sur-Seine (a Paris suburb) with uremic poisoning. Suspecting cancer, Duchamp is greatly alarmed by her condition and will write often to Roché inquiring about her state of mind and health.

June *Collection of the Société Anonyme: Museum of Modern Art 1920* is published by Yale University Press.

June 5–November 4 Librarian Maria Cimino organizes "The Fairy Tale World," an installation of Cornell's work for the Central Children's Room, New York Public Library, 42nd Street and Fifth Avenue, New York. The presentation includes seven unidentified boxes, two castles, a *Swan Lake* box, and *Ondine on Seashell.*

July Cornell designs the layout "Collage of Newport" for *Mademoiselle* (vol. 31, no. 3, pp. 70–71).

September 19 Duchamp travels to Paris to visit a gravely ill Reynolds, who will die at home on September 30. Duchamp will attend to all the funeral arrangements including her cremation, as well as emptying her house of all her possessions. Reynolds' brother, Hubachek, upon Duchamp's advice, will donate the following year her library and her bookbindings to the Ryerson Library at The Art Institute of Chicago. While in Paris, Duchamp will also arrange for the remainder of the material for approximately 180 examples of the *Boite* edition to be shipped to New York. He will return to New York on December 2.

November 28 Cornell learns of Reynolds' death when he receives a letter from Loy.[19]

December 1, 1950–January 13, 1951 "Night Songs and Other New Work–1950 by Joseph Cornell" is presented at Egan Gallery, New York. In late January 1951, The Museum of Modern Art, New York, will acquire Cornell's box *Central Park Carrousel–1950, In Memoriam* for $300 from the exhibition.

December 28 The Arensbergs sign a deed of gift, presenting their collection of twentieth-century art and pre-Columbian sculpture to the Philadelphia Museum of Art.

230 **Duchamp preparing his *Rotorelief (disques optiques)* (1935) for filming of Hans Richter's *Dreams That Money Can Buy,*** New York, 1948. Philadelphia Museum of Art, Marcel Duchamp Archive.

231 **Cornell, announcement for "Objects by Joseph Cornell"** (September 1948), Copley Galleries, Beverly Hills, California. Joseph Cornell Study Center, Natl. Museum of American Art, Smithsonian.

232 **Weekend house party** (front row, left to right: Claire Donati, Frederick Kiesler; back row, left to right: Kay Sage, Yves Tanguy, Maria Martins, Duchamp), at home of Yves Tanguy and Kay Sage, Woodbury, Connecticut, May 23, 1948. Photograph by Enrico Donati. Philadelphia Museum of Art, Marcel Duchamp Archive.

233 **Cornell's installation of "Aviary by Joseph Cornell"** (December 7, 1949–January 7, 1950), Egan Gallery, 63 East 57th Street, New York. Photograph by Aaron Siskind.

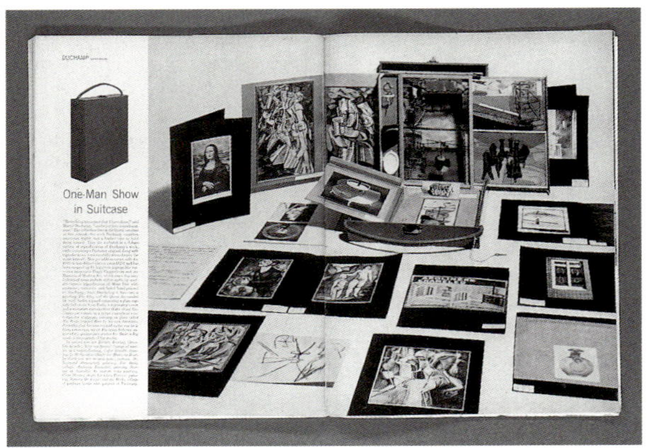

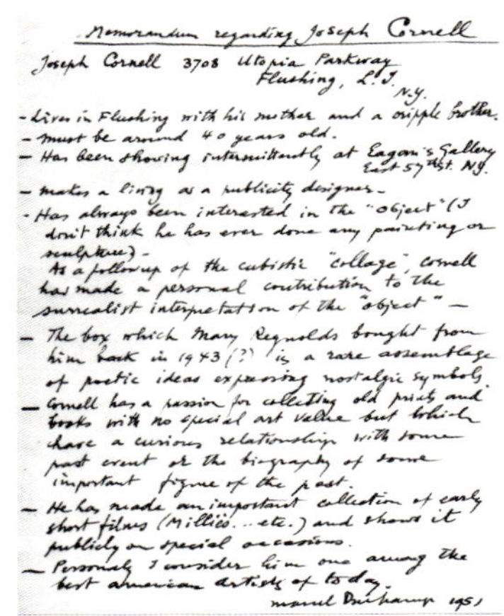
Memorandum regarding Joseph Cornell

Joseph Cornell 3708 Utopia Parkway
Flushing, L.I.
N.Y.

- Lives in Flushing with his mother and a cripple brother.
- must be around 40 years old.
- Has been showing intermittently at Eagon's Gallery
East 57th St. N.Y.

- makes a living as a publicity designer.
- Has always been interested in the "object" (I don't think he has ever done any painting or sculpture) -
As a follow up of the cubistic "collage", Cornell has made a personal contribution to the surrealist interpretation of the "object" -
- The box which Mary Reynolds bought from him back in 1943 (?) is a rare assemblage of poetic ideas expressing nostalgic symbols.
- Cornell has a passion for collecting old prints and books with no special art value but which have a curious relationship with some past event or the biography of some important figure of the past.
- He has made an important collection of early short films (Milliès... etc.) and shows it publicly on special occasions.
- Personaly I consider him one among the best american artists of today.

Marcel Duchamp 1951

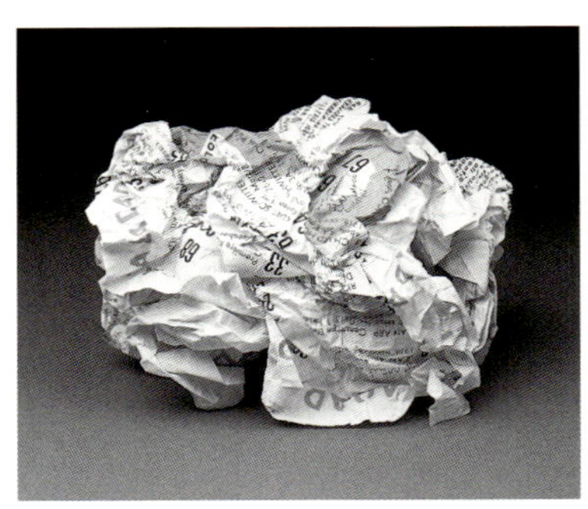

234 ***Boîte-en-valise* IX/XX reproduced in *Life*** (28 April 1952). Photograph by Eliot Elisofon.

235 Duchamp, "Memorandum regarding Joseph Cornell," 9 July 1951. Mary Reynolds Collection, The Art Institute of Chicago.

236 Duchamp, crumpled exhibition catalogue for "DADA 1916–1923" (April 15–May 9, 1953), Sidney Janis Gallery, New York. Philadelphia Museum of Art, Marcel Duchamp Archive.

237 Cornell, announcement design for "Winter Night Skies by Joseph Cornell" (December 12, 1955–January 13, 1956), Stable Gallery, New York.

238 Duchamp, Mary Reynolds book plate, 1951. Mary Reynolds Collection, The Art Institute of Chicago.

239 Duchamp and Teeny, American Federation of Arts convention, Houston, April 1957.

1951

July 9 Duchamp writes "Memorandum regarding Joseph Cornell," including "everything that came to mind," for the object files of the twentieth-century department of The Art Institute of Chicago at the request of Hubachek, who has given the museum an untitled sand tray by Cornell from his sister Reynolds' collection.[20]

Fall Duchamp renews his acquaintance with Teeny Matisse at her country house in Lebanon, New Jersey, as a weekend guest with Ernst and Tanning. Soon after, Duchamp and Teeny sublet Ernst and Tanning's apartment at 327 East 58th Street, New York, which will remain their home until 1959.

November 26 Duchamp telegrams Cornell to invite him to lunch with him and Louis Carré, the French art dealer, on Thursday, November 29, at twelve-thirty p.m.[21]

Late in year Curator Dorothy Miller asks Cornell to participate in "Fifteen Americans," an exhibition at The Museum of Modern Art, New York, scheduled to open in April of the following year; he declines the offer, stating there is not enough time to create a special environment.

1952

February Distribution of the *Boîte* edition passes to Rose Fried Gallery, 40 East 68th Street, New York, and will remain its responsibility until 1954.

March 29 Dreier dies. Duchamp is one of three executors of her will. He will take on the disbursement of her collection over the following year to numerous institutions, including Yale University Art Gallery, New Haven; The Museum of Modern Art, New York; Solomon R. Guggenheim Museum, New York; and the Philadelphia Museum of Art, to which he presents the *Large Glass.*

1953

February 10–March 28 "Night Voyage by Joseph Cornell" is presented at Egan Gallery, New York.

April 15–May 9 Duchamp has organized "DADA 1916–1923" at Sidney Janis Gallery, 15 East 57th Street, New York. He designed the catalogue/poster on a single sheet of tissue paper, which is crumpled into a ball. At the opening, the crumpled catalogues are placed in a basket near the door and visitors are asked to help themselves.

May 30 Duchamp mails Cornell a postcard of the *Mona Lisa* (DD 50).

July 12–August 30 "Joseph Cornell," organized by H. H. Arnason and presented at the Walker Art Center, Minneapolis, is Cornell's first one-person museum exhibition. Motherwell wrote an essay for the occasion, but the exhibition catalogue is not published; Motherwell's essay will remain unpublished until 1976.[22]

November Soby donates Cornell's *Taglioni's Jewel Casket* (1940) to The Museum of Modern Art, New York.

November 25 Louise Arensberg dies, followed by Walter Arensberg on January 29, 1954.

1954

Cornell publishes a limited edition of *Maria* (a pamphlet inspired by the nineteenth-century opera singer Maria Malibran-Garcia), and the following year he will publish a limited edition of *the Bel Canto Pet* (a pamphlet inspired by the nineteenth-century opera singer Julia Grisi). Comprising excerpts from the translated writings of German author Elise Polko and American author Nathaniel Parker Willis, respectively, the individual examples include collage inserts, personalized inscriptions, and Cornell's signature and a date. He will distribute them, primarily to friends, until his death.

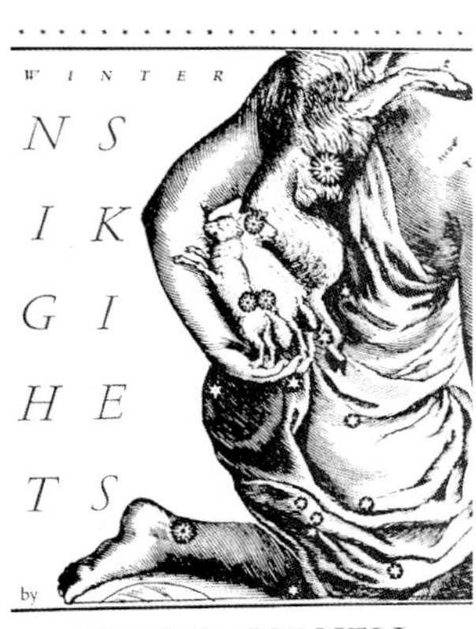

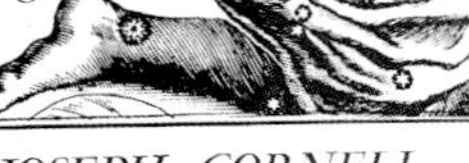
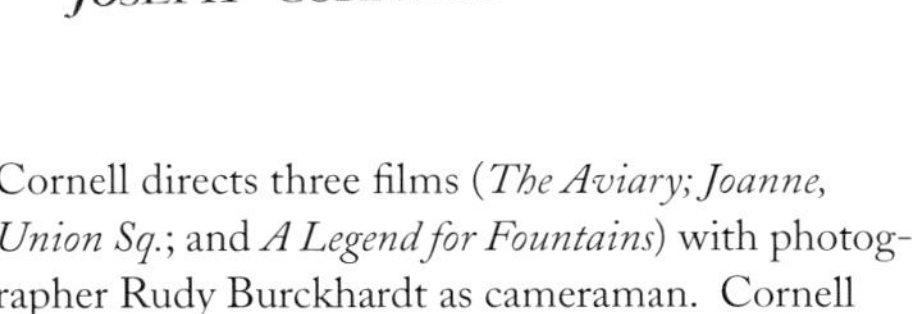

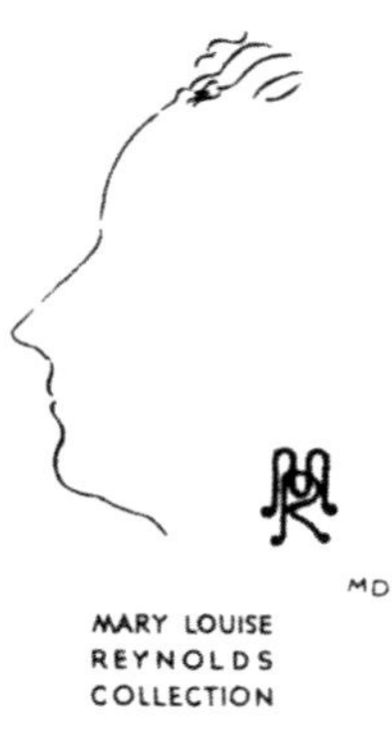

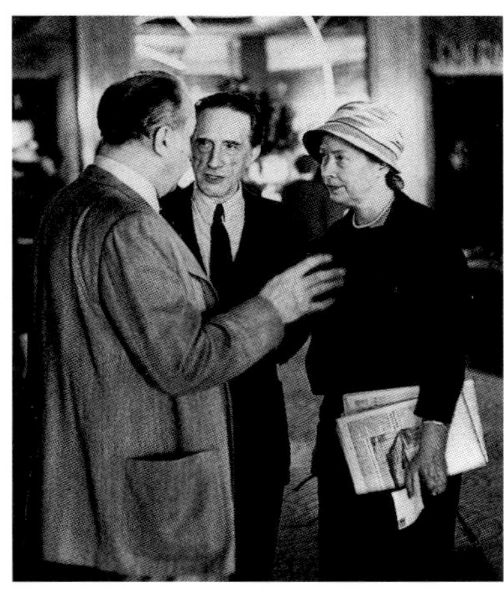

Cornell directs three films (*The Aviary; Joanne, Union Sq.*; and *A Legend for Fountains*) with photographer Rudy Burckhardt as cameraman. Cornell had met Burckhardt through Motherwell in 1949.

January 16 Duchamp marries Teeny in New York and acquires a family of three stepchildren: Jacqueline, Paul, and Peter.

January 27–February 20 Cornell begins exhibiting at Eleanor Ward's Stable Gallery, 924 Seventh Avenue, New York, in the gallery's "Third Annual Exhibition of Painting and Sculpture." Robert Rauschenberg, who had met Cornell at Egan Gallery, encouraged him to submit a box construction for the occasion.

October 15 The permanent exhibition of the Louise and Walter Arensberg Collection opens at the Philadelphia Museum of Art; a comprehensive catalogue is published. Henry Clifford installed the exhibition with Duchamp's assistance. The *Large Glass* was also installed at this time.

December Cornell designs The Museum of Modern Art's Christmas card "Constellation."

Duchamp asks publisher, author, and book designer Iliazd (Ilia Zdanevitch) to redesign the container for the *Boîte* edition. In March 1955, Duchamp will send the remaining materials for the *Boîte* edition from New York to Paris. Between March 1955 and early 1958, Iliazd will assemble thirty examples of Series C of the *Boîte* edition.

1955

Tanning, whom Cornell had met in 1943, writes Cornell from Huismes (southern France) to tell him that he "may soon get some business mail from Paris—a very nice gallery (Max's gallery too) wants to make an exhibition of the boxes and I believe Duchamp will consult with you about the choice of material."[23]

Cornell sends Duchamp a note describing his enclosed design for a "*thaumotrope à l'image à Apollinaire en travestie* [thaumotrope in the likeness of Apollinaire]." [24]

April 2–June Cornell lends boxes and memorabilia for the exhibition "Hans Christian Andersen" at the New York Public Library Children's Room.

April 3 Duchamp writes Cornell, reminding him of his promised repair to one of his boxes owned by the Hoppenots.[25]

May Cornell directs two films, *GniR RednoW [Wonder Ring]* and *Centuries of June*, respectively based on the Third Avenue el and a Flushing homestead, both scheduled for demolition. Independent filmmaker Stan Brakhage, whom Cornell met the year before through Tyler, is the cameraman.

Fall Cornell resumes making collages as independent, two-dimensional works. They are based on clippings from contemporary books, magazines, and commercial art reproductions. By 1959, his interest will escalate.

December 12, 1955–January 13, 1956 "Winter Night Skies by Joseph Cornell" is presented at Stable Gallery, New York.

December 30 Duchamp becomes a naturalized United States citizen.

1956

The Art Institute of Chicago publishes *Surrealism and Its Affinities*, a catalogue by Hugh Edwards of the Mary Reynolds Collection of rare books, periodicals, and her own bookbinding. Duchamp contributes the preface and designs the bookplate.

November 1–15 Cornell presents his "exploration" *Portrait of Ondine* in revised form at the One-Wall Gallery, Wittenborn Bookstore, 1018 Madison Avenue, New York.

1957

Cornell directs two films, *Nymphlight* and *Angel*, with Burckhardt as cameraman.

April 3–11 Duchamp delivers "The Creative Act" as part of a symposium at the American Federation of Arts convention, Shamrock Hilton Hotel, Houston. Concurrent with the convention, "Jacques Villon, Raymond Duchamp-Villon, Marcel Duchamp," an exhibition organized by Sweeney for the Solomon R. Guggenheim Museum, New York, is on view at The Museum of Fine Arts, Houston, where Sweeney has recently become director.

May 7–June 8 Cornell participates in the "Sixth Annual Exhibition of Painting and Sculpture" at Stable Gallery, New York.

December Cornell designs The Museum of Modern Art's Christmas card entitled "Carrousel." He also presents a special screening of his films to the staff of the Picture Collection, New York Public Library.

December 2–31 "Joseph Cornell: Selected Works" is presented at Stable Gallery, New York.

1958

Cornell begins to hire young people to help reorganize his work and storage areas in the house; he asks some with carpentry skills to help build the wood shells of his boxes.

Marchand du Sel, écrits de Marcel Duchamp [Salt Seller, Writings of Marcel Duchamp] (Paris: Le Terrain Vague), compiled by Michel Sanouillet, is published. It is the most comprehensive collection to date of Duchamp's writings and statements, with a bibliography by Yves Poupard-Lieussou.

Lefebvre-Foinet, Paris, a well-known supplier of artist's equipment, takes over distribution of the *Boîte* edition. It will remain their responsibility until the mid 1970s.

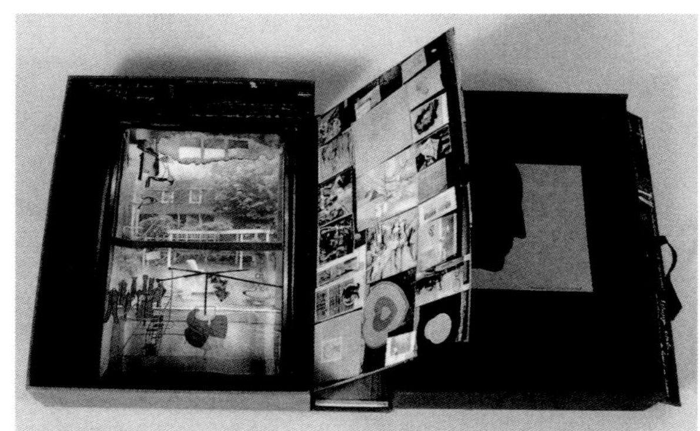

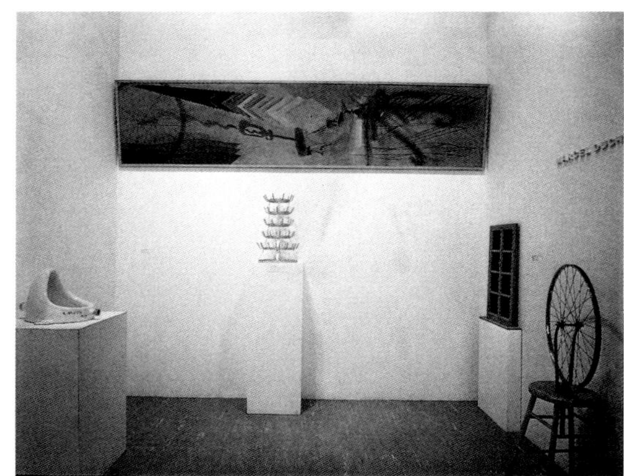

Summer Duchamp and Teeny begin to summer in Cadaqués, on the Costa Brava, Spain, with frequent visits to Paris. The wood door for the exterior of *Étant donnés* will be chosen here.

December 5, 1958–February 8, 1959 "The 1958 Pittsburgh Bicentennial International Exhibition of Contemporary Painting and Sculpture" is held at the Carnegie Institute. Duchamp and Teeny purchase an untitled sand fountain by Cornell from the exhibition.

Late in year Cornell directs the film *Seraphina's Garden* with Burckhardt as cameraman.

1959

Duchamp and Teeny move to an apartment at 28 West 10th Street, New York, which will remain their home until Duchamp's death.

Marcel Jean publishes *Histoire de la peinture surréaliste [History of Surrealist Painting]* (Paris: Editions de Seuil; an English translation follows a year later) in which he discusses both Duchamp and Cornell. Jean contacts Cornell upon Duchamp's advice and after seeing Cornell's artwork in Duchamp's apartment.[26]

January 12–February 6 Cornell and Duchamp participate in "Art and the Found Object" at the Time-Life Building, 9 Rockefeller Center, New York, an exhibition organized by the American Federation of Arts. Rauschenberg purchases a version of *Bottle Rack* (1914/1960) from the exhibition for $3.

March 2 Cornell and Duchamp both attend the opening of a René Magritte exhibition at Alexander Iolas Gallery, 123 East 55 Street, New York.

Spring Walter Hopps and Irving Blum, partners in Ferus Gallery, 723 North La Cienega Boulevard, Los Angeles, meet Cornell on separate occasions and begin buying his boxes and collages for the gallery. Ferus was opened by Hopps and Edward Kienholz in March 1957, and Blum became a third partner in 1958.

April Cornell and Duchamp both attend the opening of a Mina Loy exhibition at Bodley Gallery, 223 East 60th Street, New York.

April 6–May 2 A Duchamp one-person exhibition is presented by Sidney Janis Gallery, New York, on the occasion of the publication of *Sur Marcel Duchamp [On Marcel Duchamp]* (Paris: Trianon Press), a monograph and the first catalogue raisonné by Robert Lebel. The deluxe edition is in a box format with a facsimile readymade of a French apartment building sign: "*Eau & Gaz à tous les étages* [Water and Gas on Every Floor]."

September Italian artist Piero Dorazio facilitates Cornell's introduction to Chicago collectors Lindy and Edwin Bergman. Already actively acquiring Surrealist art and Cornell boxes, the Bergmans will become the principal patrons of his work. In 1982, the Bergmans will donate thirty-seven Cornell boxes and collages to The Art Institute of Chicago, which will open on June 8, 1983, the long-term installation "The Lindy and Edwin Bergman Joseph Cornell Collection," featuring their gift and thirty additional Cornell works from their private collection.

November 20–December 15 The exhibition "Selected Works by Joseph Cornell: Bonitas Solstitialis and an Exploration of the Colombier" is presented at Bennington College, Vermont. It is Cornell's first public opportunity to share his source materials with students, a goal he had formulated during the early 1940s.

1960

Summer In Paris, Jacqueline Matisse takes over the assembling of the *Boite* edition, completing Series D-G of the edition.

November 28, 1960–January 14, 1961 "Surrealist Intrusion in the Enchanters' Domain," organized by Duchamp and Breton, is presented at D'Arcy Galleries, 1091 Madison Avenue, New York. Duchamp, who designed the catalogue cover, is represented by *Pharmacie, Coin de chasteté [Wedge of Chastity]* (1954), and his *Environment for the Enchanter's Domain*. Duchamp also included examples of Cornell's boxes in the exhibition.

Late in year *The Bride Stripped Bare by Her Bachelors, Even* (London: Percy Lund, Humphries and Co., Ltd.), an English translation of the *Green Box* by George Heard Hamilton, is published with a typographic rendering by Richard Hamilton, in collaboration with Duchamp.

1961

Cornell hires assistants to help scout for materials, sort his papers and books, and clip magazines for his collage work.

May 17–September 3 Duchamp participates in the "Rörelse I konsten [Art in Motion]" exhibition at Moderna Museet, Stockholm. He agrees to a replica of the *Large Glass* that Ulf Linde fabricates.

October 2–November 12 "The Art of Assemblage," organized by William Seitz, is presented at The Museum of Modern Art, New York. Seitz devotes individual rooms in the exhibition to Cornell, Duchamp, and Kurt Schwitters. On October 19 Duchamp participates in a symposium at the museum in conjunction with the exhibition. Lawrence Alloway, Richard Huelsenbeck, Rauschenberg, and Roger Shattuck are panelists, with Seitz as moderator.

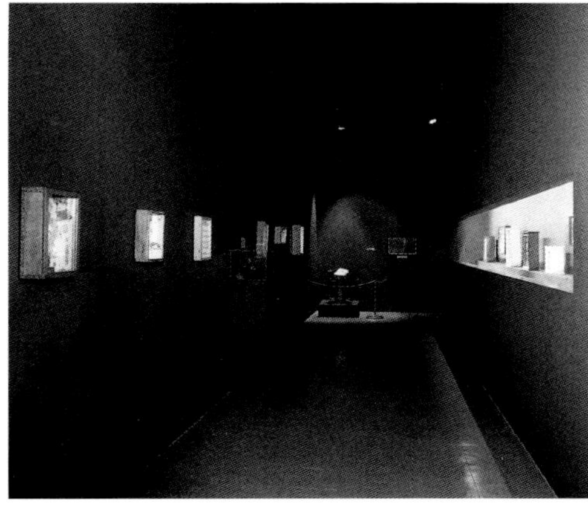

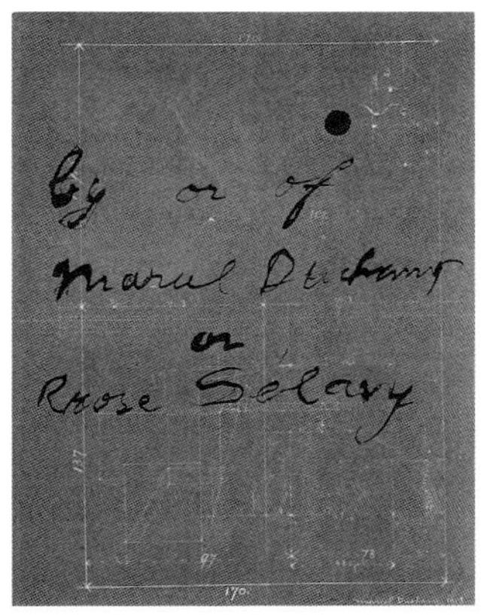

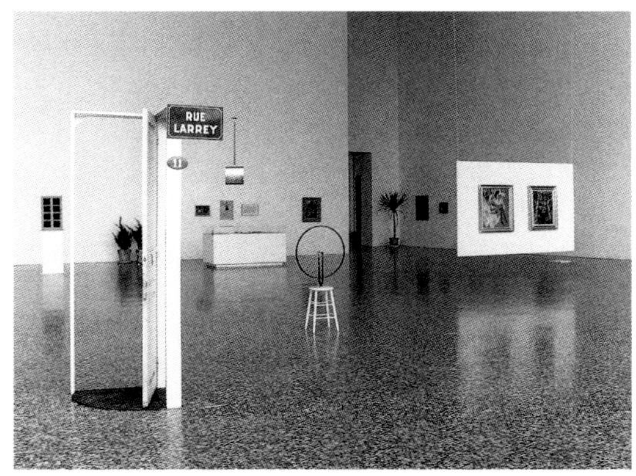

1962

December 10 "Joseph Cornell" opens at Ferus Gallery, Los Angeles, organized by Blum. By this time, Hopps has sold his share in the gallery to Blum and become a curator at the Pasadena Art Museum, Pasadena, California.

1963

April 26–27 Cornell presents "Comedy Americana: A Series of Film Programs from the Collection of Joseph Cornell" at artists Walter de Maria's and Robert Whitman's loft, 9 Great Jones Street, New York.

October 8–November 3 Hopps presents the first retrospective exhibition of Duchamp's work, "by or of Marcel Duchamp or Rrose Sélavy" at the Pasadena Art Museum, Pasadena, California. Duchamp designed the invitation, poster, and catalogue cover. Duchamp is photographed in the exhibition playing chess with a nude Eve Babitz, who will also correspond with Cornell around this time.

1964

June 5–September 30 Duchamp supervises the production of fourteen readymades in editions of eight signed and numbered copies for Galleria Schwarz, Milan, on the occasion of the exhibition "Omaggio a Marcel Duchamp."

1965

January 14–February 13 "NOT SEEN and / or LESS SEEN of / by MARCEL DUCHAMP / RROSE SELAVY 1904–1964" is presented at Cordier & Ekstrom Inc., 978 Madison Avenue, New York. For the opening dinner on January 13, Duchamp pastes a *Mona Lisa* playing card on approximately one hundred printed invitations, signing and inscribing them *rasée [shaved]*. The exhibition will travel to The Museum of Fine Arts, Houston, later in February.

February 26 Cornell's brother, Robert, dies.

March 20 Teeny Duchamp sends Cornell a condolence note on Robert's death.[27]

Late in Year Duchamp moves *Étant donnés* from the 14th Street studio to a commercial building at 80 East 11th Street, Room 403, New York.

1966

Duchamp signs *Étant donnés*, marking completion of the tableau.

January 4–29 Cornell arranges the exhibition "Robert Cornell: Memorial Exhibition, Drawings by Robert Cornell, Collages by Joseph Cornell, Related Varia" at Robert Schoelkopf Gallery, 825 Madison Avenue, New York.

June 18–July 31 "The Almost Complete Works of Marcel Duchamp," organized by Richard Hamilton, is presented at the Tate Gallery, London. Earlier in the year, Duchamp agreed to another replica of the *Large Glass* to be fabricated by Hamilton. Hamilton acquired funding for the fabrication from the Bill and Noma Copley Foundation.

October 19 Cornell's mother dies.

December 27, 1966–February 11, 1967 "An Exhibition of Works by Joseph Cornell," his first retrospective, organized by Hopps, is presented at the Pasadena Art Museum, Pasadena, California. The catalogue reprints Fairfield Porter's essay, "Joseph Cornell," which had first appeared in *Art and Literature* (no. 8, Spring 1966, pp. 8, 120–30). Cornell considers Porter's essay to be one of the few intelligent assessments of his work.

240 Robert Lebel, *Sur Marcel Duchamp* (Paris: Trianon Press), deluxe edition, 1959 (opened).

241 Duchamp gallery, "The Art of Assemblage" (October 2–November 12, 1961), The Museum of Modern Art, 11 West 53rd Street, New York.

242 Cornell gallery, "The Art of Assemblage" (October 2–November 12, 1961), The Museum of Modern Art, 11 West 53rd Street, New York.

243 Duchamp, cover design for retrospective exhibition catalogue *by or of Marcel Duchamp or Rrose Sélavy* (October 8–November 3, 1963), Pasadena Museum of Art, Pasadena, California.

244 "NOT SEEN and/or LESS SEEN of/by MARCEL DUCHAMP/RROSE SELAVY, 1904–1964" (February 24–March 28, 1965), The Museum of Fine Arts, 1001 Bissonnet Street, Houston, installation view.

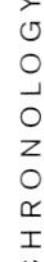

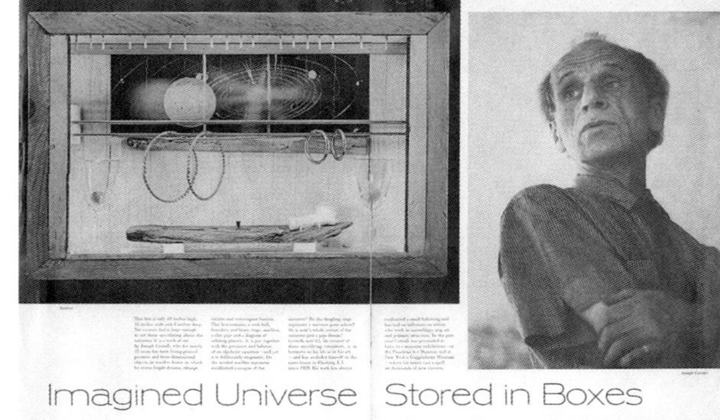

245 **Duchamp, *à l'infinitif [In the Infinitive] (White Box)* (detail), 1967.**

246 **"Imagined Universe Stored in Boxes" featuring *Sun Box* (c. 1956)** ***Life*** (15 December 1967): pp. 52–53.

247 **Duchamp,** 28 West 10th Street apartment, New York, May 1959. Photograph by Alexander Liberman.

248 **Cornell with Untitled (Bébé Marie) (c. 1943),** 3708 Utopia Parkway, Flushing, New York, 1969. Photograph by Duane Michals.

1967

Duchamp writes notes and assembles photographs for an instruction manual on dismantling and reassembling *Étant donnés.*

February 14–March 4 The exhibition "A l'Infinitif" at Cordier & Ekstrom Inc., New York, coincides with publication of a facsimile collection of Duchamp's unpublished notes from 1912 to 1920 in the limited edition box *à l'infinitif [In the Infinitive]* (New York: Cordier & Ekstrom), also known as the *White Box.*

May 4–June 25 "Joseph Cornell," a retrospective exhibition organized by Diane Waldman, is presented at the Solomon R. Guggenheim Museum, 1071 Fifth Avenue, New York. The exhibition catalogue provides the first scholarly discussion of the chronology and themes of Cornell's work.

1968

March 27–June 29 Duchamp and Cornell participate in "Dada, Surrealism, and Their Heritage," organized by William S. Rubin at The Museum of Modern Art, New York. The exhibition includes thirteen works by Duchamp and seven by Cornell, including Untitled (Pharmacy), loaned by Teeny Duchamp.

Before Summer Duchamp takes Copley to see *Étant donnés* in the 11th Street studio and expresses his desire that the completed assemblage be presented to the Philadelphia Museum of Art after his death in the name of the Cassandra Foundation (established by Copley), which acquires the work from Duchamp.

October 2 Duchamp dies at home in Neuilly-sur-Seine of heart failure after dinner with his wife, Teeny, Lebel, Man Ray, and his wife, Juliet.

October 8 Cornell, after learning of Duchamp's death on the radio, drafts a condolence note to Teeny Duchamp. His diary entries recall Duchamp's passing in Paris.[28]

October 14 Teeny Duchamp responds to Cornell's condolence note and asks him to help her circulate the following statement: *Je demande que pendant six mois il n'y ait aucune manifestation ou hommage à Marcel. Dimarche le 13 Octobre 1968 [I request that during the next six months there be no ceremony or homage to Marcel. Thursday, October 13].* The following week she will telephone Cornell, and in April of the following year, when she is next in America, she will visit him.[29]

1969

July 7 The public opening of *Étant donnés*, installed with the Arensberg Collection, is held at the Philadelphia Museum of Art. The work, which was disassembled according to Duchamp's instruction manual, has now been reassembled by Paul Matisse in collaboration with the museum staff. To celebrate the occasion, the museum publishes *Étant Donnés. . .Reflections on a New Work* (Philadelphia Museum of Art Bulletin, vol. 64, nos. 299 and 300) by Anne d'Harnoncourt and Hopps.

October 18, 1969–February 8, 1970 "New York Painting and Sculpture, 1940–1970," organized by Henry Geldzahler at the Metropolitan Museum of Art, 82nd Street and Fifth Avenue, New York, includes a room of Cornell boxes installed by Hopps.

1971

October In a book of remembrances on Guggenheim, Cornell recalls that Duchamp gave him a "mock *Valise*."[30]

1972

June Cornell undergoes surgery for prostate problems and convalesces with various family members on Long Island. He will return to his house in November.

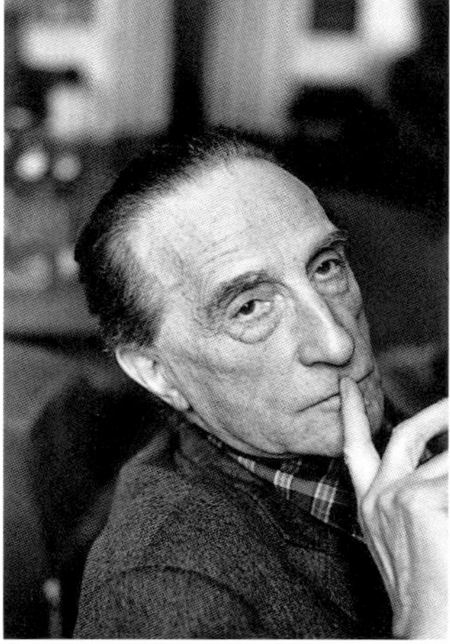

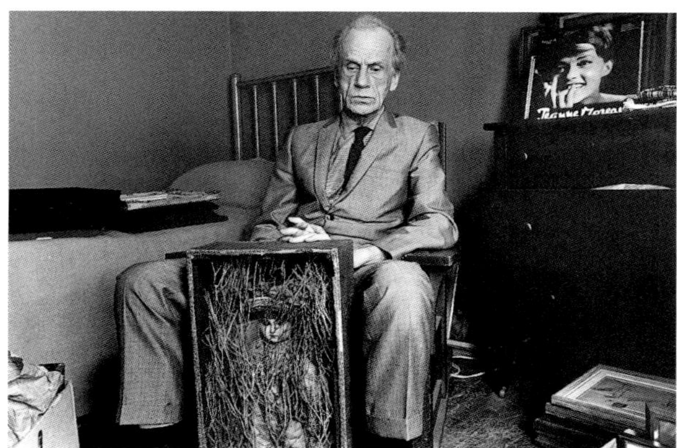

December 29 Cornell dies of heart failure at home in Flushing.

1973

Hopps encounters for the first time Cornell's *Duchamp Dossier* and Untitled Book Object *(Journal d'Agriculture Pratique et Journal de l'Agriculture)* (c. 1933–mid 1940s), among much other artwork in the effects of Cornell's house.

Mr. and Mrs. John A. Benton begin lending Cornell's papers and a selection of his source materials and library to the Archives of American Art, Smithsonian Institution, Washington, D.C.

September 22–November 11 A Duchamp retrospective exhibition, organized by d'Harnoncourt and Kynaston McShine, is held at the Philadelphia Museum of Art; it will travel to The Museum of Modern Art, New York, and The Art Institute of Chicago.

December 23, 1973–June 2, 1974 A memorial exhibition, "Joseph Cornell 1903–1972," organized by Hopps, is presented at the National Collection of Fine Arts (now National Museum of American Art), Smithsonian Institution, Washington, D.C.

1974

Dore Ashton publishes the first references to Cornell's work on Duchamp's *Boite* edition and to the *Duchamp Dossier:* "Cornell kept a box of his own filled with curiosa intended for Duchamp but somehow they were never tendered."[31]

1977

February 15–March 12 Joan Washburn opens her new gallery in the quarters once occupied by Julien Levy Gallery at 42 East 57th Street, New York.

With Levy's help, Washburn recreates the 1943 exhibition "'Through the Big End of the Opera Glass': Marcel Duchamp, Yves Tanguy, Joseph Cornell" as her inaugural show, which also marks the occasion of the publication of Levy's *Memoir of an Art Gallery* (New York: G.P. Putnam's Sons). The Museum of Modern Art, New York, will purchase Untitled (Bébé Marie) (included in the 1943 and 1977 exhibitions) in 1980.

1978

The National Museum of American Art, Smithsonian Institution, Washington, D.C., establishes the Joseph Cornell Study Center with the Bentons' donation of works by Cornell and the bulk of his source materials and library.

1980

November 17, 1980–January 20, 1981 A Cornell retrospective exhibition, organized by McShine, is held at The Museum of Modern Art, New York; the exhibition will travel internationally to London, Paris, Düsseldorf, and Chicago.

Notes by Marcel Duchamp, edited by Paul Matisse, is published (Paris: C.N.A.C. Georges Pompidou).

1982

November 19, 1982–February 27, 1983 "Joseph Cornell: An Exploration of Sources," organized by Lynda Roscoe Hartigan, is presented at the National Museum of American Art, Smithsonian Institution, Washington, D.C. The exhibition is the first posthumous investigation of Cornell's "explorations," dossiers, and source materials in conjunction with his boxes and collages.

1985

The Joseph and Robert Cornell Memorial Foundation donates the "exploration" *Portrait of Ondine* to the National Museum of American Art, Smithsonian Institution, Washington, D.C., as part of a larger gift of works to the museum.

1987

June 22–July 18 "The Crystal Cage [portrait of Berenice]" is presented at Gatodo Gallery, Tokyo, the first exhibition and catalogue devoted solely to an "exploration."

1990

The Joseph and Robert Cornell Memorial Foundation donates the *Duchamp Dossier* to the Philadelphia Museum of Art. A second gift, the "exploration" Untitled (The Life of Ludwig II of Bavaria) (1941–52) is made by the Foundation to the museum in 1997.

Notes

In addition to the primary sources consulted in preparing this chronology, secondary sources relied upon include Ecke Bonk, *The Box in a Valise: de ou par Marcel Duchamp ou Rrose Sélavy, Inventory of an Edition* (New York: Rizzoli, 1989); Joseph Cornell Papers, Archives of American Art, Smithsonian Institution, Washington, D.C.; Anne D'Harnoncourt and Kynaston McShine, *Marcel Duchamp* (New York: The Museum of Modern Art, 1973); Jennifer Gough-Cooper and Jacques Caumont, *Ephemerides on and about Marcel Duchamp and Rrose Sélavy, 1887–1968* (Milan: Bompiana, 1993); Lynda Roscoe Hartigan, "Joseph Cornell: A Biography," in *Joseph Cornell* (New York: The Museum of Modern Art, 1980); Deborah Solomon, *Utopia Parkway: The Life and Work of Joseph Cornell* (New York: Farrar, Straus and Giroux, 1997); and Calvin Tomkins, *Duchamp: A Biography* (New York: Henry Holt and Company, 1996).

1. Marcel Duchamp to Walter and Louise Arensberg, 15 June 1919, Arensberg Papers, Philadelphia Museum of Art.

2. This photograph was reproduced in the exhibition catalogue *1936 Surrealism* (New York: Zabriskie Gallery, 1986), p. 21.

3. "November 17, 1933" in *Ephemerides on and about Marcel Duchamp and Rrose Sélavy, 1887–1968,* edited by Jennifer Gough-Cooper and Jacques Caumont (Milan: Bompiana, 1993), n.p.

4. Neither the image nor the present whereabouts of this photograph are known. In 1956, it was recorded in the collection of Mary Reynolds as an unmounted photograph within the *Monsieur Phot* film scenario; see *Surrealism and Its Affinities: The Mary Reynolds Collection* (Chicago: The Art Institute of Chicago, 1956), AI 62. The Ryerson Library at The Art Institute of Chicago, which holds the Reynolds Collection, believes that the photo has been missing for some years.

5. This copy is in the Mary Reynolds Collection, Ryerson Library, The Art Institute of Chicago. Apparently Duchamp left the film scenario with Reynolds for safekeeping.

6. Photographs by James Ogle of Cornell's "Bébe Marie" are published in *Harper's Bazaar*, no. 2711, (July 1938): p. 23 and *View,* series 2, no. 4, (January 1943): p. 38.

7. It is generally understood that Duchamp advised Guggenheim on her art purchases. It is likely that he encouraged her to buy the Cornells. Joseph Cornell to Peggy Guggenheim, 12 March 1942, Peggy Guggenheim Papers, Archives of American Art, Smithsonian Institution, Washington, D.C., microfilm, ITVE I: 149.

8. Joseph Cornell to Robert Motherwell, 29 March 1942, Dedalus Foundation, New York.

9. Joseph Cornell, diary entry, Joseph Cornell Papers, Archives of American Art, Smithsonian Institution, Washington, D.C., microfilm, 1058:883.

10. Robert Cornell, diary entry, 31 July 1942, courtesy Mrs. John A. Benton.

11. Diary entry, 21 December 1942, Cornell Papers, AAA, 1058:888 and 1058:890.

12. Charles Henri Ford to Joseph Cornell, 31 January 1945, Cornell Papers, AAA.

13. *The New York Times*, 12 December 1943, section 2, p. 8.

14. Cornell Papers, AAA, 1066:1042.

15. Julien Levy, interview with Lynda Roscoe Hartigan, Bridgewater, Conn., 1977. The verso inscription on Cornell's photomontage *3/4 Bird's-Eye View of 'A Watch-Case for Marcel Duchamp'* (1944, Yale Collection of American Literature, Beinecke Rare Book and Manuscript Library) states that the original object used for the montage belonged to Mary Reynolds. The title, *Amiral Grillon (Watch),* suggests that this artwork (present location unknown) was the original object photographed. Reynolds, Duchamp, and Cornell frequently referred to one another as "Amiral Grillon."

16. Diary entry, Cornell Papers, AAA, 1058.

17. Quoted in Deborah Solomon, *Utopia Parkway: The Life and Work of Joseph Cornell* (New York: Farrar, Straus and Giroux, 1997), p. 169.

18. Mary Reynolds to Joseph Cornell, 2 October [1948], Cornell Papers, AAA, 1055.

19. Mina Loy to Joseph Cornell, 28 November 1950, Cornell Papers, AAA.

20. Marcel Duchamp to Frank Hubachek, 9 May 1951, Mary Reynolds Collection, Ryerson Library, The Art Institute of Chicago. A photocopy of "Memorandum regarding Joseph Cornell" resides with the Reynolds papers, Ryerson Library, The Art Institute of Chicago.

21. Cornell Papers, AAA, 1056:1485.

22. Robert Motherwell, "Preface to a Joseph Cornell Exhibition," in *Joseph Cornell Portfolio–Catalogue* (New York and Los Angeles: Leo Castelli Gallery, Richard L. Feigen & Co., and James Corcoran Gallery, 1976).

23. Dorothea Tanning to Joseph Cornell, Cornell Papers, AAA, 1055:73.

24. Collection of Mrs. John A. Benton.

25. Marcel Duchamp to Joseph Cornell, Cornell Papers, AAA, 1055:1547.

26. Marcel Jean to Joseph Cornell, 28 April 1958, Cornell Papers, AAA, 1055:1671.

27. Teeny Duchamp to Joseph Cornell, 20 March 1965, Cornell Papers, AAA, 1056:75.

28. Diary entry, Cornell Papers, AAA, 1063:323, 1063:333, and 1063:335.

29. Teeny Duchamp to Joseph Cornell, 14 October 1968, Cornell Papers, AAA, 1056:684, 1063:407, and 1063:860.

30. Virginia M. Dortch, ed., *Peggy Guggenheim and her Friends* (New York: Berenice, 1994), p. 97.

31. Dore Ashton, *A Joseph Cornell Album* (New York: The Viking Press, 1974), p. 75.

249 Cornell, *Duchamp Dossier*, c. 1942–53. Philadelphia Museum of Art. Gift of The Joseph and Robert Cornell Foundation.

Duchamp Dossier Pictorial Index

Duchamp Dossier Inventory

Selected Bibliography

Catalogue of Works

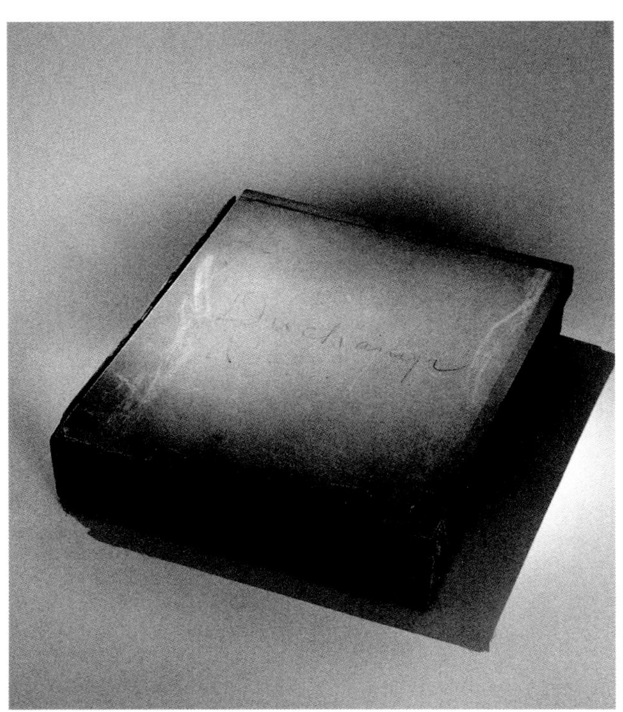

Duchamp Dossier Pictorial Index

The numbers appearing in these plates correspond to those in the *Duchamp Dossier* Inventory (pp. 304–31). The capital letters correspond to those in the upper left corner of the *Duchamp Dossier* Plates (pp. 17–59).

Duchamp Dossier Pictorial Index

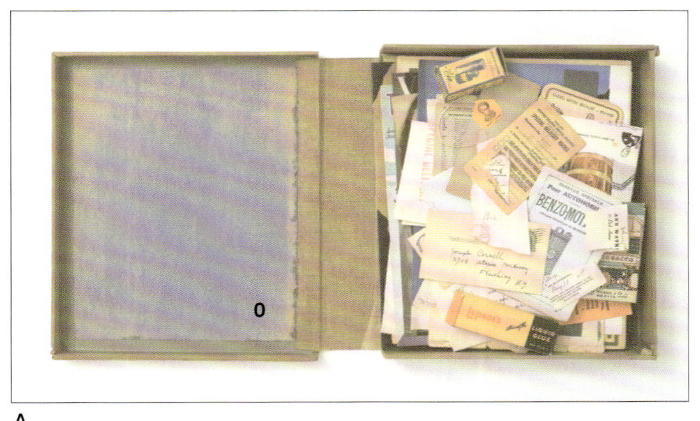

A

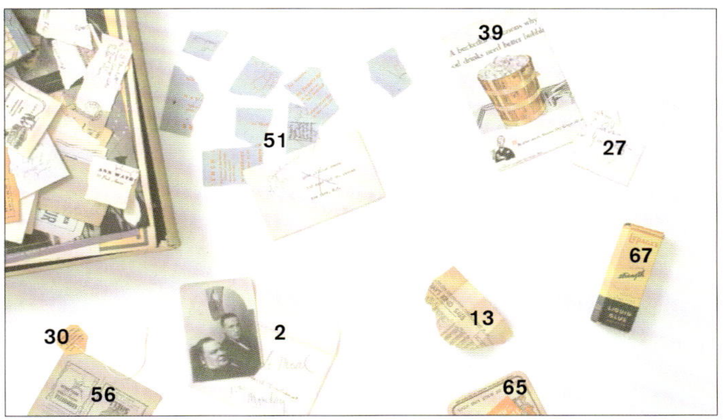

B

C

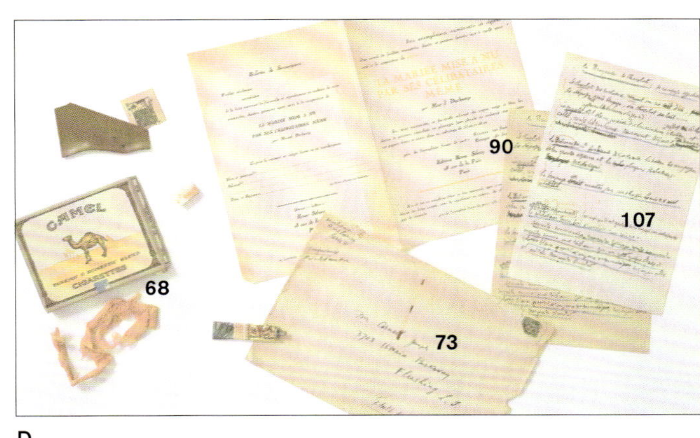

D

E

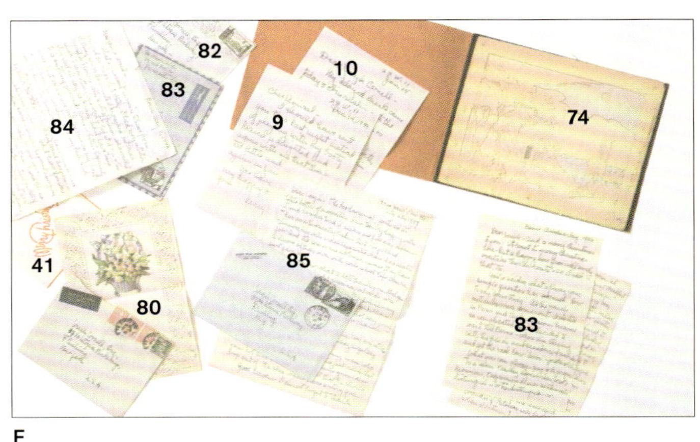

F

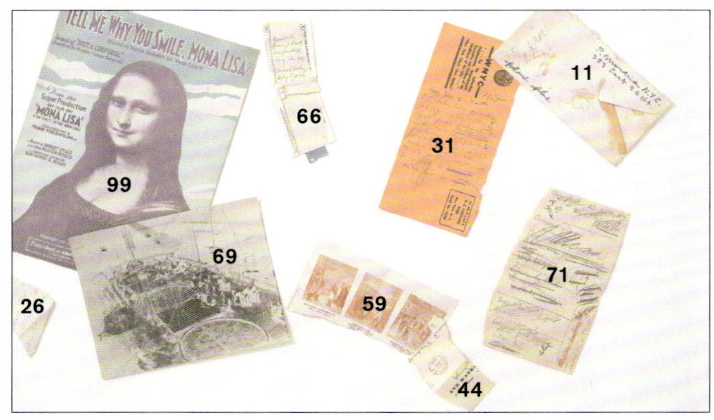

G

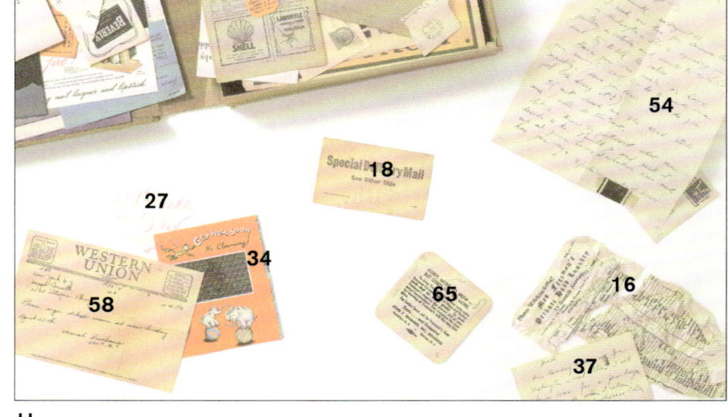

H

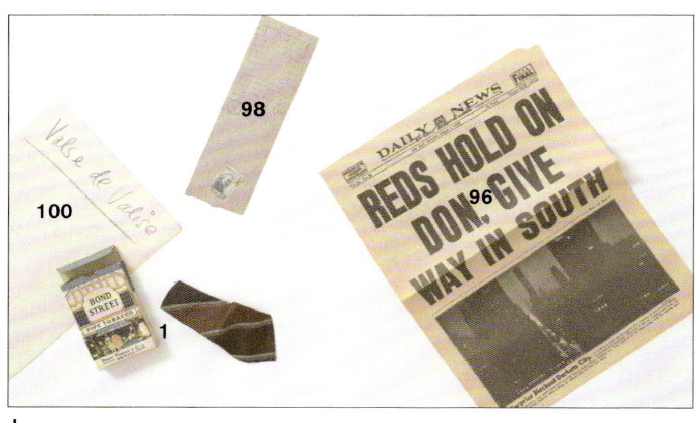

I

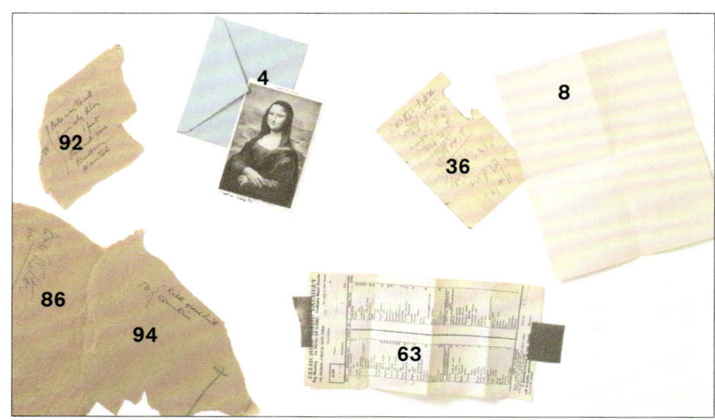

J

110
111
115

K

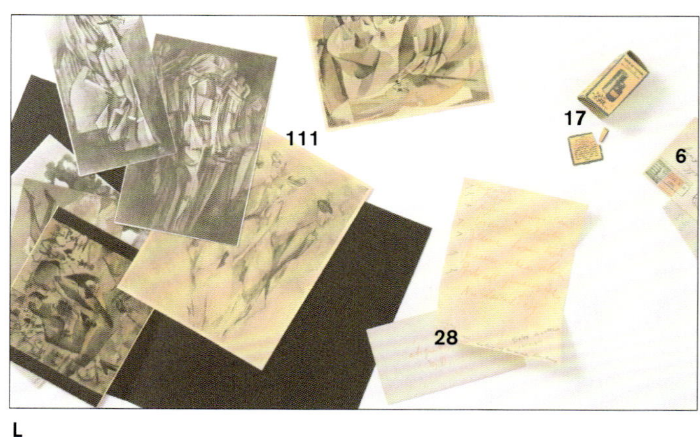

L

14
JULIEN LEVY GALLERY
76
3

M

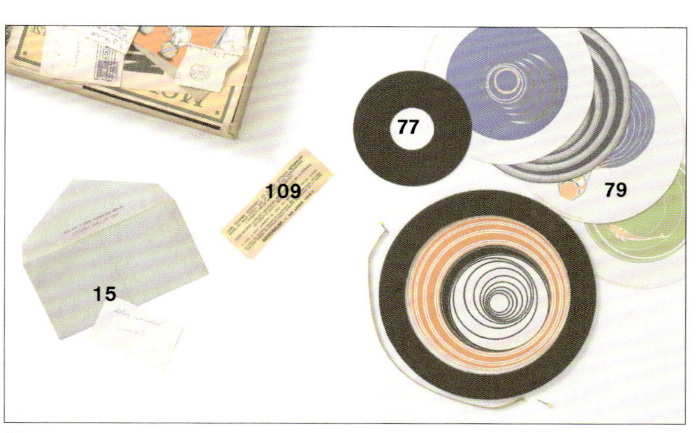

N

114
97
95
57
112
106
56
64

O

112
60
69
91
20

P

Q

18
52
105
113
78
96

R

S

67
59
66
108
5
117
57
33

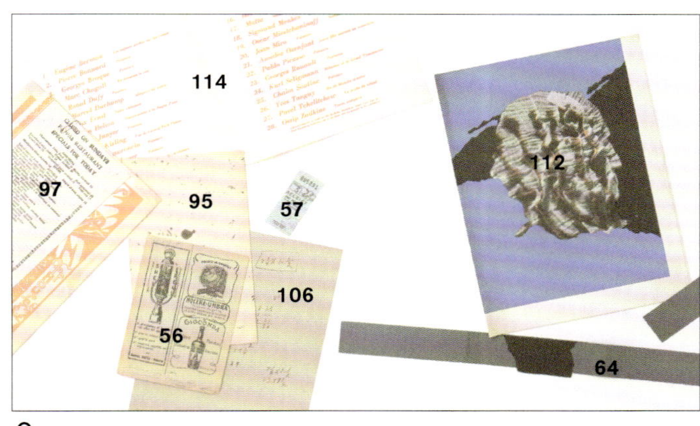

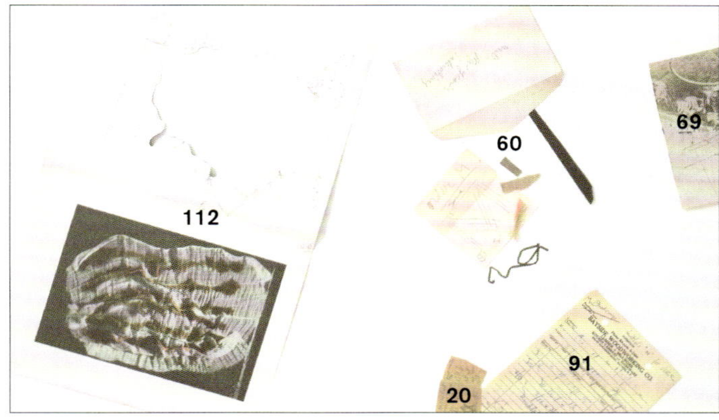

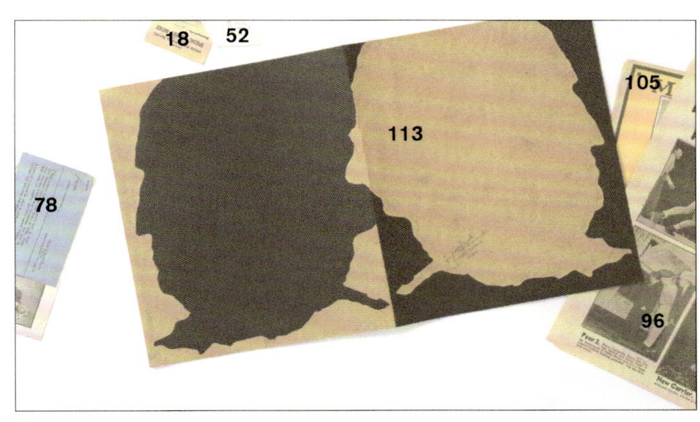

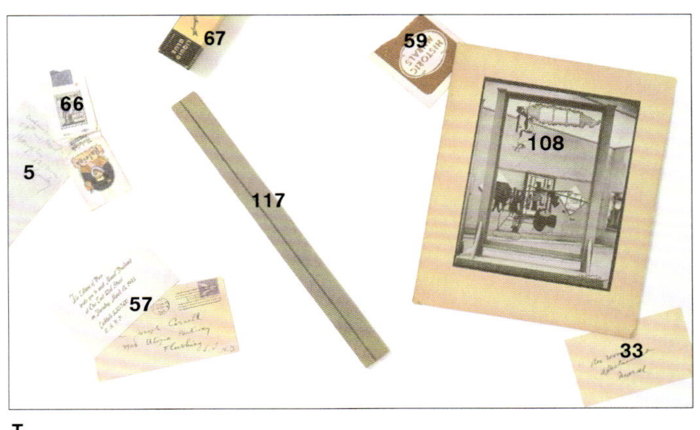

T

Cornell's assembly of the *Boîte* edition

One of the primary subjects of the *Duchamp Dossier* is Cornell's work on the assembly of Duchamp's *Boîte* edition. In July 1942, Duchamp brought an example of the *Boîte-en-valise [Box-in-a-Valise]* to Utopia Parkway to show to Joseph and Robert Cornell (Robert Cornell, diary entry, 31 July 1942, courtesy Mrs. John A. Benton). Soon after, Joseph Cornell began to assist Duchamp with the assembly of the *Boîte* edition, continuing with this work until January 1946.

Remnants, notations, drawings, and correspondence in the *Duchamp Dossier* indicate that Cornell's work included the following: assembling the precut cardboard structure of the *Boîte* edition's container with linen tape, ordering the wood sticks that formed the "M" on the lid of the box, and pasting labels and pochoir reproductions onto paper folders. Other items, such as a sketch of *Fountain*, leather fragments, and receipts, also establish that Cornell was involved in most, if not all, facets of assembling complete examples of the *Boîte* edition.

Approximately forty *Boîtes*—made from the materials sufficient for fifty examples shipped to America with Peggy Guggenheim's household goods in May 1941—could had been completed by January 1946. Before traveling to Paris in April 1946, Duchamp retrieved *Boîte* edition materials from Cornell (DD 23, 33 and 97). During the three-and-a-half-year period in which Cornell assisted Duchamp, Cornell could have been involved in the production of as many as eleven deluxe *Boîtes-en-valise* (Series A) and between twenty-five and thirty *Boîtes* (Series B). The eleven known *Boîtes-en-valise* dated to this period are nos. V, VI, VII, VIII, IX, O (Katherine Dreier), O (Arensberg), O (Kay Boyle), X, XI, and XII (Bonk, *Marcel Duchamp: The Box in a Valise*, 1989).

Duchamp Dossier Inventory

Development During Joseph Cornell's lifetime, the *Duchamp Dossier* was not publicly exhibited, published, photographed, or catalogued, and few people knew of its existence. In 1973, shortly after Cornell's death in December 1972, Walter Hopps, then curator of Twentieth-Century Art at the National Collection of Fine Arts, Smithsonian Institution (now National Museum of American Art), found the *Duchamp Dossier* among Cornell's effects in his home and studio at 3708 Utopia Parkway, Flushing, New York. Thereafter, the *Duchamp Dossier* was among the artworks comprising Cornell's estate until The Joseph and Robert Cornell Memorial Foundation gave this work to the Philadelphia Museum of Art in 1990.

Between 1981 and 1982, Janna Leepson, under the supervision of Lynda Roscoe Hartigan, founding curator of the Joseph Cornell Study Center at the National Museum of American Art, catalogued the *Duchamp Dossier*. The contents and their arrangement were documented as they existed in 1981, and the inventory presented here retains this sequence and much of the initial documentation.

For the purposes of this publication, and given the collaborative nature of this exhibition, the Philadelphia Museum of Art generously allowed the *Duchamp Dossier* to be examined at The Menil Collection in Houston. In 1997, Susan Davidson, associate curator, and Elizabeth Lunning, paper conservator, The Menil Collection, further researched the *Duchamp Dossier*'s contents, measured each item in centimeters, and standardized the format for recording this information. Ecke Bonk and Hartigan reviewed this data. Bonk and Davidson attributed authors and titles for notes and artworks, in consultation with Hartigan. Don Quaintance and Davidson wrote the annotations, in consultation with Bonk and Hartigan. Davidson assigned the cross-references. And finally, Polly Koch edited the final text and Elizabeth Frizzell placed the photo images and formatted the typography.

Treatment Each item in the *Duchamp Dossier* is attributed to its primary author. An item's amendments or annotations by another hand are excluded in its attribution and title, but recorded in its entry description (for example, Cornell regularly annotated Duchamp items with dates and comments).

Items have been given short generic titles; descriptive titles to additionally distinguish the item are given in brackets [ ]. Both Duchamp and Cornell used found paper materials to record notes. These items are simply identified as "notes" without regard to their support or medium. When an item consists of multiple parts, such as an envelope and its contents, a slash (/) separates their respective generic titles.

The date of each item is based on its inscriptions, using the earliest date when multiple dates occur. Dates that are not inscribed on an item are derived from other sources and appear in brackets [ ].

Entries include descriptions of an item's recto and verso and its inscriptions. Written inscriptions and imprinted or stamped addendums appear in italics; commercially printed text appears in Roman type.

Inventory numbers that refer the reader to related items are indicated by an arrow (**→ 11**). These cross-references emphasize shared subject matter (i.e., *Mona Lisa*, *Boîte* materials) or common dates; in other cases, they identify fragments that have been reconstructed (i.e., torn envelopes and bags). Capital letters (**→ 11, A**) refer to an item's location in the *Duchamp Dossier* Plates (pp. 17–59) and Pictorial Index (pp. 300–303).

Photos of individual items are adjacent to their entries unless items have been photographed in a reconstructed configuration. For entries without an adjacent photograph, the cross-reference identifies the item near which the reconstruction's photograph may be found; the word **(photo)** follows the appropriate inventory number. The caption for the photograph of a reconstructed configuration indicates all the inventory numbers of items appearing in the single photograph. Not all objects are illustrated recto and verso.

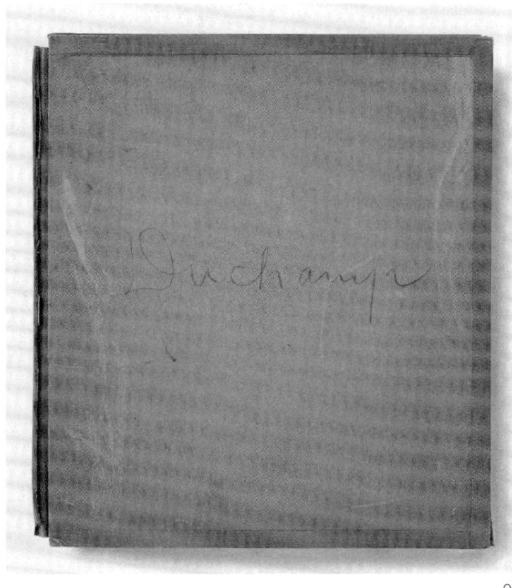

0

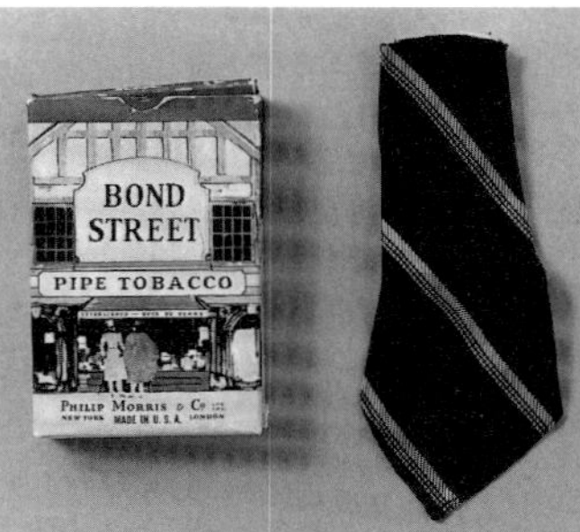

1a, b

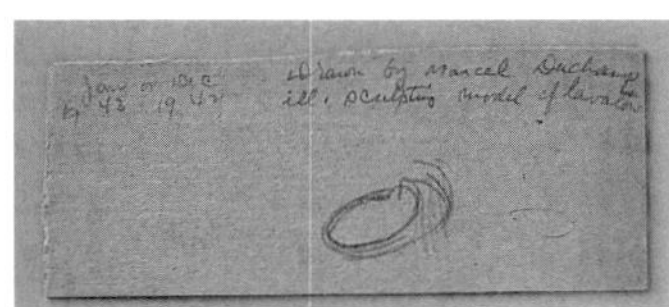

3

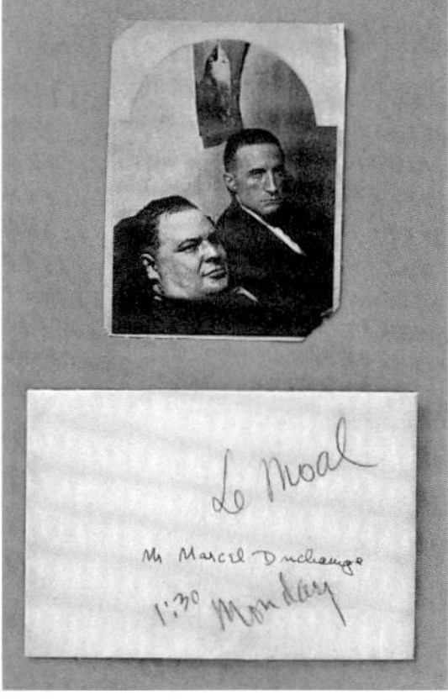

2a, b

4a, b^r

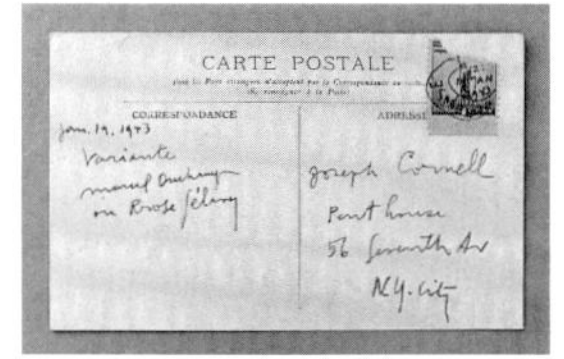

4b^v

0 Marcel Duchamp
Prototype [*de ou par Marcel Duchamp ou Rrose Sélavy*]

Handmade cardboard box with hinged lid, reinforced inside and outside with gray fabric tape. Floor of box is lined with heavy black paper. Fabric tape inside lid is colored with blue crayon overall.
Inscribed across lid exterior by Cornell in pencil: *Duchamp*
3⅜ x 14¼ x 12⅜ in. (8.2 x 36.2 x 31.4 cm)

The research of Ecke Bonk indicates that the *Duchamp Dossier* is an early, side-hinged prototype for the housing of the *Boîte* edition, brought from Marseilles to New York City and given by Duchamp to Cornell. The dimensions of the prototype are similar to the cardboard box of the *Boîte* edition, which measures 8 x 39 x 35 cm. The materials of the prototype are closely related to those of the *Boîte*: the heavy cardboard corresponds with the calendered (pressed smooth) bookbinder's stock of the *Boîte*—though it is slightly thicker—and the color, texture, and gum arabic coating of the linen tape match in both instances. For both the transatlantic voyage and various Manhattan to Flushing trips, it may have served as a temporary packing box for shuttling *Boîte* materials. Around 1970, Cornell showed the *Duchamp Dossier*, in the attic of the Utopia Parkway house, to Teeny Duchamp, who later described it as "the suitcase where he'd dump things about Marcel. A box for a valise that Marcel had rejected." Teeny Duchamp, interview with Lynda Roscoe Hartigan, Washington, D.C., 12 March 1980. Virginia [Dortch] Dorazio quotes Cornell as saying, "I have a mock *Valise* that Duchamp gave me." *Peggy Guggenheim and Her Friends*, edited by Virginia M. Dortch (Milan: Berenice Art Books, 1994), p. 97.

→ 117, A

1 Cardboard box [Bond Street Pipe Tobacco]
21 DECEMBER 1942

a Cardboard box for Bond Street Pipe Tobacco. Front and back of box has color illustration of English Tudor-style shop with two well-dressed gentlemen looking into shop window. At top and along each edge of box are blue U.S. Internal Revenue Stamps for 1.⅝ ounces of tobacco. Inscribed on bottom exterior flap by Cornell in ink: *Dec 21 1942*
Closed: 4⅝ x 2⅞ x ⅞ in. (11 x 7.3 x 2.2 cm)

b Cut and folded bottom half of striped necktie inside box.
6¾ x 2⅝ in. (17 x 6.8 cm)

Duchamp smoked Bond Street Pipe Tobacco manufactured by Philip Morris & Co.

→ I

2 Envelope [annotated] / Magazine reproduction [Man Ray photo]

a Cream-colored Cartier envelope.
recto Inscribed center by unidentified hand in ink: *Mr Marcel Duchamps* and above Duchamp's name by Cornell in pencil: *Le Moal* and below Duchamp's name: *1:30 / Monday*
3¼ x 5⅜ in. (9.7 x 13.7 cm)

b Cut black-and-white reproduction of 1920s Man Ray photograph depicting Joseph Stella and Duchamp in New York, inside envelope. Reproduction has glue residue at four corners on verso.
4⅝ x 3½ in. (11.6 x 8.3 cm)

Le Moal was a French restaurant on Third Avenue between 49th and 50th Streets, close to Duchamp's residence at the time. The *Duchamp Dossier* documents Cornell and Duchamp meeting at Le Moal for lunch three times in August 1942. The reproduction was cut from *Vanity Fair*, 23 March 1922, p. 52.

→ 24, 29, 30, 68 (item c only), B

3 Marcel Duchamp
Drawing [*Fountain*]
DECEMBER 1942

Gray cardboard having two cut edges and two torn edges with drawing in red pencil of a urinal.
recto Inscribed upper left by Cornell in pencil: *Jan or Dec / 1943 1942* and upper right: *Drawn by Marcel Duchamp / ill. sculpting model of lavator[i]e*
2⅜ x 6⅛ in. (6.3 x 15.7 cm)

This is a drawing of the sculpting model for the miniature version of *Fountain* included in the *Boîte* edition. However, here the urinal is in the orientation of *Fountain* (1917, first version) as opposed to the minature's orientation in the *Boîte* edition.

→ M

4 Marcel Duchamp
Envelope / Postcard [*Mona Lisa*]
19 JANUARY 1943

a Blue envelope, soiled with small coffee splatters.
4⅜ x 5⅝ in. (11.1 x 14.3 cm)

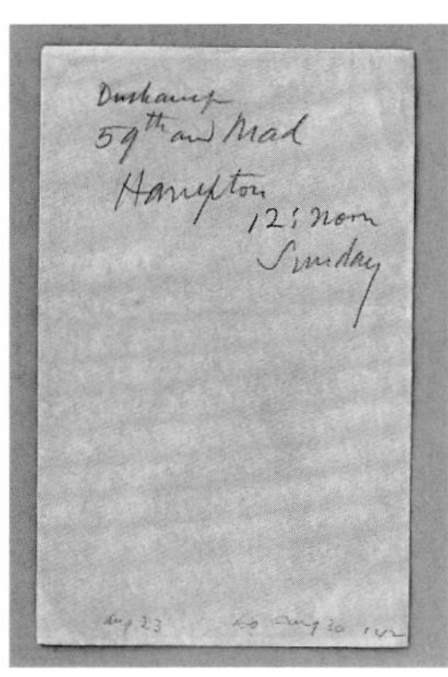

5

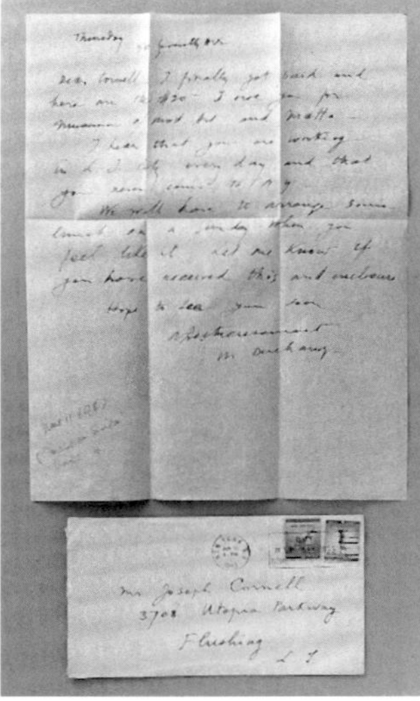

6a, b

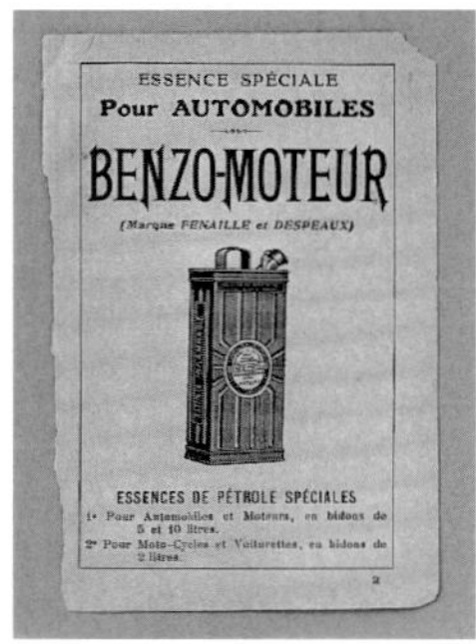

7r

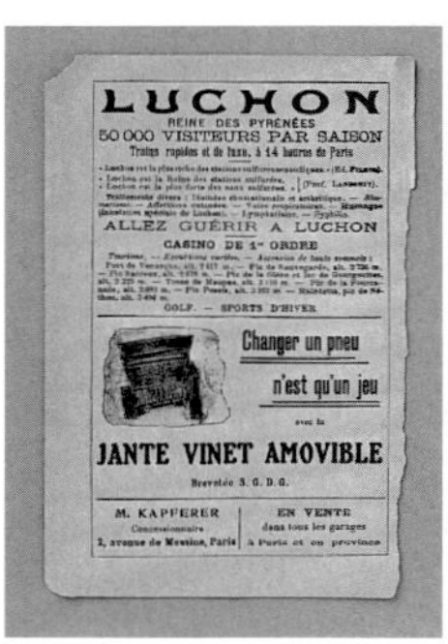

7v

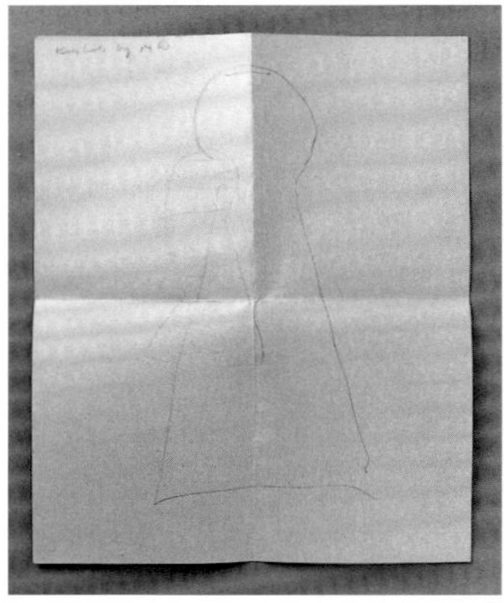

8

b Postcard from Louvre Museum printed: *LÉONARD DE VINCI. – LA JOCONDE. [Mona Lisa]* inside envelope.
recto Duchamp added small dot of blue ink on nose of *Mona Lisa.* Inscribed underneath printed text by Duchamp in blue ink: *notice nose tip*
verso Inscribed upper right on green 1¢ Statue of Liberty stamp by Duchamp in blue ink, simulating postmark: *12: / 19 Jan / 1943* and within a circle, surrounded by another semicircle: *PENTHOUSE*
Inscribed left by Duchamp in blue ink: *Jan. 19. 1943 / Variante / Marcel Duchamp / ou Rrose Sélavy* and right: *Joseph Cornell / Penthouse / 56 Seventh Av / N.Y. City*
5½ x 3⅝ in. (14 x 9.1 cm)

Duchamp "hand-delivered" the altered postcard to Cornell during a visit to Duchamp's (Frederick Kiesler's) Seventh Avenue penthouse apartment.

→ 50, 55, 56, 99, 105, J

5 Envelope [annotated]
21 AUGUST 1942

White stationery envelope lined with blue paper.
recto Inscribed laterally at right by Duchamp in pencil: *Duchamp / 59th and Mad / Hampton / 12: noon / Sunday*
Inscribed bottom left by Cornell in pencil: *Aug 23* and bottom right: *Do Aug 30 '42*
verso Inscribed on gummed surface of flap by Cornell in pencil: *Aug 21 '42*
6⅜ x 3⅞ in. (16.2 x 9.8 cm)

Hampton, a regular destination for Cornell, was a cafeteria at Madison Avenue and 59th Street, below the photography studio of George Platt Lynes and two blocks north of the Julien Levy Gallery (11 East 57th Street).

→ T

6 Marcel Duchamp
Envelope / Letter
10 JUNE 1943

a Off-white envelope, slit open at left edge, postmarked NEW YORK N.Y. / JUN 10 / 5–PM / 1943, with pink 2¢ Army Navy stamp and green 1¢ Industry Agriculture stamp. Postal cancellation reads BUY / WAR SAVINGS / BONDS & STAMPS.
recto Inscribed center by Duchamp in blue ink: *Mr. Joseph Cornell / 3708 Utopia Parkway / Flushing / L. I.*
verso Inscribed on flap by Duchamp in blue ink: *Duchamp / 56 Seventh Ave / New York ll N.Y.*
3⅝ x 6½ in. (9.2 x 16.5 cm)

b Letter on airmail tissue paper watermarked SAXON ONION SKIN MADE IN U.S.A., folded irregularly into sixths, inside envelope.
Text by Duchamp in blue ink:
Thursday / 56 Seventh Ave / Dear Cornell I finally got paid and / here are the $20– I owe you for / Museum of Mod. Art and Matta – I hear that you are working / in L. I. City every day and that / you never come to N.Y.– / We will have to arrange some / lunch on a Sunday when you / feel like it. Let me know if / you have received this and enclosure. / Hope to see you soon / Affectueusement / M. Duchamp

Inscribed diagonally bottom left by Cornell in pencil: *JUNE 11 1943 / Malibran Smile / Anne H.*
11 x 8½ in. (27.8 x 21.4 cm)

Duchamp's payment was for Cornell's work done six months earlier on two *Boîte* edition examples (The Museum of Modern Art, New York, and Matta). Maria Malibran was a nineteenth-century Italian opera singer whom Cornell honored in copious source materials and several boxes, collages, and publications. Anne H. refers to Anne Hoysio, a fellow employee Cornell met at the Allied Control Company Inc., Long Island City, on June 4, 1943.

→ L

7 Guidebook advertisement [Benzo-Moteur]

Page torn from blue French guidebook.
recto Printed advertisement for Benzo-Moteur automobile gas with illustration of gas can.
verso Printed advertisements for Luchon, Reine des Pyrénées (a bath resort), and for Jante Vinet Amovible [Vinet removable rim].
6⅛ x 4⅛ in. (15.6 x 10.2 cm)

Guide Bleu was a common French motoring and tourist publication.

→ E

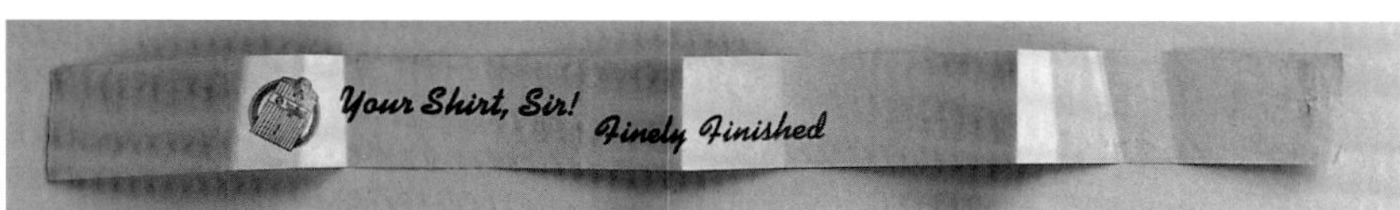

12

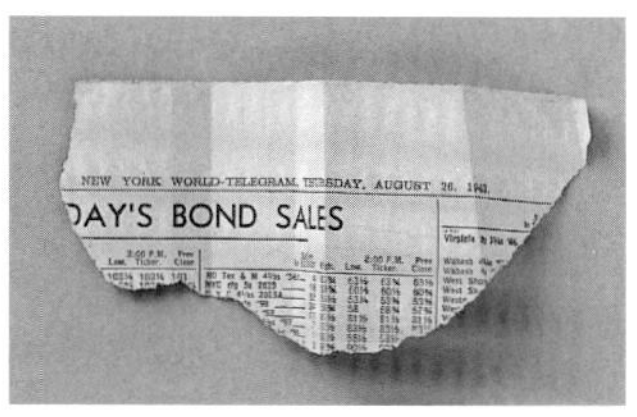

13r

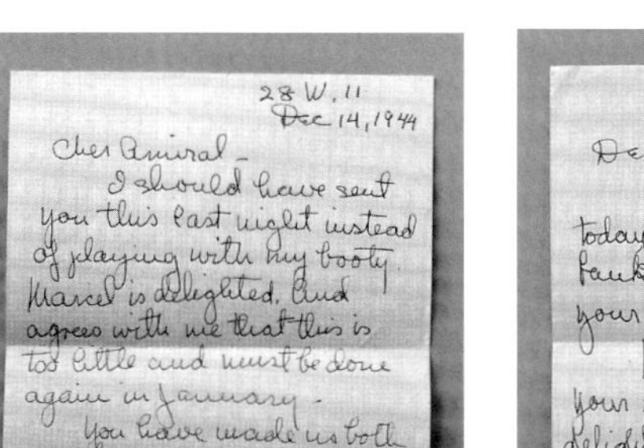
28 W. 11
Dec 14, 1944
Cher Amiral -
I should have sent
you this last night instead
of playing with my booty
Marcel is delighted. And
agrees with me that this is
too little and must be done
again in January.
You have made us both
very happy & we thank
you
Mary

9

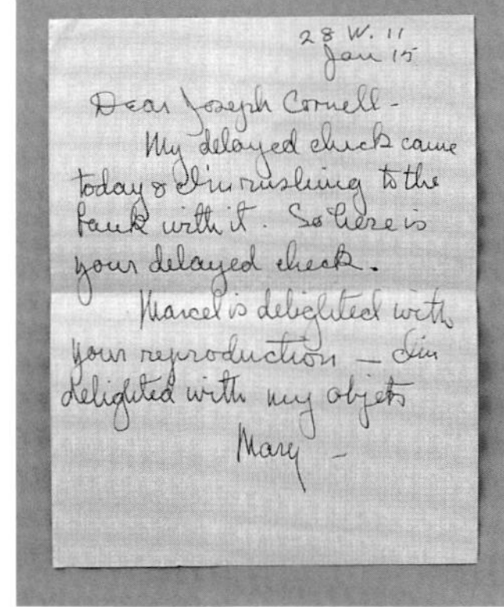
28 W. 11
Jan 15
Dear Joseph Cornell -
My delayed check came
today & I'm rushing to the
bank with it. So here is
your delayed check.
Marcel is delighted with
your reproduction - I'm
delighted with my objets
Mary -

10

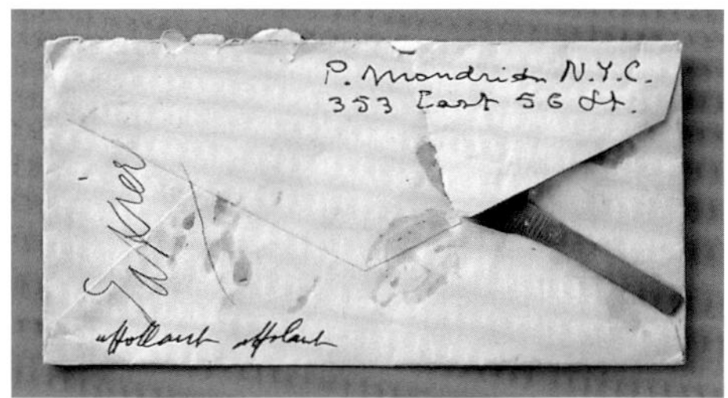

11

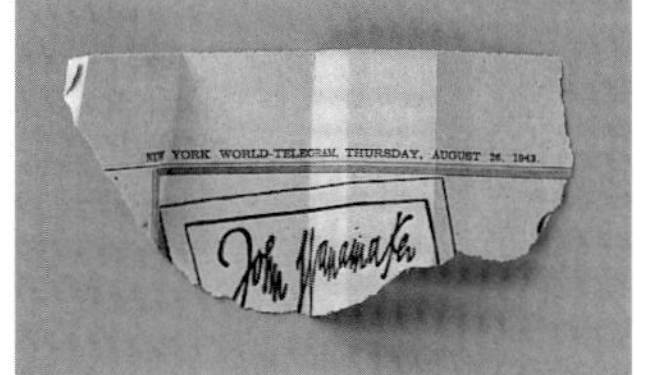

13v

8 Marcel Duchamp
Drawing [keyhole]
29 SEPTEMBER 1942

Full sheet of cream-colored paper, folded in quarters, with pencil drawing of keyhole. Smaller keyhole in perspective is repeated to its left.
recto Inscribed top by Cornell in red pencil: *Keyhole by M D*
verso Inscribed upper left quadrant by Cornell in pencil: *9/29/42*
Opened: 9⅞ x 8 in. (25 x 20.1 cm)
Folded: 5 x 4⅛ in. (12.6 x 10.2 cm)
→ J

9 Mary Reynolds
Letter
14 DECEMBER 1944

Letter on full sheet of white paper, folded in half, with blue-gray graph pattern.
Text by Mary Reynolds in ink:
28 W. 11 / Dec 14, 1944 / Cher Amiral – / I should have sent / you this last night instead / of playing with my booty. / Marcel is delighted. And / agrees with me that this is / too little and must be done / again in January. / You have made us both / very happy & we thank / you / Mary
7⅝ x 5⅞ in. (19.2 x 14.4 cm)

Mary Reynolds was an American expatriate renowned for her specialty bindings of art books. She had a liaison with Duchamp beginning in 1923 until her death in 1950. She befriended Cornell while in America (1943–45), carrying on a long correspondence with him after her return to Paris.
→ 41, 80, 84, F

10 Mary Reynolds
Letter
15 JANUARY [1945]

Letter on full sheet of white paper, folded in half, with blue-gray graph pattern.
Text by Mary Reynolds in ink:
28 W. 11 / Jan. 15 / Dear Joseph Cornell – / My delayed check came / today & I'm rushing to the / bank with it. So here is / your delayed check. / Marcel is delighted with / your reproduction – I'm / delighted with my objets / Mary
7⅝ x 5⅞ in. (19.2 x 14.4 cm)

Reynolds lived at 28 West 11th Street from January 1943 to October 1943 and again from May 1944 to July 1945.
→ F

11 Marcel Duchamp
Envelope [annotated]
19 AUGUST 1942

White envelope, slit open at top, postmarked Grand Central Station NY, N.Y. / AUG 19, 1942 / 8–PM, with magenta 2¢ ARMY & NAVY FOR DEFENSE stamp. Attached under back flap is flat wood spatula printed reverse: LePage's Glue / Made in U.S.A.
recto Inscribed center by Piet Mondrian in black ink: *M. Marcel Duchamp / 440 East 51 St. / N.Y.C.*
verso Inscribed on flap by Mondrian in black ink: *P. Mondrian N.Y.C. / 353 East 56 St.*
Inscribed bottom left by Duchamp in black ink: *affollant affolant* and along left edge: *Sakier*
3⅝ x 7½ in. (9.9 x 19 cm)

Piet Mondrian was among the artists shown by Katherine Dreier and Duchamp in a Société Anonyme exhibition and by Peggy Guggenheim at Art of This Century, 30 West 57th Street, New York. *Affolant* is the French word for bewildering, upsetting, or worrying.
→ 67, G

12 Laundry shirt band

Torn and folded blue paper seal printed: Your Shirt, Sir! / Finely Finished
1¼ x 15½ in. (3.3 x 39.3 cm)
→ 16, 63, 72, C

13 Newspaper [*New York World-Telegram*]
26 AUGUST 1943

Torn and folded fragment from top of *New York World-Telegram*, Thursday, August 26, 1943.
recto Printed bond sales.
verso Printed advertisement for John Wanamaker Department Store.
2⅝ x 5½ in. (6.6. x 14 cm)
→ 36, 66, B, C

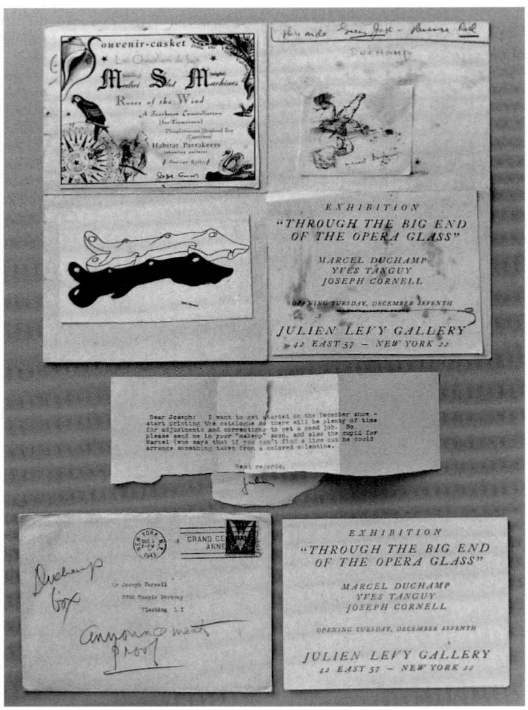

14a, b, c, d

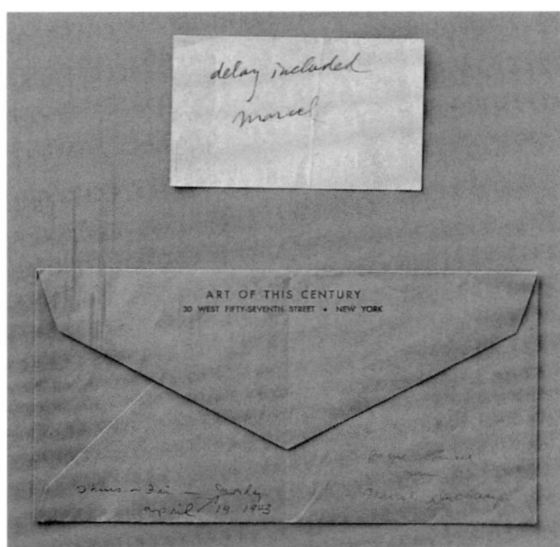

15a, b

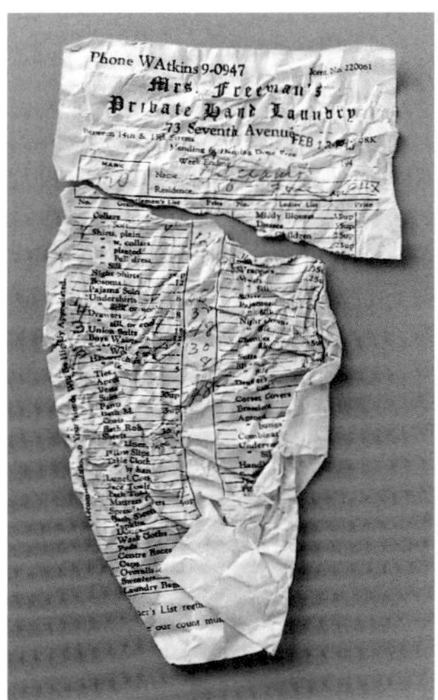

16

14 Joseph Cornell / Julien Levy
Envelope [annotated] / Exhibition announcement / Letter [Julien Levy Gallery]
2 DECEMBER 1943

a Light gray envelope, postmarked NEW YORK N.Y. / DEC 2 / 7–PM / 1943, with purple 3¢ WIN THE WAR eagle stamp. Postal cancellation reads GRAND CENTRAL / ANNEX
recto Typed center: *Mr. Joseph Cornell / 3708 Utopia Parkway / Flushing L.I.*
Inscribed left by Cornell in pencil: *Duchamp / box* and below address: *Announcement / proof*
4¾ x 6½ in. (12 x 16.4 cm)

b Sheet of cream-colored paper, folded into quarters, bearing Cornell's announcement for "Through the Big End of the Opera Glass" (December 1943) inside envelope.
recto Inscribed upper left quadrant by Cornell in pencil: *Cornell / 3708 Utopia Parkway / Flushing L I / (cut only – 4-¾ wide) / Set type to go into cut* Pasted here is printed list of Cornell artworks included in exhibition.
Inscribed upper right quadrant by Cornell in pencil: *this side Grey Ink – Reverse Red* / DUCHAMP Pasted here is printed reproduction of drawing of upside-down Cupid with bow and arrow and Duchamp's signature.
Inscribed lower left quadrant by Cornell in pencil: *Tanguy / Cut only – 4-½ wide* Once pasted here, now loose, is printed proof of signed Yves Tanguy drawing.
Inscribed lower right quadrant by Cornell in pencil: *Levy – Copy A* Once pasted here, now loose, is printed text: EXHIBITION / "THROUGH THE BIG END / OF THE OPERA GLASS" / MARCEL DUCHAMP / YVES TANGUY / JOSEPH CORNELL / OPENING TUESDAY, DECEMBER SEVENTH / ~~NINETEEN FORTY-THREE~~ / JULIEN LEVY GALLERY / 42 EAST 57 – NEW YORK 22
verso Inscribed upper left quadrant by Cornell in pencil (corresponding to Duchamp Cupid on recto): *Red Ink* Pasted here is printed reproduction of a chessboard with reverse type: White to Play and Win and below reproduction: LOOK THROUGH FROM OTHER SIDE AGAINST LIGHT.
Inscribed by Cornell in pencil: *set 8 p U & L / any type*
Opened: 9 x 11½ in. (22.9 x 29.2 cm)
Folded: 4½ x 5¾ in. (11.5 x 14.6 cm)

c Printed exhibition announcement inside envelope.
Opened: 9 x 11½ in. (22.9 x 29.2 cm)
Folded: 4½ x 5¾ in. (11.5 x 14.6 cm)

d Letter in three fragments, folded in thirds back on itself, on cream-colored paper inside envelope.
Text by Julien Levy, typed, with signature in pencil:
Dear Joseph: I want to get started on the December show – / start printing the catalogue so there will be plenty of time / for adjustments and corrections to get a good job. So / please send me in your "makeup" soon, and also the cupid for / Marcel (who says that if you can't find a line cut he could / arrange something taken from a colored valentine. / Best regards, / Julien
3⅝ x 8½ in. (9 x 21.7 cm)

Cornell designed the announcement for "Through the Big End of the Opera Glass" (December 7–28, 1943) with contributions from Duchamp and Tanguy, the other artists represented in the exhibition, which appeared at the Julien Levy Gallery. The "catalogue" referred to by Levy in his letter is actually the announcement.

→ 76, M

15 Marcel Duchamp
Envelope [annotated] / Note
19 APRIL 1943

a Gray envelope, folded in half, with printed return address verso: ART OF THIS CENTURY / 30 WEST FIFTY-SEVENTH STREET • NEW YORK
recto Three faintly incised lines form rough square on right half.
verso Inscribed lower right by Cornell in pencil: *Joseph Cornell / from / Marcel Duchamp* and lower left: *Thurs – Fri – Monday / April 19 1943* Arrow points from April to Monday.
4 x 7½ in. (9.9 x 19 cm)

b Paper fragment, torn from pad, inside envelope. Inscribed by Duchamp in blue ink: *delay included / Marcel*
2⅜ x 3¾ in. (6 x 9.5 cm)

Art of This Century presented "Exhibition of Collage," which opened on April 16, 1943, and included Duchamp and Cornell.

→ N

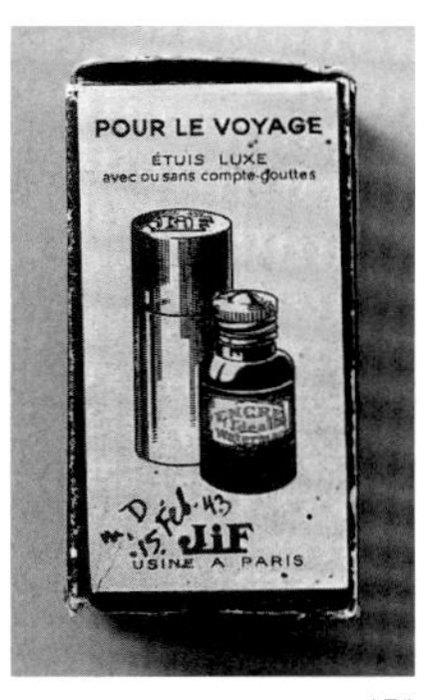

17r

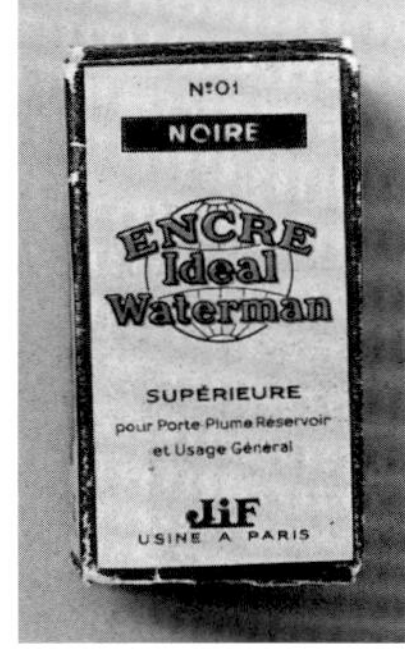

17v

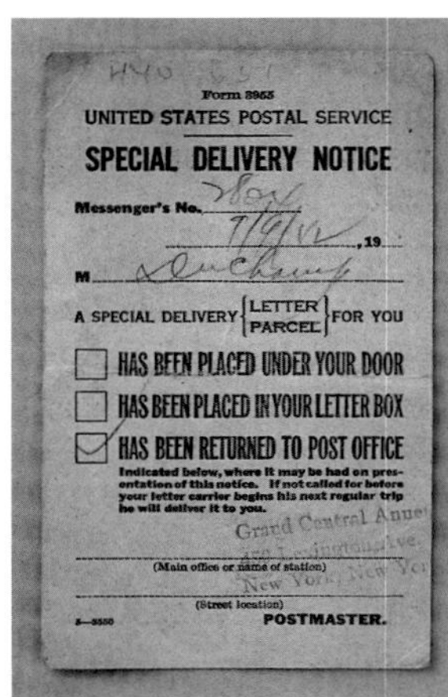

18

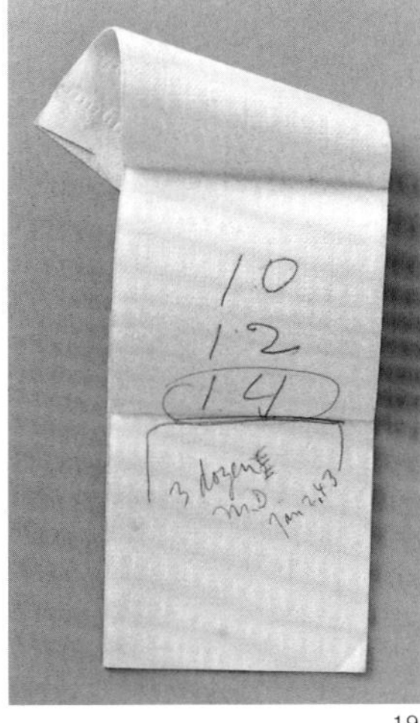

19

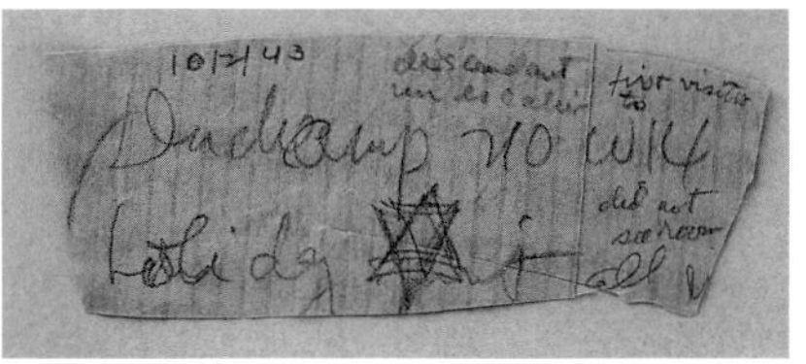

20

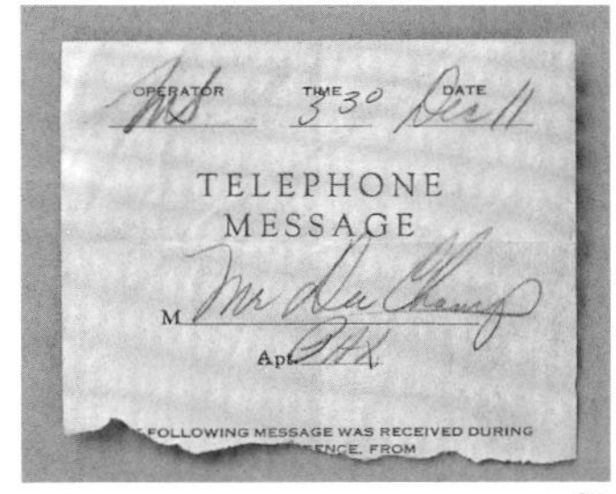

21

16 Receipt [Freeman Laundry]
13 FEBRUARY 1943

Printed on bill: Mrs. Freeman's Private Hand Laundry, 73 Seventh Avenue, Between 14th & 15th Streets. Bill is torn in two and crumpled.
recto Inscribed by unidentified hand in pencil: *Duchamp* [Name], *56 7th Ave* [Residence], *PHX* [Penthouse] [Apt.] and stamped: *Feb 13, 1943* Following items are checked and tallied for total of $2.48:

8 Shirts	*1.20*
1 Wool Undershirt	*.08*
4 Drawers	*.32*
3 Union Suits	*.48*
3 Wool Socks	*.30*
4 Handkerchiefs	*.08*

10⅜ x 5½ in. (26.2 x 14 cm)
→ **12, 63, 72, H**

17 Marcel Duchamp
Cardboard box [Encre Ideal Waterman]
15 FEBRUARY 1943

Yellow cardboard box for Encre Ideal Waterman brand of black ink. Printed French text appears in red with illustrations of ink dropper bottles with their carrying cases on left and right panels. Bottom four flaps of box have been torn off and are now placed inside.
recto Inscribed by Duchamp in ink: *M. D. / .15. Feb. / 43*
2¾ x 1½ x 1½ in. (7 x 3.6 x 3.6 cm)

Duchamp probably used Waterman ink, brought from France, to sign deluxe examples of the *Boîte* edition in the early 1940s.
→ **40, 49, 51, L**

18 Marcel Duchamp
Note
9 SEPTEMBER 1942

Printed special delivery notice from U.S. Post Office.
recto Inscribed top center by unidentified hand: *440 E 51*. Same hand has filled out in pencil: *2804* [Messenger's No.] / *9/9/42* [date] / *Duchamp* [recipient] and checked box for HAS BEEN RETURNED TO POST OFFICE. Stamped in purple at bottom: *Grand Central Annex / 450 Lexington Ave. / New York, New York*
verso Inscribed by Duchamp in pencil: *Max / Dchp / Miro / Tanguy / Hirshfield*
14⅞ x 3 in. (2.5 x 7.6 cm)

This notice of attempted special delivery was for a letter from Katherine Dreier addressed to Duchamp at Peggy Guggenheim's townhouse (440 East 51st Street), his residence at the time. Max Ernst, Duchamp, Joan Miró, Yves Tanguy, and Morris Hirshfield were all included in "First Papers of Surrealism" (October 14–November 7, 1942), organized by Duchamp and André Breton, Whitelaw Reid Mansion, 451 Madison Avenue, New York. With Duchamp's active involvement, they also appeared in the Art of This Century inaugural exhibition (October 20–late November, 1942).
→ **38, 42, 52, H, R**

19 Marcel Duchamp
Note
2 JANUARY 1943

Folded white paper napkin embossed Horn and Hardart. Folds are original.
Inscribed on opened surface by Duchamp in pencil: *10 / 12 / 14 / 3 dozens / M. D. / Jan 2 43*
Opened: 16⅝ x 3⅝ in. (42 x 9 cm)
Folded: 5 x 3⅝ in. (12.7 x 9 cm)

Cornell patronized Horn and Hardart Automats (coin-operated vending diners) at several Manhattan locations, frequently meeting friends there.
→ **E**

20 Joseph Cornell
Note
2 OCTOBER 1943

verso Inscribed upper left by Cornell in pencil: *10 /2 /43*; upper center: *descendant / un escalier* [descending a staircase]; right: *first visitors / to* [210 W 14] */ did not / see room*; and center: *Duchamp 210 W 14 / holiday spirit all* A six-pointed star has been drawn across the word *spirit*.
2 x 4¾ in. (5.1 x 12.3 cm)

Duchamp moved to a studio at 210 West 14th Street on October 1, 1943. Cornell used the six-pointed star to denote items and events of special significance.
→ **P**

21 Message [telephone]
11 DECEMBER [1942]

Torn and folded printed telephone message form filled out by unidentified hand to read: *MS* [OPERATOR] *3:30* [TIME] *Dec 11* [DATE] / *Mr Duchamp* [NAME] / *PHX* [Penthouse] [APT.]
3⅛ x 4 in. (8 x 10.2 cm)
→ **Q**

22

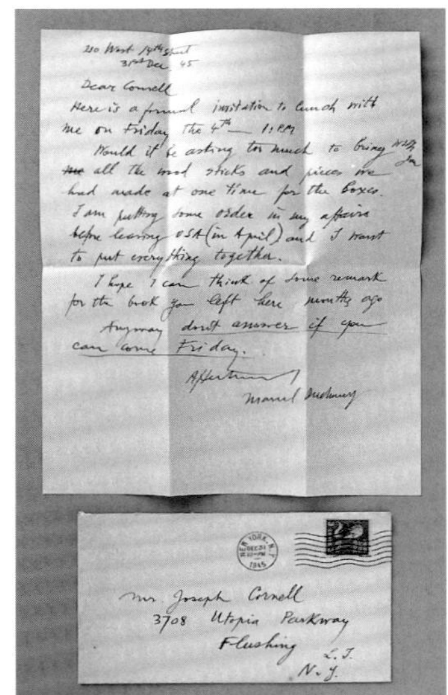
210 West 14th Street
31st Dec. 45
Dear Cornell
Here is a formal invitation to lunch with
me on Friday the 4th – 1 P.M.
Would it be asking too much to bring with you
all the wood sticks and pieces we
had made at one time for the boxes.
I am putting some order in my affairs
before leaving USA (in April) and I want
to put everything together.
I hope I can think of some remark
for the book you left here months ago
Anyway don't answer if you
can come Friday.
Affectueusement
Marcel Duchamp

Mr Joseph Cornell
3708 Utopia Parkway
Flushing L.I.
N.Y.

23a, b

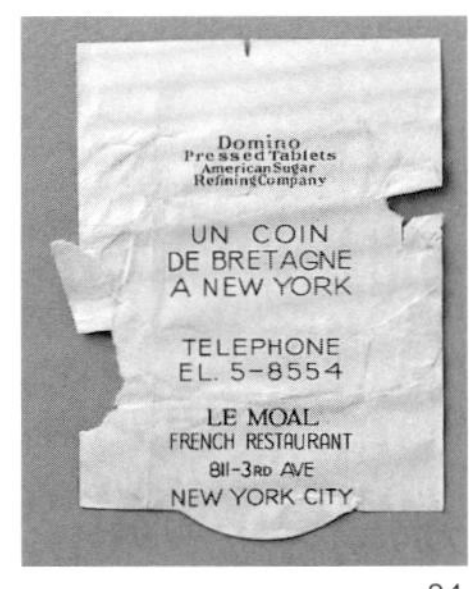
Domino
Pressed Tablets
American Sugar
Refining Company
UN COIN
DE BRETAGNE
A NEW YORK
TELEPHONE
EL. 5-8554
LE MOAL
FRENCH RESTAURANT
811-3RD AVE
NEW YORK CITY

24

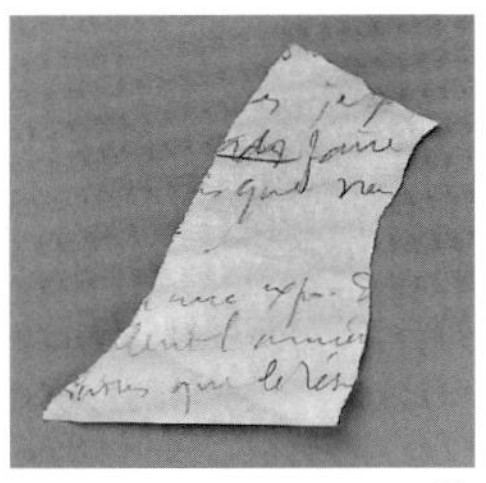

26

W. G. Brackett
c/o Samson Cordage Works
89 Broad St.
Boston, Mass.

25

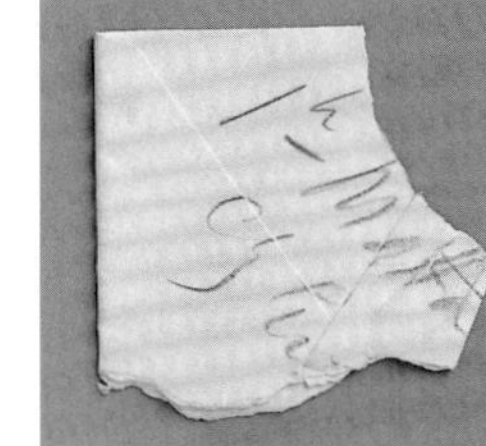

27

22 Envelope fragment

Torn fragment of large off-white envelope, folded in thirds, with watermark EAGLE BOOKLET ENVELOPE.
recto Typed (or printed by early form of addressing machine) center: *Mr. Marcel Duchamp / % Fred Kiesler / 56 7th Ave. / New York, N. Y.*
verso Printed in black, partial return address: ART / N.Y. with partial postal cancellation at left edge in blue: SEC. 562 P.
5⅝ x 7⅛ in. (14.2 x 17.9 cm)

23 Marcel Duchamp
Envelope / Letter
31 DECEMBER 1945

a Off-white envelope, slit open at top edge, postmarked NEW YORK N.Y. / DEC 31 / 10 PM / 1945, with purple 3¢ Thomas Jefferson stamp and wavy line postal cancellation.
recto Inscribed by Duchamp in blue ink: *Mr. Joseph Cornell / 3708 Utopia Parkway / Flushing / L. I. / N.Y.*
3⅝ x 6½ in. (9.2 x 16.5 cm)

b Letter on cream-colored paper watermarked SATONS 1893 LETTERPAPER HIGHLAND LINEN inside envelope.
Text by Duchamp in ink:
210 West 14th Street / 31st Dec. 45 / Dear Cornell / Here is a formal invitation to lunch with / me on Friday the 4th – 1: P.M. / Would it be asking too much to bring with you / ~~me~~ all the wood sticks and pieces we / had made at one time for the boxes. / I am putting some order in my affairs / before leaving USA (in April) and I want / to put everything together. / I hope I can think of some remark / for the book you left here months ago. Anyway don't answer if you / can come Friday. / Affectueusement / Marcel Duchamp
10 x 8 in. (25.2 x 20.3 cm)
→ 33, 60, 61, 68, 80, 91, 97, 110, 111, 115, 116, 117

24 Wrapper [Domino sugar]
14 AUGUST 1942

White paper sugar wrapper printed in blue.
recto Printed: DOMINO PRESSED TABLETS / AMERICAN SUGAR / REFINING COMPANY / UN COIN / DE BRETAGNE / A NEW YORK [a corner of Brittany in New York] / TELEPHONE / EL. 5–8554 / LE MOAL / FRENCH RESTAURANT / 811 – 3RD AVE / NEW YORK CITY
verso Inscribed by Cornell in pencil: *8/14/42*
2⅝ x 2 in. (6.7 x 5.1 cm)
→ 2, 29, 30, 68 (item c only), S

25 Envelope fragment
[Samson Cordage Works]
28 SEPTEMBER [1942]

Torn upper left corner of off-white envelope, slit open at top, postmarked BOSTON, MASS / SEP 28 / 5–PM / 19[42]
recto Inscribed upper left by unidentified hand in blue ink: *W.G. Brackett / c/o Samson Cordage Works / 89 Broad St. / Boston, Mass.*
1⅝ x 4¼ in. (4.2 x 10.7 cm)

Samson Cordage Works may have supplied the string Duchamp purchased for his installation at the exhibition "First Papers of Surrealism" (October 14–November 7, 1942), in New York.
→ 48

26 Marcel Duchamp
Note fragment

Torn white paper fragment.
recto Inscribed illegibly by Duchamp in pencil: *ije / faire / que / une expo. D / amier / que le rés*
4⅛ x 3 in. (10.1 x 7.4 cm)
→ G

27 Marcel Duchamp
Note

Torn lower right corner of envelope with partial embossed return address, verso under flap, now torn away: Inc.
recto Inscribed by unidentified hand in black ink, partial address: *champ / Ave- / ew York City* and below by second unidentified hand in pencil: *PHX*
verso Inscribed by Duchamp in red pencil, partial note: *l h – Matta / Chez Lui* [at his place]
3 x 2¾ in. (7.7 x 7 cm)
→ B, H

28 Marcel Duchamp
Envelope [annotated] / Note
19 JANUARY 1943

a Gray envelope. Inscribed center by Duchamp in red pencil: *étiquettes* [labels] / *M.D.*
3⅝ x 6½ in. (9.3 x 16.6 cm)

b Parchmentlike paper that folds either into pouch or into thirds inside envelope. Several burn marks are visible at center top and center bottom, and inside is significantly darker than outside.

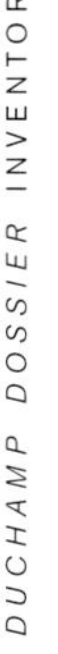

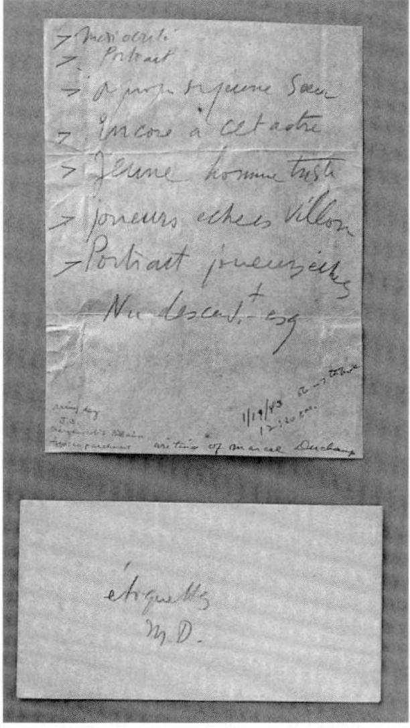
28a, b

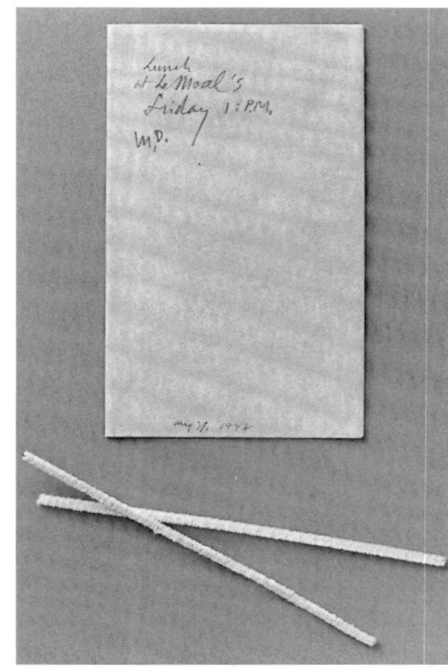
29a, b

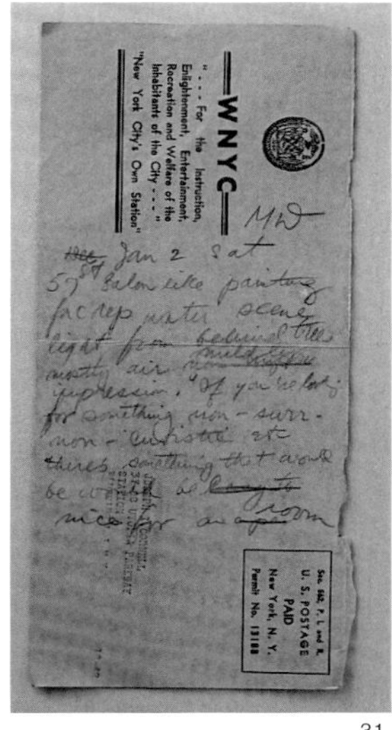
31

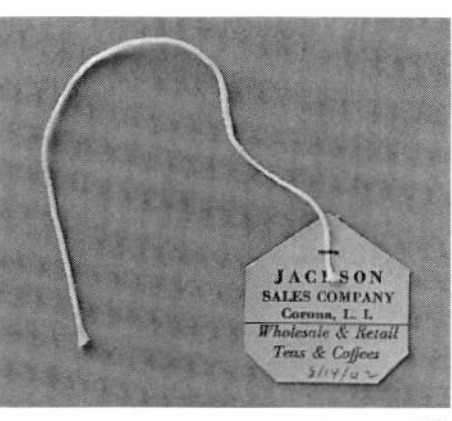
30

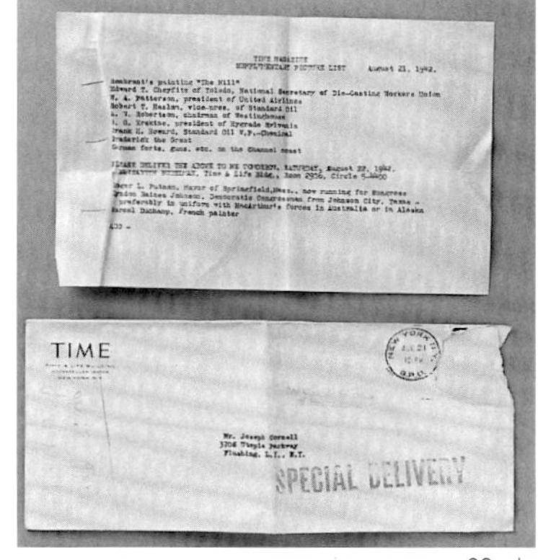
32a, b

recto Inscribed in list format by Duchamp in red pencil: *Médiocrité / Portrait / à propos de jeune soeur / Encore à cet astre / Jeune homme triste / joueurs echecs Villon / Portrait joueurs éches / Nu descendt esq.* Each item except last is checked off at left in pencil.
Inscribed lower left by Cornell in pencil: *rainy day / J.C. / Mary Reynold's Bill Aimer / tobacco parchment;* diagonally lower right in heavier pencil: *1/19 /43 56 – 7th Ave / 12:30 P.M.;* and underneath: *writing of Marcel Duchamp*
8 x 5⅝ in. (20.4 x 14.5 cm)

The titles listed correspond to eight Duchamp paintings and drawings included in the *Boîte* edition and to the eight unmounted labels in the *Duchamp Dossier.*

→ 110, 111, 115, 116, L

29 Envelope [annotated] / Pipe cleaners
21 AUGUST 1942

a White envelope lined with blue paper and stained by adhesive.
recto Inscribed laterally at left by Duchamp in pencil: *Lunch / at Le Moal's / Friday 1: P.M. / M.D.*
Inscribed lower center by Cornell in pencil: *Aug. 21, 1942*
verso Inscribed on gummed surface of flap (upside down on left side when flap is opened) by Cornell in pencil: *8-18 42*
3⅞ x 6⅜ in. (9.8 x 16.3 cm)

b Two unused white pipe cleaners inside envelope.
6 in. each, length (15.3 cm each, length)

→ 2, 24, 30, 68 (item c only), S

30 Tea tag [General Jackson]
14 AUGUST 1942

Seven-sided orange tea-bag tag with illustration verso of man labeled General Jackson Tea. Stapled to tag is white string once attached to tea bag.
recto Printed: JACKSON / SALES COMPANY / Corona, L.I. / Wholesale & Retail / Teas & Coffees
Inscribed lower center by Cornell in pencil: *8/14/42*
1⅜ x 1½ in. (3.5 x 3.3 cm)

→ 2, 24, 29, 68 (item c only), B, E

31 Joseph Cornell
Note
2 JANUARY [1943]

Printed announcement on orange card from radio station WNYC with typed address: *Joseph Cornell / 3708 Utopia Parkway / Station A / Flushing L.I. N.Y.* Verso provides table of sign-off times and announces special program beginning on Wednesday, December 2.
recto Inscribed center by Cornell in pencil: *MD / ~~Dec~~ Jan 2 Sat / 57st. Salon like painting / fac rep water scene / light from behind trees / mostly air ~~non impres~~ mildly / impression. "If you're looking / for something non-surr. / non-Cubistic etc / there's something that would / be would be ~~easy to~~ / nice for a ~~apa~~ room*
4⅛ x 10 in. (10.4 x 23 cm)

Cornell listened frequently to the classical music radio station WNYC.

→ G

32 Elizabeth Budelman
Envelope [annotated] / Time Life picture list
21 AUGUST 1942

a Off-white business envelope, folded, postmarked NEW YORK N.Y. / AUG 21 / 10–PM / GPO, with watermark FORTUNE OF TIME LIFE and printed return address upper left recto: TIME / TIME & LIFE BUILDING / ROCKEFELLER CENTER / NEW YORK, N.Y. Stamped above typed address in purple: *FEE CLAIMED BY OFFICE OF FIRST ADDRESS* and below address: *SPECIAL DELIVERY*
recto Typed center: *Mr. Joseph Cornell / 3708 Utopia Parkway / Flushing, L.I. N.Y.*
Inscribed along left edge by Cornell in pencil: *Duchamp / Wed 3:00*
verso Bottom of flap postmarked FLUSHING NY received / 22 __?__ / 1–AM
4⅛ x 9⅝ in. (10.5 x 24.3 cm)

b Folded mimeographed list from Elizabeth Budelman for *Time* magazine inside envelope. Supplementary picture list is dated August 21, 1942, and requests delivery of pictures to her tomorrow, August 22, 1942. Listed are: *Rembrant's* [sic] *painting "The Mill" / Edward T. Cheyfitz of Toledo, National Secretary of Die-Casting Workers Union / W. A. Patterson, president of United Airlines / Robert T. Haslam, vice-pres. of Standard Oil / A. W. Robertson, Chairman of Westinghouse / B. G. Erskine, president of Hygrade Sylvania / Frank H. Howard, Standard Oil V.P.-Chemical / Frederick the Great / German forts, guns, etc. on the Channel coast / . . . / Roger L. Putnam, Mayor of Springfield, Mass., now running for Congress / Lyndon Baines Johnson, Democratic Congressman from Johnson City, Texas – / preferably in uniform with MacArthur's forces in Australia or in Alaska / Marcel Duchamp, French painter*

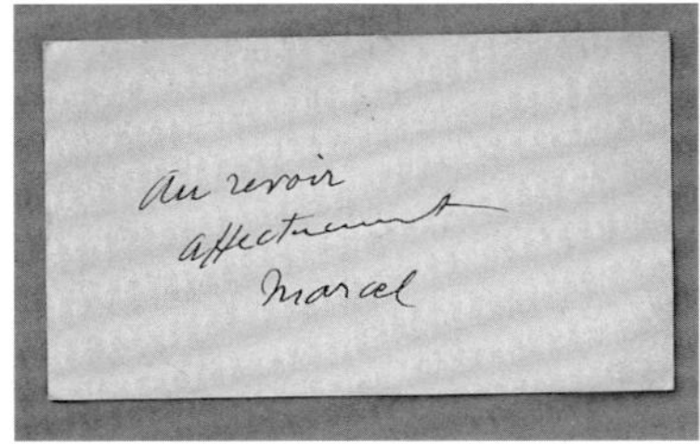

33

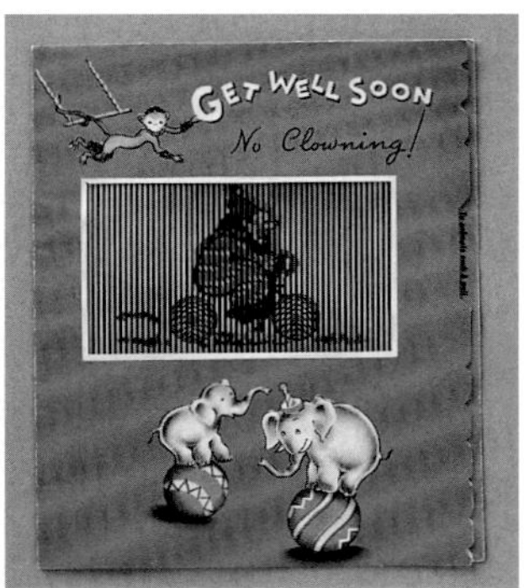

34

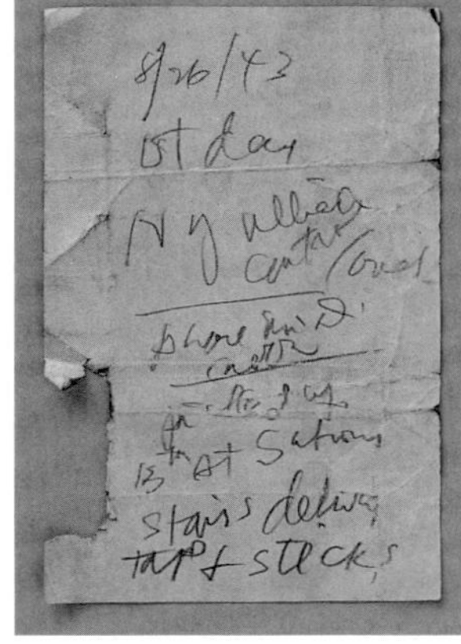
36^{r}

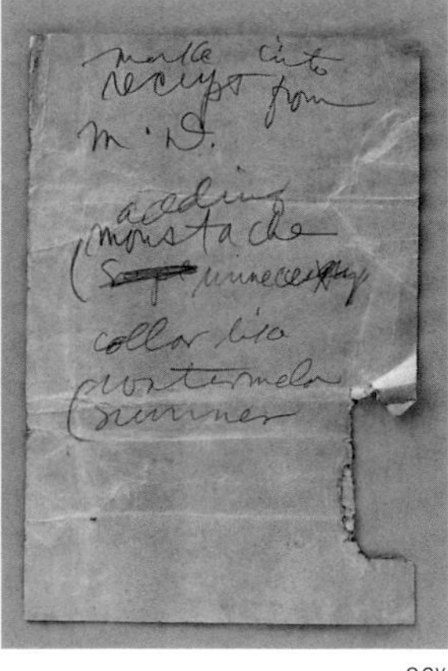
36^{v}

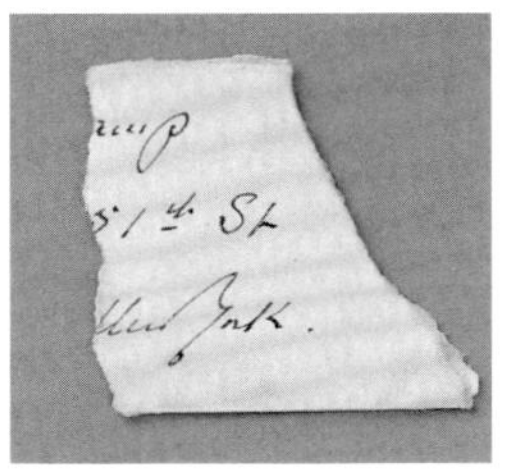
35

37

Following items are checked with long dash by Cornell in pencil: "The Mill"; Frederick the Great; Marcel Duchamp
5½ x 8½ in. (14 x 21.5 cm)

Cornell was a free-lance picture researcher for numerous periodicals, drawing upon his own vast collection of photographs, books, magazines, and printed ephemera.

→ **78**

33 Marcel Duchamp
Postcard
30 APRIL 1946

1¢ Thomas Jefferson manila-colored postcard with printed green text postmarked NEW YORK N.Y. / APR 30 / 10^{30} PM / 1946.
recto Inscribed by Duchamp in blue ink: *Joseph Cornell / 3708 Utopia Parkway / Flushing / N.Y.*
verso Inscribed center by Duchamp in ink: *Au revoir / affectueusement / Marcel*
3½ x 5½ in. (8.3 x 14 cm)

On May 1, 1946, Duchamp sailed on the SS *Brazil* to Paris where he stayed until January 1947.

→ **23, 80, 97, C, T**

34 Greeting card

Unsigned commercial greeting card with celluloid animation of clown on bicycle and two elephants balancing on balls.
recto Printed message: GET WELL SOON / No Clowning !
Message printed inside:
Here's an animated greeting / card / And it goes right into / action / To hope you're getting / better / To everyone's satisfaction!
5¾ x 4¾ in. (14.6 x 12 cm)

→ **69, H**

35 Katherine Dreier
Envelope fragment
[1942]

Torn bottom center of cream-colored envelope with watermark WRITING / BY RYTEX.
recto Inscribed by Katherine Dreier in ink, partial address: *amp / 51st Street / New York*
2¼ x 2¼ in. (5.8 x 5.8 cm)

36 Joseph Cornell
Note
26 AUGUST 1943

Folded, manufactured card (composed of black waterproofing/tarlike material), probably used as wrapper.
recto Inscribed by Cornell in pencil: *8/26/43 / 1st day / N Y Allied / control (over) / phone M.D. / noon / picked up / 13th St Subway / stairs delivery / tap & sticks*
verso Inscribed by Cornell in pencil: *make into / receipt from / M.D. / adding / moustache / (un necessary) / collar like / watermelon summer*
6⅛ x 4 in. (15.3 x 10.2 cm)

→ **13, 66, J**

37 Marcel Duchamp
Postcard
2 SEPTEMBER 1943

1¢ Thomas Jefferson manila-colored postcard with printed green text postmarked NEW YORK, N.Y. / SEP 2/6-PM/1943. Postal cancellation reads BUY/WAR SAVINGS/BONDS AND STAMPS.
recto Typed center: *Joseph Cornell / 3708 Utopia Parkway / Flushing, L.I. / New York. Flushing* has been erased and retyped.
verso Text by Duchamp in blue ink: *Jeudi* [Thursday] */ Am leaving to morrow for / Washington – and then I will / be in Conn. for a few days. / Will write when I return. / Thanks for the Chinese letter / Affect – Marcel*
3½ x 5½ in. (8.3 x 14 cm)

Duchamp went to Washington, D.C., to deliver a *Boîte* (Series B) to Caresse Crosby, who had a short-lived gallery at G Place N.W. He then went to Katherine Dreier's Connecticut home to prepare the *Large Glass* for shipment to The Museum of Modern Art, New York, for extended loan until April 1946. It was also included in the fifteenth anniversary exhibition "Art in Progress" (May 24–October 15, 1944).

→ **54, H**

38 Katherine Dreier
Envelope fragment [annotated]
[8] SEPTEMBER 1942

Torn cream-colored envelope fragment postmarked, partially illegible, H CONN / SEP / 6-PM / 1942, with 10¢ United States Postage Special Delivery stamp.
recto Inscribed by Katherine Dreier in blue ink, partial address: *Duchamp*

38, also 42, 52

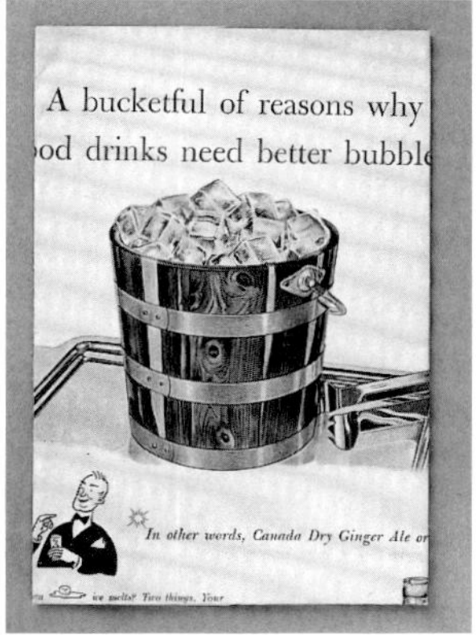

39

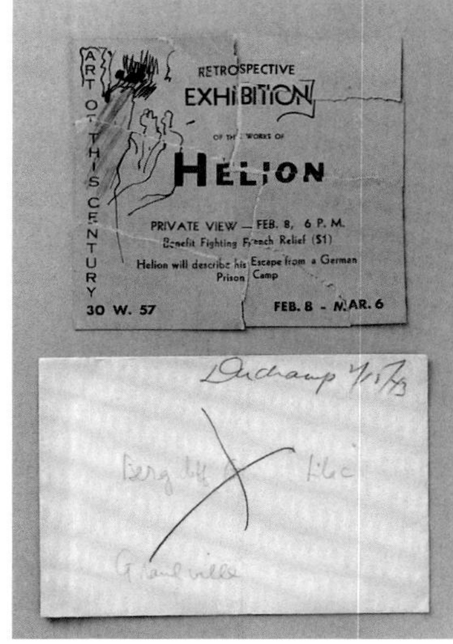

40a, b

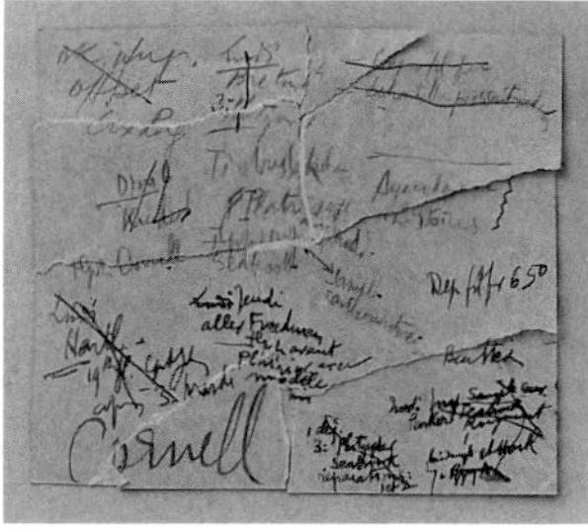

40b^v

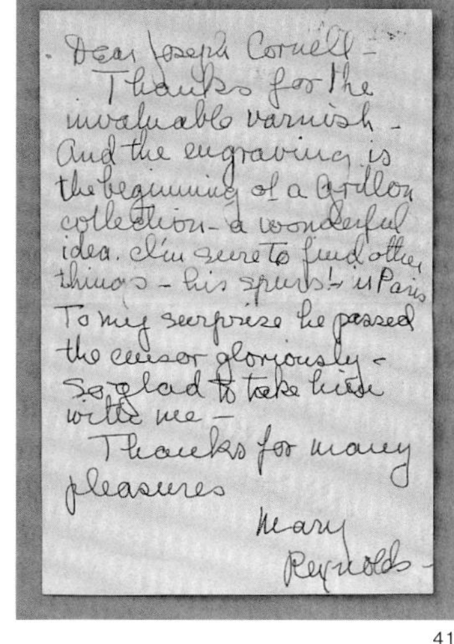
Dear Joseph Cornell –
Thanks for the
invaluable varnish –
And the engraving is
the beginning of a Grillon
collection – a wonderful
idea. I'm sure to find other
things – his spurs! – in Paris
To my surprise he passed
the censor gloriously –
So glad to take him
with me –
Thanks for many
pleasures
Mary
Reynolds –

41

verso Printed in red, partial return address: Kath / W

4⅛ x 9½ in. (10.5 x 24 cm), reconstructed

The postmark and stamp suggest that this envelope was the attempted delivery indicated by the special delivery notice.

→ 18, 42, 52, 78, E

39 Magazine advertisement [Canada Dry]
1942

Folded page (or back cover) torn from unidentified magazine.
recto Printed advertisement for 1942 Cadillac.
verso Printed advertisement for Canada Dry Pale Ginger Ale and Sparkling Water with slogan: A Bucketful of Reasons Why / Good Drinks Need Better Bubbles. Page is folded to frame illustration of bucket of ice with ice tongs on silver tray.

Opened: 11⅞ x 8⅝ in. (30 x 21.9 cm)
Folded: 6⅝ x 4⅜ in. (16.7 x 11.1 cm)

A *Green Box* note reads: "buy a / pair of ice tongs / as a Rdymade."

→ B

40 Marcel Duchamp
Envelope [annotated] / Note fragment
15 FEBRUARY 1943

a Cream-colored envelope.
recto Inscribed upper right by Cornell in pencil: *Duchamp 2/15/43* and center: *Bergdorff G. Lilac / Grandville* (later X-ed out by Cornell).

4½ x 6½ in. (11.4 x 16.5 cm)

b Printed gallery announcement on blue paper with red lettering, torn into eight fragments, inside envelope: RETROSPECTIVE / EXHIBITION / OF THE WORKS OF HÉLION / PRIVATE VIEW – FEB 8 6 P.M. / BENEFIT FIGHTING FRENCH RELIEF / Helion will describe his Escape from a German / Prison Camp / ART OF THIS CENTURY / 30 W. 57 / FEB. 8 – MAR. 6 Added along left edge recto in black ink is drawing by Duchamp of two seated figures facing wall (?), with wall shading in red pencil.
verso Inscribed (in text blocks) upper left to right, top to bottom, by Duchamp in red pencil:
Bk. imp / offset / [undecipherable]
lundi / Breton 1 h / 3 Photog
~~Couper fil fer/echantillons pressait [?] Freedman~~
Dim / Kiesler / tlph [telephone] *Cornell*
Timbres Sekula/ 8 Platrier 14th at Mad /
[undecipherable] */ Seabrook / sample couverture*
Agenda histoires
Inscribed upper left to right, top to bottom, by Duchamp in black ink: *Lundi / Hartl / 19th fl* [?]
Cptyh / apres 3 mardi
~~Lundi~~ Jeudi / aller Freedman—tlph avant
Platrier avec modéle
Dep. fil fer 6.50
B.... [undecipherable]
1 dej. / 3: Photographer / Seabrook rèparations:
1 et 2 Mardi Imp. sample couv. / Parker Seabrook
Rougemont / 6: [undecipherable] *et Hartl / 7:*
Peggy
Inscribed bottom left by Duchamp in pencil:
Cornell

5⅛ x 5½ in. (12.9 x 14 cm)

Bergdorf Goodman is a high-end department store in New York. Jean Grandville was a nineteenth-century French engraver and illustrator. Many of Duchamp's notations (both French and English) refer to the *VVV Almanac for 1943*, March, including fabricating the covers, die-cut paperboard, and chicken wire [*fil fer*] insert. Leon Hartl was Duchamp's partner in a 1920s dye shop. Authors Robert Allerton Parker, William Seabrook, and Denis de Rougemont, and artist Sonia Sekula were contributors to this issue.

→ 17, 49, 51, S

41 Mary Reynolds
Christmas card
DECEMBER [1945]

Printed red Merry Christmas note card, folded horizontally. Text by Mary Reynolds in ink: *Dear Joseph Cornell – / Thanks for the / invaluable varnish – / And the engraving is / the beginning of a Grillon / collection – a wonderful / idea. I'm sure to find other / things – his spurs! – in Paris / To my surprise he passed / the censor gloriously – / So glad to take him / with me – / Thanks for many / pleasures / Mary / Reynolds–*

Closed: 3½ x 4⅜ in. (8.8 x 11.2 cm)

Reynolds, living in occupied Paris at this time and active in the French Resistance, was appropriately circumspect about her public behavior, hence the paranoia about passing the "censors." The source of the name *Amiral* and/or *Amiral Grillon* is unknown and would recur in correspondence between Cornell and Reynolds. It also appears as an inscription in Cornell's *¾ Bird's-Eye View of 'A Watch-Case for Marcel Duchamp'* (1944) reproduce in *View* (series 5, no. 1, March 1945): p. 22.

→ 9, 80, 84, F

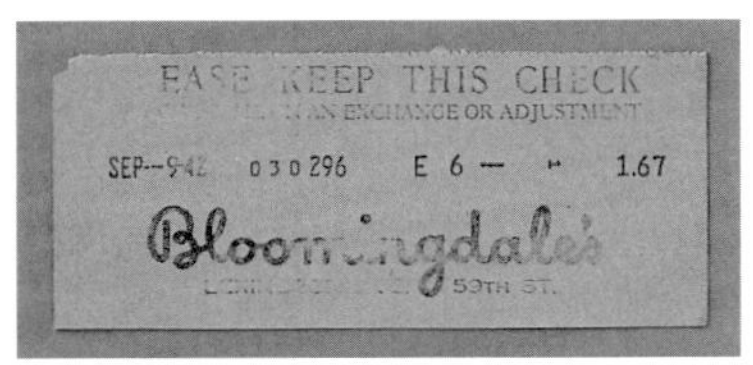

47

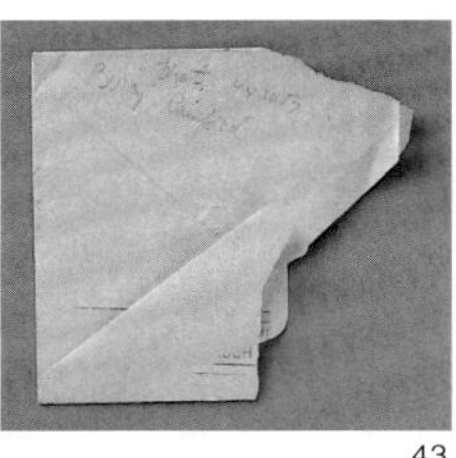

43

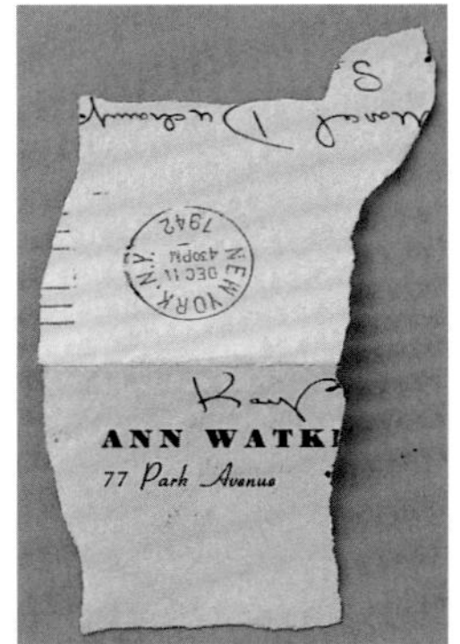

44

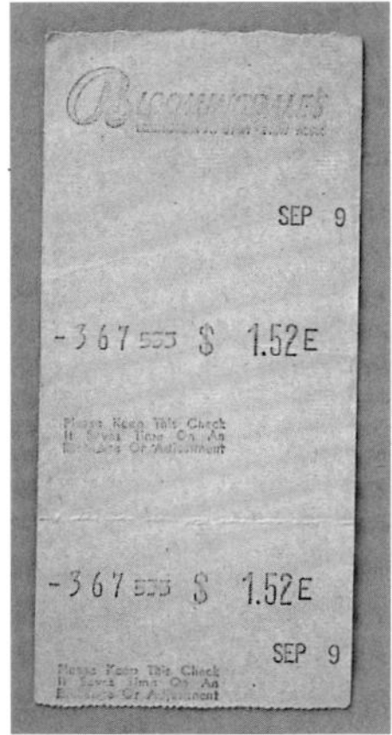

45

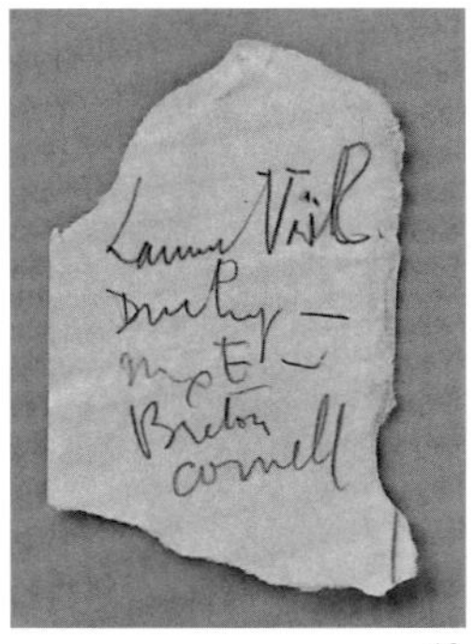

46

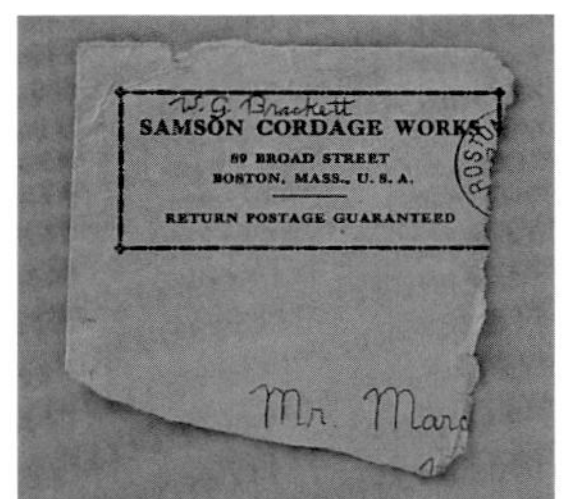

48

42 Katherine Dreier
Envelope fragment [annotated]

Torn bottom center of cream-colored envelope.
recto Inscribed by Katherine Dreier in blue ink, partial address: *Mr. Marcel / 440 East 5 / New York– N*
verso Inscribed by unidentified hand in pencil, partial note: *no answer* [underlined in purple] / *2804*

Reconstructed: 4⅛ x 9½ in. (10.5 x 24 cm)

→ 18, 38 (photo), 52, 78

43 Joseph Cornell
Note
[9] DECEMBER [1944]

Torn light gray envelope fragment partially postmarked NEW YORK / DEC / 9 3 / 1. Postal cancellation verso reads CHURCH [STREET STATION].
recto Inscribed by unidentified hand in blue ink, partial address: *M. / 210 W. / New Y*
verso Inscribed by Cornell in pencil: *phot. 44 W 57 / Percy Rainford*

4⅜ x 4⅞ in. (11.2 x 12.4 cm)

Percy Rainford was a commercial photographer who took photographs in January 1945 of Duchamp's 14th Street studio for *View* (series 5, no. 1, March 1945) and possibly of *Female Fig Leaf* (1950) for the cover of *le surréalisme, même* [*surrealism, even*] (no. 1, Winter 1956).

44 Kay Boyle
Envelope fragment
11 DECEMBER 1942

Torn top edge of light salmon envelope postmarked NEW YORK, N.Y. / DEC 11 / 430 PM / 1942, with partial watermark STRA[THMORE].
recto Inscribed by Kay Boyle in black ink, partial address: *Marcel Duchamp / Se*
verso Inscribed above printed return address by Boyle in black ink: *Kay B* Printed in black, partial return address: Ann Watk / 77 Park Avenue

2½ x 2½ in. (6.3 x 6.3 cm)

Ann Watkins was Boyle's literary agent.

→ G

45 Receipt [Bloomingdale's]
9 SEPTEMBER [1942]

Bloomingdale's cash-register receipt stamped with total ($1.52) and date (Sep 9).

4⅝ x 2⅛ in. (11.8 x 5.4 cm)

→ 47

46 Marcel Duchamp
Note
[1942]

Torn cream-colored paper fragment with partial watermark: HAMMERMILL / [B]OND / [MADE] IN USA.
recto Inscribed by Duchamp in pencil: *Laurance Vail* [sic] / *Duchamp / Max E / Breton / Cornell* Check marks in pencil accompany Duchamp's and Ernst's names.

3½ x 2¼ in. (8.9 x 5.8 cm)

All these artists exhibited at Art of This Century.

→ S

47 Receipt [Bloomingdale's]
9 SEPTEMBER [1942]

Bloomingdale's cash-register receipt stamped with total ($1.67) and date (Sep 9).

2 x 4⅝ in. (5.1 x 11.7 cm)

→ 45, C

48 Joseph Cornell
Note
[1942]

Torn upper left corner of manila envelope with printed return address: SAMSON CORDAGE WORKS / 89 BROAD STREET / BOSTON, MASS., U.S.A.
recto Inscribed above printed return address by sender in black ink: *W. G. Brackett* and below, partial address: *Mr. Marc*
verso Inscribed by Cornell in pencil: *Betty / 1/6/44*

3 x 3 in. (7.6 x 7.6 cm)

Elizabeth "Betty" Benton, Cornell's sister, accompanied him on a visit to Duchamp's 14th Street studio.

→ 25, S

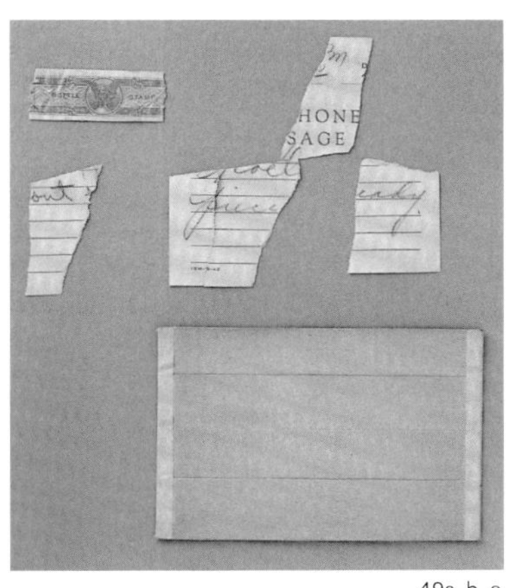
49a, b, c

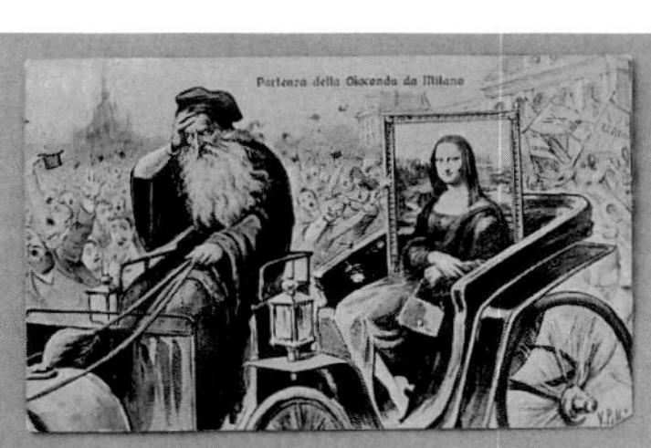
50r

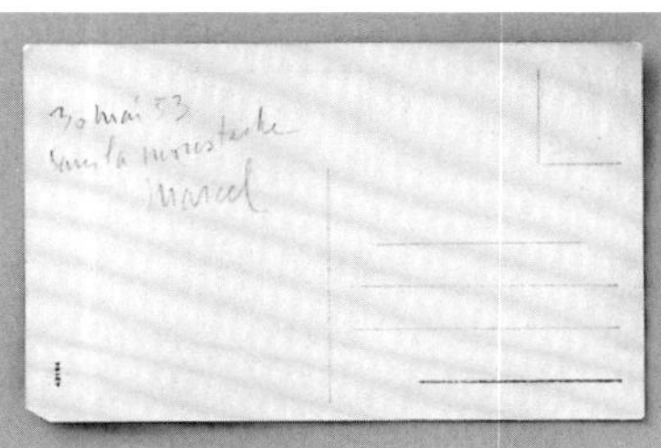
50v

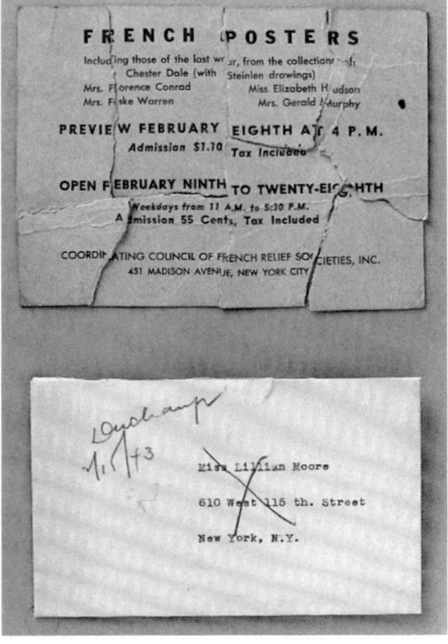

51a, br

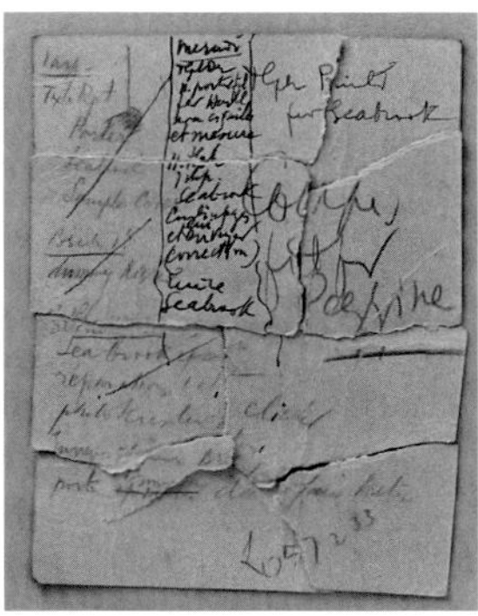
51bv

49 Message filer [telephone]
15 FEBRUARY 1943

a Three-pocket message filer constructed of manila card.
verso Inscribed top center by Cornell in pencil: *Duchamp / 2/15/43*
3⅛ x 4⅝ in. (8 x 11.8 cm)

b Red and white bottle stamp, series III, of American eagle, torn at both ends, inserted into top slot.
⅞ x 2 in. (2 x 5 cm)

c Five torn fragments of two printed phone messages on white paper with red lines inserted into bottom slot.
Printed on fragment from top center of one sheet: [P]HONE / [MES]SAGE. Writing in pencil is indecipherable.
Printed on two fragments forming lower left corner of same sheet at extreme left edge in red: 15 M–19–42. Writing across two top lines is indecipherable. Inscribed underneath by unidentified hand in pencil: *piece*
Inscribed on fragment forming lower right corner of same sheet by unidentified hand in pencil: [r]*eady. F*
Fifth fragment does not match other four fragments and appears to belong to another message due to different handwriting. Only legible word, inscribed by unidentified hand in pencil: *out*
1⅝ x 1 in. (4.2 x 2.4 cm); 1⅝ x 1¼ in. (4 x 3 cm); 1¾ x 1¼ in. (3.6 x 3.2 cm); 1⅝ x ⅞ in. (4 x 2.2 cm); 1⅝ x 1¼ in. (4 x 3.2 cm)
→ 17, 40, 51, Q

50 Marcel Duchamp
Postcard [*Mona Lisa*]
30 MAY 1953

Black-and-white Italian postcard with illustration of *Mona Lisa* in open carriage driven by bearded man in robe depicting Leonardo da Vinci.
recto Printed at top: Partenza della Gioconda da Milano [Departure of *Mona Lisa* from Milan]
verso Inscribed upper left by Duchamp in pencil: *30 Mai 53 / Sans la moustache / Marcel* [30 May 53 / Without the moustache / Marcel]
3¾ x 5⅜ in. (8.7 x 13.7 cm)

An Italian stole the *Mona Lisa* in August 1911 from the Louvre. After its recovery in Florence three years later, the painting was exhibited in Florence, Rome, and Milan, where it became a *cause célèbre* due to the question of Italian/French patrimony. The case prompted popular postcards and editorial cartoons depicting the painting's departure or arrival in various cities.
→ 4, 55, 56, 99, 105, C

51 Marcel Duchamp
Envelope [annotated] / Note fragment
15 FEBRUARY 1943

a Cream-colored envelope, slit open at top.
recto Typed center: *Miss Lillian Moore / 610 West 115 th. Street / New York, N.Y.* Address has been X-ed out. Inscribed diagonally at left of address by Cornell in pencil: *Duchamp 2/15/43*
verso Inscribed on flap by Cornell in ink: *Joseph Cornell / 3708 Utopia Parkway / Flushing*
4½ x 6½ in. (11.4 x 16.5 cm)

b Printed gallery announcement on blue paper with red lettering, torn into eight fragments, inside envelope: FRENCH POSTERS / Including those of the last war, from the collections of / Mrs. Chester Dale (with Steinlein drawings) / Mrs. Florence Conrad, Miss Elizabeth Hudson / Mrs. Fiske Warren, Mrs. Gerald Murphy / PREVIEW FEBRUARY EIGHTH AT 4 P.M. / Admisssions $1.10 Tax Included / OPEN FEBRUARY NINTH TO TWENTY-EIGHTH / Weekdays from 11 A.M. to 5:30 P.M. / Admission 55 Cents, Tax Included / COORDINATING COUNCIL OF FRENCH RELIEF SOCIETIES, INC./ 451 MADISON AVENUE, NEW YORK CITY
verso Inscribed left column by Duchamp in red pencil, partial note: *Imp / Txt. Rpt / Parker / Seabrook / Sample Cover / Breton 1h / dummy Kiesler / 8 E PH / Seabrook apres* [épreuve] / *réparations 1 et 2 / photo Kiesler à clicher / Tanguy apres Breton / porte Novelle cliche faire Breton*
Inscribed center column by Duchamp in black ink, partial note: *mercredi / Tlph / I. porte fil / fer Hartl / encre aiguille / et mesure / II. Tlph / imp. / Seabrook /* [con. . . .] */ lui / et envoyer / (correction) / Encre / Seabrook*
Inscribed right column by Duchamp in red pencil, partial note: *Tlph Printer / pour Seabrook / coupe / fil fer / Peggine* [sic] and diagonally at bottom right: *LO57233*
4¾ x 7 in. (12.1 x 17.8 cm)

Lillian Moore was a dancer and dance historian who contributed regularly to *Dance Index.* Many of Duchamp's notations (both French and English) refer to the *VVV Almanac for 1943*, March, including fabricating the covers, die-cut paperboard, chicken wire [*fil fer*] insert, and a demonstration photograph with Pegeen Vail, daughter of Peggy Guggenheim and Laurence Vail. Authors Robert Allerton Parker and William Seabrook and editor André Breton were contributors to this issue.

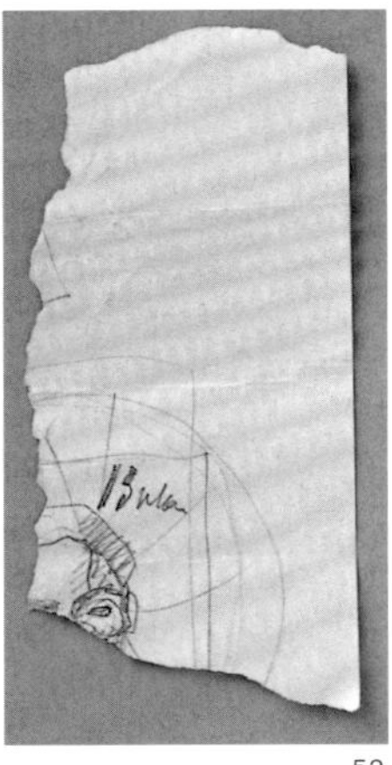
53

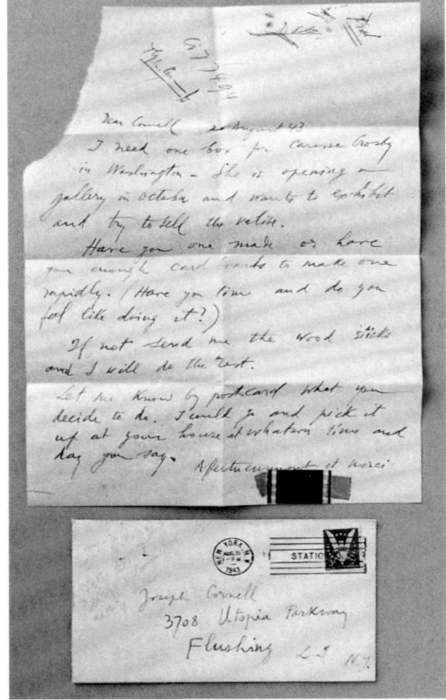
54a, b

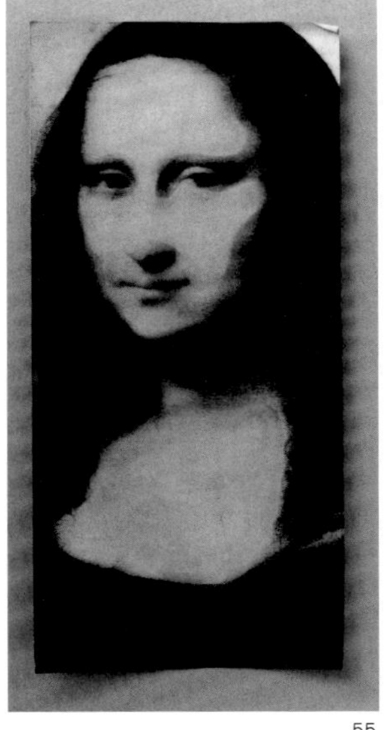
55

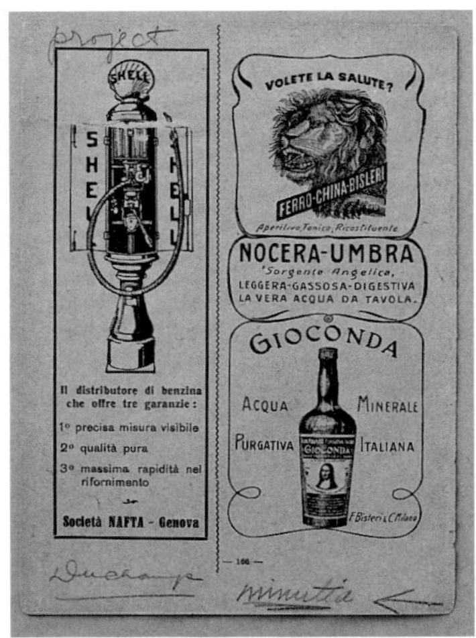

56

Frederick Kiesler collaborated with Duchamp on the back cover.

→ 17, 40, 49, B

52 Katherine Dreier
Envelope fragment [annotated]
8 SEPTEMBER 1942

Torn cream-colored envelope fragment post-marked REC'D NEW YORK, N.Y. / GRA[ND CENTRAL ANN]EX / SEP 8 / 11³⁰ PM / 1942, with partial watermark BY RYTEX.
recto Stamped: *SPECI*[AL] and inscribed along left edge by Katherine Dreier in blue ink: [co]*py of Time*
Reconstructed: 4⅛ x 9½ in. (10.5 x 24 cm)

Dreier sent Duchamp a copy of the September 7, 1942, issue of *Time*, which included an article on Duchamp, via special delivery.

→ 18, 38 (photo), 42, 78, R

53 Drawing [Portrait]

Torn off-white paper fragment folded in half, then folded in quarters, with pencil drawing by unidentified hand of man's face placed inside double-lined square and triple-lined circle. Paper is torn at nose, showing only forehead and one eye heavily outlined in circles.
recto Inscribed above drawing by unidentified hand in pencil: *13 uton*
5¼ x 2⅝ in. (13.3 x 6.6 cm)

→ E

54 Marcel Duchamp
Envelope / Letter
20 AUGUST 1943

a Beige envelope, slit open at left, postmarked NEW YORK, N.Y. / AUG 20 / 1-PM / 1943, with purple 3¢ WIN THE WAR eagle stamp. Postal cancellation reads STATION O.
recto Inscribed by Duchamp in blue ink: *Joseph Cornell / 3708 Utopia Parkway / Flushing / L.I. / N.Y.*
Inscribed upper left by Cornell in pencil: *Aug 22 / tel 5:30 / Sat appoint "living a damn fool's life" / nothing new*
verso Inscribed center of flap by Duchamp in blue ink: *Duchamp / 56 Seventh Ave / New York City*
3⅝ x 6½ in. (9.2 x 16.4 cm)

b Letter on plain paper inside envelope.
Text by Duchamp in ink:
Dear Cornell 20 August 43 / I need one box for Caresse Crosby / in Washington – She is opening a / gallery in October and wants to exhibit / and try to sell the valise. / Have you one made or have / you enough card boards to make one / rapidly. (Have you time and do you / feel like doing it?) / If not send me the wood sticks / and I will do the rest. / Let me know by postcard what you / decide to do. I could go and pick it / up at your house at whatever time and / day you say. / Affectueusement et merci.
35mm motion picture film frame of Duchamp substitutes for his signature.
Inscribed diagonally at top of page by unidentified hand in pencil: *Fred / Ci 77494 / Jsph Crn_l*
11 x 8⅜ in. (28 x 21.4 cm)

The *Boîte* version requested here was from Series B. Crosby was an author, art dealer, and publisher who with her husband, Harry Crosby, founded The Black Sun Press in 1927.

→ 37, H

55 Joseph Cornell
Photostat [*Mona Lisa*]

Photostat of *Mona Lisa*. Image was probably altered (suggested by chemical stains verso), and adhesive residue suggests that Photostat was once pasted down.
9¾ x 4½ in. (24.8 x 11.6 cm)

→ 4, 50, 56, 69, 99, 105, S

56 Joseph Cornell
Guidebook advertisement [Gioconda Acqua Minerale]

Back cover of Italian guidebook.
recto Printed advertisements for Shell gasoline featuring illustration of gas pump and three digestive remedies including Gioconda Acqua Minerale Purgativa Italiana, Ferro-China-Bisleri featuring illustration of lion, and Nocera Umbra la Vera Acqua da Tavola.
Inscribed upper left by Cornell in pencil: *project* and along bottom: <u>*Duchamp*</u> <u>*minutia*</u> ←
verso Printed table of conventional signs and principal abbreviations, and advertisements for Shell Oil and Esanofele Gharisce le Febbre di Malaria.
6⅝ x 4⅞ in. (17 x 12.2 cm)

→ 4, 50, 55, 99, 105, B, O

59r

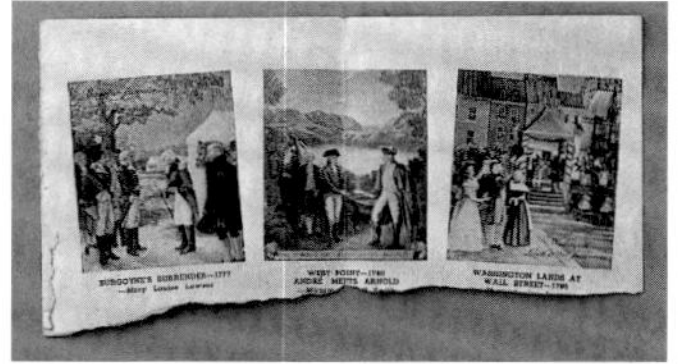

59v

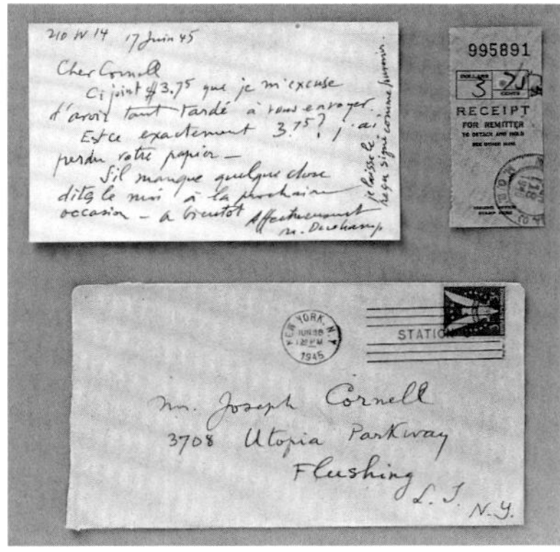

57a, b, c

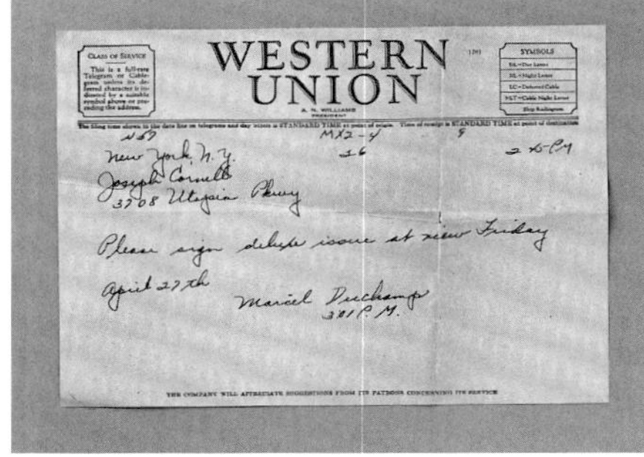

58

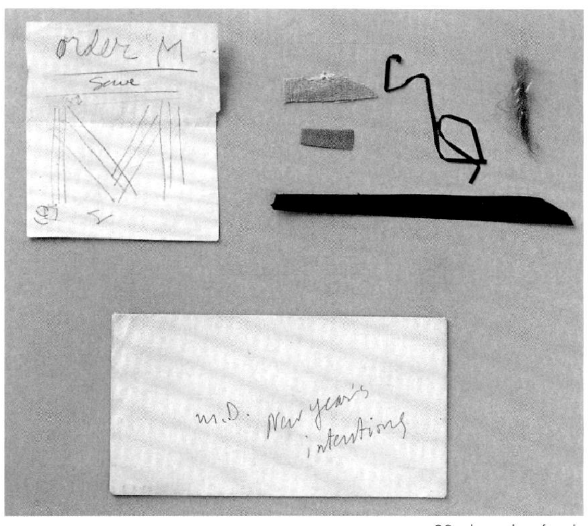

60a, b, c, d, e, f, g, h

57 Marcel Duchamp
Envelope / Note / Receipt [money order]
17 JUNE 1945

a Off-white envelope, slit open at left edge, postmarked NEW YORK N.Y. / JUN 18 / 1^{30} PM / 1945, with purple 3¢ WIN THE WAR eagle stamp. Postal cancellation reads STATION O.
recto Inscribed center by Duchamp in blue ink: *Mr. Joseph Cornell / 3708 Utopia Parkway / Flushing / L.I. / N.Y.*
3¾ x 6⅝ in. (9.4 x 16.7 cm)

b Printed announcement on off-white card inside envelope: Editors of View / invite you to meet Marcel Duchamp / at One E. 53rd Street / on Thursday March 15, 1945 / Cocktails 5:30 - 7:00 / R.S.V.P.
verso Text by Duchamp in blue ink: *210 W 14 17 Juin 45 / Cher Cornell / Ci joint $3.75 que je m'excuse / d'avoir tant tardé à vous envoyer / Este exactement 3.75 ? j'ai / perdu votre papier – / S'il manque quelque chose / dits le moi à la prochaine / occasion – à bientot / Affectueusement / M. Duchamp / je laisse le / reçu signe comme souvenir.* [210 W 14 June 17, 1945 / Dear Cornell / Here's the $3.75 that I'm sorry / has taken so long to send to you. / Is it exactly $3.75 ? I've lost your paper – / If something is still missing / tell me next time – see you soon. / Affectionately M. Duchamp / I leave the / signed receipt as a souvenir.]
3¼ x 5⅜ in. (8.3 x 13.6 cm)

c Blue postal money order receipt for $3.75 inside envelope, stamped recto: *#995891 / Jun 18, 1945*
verso Inscribed by Duchamp in blue ink: *Marcel*
3 x 1⅜ in. (7.6 x 3.4 cm)

The invitation refers to publication of the special Duchamp issue of *View* (series 5, no. 1, March 1945).
→ 66, 87, 98, O (item c only), T (items a and b only)

58 Marcel Duchamp
Telegram
26 APRIL [1945]

Western Union Telegram.
recto Inscribed by Western Union Office in black ink: *N 57 MX2-4 9 / New York, N.Y. 26 2 45 PM / Joseph Cornell / 3708 Utopia Pkwy / Please sign deluxe issue at view Friday / April 27th / Marcel Duchamp / 3:01 P.M.*
5⅝ x 8 in. (14.4 x 20.3 cm)

Cornell, a contributor to the Duchamp issue of *View* (series 5, no. 1, March 1945), was among the seventeen who signed a blank page bearing contributor signatures that was included in the one hundred copies of the deluxe edition of the issue.
→ H

59 Brochure [George Washington]

Torn fragment of printed three-panel brochure titled "Historic Murals." Brochure featured reproductions of historical paintings (left to right): Mary Louise Lawser, *Burgoyne's Surrender-1777*; Miriam __?__ Smith, *West Point-1780 / André Meets Arnold*; and Mary Louise Lawser, *Washington Lands at Wall Street-1789*.
recto Inscribed at top by Cornell in pencil: *466* [circled] *1536*
3¾ x 3⅞ in. (9.4 x 9.8 cm)
→ 64, 112, 113, 114, G, T

60 Joseph Cornell
Envelope [annotated] / Note / Material fragments
22 JANUARY 1943

a Pale gray envelope.
recto Inscribed center by Duchamp in blue ink: *M.D. / New Year's / intentions*
Inscribed lower left by Cornell in red pencil: *1943*
verso Inscribed by Cornell in pencil: *green added at gallery / Virg. Bird 1/22/43*
3⅝ x 6½ in. (9.2 x 16.5 cm)

b Cut and folded paper fragment with typed letter to Cornell's mother regarding her question to a radio (?) program for "Information Please" inside envelope.
verso Inscribed above double-lined drawing of letter M by Cornell in pencil: *Order "M"s* / *save* / ¼
Opened: 4¼ x 3¾ in. (10.8 x 9.4 cm)

c Irregular long strip of heavy black paper inside envelope.
½ x 5⅝ in. (1.3 x 14.3 cm)

d Fragment of natural linen, cut in same irregular fashion as **c**, inside envelope.
½ x 1¼ in. (1.3 x 4.7 cm)

e Strip of coated "linen" tape inside envelope.
1 x ⅜ in. (2.5 x 1 cm)

f Strip of green cellophane, possibly from cigarette or tobacco package, inside envelope.
7⅛ in., length (18 cm, length)

g Brass ring, cut irregularly, inside envelope.
⅛ in., diameter (5 mm, diameter)

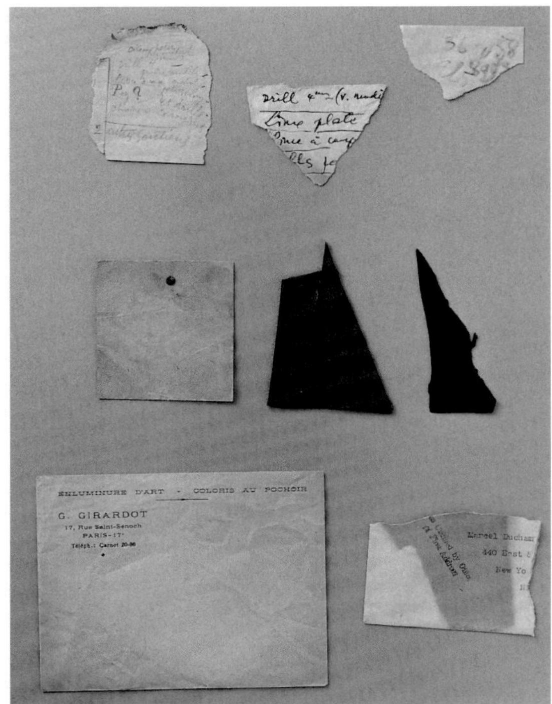

61a, b, c, d, e, f, g, h

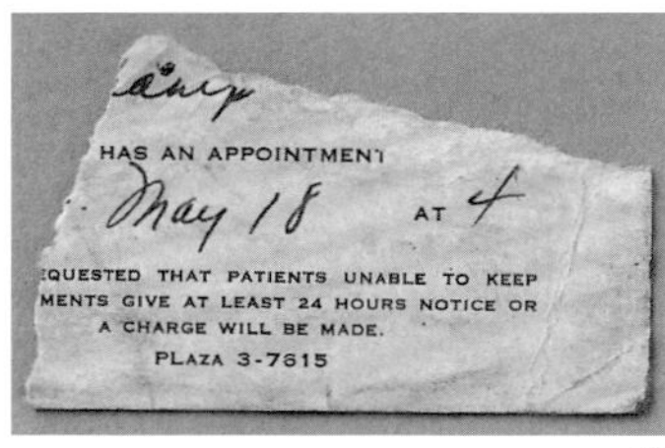
HAS AN APPOINTMENT
May 18 AT 4
QUESTED THAT PATIENTS UNABLE TO KEEP
MENTS GIVE AT LEAST 24 HOURS NOTICE OR
A CHARGE WILL BE MADE.
PLAZA 3-7615

62

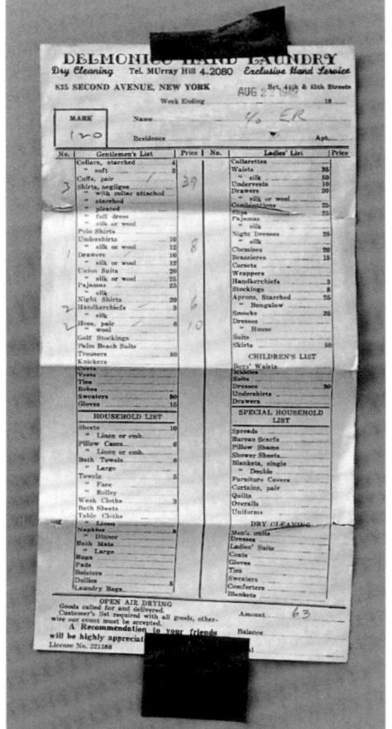

63

h Some unraveled green threads and some hot pink straight fibers inside envelope.
1½ in., length (3.8 cm, length)

The items inside the envelope relate to the assembly of the *Boîte* edition. Item b is a drawing of the wood molding used for the "M" monogram on the lid. Item c is the same black paper used for the folders. Items d and e were used in the construction of the inner container.

→ 23, 61, 68, 91, 110, 111, 115, 116, 117, P

61 Envelope / Notes / Remnants
7 SEPTEMBER 1942

a Beige envelope printed verso across top: ENLUMINURE D'ART • COLORIS AU POCHOIR with printed return address: G. GIRARDOT / 17, Rue Saint-Senoch / PARIS-17e / Téléph.: Carnot 20-66.
4½ x 5¾ in. (11.3 x 14.5 cm)

b Used fine-grain sandpaper or finishing paper manufactured by Minnesota 3 M (stamped verso) inside envelope.
2⅞ x 2¾ in. (7.3 x 6.8 cm)

c Triangular-shaped fragment of green suede inside envelope.
3⅜ x 1⅝ in. (8.6 x 4 cm)

d Roughly triangular cut fragment of brown cowhide leather inside envelope.
3½ x 2½ in. (8.7 x 6.4 cm)

e Torn fragment from Hershey's Cocoa can inside envelope.
verso Inscribed by Duchamp in pencil: *ciseaux petits / por metal / Drill 4 mm / prendre modèle / Pince à metal / petits clory / Peg ? et drille / chaine = correspondts / 2 autres soutiens*
2¾ x 2 in. (7 x 5 cm)

f Paper fragment inside envelope.
recto Inscribed by Duchamp in black ink: *Drill 4 mm (v. neodi / Line plate / Pince à coup*(e) */ Ils fe*(r)
2⅛ x 2¾ in. (5.2 x 7 cm)

g Lower left corner of second beige envelope, postmarked verso NEW YORK, N.Y. GRAND CENTRAL ANNEX REG / SEP 7 / 13-AM / 1942, inside envelope **a**.
recto Typed, partial address: *Marcel Ducham / 440 East 5 / New Yo* and stamped left of address: *Claimed by Office / of First Address*
2⅛ x 3⅜ in. (5.2 x 8.6 cm)

h Torn white paper fragment inside envelope.
recto Inscribed by Cornell in pencil: *36 W 58 / El 5 8943*
1½ x 2½ in. (3.8 x 6.3 cm)

The items relate to the assembly of the *Boîte* edition. Item a refers to the Paris pochoir studio that made the color reproductions between 1935 and 1941. Items b, c, and d are fragments of materials used in the assembly. Items e and f are notations about the assembly process.

→ 23, 60, 68, 91, 110, 111, 115, 116, 117, 118, Q

62 Marcel Duchamp
Note
18 MAY

Printed doctor or dentist appointment card.
recto Inscribed by unidentified hand in blue ink: [Duc]*hamp / May 18* [at] *4*
verso Inscribed upside-down to recto orientation by Duchamp in black ink, partial note in French: *ansoft / en in Camp / lag 122 / èse*
1⅝ x 2⅝ in. (4.2 x 6.6 cm)

→ E

63 Receipt [Delmonico Hand Laundry]
22 AUGUST 1942

Folded laundry bill with dark blue-gray paper tabs at top and bottom from Delmonico Hand Laundry, 835 Second Avenue, New York, stamped: *Aug 22 1942*.
verso Inscribed where name should appear in pencil: *40 ER*
Following items totaling $.63 are inscribed by unidentified hand in pencil:

3	Shirts	*39*
1	Drawers	*8*
2	Handkerchiefs	*6*
2	Hose, pair	*10*

10⅞ x 6 in. (27.6 x 13.5 cm)

→ 12, 16, 72, J

64

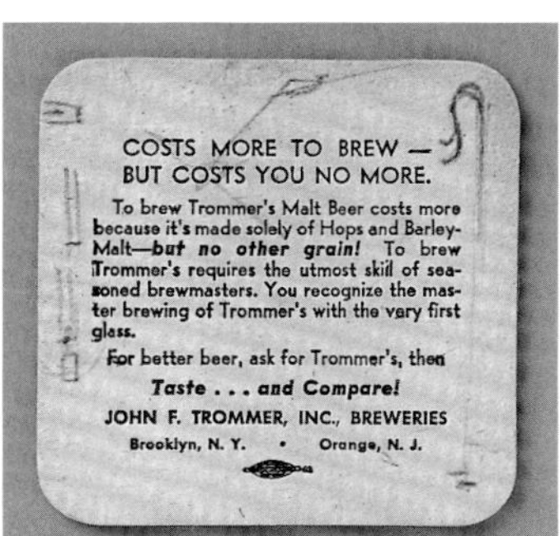

65

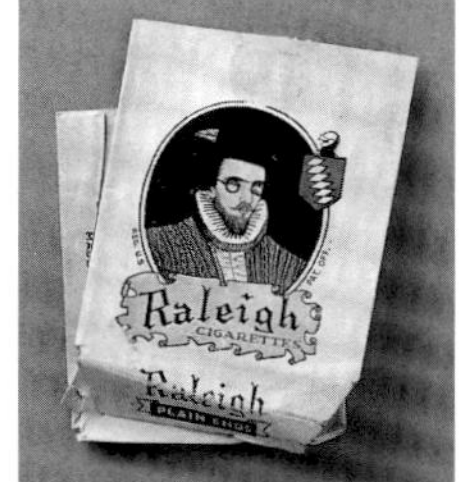

66r

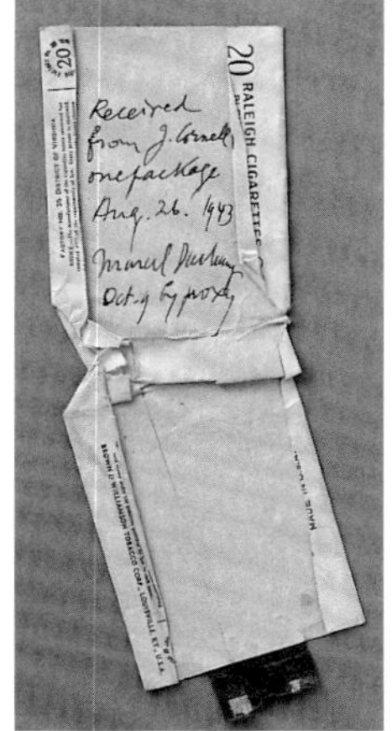

66v

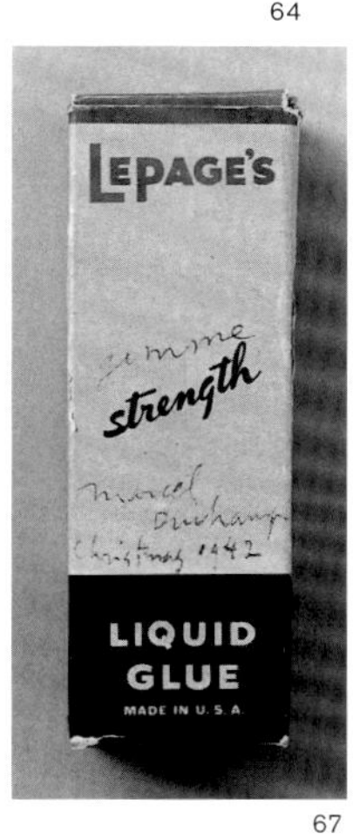

67

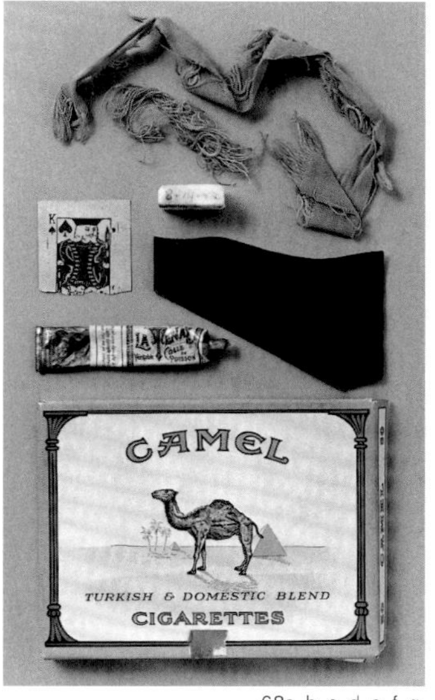

68a, b, c, d, e, f, g

64 Marcel Duchamp
Paper fragment [*Allégorie de genre*]

Fragment of black paper silhouette of map of Mexico with faint pencil marks, mounted at center on blue-black construction paper, folded in half, then in quarters.
1½ x 24⅜ in. (3.8 x 61.9 cm)

The shape of this black paper scrap is similar to the silhouette of the map of Mexico in Duchamp's *Allégorie de genre* (1943).
→ 59, 112, 113, 114, O

65 Marcel Duchamp
Drawing [*Boîte* edition]

Paper coaster with rounded corners advertising Trommer's The Malt Beer, featuring two dwarfs holding mugs.
recto Printed text advertising beer's quality with pencil line drawings by Duchamp at top and along left and right sides.
verso Printed: Tastes Better Because – Brewed / Solely of Malt and Hops / There's an interesting message on the other side
4 x 3⅞ in. (10 x 10 cm)

These line drawings relate to structural elements involved in assembling the *Boîte* edition. The hooked line drawing at right is of a metal hinge rod.
→ B, H

66 Marcel Duchamp
Receipt [Raleigh cigarette package]
9 OCTOBER 1943

Cut and opened package for Raleigh-brand unfiltered cigarettes featuring illustration of Sir Raleigh in Brisk costume. Blue U.S. tax stamp for class A 20 cigarettes is attached at top. Printed on opposite side: FOR VICTORY / BUY UNITED STATES / WAR BONDS / AND / STAMPS.
recto Inscribed by Duchamp in ink: *Received / from J. Cornell / one package / Aug. 26. 1943 / Marcel Duchamp / Oct. 9 by proxy*
verso Drawing of pair of reading glasses over Sir Raleigh's eyes by Duchamp in ink.
6⅜ x 2¼ in. (16 x 5.6 cm)

Dating links this receipt to an earlier delivery. It is implied that Sir Walter Raleigh is exercising the proxy.
→ 13, 36, 57, 87, 98, G, T

67 Marcel Duchamp
Cardboard box [Gimme Strength]
21 DECEMBER 1942

Yellow and black cardboard box with red and black lettering for LePage's Liquid Glue.
recto Inscribed above printed word "strength" by Duchamp in ink: *gimme* and below printed word "strength": *Marcel / Duchamp / Christmas 1942*
4⅝ x 1⅝ x 1 in. (11.7 x 4.0 x 2.6 cm)

Cornell described this birthday/Christmas gift from Duchamp in his diary for December 21, 1942, as a "readymade 'gimme strength' a glue box empty." Joseph Cornell Papers, AAA, 1058:890.
→ 11, B, T

68 Cardboard box [Camel cigarettes] / Materials / Fragments
14 AUGUST 1942

a Cardboard box for fifty Camel cigarettes. Bottom of box bears factor imprint for No. 4 / District of North Carolina, and inside lid is printed: Camel / The Better Cigarette manufactured by R.J. Reynolds Tobacco Company / Winston-Salem, N.C. U.S.A. Remnant of blue tax stamp is attached at center bottom.
4⅝ x 5¾ x ⅝ in. (11.6 x 14.8 x 1.5 cm)

b Torn fragment of miniature playing card of the King of Spades inside box.
verso Inscribed by Cornell in pencil: *57 & 8th / Sun – / Sep*
1¾ x 1⅝ in. (4.4 x 4 cm)

c Lump of sugar inside box.
Inscribed on long edge by Cornell in pencil: *8-14-42*
1⅛ x ¾ x ⅜ in. (2.8 x 1.9 x .9 cm)

d Crumpled strip of pink frayed cotton fabric inside box.
1⅜ x 1 in. (3.5 x 2.4 cm)

e Clump of pink threads inside box.
4 x 2⅜ in. (10.2 x 6 cm)

f Roughly triangular cut fragment of brown cowhide leather with two small holes inside box.
3⅜ x ¾ x ⅜ in. (8.5 x 2.1 x 1.1 cm)

g Lead tube (missing cap) of French fish glue, printed: La Tenax / Véritable / Colle de Poisson, inside box.
3 x ¾ in. (7.6 x 1.9 cm)

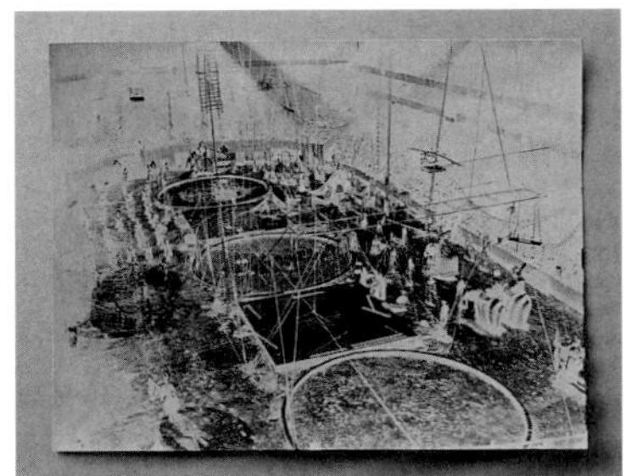

69

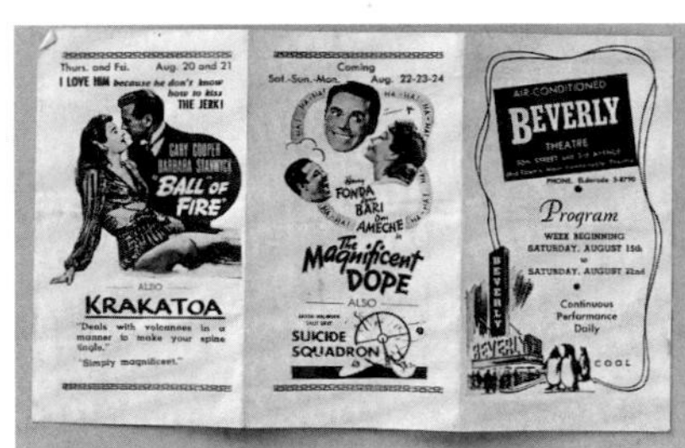

70

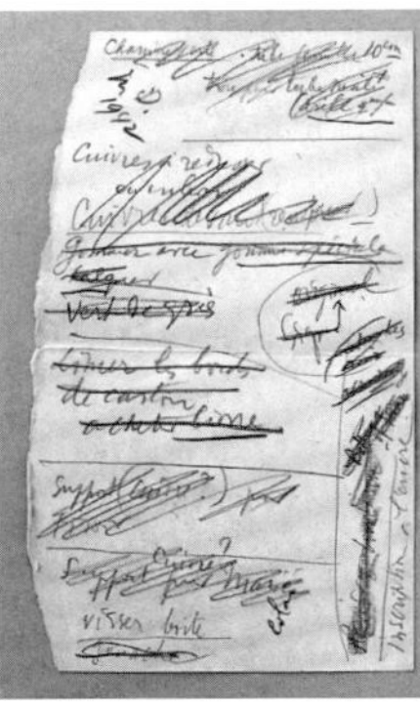

71

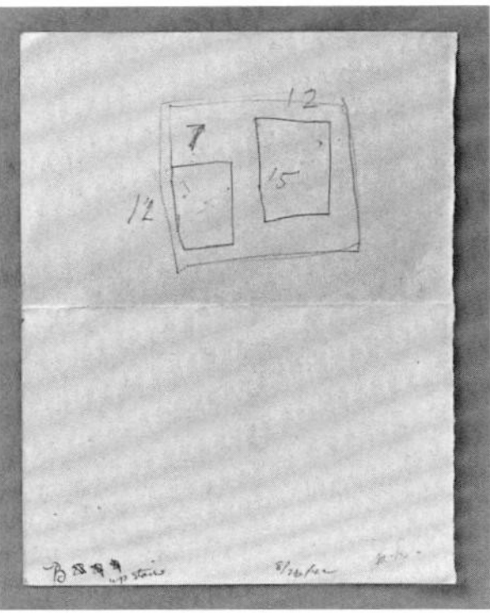

72

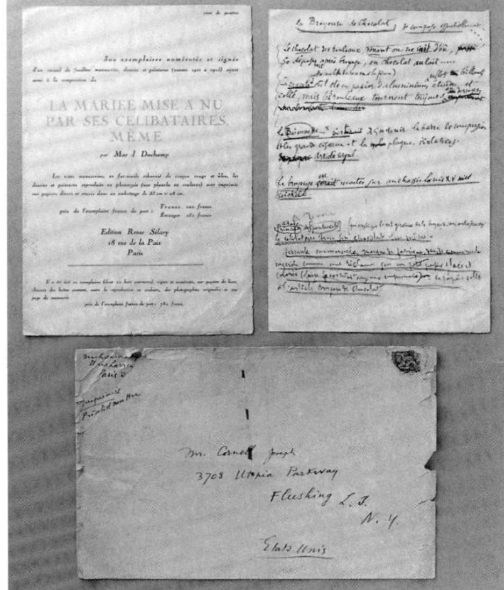

73, also 90a, b

Items f and g relate to the assembly of the *Boîte* edition. Among the destinations located at 57th Street and Eighth Avenue is a Horn and Hardart Automat.

→ 2, 24, 29, 30, 61 (item c only), D

69 Joseph Cornell
Photostat [circus]

Photostat (positive printed as negative) of grand parade in a three-ring circus.

6¾ x 8½ in. (17.2 x 21.6 cm)

→ 34, 55, G, P

70 Brochure [Beverly Theatre]
15 AUGUST [1942]

Folded brochure for Beverly Theatre, 50th Street and Third Avenue, listing movie program for week beginning Saturday, August 15: *King's Row* and *Fantasia* on Saturday, Sunday, and Monday, August 15, 16, and 17; *The Little Foxes* and *The Adventures of Chico* on Tuesday and Wednesday, August 18 and 19; and *Ball of Fire* and *Krakatoa* on Thursday and Friday, August 20 and 21. Also listed are movies for coming week: *The Magnificent Dope* and *Suicide Squadron* on Saturday, Sunday, and Monday, August 22, 23, and 24.

Opened: 5½ x 8⅝ in. (13.8 x 21.8 cm)
Folded: 5½ x 2⅞ in. (13.8 x 7.3 cm)

The Beverly Theatre was near Le Moal restaurant where Cornell and Duchamp ate lunch the day before this schedule began.

→ E

71 Marcel Duchamp
Note
[AUGUST] 1942

Torn and folded sheet of paper.
recto Inscribed diagonally top left by Duchamp in pencil: *M. D. / 1942*
Inscribed by Duchamp in different pencil with all words crossed out: *chamois verte. tube feuille 10 cm / trou pour tube viats nails / (drille 4 mm) / Cuivres à redoir / ou enlerer / Cuivres des ant (renprear) / gommier avec gomme speciale / calques / vert le gris / Limer le bords / de carton / acheter bione luime / support (cuivre?) pour / Tiroi(r) / support cuivre? pour Mariée / colorée / visser boite / gouache / original / Signed / recherches / air /* [undecipherable] */ Raisser bonbinn Ball of twine / inscription a l'encre*
verso Line drawing by Duchamp in pencil.
Inscribed lower left by Cornell in pencil: *Bernard Reis*

8¼ x 4¼ in. (20.1 x 10.8 cm)

The notations refer to the assembly of the *Boîte* edition. The line drawing represents the leather frame, showing the placement of the original artwork in the inner lid of each deluxe edition example (in this instance, the *coloriage original* of *Mariée* in number V/XX for Bernard Reis, the first *Boîte-en-valise* completed in the United States). Reis was a CPA who was one of the people involved in the process of obtaining Duchamp's exit papers for emigration to the United States in 1942 and was also the financial supporter of the magazine *VVV*.

→ G

72 Marcel Duchamp
Drawing [*Boîte* edition]
26 AUGUST 1942

Torn and folded sheet of paper.
recto Inscribed by unidentified hand in pencil: *Shurts* [sic] *= 3 / drawers 1 / stockins* [sic] *2 Pairs / Handkerchif* [sic] *2*
verso Drawing by Duchamp in pencil: double-lined drawing of rectangle with number 12 at top and at left, and two boxes inside, left with number 7 above, and right with number 15 inside.
Inscribed lower left by Cornell in pencil: *B *** upstairs* and lower right: *8/26/42 M. D.*

Opened: 8 x 6 in. (20.1 x 15.1 cm)

→ 12, 16, 63, Q

73 Marcel Duchamp
Envelope [*Green Box*]
[SEPTEMBER 1934]

Large cream-colored envelope with detached flap, green 30 centième postage stamp, and partially legible postmark.
recto Inscribed upper left by Duchamp in blue ink: *Duchamp / 11 rue Larrey / Paris V*; center: *Mr. Cornell Joseph / 3708 Utopia Parkway / Flushing L.I. / N.Y. / Etats Unis*; and beneath return address: *imprimeur / Printed matter*

7¾ x 11¾ in. (19.8 x 29.9 cm)

The envelope contained the subscription bulletin for Duchamp's *Green Box* issued in September 1934.

→ 90, 107, D

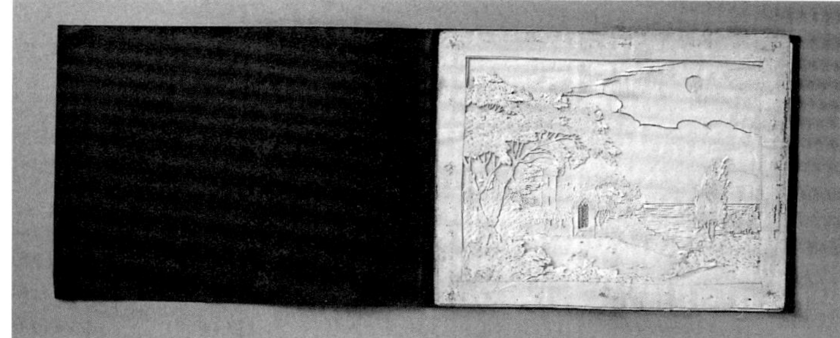

74

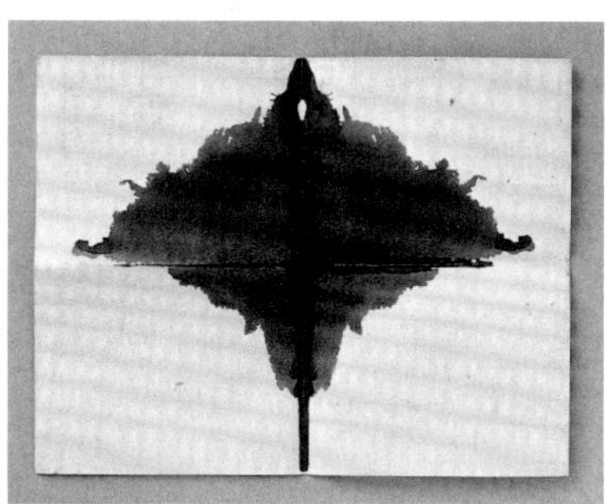

75

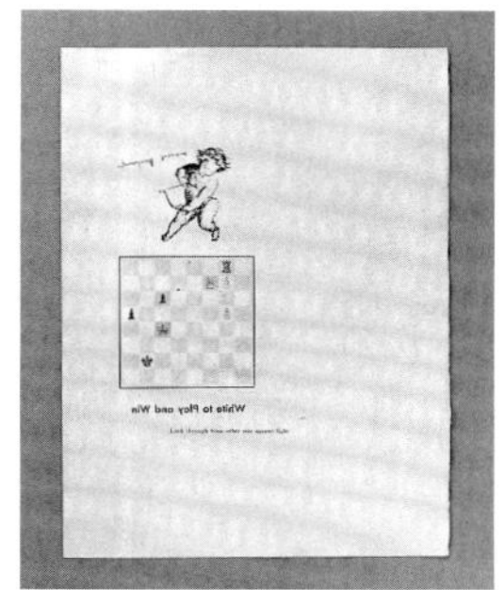

76

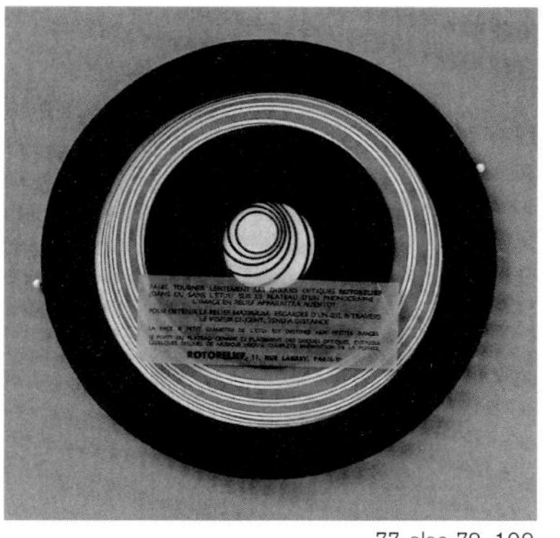

77, also 79, 109

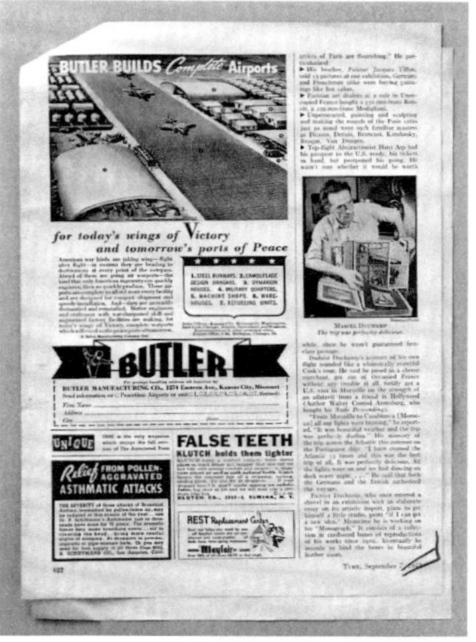

BUTLER BUILDS Complete Airports

for today's wings of Victory and tomorrow's ports of Peace

BUTLER

FALSE TEETH

ASTHMATIC ATTACKS

78a

74 Cut Paper Landscape
[DECEMBER 1947]

Red construction paper folio. Inside folio is single sheet of black paper with embossed watermark LES-ANNONAY ANG . . . and bound late nineteenth-century multilevel cut paper tableau of castle ruins and Gothic chapel in grove of trees by water.
verso Inscribed on folio at top by Mary Reynolds in pencil: *Dear Joseph – This is a romantic / trophy of the Duchamp family which I / think would be better treated chez vous que / chez mois* [with you rather than me] – *and a way to wish you / all good things for 1948 / Mary*
Folio: 7¼ x 9½ in. (18.2 x 24 cm)
Sheet: 7¼ x 9¼ in. (18.2 x 23.4 cm)
Landscape: 7⅛ x 8⅞ in. (18 x 22.4 cm)
→ F

75 Drawing [inkblot]
18 AUGUST 1942

Folded cream-colored sheet of paper with printed black square grid recto, used under transparent writing paper as guide.
recto Inscribed upper right in individual square by Cornell in pencil: *8 18 42*
verso Drawing in blue ink of inkblot.
Opened: 9⅞ x 7⅞ in. (24.9 x 20 cm)

Although both Cornell and Duchamp used the inkblot drawing technique associated with the Rorschach test, the attribution of this example is uncertain.
→ E

76 Marcel Duchamp
Printer's proof
[Julien Levy Gallery exhibition]
1943

Black-and-white proof print of Duchamp's design for his section of announcement for exhibition "'Through the Big End of the Opera Glass': Marcel Duchamp, Yves Tanguy, Joseph Cornell," Julien Levy Gallery (December 7–28, 1943).
11 x 8⅛ in. (27.8 x 20.5 cm)

The proof varies from the printed announcement because the Cupid and chessboard appear here on the same side of the sheet.
→ 14, M

77 Marcel Duchamp
***Rotorelief* (*disques optiques*)**
1935

Circular black pressboard viewer for *Rotorelief (disques optiques)*.
5⅜ in., diameter (13.5 cm, diameter)
→ 79, 109, N

78 Magazine article [*Time*] / Memo
7 SEPTEMBER 1942

a Stapled and folded pages 100–102 of anonymous article "Artist Descending to America" from *Time* (vol. 60, no. 10, 7 September 1942).
11⅝ x 8¼ in. (29.5 x 21 cm)

b Blue printed desk memo from ARTHUR NORTHWOOD, JR. / Bureau of Special Services / TIME, INC. / ROCKEFELLER CENTER, NEW YORK CITY attached.
Typed memo by Northwood:
I feel pretty certain you won't want to miss / this article from the new issue of TIME. *Prob- / ably you would have seen it anyway, but just to / make sure I'm sending you this marked folio. / Naturally I would be glad to pass along to the / editors any comments you might care to make.*
3⅝ x 5⅝ in. (9 x 14.1 cm)

The article discusses Duchamp's arrival in New York City from occupied France, wartime conditions for European artists, and Duchamp's current project, the *Boîte* edition. He is pictured in Peggy Guggenheim's townhouse with a *Boîte-en-valise* [in progress], the work's first popular publication following its appearance in the Art of This Century catalogue (August 1942). Northwood sent identical tear sheets and typewritten copy on blue notepaper to the Arensbergs. Arensberg Archives, Philadelphia Museum of Art.
→ 32, 38, 42, 52, C, R

79 Marcel Duchamp
***Rotorelief* (*disques optiques*)**
1935

One of original edition of five hundred unnumbered and unsigned sets of Duchamp's *Rotorelief (disques optiques)* to be viewed at 33⅓ revolutions per minute: six cardboard discs, printed on both sides in letterpress, have been placed in circular holder secured with cardboard strip held by yellow pins to sponge rubber. Two black

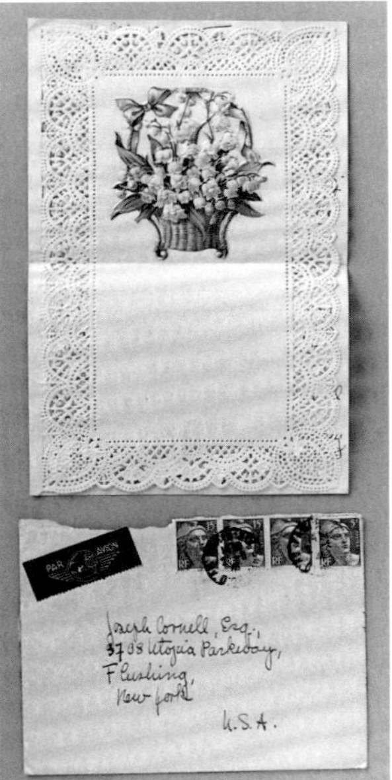

80a, b

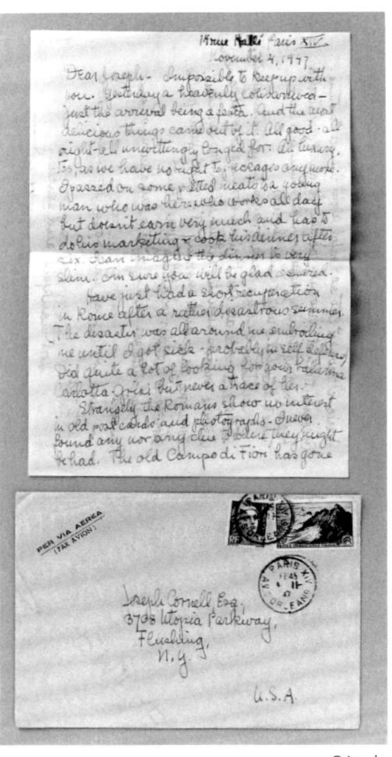

81a, b

cardboard rings are sandwiched in holder with black sponge rubber.

Holder: 9¾ in., diameter (25 cm, diameter)
Disks: 7⅞ in., diameter (20 cm, diameter)

The autographed magazine reproduction of the *Large Glass* (inscribed January 1934), the *Green Box* subscription bulletin (September 1934), and the *Rotorelief (disques optiques)* (late summer 1935) are the earliest items in the *Duchamp Dossier*.

→ 77 (photo), 109, N, Q

80 Mary Reynolds
Envelope / Letter
1 MAY 1946

a Cream-colored envelope, lined in thin purple paper, postmarked PARIS XIV A.V. D'ORLEANS / 14 30 / 2–5 / 46, with three 15 franc Republic of France stamps and one 5 franc Republic of France stamp.
recto Inscribed center by Mary Reynolds in black ink: *Joseph Cornell, Esq., / 3708 Utopia Parkway, / Flushing, / New York / U.S.A.*

4⅜ x 5¾ in. (11 x 14.6 cm)

b Letter on paper folio, front page stamped and cut scalloped lace pattern with embossed die-cut lily of the valley, inside envelope.
Text by Reynolds in ink:
14 rue Hallé Paris XIV May 1, 1946 / Dear Joseph Cornell. / I was surprised delighted and / abashed (if I know what that means) / by the perfect package from you. It / arrived at the same time as a wire from / Marcel saying he was really sailing. / So we will share the contents. Except / the tomato sauce which will make / of spaghetti a regal dinner for 5 / Tomorrow. / Did you know or divine that / ginger bread mix and onion / flakes & currants have been my / dream for a year – especially the / G.B. Mix – and no one has sent / them to me. With courage fortitude / and unparallelled [sic] *generosity I shall / wait for Marcel to MIX – / I'm also looking forward to having / again two of your boxes I thought I / had not to take with me when I came / – the war still being on & they had a / spyish look to them. The Amiral / & the box with ring & black powder are / here before me. Tho I've made myself an / almost perfect life – hardly allowing / anyone in the house I don't approve – / there have yet been inquiries about the / box – What is it? How do you play it?" / I feel very much touched that / you should remember me and go / to so much trouble to send that / delicious box. I can't think how / to thank you. Here are the May- / day lilies of the valley to bring to* [you] */ luck and all my best wishes / and thanks – / Mary–*

8¼ x 5⅜ in. (21 x 13.5 cm)

During and immediately after World War II, Cornell regularly sent care packages to friends and pen pals (acquired through *The Christian Science Monitor*) in Europe. Reynolds owned four Cornell works purchased during her residence in New York City (1943–45). She implies that Duchamp will bring to Paris two examples she left behind; she returned to Paris with a sand tray (The Art Institute of Chicago, pl. 88) and an object, *Amiral Grillon (Watch)*.

→ 9, 23, 33, 41, 84, F

81 Mary Reynolds
Envelope / Letter
4 NOVEMBER 1947

a Blue-gray airmail envelope postmarked twice PARIS XIV A.V. D'ORLEANS / 11 45 / 4 11 / 47 (second postmark not legible, but appears to be same), with watermark FABRIANO, and one 5 franc Republic of France stamp and one 20 franc Pointe du Raz Finistere stamp.
recto Inscribed center by Mary Reynolds in ink: *Joseph Cornell, Esq., / 3708 Utopia Parkway, / Flushing, / New York / U.S.A.*

4½ x 6⅜ in. (11.5 x 16.3 cm)

b Folded four-page letter on cream-colored tissue paper with same watermark inside envelope.
Text by Reynolds in ink:
14 rue Hallé Paris XIV / November 4, 1947 / Dear Joseph – / Impossible to keep up with / you. Yesterday a heavenly colis [parcel] *arrived – / just the arrival being a festa* [feast]. *And the most / delicious things came out of it. All good. all / right – all unwittingly longed for. All luxury, / too, as we have no right to packages anymore. / I passed on some potted meats to a young / man who was here who works all day / but doesn't earn very much and has to / do his marketing & cook his dinner after / six. I can imagine the dinner is very / slim. I'm sure you will be glad I shared. / Have just had a short recuperation / in Rome after a rather disastrous summer. / The disaster was all around me embroiling / me until I got sick – probably in self defense / Did quite a lot of looking for your ballerina / Carlotta – Grisi but never a trace of her. / Strangely the Romans show no interest / in old postcards and photographs – I never / found any nor any clue to where they might / be had. The old Campo di Fiori has gone / so far as amusing things are concerned – / just vegetables combs hair pins ribbons etc. / But surely there is something left somewhere / in Rome and next visit will unearth it perhaps. / I wonder where on earth you got those / old films – and if there is anything you / haven't? And where you keep all your / treasures and if you know*

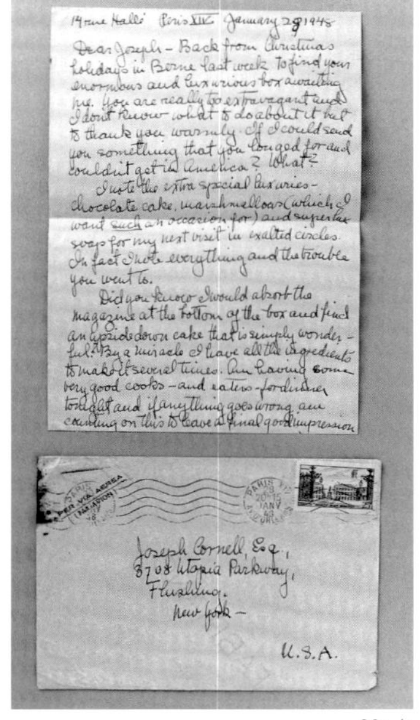

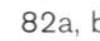

82a, b

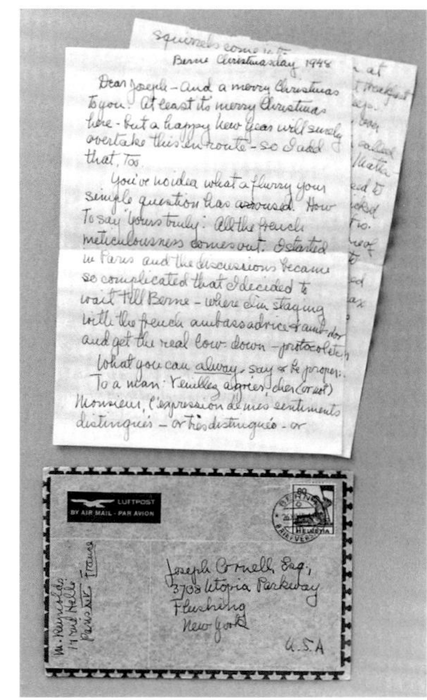

83a, b

what you / have and where it is? I have an / undisciplined magpie nature but have / lost track of a lot of things and often turn / up surprises. But of course my collecting / is like the little boy's pockets and I've had / more years to do it in than you. For years / have aspired to a room lined with closets & / the closets full of shelves and all the odds / and ends laid out in plain sight. And / a carpenter's bench with all tools in order over / it & the nails hooks brads tacks hinges / screw bolts rivets sorted. / In spite of fears in some quarters that / de Gaulle will start a revolution and the / constant echo of the american panic over / Russia – I have not felt so hopeful about life in a long time. / Of course it is just personal – probably because I've started / book-binding, timidly, again – the first time I've had / time to do what I want since the war. / And then I came back to Paris during the transportation / strike and rode all over Paris in commandeered cassions. / A strike sounds sinister but the effect was carnival. / Everyone gay and enjoying it – unless perhaps the / strike[r]*s. I wonder what they were doing? / My bottles are still a joy – to me and many other / people. / And now I shall make some Cornell tea before I / go to bed. / Most thankfully and sincerely / Mary – / Peggy seems fluttering over something like 33 palazzi / and rushing to cover whenever Tito is mentioned. She has now / taken Lawrence (and Genie) to Venice to choose for her. / I think if anyone can make up her mind it will be Lawrence / who spent his childhood in Venice.*

Opened: 11⅞ x 8⅝ in. (30.2 x 21.9 cm)

Cornell frequently asked overseas friends to scout for source material. Grisi was a nineteenth-century ballerina. Reynolds mentions Peggy Guggenheim, Laurence "Lawrence" [sic] Vail (Guggenheim's husband from 1922–28), and Jean "Genie" [sic] Connolly (Vail's third wife).

→ 85

82 Mary Reynolds
Envelope / Letter
28 JANUARY 1948

a Blue-gray airmail envelope postmarked PARIS XIV A.V. D'ORLEANS / 20 15 / Jan V / 48, with watermark FABRIANO, one 25 franc Nancy-Place Stanislaus stamp, and wavy line postal cancellation.
recto Inscribed center by Mary Reynolds in blue ink: *Joseph Cornell, Esq., / 3708 Utopia Parkway, / Flushing, / New York – / U.S.A.*

4⅝ x 6⅜ in. (11.6 x 16.2 cm)

b Folded one-page letter on thin beige paper inside envelope.
Text by Reynolds in blue ink:
14 rue Hallé Paris XIV January 28 1948 / Dear Joseph – Back from Christmas / holidays in Berne last week to find your / enormous and luxurious box awaiting / me. You are really too extravagant and / I don't know what to do about it but / to thank you warmly. If I could send / you something that you longed for and / couldn't get in America? What? / I note the extra special luxuries – / chocolate cake, marshmallows (which I / want such an occasion for) and superlux / soap for my next visit in exalted circles. / In fact I note everything and the trouble / you went to. / Did you know I would absorb the / magazine at the bottom of the box and find / an upsidedown cake that is simply wonder- / ful? By a miracle I have all the ingredients / to make it several times. Am having some / very good cooks – and eaters – for dinner / tonight and if anything goes wrong am / counting on this to leave a final good impression / For mysterious reasons I believe / 1948 will be the beginning of a better era. / Or is it something I half remember from / the great Pyramid? At any rate it has / begun well for me and there are only / eleven more months to go. / I would love to know how it is / with you and what are your activities. / Marcel writes me with exemplary regularity / and manages never to give me news of / friends. / With all my appreciation and / thanks and best wishes / Sincerely / Mary Reynolds / I would be so happy to do / any errands you might think of – / in France, Switzerland or Italy.

8⅛ x 5¾ in. (21 x 14.8 cm)

→ F

83 Mary Reynolds
Envelope / Letter
25 DECEMBER 1948

a Blue airmail envelope postmarked BERNE / 26.XII.48.14 – / BRIEFVERS__?__, with watermark GES.GESCH. – DEPOSÉ and one 80 franc Swiss stamp.
recto Inscribed left edge by Mary Reynolds in blue ink: *M. Reynolds / 14 rue Hallé / Paris XIV France* and center: *Joseph Cornell, Esq., / 3708 Utopia Parkway / Flushing / New York / U.S.A.*

4⅜ x 6⅛ in. (11 x 15.5 cm)

b Two-page letter on cream-colored paper with circular watermark inside envelope.
Text by Reynolds in black ink:
Berne Christmasday 1948 / Dear Joseph – And a merry Christmas / to you. At least it's merry Christmas / here – but a happy New Year will surely / overtake this en route – so I add / that, too. / You've no idea what a flurry your / simple question has arroused [sic]. *How / To say "Yours truly." All the french / meticulousness comes out. I started / in Paris and the discussions became / so complicated that I decided to / wait till Berne – where I'm staying / with the french ambassadrice & amb*[assa]*dor / and get the real low-down – protocolete. / What*

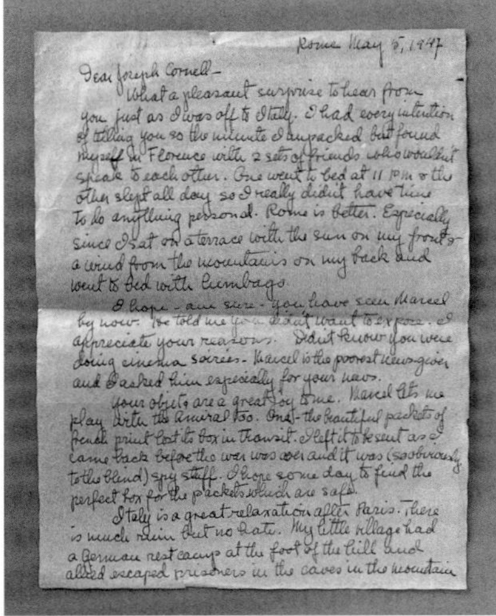

84

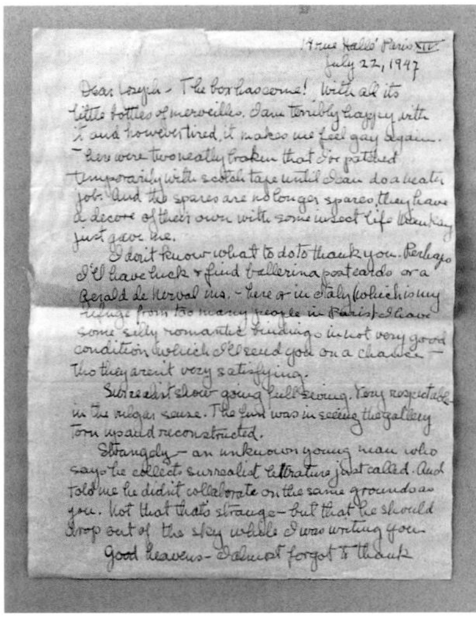

85

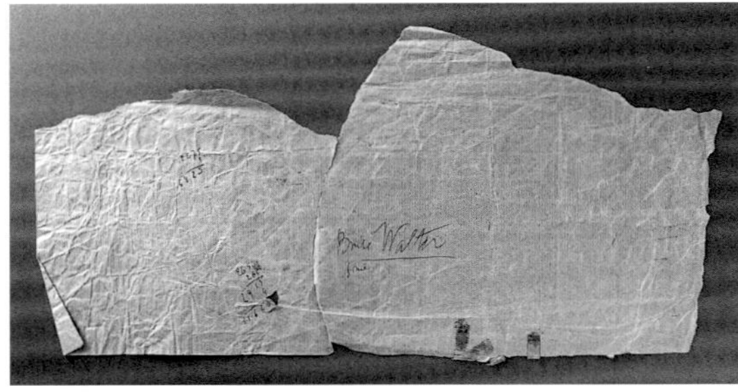

86ʳ, also 89ʳ

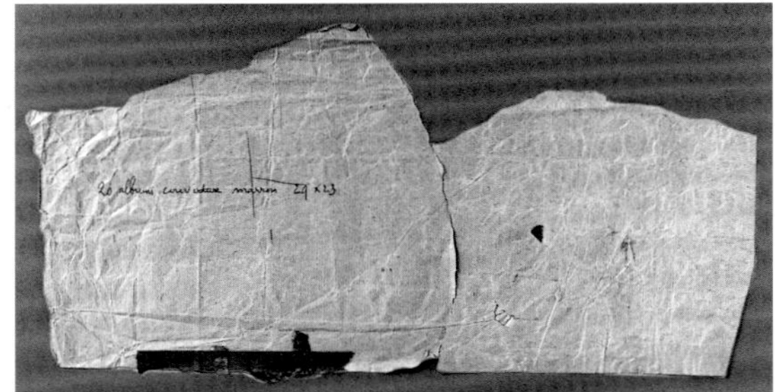

86ᵛ, also 89ᵛ

you can always say & be proper: / To a man: Veuillez agrier, cher (or not) / Monsieur, l'expression de mes sentiments / distingués – or très distingués – or / ~~sypo~~ sympatique – or more friendly – mes meilleurs sentiments. / To a woman / Veuillez agréer, chére Madame / l'expression de mes sentiments / respectueux. / Very chummy / Sincerement votre / amicalement votre / And the conclusion is that as / a foreigner you can say anything / that enters your head! / I'm rather worried about that / "sympatique" – can't spell any- / thing this morning & no dictionary / Last night after the petit Jésu had made / his midnight visit I doggedly finished / a detective story – which also was full / of misspelling – And as a group of / squirrels come into my room at / 8:30 promptly for their walnut breakfast / there's no making up lost sleep. / I worked myself into a fury over / the "Matta case" with a character called / Heisler. As you probably know Matta – / and 6 other surrealists who refused to / sign against him – has been kicked / out of the clan – party whatever it is. / Based on the poison pen letters of one of / our "friends." I was mad enough to / spit at the 2nd hand gossip relayed / with such zest by H. and the climax / came when he said – "Nous croyons / savoir que Marcel Duchamp est / d'accord. [We believe that Marcel Duchamp is in agreement.]" *I can never put my anger / over properly – but I think he then / gathered I was quite annoyed. / Wonder if Patricia will be in Paris / when I return? / Can you imagine anything more / enraging than being so angry you have / indigestion for a week and no one has / noticed? / I hope you have nice people in / your rooms. If only we were all / citizens of the world you could take / your pick. As it is there's a small / visa difficulty. I shall be dread- / fully ashamed when I go to the / Embassy Jan 20th to ask for a / new passport. No wonder a few / big bullies can make wars when / the majority of people are cowards / like me – / Must help prepare my agony – a / big Christmas reception which makes / my knees weak to fore feel – / All best wishes to you / Annealement / Mary –*

8¼ x 5¾ in. (20.8 x 14.6 cm)

Reynolds refers to the wrenching divisions caused by André Breton's banishing Matta from the Surrealist group following Frederick Kiesler's accusation that Matta was responsible for Arshile Gorky's suicide. Reynolds mentions Patricia Kane O'Connell, Matta's second wife, whose involvement with Gorky precipitated the scandal, and Jindrich Heisler, a Czech Surrealist poet and artist, who worked on the Paris exhibition "Exposition Internationale du Surréalisme."

→ F

84 Mary Reynolds
Letter
5 MAY 1947

Folded one-page letter on cream-colored paper with partially legible watermark TENAX (?) EXTRA.
Text by Mary Reynolds in blue ink:
Rome May 5, 1947 / Dear Joseph Cornell – / What a pleasant surprise to hear from / you just as I was off to Italy. I had every intention / of telling you so the minute I unpacked but found / myself in Florence with 2 sets of friends who wouldn't / speak to each other. One went to bed at 11 PM & the / other slept all day so I really didn't have time / to do anything personal. Rome is better. Especially / since I sat on a terrace with the sun on my front & / a wind from the mountains on my back and / went to bed with lumbago. / I hope – am sure – you have seen Marcel / by now. He told me you didn't want to expose. I / appreciate your reasons. Didn't know you were / doing cinema soirées – Marcel is the poorest news-giver / and I asked him especially for your news. / Your objets are a great joy to me. Marcel lets me / play with the Amiral too. One – the beautiful packets of / french print lost its box in transit. I left it to be sent as I / came back before the war was over and it was (so obviously / to the blind) spy stuff. I hope some day to find the / perfect box for the packets which are safe. / Italy is a great relaxation after Paris. There / is much ruin but no hate. My little village had / a German rest camp at the foot of the hill and / allied escaped prisoners in the caves in the mountain / behind. They were so sorry for the poor tired Germans. / and risked their lives to share their scanty food / with the poor prisoners! And miraculously not a / child betrayed the prisoners to the Germans. Incredible / people – antiquity does it. / I shall always remember the wonderful box / you sent me when life was difficult. You were / the only person who divined that I longed for / gingerbread mix and tooth paste! / I wish you could come over and discover / things in Paris – most sincerely / Mary Reynolds – / Would you let me go to the Marché aux Puces /with you?

10¼ x ⅜ in. (25.9 x 18.8 cm)

Reynolds' comment "you didn't want to expose" refers to Cornell's decision not to participate in the Paris exhibition organized by Duchamp, "Exposition Internationale du Surréalisme." The Cornell work Reynolds describes as "beautiful packets of french print" refers to a group of artworks Cornell placed inside found wooden chests or pharmaceutical boxes. In her next letter (DD 85), Reynolds' description of this object suggests her pillbox was covered with marbleized paper. "Cinema soirées" were Cornell's presentations of his films at various New York City venues, such as those on March 2 and 16, 1947, at Norlyst Gallery, just prior to this letter.

→ 9, 41, 80, 85, F

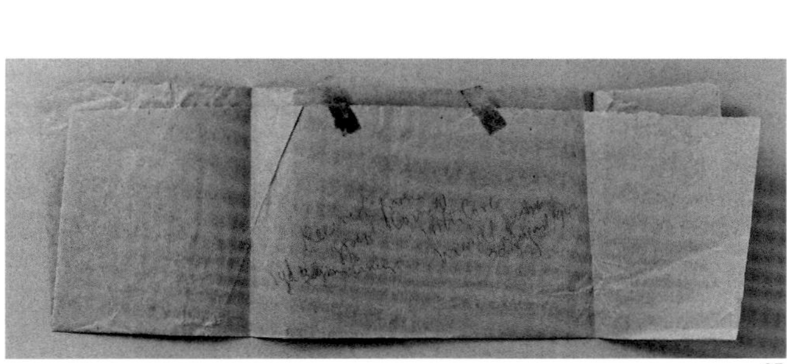

87

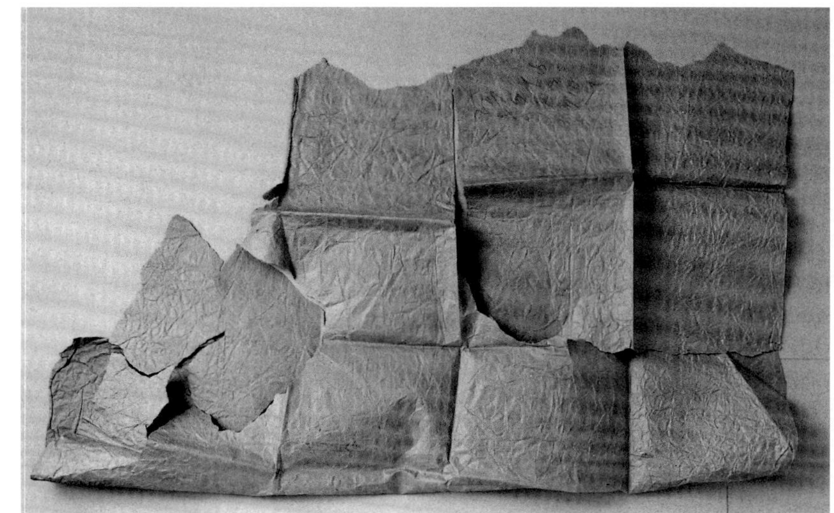

88, also 93, 101, 102

85 Mary Reynolds
Letter
22 JULY 1947

Folded one-page letter on cream-colored paper with partially legible watermark TENAX (?) EXTRA.
Text by Mary Reynolds in blue ink:
14 rue Hallé Paris XIV / July 22, 1947 / Dear Joseph – The box has come! With all its / little bottles of merveilles. I am terribly happy with / it and however tired, it makes me feel gay again. / There were two neatly broken that I've patched / temporarily with scotch tape until I can do a neater / job. And the spares are no longer spares, they have / a decor of their own with some insect life Man Ray / just gave me. / I don't know what to do to thank you. Perhaps / I'll have luck & find ballerina postcards or a / Gerald de Nerval ms. – here or in Italy (which is my / refuge from too many people in Paris). I have / some silly romantic bindings in not very good / condition which I'll send you on a chance – / tho they aren't very satisfying. / Surrealist show going full swing. Very respectable – / in the vulgar sense. The fun was in seeing the gallery / torn up and reconstructed. / Strangely – an unknown young man who / says he collects surrealist literature just called. And / told me he didn't collaborate on the same grounds as / you. Not that that's strange – but that he should / drop out of the sky while I was writing you. / Good heavens – I almost forgot to thank / you for the cigarettes which are a god send and / will accompany many breakfasts – the best / moment in daily life. / And the pill box is perfect for the paquets / which I didn't dare bring in in 1945 as they / would have certainly been considered spy-stuff. / Am considering covering it with marbled paper / like the original. I have a lot left from the / dear dead days when I had time to bind / books. Would you like some? Is it current in / America? / Again many many thanks for the / boite a merveilles. It makes me feel as I did / when I first heard fairy tales instead of / just plain / Mary –
10⅛ x 7½ in. (25.8 x 19.0 cm)

In 1947, Reynolds bought the "boîte a merveilles" [box of marvels] *Petit musée*, possibly directly from Cornell (private collection; see pl. 84).
→ 81, 84, F

86 Marcel Duchamp
Wrapping paper [annotated]
[1941]

Torn fragment of European lined brown paper with strip of green paper tape and two pieces of cellophane tape at bottom edge.
recto Inscribed center left by Duchamp in blue ink : *Boite Walter / finie*
verso Inscribed by Duchamp in blue ink: *20 albums couverture marron* [20 albums covered in maroon] *29 x 23*
10¼ x 11¾ in. (26 x 29.6 cm)

Duchamp used this type of paper to wrap the unassembled materials for fifty examples of the *Boîte* edition shipped with Peggy Guggenheim's "household effects" from Grenoble to New York City in 1941. The inscription confirms that the Arensbergs' *Boîte-en-valise* 0/XX was essentially complete by this date, lacking only its valise and some details (as also noted in Duchamp's letter to Arensberg, 22 July 1942, Arensberg Archives, Philadelphia Museum of Art).
→ 89, 92, 94, J

87 Marcel Duchamp
Receipt [annotated wrapping paper]
30 AUGUST 1942

Torn and folded sheet of brown wrapping paper with two tabs of cellophane tape at top.
recto Inscribed center by Duchamp in pencil: *Received from / Joseph Cornell 1 yd Belgian linen / with love / Marcel Duchamp / 30th August 1942*
13¼ x 18 in. (33.4 x 45.5 cm)
→ 57, 66, 98

88 Marcel Duchamp
Wrapping paper [annotated]

Torn fragment of brown wrapping paper.
recto Inscribed center by Duchamp in blue ink: *3 Gd Verre / 3 M*
4⅞ x 8⅝ in. (12.4 x 22 cm)

The note on the wrapping paper refers to three reproductions of the *Grand Verre* [*Large Glass*] and three "M" monograms for the *Boîte* edition.
→ 93, 101, 102, E

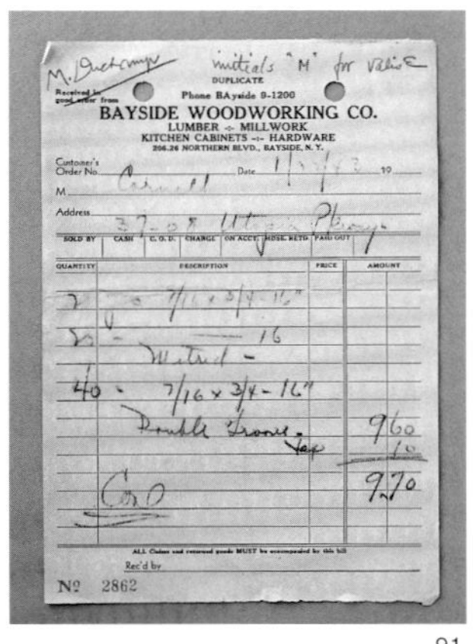

91

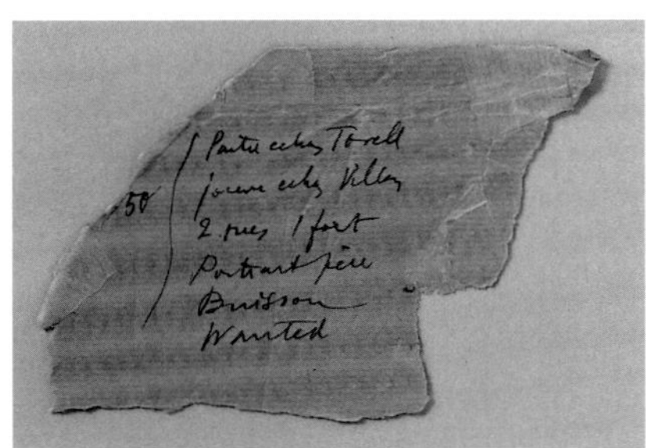

92

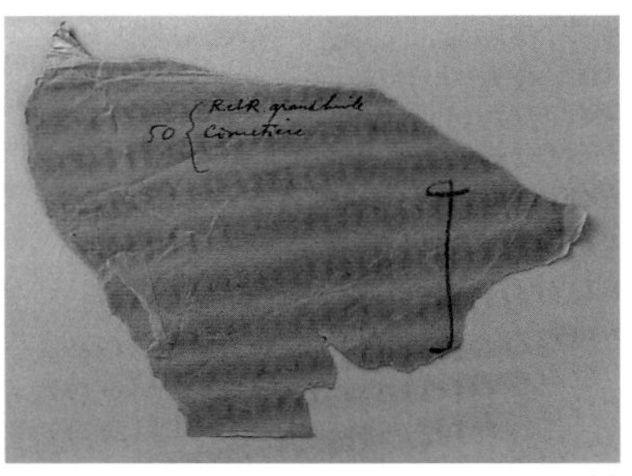

94

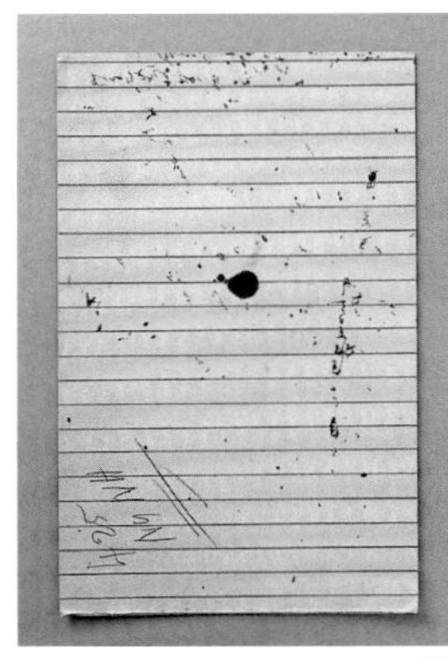

95

89 Marcel Duchamp
Wrapping paper [annotated]
[1941]

Torn and cut fragment of European lined brown paper.
recto Inscribed by Duchamp in blue ink:

2275	2650
3	265
6825	2915

4
11660

7⅛ x 8⅞ in. (17.9 x 22.5 cm)
→ 86 (photo), 92, 94

90 Marcel Duchamp
Subscription bulletin / Specimen page [*Green Box*]
SEPTEMBER 1934

a Four-page cream-colored paper folio with watermark MUSÉE DE LIVRE announcing, in French, publication of three hundred signed and numbered copies of manuscripts, drawings, and paintings comprising *La Mariée mise à nu par ses célibataires même* [*The Bride Stripped Bare by Her Bachelors Even*] *(Green Box)* by Duchamp, Edition Rrose Sélavy, 18 rue de la Paix, Paris. Verso page is perforated for subscription reply form.
11¼ x 7⅝ in. (28.4 x 19.2 cm)

b Facsimile specimen page on manila paper of *Green Box* note referring to *Broyeuse de chocolat* [*Chocolate Grinder*], printed in collotype and colored in pochoir, inside folder.
10¾ x 7¼ in. (27.2 x 18.4 cm)

Each subscription bulletin contained one example of a facsimile note included in the *Green Box*.
→ 73 (photo), 107, D

91 Joseph Cornell
Receipt [Bayside Woodworking Co., annotated]
22 JANUARY 1943

Carbon-copy receipt No. 2862 from Bayside Woodworking Co., 206–26 Northern Blvd., Bayside, N.Y., that has been filled out by unidentified hand: *1/22/43* [Date] / *Cornell* [M] / *37-08 Utopia Pkwy.* [Address] / *20 pcs 7/16 x 3/4 -16"* / *20-16 / Mitred– / 40-7 /16 x 3/4-16" / Double Groove.– 9.60 / tax 10 / 9.70 / CASH*
recto Inscribed diagonally top left by Cornell in pencil: *M. Duchamp* and top right: *initials "M" for Valise*
8⅜ x 5¾ in. (21.3 x 14.4 cm)

Cornell used this supplier to order wood molding for ten "M" monograms for the *Boîte* edition, composed of twenty vertical elements and twenty mitered diagonal elements; all forty were double grooved. This molding, originally a stock item (readymade) from a French electrical supply, had to be custom milled in America to match those made earlier in France.
→ 23, 60, 61, 68, 110, 111, 115, 116, 117, P

92 Marcel Duchamp
Wrapping paper [annotated]
[1941]

Torn fragment of European lined brown paper with four pieces of brown packing tape.
recto Inscribed center by Duchamp in blue ink: *50 / Partie d'echecs Tovell / Joueurs echecs Villon / 2 nues 1 fort / Portrait pére / Buisson / Wanted*
4⅝ x 5⅜ in. (11.8 x 13.6 cm)

The note on the wrapping material refers to fifty (50) reproductions of each of six Duchamp artworks listed for inclusion in the *Boîte* edition.
→ 86, 89, 94, J

93 Marcel Duchamp
Wrapping paper [annotated]

Torn fragment of brown wrapping paper.
recto Inscribed center by Duchamp in blue ink: *FRAGILE*
5 x 10¼ in. (12.6 x 26 cm)

This fragment is from the wrapping material used for item(s) relating to the *Boîte* edition.
→ 88 (photo), 101, 102, E

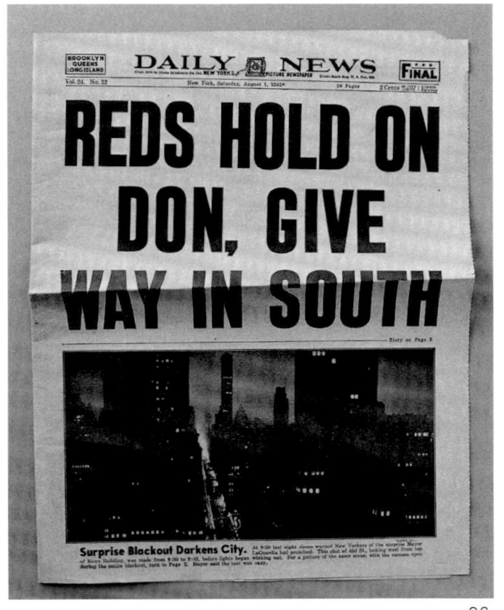
DAILY NEWS FINAL

REDS HOLD ON DON, GIVE WAY IN SOUTH

Surprise Blackout Darkens City.

96

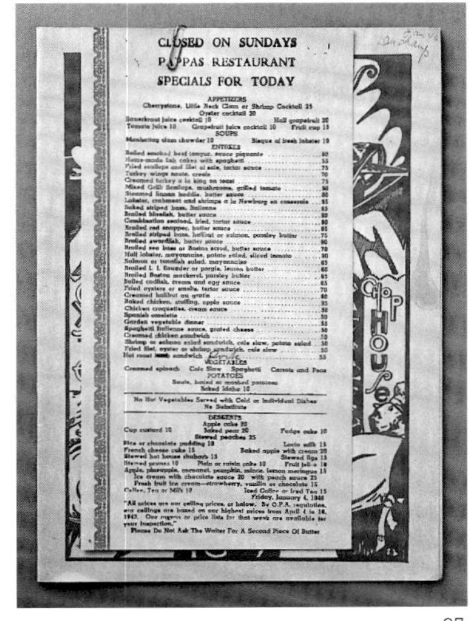
CLOSED ON SUNDAYS
PAPPAS RESTAURANT
SPECIALS FOR TODAY

97

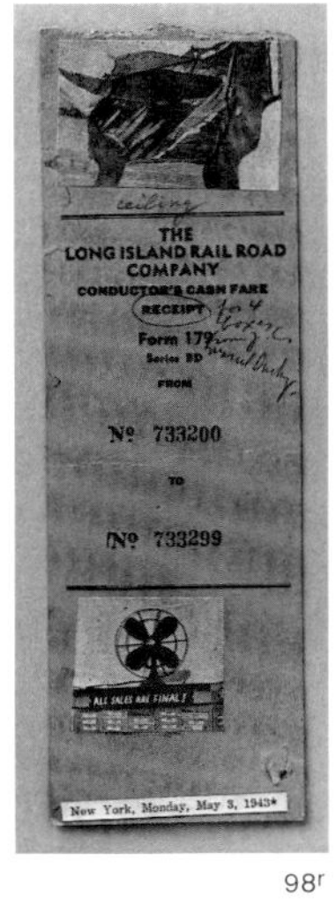

THE
LONG ISLAND RAIL ROAD
COMPANY
CONDUCTOR'S CASH FARE
RECEIPT
Form 179
Series BD
FROM
№ 733200
TO
№ 733299

New York, Monday, May 3, 1943

98r

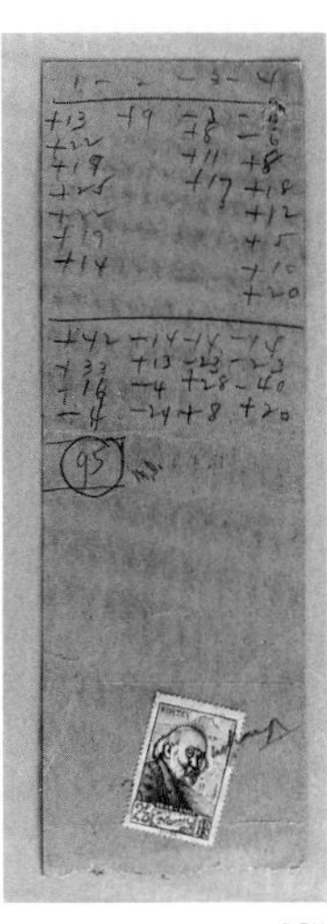

98v

94 Marcel Duchamp
Wrapping paper [annotated]
[1941]

Torn fragment of European lined brown paper with brown packing tape center left edge and a drawing at right edge in pencil of height measurements.
recto Inscribed center top by Duchamp in blue ink: *50 / R et R. grandhuile / cimetière*
7⅛ x 10⅛ in. (18 x 25.6 cm)

The note on the wrapping material refers to fifty (50) reproductions of *Le roi et la reine entourés de nus vites* (1912) and *Cimetière des uniforms et livrés* (1913) for inclusion in the *Boîte* edition.

→ 86, 89, 92, J

95 Marcel Duchamp
Note
18 AUGUST 1942

Sheet of cream-colored paper with printed gray lines verso, torn from pad once used to blot ink.
recto Inscribed diagonally top right by Duchamp in pencil: *425 / NY NH* Inscribed lower right by Cornell in pencil: *8/18/42*
verso Inscribed top by Duchamp in pencil: [undecipherable] *au claire de la lune Bretons / asleep in the woods*
5½ x 9⅛ in. (14 x 23 cm)

"NY NH" refers to the New York-to-New Haven railroad line that Duchamp rode when visiting Katherine Dreier at The Haven, her home in West Redding, Connecticut.

→ O

96 Newspaper [*Daily News*]
1 AUGUST 1942

Folded newspaper tabloid, pages 1, 2, 27, and 28 of *Daily News*, Saturday, August 1, 1942. Front-page headline reads: Reds Hold On / Don, Give / Way in South
Below headline is photograph of New York City blacked out with printed caption: Surprise Blackout Darkens City.
15⅛ x 11⅝ in. (38.8 x 29.4 cm)

Cornell's newspaper clippings during World War II focused on the war's effect on New York City. The front-page headline refers to the Russian army's holding out against the Germans at the Don River in Russia, and the picture shows an unannounced air raid blackout drill in New York City. The back page features a photograph of Mayor LaGuardia visiting Flushing to inspect a bomb removal truck.

→ I, R

97 Menu [Pappas]
[4] JANUARY 1946

Menu for Pappas Restaurant Chop House, 254 West 14th Street, with second paper-clipped menu printed: SPECIALS FOR TODAY.
recto Inscribed upper right by Cornell in pencil: *Jan 46 / Duchamp*
Menu: 11¾ x 8¼ in. (29.7 x 21 cm)
Specials: 11 x 5½ in. (28 x 14 cm)

Duchamp and Cornell met for lunch at Pappas near Duchamp's 14th Street studio so Cornell could return materials he had used in assembling the *Boîte* edition.

→ 23, 33, O

98 Marcel Duchamp
Receipt [Long Island Railroad]
3 MAY 1943

Blue-gray conductor's receipt book cover, torn at top, printed: THE / LONG ISLAND RAILROAD / COMPANY / CONDUCTOR'S CASH FARE / RECEIPT / Form 179 / Series BD / FROM / N° 733200 / TO / N° 733299. Pasted at top recto is newspaper photograph of collapsed ceiling. Pasted at bottom is newspaper photograph of large table fan on top of series of boxes with sign ALL SALES ARE FINAL! Below this, pasted from newspaper is printed dateline: New York, Monday, May 3, 1943*. Pasted bottom verso is green 2 franc 25 centième French postage stamp of Paul Cézanne.
recto Inscribed beneath upper photo by Duchamp in pencil: *ceiling* Word "receipt" has been circled and inscribed at right by Duchamp in pencil: *for 4 / boxes / from J.C. / Marcel Duchamp*
verso Inscribed above and below pencil line by Duchamp in pencil is series of numbers. Numbers below line may be a type of mathematical game with each line equaling 0 and first vertical column equaling 95. 95 is circled.

+ 42 - 14 - 14 - 14
+ 33 + 13 - 23 - 23
-16 - 4 + 28 - 40
- 4 - 24 + 8 + 20
95 M.D.

Inscribed diagonally across Cézanne stamp by Duchamp in pencil: *Marcel Duchamp*
9¼ x 2⅞ in. (23.4 x 7.2 cm)

The Cézanne stamp also appears on the April page of the calendar section in *VVV Almanac for 1943*, March, to which Duchamp contributed. Cornell's house in Flushing was near the Auburndale station of the Long Island Railroad.

→ 57, 66, 87, C, I

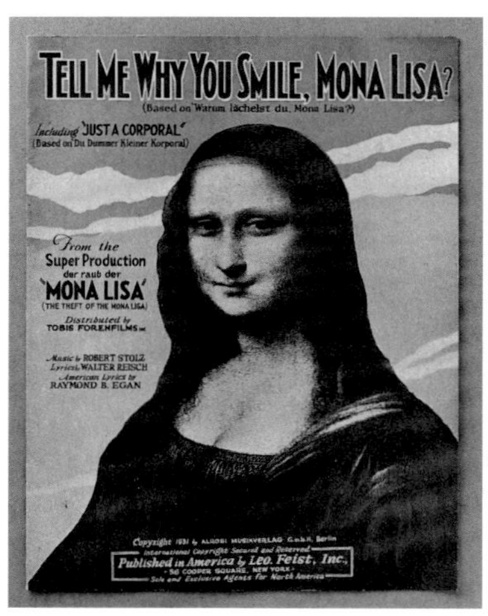

99

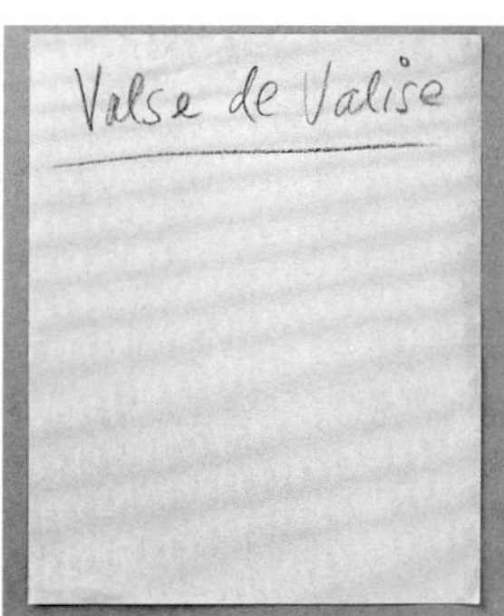

100

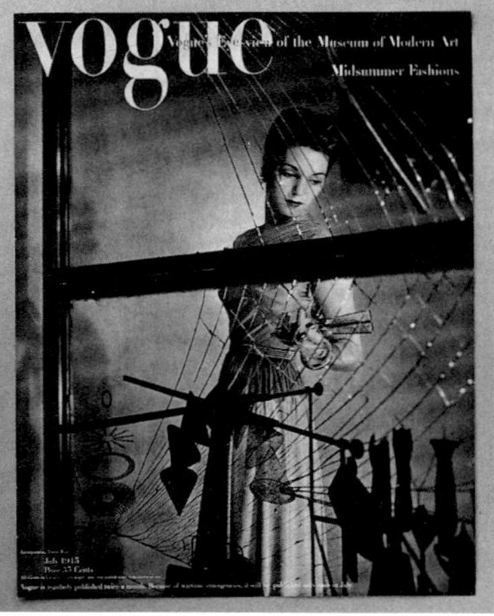

103, 104

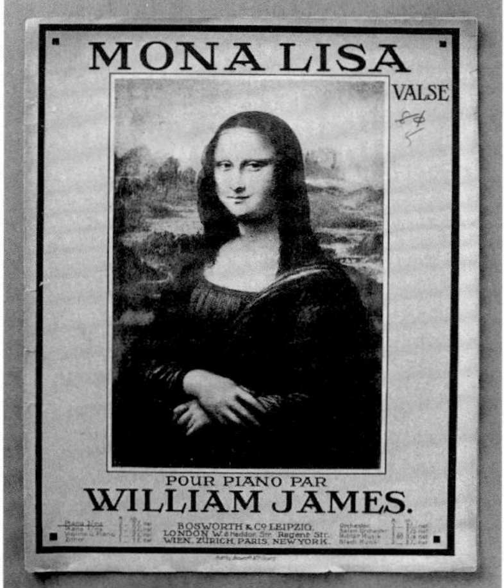

105

99 Sheet music [*Mona Lisa*]
1932

Eight-page folio of sheet music for *Tell Me Why You Smile, Mona Lisa? (based on Warum lachelst du Mona Lisa?)*, copyright 1931 by Alrobi Musikverlag, Berlin, published 1932 by Leo Feist, N.Y. Music is from 1931 super film production *Der Raub der Mona Lisa [The Theft of the Mona Lisa]* distributed by Tobis Forenfilms. Front cover, printed in violet on turquoise background, depicts reproduction of *Mona Lisa*. Folio also includes *Just a Corporal*.
12¼ x 9⅛ in. (30.9 x 23 cm)
→ 4, 50, 55, 56, 105, G

100 Joseph Cornell
Note

Sheet of cream-colored manila paper.
recto Inscribed top by Cornell in black crayon: *Valse de Valise [Waltz of the Suitcase]*
11 x 8½ in. (28 x 21.6 cm)
→ I

101 Marcel Duchamp
Wrapping paper [annotated]

Torn and folded sheet of brown wrapping paper, badly wrinkled.
recto Inscribed diagonally along center fold by Duchamp in pencil: *Coudures / 3 rue Faser / St. Jean du / Var*
17 x 17⅝ in. (43 x 44.7 cm)

St. Jean du Var is near Sanary-sur-Mer in the south of France, where Duchamp's sister Suzanne Crotti had a house. He stayed there in 1941 and 1942 during the process of obtaining his visa to America. *Coudures* is not a known French word.
→ 88 (photo), 93, 102, E

102 Wrapping paper

Torn and folded sheet of brown wrapping paper, badly wrinkled, with two pieces of cellophane tape and two pieces of masking tape attached to edge at bottom center.
38¼ x 31⅛ in. (97 x 79 cm)
→ 88 (photo), 93, 101

103 Magazine [*Vogue*]
JULY 1945

Front cover of *Vogue*, July 1945, issue devoted to "Vogue's Eye-view of The Museum of Modern Art," which shows a model standing behind Duchamp's *Large Glass*.
verso Printed advertisement for Chen-Yu nail lacquer & lipstick with slogan: Frozen Fire
12¼ x 9⅜ in. (31 x 23.6 cm)

Katherine Dreier placed the *Large Glass* on extended loan to The Museum of Modern Art, New York, from September 1943 until April 1946.
→ 104, Q

104 Magazine [*Vogue*]
JULY 1945

A second example of front cover of *Vogue*, July 1945, issue devoted to "Vogue's Eye-view of The Museum of Modern Art," which shows a model standing behind Duchamp's *Large Glass*.
verso Printed advertisement for Chen-Yu nail lacquer & lipstick with slogan: Frozen Fire
12¼ x 9¼ in. (31 x 23.2 cm)
→ 103, S

105 Sheet music [*Mona Lisa*]

Ten-page folio of sheet music for *Mona Lisa Valse* by William James, published by Bosworth and Co., Leipzig, copyright 1913. Front cover (reproducing the *Mona Lisa*) now separated from folio.
recto Inscribed top right edge by unidentified hand in pencil: ~~*84*~~ */ 5*
Inscribed bottom of page 10 by Duchamp in pencil:
12 14 1/4 2 + 1
and near center right edge:
2 1/2 12 [12 written over 13]
13¼ x 10½ in. (33.7 x 26.6 cm)

This sheet music was published during the period that the *Mona Lisa* was receiving further notoriety due to its theft from the Louvre.
→ 4, 50, 55, 56, 99, R

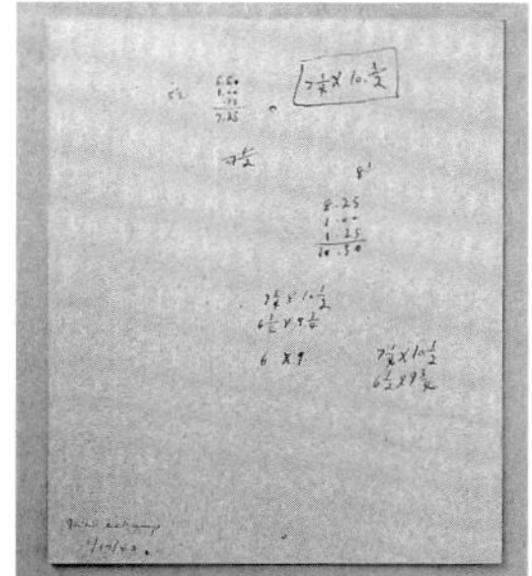

106

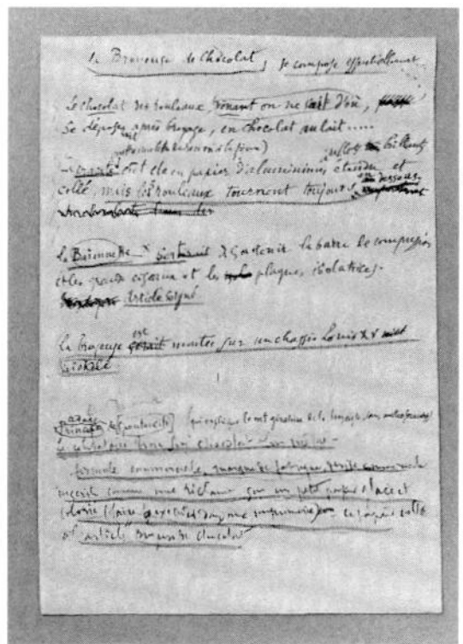

107

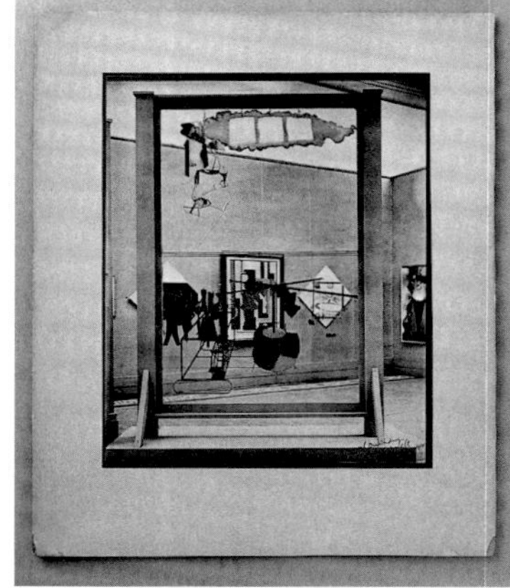

108r

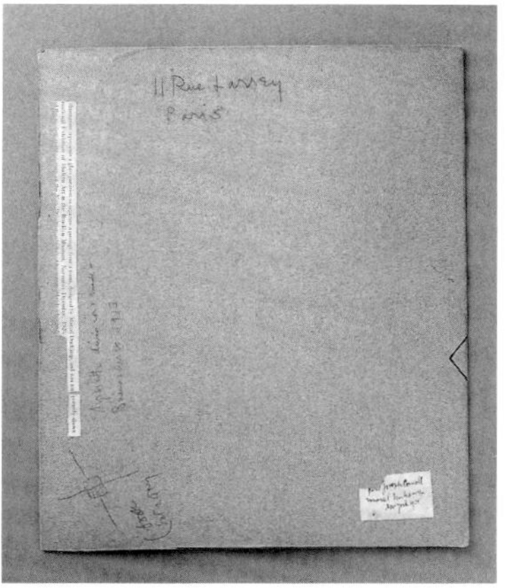

108v

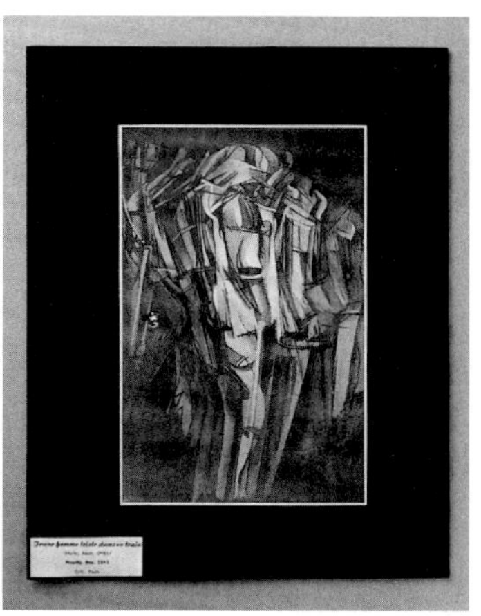

110

106 Marcel Duchamp
Note
19 JANUARY 1943

Sheet of cardboard with two circular stamped holes (1 mm in diameter), one above the other, both just above center.
recto Inscribed by Duchamp in ink are five groups of additions and multiplications.
Inscribed bottom left by Cornell in pencil: *Marcel Duchamp / 1/19/43*
10 x 8 in. (25.2 x 20.2 cm)
→ O

107 Marcel Duchamp
Specimen page [*Green Box* note]
[SEPTEMBER 1934]

A second example of facsimile specimen page on manila paper of *Green Box* note referring to *Broyeuse de chocolat [Chocolate Grinder]*, printed in collotype and colored in pochoir.
10⅞ x 7⅜ in. (27.6 x 18.6 cm)
→ 73, 90, D

108 Marcel Duchamp
Magazine reproduction [*Large Glass*]
JANUARY 1934

Printed reproduction of unattributed photograph cut from *Art News* (vol. 25, 14 May 1927, n.p.) depicting Duchamp's *Large Glass* installed at Société Anonyme exhibition, Brooklyn Museum (November 19, 1926–January 1, 1927). Reproduction is mounted on black construction paper and again on manila paperboard, probably by Cornell, with drawing verso, by unidentified hand, of suspended book, inscribed in pencil: *Book balcony*
recto Inscribed lower right by Duchamp in blue ink: *Marcel Duchamp / for Joseph Cornell / New York Jan 1934*
verso Inscribed near center by unidentified hand in pencil: *11 Rue Larrey / Paris*
Inscribed left by Cornell in pencil: *book / balcony / Separate divisions made in / Buenos Aires 1913* [sic]
Printed text, also cut from *Art News* (vol. 25, 14 May 1927, n.p.), is pasted along left side running vertically: "illustration represents a glass partition to separate / a passage from a room, designed by Marcel / Duchamp, and was temporarily shown / [Inte]rnational Exhibition of Modern Art at the Brooklyn Museum, / November – December, 1926, / . . . and the modern point of view of the New Primitives which had"
Inscribed lower right on pasted cut section of white coated paper by Duchamp in blue ink: *pour Joseph Cornell / Marcel Duchamp / New York 1934*
12⅝ x 10 in. (32 x 25.5 cm)

The phrase "Book balcony," the drawing, and Cornell's inscription refer to the *Ready made malheureux* (1919) conceived by Duchamp in Buenos Aires as a wedding present to his sister Suzanne and Jean Crotti. Realized by the newlyweds according to Duchamp's instructions, it is documented in a photograph (1920) and a painting, *Le Ready made Malheureux de Marcel* (1920), both by Suzanne. The Suzanne Crotti photograph, in a retouched version, appears in the *Boîte* edition. 11 Rue Larrey was Duchamp's address in Paris.
→ T

109 Marcel Duchamp
Label [*Rotorelief (disques optiques)*]
1935

Explanatory note, printed in French on waxed paper, for operating *Rotorelief (disques optiques)* on a phonograph.
2½ x 5¾ in. (6.2 x 14.4 cm)
→ 77 (photo), 79, N

110 Marcel Duchamp
Folder [*Boîte* edition]
[1942–43]

Four-page black paper folio.
recto Mounted collotype reproduction of Duchamp's *Nu descendant un escalier* with white paper label pasted lower right: *Nu descendant un escalier / – esquisse – / (Huile, carton; haut. 0m95) / Neuilly, Déc. 1911 / Coll. Arensberg*
Mounted collotype reproduction of Duchamp's *Jeune homme triste dans un train* with white paper label pasted lower left: *Jeune homme triste dans un train / (Huile; haut. 0m81) / Neuilly, Déc. 1911 / Coll. Pach*
verso Mounted collotype reproduction with pochoir coloring of Duchamp's *Joueurs d'échecs* with white paper label pasted lower right: *Joueurs d'échecs / (Huile; haut. 0m54) / Neuilly Déc. 1911 / Coll. Villon*
Mounted collotype reproduction of Duchamp's *Portrait de joueurs d'échecs* with white paper label pasted lower left: *Portrait de joueurs d'échecs (Huile; 0m97 x 0m97) / Neuilly Oct. Nov. 1911 / Coll. Arensberg*
Opened: 12⅞ x 19⅝ in. (32.6 x 49.9 cm)
Closed: 12⅞ x 10¼ in. (32.6 x 26 cm)

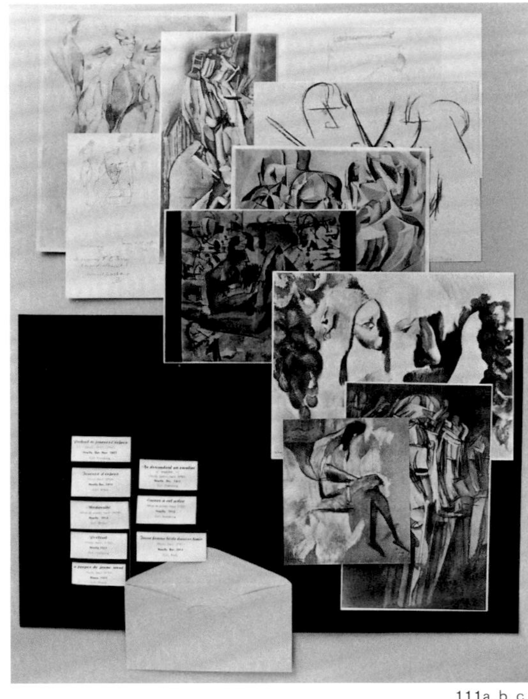

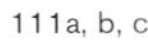
111a, b, c

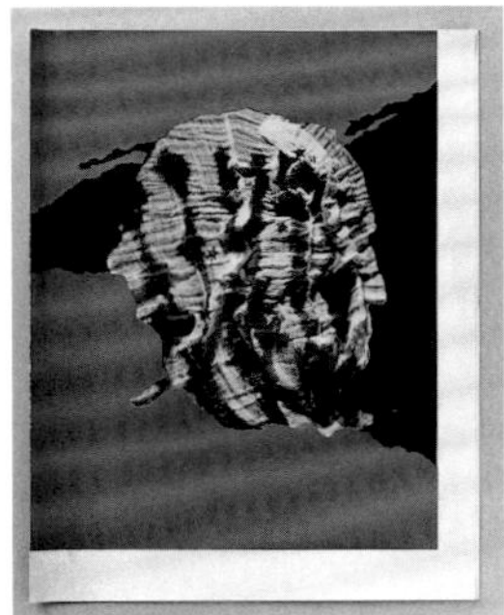
112r

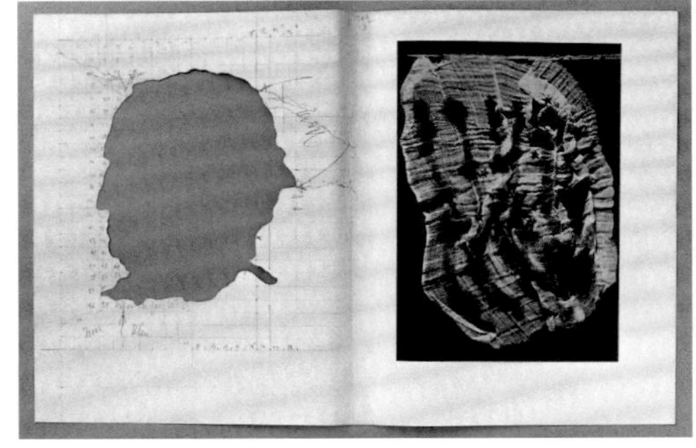
112v

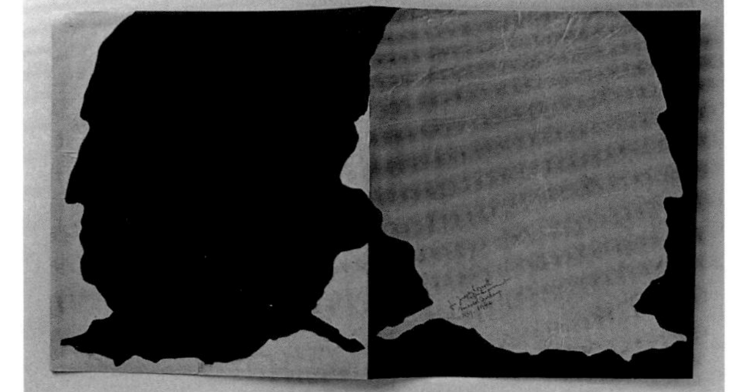
113

These are rejected folders from the assembly of the *Boîte* edition. This example of folder 3 is missing *Joueurs d'échecs*, an ink and charcoal drawing included in the finished boxes.

→ 23, 28, 60, 61, 68, 91, 111, 115, 116, 117, K

111 Marcel Duchamp
Folder / Labels / Reproductions
[*Boîte* edition]

a Four-page black paper folio with blue envelope inside.

b Eight white paper, letterpress-printed labels, cut askew to indicate cut lines, with gummed versos, inside envelope inside folio:
Nu descendant un escalier / – esquisse – /(Huile, carton; haut. $0^{m}95$) / Neuilly, Déc. 1911 / Coll. Arensberg
Portrait de joueurs d'échecs / (Huile; $0^{m}97$ x $0^{m}97$) / Neuilly Oct. Nov. 1911 / Coll. Arensberg
Joueurs d'échecs / (Huile; haut. $0^{m}54$) / Neuilly Déc. 1911 / Coll. Villon
Médiocrité / (Mine de plomb; haut. $0^{m}14$) / Neuilly, 1912 / Coll. Breton
Portrait / (Huile; haut. $1^{m}45$) / Neuilly 1911 / Coll. Arensberg
Jeune homme triste dans un train / (Huile; haut. $0^{m}81$) / Neuilly, Déc. 1911 / Coll. Pach
à propos de jeune soeur / (Huile; haut. $0^{m}70$) / Rouen, 1911 / Coll. Roché
Encore à cet astre / (Mine de plomb; haut. $0^{m}23$) / Neuilly, 1912 / Coll. Arensberg

c Ten collotype reproductions, each identified by verso stamps, inside folio:
Nu descendant un escalier / – esquisse – / (Huile, carton; haut. $0^{m}95$) / Neuilly, Déc. 1911 / Coll. Arensberg Stamp has been placed upside down.
Portrait de joueurs d'échecs / (Huile; $0^{m}97$ x $0^{m}97$) / Neuilly Oct. Nov. 1911 / Coll. Arensberg Reproduction has been hand-touched in ink at top.
Joueurs d'échecs / (Huile; haut. $0^{m}54$) / Neuilly Déc. 1911 / Coll. Villon
Médiocrité / (Mine de plomb; haut. $0^{m}14$) / Neuilly, 1912 / Coll. Breton
Portrait / (Huile; haut. $1^{m}45$) / Neuilly 1911 / Coll. Arensberg
Jeune homme triste dans un train / (Huile; haut. $0^{m}81$) / Neuilly, Déc. 1911 / Coll. Pach
Joueurs d'échecs / (Huile; haut. $0^{m}54$) / Neuilly Déc. 1911 / Coll. Villon
Yvonne et Magdeleine déchiquetées / (Huile; long. $0^{m}70$) / Veules, Sept. 1911 / Coll. Arensberg
à propos de jeune soeur / (Huile; haut. $0^{m}70$) / Rouen, 1911 / Coll. Roché Verso stamp is missing.
Encore à cet astre / (Mine de plomb; haut. $0^{m}23$) / Neuilly, 1912 / Coll. Arensberg

Opened: 12⅞ x 19⅝ in. (32.6 x 49.9 cm)
Closed: 12⅞ x 10¼ in. (32.6 x 26 cm)

Items relate to the assembly of the *Boîte* edition: the folio is a rejected folder containing no mounted reproductions; labels are from folders 2, 3, and 10; and reproductions are from folders 2 and 3.

→ 23, 28, 60, 61, 91, 110, 115, 116, 117, K, L

112 Marcel Duchamp
***VVV* offprint [*Allégorie de genre*]**
[FEBRUARY 1944]

Untrimmed photolithograph of die-cut sheet folded over embossed sheet depicting Duchamp's *Allégorie de genre* with white border at right and bottom edge.
verso Inscribed by Duchamp in pencil are a series of consecutive numbers from 1 to 18 across top and bottom, and 1 to 63 switchbacking along left edge of cutout as well as color notations, both done after die-cut.
Printed on last page of folio: *Allegorie de Genre*, Marcel Duchamp
Inscribed lower left by Duchamp in pencil is a group of mathematical measurements with fractions, some crossed out.

Image: 11⅜ x 8¾ in. (28.8 x 22.0 cm)
Sheet: 13 x ⅝ in. (31.8 x 24.0 cm)

Allégorie de genre (1943, Musée National d'Art Moderne, Centre Georges Pompidou, Paris) was executed for *Vogue*, February 1, 1943, but rejected. For reproduction in *VVV* (no. 4, March 1944), Duchamp created another version, composed of two elements: a die-cut and printed sheet of George Washington's profile laid over the second element, a photograph of gauze, iodine, and stars (different configuration from the original work). At some time after production of the die-cut leaf, the verso of this was gridded and numbered in pencil in a system similar to that used by Duchamp in the preliminary drawing for *Jacquette* (1956) and on the photograph of the bricks for *Étant donnés* reproduced in its instruction manual.

→ 59, 64, 113, 114, 116, O, P

113 Marcel Duchamp
Collage [*Allégorie de genre*]
[1944]

Additional version of *Allégorie de genre*. Positive and negative portions of mirror cutout from brown wrapping paper with pencil traces have been pasted on heavy black paper. Brown wrapping paper bleeds over and wraps around black

117

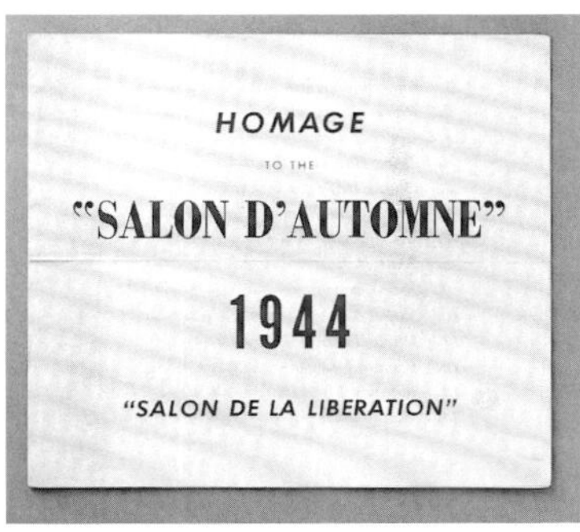

114

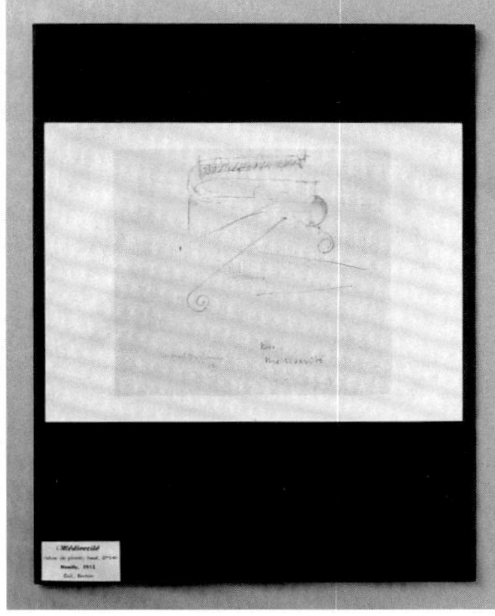

115

116

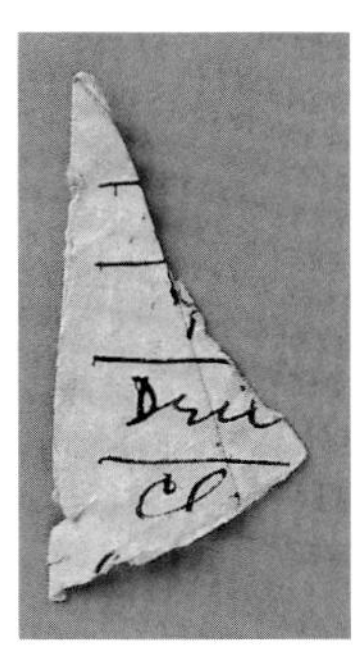

118

paper at left, bottom left, and top right.
recto Inscribed lower left by Duchamp in pencil: *for Joseph Cornell / Affectueusement / Marcel Duchamp / N.Y. 1944*

Opened: 13⅜ x 24 in. (34 x 58.5 cm)
Closed: 13⅜ x 11½ in. (34 x 29.2 cm)

This additional version of the *Allégorie de genre* depicts the George Washington silhouette in mirror images flopped horizontally. The positive and negative elements are cut out of a single sheet of brown wrapping paper. The black paper ground is the same as that used in the folders of the *Boîte* edition. The silhouette was first traced in pencil onto the brown paper using either the cutout from the Pompidou version or its cutting template: the shape and dimensions of the original silhouette and this additional version match. It is unknown if this version was made before or after the one printed in *VVV* (no. 4, March 1944). A recently documented work, the original item in the Orin Raphael *Boîte-en-valise* (XI/XX, also 1944), is another version of the black silhouette map of the United States (see pl. 29).

→ **59, 64, 112, 114, R**

114 Exhibition announcement [Pierre Matisse Gallery]

9 DECEMBER 1944

Four-page printed announcement: HOMAGE / TO THE / SALON D'AUTOMNE / 1944 / "SALON DE LA LIBERATION"
verso Printed: PIERRE MATISSE GALLERY / 41 EAST 57TH ST. N.Y. / THROUGH DECEMBER 1944 / OPENING SAT. DEC 9 FROM 4 UNTIL 6 P.M.

8 x 9 in. (20.2 x 22.8 cm)

This is the first exhibition of Duchamp's *Allégorie de genre* (1943), no. 6 of twenty-eight artworks on the checklist.

→ **59, 64, 112, 113, O, Q**

115 Marcel Duchamp Folder [*Boîte* edition]

Four-page black paper folio.
recto Mounted collotype reproduction of Duchamp's *Encore à cet astre* with white paper label pasted lower right: *Encore à cet astre / (Mine de plomb; haut. 0m23) / Neuilly, 1912 / Coll. Arensberg*
Mounted collotype reproduction of Duchamp's *Médiocrité* with white paper label pasted lower left: *Médiocrité / (Mine de plomb; haut. 0m14) / Neuilly, 1912 / Coll. Breton*
verso Mounted varnished collotype reproduction of Duchamp's *Portrait* with white paper label pasted lower right: *Portrait / (Huile; haut. 1m45) / Neuilly 1911 / Coll. Arensberg*
Mounted collotype reproduction of Duchamp's *à propos de jeune soeur* with white paper label pasted lower left: *à propos de jeune soeur / (Huile; haut. 0m70) / Rouen, 1911 / Coll. Roché*

Opened: 12⅞ x 19⅝ in. (32.6 x 49.9 cm)
Closed: 12⅞ x 10¼ in. (32.6 x 26 cm)

Folder 2, related to the assembly of the *Boîte* edition, is missing *Yvonne et Magdeleine déchiquetées*, included in the finished boxes.

→ **23, 28, 60, 61, 68, 91, 110, 111, 116, 117, K**

116 Marcel Duchamp Folder [*Boîte* edition]

Empty four-page black paper folio.

Opened: 12⅞ x 19⅝ in. (32.6 x 49.9 cm)
Closed: 12⅞ x 10¼ in. (32.6 x 26 cm)

→ **23, 28, 60, 61, 68, 91, 110, 111, 112, 115, 117**

117 Marcel Duchamp Structural element [*Boîte* edition]

Gray cardboard strip with two narrow cardboard strips adhered to form groove.

3 x 14¼ x 12¼ in. (7.6 x 36.2 x 31.1 cm)

This is a rejected support strip for the right wing of the *Boîte* edition.

→ **0, 23, 60, 61, 68, 91, 110, 111, 115, 116, T**

118 Marcel Duchamp Note

Torn fragment of white envelope.
recto Inscribed by Duchamp in black ink: ____ / ____ / <u>Drill</u> / *cl.*

2½ x 1⅛ in. (6.2 x 3 cm)

→ **61, E**

Catalogue of Works

The sequence presented here corresponds to that of the plate section (pp. 112–219) and is not strictly chronological. The catalogue of works is divided by artist, Marcel Duchamp and Joseph Cornell, respectively. Ephemera such as gallery announcements and periodicals is attributed to the principal designer. All works in the exhibition are illustrated in the plate section. A dagger (†) indicates works illustrated in the plate section that were not available for the exhibition at the time of printing.

Titles and dates of works reflect current research and primary documentary evidence and may differ from those published elsewhere. Works are designated as Untitled in the absence of a title inscribed by the artist. Titles of a series (or related bodies of work) and working titles that do not appear on the artwork follow primary titles and appear within parentheses ( ). Descriptive titles not ascribed by the artist appear within brackets [ ].

The probable date of execution of an undated work is designated as a circa (c.) date. A hyphenated date (e. g., 1943–45) indicates an intermittent period of execution. A comma between dates indicates that the artist worked on the object during separate and distinct periods (Cornell used this convention when placing dates on some works). The date of execution is provided for all gelatin-silver prints.

An attempt has been made to describe accurately the medium of each artwork; approximations remain where technical examination has not been possible.

Height precedes width precedes depth. Dimensions for dossiers, boxes, and book objects document their closed state.

Marcel Duchamp

1 ***Box of 1914*** 1913–14
Commercial photographic supply box containing photographic facsimiles of sixteen manuscript notes and the drawing *Avoir l'apprenti dans le soleil [To Have the Apprentice in the Sun]* (1914), mounted on mat boards
Edition of five, plus box with original documents
1½ x 7½ x 9⅞ in. (3.8 x 25 x 19 cm)
Philadelphia Museum of Art. Gift of Mme. Marcel Duchamp

2 ***A Bruit Secret***
[With Hidden Noise] 1916
Assisted readymade: ball of twine (containing small unknown object added by Walter Arensberg), brass plates, metal screws, and paint
4½ x 5⅛ x 5⅛ in. (11.4 x 13 x 13 cm)
Philadelphia Museum of Art. The Louise and Walter Arensberg Collection

3 ***Apolinère Enameled*** 1917
Rectified readymade: gouache and pencil on painted tin, mounted on cardboard
9⅝ x 13⅜ in. (24.4 x 34 cm)
Philadelphia Museum of Art. The Louise and Walter Arensberg Collection

4 ***Air de Paris***
[50cc of Paris Air] 1919
Readymade: glass ampoule (broken and later restored)
5¼ x 8⅛ in., diameter (13.5 x 20.5 cm, diameter)
Philadelphia Museum of Art. The Louise and Walter Arensberg Collection

5 ***L.H.O.O.Q.*** 1919 †
Rectified readymade: pencil on printed reproduction of Leonardo da Vinci's *Mona Lisa*
7¾ x 4⅞ in. (19.7 x 12.4 cm)
Private collection

6 ***L.H.O.O.Q.*** 1930 †
Readymade: pencil on printed reproduction of Leonardo da Vinci's *Mona Lisa* for Louis Aragon's "La Peinture au défi," published in *Exposition de Collages* (Paris: Galerie Goemans, 1930)
25½ x 19 in. (64.7 x 48.2 cm)
French Communist Party

7 ***L.H.O.O.Q.: Mustache and Beard*** 1941
Pochoir and graphite on paper
Edition of 200
1½ x 2½ in. (4.8 x 6.3 cm)
Collection of Virginia Green, New York

8 ***L.H.O.O.Q rasée***
[L.H.O.O.Q shaved] 1965
Readymade: Leonardo da Vinci's *Mona Lisa* playing card mounted on printed dinner invitation, with ink
8½ x 5½ in. (21 x 13.8 cm)
Collection of Alice Saligman, New York

9 ***Why Not Sneeze Rose Sélavy?*** 1921
Assisted readymade: painted bird cage with paper tape lettering, containing marble cubes, thermometer, wood, and cuttlebone
4½ x 8⅝ x 6¼ in. (11.4 x 22 x 15.8 cm)
Philadelphia Museum of Art. The Louise and Walter Arensberg Collection

10 ***Fresh Widow*** 1920/3rd version 1964
Miniature French window made by a carpenter according to Duchamp's specifications: painted wood frame with paper tape lettering and glass panes covered in black leather
Edition of eight
31 x 21 x 4 in. (78.7 x 53.3 x 10 cm)
Staatliches Museum Schwerin

11 ***La bagarre d'Austerlitz***
[The Brawl at Austerlitz] 1936 †
Printed reproduction with cellophane as included in the *Boîte* edition. Initially executed for André Breton's *Au Lavoir Noir* (Paris: Editions G.L.M., 1936)
9 x 4⅛ in. (23 x 10.6 cm)
Private collection

12 ***La bagarre d'Austerlitz***
[The Brawl at Austerlitz] 1921 †
Miniature window made by a carpenter according to Duchamp's specifications: paint on wood and glass
26¾ x 13 x 8 in. (66 x 33 x 20.3 cm)
Staatsgalerie Stuttgart

13 **Cover for *Minotaure*** 1934 †
Printed publication (no. 6, Winter 1935)
12⅜ x 9½ in. (31.4 x 24.1 cm)
Courtesy Laurence McGilvery, La Jolla, California

14 **Marcel Duchamp, Man Ray, and Marc Allégret**
Anémic Cinéma 1926
Stills from seven-minute black-and-white film
The Museum of Modern Art Film Library

15 ***Box of 1932*** 1932
Commercial cardboard box containing typed and handwritten manuscripts, proofs, and diagrams for *L'Opposition et les cases conjuguées sont réconciliées [Opposition and Sister Squares Are Reconciled]* (Brussels: L'Echiquier, 1932) and one drawing *The King Checked by the Queen*
3¼ x 18¼ x 11¾ in. (9 x 46.5 x 30 cm)
Philadelphia Museum of Art. Gift of Marion Boulton Stroud in memory of Mme. Alexina Duchamp

16 ***La Mariée mise à nu par ses célibataires même [The Bride Stripped Bare by Her Bachelors Even] (Green Box)*** 1934 †
Cardboard box covered in green flocked paper, containing ninety-three facsimiles of notes, drawings, and photographs dating from 1912–23, plus one color reproduction of *9 moules mâlic [9 Malic Molds]*
Edition of 300
1 x 11 x 13⅛ in. (2.5 x 28 x 33.4 cm)
Collection of Virginia Green, New York

17 ***La Mariée mise à nu par ses célibataires même [The Bride Stripped Bare by Her Bachelors Even] (Green Box)*** 1934
Cardboard box with copper initials, containing ninety-three facsimiles of notes, drawings, and photographs dating from 1912–23, plus one color reproduction of *9 moules mâlic [9 Malic Molds]* and one original note: *Bouteille de Bénédictine [Bottle of Benedictine]*
Deluxe edition VI/XX, inscribed by perforation: Bernard Reis
1 x 11 x 13⅛ in. (2.5 x 28 x 33.4 cm)
The Menil Collection, Houston

18 ***Rotorelief (disques optiques) [Rotorelief (Optical Disks)]*** 1935
Set of six double-sided letterpress cardboard disks in heavy cardboard holders, with two plastic-head pins, cellophane label, and waxed paper instructions
Edition of 500
7⅞ in., diameter, each (20 cm, diameter, each)
Philadelphia Museum of Art. The Louise and Walter Arensberg Collection

19 **Display folder for *Rotorelief (disques optiques) [Rotorelief (Optical Disks)]*** 1953 †
Printed text and reproduction mounted on cardboard
½ x 9¾ x 4½ in. (1.3 x 24.8 x 11.4 cm)
The Menil Collection, Houston

20 **Subscription bulletin for *de ou par Marcel Duchamp ou Rrose Sélavy [by or of Marcel Duchamp or Rrose Sélavy]*** 1941
Printed card with detachable coupon
8⅞ x 5⅜ in. (22.5 x 13.5 cm)
Collection of Ronny Van de Velde, Antwerp, Belgium

21 ***de ou par Marcel Duchamp ou Rrose Sélavy [by or of Marcel Duchamp or Rrose Sélavy]*** 1935–41
Series A, V/XX for Bernard Reis, 1942
Leather valise containing sixty-nine miniature replicas and printed reproductions and one original: *Mariée [Bride]*, 1937
3 x 14 x 15 in. (8 x 35 x 39 cm)
Collection of Jose Mugrabi

22 ***de ou par Marcel Duchamp ou Rrose Sélavy [by or of Marcel Duchamp or Rrose Sélavy]*** 1935–41
Series A, O/XX for Walter Arensberg, 1943
Leather valise containing sixty-nine miniature replicas and printed reproductions and one original: *Vierge [Virgin]*, 1938
3 x 14 x 15 in. (8 x 35 x 39 cm)
Philadelphia Museum of Art. The Louise and Walter Arensberg Collection

23 ***À la manière de Delvaux [In the Manner of Delvaux]*** 1942 †
Collage: tinfoil and cut photograph mounted on cardboard
13⅜ x 13⅜ in. (34 x 34 cm)
The Israel Museum, Jerusalem. Gift of Arturo Schwarz

24 **Cover for *First Papers of Surrealism*** 1942
Printed exhibition catalogue
10½ x 7¼ in. (26.7 x 18.4 cm)
Philadelphia Museum of Art. Marcel Duchamp Archive, Gift of Jacqueline, Paul and Peter Matisse in memory of their mother, Alexina Duchamp

25 **Cover for *VVV Almanac for 1943*** 1943
Printed publication (nos. 2–3, March)
11⅛ x 8¾ in. (28.2 x 22.2 cm)
The Menil Collection, Houston

26 ***de ou par Marcel Duchamp ou Rrose Sélavy [by or of Marcel Duchamp or Rrose Sélavy]*** 1935–41
Series A, X/XX for Julien Levy, 1944 †
Leather valise containing sixty-nine miniature replicas and printed reproductions and one original: *La fourchette du cavalier [The Knight's Fork]*, 1943
3 x 14 x 15 in. (8 x 35 x 39 cm)
Mono Art Gallery, Tokyo

27 **Cover for *Young Cherry Trees Secured Against Hares*** 1946
Printed publication of André Breton's book of poems (New York: View, 1946)
9¼ x 6¼ in. (23.5 x 15.9 cm)
The Menil Collection, Houston

28 **Invitation for blindfold chess games during "The Imagery of Chess"** 1945
Printed announcement for Julien Levy Gallery, New York
7¾ x 5 in. (18.7 x 12.7 cm)
The Young-Mallin Archive, New York. The Julien Levy Papers

29 ***de ou par Marcel Duchamp ou Rrose Sélavy [by or of Marcel Duchamp or Rrose Sélavy]*** 1935–41
Series A, XI/XX for Orin Raphael, 1944
Leather valise containing sixty-nine miniature replicas and printed reproductions and one original: Untitled, 1944
3 x 14 x 15 in. (8 x 35 x 39 cm)
Private collection

30 **Untitled *(Allégorie de genre) [Allegory of Genre]*** 1944
Collage: cut black construction paper pasted on brown wrapping paper, with pencil
13⅜ x 23⅛ in. (34 x 58.7 cm)
From Joseph Cornell, *Duchamp Dossier*, c. 1942–53 (DD 113)
Philadelphia Museum of Art. Gift of The Joseph and Robert Cornell Memorial Foundation

31 ***Allégorie de genre [Allegory of Genre]*** 1944
Photolithograph and die-cut folded over embossed sheet, with pencil. Off-print reproduced in *VVV*, no. 4, March 1944, pp. 65–66
13 x 9⅜ in. (33 x 24 cm)
From Joseph Cornell, *Duchamp Dossier*, c. 1942–53 (DD 112)
Philadelphia Museum of Art. Gift of The Joseph and Robert Cornell Memorial Foundation

32 ***Allégorie de genre [Allegory of Genre]*** 1943
Collage: gauze soaked in iodine with thirteen gilt stars and painted nails, mounted on board overlaid with cut black construction paper and cut-and-painted paper in wood frame
21 x 16 in. (53.3 x 40.6 cm)
Musée National d'Art Moderne, Centre Georges Pompidou, Paris

33 Man Ray
Untitled [setup for *View* cover] c. 1945
Vintage gelatin-silver print
10 x 8 in. (25.4 x 20.3 cm)
Philadelphia Museum of Art. Marcel Duchamp Archive, Gift of Jacqueline, Paul and Peter Matisse in memory of their mother, Alexina Duchamp

34 *View* 1945
Deluxe edition of printed publication (vol. 5, no. 1, March) with seventeen contributors' signatures in ink and printed and signed reproduction of *Pharmacie [Pharmacy]*
12 x 9 in. (30.5 x 22.8 cm)
Philadelphia Museum of Art. The Louise and Walter Arensberg Archives

35 Cover for *View* 1945
Printed publication (vol. 5, no. 1, March)
12 x 9 in. (30.5 x 22.8 cm)
The Menil Collection, Houston

36 Study for *Étant donnés: 1° la chute d'eau / 2° le gaz d'éclairage [Given: 1. The Waterfall / 2. The Illuminating Gas]* c. 1947
Textured wax and ink on paper and cut gelatin-silver prints, mounted on board
17 x 12¼ in. (43.2 x 31.1 cm)
Private collection, on loan to Philadelphia Museum of Art

37 Study for *Étant donnés: 1° la chute d'eau / 2° le gaz d'éclairage [Given: 1. The Waterfall / 2. The Illuminating Gas]* 1948–49 †
Pigment and graphite on vellum over gesso with velvet, mounted on cardboard
19¾ x 12¼ in. (50.2 x 31.1 cm)
Moderna Museet, Stockholm

38 Study for *Prière de toucher [Please Touch]* 1947
Plaster mounted on velvet in wood and glass frame
16 x 16 x 4 in. (40.6 x 40.6 x 10.2 cm)
Philadelphia Museum of Art. Gift of Enrico Donati

39 Marcel Duchamp and Enrico Donati
Cover for *Le Surréalisme en 1947* 1947 †
Printed exhibition catalogue; cover photograph by Rémy Duval
9¼ x 8 in. (23.5 x 20.3 cm)
The Menil Collection, Houston

40 Marcel Duchamp and Enrico Donati
Cover for *Le Surréalisme en 1947* 1947
Printed exhibition catalogue; deluxe edition with *Prière de toucher [Please Touch]*
9¼ x 8 in. (23.5 x 20.3 cm)
Philadelphia Museum of Art. Purchased with the Gertrud A. White Memorial Fund

41 *de ou par Marcel Duchamp ou Rrose Sélavy [by or of Marcel Duchamp or Rrose Sélavy]* 1935–41
Series A, XVIII/XX for Hélène and Henri Hoppenot, 1949
Leather valise containing sixty-nine miniature replicas and printed reproductions and one original: *Réflection à main [Hand Reflection]*, 1948
3 x 14 x 15 in. (8 x 35 x 39 cm)
Private collection

42 Marcel Duchamp and unidentified photographer
Untitled *(Étant donnés: 1° la chute d'eau / 2° le gaz d'éclairage) [Given: 1. The Waterfall / 2. The Illuminating Gas]* c. 1948
Vintage gelatin-silver print
9¼ x 7½ in. (23.5 x 29 cm)
Achim Moeller Fine Art, New York

43 *Moonlight on the Bay at Basswood* 1953
Ink, pencil, crayon, talcum powder, and chocolate on blue blotting paper in wood frame
10⅜ x 7¼ in. (26.4 x 18.4 cm)
Philadelphia Museum of Art. Gift of Mr. Frank Brookes Hubachek

44 *Étant donné: 1° la chute d'eau / 2° le gaz d'éclairage [Given: 1. The Waterfall / 2. The Illuminating Gas]* 1946–66 †
Assemblage: wood door, bricks, velvet, wood, painted leather stretched over metal armature, gouache on cut gelatin-silver prints, mounted on frosted glass, twigs, leaves, aluminum, iron, glass, Plexiglas, linoleum, cotton, electric lights, Bec Auer-type fixture, and motor
96 x 70½ x 118⅛ in. (243.8 x 179 x 300 cm)
Philadelphia Museum of Art. Gift of the Cassandra Foundation

45 *à l'infinitif [In the Infinitive] (White Box)* 1967
Plexiglas-covered box with silkscreen of *Glissiere contenant un Moulin à Eau (en métaux voisins) [Glider Containing a Water Mill (in Neighboring Metals)]*, containing seventy-nine facsimile notes from 1912–23
3 x 13⅛ x 11½ in. (7.6 x 33.3 x 29.2 cm)
The Menil Collection, Houston

Joseph Cornell

pp. 17–59
Duchamp Dossier c. 1942–53
Lidded cardboard box containing typed and handwritten notes, letters, and postcards, Photostats, paper, newspaper and magazine clippings, exhibition announcements, printed papers, printed reproductions, and drawings, objects, and readymades by Duchamp and Cornell
3⅜ x 14¼ x 12⅝ in. (8.2 x 36.2 x 31.4 cm)
Philadelphia Museum of Art. Gift of The Joseph and Robert Cornell Memorial Foundation

46 *Jouet Surréaliste [Surrealist Game]* c. 1932
Steel line engravings, paper, paint, and ink on paperboard and metal
7/8 x 4⅛ x 3⅞ in. (.9 x 10.5 x 9.9 cm)
National Museum of American Art, Smithsonian Institution. Gift of Mr. and Mrs. John A. Benton

47 *Le Voyageur dans les Glaces [The Traveler in the Mirrors]* c. 1932
Steel line engravings, paper, paint, and ink on paperboard and metal
1⅛ x 3¾ x 3¾ in. (2.8 x 9.5 x 9.5 cm)
Collection of Lindy Bergman, Chicago

48 Cover for *Surrealism* 1936 †
Printed publication of Julien Levy's anthology (New York: The Black Sun Press)
9¾ x 7½ in. (24.8 x 19 cm)
The Menil Collection, Houston

49 Exhibition announcement for "Surréalisme" 1932
Printed announcement for Julien Levy Gallery, New York
5½ x 4⅛ in. (14 x 10.5 cm)
Joseph Cornell Study Center, National Museum of American Art, Smithsonian Institution. Gift of Mr. and Mrs. John A. Benton

50 *Monsieur Phot* 1933, no. 12 †
Film scenario in black construction paper folder with thirteen pages of typed text on red paper interspersed with five stereopticon photographs, all mounted on black construction paper
¼ x 9 x 11¼ in. (15.8 x 22.8 x 28.6 cm)
The Art Institute of Chicago. Mary Reynolds Collection

51 **Untitled Book Object *(Journal d'Agriculture Pratique et Journal de l'Agriculture)*** c. 1933–mid 1940s
Printed publication (vol. 22 [Paris: Librairie Agricole de la Maison Rustique, 1911]) altered with collage, paper inserts, cutouts, ink, and pencil; loose folder containing seventeen collages
1¾ x 7⅜ x 10⅝ in. (4.4 x 18.7 x 27 cm)
The Joseph and Robert Cornell Memorial Foundation

52 ***Cabinet of Natural History (Object)*** 1934, 1936–40
Stained and papered wood chest with eight papered wood cylinders, twelve glass strips, two mounted photographs, and fifty-five glass bottles and vials with glass and cork stoppers, housing various objects, materials, and colored liquids
3¼ x 9¾ x 7⅜ in. (8.3 x 24.8 x 18.7 cm)
Private collection

53 **Untitled (Soap Bubble Set)** c. 1936 †
Glass-paned, stained wood box with printed reproductions, wood, glass, fabric, paint, bronze paint, composition head and egg, and clay pipe
15¾ x 14¼ x 5½ in. (40 x 36.2 x 13.9 cm)
Wadsworth Atheneum, Hartford, Connecticut. Gift of Henry and Walter Keney

54 ***The Crystal Cage [portrait of Berenice]*** c. 1934–67
Papered wood valise, with sepia photograph mounted inside lid containing photographs, excerpts from books and magazines, printed and photomechanical reproductions, newspaper clippings, handwritten and typed notes, exhibition announcements, copies of Cornell's pamphlets *Maria* (1954) and *the Bel Canto Pet* (1955), and a collage
4⅜ x 15⅝ x 19⅞ in. (11.1 x 39.7 x 50.3 cm)
Collection of Richard L. Feigen, New York

55 ***Rose Hobart*** c. 1936
Stills from nineteen-minute black-and-white film, projected through deep-blue filter
Anthology Film Archives, New York

56 ***Object (Hotel Theatricals by the Grandson of Monsieur Phot Sunday Afternoons)*** 1940
Glass-paned, painted wood cabinet with photomechanical reproductions, Photostat of typescript, wood, paper, velvet, and eleven glass marbles
11¾ x 7⅞ x 2⅝ in. (29.8 x 20 x 6.7 cm)
Yokohama Museum of Art

57 **Untitled [Hommage to the Romantic Ballet]** c. 1940–42
Stained wood chest with twelve clear glass cubes in velvet-lined tray, blue glass, two glass bead necklaces, sand, rhinestones, glass chips, tulle, and mirror
5 x 11½ x 8 in. (12.7 x 29.2 x 20.3 cm)
Private collection

58 **Untitled Object *[Mona Lisa]*** c. 1940–42
Lidded and papered cylindrical cardboard box sealed with painted clear glass, containing photographic reproductions, sequins, hairpin, glass beads, and black paper fragment
1⅜ x 3 in., diameter (3.5 x 7.6 cm, diameter)
The Joseph and Robert Cornell Memorial Foundation

59 ***Portrait of Ondine*** c. 1940–late 1960s
Lidded paperboard slipcase containing mounted and unmounted photomechanical reproductions, watercolors, typed and handwritten notes, book excerpts, and pamphlets
2½ x 10¾ x 12¾ in. (5 x 27.3 x 32.4 cm)
National Museum of American Art, Smithsonian Institution. Gift of The Joseph and Robert Cornell Memorial Foundation

60 **Exhibition announcement for "Exhibition of Objects (Bilboquet) by Joseph Cornell"** 1939
Printed announcement for Julien Levy Gallery, New York
3⅞ x 6⅛ in. (9.7 x 15.6 cm)
Joseph Cornell Study Center, National Museum of American Art, Smithsonian Institution. Gift of Mr. and Mrs. John A. Benton

61 **Exhibition announcement for "Joseph Cornell: Exhibition of Objects"** 1940
Printed announcement for Julien Levy Gallery, New York
4 x 6⅛ in. (10.2 x 15.6 cm)
Collection of Dr. and Mrs. M. Michael Eisenberg

62 ***Object*** 1940
Printed publication *(Bibliothèque du Médecin-Praticien,* vol. 12 [Paris: J.B. Baillière, 1850]) with interior glued en bloc and altered with marbleized paper, painted clear glass, and metal coil
8⅞ x 5⅞ x 1½ in. (22.5 x 14.9 x 3.8 cm)
The Joseph and Robert Cornell Memorial Foundation

63 **Joseph Cornell and unidentified photographer Untitled (preparatory photomontage for *"Enchanted Wanderer": Excerpt from a Journey Album for Hedy Lamarr)*** 1941
Vintage gelatin-silver print
8⅝ x 7 in. (22 x 17.9 cm)
Joseph Cornell Study Center, National Museum of American Art, Smithsonian Institution. Gift of Mr. and Mrs. John A. Benton

64 ***"Enchanted Wanderer": Excerpt from a Journey Album for Hedy Lamarr*** 1941–42
Layout with printed photomontage and text *(View,* series 1, nos. 9/10, December 1941/January 1942, p. 3)
15 x 10½ in. (38.1 x 26.7 cm)
Joseph Cornell Study Center, National Museum of American Art, Smithsonian Institution. Gift of Mr. and Mrs. John A. Benton

65 **Exhibition announcement for "Objects by Joseph Cornell; Marcel Duchamp: Box-Valise; Laurence Vail: Bottles"** 1942
Printed announcement for Art of This Century, New York
5¾ x 4¾ in. (14.6 x 12 cm)
The Young-Mallin Archive, New York. P. Guggenheim Papers

66 **Joseph Cornell with Marcel Duchamp and Yves Tanguy Exhibition announcement for "'Through the Big End of the Opera Glass': Marcel Duchamp, Yves Tanguy, Joseph Cornell"** 1943
Printed announcement for Julien Levy Gallery, New York
4½ x 5¾ in. (11.5 x 14.6 cm)
The Jean-Noël Herlin Archive, New York

67 **Untitled (The Life of Ludwig II of Bavaria)** c. 1941–52
Papered wood valise with sepia photograph mounted inside lid containing one bound book, one printed folio of photographic reproductions, two rectangular boxes with clear glass miniature swans, two cylindrical boxes with broken glassware, crockery shards (with swan images), and two swan bones, and one paper file folder with printed and photomechanical reproductions, documents, newspaper clippings, and photographs
3⅝ x 11 x 14½ in. (9.2 x 28 x 36.8 cm)
Philadelphia Museum of Art. Gift of The Joseph and Robert Cornell Memorial Foundation

68 ***Mémoires inédits de Madame La Comtesse de G. [Unpublished Memoirs of Comtesse de G.]*** c. 1942
Lidded and papered cylindrical cardboard box ringed with velvet and sealed with clear glass pane, and containing strips of printed French text, blue sand, ball, and ribbon
1⅞ x 4¼ in., diameter (4.8 x 10.8 cm., diameter)
The Joseph and Robert Cornell Memorial Foundation

69 ***Mémoires inédits de Madame de Rochejaquelein [Unpublished Memoirs of Madame de Rochejaquelein]*** 1943
Lidded and papered cylindrical cardboard box, sealed with clear glass pane, lined with photomechanical reproduction in negative, and containing glass strips with printed French sentence fragments, sand, beads, and fabric
2 x 4¼ in., diameter (5 x 10.8 cm, diameter)
San Francisco Museum of Modern Art. Gift of Leo Castelli, Richard L. Feigen, and James Corcoran

70 **Untitled (Pharmacy)** 1943
Glass-paned, stained wood cabinet lined with mirror and containing twenty glass apothecary bottles, housing various objects, materials, and colored liquids
15⅞ x 11⅞ x 4⅜ in. (40.3 x 30.2 x 11.1 cm)
The Menil Collection, Houston. Gift of Alexander Iolas

71 ***Object (Roses des Vents) [Object (Compass Roses)]*** 1942–53
Stained wood box with tripartite hinged lid containing removable panel holding twenty-one compasses, printed reproductions, wood, metal spirals and spring, glass marbles and balls, plaster chips, seeds, shells, beetle, sequins, paper, pins, and colored glass
2⅝ x 21¼ x 10⅜ in. (6.7 x 54 x 26.4 cm)
The Museum of Modern Art, New York.
Mr. and Mrs. Gerald Murphy Fund

72 **Cover and layout for *View* ["Americana Fantastica" issue]** 1943
Printed publication (series 2, no. 4, January)
10⅜ x 7¼ in. (26.3 x 18.4 cm)
The Menil Collection, Houston

73 ***Beehive (Thimble Forest)*** 1943–48
Stained, lidded, cylindrical wood box with peephole, lined with mirrors and containing two colored wood balls and five metal thimbles on sawdust-covered wood platform
3½ x 7½ in., diameter (8.9 x 19 cm, diameter)
Collection of Richard L. Feigen, New York

74 **Joseph Cornell and unidentified photographer *¾ Bird's-Eye View of 'A Watch-Case for Marcel Duchamp'*** 1944
Photomontage
5¾ x 8¼ in. (14.6 x 21 cm)
Yale Collection of American Literature, Beinecke Rare Book and Manuscript Library

75 **Joseph Cornell and unidentified photographer Untitled (preparatory photomontage for *¾ Bird's-Eye View of 'A Watch-Case for Marcel Duchamp'*** c. 1944 †
Gelatin-silver print reproduced as *Appartient à M. Grillon,* c. 1942, in *Art News,* December 1957, p. 26

76 ***GC 44*** c. 1944–70
Mounted and unmounted photomechanical reproductions, photographs, postcards, and typed and handwritten notes, loose or stored in folder, paper bags, and envelopes
3½ x 9½ x 11 in. (8.9 x 24.1 x 27.9 cm)
Joseph Cornell Study Center, National Museum of American Art, Smithsonian Institution. Gift of Mr. and Mrs. John A. Benton

77 ***Palace*** c. 1943
Glass-paned, painted wood box with photomechanical reproduction, mirror, spray-painted twigs, wood, and shaved bark
10½ x 19⅞ x 5⅛ in. (26.7 x 50.5 x 13 cm)
Collection of Christophe de Menil

78 **Untitled (Pink Palace)** c. 1948
Glass-paned, painted wood box with photomechanical reproduction, mirror, spray-painted twigs, and glass chips
10 x 16½ x 3¾ in. (25.4 x 41.9 x 9.5 cm)
Collection of Mr. and Mrs. Robert Lehrman, Washington, D.C.

79 **Joseph Cornell and James Ogle Untitled (Bébé Marie)** 1938
Vintage gelatin-silver print, touched by unidentified hand with gouache and black ink
9½ x 7¼ in. (24.1 x 18.4 cm)
Collection of Michael Senft, New York

80 **Exhibition announcement for "Romantic Museum at the Hugo Gallery / Portraits of Women: Constructions and Arrangements by Joseph Cornell"** 1946
Printed announcement for Hugo Gallery, New York
11⅝ x 9 in. (29.5 x 22.9 cm)
Joseph Cornell Study Center, National Museum of American Art, Smithsonian Institution. Gift of Mr. and Mrs. John A. Benton

81 **Untitled (Bébé Marie)** c. 1943
Glass-paned, painted, and papered cardboard box with nineteenth-century doll in linen dress and straw hat and spray-painted twigs
23½ x 12⅜ x 5¼ in. (59.7 x 31.5 x 13.3 cm)
The Museum of Modern Art, New York. Acquired through the Lillie P. Bliss Bequest

82 ***Habitat Group for a Shooting Gallery*** 1943 †
Stained and painted wood cabinet with shattered clear glass pane between intact clear glass panes, with chromolithographic cutouts, photomechanical reproductions, paper, newsprint, feathers, and dried weeds
15½ x 11⅛ x 4¼ in. (39.4 x 28.3 x 10.8 cm)
Des Moines Art Center, Iowa. Purchased with funds from the Coffin Fine Arts Trust; Nathan Emory Coffin Collection

83 **Untitled (The Hotel Eden)** c. 1945
Glass-paned, stained, and painted wood box with chromolithographic cutouts, wood, metal, glass, printed reproductions, music box, cord, and newspaper
15⅛ x 15¾ x 4¾ in. (38.4 x 40 x 12.1 cm)
National Gallery of Canada, Ottawa

84 ***Petit musée [Small Museum]*** 1947 †
Stained wood chest with Photostats of typed text and eleven fabric-capped glass bottles housing various objects, materials, and printed papers
7 x 7⅞ x 5½ in. (17.8 x 20 x 14 cm)
Private collection

85 ***Museum*** c. 1944–48
Stained wood chest with Photostats of type and typeset text, and twenty fabric-capped, cork-stoppered glass bottles housing various printed papers, objects, materials
2¼ x 8⅝ x 7 in. (5.7 x 22 x 17.8 cm)
The Menil Collection, Houston. Bequest of Jermayne MacAgy

86 **Untitled *(Penny Arcade Portrait of Lauren Bacall)*** 1945–46 †
Glass-paned, painted wood cabinet with Masonite panel, panes of blue and clear glass, mirror, photomechanical reproductions, photographs, wood, gears, and thread
20½ x 16 x 3½ in. (52 x 40.6 x 8.9 cm)
Collection of Lindy Bergman, Chicago

87 ***Penny Arcade Portrait of Lauren Bacall (Working Model Based Upon "To Have and Have Not")*** c. 1945–70
Paperboard folder containing magazine excerpts, photographs, photomechanical reproductions, pamphlet, and handwritten and typed notes
3/4 x 8¾ x 12 in. (2 x 22.2 x 30.5 cm)
Collection of Lindy Bergman, Chicago

88 **Untitled (Sand Box)** c. 1944 †
Glass-paned, painted wood box with black sand, metal ring, and ball bearings
1⅞ x 10¼ x 7 in. (4.8 x 26 x 18 cm)
The Art Institute of Chicago. Gift of Frank B. Hubachek

89 Untitled (Sand Fountain) c. 1958
Glass-paned, painted wood box with yellow sand, glass, cork, and wood
13¼ x 8⅜ x 4¾ in. (33.7 x 21.3 x 12.1 cm)
Collection of Jacqueline Matisse

90 Untitled [Window Facade] c. 1950–52
Glass-paned, painted wood box with wood, cracked glass, and mirror
18⅝ x 12⅜ x 3½ in. (47.3 x 31.4 x 8.9 cm)
The Menil Collection, Houston

91 Untitled (Rattle and Music Box) c. 1955
Fiberboard box papered with postage stamps and printing stamps housing concealed wood ball and toy xylophone
3⅛ x 10⅛ x 7¼ in. (7.9 x 25.7 x 18.4 cm)
The Menil Collection, Houston. Bequest of Jermayne MacAgy

92 Untitled [Owl Habitat] 1946
Glass-paned, stained wood box with chromolithographic cutout, wood, colored glass, lichen, dried seed pod, twigs, and bark
12 x 8⅛ x 4¼ in. (30.5 x 20.6 x 10.8 cm)
Collection of Arno Schefler

93 *Neptun au Lac* c. 1953
[Neptune at the Lake]
Blue glass-paned, stained, and crackled wood box with chromolithographic cutout, painted lichen, bark, and electric light
13 x 8½ x 4½ in. (33 x 21.6 x 11.4 cm)
The Joseph and Robert Cornell Memorial Foundation

94 Untitled (Renée Jeanmarie in *la belle au bois dormant)* *[Sleeping Beauty]* 1949
Blue glass-paned, stained, and papered wood box with photomechanical reproduction, bark, glitter, and electric light
14½ x 11⅞ x 6¾ in. (36.8 x 30.2 x 17.1 cm)
Private collection

95 Untitled [Sequestered Bower] c. early 1950s–early 1960s
Amber glass-paned, painted, and papered wood box with plastic doll, wood, bark, twine, wire, dried plants, mirrors, and sawdust
15½ x 12 x 4⅞ in. (39.4 x 30.5 x 12.4 cm)
The Art Institute of Chicago. The Lindy and Edwin Bergman Joseph Cornell Collection

96 Untitled [Landscape with Reclining Nude and Castle] late 1950s †
Cut and pasted photomechanical reproductions on Masonite in wood frame
13⅞ x 10½ in. (35.3 x 26.7 cm)
Private collection, courtesy PaceWildenstein, New York

97 Untitled (Mélisande) c. early 1950s–early 1960s †
Glass-paned, stained wood box with plastic doll and spider, Masonite, wood, sawdust, lichen, and bark
18⅛ x 11⅞ x 5⅞ in. (46 x 30.8.1 x 15 cm)
Private collection

98 Untitled [Doll Habitat] c. early 1950s–1965
Glass-paned, painted wood box with plastic doll in Diamond match box, bark, lichen, and sawdust
9⅝ x 6½ x 4⅜ in. (24.5 x 16.5 x 11.1 cm)
Collection of Janice and Mickey Cartin

99 *Sorrows of Young Werther* c. 1966
Cut and pasted photomechanical reproductions on Masonite
8¼ x 11¼ in. (21 x 28.6 cm)
Hirshhorn Museum and Sculpture Garden, Smithsonian Institution. Gift of Joseph H. Hirshhorn

100.1 Shoe box of "Medici Slot Machine" working materials c. 1940s–1950s
Painted shoe box with mounted and unmounted photomechanical reproductions, and wood cubes and discs in various states of decoration
5⅜ x 13½ x 6⅞ in. (13.7 x 34.3 x 17.5 cm)
Joseph Cornell Study Center, National Museum of American Art, Smithsonian Institution. Gift of The Joseph and Robert Cornell Memorial Foundation

100.2 "Medici Slot Machine" source material files c. late 1930s–1966
Folders containing book and magazine excerpts, photomechanical reproductions, and newspaper clippings
2 x 8½ x 11 in. (5 x 21.6 x 28 cm)
Joseph Cornell Study Center, National Museum of American Art, Smithsonian Institution. Gift of Mr. and Mrs. John A. Benton

Selected Bibliography

compiled by RACHAEL ARAUZ

Joseph Cornell

Ashton, Dore. *A Joseph Cornell Album*. New York: The Viking Press, 1974.

Blair, Lindsay. *Joseph Cornell's Vision of Spiritual Order*. London: Reaktion Books, 1998.

Caws, Mary Ann, ed. *Joseph Cornell's Theater of the Mind: Selected Diaries, Letters and Files*. New York: Thames and Hudson, 1993.

Hartigan, Lynda Roscoe. *Joseph Cornell: An Exploration of the Sources*. Washington, D.C.: National Museum of American Art, Smithsonian Institution, 1982.

Hopps, Walter. *An Exhibition of Works by Joseph Cornell*. Pasadena, Calif.: Pasadena Art Museum, 1966.

Joseph Cornell. Kamakura: The Museum of Modern Art, 1992. Essay by Sandra Leonard Starr.

Joseph Cornell: Box Constructions and Collages. New York: C & M Arts, 1996. Essay by Donald Windham.

Joseph Cornell Papers. Archives of American Art, Smithsonian Institution, Washington, D.C.

Joseph Cornell Portfolio. New York: Castelli, Feigen, Corcoran, 1976. Essays by Julien Levy, Robert Motherwell, Sandra Leonard Starr, et al.

McShine, Kynaston, ed. *Joseph Cornell*. New York: The Museum of Modern Art, 1980. Essays by Dawn Ades, Carter Ratcliff, P. Adams Sitney, and Lynda Roscoe Hartigan.

Michelson, Annette. "Rose Hobart and Monsieur Phot: Early Films from Utopia Parkway." *Artforum* (June 1973): pp. 47–57.

Solomon, Deborah. *Utopia Parkway: The Life and Work of Joseph Cornell*. New York: Farrar, Straus and Giroux, 1997.

Starr, Sandra Leonard. *Box Constructions & Collages by Joseph Cornell* and *The Crystal Cage [portrait of Berenice]*. Tokyo: Gatodo Gallery, 1987.

Tashjian, Dickran. *Joseph Cornell: Gifts of Desire*. Miami Beach, Fla.: Grassfield Press, 1992.

Waldman, Diane. *Joseph Cornell*. New York: The Solomon R. Guggenheim Museum, 1967.

Marcel Duchamp

Adcock, Craig. *Marcel Duchamp's Notes from the "Large Glass": An N-Dimensional Analysis*. Ann Arbor: UMI Research Press, 1983.

Bonk, Ecke. *Marcel Duchamp: The Box in a Valise*. New York: Rizzoli, 1989.

Cabanne, Pierre. *Dialogues with Marcel Duchamp*. Translated by Ron Padgett. New York: Viking Press, 1971.

Camfield, William A. *Marcel Duchamp/Fountain*. Houston: Menil Collection, Houston Fine Arts Press, 1989.

Clair, Jean, ed. *Marcel Duchamp*. Paris: Musée National d'Art Moderne Centre Georges Pompidou, 1977.

d'Harnoncourt, Anne, and Kynaston McShine, eds. *Marcel Duchamp*. New York and Philadelphia: The Museum of Modern Art and Philadelphia Museum of Art, 1989. Essays by Anne d'Harnoncourt, Michel Sanouillet, Richard Hamilton, Lawrence D. Steefel, Jr., Arturo Schwarz, David Antin, Lucy Lippard, Kynaston McShine, Robert Lebel, Octavio Paz, and John Tancock.

d'Harnoncourt, Anne, and Walter Hopps. *"Étant Donnés: 1. La Chute d'eau, 2. Le Gaz d'éclairage": Reflections on a New Work by Marcel Duchamp*. Philadelphia: Philadelphia Museum of Art, 1987.

Duchamp, Marcel. *Manual of Instructions for "Étant Donnés."* Philadelphia: Philadelphia Museum of Art, 1987.

Duve, Thierry de, ed. *The Definitively Unfinished Marcel Duchamp*. Cambridge: MIT Press, 1991.

Gough-Cooper, Jennifer, and Jacques Caumont. *Ephemerides on and About Marcel Duchamp and Rrose Sélavy, 1887–1968*. Milan: Bompiani, 1993.

Henderson, Linda Dalrymple. *Duchamp in Context: Science and Technology in the "Large Glass" and Related Works*. Princeton, N.J.: Princeton University Press, 1998.

Hopps, Walter. *By or of Marcel Duchamp or Rrose Sélavy*. Pasadena, Calif.: Pasadena Art Museum, 1963.

Hopps, Walter, Ulf Linde, and Arturo Schwarz. *Marcel Duchamp Ready-Mades, etc. (1913–1964)*. Paris: Le Terrain Vague, 1964.

Kuenzli, Rudolph, and Francis Naumann, eds. *Marcel Duchamp: Artist of the Century*. Cambridge: MIT Press, 1989.

Lebel, Robert. *Marcel Duchamp*. English translation of *Sur Marcel Duchamp* by George Heard Hamilton. New York: Grove Press, 1959.

Sanouillet, Michel, and Elmer Peterson, eds. *Salt Seller: The Writings of Marcel Duchamp*. New York: Oxford University Press, 1973.

Schwarz, Arturo. *The Complete Works of Marcel Duchamp*. New York: Delano Greenidge Editions, 1996.

Sweeney, James Johnson. "A Conversation with Marcel Duchamp...." In *Wisdom: Conversations with the Elder Wise Men of Our Day*, edited by James Nelson. New York: W.W. Norton, 1958.

Tomkins, Calvin. *Duchamp: A Biography*. New York: Henry Holt and Company, 1996.

General

Ades, Dawn. *Surrealist Art: The Lindy and Edwin Bergman Collection at the Art Institute of Chicago.* Chicago and London: The Art Institute of Chicago and Thames and Hudson, 1997.

Altshuler, Bruce. *The Avant-Garde in Exhibition: New Art in the 20th Century.* New York: Abrams, 1994.

André Breton: La beauté convulsive. Paris: Musée National d'Art Moderne Centre Georges Pompidou, 1991.

Barr, Alfred H., Jr., ed. *Fantastic Art Dada Surrealism.* New York: The Museum of Modern Art, 1936.

Bogner, Dieter. *Friedrich Kiesler 1890–1965: Inside the Endless House.* Vienna: Biesler, 1997.

Breton, André. *Surrealism and Painting.* Translated by Simon Watson Taylor. New York: Harper & Row, Publishers, 1972.

Breton, André, ed. *VVV.* 1942–44.

Burke, Carolyn. *Becoming Modern: The Life of Mina Loy.* New York: Farrar, Straus and Giroux, 1996.

Dortch, Virginia M., ed. *Peggy Guggenheim and Her Friends.* Milan: Berenice, 1994.

Edwards, Hugh. *Surrealism & Its Affinities: The Mary Reynolds Collection.* Introduction by Marcel Duchamp. Chicago: The Art Institute of Chicago, 1956.

Ernst, Jimmy. *A Not-So-Still Life.* New York: St. Martin's, 1984.

First Papers of Surrealism. New York: Coordinating Council of French Relief Societies, Inc., 1942.

Ford, Charles Henri, ed. *View.* 1940–47. Especially "Americana Fantastica" Issue, series 2, no. 4 (January 1943), and "Marcel Duchamp" Issue, series 5, no. 1 (March 1945).

Ford, Charles Henri, ed. View: *Parade of the Avant-Garde: An Anthology of* View *Magazine (1940–1947).* Compiled by Catrina Neiman and Paul Nathan. New York: Thunder's Mouth Press, 1991.

Frederick Kiesler: Artiste-architecte. Paris: Musée National d'Art Moderne Centre Georges Pompidou, 1996.

Guggenheim, Peggy. *Art of This Century Objects–Drawings–Photographs–Paintings–Sculpture–Collages 1910 to 1942.* New York: Art of this Century, 1942.

Guggenheim, Peggy. *Out of This Century: Confessions of an Art Addict.* 1946. Reprint. New York: Universe Books, 1979.

Janis, Sidney. *Abstract & Surrealist Art in America.* New York: Reynal & Hitchcock, 1944.

Jean, Marcel. *The History of Surrealist Painting.* Translated by Simon Watson Taylor. New York: Grove Press, 1960.

Levy, Julien. *Memoir of an Art Gallery.* New York: Putnam, 1977.

Levy, Julien. *Surrealism.* New York: Black Sun Press, 1936.

Lynes, Russel. *Good Old Modern: An Intimate Portrait of The Museum of Modern Art.* New York: Atheneum, 1973.

Maria: The Surrealist Sculpture of Maria Martins. New York: André Emmerich Gallery, 1998.

Mary Reynolds and the Spirit of Surrealism. Museum Studies, vol. 22, no. 2. Chicago: The Art Institute of Chicago, 1996.

Morris, Jan. *Manhattan '45.* New York: Oxford University Press, 1987.

Myers, John Bernard. *Tracking the Marvelous: A Life in the New York Art World.* New York: Random House, 1983.

Phillips, Lisa. *Frederick Kiesler.* New York and London: Whitney Museum of American Art and W. W. Norton & Company, 1989.

Polizzotti, Mark. *Revolution of the Mind: The Life of André Breton.* New York: Farrar, Straus and Giroux, 1995.

Rudenstine, Angelica Zander. *Peggy Guggenheim Collection, Venice, Solomon R. Guggenheim Foundation.* New York: Harry N. Abrams, Inc., 1985.

Sawin, Martica. *Surrealism in Exile and the Beginning of the New York School.* Cambridge: MIT Press, 1995.

Schaffner, Ingrid, and Matthias Winzen. *Deep Storage: Collecting, Storing, and Archiving in Art.* New York: Prestel, 1998.

Schaffner, Ingrid, and Lisa Jacobs, eds. *Julien Levy: Portrait of an Art Gallery.* Cambridge: MIT Press, 1998.

Tacou-Rumney, Laurence. *Peggy Guggenheim: A Collector's Album.* Paris and New York: Flammarion, 1996.

Tashjian, Dickran. *A Boatload of Madmen: Surrealism and the American Avant-Garde, 1920–1950.* New York: Thames and Hudson, 1995.

Weld, Jacqueline Bogard. *Peggy: The Wayward Guggenheim.* New York: E.P. Dutton, 1986.

Index

Photography Credits

Specific sources, Photographer credits, and copyrights are noted below; otherwise, photographic material has been supplied by the owner

Berenice Abbott / Commerce Graphics Ltd., Inc.: figs. 5, 42, 43, 44, 98, 184, 201, 214, 250

Courtesy Acquavella Galleries: fig. 172

Archives of American Art, Smithsonian Institution: figs. 40, 121, 146

Courtesy Archives of American Art, Smithsonian Institution: fig. 177

Argonne National Laboratory: fig. 62

The Art Institute of Chicago: fig. 204

Oliver Baker, courtesy Sidney Janis Gallery, New York: fig. 175

Courtesy Joshua Beadle and Time Inc.: fig. 94

Bibliothèque Municipal, Rouen: fig. 147

Ben Blackwell: pl. 69

Courtesy Bogner + Lord, Vienna: figs. 87, 141, 193

Rudy Burkhardt: fig. 183

Michael Cavanaugh: pl. 10

Corbis-Bettman: fig. 39

Joseph Cornell Study Center, National Museum of American Art, Smithsonian Institution: pls. 51, 63, 64, 100.1, 100.2; figs. 99, 100, 103, 104, 106, 107, 108, 110, 111, 112, 113, 119, 120, 122, 123, 124, 125, 126, 135, 137, 143, 208, 210, 220, 227, 231

Courtesy Joseph Cornell Study Center, National Museum of American Art, Smithsonian Institution: figs. 26, 105, 117, 118, 130, 131, 132, 133, 176, 192, 209, 233

Prudence Cuming Associates Ltd., London: pl. 29

D. James Dee, New York, courtesy Shirmer Mosel Verlag, Munich: pl. 21.1

Studio Duttman, Hamburg, courtesy Schirmer-Mosel Verlag, Munich: pl. 26; figs. 81, 82, 83

Courtesy Betty Factor: fig. 24

Allan Grant, *Life* © Time Inc.: fig. 155

Hachette Publications, Paris: fig. 136

© Denise Brown Hare, courtesy Philadelphia Museum of Art: fig. 19

Robert Hashimoto, courtesy The Art Institute of Chicago: pl. 88.

David Heald, New York: pl. 92

Rich Heki, Des Moines: pl. 82, fig. 9

Hester + Hardaway: pages 19–59, 301–303, 305–331; pls. 3, 13, 17, 18, 19, 24, 25, 27, 30, 31, 35, 39, 45, 48, 72, 79; figs. 29, 38, 47, 61, 67, 68, 72, 74, 75, 80, 85, 86, 90, 97, 139, 142, 144, 145, 156, 158, 160, 169, 219, 240, 243, 245, 249

Hickey-Robertson, Houston: pls. 8, 57, 70, 77, 85, 90, 91, 94; fig. 159

George Hixson, Houston: pl. 67 (left)

© 1973, The Estate of Peter Hujar: figs. 56, 60

Courtesy Lillian Kiesler, New York: figs. 93, 223

Alexander Liberman: figs. 8, 12, 247

Courtesy The Menil Collection, Houston: figs. 15, 22, 53, 54, 55, 59, 114, 116, 127, 157, 166, 173, 174, 189, 199, 213, 216, 224, 234, 237, 239, 244, 246

Duane Michals, courtesy Sidney Janis Gallery, New York: frontispiece (page 5), 10, 14, 101, 248

Philippe Migeat, Paris: pl. 32

© Lee Miller Archives, Chiddingly, England: figs. 178, 197, 198

Eric Mitchell, courtesy Philadelphia Museum of Art: pl. 22 (page 137)

© Museum of the City of New York: figs. 4, 48, 185

The Museum of Fine Arts, Houston: fig. 244

© 1998 The Museum of Modern Art, New York: pls. 71, 81; figs. 49, 50, 51, 128, 191, 221, 241, 242

© Hans Namuth, 1990: figs. 31, 95, 96, 164

National Museum of American Art, Smithsonian Institution: pls. 46, 49, 59, 60, 76,80; figs. 109, 111, 113

Courtesy National Museum of American Art, Smithsonian Institution: figs. 71, 140

Lusha Nelson, Courtesy Vogue, © 1934 (renewed 1962, 1990) by The Condé Nast Publications, Inc.: fig. 2

Otto Nelson, courtesy National Museum of American Art, Smithsonian Institution, Washington, D.C.: fig. 207

© Arnold Newman: fig. 92

New York Public Library Archives: figs. 11, 163

Courtesy The Cartoon Bank: fig. 37

James Ogle: figs. 1, 102, 149

Bill Orcutt, New York: pl. 16

Edward Owen, courtesy Joseph Cornell Study Center, National Museum of American Art, Smithsonian Institution: pl. 86; fig. 134

Courtesy Jürgen Pech, Bonn: fig. 57

Philadelphia Museum of Art: pls. 2, 3, 4, 9, 44; figs. 45, 91, 161, 212

Philadelphia Museum of Art, Marcel Duchamp Archive, Gift of Jacqueline, Paul and Peter Matisse in memory of their mother, Alexina Duchamp: frontispiece (page. 6), figs. 13, 169, 187, 202, 226, 236

Courtesy Philadelphia Museum of Art: pl. 42

Courtesy Philadelphia Museum of Art, Marcel Duchamp Archive, Gift of Jacqueline, Paul and Peter Matisse in memory of their mother Alexina Duchamp: figs. 17, 151

Tom Powell, New York: pls. 58, 62, 68, 93

Mary Reynolds Collection, The Art Institute of Chicago: figs. 195, 200, 235

Harry Roseman: figs. 3, 27, 150, 180

Lynn Rosenthal, courtesy Philadelphia Museum of Art: pls. 33, 43

Lynn Rosenthal, courtesy Philadelphia Museum of Art, Marcel Duchamp Archive, Gift of Jacqueline, Paul and Peter Matisse in memory of their mother Alexina Duchamp: figs. 41, 148, 162, 167, 168, 179, 190, 215, 225, 228, 230

Courtesy Martica Sawin: fig. 211

Courtesy Ingrid Schaffner: fig. 36

Courtesy Schirmer-Mosel Verlag, Munich: fig. 84

Oren Slor, New York: pl. 66

Courtesy Sotheby's: fig. 73

Courtesy Mrs. Soichi Sunami: fig. 35

Gregory R. Staley, Washington, D.C.: pl. 52; figs. 129, 138

Dorothea Tanning, New York: fig. 222

John Tennant: pl. 99

Frank J. Thomas Archives: figs. 20, 21

Michael Tropea, Chicago: pls. 47, 87

Anna Maria Martins Turner, courtesy André Emmerich Gallery, New York: fig. 217

the typosophic society, Primersdorf: figs. 18, 64, 65, 70, 76, 77

Courtesy the typosophic society, Primersdorf: pl. 11; figs. 66, 78, 79, 153, 234

University of London, The Warburg Institute: figs. 88, 89

UPI / Corbis-Bettman: figs. 6, 7, 30, 32, 52, 58, 181, 182, 186, 194, 206

Courtesy Daniel Varenne, Geneva: pls. 84, 97

Laura Voight, courtesy Philadelphia Museum of Art, Marcel Duchamp Archive, Gift of Jacqueline, Paul and Peter Matisse in memory of their mother Alexina Duchamp: figs.232

Courtesy Wadsworth Atheneum, Hartford: pl. 98

© 1963 Julian Wasser: figs. 23, 25

Graydon Wood, courtesy Philadelphia Museum of Art: pl. 1, 15, 22 (pages 138–39), 34, 36, 38, 40, 67; figs. 63, 69, 188

Matt Wrbican: figs. 170, 171

Sue Wrbican: pls. 28, 65; figs. 154, 196, 229

The Young–Mallin Archive, New York: fig. 218